Gestures

This volume has emerged from a collaboration among:

The NWO Research Council for the Humanities (GW),
The NWO Research Council for Social Sciences (MaGW), and
The Netherlands Foundation for the Advancement of Tropical Research (WOTRO).

International Advisory Board

Veena Das, Chair
Christoph Auffarth
Peter Clarke
Galit Hasan-Rokem
Michael Lambek
Regina M. Schwartz

THE FUTURE OF THE RELIGIOUS PAST

Hent de Vries, General Editor

In what sense are the legacies of religion—its powers, words, things, and gestures—disarticulating and reconstellating themselves as the elementary forms of life in the twenty-first century? This sequence of five volumes publishes work drawn from an international research project that seeks to answer this question.

Editorial Board

Meerten ter Borg
Jan Bremmer
Martin van Bruinessen
Jan Willem van Henten
Dick Houtman
Anne-Marie Korte
Birgit Meyer

Gestures

THE STUDY OF RELIGION AS PRACTICE

MICHIEL LEEZENBERG, ANNE-MARIE KORTE
and MARTIN VAN BRUINESSEN

Editors

FORDHAM UNIVERSITY PRESS NEW YORK 2022

Frontispiece: Courtesy of pexels / Roman Odintsov

Copyright © 2022 Fordham University Press

All rights reserved. No part of this publication may be reproduced, stored in a retrieval system, or transmitted in any form or by any means—electronic, mechanical, photocopy, recording, or any other—except for brief quotations in printed reviews, without the prior permission of the publisher.

Fordham University Press has no responsibility for the persistence or accuracy of URLs for external or third-party Internet websites referred to in this publication and does not guarantee that any content on such websites is, or will remain, accurate or appropriate.

Fordham University Press also publishes its books in a variety of electronic formats. Some content that appears in print may not be available in electronic books.

Visit us online at www.fordhampress.com.

Library of Congress Cataloging-in-Publication Data

Names: Leezenberg, Michiel, editor. | Korte, Anne-Marie, 1957– editor. | Bruinessen, Martin van, editor.
Title: Gestures : the study of religion as practice / Michiel Leezenberg, Anne-Marie Korte, and Martin van Bruinessen, editors.
Description: New York : Fordham University Press, 2022. | Series: The future of the religious past | Includes bibliographical references and index.
Identifiers: LCCN 2021056784 | ISBN 9780823299614 (hardback) | ISBN 9780823299621 (paperback)
Subjects: LCSH: Religious life.
Classification: LCC BL624 .G4824 2022 | DDC 204/.4—dc23/eng20220311
LC record available at https://lccn.loc.gov/2021056784

Printed in the United States of America

24 23 22   5 4 3 2 1

First edition

To the memory of
Helen Tartar
(1951–2014)

Contents

List of Illustrations — xiii
List of Credits — xv
Preface — xvii

Introduction: Practice Turns in the Study of Religion
MICHIEL LEEZENBERG — 1

I. RELIGIOUS PERFORMANCE AND PERFORMATIVITY

1. Gesturing Toward Sacrifice:
   Aping the Scapegoat and Monkeying
   Around with the Lamb
   YVONNE SHERWOOD — 47

2. Unpacking "Performance":
   Felicity Conditions, Efficacy, and Indexicals
   in Islamic Actions
   JOHN R. BOWEN — 106

3. "Thou Shalt Not Freeze-Frame":
   How Not to Misunderstand the Science
   and Religion Debate
   BRUNO LATOUR — 119

4. Dorsal Monuments:
   Messiaen, Sellars, and Saint Francis
   SANDER VAN MAAS — 141

II. EMBODIMENT AND MATERIALITY

5. From Kama to Karma:
   The Resurgence of Puritanism
   in Contemporary India
   WENDY DONIGER — 173

6. Bodies in Alliance and the Politics of the Street
   JUDITH BUTLER — 194

7. Divine Impersonations:
   Transgressive Gestures in Hindu Devotion
   ROKUS DE GROOT — 215

8. Islamic Dress and Fashion:
   A Religious and a Sartorial Practice Revisited
   ANNELIES MOORS — 235

9. On Spirit Writing:
   Materialities of Language and the Religious
   Work of Transduction
   WEBB KEANE — 249

III. EVERYDAY RELIGION

10. The Quotidian Turn:
    Interpretive Categories and Scholarly Trajectories
    THOMAS A. TWEED — 279

11. Rhythms of Roots:
    Identity Politics in Religious Dance
    Processions in Bolivia
    SANNE DERKS, CATRIEN NOTERMANS,
    AND WILLY JANSEN — 303

12. State Rituals in Turkey:
    Commemorating the Gazi and Kubilay the Martyr
    UMUT AZAK — 322

13. Second Thoughts About the Anthropology of Islam
    SAMULI SCHIELKE — 348

IV. TRANSGRESSIVE ACTS: HERESY AND BLASPHEMY

14. Eventual Blasphemies:
    Setting the Offensive Work of Art in Time
    S. BRENT PLATE — 375

15. The Political Gesture of "Blasphemous" Art:
    Facing Pussy Riot's Punk Prayer
    ANNE-MARIE KORTE — 391

16. On Silencing and Public Debates
    about Religiously Offensive Acts
    CHRISTOPH BAUMGARTNER — 417

17. Offending Muslims:
    Provocation, Blasphemy, and Public Debate
    in the Netherlands
    MARTIJN DE KONING — 445

V. VIOLENT RELIGIOUS PERFORMANCES: SACRIFICE AND MARTYRDOM

18. Sacrifice and the Problem of Beginning:
    Meditations from Sakalava Mythopraxis
    MICHAEL LAMBEK — 475

19. The Mass and the Theater: *Othello* and Sacrifice
    REGINA M. SCHWARTZ — 502

20. Martyrdom, Religion, and Nation
    in Kurdish Literature
    MARIWAN KANIE — 524

21. Suicide Terrorism and the Modern Nation-State:
    Antiliberal Protest or Biopolitical Performance?
    MICHIEL LEEZENBERG — 546

VI. SECULARISM AND POSTSECULARISM

22. Good Religion, Bad Religion:
    Beyond the Secularity-Religion
    and Secularity-Piety Binaries
    YOLANDE JANSEN — 579

23. Human Rights, Muslim Communities,
    and the Unintentional Secularization of Canada
    ALI HASSAN ZAIDI   605

24. The Distinctiveness of Indian Secularism
    RAJEEV BHARGAVA   623

List of Contributors   651
Index   657

List of figures

1.1	Bulwer's manual alphabet	61
1.2	Chirogram for the "speaking action"	63
1.3	Caravaggio's 1603 sacrifice of Isaac	69
1.4	Rembrandt, *Sacrifice of Isaac*	70
1.5	David Aronson, *Sacrifice of Isaac*	86
1.6	Samuel Bak, *Dress rehearsal*	89
1.7	Paul Fryer, *The Privilege of Dominion*	93
3.1	Philippe de Champaigne, *La Sainte Face*	135
3.2	Pieta (fifteenth century)	136
7.1	Inspector General Devendra Kumar Panda	216
7.2	*Radha and Krishna Walk in a Flowering Grove*	218
7.3	Mirabai singing to Krishna	225
7.4	Indira Devi (1920–98)	227
12.1	"Dear Atatürk	325
12.2	Some "reactionaries"	330
12.3	Commemoration at the Kubilay monument	335
12.4	Portrait of Kubilay in front of the monument	339
12.5	"The Republic of Turkey cannot be a country of shaykhs, dervishes and disciples"	340
14.1	Stills from David Wojnarowicz, *A Fire in My Belly*	381
15.1	Pussy Riot performs a punk prayer in the Cathedral of Christ the Saviour in Moscow	399
15.2	Pussy Riot members in court	402
15.3	Pussy Riot at Lobnoye Mesto on Red Square	406

Part I illustration courtesy of pexels / Prabhala Raguvir
Part II illustration courtesy of pexels / Jonathan Borba
Parts III and V illustrations courtesy of Martin van Bruinessen
Part IV illustration courtesy of pexels (anonymous)
Part VI illustration courtesy of pexels / José Aragones

Credits

The editors thank authors and publishers for permission to reprint the following previously published articles:

Rajeev Bhargava, "The Distinctiveness of Indian Secularism," *Critique internationale* 35, no. 2 (2007): 121–147.

Judith Butler, "Bodies in Alliance and the Politics of the Street," *Transversal texts* (September 2011), https://transversal.at/transversal/1011/butler/en.

Wendy Doniger, "From Kama to Karma: The Resurgence of Puritanism in Contemporary India," *Social Research* 78, no.1 (2011): 49–74.

Webb Keane, "On Spirit Writing: Materialities of Language and the Religious Work of Transduction," *Journal of the Royal Anthropological Institute* (N.S.) 19, no. 1 (2013): 1–17.

Michael Lambek, "Sacrifice and the Problem of Beginning: Meditations from Sakalava Mythopraxis," *Journal of the Royal Anthropological Institute* (N.S.) 13, no. 1 (2007): 19–38.

Bruno Latour, "Thou Shall Not Freeze-Frame" or How Not to Misunderstand the Science and Religion Debate," in James D. Proctor (ed.), *Science, Religion, and the Human Experience* (Oxford University Press, 2005). DOI:10.1093/0195175328.003.0003

Samuli Schielke, "Second Thoughts About the Anthropology of Islam," Working paper (Zentrum Moderner Orient, Berlin, 2010).

Preface

This book has its origin in the conference *Gestures: Religion as Performance* at Utrecht University, June 9–10, 2008. The conference was held within the framework of the research program The Future of the Religious Past, which was sponsored by the Netherlands Organization for Scientific Research (NWO). The program's ambition was to map new and unprecedented forms of religious life in the early twenty-first century and to encourage conversations among the full range of approaches to the study of religion. The program funded fifteen research projects, which had been selected for relevance and originality by the program's committee and an international advisory board, and which were carried out by teams of three or four members.

The conference focused especially on practice, performance, and the performative aspects of religion: embodiment, sacrifice, blasphemy and public expression of religion, and contestations of secularism and the secular. As in earlier conferences, the contributions were an equal mix of presentations by the Dutch research teams and invited international guests. For the purpose of this book, the most relevant and innovative conference presentations have been selected, revised where necessary, and complemented with a number of additional essays to achieve a balanced coverage of the full range of subjects and approaches. Several papers included in this collection were sponsored by the NWO as part of the following research projects: The Power of Marian Pilgrimage (Derks, Jansen, and Notermans); New Music and the Turn to Religion (De Groot and Van Maas); and The Sacred and the Secular: Genealogies of Self, State, and Society in the Contemporary Islamic World (Jansen, Kanie, and Leezenberg). This funding, too, is gratefully acknowledged.

We thank our colleagues of the Dutch program committee and the members of the international advisory board, especially Michael

Lambek and Regina M. Schwartz, for their intellectual input in the conference, and Marc Linssen and the other staff officers of NWO for their unyielding support for this huge and complex program. NWO is to be commended for sponsoring an interdisciplinary research program of the scope and ambition of The Future of the Religious Past, which has been a rare and unique experience for all involved. It is our hope that this volume will transmit to the reader the sense of being on a voyage of discovery.

While editorial work on the volume was in progress, we received the shocking news of Helen Tartar's untimely death in a traffic accident. Helen had been involved in the research program on behalf of Fordham University Press almost from the beginning. She had been present at all the conferences, had spoken to most of the contributors, and had been working with the editors of each of the books in this series in a most stimulating way. Like the earlier books in this series, this volume, too, owes much to Helen's dedication and professionalism. We have lost a friend with whom it was a pleasure and a privilege to work, and we regret that she has not been able to see the entire series to completion. We dedicate this volume to her memory.

Introduction

Practice Turns in the Study of Religion

Michiel Leezenberg

The book series of which you are now holding the final installment is informed by a sense of the continuing, recurrent, and indeed increasing relevance of religion for today's world. This volume is devoted to the study of religion as practice; as such, it is informed by what has been called the *practice turn* in the humanities and social sciences. This is not so much a new theory or paradigm to the exclusion of others but rather an array of broadly similar approaches that focus primarily on how religious traditions function rather than on what they are; on what people *do* when engaging with religion rather than on what they believe; on everyday devotions rather than on sacred texts; on outward acts rather than on inner states or subjective aspects of faith, belief, or religious experience; and on ritualized practices and informal negotiations rather than on institutionalized phenomena such as churches and religious hierarchies. This introduction sketches some of the main conceptual dimensions of this practice turn, briefly traces its origins, discusses some of its empirical consequences, explores how it affects the historical study of religion, and discusses some of its normative implications.

The shift from doctrine to practice, from text to act, and from inner experience to outward behavior invites us to conceptualize religion anew, thus further complicating a term with an already complex background and history. One hardly needs to belabor the oft-made point that the concept of religion is notoriously difficult to grasp. In his introduction to the first volume of this series, significantly titled *Religion: Beyond a Concept*, Hent de Vries argues that religion still eludes classificatory regimes, and that it is impossible to distill the necessary and sufficient features of phenomena called "religious," or of the category "religion"; hence, he recommends a "deep pragmatism" in our approaches of religion, which reflects the need to be resolutely strategic, selective, and inventive in our dealings with it and which systematically spurns the conceptual confines of any strict definitions and a priori assumptions about what religion really is.

In fact, beliefs, institutions, and actions commonly labeled "religious" vary so widely as to be practically incommensurable; moreover, the very attempt to subsume this variety under a single universally applicable rubric or category of religion has been criticized on more principled grounds. Thus, William Cantwell Smith has famously argued that we should drop both the word and the concept of *religion* from our theoretical vocabulary, as they fail to help us understand either our own individual faith or the traditions of others. He argues that the labels for the various "world religions"—such as Buddhism, Hinduism, and Confucianism—are of a remarkably recent date (first occurring in, respectively, 1801, 1829, and 1862) and lack any premodern equivalents or near-equivalents in their home languages; furthermore, the very category of religion itself, in anything like its current meaning, did not exist until the nineteenth century.[1] As is well known by now, the notion that the essence of religion lies in inner faith or belief rather than in external or public ritual practice or institutional organization is of a Protestant origin.[2] Yet, as I will show below, this assumption continues to inform various recent discussions of religion to a greater or lesser extent.

The previous volumes in this series have tried to redress the balance in various ways. The first volume set the stage with a broad array of both conceptually and empirically motivated discussions of the concept of religion in general; subsequent volumes addressed, respectively, questions of power and powerlessness in matters religious; the materiality of religion; and the religious roles and importance of words, language, or discourse. Jointly, they attempt to capture the richness and complexity of religion in the late twentieth and early twenty-first centuries. In this final volume, we present a broad collection of papers that all, in their radically different ways, approach religion as practice. Such a practice perspective may be said to subsume the themes of the earlier installments: it stems from a resolutely anti-essentialist attitude that rejects the idea of universally applicable concepts; it systematically poses questions of how power and authority may be articulated or contested in religious practices; it sees practices as embodied, public, and material rather than as inner, subjective, and spiritual; and it emphasizes the—possibly irreducible—verbal or discursive character of religious practice. Thus, although this volume can hardly pretend to constitute anything like a conclusion to the whole series, the questions, themes, and concerns of earlier volumes do reappear here within the context of practices more generally.

In the following sections, I first present a brief characterization of what practices in general are and sketch out some of the possible implications of a practice approach to the study of religion. Next, I discuss a number of specific practice-related themes and issues that inform the essays in this volume. These themes may be broadly grouped as conceptual, empirical, historical, and normative. Conceptually, they primarily concern the question of exactly what practices, and more specifically religious practices, amount to. Empirically, they explore which phenomena or aspects of religion are investigated anew. Historically, they involve not only reappraisals of the famous secularization thesis but also explorations of how the category of religion has been and continues to be shaped and reshaped by phenomena specific to the modern world, in particular the nation-state, colonial rule, decolonization, and more recently globalization. Normatively, they primarily concern questions of how secularist assumptions that religion is and should be primarily or exclusively a matter of private faith rather than public powers continue to shape both empirical analyses and normative discussions. I will briefly address each of these themes in turn without in any way pretending to be complete or comprehensive.

Conceptual Questions: What Are Practices?

First, I present a rough general characterization of the notion of a practice, bearing in mind that this concept can no more pretend to have a universal applicability than, say, religion or reason. As a first approximation, practices may be characterized as everyday activities of restricted scope and radical geographical and historical variability. This variability already indicates that it may be difficult if not principally impossible to provide a general definition of them: famously, Ludwig Wittgenstein emphasized that the (linguistic) practices he calls "language games" do not have any feature or set of features that may serve as their essence but at most display a set of overlapping features, or "family resemblances."[3] Even the everyday character and restricted scope claimed to be typical for practices can be contested in the case of religious practices, as religion is often characterized precisely as transcending the everyday, and as many—though by no means all—religions aspire to universally valid statements or values.

Although practices are by no means easier to define than religion, it may be useful to state a few recurring features, especially insofar as they will reappear in the following pages. The first, and perhaps crucial, feature is that practices are *public* or *social*: they are either collective, visible, or accessible to others, unlike purely individual or private experiences or beliefs. A concomitant aspect of this public or social character of practices is that human agency, subjectivity, or intentionality does not have a basic explanatory role in them. Although obviously the work of human actors in some generic sense, practices are not conceptually or logically posterior to human agency or subjectivity. In line with Wittgenstein's argument, one may argue that it is not human intentions or other mental states that explain linguistic and other practices, but the other way around. Further, and in line with Bourdieu and Foucault, one may argue that subjects are generally not fully autonomous agents, that is, fully conscious and rational intentional actors who are fully sovereign over their own actions. Rather, human agency or subjectivity is constituted by and in practices as much as the other way around. Accordingly, practice perspectives also crosscut the apparently unbridgeable gap between structure and agency, between institutions and consciousness, and between macrosocial facts and subjective meanings. Although they are public in principle, the actual access to particular religious practices may, of course, be severely restricted, for example, by the use of sacred languages that are seen as and kept distinct from the spoken languages of the laity, or by taboos or rituals that screen religious materials from outsiders. This suggests that even distinctions like those between public and private are practically constituted rather than conceptually given.

Second, practices are typically if not irreducibly *linguistically articulated*. Not only are what Wittgenstein called "language games" the prototypical kind of everyday practice under consideration; the public character of practices discussed here also inverts the long-held assumption that inner experience is prior to and independent from public linguistic expression. As such, practice approaches upset long-held phenomenological assumptions about the transcendental subject and the irreducible and primary character of experience. This is not the place to discuss the question of whether practices are *irreducibly* linguistic in kind; suffice it to say that a systematic attention to language use is a widespread feature of practice approaches. The linguistic character of practices should not, however, tempt us into elevating a reified notion of language to a transcendental condition of possibility of practices. Language is but one feature of practices, perhaps a particular status but equally variable as others. Moreover, practices involve not only variable *uses* but also different *ideologies* of language, that is, folk explanations and rationalizations of what words are and do. Over the years, the study of linguistic—or, more generically, semiotic—ideologies has taken a high flight in linguistic anthropology; more recently, their relevance has also been acknowledged for the anthropological study of religion.[4] Practices are not just generally linguistic in character; they may also more specifically be *performative*, that is, they may bring about, or help to bring about, the very social realities they represent, as had been argued for speech acts such as "I hereby baptize this ship the *Lady Gaga*."[5] For religious practices, this notion has first been applied to ritual,[6] but, as will be seen below, its potential relevance and applications reach far wider.

Third, practices are *material*, and more specifically *embodied*. That is, a practice approach refocuses our attention from questions concerning ideas, ideals, ideologies, dogmas and doctrine to questions of observable, exterior embodied action and material objects and artifacts. Religion has, of course, long been seen as, by definition, going beyond or antithetical to the material world; but more recently, research has shifted to how religion interacts with things, that is, with the materiality of the everyday world. In their introduction to the volume *Things*, Birgit Meyer and Dick Houtman already observe that the protestant focus on faith and the inner has tended to block attention to the embodied and physical aspects of religious practice; but this materiality also has another dimension: practices involve an engagement with material objects, such as the locations and objects of religious worship, in various ways. They are also embodied insofar as they are generally not fully conscious actions; as Bourdieu has suggested, practice may be driven less by conscious decisions or calculations than by what he calls a habitus, or "bodily hexis," that is, a disposition to move one's body in particular ways rather than in others. One theoretically significant aspect of the embodied character of practices is the fact that, by calling attention to gendered human bodies, it allows us to reframe questions of gender and sexuality in studies of religion. Likewise, it allows us to treat emotions not as simply inner or subjective but as practically constituted and contested. These questions of sexuality and affect are discussed in more detail below.

Further, and only apparently in contradiction with the preceding point, practices are *mediated*: the relation or confrontation between the individual and the world they involve is not given—that is, natural, direct or innate—but socially acquired or culturally transmitted. Conceptually, this rejection of the "myth of the given" proceeds from the—ultimately Hegelian—revolt against the empiricist idea that knowledge is construed out of the unmediated contact between the individual knowing subject and the outside world, and that our perceptual knowledge does not presuppose any concepts and is not learned or acquired in any way. Against this, it is argued that even perceptual knowledge is in an important sense acquired, insofar as it is irreducibly linguistic and conceptual in character, and as such mediated by the use of language, that is, by social practices.[7] Empirically, the emphasis on the mediated character of practices directs us to the crucial, and perhaps constitutive, role of media such as writing, print, television, and more recently the Internet. Thus, in the study of religion, one may also witness a steadily increasing, and increasingly systematic, attention to religion in film or other media and to phenomena such as television evangelism and Internet religion.[8] Contradicting the suggestion implicit in the very term *media*, one may even argue that mediatization is in fact constitutive of religious experience and practice.

Fourth, practices are typically, if not inherently, *normative*; as such, they are *power-saturated* and may articulate, involve, or imply different kinds of *violence*. They are normative in that there are correct and incorrect ways of, say, speaking a language or performing a ritual. In language usage, the normativity involved is not only grammatical correctness but may also concern the appropriate dialect, register, or vocabulary; in religious practices, it may concern demands of ritual purity, orthodoxy, and the like. Wittgenstein has famously argued that this normativity is irreducible; such a claim militates against the reduction of practices to purely causal processes, even though Wittgenstein himself saw his own account as "naturalistic" in a wider sense.[9] This normativity also implies that practices are, equally crucially, power-saturated insofar as they involve particular individuals, groups, or institutions having the legitimate authority to determine which acts or usages are correct. Such questions of power, authority, and legitimacy, however, were overlooked entirely by Wittgenstein and almost entirely by Austin; but Bourdieu and Foucault (and, in a way, even Mikhail Bakhtin) have emphasized their importance. Extending this point even further, one might explore the different kinds of violence that may be involved in particular religious practices, be they physical, structural, discursive, or symbolic. So-called genealogical approaches emphasize that religious practices and values involve various kinds of power relations such as the obvious doctrinal or ritual authority of religious specialists or clergymen as opposed to the laity or the less visible powers implicated in particular regimes of language or knowledge. Such genealogical approaches—first formulated concerning (Christian) religious morality by Friedrich Nietzsche and reformulated concerning human-scientific knowledge by Foucault—have in recent years become more popular in the study of religion.

Obviously, these characteristics no more pretend to capture the essence of practices than a practice perspective can pretend to capture the essence of religion, language, or any other phenomenon. On the contrary, as noted above, the point of many practice approaches is precisely that there is no such essence in the first place, but at best a series of overlapping features or "family resemblances" shared by many, but not all, practices alike. Taken together, however, they do provide a distinct set of lines of investigation that may help to reorient our research, raise new questions, or reformulate familiar questions in new terms and consequently also to come up with new answers. One could also suggest that the practice turn in the social sciences subsumes or anticipates both the linguistic and the material focus as well as the systematic attention for questions of power that are characteristic of the earlier volumes in this series.

Religion and/as Practice: A Short History

Needless to say, approaching religion in terms of practice should not be seen as the sole path to methodological salvation; but it does seem to provide a fruitful complement, counterweight, or alternative to earlier frameworks. Practice-based accounts take us beyond the familiar phenomenological claim that embodied experience is basic, and logically prior to the allegedly purely mental and disembodied activity of rational thought; they treat human agency as itself emerging from, rather than sovereign over, practices, without thereby reducing the latter to objective social conditions or transcendental structures. Thus, the practice turn crosscuts the long-standing opposition between phenomenological and structuralist accounts of religion. Perhaps even more importantly, practice approaches have also replaced philological methods as the self-evident way to approach religion. For example, Clifford Geertz famously characterized religion as a "system of symbols," that is, basically as a text or script to be read and interpreted by the social scientist;[10] but more recently, the anthropological study of religion has shifted attention away from symbols and the meanings they express toward practices and the powers they involve. They also allow for a reframing of the long-standing debate, or polemic, concerning the relation between science and religion, which can now be reformulated not so much in terms of faith versus knowledge or revelation versus reason but rather in terms of the different forms of practice and their distinct conditions and effects.[11] The details of how what has come to be known as practice theory emerged historically are complex and need not concern us; here, I merely discuss some of the main protagonists of a practice framework, especially with an eye to their implications for or explicit statements on religion.

One of the first and most influential advocates of a practice approach was Ludwig Wittgenstein, who in his *Philosophical Investigations* explained private mental states in terms of irreducibly public and normative practices, rather than vice versa. Famously, he concluded his argument against the possibility of private languages: "And hence also 'obeying a rule' is a practice. And to *think* one is obeying a rule is not to obey a rule. Hence it is not possible to follow a rule 'privately': otherwise thinking one was obeying a rule would be the same as obeying it."[12] This claim has often been read as a proclamation of a philosophical behaviorism that rejects the explanatory relevance, if not the very existence, of private mental states. As such, it has major implications for the study of religion as belief, where belief is traditionally taken as precisely such a mental state. However, it concerns less the priority of the public over the private than the priority of practice over structure. Wittgenstein repeatedly calls these practices "language games." Although his use of this term varies, it generally indicates a specific and restricted practice of language use, such as giving orders, telling jokes, or translating from one language into another (§23), in short, something much like what John Langshaw Austin would call speech acts. Unlike Austin, however, Wittgenstein emphasizes that the number of different language games is infinite and indeterminate: his claim that there is no common feature or essence of these language games (§§66–67) also militates against any hope that we can provide a typology or classification of such practices. In other words, the practice account of language sketched by Wittgenstein is resolutely anti-essentialist.

The application of these ideas to religion is tempting but elusive. In fact, Wittgenstein himself hardly linked his philosophical analysis to his religious concerns. He did write several critical remarks on James George Frazer's *The Golden Bough* and its account of magic and "primitive religion" in 1931, and he gave three lectures on religious belief in 1938; both, however, long antedate the final draft of the *Investigations* and hardly if at all anticipate its practice-oriented tenets: thus, the lectures, as their title indicates, are concerned more with belief than with practices. Likewise, Wittgenstein's famous remarks on Frazer's *The Golden Bough* are more concerned with the apparent irrationality of the magical beliefs of the adherents of "primitive religions" than with religious or magical practices as such.[13] Thus, the notion of a language game may invite us to look at everyday, mundane religious activities; but Wittgenstein's own writings on religion do not yet achieve such a shift.

Questions of power and conflict, or of the contested interpretation of signs, figure hardly if at all in Wittgenstein's writings. Such matters are taken up by Pierre Bourdieu and Michel Foucault. The sociologist Bourdieu was in many ways indebted to the later Wittgenstein; he not only greatly expands the concept of practice and emphasizes its theoretical centrality but also grounds it in social theory rather than the philosophy of language.[14] The key insight of his many and evolving writings is that we should not treat social action as guided by the fully conscious and goal-directed intentions of goal-rational actors but rather as generated by a set of embodied, semiautomatic, and at most semiconscious dispositions to act in specific ways; this set of dispositions he famously calls *habitus*. Further, he argues that symbolic systems such as religion, art, and even language itself cannot be reduced to a struggle for political power or a competition for economic resources but have their own form of "capital" (i.e., roughly, their own kind of prestige or honor). Hence, they may be considered as distinct *fields* of social action: they do not follow the rules of economic capital but have their own logic. Bourdieu thus accounts for action in terms of the interaction between habitus and field.

Undoubtedly, this is a fruitful perspective on religious practices that takes us far beyond the famous characterization of religion as an instrument of both knowledge and social integration as Émile Durkheim and Max Weber argued; but Bourdieu himself appears more concerned with elaborating general theoretical notions of symbolic capital and symbolic power than with the study of religion as such. More consistently than Wittgenstein, he analyzes phenomena like language and religion in terms of power-saturated practices; but he runs the risk of *reducing* religion to other dimensions of social action and pays little if any attention to what is specific to religion. This tendency appears clearly in a relatively early article on the genesis and stricture of the "religious field," where he characterizes religion as a relatively autonomous field of social action with its own unequal distribution of "properly religious capital of authority," or alternatively, as a market of "goods of salvation."[15] Bourdieu pits his own practice approach against the treatment of religion as a language (or more generally, a symbolic system) along the lines suggested by Wilhelm von Humboldt and Ernst Cassirer: such an approach, he argues, takes symbols out of the social context in which they were produced and ignores the symbolic power exercised in achieving and maintaining the apparent consensus concerning the meaning of religious signs and symbols.

Historically, Bourdieu traces the emergence of the "grand universal religions" (i.e., the monotheistic, script-based religions that employ a body of religious specialists) to the rise of cities, with their increasingly complex division of labor. Thus, he strictly distinguishes urban religion and the magical forms of religion found in "primitive," that is, nonurbanized, socially undifferentiated, and illiterate societies. In a class-based society, Bourdieu argues, the system of religious representations and practices contributes to the reproduction of social order.[16]

Historically, he sees the rise of institutions like that of the church as reflecting more general macrohistorical processes of bureaucratization and institutionalization of religion, arguing that every successful religious sect tends to become a church—a repository and guardian of orthodoxy characterized by its specific hierarchy and dogmas. Put more theoretically, he analyzes religious authority in terms of the monopolization of symbolic power and of the latter's interaction with other forms and spheres of domination; thus, he claims, in regulating and reaffirming an existing symbolic order, religion also contributes to the reproduction of the political order and to the misrecognition of the latter as natural or as cosmologically legitimated.

Despite his explicit rejection of economic reductionism, Bourdieu's analyses are phrased in a clearly Marxist-inspired language of monopolization, domination, competition, and capital, and of the ideological transformation of a contingent state of social inequality into a natural state of affairs, if not a cosmological necessity. Moreover, although his focus is on practices rather than institutions, Bourdieu generally discusses institutionalized and legitimate forms of religion—especially as sanctioned by or in collusion with the state—and pays rather less attention to religious conflict and contestation and to forms of historical change other than the linear concentration of different powers and evolutionary progress marked by urbanization, bureaucratization, or the rise of capitalist societies. Thus, one may ask whether this focus on institutionalized churches and reified religious fields does not amount to a tacit relapse into an institutionalist account that, moreover, seems to focus on the development of the Catholic Church in France; as such, one may ask to what extent it is applicable to other traditions. Moreover, apart from his evolutionist view on "primitive" and "urban" religions, Bourdieu sees an analogy, homology, or mutual reinforcement of the binary oppositions between the powerful and the oppressed, between male and female, and in religious matters between religion and magic: "We find in fact in the political sphere the same division of labor which entrusts religion—public, official, solemn and collective—to the men, and magic—secret, clandestine, and private—to the women."[17] Subsequent research has not only questioned the strictly binary character of Bourdieu's oppositions; it also implies that the religious and the political are more deeply mutually implicated than this apparently neat conceptual division into autonomous fields suggests.

Foucault's writings on practice and religion have been perhaps even more influential than those of Wittgenstein or Bourdieu. Around 1970, Foucault gradually shifted from the archaeological study of systems of human-scientific knowledge to the genealogical study of discursive and nondiscursive practices. Although

Foucault had intensively studied the ordinary language philosophy of thinkers such as Wittgenstein and Austin, this particular practice turn appears to have been inspired by Nietzsche and Deleuze as much as by any analytical philosopher.[18] This change involved a shift from the (Neo-)Kantian study of the changing conditions of possibility of particular forms of knowledge to a more Nietzschean investigation of the forms of power that shaped both knowledge and the human beings figuring as either subject and object of that knowledge. It is also specifically meant to call attention to forms of conflict and violence that tend to be downplayed in institutional analyses, which emphasize social peace, stability, and consensus. This practice approach, which Foucault also applies in *Discipline and Punish*, suggests that the specifically modern discursive practices of human sciences such as criminology and medicine are closely related to modern nondiscursive practices of, for example, punishing or curing; both kinds of practice, Foucault famously suggests, involve a specifically modern modality of power he calls *discipline*: he argues that this power, as opposed to sovereign power, is not directly exercised by the state, and is generally not even visible as such; further, it also involves a specific kind of normativity focusing on the opposition between normal and abnormal rather than on that between morally right or wrong.[19]

Although Foucault by and large seems to share and reproduce the assumption of the modern state as secular, he does have an original view on secularization, which—Foucault being Foucault—is virtually the opposite of the more familiar secularization thesis that the social power of religious institutions like the church has diminished and that religion has increasingly been restricted to the private sphere in the process of modernization. He analyzes the rise of the modern disciplinary society after 1800 not in terms of the progressive separation of church and state or the withdrawal or banishment of religion to the private sphere, but as involving the spread and multiplication of disciplinary forms of power that had hitherto been confined to religious institutions like the church and the monastery, across the social body as a whole; or, put differently, as involving the etatization of religious modes of power.[20] For the most part, however, Foucault appears to be concerned less with religious practices in their own right than with their effects in society at large.

The notion of the religious origins of (secular) modernity is even more explicit in Foucault's notion of "pastoral power," which is a form of power exercised over a flock or group of people rather than a territory and aims at its salvation or well-being; according to Foucault, the modern (Western) state involves a unique blend of sovereign power and a new form of pastoral power no longer exercised by church-related institutions and aiming at the population's well-being in this world rather than the hereafter.[21] Thus, religion plays an important, if undertheorized, aspect of Foucault's explorations. Except for a few short articles on Zen Buddhism and the 1979 Islamic revolution in Iran, he nowhere addresses the phenomenon of religion in the modern world and appears to tacitly assume that modernity does involve *some* form of secularization.[22]

In short, philosophers who call our attention to practice rarely zoom in on religion (the following section highlights the major thinkers who do discuss religion rarely have a systematic focus on practice). This also holds for two of the most influential contemporary thinkers, Charles Taylor and Jürgen Habermas, who have tried to come to grips with the presence of religion in contemporary society.

Empirical Applications: Ritual, Gender, Affect

A greater emphasis on practice has clearly led to important shifts in theoretical and philosophical discussions of religion, although obviously nothing like a theoretical or methodological consensus has emerged. In the empirical study of religion, too, the practice turn has led to major innovations. The following looks at three areas where a focus on practices has led to significant changes.

First, the practice turn has led to a reappraisal of religious ritual. Although a crucial aspect of most if not all religious traditions, ritual—in the sense of a fixed sequence of stylized actions—is not in itself a religious category, witness Erving Goffman's famous studies of interaction rituals; instead, one may fruitfully focus on the contested boundary between the religious and the nonreligious in ritual.[23] As noted above, ritual has long been seen as not belonging to "real" religion, due in part to a pronounced anti-ritualistic strain in Northern European and Anglo-Saxon Protestantism, which characterized the essence of religion in terms of an inner mental state of faith rather than in outward behavior. As a result, early social scientists such as Durkheim, Marcel Mauss, and Arnold van Gennep generally associated ritual with non-Western or "primitive" forms of religion.

Many, though not all, rituals mark a passage or transition, for example, between life and death, as in rituals surrounding birth and ritual, or between childhood and adulthood, as in rites of initiation or marriage. Famously, Van Gennep has argued that such rites of passage generally have a clear sequential structure, involving, first, the separation of the individual from their social surroundings (for example, by their physical seclusion or by a visible purification of the body); second, the liminal stage, in which the individual's body or soul is transformed; and third, the individual's reincorporation into society with a new social status. Equally famously, Victor Turner has zoomed in on the notion of liminality.[24] In *The Ritual Process*, he emphasizes that liminal persons and entities are ambiguous and indeterminate and "between the positions assigned and arrayed by law, custom, convention, and ceremonial."[25] Hence, against Durkheim's idea that in ritual, a given social order or structure legitimizes and reaffirms itself, Turner argues that in the liminality of ritual, a more spontaneous, immediate, and concrete form of *communitas*, or anti-structure, is created which is not institutionalized or shaped by existing norms. Rather, in the liminal space between ordered structures, alternative social arrangements may be imagined and generated. Liminal social action, he emphasizes, cannot be characterized as the execution of an antecedently given program or script; thus, despite his emphasis on the role of the symbols, metaphors, and paradigms in actors' heads, Turner marks a practice turn of sorts against structural-functional approaches to ritual, still dominant in his time, that emphasize actor-transcendent structure and social integration.[26]

Turner and others paved the way for a more substantial practice turn in the study of ritual and hence for a reappraisal of the importance of ritual in religious studies. Thus, the late twentieth century marked the rise of the new interdisciplinary field of *ritual studies*, pioneered by Ronald Grimes and Catherine Bell.[27] Bell rejects both the bifurcation of thought and action implicit in earlier theoretical discourse about ritual and the tacit assumption of ritual action as essentially expressive, noninstrumental, and irrational. Instead, she analyzes "acting ritually" as a particular cultural *strategy*. Ritual, she argues, should not simply be approached as a mechanism of social control: it is a strategic arena for the embodiment of power relations. Ritualization is a strategy for the construction of rather than an instrument for the reproduction of particular power relations that may or may not be effective. Thus, she develops a practice approach to ritual that studies rituals in their real context rather than as an a priori category of action. In doing so, she not only traces the genealogy of ritual as a theoretical construct but also uncovers some of the hidden practices that may generate a body of theoretical knowledge. Thus, she shows how practice approaches also involve an increasing critical methodological self-awareness.

A second aspect of the study of religion that has benefited from a practice turn is that of gender and sexuality. A major insight of recent practice-theoretical approaches has been that gender and sexuality are neither biologically given nor simply part of an individual's inner subjectivity or identity.[28] Rather, they are constituted in part by changing forms of knowledge and social norms; moreover, they are performatively enacted, and as such, they are public—even political—as much as they are private. Famously, Michel Foucault has argued that sexuality as a biological or medical category is of a relatively recent origin. The rise of the modern science of sexuality, he argues, marks a shift away from sexual practices as a source of moral, and hence religious, concern to sexuality as a normal or pathological condition of the individual. Equally famously, Foucault has noted the connections between sexuality and religion, especially through his already mentioned notion of "pastoral power," which he sees as embodied in the institutionalized and ritualized practice of confession in the medieval Catholic Church, in which the truth about the individual's sexuality is produced with an eye to their salvation in the hereafter. Thus, Foucault has explored entirely novel ways of studying the relation between religion, sexuality, and power. Hitherto, various authors of a secularist bent had dismissed all religious traditions as essentially patriarchal and as repressive of women and of deviant forms of sexual behavior; others had created an orientalist opposition between the alleged oppressiveness of Western monotheistic religions and Eastern traditions seen as essentially permissive, such as Hinduism and (Tantric) Buddhism. The detailed study of practices of sexuality and the different forms of power implied in them, which has emerged in the wake of Foucault's early writings, has greatly nuanced such sweeping characterizations; most importantly, it has emerged that practices of and attitudes to sexuality in all religious traditions have changed dramatically over the centuries, and especially in the modern period. Various authors have argued that the rise of the modern nation-state and colonial domination have led to major changes in gendered subjectivity and, by extension, to traditional religiously sanctioned forms of sexual morality. As is well known, the nineteenth century saw the rise of modern states with a centralized bureaucracy and newly governmentalized responsibilities for the health, education, and well-being of the population; the twentieth century witnessed the worldwide creation of nation-states. These were based in theory if not always in practice on popular sovereignty and on constitutions, which defined and codified the individual and collective rights of their citizens—and in the same gesture, constituted them as rights-bearing individuals or subjects of law. But not only the citizens' subjectivity was redefined against the background of the modern secular nation-state; their religious and gendered identities, too, were rearticulated. Thus, concomitant with the rise of the nation-state, we may witness a dramatic—and to all practical purposes virtually universal—change in gendered subjectivity and new regimentations of sexuality in naturalistic medical terms of normality and perversion rather than traditional religious vocabulary of sin or taboo.[29]

Third, the study of religion has also benefited from practice approaches to the emotions, such as affect theory, as developed by Sarah Ahmed and others. For centuries, Western philosophers have thought of the emotions, or passions, as belonging to an inferior faculty of the soul, which should be governed by a higher faculty of reason. Moreover, thinkers from Plato to Spinoza not only distinguish between "good" and "bad" emotions but also characterize some as typically feminine and others as typically masculine. This already indicates that thinking about emotions is intimately linked to questions of gender, and hence of power and domination. Emotions have long been treated as inner psychological states, and more specifically as intentional states, directed to a particular object: love is generally love *for* somebody, fear is generally fear *of* something. As a result, the interiority and intentionality of emotions—and with it the distinctions between inner and outer and between subject and object—have long been assumed as given. In recent decades, however, social scientists have moved away from these assumptions and analyzed emotions primarily in terms of social practices. In doing so, they do not simply revert the relation between the mental and the social; rather, they explore how emotions help to create the very boundaries between inner and outer and between *I*, *we*, and *they*. This suggests that emotions may, at least in part, be the performative effects of the very naming of those emotions.[30] Thus, the emotion of disgust in part results from *describing* something or someone as disgusting, and such labels have to be made to stick to particular objects. Such emotions are often characterized in terms of the psychoanalytical notion of abjection, especially as it was developed by Julia Kristeva.[31] According to Kristeva, who frames her discussion of abjection in terms of Lacanian psychoanalysis, the abject falls outside the symbolic order of language and norms; hence, the experience of the abject is inherently traumatic for the superego as the representative of that order. In the study of religion, this perspective is particularly fruitful in the study of marginalized groups, such as women, homosexuals, and religious minorities or heterodox groups which may be represented as in a state of abjection. Thus, emotions of affect and disgust play an important role in religious perspectives on homosexuality; they also appear in the context of blasphemy, which in recent years has gained a worldwide new attention in the light of, among others, the Danish "cartoon affair" concerning allegedly sacrilegious or blasphemous drawings of the prophet Muhammad and of several incidents on the Indian subcontinent. Some of the following essays address the practical construal of religious emotions in different blasphemy cases.

Historical Dimensions: The Secularization Thesis

One of the questions that have most vexed philosophers and social scientists alike is that of the changing status of religion in the modern world. For a long time, the belief that modernity would inevitably lead to a decline in religiosity held sway; this famous "secularization thesis" was first formulated by Émile Durkheim and Max Weber. The thesis is surrounded by confusion, however, much of which arises from a tacit blurring of the distinctions between the descriptive concept of the secular (as opposed to the sacred or the religious), the normative doctrine of secularism, and the historical thesis of secularization: as often as not, the identification of modernization and secularization betrays a normative *parti-pris*, if not polemical stance, rather than a purely descriptive position. Moreover, various authors have either implicitly assumed or explicitly claimed that modernization-as-secularization is a uniquely Western phenomenon, likened to a normative and ethnocentric view that the non-Western world is not fully or unproblematically "modern" and hence has not successfully secularized.

Even if we confine ourselves to its descriptive dimensions, we must explicate exactly what we mean by the secularization thesis. Thus, José Casanova has argued that we should distinguish three phenomena that have often been conflated in generic claims about secularization, and that we should evaluate each of them separately for a more balanced assessment of the secularization thesis.[32] Secularization may be seen as involving, first, a decrease in church attendance, which was especially visible in post–World War II Western Europe. This claim is only partially correct, Casanova argues: in its emphasis on traditional institutions like established churches, it risks overlooking the rise of new evangelical movements in the West, and the growth of movements such as Pentecostalism and Salafi Islam elsewhere in the world. Second, secularization may be said to involve the functional differentiation of distinct spheres of social action such as politics, law, and religion. According to Casanova, this variant of the secularization is no more plausible than its first guise: it implies that any reappearance or rearticulation of religion in, say, the political sphere is, strictly speaking, anomalous. Third, secularization may be said to involve the privatization of religious faith and the decreasing role of religion in society. It is only in the third sense, Casanova argues, that the secularization thesis can be maintained; accordingly, he speaks of the twentieth-century religious revivals and reassertions as involving a *deprivatization* of religion. As a worldwide catchphrase, however, even this term may be problematic: how can we speak of deprivatization in areas where there was no prior secularization-as-privatization in the first place? Thus, Casanova admits that Confucianism and Taoism have hardly witnessed anything that can be called secularization in the strict sense, as they know neither a conceptual distinction of religion as against the world and the worldly nor any strict ecclesiastical organization.[33] On the other hand, such differences should perhaps not be overstated. For example, the thesis that only Christianity knows an ecclesiastical organization or institutionalized church in the strict sense of the word should not blind us to the fact that various other religious traditions have had, or developed, broadly similar corporate bodies of specialists in religious learning. In the case of the Islamic world, or more specifically the Ottoman Empire, secularization boiled down to the replacement, or redefinition, of the religious law, or shariah, in a codified and more strictly state-implemented juridical system, or, in the words of Sami Zubaida, the etatization of law. The institution of the state itself, however, was undergoing an equally radical transformation both in the Ottoman Empire and elsewhere—what Foucault has called a *governmentalization of the state*: not so much the shift of legal from one unitary institution to another but the transformation of the tasks and technologies of government associated with the composite reality we usually label "the state" and of the forms of knowledge instrumentalized in governing.[34]

In China, modernist and later communist activists agitated against the Confucian heritage, which, although perhaps not a religion in the modern and strict sense of the word, did know institutionalized forms of hierarchy and doctrinal authority that may be broadly compared to the Catholic Church in the Christian world, especially through the famous exam system. Likewise, in the nineteenth century, a secular Zionism arose that reacted against the entrenched and institutionalized religion of rabbinic Judaism and its premodern traditions of learning.[35] Even if no tradition witnessed a secularization in precisely the sense that is claimed for the Western (or even the Western European) Christian world, we may witness similar movements against traditional or premodern forms of learning and authority that had often been articulated and legitimized in religious terms. A practice approach to these questions may be valuable in turning our attention away from possibly superficial or misleading institutional differences, like the presence or absence of a formal church, to questions of how doctrinal and ritual authority may be claimed, contested, or redefined in the transition from premodern to modern practices of religious learning. Thus, one may argue with good reason that although traditions such as Buddhism, Hinduism, and Confucianism *are* no religions (in involving no concept of a creator and no clergy or church), they have *become* religions in the nineteenth century, in that they were redefined in terms of similarities and differences with Christianity; subsequently, they may be said to display broadly comparable patterns of secularization, in the sense of a decrease of religious authority in the early twentieth century and a subsequent desecularization, or deprivatization, of religion in the later twentieth and early twenty-first century. I will return to this point below.

It is unclear how these various non-Western experiences affect the argument of one of the most influential contemporary authors writing on secularization, Charles Taylor, who explicitly limits his discussion to the modern Western Christian experience. In his voluminous *A Secular Age*, some of the central theses of which appeared in a preliminary form in an earlier volume of this series, Taylor explores the topic of modernity-as-secularity, self-consciously restricting himself to the Western, or as he calls it North Atlantic, experience, while arguing that the issues he is discussing, although dealt with "within a regional compass," are of a universal human concern.[36] In the Middle Ages, he argues, it was virtually impossible *not* to be a believer; but by the twentieth century, religious belief or faith had largely lost this self-evident status. How and why, then, did religious faith turn from an inevitable and self-evident mode of being into something optional? Taylor is not satisfied with the familiar accounts concerning the rise of modern natural science or the rationalization of society: after all, he notes, early modern science was not even claimed by its protagonists to be anti-religious in its main tenets. In his view, it was not until the late nineteenth century that modern natural science (in particular in the wake of Darwin's evolutionary theory) was consciously and polemically pitted against religion. Moreover, he sees modernity as characterized by what he calls the "affirmation of ordinary life," that is, by the value newly attached to everyday practical concerns (e.g., those of making a living or creating and maintaining a family) as opposed both to a purely passive life of contemplation or *theôria* and to the active life of the classical citizen.[37] Under such conditions, he argues, religious morality is *experienced* in a wholly new way. Thus, Taylor formulates his analysis neither in terms of changing beliefs (for example, the decline of religious faith and the rise of a scientific worldview inspired by the natural and social sciences) nor in terms of changing institutions (such as a decline in the societal and/or political power of churches) but rather in terms of changing *conditions* of religious belief and experience. In line with this, he characterizes religious faith not as a set of beliefs but as a lived condition.

This shift away from belief to the conditions of belief is certainly refreshing. Oddly, however, Taylor here appears to fail to live up to the practice turn in the study of religion that he himself had recommended earlier. Thus, in his 2003 *Varieties of Religion Today*, Taylor already formulates a Wittgensteinian argument against William James's characterization of religion as involving primarily an individual, inner experience.[38] Against the latter's line of reasoning, he argues that all individual experience, whether religious or not, requires a vocabulary and hence presupposes the possession and use of a language. Language use, however, he continues, is an irreducibly public normative practice rather than a purely causal inner mental state or event; hence, even such allegedly irreducible inner states as religious experience, faith or belief should be characterized in terms of public linguistic practices.

In itself, this line of reasoning is not new: in his "Interpretation and the Sciences of Man," Taylor had already argued along similar lines for the conceptual priority of a linguistic, cultural, or moral community; but here, the question becomes how this communitarian claim applies to the study of religious experience. At the very least, it appears to cast doubt on the assumption of religious experience as irreducible, which informs many phenomenological approaches to religion. It is also unclear exactly what are the practical implications of this linguistic and practical turn concerning religious experience for the argument of *A Secular Age*. The latter is generally framed and phrased in terms of changing conditions of experience and faith rather than changing conditions of linguistic and embodied religious practice. In short, a practice turn has complex implications for the once uncontroversial secularization thesis; the contributions in this book reveal many such complexities.

Religion between Empire, Nation-State, and Globalization

A focus on practices also invites us to rethink other received views on the historical development of religion, especially in the modern and contemporary periods. As has already emerged from the preceding discussion, in practice approaches, the microlevel phenomena of practices—or of "real people doing real things," as Sherry Ortner famously characterized them[39]—interact in complex ways with macrolevel factors without necessarily reducing either to the other. In this, they differ from, among others, phenomenological approaches, which take individual and inner experience as a basic explanatory notion, and Marxist approaches, which generally attempt to explain such individual and ideological phenomena in terms of macro factors of the political economy. Here, I will briefly discuss the interaction of three such macro factors with changing religious practices: the rise of the nation-state, colonialism, and globalization.

The modern nation-state is often seen as by definition secular, and with good reason: many nineteenth-century national movements defined themselves in explicit opposition to religious forces or authorities, which tended to be socially dominant in premodern empires and were seen by many nationalist activists as obstacles to national self-identification. In various other cases, however, it was precisely religious groups or movements that provided organizational networks or successfully claimed to represent, embody, or protect the national identity or national soul. Hence, it has been argued that modern nationalism involves a more complex rearticulation of the religious than earlier secularist and modernization-theoretical accounts such as Gellner's and Anderson's had suggested.[40] Earlier, nationalism had been characterized as a "civic religion," and the nation has often enough been conceived of as itself possessing a sacral character; but modern nationalism probably involves not only a relocation but also a more radical redefinition of the sacred. Thus, Talal Asad argues that by the secularization of the state, religion was conversely liberated from the confines of worldly power; thus, the creation of the modern nation-state involved not only the rise of newly governmentalized forms of power, but also a "redefinition of the essence of 'religion' as well as of 'national politics.'"[41] In other words, modernity, in the guise of the nation-state, has not so much marginalized as redefined religion. Not only did the modern nation-state that emerged in the nineteenth century take over various tasks and responsibilities that for long had been associated with the church or with similar religious institutions—such as education, health care, and welfare—its rise also implied a redefinition of religion itself. It may be difficult to account for these dimensions within conceptual and normative frameworks that a priori assume the spheres of religion and politics as given, stable, or essentially distinct from each other.

One important aspect of the rise of the modern nation-state is the complex interaction between religion and language. Virtually all over the world, the institutional environment of religion has changed dramatically. In the world of Western Christianity, the traditional churches have become increasingly marginalized, and new religious movements have gained in importance. In the Islamic world, medrese education was either completely replaced or at least marginalized by state-based institutions of modern education. In India, the classical Sanskrit tradition disappeared equally dramatically as a dominant form of learning, leading one scholar to speak, with some slight overstatement, of the "death of Sanskrit" as a language of literature and learning;[42] and in the nineteenth century, Persian was equally replaced as a language of learning for the Indian elites by English and the European classical languages, Greek and Latin, and, perhaps even more importantly, by Urdu, which was increasingly used in newly printed texts. These new literate practices as well as the new contact with assertively proselytizing forms of Christianity may even have led to major doctrinal reformulations in Hinduism, which acquired a more pronouncedly monotheistic character during this period.

In many traditions, religious authority was articulated in terms of long-standing institutions and practices of religious learning, which typically involved sacred classical languages such as Latin, Koinè Greek, Church Slavonic, Hebrew, Arabic, Sanskrit, or classical Chinese. Over the centuries, these sacred languages had become more and more isolated from the locally spoken language varieties. The early modern and modern periods witnessed clear shifts away from these classical or sacred languages to the spoken vernaculars as means of education and learning, whether religious or other. These shifts, which occurred in various places during the eighteenth and nineteenth centuries, anticipated the rise of modern nationalism and the nation-state, which defines people or nations precisely in terms of such spoken vernaculars. In the wake of this shift in religious language and authority, one may witness a gradual replacement, or ousting, of traditions of religious learning by new state-sponsored institutions of education.

Thus, the nineteenth-century shift in religious practices is both linguistic and institutional in kind: the modern nation-state's population consists not only of a sovereign people in the political sense but also of a laity in the religious sense. The rearticulation of language both religious and secular, and the concomitant redefinition of religious authority, was accompanied by the rise of the laity, as opposed to the traditional learned elites, as subjects of religious discourse and practice. One main reason for this rise was the great and virtually worldwide increase in possibilities for education and increasing literacy rates and the concomitant growth of the reading public in the later nineteenth and early twentieth centuries. In other words, the newly available technology of printing not only led to new imaginings of national communities, as has famously been argued by Benedict Anderson, but also made possible new *religious* imaginaries.[43] Moreover, the evidence suggests that, *pace* Anderson, it is not simply the availability of such new technologies or the appearance of new institutions such as schools that leads to changes in consciousness or imaginary; rather, the practical *uses* made of such technologies and institutions are what mark the real change. One may therefore argue that modern conceptions of religion not only involve the modern concept and institution of the nation-state but also particularly modern conceptions of the self. Taylor has noted as much but has confined his discussions to the modern Western, or Western Christian, experience.[44]

In short, changing practices of religion, language, knowledge, and government brought along major institutional and even doctrinal changes in virtually all religious traditions. Religious authority was redefined and renegotiated; creeds and catechisms were written in vernacular languages, and became accessible to much larger audiences than the sacred classical languages had ever been; and through the new technology of printing, they gained even wider circulation.

More recently, it has been argued that studies of nationalism and the rise of the nation-state should not ignore or downplay the crucial and in many ways destructive impact of colonialism. Thus, Partha Chatterjee has raised objections against often tacit world-historical assumptions about modernization that inform much writing about nationalism, arguing that the colonial state has a distinct and distinctly violent character and marks a radical rupture with the precolonial past.[45] Although colonial relations were perhaps more variable than Chatterjee appears to allow for, the question of an increasing Western domination clearly becomes central in the course of the nineteenth century, especially also for the rise of the notion of "world religions."

As noted above, the nineteenth century, especially its second half, has long been seen as marking a steady decline of religion in favor of more secular and scientific worldviews. More recently, however, it has been argued that this period in fact witnessed a dramatic and worldwide religious *expansion*; most immediately visible from a European perspective, Christian missionaries associated with various churches, and often supported or protected by some form of colonial rule, spread all over the non-Western world; this missionary activity increased significantly after 1860.[46] In various places, this newly pervasive and self-confident presence of Christian missionaries led to redefinitions or reassertions of Buddhist, Confucianist, Islamic, and Hindu doctrine; but these developments cannot be explained as simply a reaction against early Christian missionary activity. An increase in Islamic proselytizing—often led by Sufi orders or tarîqas but also by anti-Sufi movements such as, most famously and influentially, the Wahhâbî movement—had actually preceded the spread of Christian colonial and missionary influence and had already led to a dramatic expansion of Islam in Sub-Saharan Africa, Central Asia, and Southeast Asia immediately prior to the nineteenth century. Likewise, in the Indian subcontinent, a newly essentialized Hinduism was also becoming a more actively proselytizing religion and was in particular trying to win back lower-caste converts to Islam. In China, Kang Youwei propagated the redefinition of Confucianism (as noted, a novel category in itself) as the religious essence of the Chinese people. In Japan, from the 1870s onward, Shintoism was redefined as the state religion, involving, in particular, a novel cult of the emperor. Combined, the rearticulation of religious authority, and the reformulation of religious doctrine led to more uniform and regimented religious traditions which, paradoxically, precisely in stating their mutual doctrinal differences more clearly and explicitly than ever before, became more alike as rivals in a common and commensurable field or arena characterized as religious. Outright atheism remained an elite phenomenon during this period, both in Europe and elsewhere. This was to change in the twentieth century, most importantly with the rise to political prominence of radically anti-religious forms of Marxism (and to a lesser extent, modernist nationalism); but even here one may ask to what extent repressive state policies had any enduring effects, witness the rapid spread of various religious movements following the collapse of the Soviet-led Eastern Bloc in 1989.

The category of world religions was distinguished in an evolutionary manner from "primitive" forms of religion such as magic and animism, based on literate traditions, possessing "holy books" of some sort, and universal in their aspirations. Tomoko Masuzawa has even argued that the very notion of world religions was shaped by Western secular modernity and tacitly reproduces a sense of Western and Christian superiority in the language of pluralism.[47] These analyses have met with substantial criticisms; but whether Masuzawa's thesis is correct in general need not concern us here. The most relevant point in the present context is that world religions were defined as faiths rather than practices. Arguably, then, modern conceptions of religion, including the category of world religions—formulated in terms of doctrine, faith, or inner experience—have not only tended to downplay the practical aspects of religion but may in fact have their roots in the ultimately Protestant rejection of public and ritualized practice as not belonging to the essence of religion, or, more polemically, as examples of idolatry rather than genuine religiosity. Thus, the distinction between faith and ritual not only has a specifically modern Western background, it also presupposes conceptual oppositions such as those between public and private or between state and civil society which are Western and, more specifically, liberal and secular in origin.

This brings us to the religious aspects and implications of contemporary globalization. It has often been observed that the collapse of the Soviet Bloc and the concomitant delegitimation of Marxism-Leninism as a challenge to world capitalism, more than anything else, has opened up the prospect of a unified world market, characterized by the deregulation of national economies and of international financial transactions. Initially, this led to (over-)enthusiastic claims about the "end of history" and of globalization as a bringing worldwide affluence in a process that was presented as both actorless and inescapable. Not only did many observers predict an end to poverty but also a deterritorialization of cultural flows and the demise of the nation-state, and with them, the demise of any kind of identity politics. Yet, in fact, and with the benefit of two decades of hindsight, globalization appears to have had rather more complex, if not contradictory consequences. Here, only the religious consequences can be addressed.

An early aspect of globalization is a novel appreciation of "oriental," or more generally non-Western, religions in some circles in Western Europe and America. This process started already in the late nineteenth century, as evident by the fin de siècle popularity of what came to be called "oriental wisdom" and of the theosophical movement, which discursively pitched an essentialized spiritual East against a Western world construed as materialistic in both the economic and the metaphysical sense. In the twentieth century, and especially after World War II, Eastern philosophies and religions gained even more popularity, as seen, perhaps most spectacularly, by the rise of Zen Buddhism in America from the 1950s onward as well as the increasing popularity of new religious movements such as the Bhagwan or Rajneesh movement, transcendental meditation, and Western forms of Sufism.

One striking feature of the globalization of information is the fact that religious challenges and conflicts may travel across the globe very quickly and that people may be quickly mobilized across political, linguistic, and religious boundaries. A first indication of this was the so-called Rushdie Affair, which started when protests against Rushdie's novel *The Satanic Verses* erupted in South Africa in late 1988, then spread to India and Pakistan, and notoriously culminated in the death sentence pronounced against Rushdie by Ayatollah Khomeini in February 1989. More recently, the Danish cartoon affair quickly acquired international dimensions when a local Muslim cleric, after failing to secure an audience for his protests against a series of cartoons about the Prophet, Muhammad, in the Danish daily *Jyllands Posten*, took his case abroad; soon, states such as Syria and Iran became involved in the affair and severe unrest broke out in several cities in the Islamic world. Likewise, in early 2014, Penguin Books announced it would pulp the Indian edition of Wendy Doniger's *The Hindus: An Alternative History* (2010) in the face of pressure from Hindu nationalist lobby groups, which had been mobilizing protests against Doniger's work in India, Europe, and the United States. And governments on the African continent have been encouraged and supported by American evangelical groups to adapt tougher laws against homosexuality.

What are we to make of these globalizations of religious conflict? What are the peculiar consequences of globalization for religion? Several rather different answers have been given. A first group of scholars, which was especially influential in the years immediately following the collapse of the Soviet Bloc, emphasized the hybridizing and creolizing effects of globalization. Authors such as Arjun Appadurai, Ulf Hannerz, Homi Bhabha, and others argued—somewhat overoptimistically, seen with the benefit of hindsight—that all fixed national and local identities, and, by implication, religious identities as well, were in the process of becoming thoroughly problematized and delegitimized. Famously, Appadurai, writing in 1996, argued that the nation-state was in crisis and was apparently becoming increasingly obsolete; in its place, a "postnational" constellation was gradually emerging.[48] Appadurai hardly addressed religious, as distinct from national, identities; but his rejection of the teleological assumptions of modernization theory might also imply a rejection of the modernization-theoretical and teleological assumptions of the secularization thesis. Arguing along Appadurai's lines, one might claim that, corresponding to the cultural hybridization it brings along, globalization may also lead to the emergence of new forms of religious syncretism. Would an extension of Appadurai's claims imply that global modernity undermines religious identities as much as national ones? Subsequent developments do not immediately seem to confirm such bold claims: the nation-state and nationalism did not seem to be appreciably weaker in 2014 than they were in 1994; and religious identities appear to have strengthened rather than weakened or become more hybridized or syncretistic.

Hence, another group of scholars argued that globalization, far from weakening or dissolving older identities, has actually led to the strengthening or reassertion of identity politics. In the field of religious studies, the most sophisticated of these voices is perhaps Olivier Roy. In the early 1990s, Roy had become famous with his analysis of what he called the "failure of political Islam," as the revolutionary attempt to Islamize the state, as opposed to the neo-fundamentalist drive to Islamize society, and of the rise of new, globalized, and deculturalized forms of Islam. More recently, he has argued that globalization has led to a more general deterritorialization and deculturation of religion, without this necessarily implying new forms of hybridity or syncretism. Using as evidence the contemporary phenomenon of conversion—for example of young European Muslims to Salafism and of Westerners of Christian backgrounds to Buddhism or shamanism, not to mention the mass conversions to Protestant Evangelicalism and Pentecostalism in places as far apart as Africa and Brazil—Roy argues that globalization has led to a fundamentalist religious reassertion rather than to either secularization or syncretism. Such conversions, he holds, are a key for understanding the severing of the traditional links between religion and culture that results from processes of globalization. With the emergence of a globalized religious market, Roy claims, different religions are reformatted along increasingly similar lines, leading to a convergence of forms of religiosity (involving an increasingly individualized spiritual quest and individual self-improvement); as a result, religions are redefined as purely normative systems abstracted away from any specific doctrinal or cultural content. In fact, he claims, religious fundamentalism (whether or not militant and politicized) is the religious form most suited to globalization precisely "because it accepts its own deculturation and makes it the instrument of its claim to universality."[49] Thus, on his analysis, the globalized present is characterized by deculturation and deterritorialization and marks not so much the revival as the transformation of religion. One may ask, however, if Roy does not overstate the case for the emergence of an "identity communitarianism, based on religion rather than ethnicity or culture."[50] After all, globalization has been claimed to reinforce both religious and secular (especially nationalist) forms of identity politics; and the nation-state, far from having been durably undermined by globalization, appears to be not only one of its main initiators but also one of its main beneficiaries. Hence, other scholars have argued that globalization is in fact marked by a rearticulation and reaffirmation rather than by the weakening or delegitimation of identities, whether national, local, sexual, or religious.

In conclusion, one may state that from the nineteenth century onward, we can see a worldwide increase and indeed interlocking process of not only the steady expansion of religious practices but also of their redefinition *as* religions, or even as world religions, that are commensurable in their differences as sets of doctrines with an essentially moral, cosmological, and eschatological content. The comparable, if not converging, experiences of these different parts of the world provide just one more reason for not overemphasizing the role of institutions such as the church and the state and instead to look for increasingly common and converging practices and powers. It remains to be seen how recent developments usually headed under the rubric of globalization will affect religions across the world; but the contributions to this volume will show that approaching these phenomena in terms of practices rather than doctrines, institutions, or experiences, has much to offer.

Normative Implications:
Liberalism, Communitarianism, and Genealogy

The public appearance of religious convictions, claims, and practices raises several normative questions, many of which center on the notion of secularism, that is, the view that religion has no legitimate place in public life or at least should be subordinated to strict state control. Needless to say, secularism can, and does, take various forms in different liberal democracies. The constitution of the United States is staunchly secular; but it is at present virtually impossible, not to say unthinkable, for an openly atheist American to become president. In France, by contrast, and in Turkey until the rise of the Islamist AKP government in 2002, a very different form of secularism or *laicité* (Turkish: *laiklik*), held sway that implies the strict subordination of all religion to the state and the banishment of visible religious symbols—such as Christian crosses worn on neck chains, Jewish kippas, and Islamic headscarves—from schools and other public institutions. Germany and the Netherlands, again, are secular states; but they allow for the public and political organization of religion, in particular in the form of so-called Christian Democrat parties, which subordinate their religious morality to the rules of the game of pluralistic party politics.

In recent years, normative political doctrines of secularism have come to be hotly debated. Broadly, one can distinguish three dominant positions in such academic debates, which for the sake of convenience may be labeled liberal, communitarian, and genealogical. The following sections briefly discuss a few of the most influential representatives of each.

Liberalism and (Post-)Secularism: Rawls and Habermas

The first and perhaps the most influential position is the liberal one. For the sake of convenience, discussion here is limited to the positions of John Rawls and Jürgen Habermas. Ever since Kant turned against the societal power of the church in his famous essay "What Is Enlightenment?," liberal authors have tended to be anticlerical to some degree. In the second half of the twentieth century, much liberal political theory was almost secularist by default, assuming not only that contemporary Western societies had effectively been secularized with the churches' steady loss of membership and influence but also that the social marginalization of religion was a good thing. In liberal ethical and political theorizing, churches and other institutions were widely seen, at best, as channels of private convictions that had no legitimate place in public debate and, at worst, as a detriment to individual liberty and autonomy. Arguably, a similar secularism-by-default also informs Rawls's *A Theory of Justice* (1971), which does not address religion in detail, let alone religious challenges to liberal-secular values. In this early work, Rawls assumes a liberal society to have a broad consensus over basic moral values; but in his later *Political Liberalism* (1993), he attempts to come to grips with the fact that in modern democratic societies, a plurality of irreconcilable religious, moral, and philosophical doctrines do and must coexist.[51] Whereas in his earlier work, he had assumed a broad societal consensus concerning basic moral values, he now comes to emphasize the presence of mutually irreconcilable worldviews or, as he calls them, "comprehensive doctrines," such as (different forms of) Christianity, Islam, and atheism; as different as they are, however, these doctrines display an "overlapping consensus" that provides the basis for a purely political and purely procedural form of justice.

Rawls emphasizes that his own liberal position, and in particular the doctrine of justice he develops in the latter work, is procedural rather than metaphysical in nature and that this "political liberalism" is not itself a comprehensive doctrine. This becomes particularly clear in his discussion of what he calls "well-ordered societies," which are not liberal but nonetheless rationally defensible. On his account, well-ordered societies are assumed to consist of free, equal, and above all rational citizens displaying an overlapping consensus of reasonable doctrines; but what if a particular comprehensive doctrine claims to be divinely revealed and nonnegotiable and explicitly denies that all humans are free, equal, or rational?

Much like Rawls, the German philosopher Jürgen Habermas, whose views are applied or discussed in several of the essays in this book, has turned his attention to religious matters in political philosophy around the turn of the century. Whereas his earlier work had been secularist by default, in a 2001 lecture, he introduced the notion of a "postsecular" society as involving the "persistence of religious groups in a secularized environment." In a later work, published in 2008, he characterizes the postsecular society in terms of a change in *consciousness*, in particular the loss of the certainty, hitherto allegedly prevalent among secularized populations, that religion is a thing of the past and will in time disappear completely as a societal force to be reckoned with. Despite his repeated talk of practices of justifying religious claims with secular arguments and of mutual "learning processes," Habermas thus appears to fall back on a philosophy of consciousness of the kind he himself had rejected as inadequate in his earlier work and had attempted to replace by a linguistic philosophy.[52]

Habermas proceeds from a firm and continued belief in a version of the secularization thesis and from a normative standpoint that in many respects remains roundly secularist. He is aware, of course, of the numerous objections that have been raised against the thesis; but despite the well-known criticisms of the thesis, even as restricted to Western Europe, he calls the evidence for it "remarkably robust" and continues to view the European *Sonderweg* as a conceptual if not normative standard. Habermas defines secularization as a societal process of "functional differentiation," that is, as the progressive (and in principle irreversible) separation and becoming autonomous of distinct spheres or subsystems, such as law, politics, education, and welfare. He sees the individualization and interiorization of religious practice as natural correlates of this functional specification of the religious subsystem. Incidentally, similar forms of interiorization may also be witnessed in other traditions. Thus, Batnitzky emphasizes that Judaism has historically been conceived of as a religion of law, and hence of practice; as a result, concerns were generally more with the public adherence to this law than with inner faith or belief; much the same may be said of premodern Islam. Both traditions saw significant changes in these respects in the nineteenth and twentieth centuries.

Habermas's analysis of secularization in terms of the functional differentiation of societal spheres, however, is shaped by an implicit teleological and normative assumption that each such sphere has a "proper function" (*genuine Funktion*) or "core function" (*Kernfunktion*), or put differently, that religion is a societal sphere with a distinct essence. Such assumptions, however, almost automatically turn the deprivatization of religion or desecularization—in which the spheres of the religious, the social, the moral, and the political are blended and rearticulated anew—into a conceptually and normatively anomalous as well as historically atavistic phenomenon.[53]

There are good reasons to think this analysis cannot be maintained even for the European case, let alone the rest of the world. Regarding the latter, Habermas rather too sweepingly characterizes, for example, the contemporary Islamic world as "traditional," that is, as not yet modernized and secularized, and hence by definition as not yet in a position to enter a postsecular phase. These claims fly in the face of virtually everything that is known about the nineteenth- and twentieth-century experience of the Islamic world; it completely overlooks, for example, the radical, and in many respects successful, secularization of the Ottoman Empire and the subsequent Republic of Turkey.[54] In short, for a practice approach to religion, the most immediately relevant points are, first, that Habermas—much like Taylor—repeatedly appears to relapse into a phenomenological or subjectivist vocabulary of belief, consciousness, and experience and, second, that his analysis in terms of spheres or subsystems almost a priori excludes any conflict over or contestation of the boundaries between these spheres as conceptually or normatively marginal, if not based on an outright category mistake. Thus, it remains to be seen how a more practice-oriented perspective would affect the normative argument Habermas is trying to make.

Finally, Habermas assumes a concept of reason that he sees as unproblematically and universally valid; thus, in "Faith and Knowledge," he argues that religious objections against, for example, abortion or genetic manipulation should not be based on scriptural authority but should first be reformulated as rationally defensible claims about the freedom and dignity of humans as rational and autonomous beings. Here, Habermas seems to make a similar argumentative move as Rawls: on this account, religious doctrines first have to be reformulated as, or translated into, the terms of rational political debate for them to have a valid place in public debate. On such an account, it seems, religious claims can never *as such* legitimately figure in public debate: for Habermas, they are admissible only insofar as they are reformulated as reasonable doctrines or can be translated into a language of rational debate.

Communitarianism and Religious Tradition: MacIntyre and Taylor

Both Rawls and Habermas assume a notion of public reason as neutral and as universally valid; but this notion in fact stems from the very particular tradition of the European Enlightenment, the universalization of which is highly problematic. Such, at least, is the general tenor of a converging line of philosophical criticism of liberal assumptions, especially as they appear in Rawls's work, that came to the fore in the 1980s. Collectively, these criticisms have come to be known as communitarianism.[55] The most directly relevant authors in the context of religion are Alisdair MacIntyre and Charles Taylor; hence, the discussion below is restricted to their varieties of communitarianism.

In several works, most importantly his 1981 study *After Virtue*, MacIntyre argues that the liberal assumption of the self as atomic and autonomous overlooks the central importance of tradition and communal life for the individual.[56] Modern liberal democracies, he argues, are marked by the coexistence of compatible, and indeed incommensurable, moral views. Particular moral claims may be rationally justified *within* each of these competing moral frameworks; but the frameworks themselves do not allow for any such rational justification. Thus, they seem to be arbitrary personal preferences. MacIntyre finds this emotivist or expressivist account of moral judgment unsatisfactory, however: he sees the impossibility of rationally choosing between frameworks as a major failure of the entire Enlightenment project of trying to justify morality. Against what he calls this emotivist view of the self and of morality, MacIntyre then places an Aristotelian view of morality, which distinguishes man as a natural being from man as a social being (*zôon politikon*); it is only within the community, he argues, that the human virtues are exercised. Moreover, he argues, the moral practices of any given community are historically specific: "I inherit from the past of my family, my city, my tribe, my nation, a variety of debts, inheritances, rightful expectation and obligations. These constitute the given of life, my moral starting-point. This in part is what gives my life its moral particularity."[57] In other words, one's individual moral outlook is crucially shaped by one's membership of a tradition; without the framework provided by tradition and community, there can be no morality as a rational enterprise.

A similar line of argument may be found in the writings of Charles Taylor. In his *Sources of the Self* (1989), Taylor argues that assumed moral frameworks are not optional and arbitrary choices or preferences but an inescapable way to find our bearings in life; as such, he claims, the self is in part constituted by its sense of the meaning or significance of the persons, objects, and situations one encounters. Human beings are selves only to the extent that they seek—and find—an orientation to the good, he continues; and to do so requires one's being embedded in a community. First, self-understanding requires a vocabulary, which only exists in a language community; second, one cannot be a self on one's own, but only in relation to interlocutors who are essential to the self's self-definition. Put differently, "one cannot be a self on one's own . . . a self only exists within what I call 'webs of interlocution.'"[58] On this account, Taylor's view that humans are self-interpreting animals entails the claim that the relation to one's community is constitutive of an individual's identity.[59] Thus, arguing along rather different lines, Taylor comes close to MacIntyre's claim that communities are essential for and constitutive of individual selves.

MacIntyre and Taylor appear to frame their arguments in terms of specifically *religious* communities and moral traditions. Thus, Taylor assimilates the moral to what he calls "the spiritual," that is, to "questions about what makes our lives meaningful, fulfilling . . . and worth living."[60] Obviously, until relatively recently, many if not most Europeans sought and found the answers to such moral-spiritual questions in religion. More importantly, both appear to assume traditions and communities as, in a sense, basic; thus, MacIntyre explicitly identifies communities as "the given of life." The constitution and reproduction of communities, however, are as historically variable and as power-saturated a process, or practice, as any. It remains unclear what implications acknowledging the conceptual and normative relevance of such power relations would have for the view of the self as communally constituted and of the community as, in essence, anonymous, actorless, and apolitical. On closer inspection, communitarians appear to make substantial assumptions about temporality, seeing moral traditions as essentially continuous and unchanging; and to presume a consensus-oriented view of communities as harmonious, and geared toward social integration. Neither of these assumptions is obviously true or even necessarily a priori plausible.

Another line of criticism, rooted less in conceptual considerations than in the empirical study of religious traditions outside the Western world, is that both MacIntyre and Taylor base their arguments on a specifically Western experience, with an emphasis on the traditions of Aristotelianism, Christianity, and the Enlightenment. It is not at all obvious, however, that these arguments can be generalized to, say, premodern and early modern India or China, where we not only find very different articulations of so-called tradition, culture, and community, but where, at least in premodern times, also the very vocabulary to speak of culture, religion, or tradition in communitarian terms is virtually absent. Moreover, when, in modern times, such a vocabulary was developed, this was typically done under conditions of increasing contact with colonizing Western powers, which constituted these local experiences as so-called religions or religious traditions in the first place.⁶¹ Thus, communitarians may face intriguing and nontrivial challenges from a non-Western and, more specifically, a postcolonial perspective.

Genealogy and Secular Reason: Foucault and Asad

A third normative position is the genealogical one, which calls attention to various forms of power at work in religious practices as well as in the creation and reproduction of religious communities. From this position, one may formulate a critique of the liberal assumption of individual liberty for overlooking the power relations that constitute the modern, rational, and autonomous self as well as of the communitarian assumption of a constitutive role for tradition and community, for overstating the continuity and coherence of traditions, and for representing the formation of communities to be an essentially harmonious apolitical or pre-political process. This form of genealogical critique originates, of course, with Friedrich Nietzsche. In particular in *Beyond Good and Evil* and *The Genealogy of Morals*, Nietzsche set out to unmask morality as a mere surface effect of an underlying will to power; more specifically, he attacked Christian morality as shaped by resentment. The secularist, anticlerical, and indeed anti-religious thrust of Nietzsche's criticisms is obvious: although he occasionally mentions Judaism and Buddhism and, to a lesser extent, Hinduism and Islam, it is clear that his main target is Christianity morality.

A second form of genealogical critique, which is even more influential in the present-day humanities and social sciences than Nietzsche's, is formulated by Michel Foucault. As noted above, around 1970 Foucault abandoned his earlier archaeological explorations of the historically variable conditions of possibility for human-scientific knowledge in favor of a more properly genealogical critique that unmasked the modern human sciences as the product of a violent "will to knowledge." Later, he analyzed how such forms of knowledge were inextricably linked to and, in part, constituted by specifically modern modalities of power. The most well-known of these modalities are the individualizing power he calls "discipline," which produces individuals as free, rational, and productive subjects, and the generalizing power he calls "biopolitics," which targets populations conceived of as groups of living beings rather than a corporate body of citizens.

Unlike Nietzsche, Foucault traces the genealogy not of religious morality but of modern human-scientific knowledge. Hence, his writings appear to rest on a number of residual secularist assumptions; but they may also be read as implying a genealogy of modern Western secular reason. This genealogy becomes much more pronounced in anthropological authors such as Talal Asad, who argues that the modern Western concept of religion presupposes not only a particular Western history but, more specifically, a particular history of power.[62] This theoretical and power-ridden background, he argues, militates against the very possibility of any universal concept of religion. In later works, Asad has similarly traced the genealogy of the specifically Western post-Enlightenment concept of the secular.

Asad's analysis of the concepts of religion and the secular appears to be roundly genealogical insofar as it links these notions to the history of the expansion of Western political, economic, and epistemological influences over the non-Western world; on closer inspection, however, his work appears to have a clear communitarian strain as well.[63] More specifically, one may signal an asymmetry in his writings: regarding the Western concepts of religion and the secular, Asad is a convinced genealogist; but regarding Islam, he appears an unabashed communitarian. This kind of communitarianism becomes particularly visible in his proposal to treat Islam as a "discursive tradition," that is, as "simply a tradition of Muslim discourse that addresses itself to conceptions of the Islamic past and future, with reference to a particular Islamic practice in the present."[64] Such a tradition, he argues against modernist critics, is neither invented nor necessarily homogeneous; it involves power and resistance as well as argument and contestation. Yet, Asad argues, Islam is a single tradition rather than a plurality of local traditions; moreover, it is essentially continuous over time: "for analytical purposes, there is no essential difference . . . between 'classical' and 'modern' Islam."[65] Thus, the notion of a discursive tradition appears to be a curious amalgam of Foucault's concept of discursive practices, which sets out to expose power relations and discontinuities, and MacIntyre's concept of a tradition, which emphasizes rationally defensibility and continuity. It is unclear whether these two modes of historical inquiry are logically compatible, let alone what the normative implications of such an amalgamation are.

Thus, the liberal, communitarian, and genealogical positions concerning questions of religion and secularism all have their conceptual and normative difficulties; moreover, all of them can benefit from a confrontation of rich empirical material originating in both Western and non-Western settings. It is to be hoped that the contributions to this volume will help in presenting such materials and thus in providing food for the further study of the conceptual, empirical-historical, and normative study of religious practices of religion.

Notes

1. William Cantwell Smith, *The Meaning and End of Religion* (New York: Macmillan, 1963), 50, 60–63. Talal Asad has subsequently discussed and criticized Smith's original

thesis in "Reading a Modern Classic: Smith's *The Meaning and End of Religion*," *History of Religions* 40, no. 3 (1997): 205–222.

2. On the Protestant dislike of outward ritual and its vicissitudes in mission efforts in the Dutch East Indies, see Webb Keane, *Christian Moderns: Freedom and Fetish in the Christian Missionary Encounter* (Berkeley: University of California Press, 2007).

3. Ludwig Wittgenstein, *Philosophical Investigations* (Oxford: Blackwell, 1953), §§66–67.

4. The notion of linguistic ideologies was originally spread by Michael Silverstein, "Language Structure and Linguistic Ideology," in *The Elements: A Parasession on Linguistic Units and Levels*, ed. P. Clyne et al. (Chicago: Chicago Linguistic Society, 1979), 193–247. For the use of linguistic or semiotic ideologies in the study of religion, see, for example, Keane *Christian Moderns*, chap. 2; see also Keane's contribution to this volume.

5. See J. L. Austin, *How to Do Things With Words*, 2nd ed. (Oxford: Oxford University Press, 1975).

6. S. A. Tambiah, "A Performative Approach to Ritual," *Proceedings of the British Academy* 65 (1971): 113–169; reprinted in Tambiah, *Culture, Thought, and Social Action* (Cambridge: Cambridge University Press, 1985), 123–166.

7. In analytical philosophy, this Hegelian point has been made famous by Wilfrid Sellars's "Empiricism and the Philosophy of Mind," *Minnesota Studies in the Philosophy of Science* 1 (1956): 253–329; but already in his review of the *Philosophical Investigations*—in *Mind* 63 (1954): 70–99, esp. 90—Peter Strawson had also noted Wittgenstein's "hostility to immediacy."

8. See also, for example, Samuel Weber and Hent de Vries, eds., *Religion and Media* (Stanford, CA: Stanford University Press, 2001). For a useful overview, see Jeremy Stolow, "Religion and/as Media," *Theory, Culture & Society* 22, no. 4 (2005): 119–145.

9. Wittgenstein, *Philosophical Investigations*, §§25, 202.

10. Clifford Geertz, "Religion as a Cultural System," in *The Interpretation of Cultures* (New York: Basic Books, 1973), 87–125, esp. 90–123. See also Geertz's characterization of religion as a particular set of ideas, or a "transtemporal conception of reality," sustained by particular ideas, practices and institutions, or put differently, by particular symbolic forms and social arrangements, in *Islam Observed* (Chicago: University of Chicago Press, 1968), 2.

11. For an early overview of the practice turn, see Sherry Ortner, "Theory in Anthropology Since the Sixties," *Comparative Studies in Society and History* 26, no. 1 (1984): 126–166; for Ortner's more recent reflections on practice theory, see her *Anthropology and Social Theory: Culture, Power, and the Acting Subject* (Durham, NC: Duke University Press, 2006). See also Karin Knorr Cetina, Theodore Schatzki, and Eike von Savigny, eds., *The Practice Turn in Contemporary Theory* (London: Routledge, 2001).

12. Wittgenstein, *Philosophical Investigations*, §202.

13. Ludwig Wittgenstein, *Lectures and Conversations on Aesthetics, Psychoanalysis, and Religious Belief*, ed. by C. Barrett (Oxford: Blackwell, 1966); "Bemerkungen über Frazers *The Golden Bough*/Remarks on Frazer's *The Golden Bough*," reprinted in

Wittgenstein, *Philosophical occasions 1912–1951*, ed. by J. C. Klagge (Indianapolis, IN: Hackett, 1993), 115–155.

14. Pierre Bourdieu, *Outline of a Theory of Practice* (Cambridge: Cambridge University Press, 1977); on Wittgenstein's influence on Bourdieu, see Bourdieu, "Fieldwork in Philosophy," in *In Other Words: Essays Towards a Reflexive Sociology* (Cambridge: Polity Press, 1990), 3–33.

15. Pierre Bourdieu, "Génèse et structure du champ réligieux," *Revue française de sociologie* XII (1971): 295–334, esp. 319–320; translated into English as "Genesis and Structure of the Religious Field," *Comparative Social Research* 13 (1991): 1–44. See also Terry Rey, *Bourdieu on Religion: Imposing Faith and Legitimacy* (London: Equinox, 2007) for a more detailed attempt to operationalize Bourdieu's theoretical framework for the study of religion.

16. Bourdieu, "Génèse," 315.

17. Bourdieu, *Outline*, 41.

18. Some may object that Foucault owes his concept of practice primarily to Marxist authors, in particular his mentor Louis Althusser, whose *Pour Marx* (1965) he is known to have studied intensively around this period. It is certainly true that Althusser, too, focuses on practice in an attempt to move away from a philosophy of consciousness and the subject; but this should not obscure the important differences between the two. Whereas Althusser generally and generically speaks of *practice* or *praxis* in the singular, and primarily as the opposite of an equally generic theory, Foucault consistently explores specific *practices* in the plural, as concrete and delimited in time and space; hence, the latter are rather closer to what Wittgenstein calls games.

19. See Foucault's provocative characterization of the soul as the "prison of the body" in *Discipline and Punish* (New York: Pantheon, 1978), 30.

20. Foucault, 137; 215–216.

21. For a famous but brief statement of the notion of pastoral power, see "The Subject and Power" in Dreyfus and Rabinow, *Michel Foucault: Beyond Hermeneutics and Structuralism*, 2nd ed. (Berkeley: University of California Press, 1983), and "Omnes et singulatim: Towards a Criticism of Political Reason," in S. McMurrin, ed., *The Tanner Lectures on Human Values* (Salt Lake City: University of Utah Press, 1980). For a more detailed discussion of the classical pastorate, see lectures 5 through 9 of Foucault's *Society, Territory, Population* (Basingstoke: Palgrave Macmillan, 2007).

22 However, in the recently published *Confessions of the Flesh*, volume 4 of *The History of Sexuality*, Foucault discusses the early Christian backgrounds of the modern Western view of sexuality, focusing on church fathers such as Cassian and Augustine.

23. Against the still widespread assumption of ritual as fixed, ordered, and invariant, Gavin Brown emphasizes the "condition of indeterminacy" that, he claims, lies at the heart of ritual form, in "Theorizing Ritual as Performance: Explorations of Ritual Indeterminacy," *Journal of Ritual Studies* 17, no. 1 (2004): 3–18.

24. Arnold van Gennep, *Les rites de passage* (Paris: Émile Nourry, 1909); translated as *The Rites of Passage* (London: Routledge and Kegan Paul, 1960); Victor Turner, *The*

Ritual Process: Structure and Anti-Structure (Chicago: Aldine, 1969); Turner, *Dramas, Fields, and Metaphors: Symbolic Action in Human Society* (Ithaca, NY: Cornell University Press, 1974).

25. Turner, *Ritual Process*, 95.

26. To the extent that he emphasizes the immediacy of *communitas* and of anti-structural and liminal experience (e.g., in *Dramas, Fields, and Metaphors*, 274, 288), Turner may show traces of a residually phenomenological position that assumes the primacy and irreducibility of immediate experience as well as the givenness of community.

27. For some of the most important early statements, see, for example, Ronald Grimes, *Beginnings in Ritual Studies* (Washington, DC: University Press of America, 1982, rev. 1994); "Ritual Studies," in *Encyclopedia of Religion*, vol. 12, ed. M. Eliade (New York: Macmillan, 1987), 422–425; Catherine Bell, *Ritual Theory, Ritual Practice* (New York: Oxford University Press, 1992); and Bell, *Ritual: Perspectives and Dimensions* (New York: Oxford University Press, 1997).

28. The *locus classicus* for the modern practice-theoretical reconceptualization and normalization of sexuality is, of course, Michel Foucault, *The Will to Knowledge: The History of Sexuality*, vol. 1 (New York: Random House, 1978); but Foucault nowhere touches on the role of either contemporary religion or nationalism in the development of modern sexuality—nor for that matter, does he discuss gender in detail. Judith Butler, taking off from Foucault's theories, has emphasized the performative character of gender identities, most famously in *Gender Trouble* (London: Routledge, 1990). For a recent collection of articles on religion, gender, and sexuality, see, for example, Peter Nynäs and Andrew Kam-Tuck Yip, eds., *Religion, Gender, and Sexuality in Everyday Life* (Farnham, UK: Ashgate, 2012).

29. See, for example, Joseph Massad, *Desiring Arabs* (Chicago: University of Chicago Press, 2007) for the modern Arab-Islamic world. Wendy Doniger's *The Hindus: An Alternative History* (London: Penguin Books, 2010) devotes much attention to changing practices of and attitudes toward gender and sexuality in India.

30. Sarah Ahmed, *Queer Phenomenology: Orientations, Objects, Others* (Durham, NC: Duke University Press, 2006), 13.

31. Julia Kristeva, *Powers of Horror: An Essay on Abjection* (New York: Columbia University Press, 1982).

32. José Casanova, *Public Religions in the Modern World* (Chicago: University of Chicago Press, 1994).

33. José Casanova, "Public Religions Revisited," in *Religion: Beyond a Concept*, ed. Hent de Vries (New York: Fordham University Press, 2008), 105.

34. Sami Zubaida, *Law and Power in the Islamic World* (London: I.B. Tauris, 2003), chap. 4; Michel Foucault, "Governmentality," in *Power: Essential Works*, vol. 3 (Harmondsworth, UK: Penguin, 2002), 201–222.

35. See Leonora Batnitzky, *How Judaism Became a Religion: An Introduction to Modern Jewish Thought* (Princeton, NJ: Princeton University Press, 2011).

36. Charles Taylor, *A Secular Age* (Cambridge MA: Harvard University Press, 2007), 21–22.

37. Taylor, *A Secular Age*, 370–373; see also Charles Taylor, *Sources of the Self: The Making of the Modern Identity* (Cambridge, MA: Harvard University Press, 1989), chap. 11.

38. Charles Taylor, *Varieties of Religion Today* (Cambridge, MA: Harvard University Press, 2003), 24–26.

39. Ortner, "Theory in Anthropology Since the Sixties," 126–166.

40. Peter van der Veer, *Religious Nationalism: Hindus and Muslims in India* (Berkeley: University of California Press, 1994).

41. Talal Asad, "Secularism, Nation-State, Religion," in *Formations of the Secular* (Stanford, CA: Stanford University Press, 2003), 128.

42. Sheldon Pollock, "The Death of Sanskrit," *Comparative Studies in History and Society* 43, no. 2 (2001): 392–426.

43. Benedict Anderson, *Imagined Communities: Reflections on the Origin and Spread of Nationalism*, rev. ed. (London: Verso Books, 1991).

44. Taylor, *Secular Age*, 21 and note acknowledges as much.

45. Most importantly in Chatterjee, *The Nation and Its Fragments* (Princeton NJ: Princeton University Press, 1993), chap. 2.

46. C. A. Bayly, *The Birth of the Modern World, 1789–1914: Global Connections and Comparisons* (Oxford: Blackwell, 2004), 348.

47. Tomoko Masuzawa, *The Invention of World Religions, or, How European Universalism was Preserved in the Language of Pluralism* (Chicago: University of Chicago Press, 2005).

48. Arjun Appadurai, *Modernity at Large: Cultural Dimensions of Globalization* (Minneapolis: University of Minnesota Press, 1996); see also Ulf Hannerz, *Cultural Complexity: Studies in the Social Organization of Meaning* (New York: Columbia University Press, 1992).

49. Olivier Roy, *Holy Ignorance* (New York: Columbia University Press, 2010), 5; see also Olivier Roy, *Globalized Islam: The Search for a New Ummah* (New York: Columbia University Press, 2004).

50. Roy, *Holy Ignorance*, 119.

51. John Rawls, *A Theory of Justice* (Cambridge, MA: Harvard University Press, 1971); Rawls, *Political Liberalism* (New York: Columbia University Press, 1993).

52. Jürgen Habermas, "Faith and Knowledge," in *The Future of Human Nature* (Cambridge: Polity Press, 2003), 101–115; Habermas, "Secularism's Crisis of Faith: Notes on Post-Secular Society," *New Perspectives Quarterly* 25, no. 4 (2008): 17–29. For the philosophical motivation of the shift of founding social theory not on a philosophy of consciousness but on philosophy of language, see in particular Habermas's 1971 Gauss lectures, reprinted in Habermas, *On the Pragmatics of Social Interaction* (Cambridge MA: MIT Press, 2001), 1–103.

53. See Habermas, "Secularism's Crisis of Faith," 34, 36.

54. Two further features of Habermas's account stand out: first, he pays little if any sustained attention to recent processes of globalization, which have not only increased the global flow of religious information but also created new arenas for religious conflict; second, he repeatedly characterizes secularization as a dialectical process but does not spell out exactly what this dialectic amounts to. His own remarks suggest that we should not take this term in a Marxist or Hegelian sense but more generically as pointing to a process that is broadly linear but beset with difficulties, challenges, and relapses.

55. For an overview of the liberalism-communitarianism debate as it stood in the wake of Rawls's 1993 publication of *Political Liberalism*, see Stephen Mulhall and Adam Swift, *Liberals and Communitarians*, 2nd ed. (Oxford: Blackwell, 1996). For a comparison of liberalism, communitarianism, and genealogy from a communitarian perspective, see Alisdair MacIntyre, *Three Rival Versions of Moral Enquiry* (London: Duckworth, 1990).

56. Alisdair MacIntyre, *After Virtue: A Study in Moral Theory*, 2nd ed. (London: Duckworth, 1984).

57. MacIntyre, *After Virtue*, 220; quoted in Mulhall and Swift, *Liberals and Communitarians*, 89.

58. Taylor, *Sources of the Self*, 36.

59. See Mulhall and Swift, *Liberals and Communitarians*, 113.

60. Taylor, *Sources of the Self*, 4

61. For a discussion of the problematic and power-saturated origins of such seemingly neutral analytical concepts as language, culture, and tradition, see Richard Bauman and Charles Briggs, *Voices of Modernity: Language Ideologies and the Politics of Inequality* (Cambridge: Cambridge University Press, 2002). For some of the twists and turns by which a Western philosophical vocabulary was assimilated in nineteenth-century India, see Wilhem Halbfass, *India and Europe* (Albany: State University of New York Press, 1988).

62. Talal Asad, "The Construction of Religion as an Anthropological Category," in *Genealogies of Religion* (Baltimore, MD: Johns Hopkins University Press, 1993), 27–54.

63. David Scott discusses this tension between the genealogical and the communitarian strains (or, as he calls it, between genealogy and tradition) in Asad's work. In his reply, Asad hardly addresses this tension, elaborating instead on the category of the tragic. See David Scott, "The Tragic Sensibility of Talal Asad," in *Powers of the Secular Modern*, ed. D. Scott and C. Hirschkind (Stanford, CA: Stanford University Press, 2006), 134–153; for Asad's reply, see *Powers*, 233–235.

64. Talal Asad, *The Idea of an Anthropology of Islam* (Washington, DC: Occasional Papers Series, Georgetown University Center for Contemporary Arab Studies, 1986).

65. Asad, 15.

Part I

Religious Performance and Performativity

The 1990s witnessed the rise of both performance theory and the concept of performativity as a master trope in the human sciences. Although these two notions are often conflated in the literature, it is good to keep them analytically separate. *Performance* emphasizes the theoretical autonomy of practice in general; it militates against the structuralist idea that practice is merely the implementation or acting out of an antecedently and independently given script. *Performativity* calls attention to one characteristic that some kinds of practice (or, according to some, all practices) possess; originating with J. L. Austin's speech act theory, it expresses the idea that some utterances may bring about the very state of affairs or (social) fact they purport to represent or describe, as in "I hereby baptize this ship the *Queen Elisabeth II*." In subsequent decades, this idea was generalized from speech actions to various other kinds of embodied practice. Most influentially, Judith Butler, alongside Eve Sedgwick, has argued that gender identities are neither biologically given nor socially constructed but performative in character. However, following Derrida, Butler argues that gender identities are not fixed once and for all but have to be reaffirmed, and can be challenged, by being iterated or quoted out of context (most famously, characterizing drag as involving a "parody" of gender and thus suggesting that there is no inner essence to the latter). Most importantly, the logic of iteration systematically undermines the idea of speakers' intentions as sovereign over their actions and, by extension, the still predominant view of power as primarily *sovereign* power. Authors working in the wake of Butler's theories also have interesting applications in the study of religion, as the contributions to this section make clear. (Austin's speech act theory and its offshoots also inform Baumgartner's, Leezenberg's, and De Koning's essays in this volume.)

Yvonne Sherwood's "Gesturing Toward Sacrifice" is a fitting opening of this collection, both in its scope and in its detailed analytical attention to gestures. Sherwood sees the turn toward embodiment, performance, and materiality in the study of religion as part of a larger recoil in the humanities at large, away from Derridean and other forms of linguistic constructivism that reduce practices to texts. She suggests that the early modern birth of the study of gestures or "manual discourse," as seen in John Bulwer's 1644 *Chirologia*, coincides with the rise of religion as a distinct category. She then sets out on a rich exploration of the ambiguities of the term *gesture*, which for her denotes a weak, ironic, or incomplete action—comparable to the nonserious speech acts famously discussed by J. L. Austin and Jacques Derrida—in exposing the inherently unstable and vulnerable character of all (speech) acts. Furthermore, she sees gestures as ephemeral, apparently trivial, and individual rather than collective; "as a word is to a paragraph or book," she adds, "so a gesture is to a performance or act."

In Sherwood's view, both gesture and religion are fundamental and natural phenomena that escape language, or rather, militate against the strict dichotomy between texts and acts. Following Derrida, Sherwood characterizes sacrifice as a theatrical act, or more precisely as a *gesture*: a trivial, ineffective act, which necessarily remains nonserious and incomplete. She pursues this line of argument through a detailed discussion of Caravaggio's and Rembrandt's paintings of Abraham's interrupted sacrifice of his son Isaac. Abraham's gesture, she argues, is an incomplete act of sacrifice: just as he is about to strike, an angel holds back the knife in his hand. Moreover, this sacrificial gesture falls between the act as law, that is, as the execution of a rule or script commanded by God, and the act as a transgressive one-off event, that is, as the ultimate *violation* of the Law. In conclusion, she provocatively invites us to consider the gestural dimensions of Abraham's sacrifice, the crucifixion of Christ, and even the September 11 attacks. The latter, she argues, were not a mere gesture to religion that failed to be religious in itself; rather, such blasphemous gestures are the ones that take the sacred text *too* seriously and *too* literally. (You will find similar views on the ambiguity of sacrifice in Regina Schwartz's reading of *Othello* in "The Mass and the Theater" in this volume.)

John Bowen takes his starting point from J. L. Austin's famous distinction between performative and constative, or descriptive, acts. In his densely argued "Unpacking 'Performance,'" Bowen claims that the meaning of religious practice is performative rather than propositional in character. Moreover, he argues, it involves a particular *kind* of signs, viz., indexical signs, which refer to a particular aspect of the context of utterance rather than symbols, which represent their object and signify in a general manner, or icons, which refer in virtue of a similarity or likeness with their referent. By their acts of worship, he suggests, individual actors may index their socioreligious status among their co-believers; more specifically, religious acts may amount to what he calls "diacritic indexicals," which mark off one religious position or group with respect to others. For example, in Northern Nigeria, Muslim worshippers could index their membership of a reformist Sufi group or a messianic movement and, later, of a particular ethnic group such as the Yoruba or Hausa by crossing their arms during worship instead of letting them hang at their sides.

The indexical aspects of performative acts involving religion, however, go far beyond their immediate social context: in fact, various other aspects of religious practice may be analyzed in terms of speech acts, performativity, and indexicality. Thus, by demanding the right to have divorce pronounced in Islamic rather than in civil courts, Muslims in Western liberal secular states may index their religious attachment; conversely, attempts by French officials to ban headscarves from public space can be semiotically analyzed as indexing the distinctness and superiority of secular space with respect to religious practice. Disputes concerning the legitimate authority to perform religiously sanctioned actions such as divorce ceremonies may equally be analyzed as contestations over the felicity conditions of particular religious performatives, that is, over the question of who may legitimately and successfully pronounce divorces. Because of this theoretical perspective that focuses on indexical signs and semiotic ideologies, Bowen's essay shines an interesting light on some of the other contributions in this volume, in particular on those dealing with religious rights and identity of immigrant minority communities such as Zaidi's, Baumgartner's, and De Koning's contributions.

Like other authors in this volume (most notably Butler and Van Maas), Bowen also complicates the temporality of performatives, rejecting the intuitive idea that speech acts are simply driven by logically and chronologically prior speakers' intentions. Inner mental states, he argues, may be part of the felicity conditions for religious acts of worship; conversely, such acts may precisely aim at *creating* such states of mind, for example, a state of inner sincerity or faith.

Bruno Latour's "Thou Shalt Not Freeze-Frame" is an even more suggestive and thought-provoking variation on Austinian themes. Pursuing a "weak analogy" with Austin's speech act theory, Latour sets out to map the felicity conditions of religious as opposed to scientific, political, and juridical forms of truth production. The concept of religious belief, he argues, is patterned after a mistaken idea of science. In unpacking this misunderstanding, he exposes the semiotic ideology of what he calls "double-click communication," that is, the belief in information as transparent and unmediated access to the outside world. On his own account, neither scientific nor religious truth can be construed as an unmediated correspondence between world and words or between original and copy. Religious talk, he argues, is not informative but transformative: it does not referentially or descriptively talk *of* things but performatively speaks *from* things, and—a bit like love talk—tries to elicit what it talks about. Put differently, religious talk does not try to describe a distant reality *beyond*; rather, it tries to represent the "presence of the Word incarnate": it does not aim at truthfully describing some distant state of affairs but at bringing people and what they say closer to each other, thus drawing attention to what is present or nearby. In his account, the "belief in belief," that is, the idea that religious faith is a belief in a particular state of affairs, is a serious, if widespread, category mistake. Scientific talk, by contrast, does not, as is usually thought, deal with the visible, the immediate, or with so-called matters of fact; it does not establish any immediate relation between words and the world but, on the contrary, builds long chains of reference mediated by experiments and laboratories.

Finally, Latour links these ideas to the question of image-making in religion, science, and art and the iconoclastic reactions against images as mediating between the human and the divine that it may provoke. Religious icons do not turn the religious worshipper's mind to a distant prototype or original, he argues; rather, precisely by breaking the viewer's habitual way of looking, they draw their attention to what is present. He then illustrates these claims with a discussion of a number of famous Renaissance artworks, including a fresco by Fra Angelico and Piero della Francesca's *Annunciation*. This links his discussion to his famous notion of "iconoclash," which calls attention to the uncertainty to what extent images are human-made.

Sander van Maas's "Dorsal Monuments" takes us from the visual arts to music. Like Bowen, Van Maas thematizes the linear temporality often tacitly assumed in commonsensical views of musical performance. Van Maas considers what he calls "dorsality"—that is, a looking or turning back or reverting that leads to both the production and the undoing of presence—as the "master gesture" at work in Olivier Messiaen's work and in an adaptation of that work by director Peter Sellars. He opens his argument by analyzing how Messiaen's compositions both produce and problematize presence in the sense of overwhelming lived experience (*Erlebnis*). The monumentality and grand (sonic) gestures of, in particular, Messiaen's compositions of the 1960s are intended to create a sense of being overwhelmed by the divine in the audience. Although several compositions are written in honor of the dead, they do not commemorate the past as much as eschatologically anticipate the future. Van Maas especially sees what he calls a "logic of dorsality" at work in Sellars's 1990s production of Messiaen's opera *Saint François d'Assise* (1983). In Sellars's staging, dramatic gesture rather than Messiaen's music or the libretto text is central; moreover, Sellars turns from religion and spirituality toward the social and political world (or, at the very least, toward a more immanent, this-worldly form of spirituality), thereby turning the opera's monumental anticipation of the future toward the present, or, more precisely, into a monument to the power of lived experience. Yet, Van Maas claims, in an argument that owes much to Derrida's writings on the work of mourning, even this turn is marked by a dorsal movement: *Saint François* being an opera rather than a religious ritual ultimately sacrifices both religion and ritual to the principles of artistic creation in Sellars's adaptation as in Messiaen's score. Thus, the logic of dorsality implies an unending turning back rather than a unitary turn toward either the divine or the present.

CHAPTER 1

Gesturing Toward Sacrifice

Aping the Scapegoat and Monkeying Around with the Lamb

Yvonne Sherwood

Between the motion
And the act
Falls the Shadow

—T. S. Eliot, "The Hollow Men"

Gesture. An action performed to convey a feeling or intention . . . an action performed for show in the knowledge that it will have no effect.

—*Oxford Dictionary of English*, 2nd ed.

The turn to gesture summoned by this volume may well strike us as timely, uncontroversial, and incidental. It could look like a welcome little supplement to the now well-established effort to bring us to our senses, to our bodies, to the skin of what is called religion. It may appear as no more than a little appendix, or appendage, to the already well-established move from religion's words to religion's performances, practices, and acts. Triviality seems to be built into the very word *gesture*. A gesture is like an act but smaller: it tends to be identified with an individual rather than a group and confined to a fleeting moment. It seems that as a word is to a paragraph or book, so a gesture is to a performance or act.

In this essay I argue that gesture is far more than a passive supplement or diminutive act. It has the potential to disturb assumptions that undergird the turn to act. This is because *gesture* is one of those commonplace words that we have used (often without being aware of it) to register fundamental philosophical problems in shorthand. The very word *gesture* stages, and indeed insists on, fundamental theoretical problems that haunt religious studies. The deeply conflicted senses packed into this strange little word foreground all the problems that we usually push to the side when we talk of act.

The Conflicted Soul of Religious Studies

> The anxiety, the desire to see, touch, and eat the body of God, to be that body and nothing but that, forms the principle of Western (un)reason. That's why the body, bodily, never happens, least of all when it's named and convoked. For us, the body is always sacrificed: eucharist.
> —Jean-Luc Nancy, *Corpus*

The recent turn to what we call, variously, embodiment, emplacement, performance, or material religion is part of a larger recoil in the humanities away from what has been seen as an all-pervasive linguistic constructivism. At its extremes this allegedly made (to quote some parodies of Derrida) all the world a "text."[1] The compensating, if admittedly difficult, dream for some is now to "unearth experience from the thick sedimentary strata of language covering it."[2] This is another version of the Enlightenment drama of liberating ourselves from shackles (here language) into the expanding sphere of truth and freedom—a drama that has traditionally taken tradition and, particularly, religious tradition as its foil.

In the field of religious studies, the emancipatory desire to get out from under the thick sedimentary strata of language has proved even more alluring than in other subjects in the humanities because religious studies has particular baggage in relation to the text. Religious studies has often defined itself by disciplinary autobiography. As a teenager, it once broke free from strict, text-devoted and often embarrassing parents: Protestant biblical hermeneutics and Christian theology.[3] No surprise that the disciplinary offspring of such parents found the dream of breaking through thick piles of mediation particularly compelling. The parent disciplines were, and continue to be extremely, if not absurdly, bookish. They like nothing better than piling carefully finessed nuance around the Trinity or patiently teasing out (as if with tweezers) the sedimented strata of a small square of biblical text.

Religious studies dreamt, therefore, of being the zone of comparative immediacy, beneath projection and mediation. But equally fervently and passionately, the heart of religious studies qua religious studies has been defined as the realm of acknowledged constructivism and projection. The field of religious studies was founded on a split creed: a founding belief in projection and its equally emphatic repudiation and denial. One strong proof of religious studies as religious studies has been its willingness to dish out the hard truths of demystification, even when it hurts. The religious studies scholar is precisely the one (and, allegedly, the only one on the religion and theology corridor) who is prepared to say that religion does not exist—except as a scholarly construct or a sociological or a psychological special effect.

The religious studies scholar is the austere one: the one who habitually (indeed as a matter of self-definition) insists that religion is a specter projected by societies, economies, subjects. But this is an exhausting work: as hard and noble as the philosophical spiritual exercises of a Descartes or a Kant.[4] So it is hardly surprising that religion scholars find themselves sinking back into and trying to touch experience or "the material." Trying to grasp the body—the "body that never happens, least of all when it's named and convoked"[5]—we try to conjure it using, as a mantra, words such as *embodiment* and *flesh*. Feeling guilty of sins of solipsism, we find ourselves chasing the holy grail of the really real or (at least) the relatively real, in order to restore what we (not by accident, but as a matter of disciplinary self-definition) have taken away. Religious studies then becomes, equally compellingly and by way of compensation, the place where we believe that (unlike the theologians or the biblical scholars, whom we so regularly call on, for contrast) we are deducing from a form of empirical presence that can be (almost) touched, or that at the very least is closer to "the real" than a mere text.

What is often termed lived or embodied religion typically splits. It functions as a repository for the material (in the sense of that which is more real than scholarly projections) and a sign of the surplus beyond the merely material. Religion and its vocabularies become the terms for conjuring, and humbling, the empirical and the concrete. They bring it "here" (somehow), and, in the same gesture, relativize it as "mere." In his essay "The Problem of the Holy," Robert Orsi demonstrates the double gesture or double bind perfectly. "The holy" is a mode of sensation in which the presence of Jesus can be "as real as a kitchen table and arthritis." But it is also that which exceeds the (mere) reality of things such as tables and arthritis—the mystical algorithm that means that (systematically, and by way of the production of religion) $2 + 2 = 5$.[6]

Religious studies is the most typical modern discipline in the sense that it most perfectly expresses, and compresses, the founding aporiae of Western philosophy. This is not by accident or because religion scholars were not paying attention or were particularly dim. Because religion served as the bogeyman and ghost of Enlightenment discourse and therefore the foil of "freedom," the discipline that took religion as its ostensible object was squeezed into a particularly tight and contradictory corner. It was forced to dramatize and compress the conceptual conflicts at the heart of modernity in particularly revealing ways, as it strove (starting on the back foot) to show how the study of religion was, in fact, "free," factual and not *completely* spectral or unreal.

As soon as we start to think about how we operate as analysts, observers, or scholars, we find ourselves caught in the shadow between construction/projection and the given, subjecthood and subjection, passivity and agency, the inside and the outside. In old currency this was thought of as the distinction between thinking stuff and extended stuff or the abyss between mind/soul/subject and world/body/things. We can denounce bad old Plato, bad old Descartes, and bad old Kant to help give us some sense of easy emancipation from the fundamental problems of ontology and epistemology, but in getting out of their old binaries, we find ourselves constructing more binaries: for example, theory and praxis, word and flesh, words and acts, language and performance, language and experience, all of which are haunted by their opposite and the anxious shadowlands in between. Leaning hard into one we cannot help, sooner or later, making compensatory gestures to the other—whether this comes in our next caveat or sentence or the next compensatory move in the fickle *Zeitgeists* of the academy. Religious studies performed this violent oscillation more intensely than any other discipline. Its very object, religion, was dispelled as mere projection and constantly reinstated. Suspended in the shadowlands of Western philosophy, religion perpetually did and did not exist.

But it is wearisome to constantly think like this. The desire to get on with things and *do* something—starting from solid (uncontested) ground—soon kicks in. While the self-constituting aporiae at the heart of religious studies remain unresolved, rallying points of political-moral virtue often substitute for a slow acknowledgment of the conflicting ideas and positions at the heart of what the discipline is or aspires to be. Down beneath the sophisticated discourse of methodologies, scholars often present new moves in religious studies as forms of emancipation. And what could be more attractive to moderns than new ways of becoming free?

Religious studies is often presented as a youthful rebellion against the old fathers and the place of emancipation from the shackles of scripts and doctrines. Thus, religious studies appears as relatively unmediated and free. It is often presented as liberation from the kind of truth that is administered in an oppressive, top-down fashion. Religious studies is presented as the space that has secured independence from colonial administrators, archbishops, theologians, and all the heavenly hierarchies.[7] Lived/performed/material religion is the kind of religion practiced or performed "by human beings, not angels."[8] (Angels are useful focal points to organize oneself against, heavenly figures that do not exist.) Praxis, performance, or lived religion seem more solid—almost tangible—when juxtaposed with the esoteric mists of theory or the speculative paper projections of the excessively bookish.[9] The "sonic, tactile, olfactory, gustatory, and kinetic dimensions" of religion seem almost tangible, audible, smellable when the paper on which they are printed declares itself so ardently against text, reason, or belief.[10]

Often, in ways that would have been unthinkable for Kant or Calvin, reason and belief are conjoined and added to text as the others of religious studies. Together, reason and belief evoke control/dogma and illusion, excessive reason, and excessive unreason: that which is entirely unvalidated, untrue (a matter of belief, not knowledge), and that which is substantiated and limited through reason's truth machines. The linked enemies are opposites. They evoke bad memories of the excessive control and repression of religion (allowing religious studies to be the place that allows the ghosts and powers of the religious to return) and, conversely, excessive superstition (allowing religious studies to be the space of the epiphany of the relatively real). The divided theoretical ground of religious studies would be impossible to articulate with any philosophical coherence. But we can almost believe in it, feel it, when we rally against its opposite opposites: "reason and belief." We can get a real sense that we are moving closer to the real, beating heart of religion by refuting the unreal machinations of reason and its dead letters, and, conversely, the old ghost of belief.

Unsure as to where it is or where it believes the holy grail of the really real to be, religious studies stabilizes itself by conjuring (as its opposite) angels, text, and the vaguely (newly) amalgamated forces of reason and belief. This lends a new sense to the phrase "comparative religion." By comparison and contrast with religions as controlled, scripted, and managed by philologists, professors, and angels, the new religion of religious studies appears as comparatively free and comparatively real.

I do not mean to question the importance of critiquing text-centered, elitist, or colonial constructions of religion. My point is rather that political/moral self-evidence and virtue are being used to conjure—and substitute—for a different kind of solidity, that of the more or relatively living, the more or relatively free. I feel myself closer to the real of religion when I read these calls; I feel so close I can really feel it, touch it, touch experience or the lived. But maybe the bodies that I am touching here (or think I am almost touching) are those of the religion scholars who have congregated here for the same reason as I have. Without thinking about it and without having to think about it, we congregate at the meeting point marked as "not angels and arcane theologies," "not philology," "not text," "not reason and belief." This social banding-together, this meeting point of political-moral virtue, lends a compelling force of affect and solidity to the place that we call the place of performance and the sensual (the sonic, tactile, gustatory, and kinetic). Polemic, solidarity and the quest for freedom lead us here, to this place which is so much harder to access conceptually and philosophically. Political-moral virtue substitutes for the certainty and self-evidence that are always denied us around the so-called real. On clear political and moral grounds, we can feel the exhilaration of a new space, a freer space, a more expansive space (the space of religions plural), closer to the body and the real. But the study of religions may be most Christian in its quest for world and tangibility. This almost desperate quest for the body (*Hoc est corpus meum*) and this campaign against the dead letter seem to betray more than a little debt to Christianity and the forces of globalatinization from which we seek to be released.[11]

Writing Acts

There is something of a sleight of hand about this turn to acts, hands, and gestures as a turn to authenticity and freedom from scripts. The very words *acts* and *performance* belie this hope. *Act* means an action, a thing done, a law (as in Act of Parliament), but also a pretense and a section of a play. The very word begs the question of truth, pointing to that which was definitely done, and definitively passed, but also to the scripted and the fake. Similarly, the word *performance* offers no more guarantee of freedom than the word *text*. As Catherine Bell deftly simplifies, *performance* has (at the very least) a threefold meaning: "the accomplishment or execution of a specified action, most notably a command or a promise" (I will return to this "command or promise"); "the enactment of a script or a score, as in a theatrical play or a musical recital"; and an "unscripted event."[12]

When religion scholars write up the turn to performance or act, they tend to underplay the senses of a pregiven script, rite, or law and the mediated, inauthentic, and fake. In her important article "Practicing Religion," Courtney Bender attempts to push our understanding of religious practice beyond the religious actors presumed to be the "keepers or containers of religion."[13] This is an analysis of gestures—and all the individuality, triviality, and tangents that we associate with the word *gesture*. The topic is a chance encounter, an act of social improvisation, at several removes from what we might imagine to be the operational center of religious acts. Yet this *ad hoc* encounter is written up in a highly prescripted fashion as in "the enactment of a script or a score."[14] The setting is firmly located in the coordinates of reality: a train from Newark to Philadelphia. The style is journalistic. Using concrete (not abstract) nouns and verbs and eschewing the adjectives that would make the piece overtly literary or tendentious, the article seems to run like a train, moving with precision on a particular track. The conversation to which Bender "idly listen[s]" is reported verbatim, as if recorded.[15] (Was it recorded? Did Bender set up a digital microphone to listen in on this accidental encounter? At what point did she press Record?) The actors, or improvisers, are a "heavyset woman in her early thirties . . . in loose fitting sweatpants, a long-sleeved white shirt, white sneakers and a bandana," and a man of similar age wearing "sunglasses, sneakers, jeans, and a T-shirt and vest that identified him as a member of a train workers' union."[16] The detail is also heavyset, as if the density of detail were designed to create an illusion of a solidity of the world. The concentration on details of clothing and age mimics the structure of newspaper court reports. As a consummate academic act, the article seems to imagine itself being performed in the forums where we perform our most intense trials of truth and witnessing: the courts and witness statements to the police.

"I know of no writing that doesn't touch. Because then it wouldn't be writing, just reporting or summarizing," writes Jean-Luc Nancy. "Writing in its essence touches upon the body"; writing attempts to "make of meaning a touch."[17] Bender uses genre conventions that signal dispassionate witnessing, raw truth, stripped of all projection or construction. At the same time that it seeks to meticulously preserve the code and truth of witnessing, the article seeks to touch the truth of the body. Gesture is meticulously recorded and deciphered, even though it is also clichéd, maybe ritualized, as in a theater script. When the woman reveals that her husband is Muslim, the man "blinks." (Did Bender look at him directly, face-to-face?) He speaks in a "stammered tone" and a "worried look passe[s] over his brow."[18] The implication is that these secrets and revelations are more authentic for having been seen, heard, witnessed, or written on the flesh. And yet the man becomes a character in a play as soon as his motions are recorded so meticulously as in a theatrical script.

Robert Orsi's article revising the old concept of "the holy" models different ways of organizing the relation between witnessing, authenticity, and the desire to touch. The setting carries even more promise of reality than a train between Newark and Philadelphia. The acts and artifacts are dug up from the place least associated with transcendence and escapes from reality: the Bronx. Working upward from the raw experience of an uncle with cerebral palsy, this meditation on the holy is stubbornly embodied. Indeed, it is centered on the "insistence of the body" in the life of "men and women with twisted limbs, who had difficulty speaking, and who needed assistance with the most basic life functions—eating, drinking, going to the bathroom."[19] These are insurmountable, insistent bodies that cannot possibly dream of any Cartesian escape. The forces of attraction-repulsion that converge "around the holy cripple" and his intimate relation with the broken body of Jesus lead to reflections about the holy as a force field of "sentimentality, horror, titillation, awe and disgust."[20] New senses of the holy are compiled around the living corpus of the body and the (mediated) memory of gesture. "Cripples are holy people, the well-intentioned ambulatory announced to the 'cripples,' who nodded their heads but kept their thoughts mostly to themselves, although my uncle occasionally made his amusement at being cast in the role of holy object known to me by subtle signs."[21]

Orsi's interpretation (deduction?) of the holy relies on an archive of memories, represented as a very different kind of repository to, say, a religious text. He invites us to examine, with him, his deceased uncle's things, crammed into a small cardboard carton: an incredible number of rosaries; a statue of the Blessed Margaret of Citta di Castello; many chewed and broken cigarette holders; and prayer books stuffed with brightly colored holy cards and bound with wide, red, rubber bands. We are invited to handle the possessions, to touch, with Orsi, the things his uncle had handled "all jumbled together and smelling sweetly of tobacco, after his death."[22] The density of the authentic comes from compression. Instead of roaming the heavens, soaring with liturgies and angels, the article confines itself to church hall lunches and artifacts to be handled and smelled. Immersion in the concrete is reinforced by calling on the "gustatory" and "olfactory" (as Vasquez puts it, using those strangely distancing academic words for the senses that promise more intimacy and authenticity than eyes and texts). The chimera of the real clings more intensely to the everyday, the workaday, the banal and profane. The solidity of the secular is made from stuff like tables, arthritis, rubber bands, solid nouns, and sensations. When religious studies brings religion back in, it brings in the kind of tangible religion we can believe in; the kind of religion that stays close to tables, beer, and cigarettes. Touching and smelling suggests something more immediate than a merely textual encounter. In its smells and its lingering materiality, the uncle's body has a (modest) afterlife. It persists and insists and points, deictically, to some conflicted meanings of the holy, even after death.

Orsi's article is overtly interpretative—even exegetical. He calls on the truth of the body to underwrite what he projects, deduces, feels, and intuits (from memory) as the force field of "sentimentality, horror, titillation, awe and disgust."[23] Bender's article concentrates on the "capillary working of power in and through our bodies and speech, normalizing and naturalizing the relations that make our worlds."[24] Neither writer would be surprised by the bland little revelation (which is not what I am after here) that "all acts are mediated." Nor would they always claim a naïve correlation between interior, secret truth and the movements of the body. The "worried look" observed by Bender signifies, well, worry, but Orsi's "cripples" clearly dissent, even as they nod their heads.[25] But both writers are also caught in the impasse of trying to touch upon the foreign body in writing in ways that do not just make it signify—while also making it signify. By calling up a lexis of the fleshy and the concrete, they create a real sensation of revelation that feels more immediate than the lifeless text. Both texts, in different ways, attempt to get closer to the holy grail of the real, split between the surplus of "religion" and the incontrovertible (mundane) reality of sneakers, church halls, beer, and cigarettes.

Gesture and Religion as Sites of Faith and Doubt

> Man himself acts [*handelt*] through the hand [*Hand*]; for the hand is, together with the word, the essential distinction of man.
> —Martin Heidegger, *Parmenides* (1942–1943)

Leafing through our dictionaries, certain commonplace words stand out as little cultural drawers that have been used to store opposing observations. (It is not that we did not notice the problems or that they were dreamt up by the philosophers and theorists looking to keep themselves in work. We noticed them and stored them, as if we needed an operative expression of the contradictions in shorthand.) Some words seem designed for maximal functionality, slick action. Others seem designed to register dysfunction or inject a pause. Perversely, it seems that these pauses and competing nuances have been stored in those words that we use for doing things and getting things done, as if doing/performing becomes complex as soon as it is thought.

I have already noted some of the ambiguities in the words *act* and *performance*. These are mild compared to those packed into that strange little word *gesture*. *Gesture* seems particularly, whimsically, perverse. It is as if it has been deliberately designed to bring two questions to the fore. Firstly, *gesture* carries the connotations of a weak, partial, or even hypocritical or ironic action. Therefore, every time we use it, it begs the question of the effectiveness or sincerity of the act. Secondly, *gesture* has been used to mean an act that functions precisely like a word. Thus, it foregrounds the question that we try to mask in our clear antitheses between lived and archived religion: words and worlds, texts and acts.

Gesture is a word that seems to have been manipulated to describe those acts that only reach, impotently, half-heartedly, or ironically toward their ostensible end. Hence the phrase *gesturing toward* or even (putting even more words and distance between the actor and the outcome) *making a gesture toward*. Gesture implies the deliberate failure of hypocrisy or irony, as in "Donald Trump made a gesture toward combating racism by appointing Ben Carson as secretary of housing and urban development." The *Oxford Dictionary of English* renders one of the many senses stockpiled in *gesture* as "an action performed for show in the knowledge that it will have no effect." An act already compresses the senses of serious performance and staged performance, proper and improper.[26] But *gesture* goes further—or rather not so far. It signals a weak act, an act that does not have enough force to go through with itself. This can be an effect of hypocrisy (a deliberate split between will and force) or an effect of a lack of power. *Gesture* is regularly used to gesture to the kind of act that cannot, despite its best efforts, do what it wants to get done. *Gesture* is a word that can be qualified (sometimes tautologically) by the word *helpless*, unlike *performance* or *act*. *Gesture* is regularly preceded by the qualifier *mere*. This makes it unlike actions and more like words or scripts. In its "mereness" or its ability to be qualified in terms of lack of power, the word *gesture* seems to deliberately break through the border that separates acts and scripts.

Gesture is like a drawer crammed with our conceptual odds and ends. It has been used to gesture to the disjunction between intention and outcome or the space between act and will. It has been used to express the weak act that (for various reasons) fails. Since one of the many kinds of weak acts stashed in the idea of *gesture* is the feigned act, gesture draws attention to the space between act and meaning or intention. *Gesture* foregrounds the fact that there may be a faulty connection between the will and the execution and between the act and its decipherment. Thus, a gesture is a kind of act that is particularly vulnerable to being misread.

But, at the same time—and this is where *gesture* becomes particularly interesting because particularly conflicted—gesture has been used to bear the sense, quite precisely, of a particular kind of action that can be read. *Gesture* is a word we use for an act that functions like a word. Historically, *gesture* has been used to indicate actions that clearly indicate: movements that are wired in a mechanical way to will, intention, and effect. But at the same time, and equally pointedly, *gesture* explicitly points to the act that ended up as a mere gesture because it was not powerful enough or because it was never really meant.

I want to explore the tensions and potential of gesture and also trace a persistent pairing between gesture and religion by looking at that tragically underread classic of 1644: John Bulwer's *Chirologia: or the Naturall Language of the Hand, Composed of the Speaking Motions, and Discoursing Gestures Thereof. Whereunto is added Chironomia: Or, the Art of Manuall Rhetorike, Consisting of the Naturall Expressions, digested by Art in the Hand, as the chiefest Instrument of Eloquence, By Historicall Manifestos Exemplified*—hereafter, less verbosely, *Chirologia*. This massive and tedious archive of gesture seems to deliberately foreground the ambiguities of the author's own gesture. Published by J. A. Gent.o.Philochirosophus, the book questions the sincerity of the gesture in its labored puns, its self-conscious theatricality, and its hyperbolic devotion to the task.

In an approach that is hardly going to endear him to modern scholars of religion, Bulwer searches assiduously through the "scattered glances and touches of Antiquity" (that is, the Bible and the classics), to produce a Eurocentric archive of gesture which he then presents as a veritable bible of the hand.[27] This scripture of gesture puns on various organizational devices and tropes of Christian scripture: Chirologia; Chironomia; Indigitatio, the Canons of the Fingers; and the Apocrypha of Action. Tabular chirograms collate all the "typical significations" and are "so ordered to serve for privy ciphers to any secret intimation."[28] Laid out as a quasi-alphabet from A to Z, alpha to omega, and accompanied by explanatory apparatus and garrulous exegesis, the chirograms are the essential vocabulary of the hand.

Written in 1644, *Chirologia* was penned at roughly the same time that Lord Herbert of Cherbury (1583–1648) was busy distilling the essence of natural religion, and René Descartes (1596–1650) was locating the touching point between thinking stuff and extended stuff in the soul as pineal gland. Like the more famous writings of Herbert and Descartes, *Chirologia* can be read as a work that resonates with contemporary concerns and impasses, as well as a curio from the early modern past. As contemporary scholars attempt to "unearth experience from the thick sedimentary strata of language covering it,"[29] so Bulwer attempts to strip back the accretions of language to touch the primary language of gesture and the hand.[30] Echoing, from a distance, what is hoped for in the contemporary turn from a top-down administration (the religion of elites and angels) to the lived and embodied, Bulwer apostrophizes the nonsovereign, proto-democratic hand. The hand bespeaks body, is a metonym for body, indeed a member of parliament for the body. It "speaks for all the members [of the body], denoting their suffrages and including their votes."[31] Closing the gap between the material and the immaterial, the hand is envisioned as a kind of embodied soul, a figure for the elusive meeting point between immaterial and material, inside and outside, rather like Descartes's pineal gland.

Bulwer's quest for an essential "manual discourse" coincided with the birth of religion as an independent sequestered category and the quest for the essentials of natural (universal) religion and natural (universal) law.[32] Empire and discovery provided the context and the stimulus for these enterprises that went hand to hand. Bulwer references this directly when, bragging that he is the first to "handle gesture,"[33] he presents himself as the first pioneer cartographer to visit that "one Province not to have been visited, the land of Gesture," in order to bring back the precious treasure which, like all colonial treasures, will benefit "men in all regions of the habitable world."[34]

Missionary endeavors in New Worlds had forced home the paradox that European languages and alphabets were (of course) superior but also tragically localized and secret. As the Spanish Jesuit José de Acosta fretted (in Spanish) "when the word *sol* is written; neither Greek nor Hebrew knows what it means, for these languages do not know the Latin word itself."[35] Or as Bulwer puts it, (somewhat optimistically) "by speech we are only understood by people of our own country and lingua; but by gesture, we render our thoughts and our passions intelligible to all Nations, indifferently, under the sun."[36] The perceived parochialism and failure of language led to a renewed faith in gesture. But falling back into the fundamental language of gesture led, in turn, to an acute sense of the failed or ineffective act that is shelved at the forefront of the word gesture. Fray Juan de Torquemada reports how Christian basics were "taught by the holy religious men in pantomime, and only in signs; in signaling to the sky and saying that they ought to believe that the only God was there; and turning their eyes to the earth, they signified that there was hell, wherein walked the likeness of toads and serpents. These were the demons tormenting the condemned souls."[37] (I would have paid good money to have witnessed this evangelistic dumbshow. Having attempted my own gauche improvisations of the relatively simple desire for a bill or an ice-cream, I marvel at the audacity of attempting to gesture to a Boschian hell.) Columbus seems blithely oblivious to the problems with his methodology in his fact-finding mission in Cuba: "I thought that it was a temple and I called [the natives] and asked by signs if they said prayers in it. They said no." Which universal gestural sign did he use to communicate prayer?[38]

As his contemporary Lord Herbert of Cherbury was busy distilling the essence of natural religion and the Salamanca theologians and their followers were busy working out the essentials of the law of nations, Bulwer was hard at work distilling the international essence of communication. The quest for the ur-language, the ur-religion, and the primal essential law were motivated by the same desire for security, transparency, and nostalgia—and manipulation. They all participated in a mystical-rational dream of touching, through the natural, the Origin and the One. Bulwer argues that the motions and habits of the hand are "purely natural, not positive"—just like natural religion, or natural law.[39] The idea is that we can touch the One and one another through the primary *Chironomia* or laws of the hand. However, as with the law of nations, there is something coercive and manipulative about the outstretched hand.[40] Faced with the difficult task of persuading readers to plod through his laborious inventory of gesture, Bulwer offers the incentive that those who master the universal lexis of the hand will have the upper hand in trade. Like natural law and natural religion, the language of the hand is fundamentally benign and available to all. It "speaks all languages" and has the "universal character of reason," being "generally understood and known by all nations among the formal differences of their tongue."[41]

Strange early modern texts and obsessions intersect with contemporary reflections on tension between the given and the constructed. This tension is intrinsic to (and managed by) the concepts of natural (gestural) language, natural religion, and natural law. The promise of managing such a fundamental tension helps to explain why we have been so addicted to concepts such as natural language, religion, and law. All three are described as fundamental, given, prior to all deductions and projections—and yet all have to be learned and recovered. The origin, the fundamental, is out there, back there. We just have to get closer to it. We need to recover the natural/given though it is known by all. Luckily, the Christian-biblical archive has devices for articulating and managing this paradox of the given and the (re)constructed, just like contemporary religious studies (though the devices are, of course, very different). The explanatory mechanism is: "We had it; we touched it; but we lost it." This is the meaning of those versatile and important myths of Babel and the Fall. The power of these myths is that they help us live with the tension and go on laboring and producing within it. We have had our cake and eaten it, had our givenness and naturalness and made it, thanks to the beautifully flexible structures of Babel and the Fall.

Bulwer performs this productive tension when he claims that the language of the hand was lost, or "partly lost,"[42] with Adam, but that, on the other hand, the language of the hand survived the catastrophe of Babel as a purely linguistic fall. The natural language of the hand is "purely natural, not positive."[43] It is given, not constructed. But because it was lost, or partly lost, Bulwer must work at (re) constructing "the kind of knowledge that Adam partly lost with his innocency, yet might be repaired in us."[44] The "natural language of the hand" had the "happinesse to escape the curse at the confusion of Babel," and moreover "hath since been sanctified by the expressions of our Saviour's Hands."[45] Thus gesture is simultaneously on one side of the Fall and the other. It dramatically embodies the tension that is also intrinsic to natural religion and natural law.

The opening statement of *Chirologia* is effectively: *En archē ēn ho cheirologos* (cf. John 1.1). The argument is based on a theology of manual incarnation and redemption. Bulwer sets about recovering a fundamental language, which is not split like verbal language but still has to be recovered, and indeed which varies between nations. (Gesture has fallen into disuse among the more moderate English and Germans, while "in France he is not *a la mode*, and a *compleat Mounsieur*, who is not nimble in the discoursing garbe of his hand."[46]) The task is to work out which gestures are primal and which are superfluous; which are positive and which are natural. The same (unending) process applies to natural religion and natural law. At the end of the quest is the promise that one can touch the origin and the universal and break back through the conceptual, postlapsarian shadows that haunt us. (Think of the almost touching fingertips in Michelangelo's *Creation of Adam*.) Trying to think of the terms that would take them closest to the fundamental, early moderns sank back into the solidity of religion, gesture (body), and law.

In *Chirologia*, primal gesture and religion are virtually synonymous. Bulwer's hand is rather like the god function in Cartesian philosophy. It is embodied soul: the point where the invisible and the material touch. Gesture and religion also touch in the primary gesture envisaged as prayer. The first four letters of Bulwer's manual alphabet are *Supplico*, *Oro*, *Ploro*, and *Admiror* (fig. 1.1).

The hands in the fundamental gestural ABCD are all reaching upward. It is as if Bulwer believes that reaching upward is somehow *the* primal gesture. (Presumably this was the "universal" gesture used by Columbus in Cuba to ask the natives if this "temple" was where they said their prayers.) The raised hands in the first line are in marked contrast to the horizontal social gestures in the next line: *applaudo, indignor, explodor*.[47] Prayer is the exhibition of "our great infirmity," our inability to move our "soaring thoughts . . . beyond the centre of our bodies." In prayer, the hands "supplying the place of wings, help our hearts in their flight upward."[48] *Gestus* II, *Oro*, seems to be taken as the primal gesture, insofar as it expresses the limits of our powers, the desire to extend ourselves beyond the edges of ourselves. Prayer appears as the fundamental gesture because it is the gesture of infirmity. Summoning prayer (*oro*, *supplico*) as the fundamental gesture seems to equate gesture, at source, with a lack of power. The hands that reach upward convey the same impotence as the phrase *gesturing toward*. Nothing seems to embody the weakness and precariousness of gesture as starkly as prayer. The word *precarious*, coined in the 1640s when Bulwer was writing *Chirologia*, was first used as a legal term to describe the condition of being "held through the favor of another." The derivation was from Latin *precarius* "obtained by asking or praying," from *prex* (genitive *precis*) "entreaty, prayer." Prayer, gesture, and precariousness touch at the point where we attempt to mark (or gesture toward) the limit or insufficiency of power, will, or action. Perhaps the most fundamental point about gesture is the place where the fingertips end.

The belief in prayer as the fundamental gesture is a common thought-reflex, found in dictionaries, philosophies—and Bulwer's *Chirologia*. Heidegger, like Bulwer, begins his reflections on the hand with prayer. "Through the hand can occur both prayer and murder, greeting and thanks, oath and signal, and also the 'work' of the hand."[49] Like the connotations of the word *gesture*—though in a more complex and idiosyncratic fashion—Heidegger also links words and hands

A Corollary of the Speaking Motions

FIGURE 1.1 Bulwer's manual alphabet, starting with the four fundamental gestures of prayer and worship (A–D) before moving to the social realm.

and sees words and hands as the "essential distinction of man": "The hand sprang forth only out of the word and together with the word. Only a being which, like man, 'has' the word can and must 'have' 'the hand.'"[50] *Have* is in inverted commas because the hand, like the word, is never a simple tool of agency but a force of dispossession. "Man does not 'have' hands, but hands hold the essence of man."[51] Perhaps this is why prayer appears so primary, because it is a gesture of dispossession, supplication, lack of power.

Modern dictionaries also begin with prayer. The *Oxford English Dictionary* defines gesture as "a manner of placing the body; position, posture, attitude, *esp. in acts of prayer and worship*." There is a special and privileged relation between gesture and acts of worship and prayer. In seeking out our primal gestures, the *New Dictionary of the History of Ideas* calls on religion and the military. Gesture is best exemplified in "the gestures of kneeling and folding the hands in prayer," "the movements of the priest officiating at Mass, especially in the elevation of the host and in other religious rituals," and the military "gait" and "salute."[52] Out of habit, we imagine the most precise choreographers of our bodies to be gods, military commanders and priests.

Gesture has operated as a strange word through which we summon (or supplicate or pray to) that which is beyond us, just out of reach, which is to say in the traditional space of the God of Christianity. In its primal state and maybe at its origin (so the *Oxford English Dictionary* and Bulwer lead us to believe), it seems that *gesture* gestures toward the ineffable: that which, as Samuel Beckett said, "cannot be effed." Gesture is also the place where the grasping for the security and solidity of body instantly turns back on itself. Gesture seems to carry something of the Reformation contrast between faith and *mere* works—works being another kind of action that, like gesture, can be qualified by *mere*. Calvin and the Reformers did a great deal to drain the sincerity from *gesture*. "There is eachwhere too much of pompes, ceremonies and gesturings," Calvin complained.[53] Even works with pure intention, works that avoid the hypocrisy of *gesture*, are impotent. In strong Reformation theology works can do nothing; they aim for an end that only God can accomplish. According to this logic, people make futile gestures but only God acts. Human acts are *precarious* in the original sense of "dependent on the will of another." *Gesture* embodies this dependence: this act that (alone) cannot work or fulfill itself.

On the other hand, Bulwer's chirograms also express a fantasy of perfect manipulation; hyper-agency concentrated in the hand. In a beautifully naïve pathway from interior will to exterior gesture, hands express the soul within and perfectly control the force field of affect. For example, were you to "shut in your two inferior fingers, and present your other three in an eminent posture in the extended Hand" in a gesture as precise and awkward as Fleming's left-hand motor rule, you would have perfectly executed (with mechanical efficiency) the "speaking action, significant to demand silence, and procure audience" (fig. 1.2).[54] (Try this when you are next giving a public talk.) Ebulliently performing the dream of gesture as visible word at maximal legibility, Bulwer offers the "candid and ingenious reader" (would that we still flattered our readers thus!) nothing less than a "rhetorical alphabet of manual significations" and a "manual text of utterance," in which the hand can be read off as the "instrument of the will."[55] This stubborn logic runs from Quintilian to semiologists in the relatively recent field of gesture studies, where gesture is "visible action" used as an "utterance."[56] (The move is naïve but insurmountable. How to say anything about gesture without treating it, in some sense as utterance, or without assuming that "a gesture is a combination of a body movement (or a bodily posture) and a meaning"?[57]) In fact, in gesture studies gesture must be (at least for academic purposes so that we can construct our sign systems) "an action over which we exercise at least some degree of voluntary control."[58]

Bulwer adheres less strictly to the orthodoxy of agency than contemporary practitioners of gesture studies. He allows for involuntary gestures such as crying and involuntary expressions of despair. And even as a dream of hyper-agency is

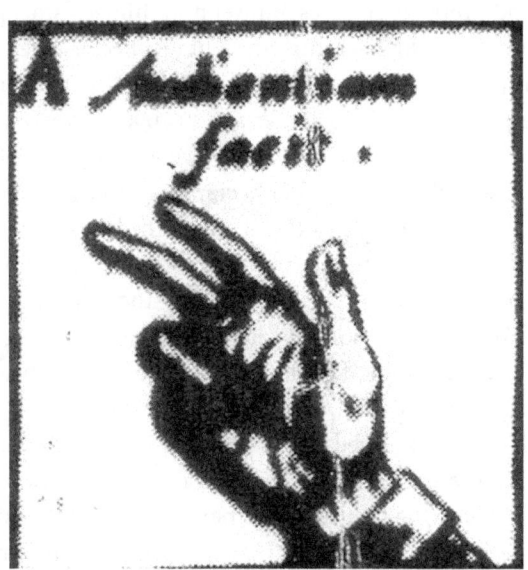

FIGURE 1.2   Chirogram for the "speaking action" of demanding silence and compelling the audience to pay attention.

concentrated in the hand, as a metonym of body, it collapses into convoluted exegeses and expressions of lack of faith. Interpretation becomes insecure at the level of decipherment (between gesture and observer) and at source (between the gesturer's motions and his or her soul or will). Words and gestures are caught in paradoxes of mutual dependency and mutual mirroring. In a simple incarnational, platonic theology of gesture, the hand is the ambassador of the soul; the "substitute and vice-regent of the tongue."[59] And yet (and the twist is so intrinsic to the history of Western philosophies and scriptures that it is entirely unsurprising) there is no sovereign without the supplement, visible vice-regent, or mediator. If Bulwer's hand serves as a kind of pineal gland, a point where the material and the immaterial touch, then all the usual impasses flow from the attempt to imagine such an impossible point. The paradoxes are generated automatically, without any intentional gesture on Bulwer's part, from the binaries in which he—and we—are inscribed.) The hand is deputy; and the hand is sovereign. Without the hand, the soul cannot make contact. "The soul being invisible, unless she show herself by demonstration of gesture, the hand was instituted surrogate, and vicar of the heart."[60]

As soon as you gesticulate, you need to articulate. And at once the fantasized point of solid, simple contact becomes a chain of "manual significations" that are garrulous, ambiguous, insecure, and potentially insincere. In his attempt to exegete, clarify, and canonize gestures, Bulwer finds himself stockpiling numerous potential meanings for a single gesture and not just because he is a citizen of the seventeenth century, with a penchant for numerous subclauses and sentences that are ten or twelve lines long. What is intended as an alphabet of gesture becomes a dictionary. Early modernity was the birthplace for the concept of religion and the dictionary.[61] A simple gesture often becomes a meeting point for opposites, just like the word *gesture*. For example, "To apply the hand passionately unto the head is a sign of anguish, sorrow, grief, impatience, and lamentation, used also by those who *accuse* or *justify* themselves."[62] The stockpiled nuances, pulling in different directions of accusation and justification seem to touch, across the centuries, Orsi's decipherment of the body language of the holy as a revelation of "sentimentality, horror, titillation, awe and disgust."[63]

Chirologia is fascinating because it performs, so overtly, the paradoxes of gesture as the dream of perfect correlation of intention, action, and utterance, but also the space where the failure of this perfect correlation cannot be denied. Absolute faith in gesture is constantly asserted—and qualified and undermined. The confidence of gesture is decomposed by the two fundamental doubts and lacks intrinsic to the very idea of "gesture": hypocrisy and the insufficiency of human power. Both of these find their focal point in religion. As the fundamental "letter A" of gesture is occupied by prayer and the rites of religion, so religion and particularly prayer are also the primary site of doubt. Indeed the doubt intrinsic to the very idea of gesture seems to spiral out from Christian/biblical invective against idolatry and hypocrisy (from *hypokrites*: actor), amplified by Reformation theologies of the ineffective and often insincere act.[64] Caught between profound suspicion and profound belief in gesture, Bulwer warns us to beware of the "idolaters who are apes" and the hypocrites who can "extend their arms and hands" when "their hearts belie their hands."[65] Religion is the source of faith in gesture and profound anxiety about gesture. Gesture becomes the guarantor of the real, the primary, the natural, the One (so close we can almost touch it)—and also that which we are well-advised to doubt.

Tactile Scriptures and Abraham's Hand

> Gestus XXXIV: Castigo, "I chastise": To shake or hold the stretched and raised hand over any is their expression who offer to chastise and show a willingness to strike or take revenge. Hence the prohibition of the angel to Abraham (about to sacrifice his son, after he had stretched out his hand) to that intent: "Lay not thine hand upon the child."
>
> —John Bulwer, *Chirologia*

Strangely, Bulwer is more open about the vacillation between faith and doubt than some contemporary scholars of religion, who seem more able to put their faith in the purity and legibility of the act. Modern scholars tend to make performance relatively reliable through those acts of "comparative religion," discussed earlier.[66] By calling on the foil of scripture and the biblical scholars, they stabilize and securitize the relative confidence of "act." Often scripture is portrayed as a straw or paper man confined in his natural habitat: the study. In a very strange summary, Orsi describes the kind of religion that has its head in scripture (or its head stuck up its scripture) as "private and interior" rather than "shamelessly public," and "intellectually consistent and reasonable" rather than "ambivalent and contradictory."[67]

Orsi is arranging his binaries so as to make the nonscriptural space look more solid, wild, and enticing. Taking the Hebrew Bible/Old Testament, for example, we can concede that there might be some truth (but still only some) in this, if we are referring only to the smoothed down Bible of the systematic theologians or biblical scholars.[68] But even this is only partly true. For those who work on the Hebrew Bible are most acutely aware of the Bible as a "box containing heterogeneous materials,"[69] with the emphasis on material. They know that writing does not function as signs absorbed into paper or papyrus. Writing is conceived of as a storage box, not unlike the ark of the covenant. Scripture is a place for preserving monuments, names, events, sites, things, and nouns. The stylistic codes are different, but biblical writers show the same kind of determination as an Orsi or a Bender to touch us, if not assault us, with the visceral and the "truth" of the body. They pack detail dense and thick to conjure the solidity of the real. The book/box stores long inventories of the materials and dimensions of a temple or tabernacle. (It's as if it is buried there, like instructions for an Ikea flat pack, so that one day it can be built again from scratch.) Tedious genealogies and the precise ingredients and rituals of sacrifice attempt to preserve the presence of a people and their temple, as if to keep it/them and keep it/them "real." Somber records of the cut, length, and color of the high priest's garment create a density of worldliness, as in Bender's thick-set sentence about the "heavyset woman in her early thirties . . . in loose fitting sweatpants" and "a long-sleeved white shirt."[70] And as Elaine Scarry famously noted, there is a relentless emphasis on externalization: tools, weapons, labor, wounds, bodies—and hands.[71] There is an almost Heideggerian obsession with the hand. It's as if the texts are seeking to outdo Orsi and Vasquez in their determination to get at the sonic, tactile, kinetic, olfactory, and gustatory (all of which change, of course, in their transformation into text). Even God enjoys the sweet smell of sacrifice (Gen. 8.21), as if to compete with Orsi's lingering smell of cigarettes. The prophetic word or scroll is often eaten or turned into a gustatory experience (Ezek. 3.1–3; Rev. 10.9–10). It then manifests itself in strange symptoms which are, contra Orsi, "shamelessly public."[72] Prophets go naked and barefoot and have sex with prostitutes. They complain that they have been raped and violated by the word of God which has forced them into bizarre acts such as eating revolting cakes baked over dung or being bound by a yoke of straps and bars (Jer. 13; Hosea 1–1; Ezek. 4 and 5; Jer. 27 and 28).[73] A long way from a Protestant model of serene and private reading (orientated around the soul, mind, and "reason and belief"), the texts keep forcing us back into the corporeal by incorporating details about bodies writhing on too short beds with too short covers (Isa. 28.19); bodies slopped like liquid from one container to another (Jer. 48.11); bodies covered in shit, swimming in milk and honey, or being digested or vomited out of the land (Jer. 51). Famously even God is radically anthropomorphic. He has a back, regrets, and hands. Even Bulwer finds this a bit too much. He ingeniously gets around the problem by falling back on the device of accommodation.[74] "God is pleased to condescend to the capacity of man" and thereby "contribute to the advancement of the dignity and reputation of the Hand."[75] In a lovely gesture based on the paradox of word/act at the heart of gesture, it turns out that God only *said* he had a hand because he wanted to act as a divine patron for Bulwer's important project on the hand.

To show that God is not alone in the Bible in his commitment to gesture, Bulwer itemizes all the "Hebraismes and mysterious notions resulting from the property of the hand."[76] Helpfully contributing to the primer of gesture, the prophet Ezekiel models how to smite hand to hand in grief. The prophet Jeremiah holds up his hand to the loins, as a gesture of melancholy (apparently).[77] The rude gesture of the extended middle finger meaning "I provoke an argument" is obligingly demonstrated by the prophet Isaiah.[78] Explaining how the gesture "to shake or hold the stretched and raised hand" is (in a typically ambidextrous, verbose, conflicting exegesis) an expression of chastisement or the "willingness to strike or take revenge," Bulwer adds "Hence the prohibition of the angel to Abraham (about to sacrifice his son, after he had stretched out his hand) to that intent: 'Lay not thine hand upon the child.' (Gen. 22.12)."[79] The idea that the angel is going to *chastise* Abraham for obeying God is strange, and extremely strange for the 1640s. (Compare the gesture "Naughty Abraham!" in fig. 1.5). Even more curious, in fact completely anomalous, is the notion that the angel may want to strike Abraham or take revenge.

Bulwer's response highlights how scripture—and this piece of scripture in particular—is deeply "ambivalent and contradictory" or, better, ambidextrous. For Abraham's sacrifice is a fragment from the good old book that focuses relentlessly on the body and the conflicting gestures of the hand. Artists register this (albeit subliminally) as they embody the text as frozen posture, remembering the climactic scene of the son sprawled out on the altar with the father's hand perpetually suspended above him. The story becomes similarly gestural in the Koran (Sura 37), where the son puts his forehead down to the ground modeling the posture of prayer (*salat*).

I want to use Genesis 22 to explore how we might liberate a biblical text from static models of textuality and late modern Protestant and academic models of reading, and so overcome a reductive dichotomy between texts and acts. This is a text that insists on its materiality (wood, fire, body, knife) and that seeks to archive and preserve the act qua act. As one of the many origin stories, and new beginnings, in Genesis, the text narrates (as if with a nod to Heidegger), the creation of the nation and "man" through the word and the hand, as if word and hand constituted the essence of man.[80] Elaine Scarry analyzes how the Old Testament and Hebrew Bible conscript labor and material—primarily *human material*—for the arduous task of giving body and presence to the invisible God. God is gestured to in miraculously reproducing bodies, temples (with all their belabored artifacts and interiors) and bodies that receive pain from and for God. At the summit of the labor of divine representation stands Abraham. As the most extreme act of witness, human sacrifice goes into the furthest recesses of the body. By "turning his insides out" and putting his son and future under the knife, Abraham does everything he can possibly do to testify to, and concretize, God.[81]

As Erich Auerbach insists, the text belabors physical action, while occluding interior secrets.[82] It is not simply that the narrative is agnostic about the "faith" ascribed to it in the New Testament and massively amplified by Luther and Kierkegaard. It lacks inner life and effects the complete sacrifice of inner life, irrespective of the technicality that nobody ever actually goes under the knife. This text is the very opposite of all the caricatures we lazily pile on text. It has nothing to say about mind, soul, reason, or belief. Putting all interiority on the altar, eschewing background, the text is nothing but an inventory of tools (knife, wood, fire) and an account of work for hands (and feet). It is, we could say, prosaic or "pedestrian," in that metaphor for the commonplace that we take not from hands but feet.

In a laboriously accumulating pile of action that reads like a recipe for human sacrifice told by someone with an eye for every pedantic, tactile detail, we are forced to watch the old robotic patriarch get everything together, as if getting ready for a barbecue. We watch him saddle his donkey, cut wood, carry knife and fire (fire in one hand and knife in the other, presumably?), then lay the wood on the son's back—most likely because he himself only had two hands rather than because he wanted to begin to craft a typology for Christ. In a literally pedestrian concentration on the journey, we watch father and son "walk together" (reiterated twice) and walk for three days, together with the servants they take with them, in order to open up a space for awkward conversation when they leave the servants behind. As Erich Auerbach noted, the *structure* of the text is sacrificial, pleasure-denying, for both characters and readers. It is rather like listening to a pedantic relative report all the details of the bus, train, or car journey to the seaside as if unable to distinguish (or distinguishing differently) between the trivia and the main event.

Sharing a sense of labor and ordeal, the reader trudges to the top of the mountain, with his or her eyes on pedestrian details: wood, knife, hands, and feet. At the climax we get to watch Abraham build an altar, lay the wood in order, lay the son on top of the wood—then reach out his hand to take the knife to slaughter the son (Gen. 22.10). The hand and the reaching-out are surely redundant. How else would one take a knife but in the hand? How could one take a knife without putting out the hand? This is not just a tactic of retardation to highlight the climactic moment. It is a tactic of making us feel the tactile. The hand extends itself, insists on itself, as if trying to take over the narrative and force itself through the ripped page. And then the messenger of God intervenes and says (appropriately enough), "Do not lay a hand."

In the biblical text the angel speaks, gives a countermand. He does not grab or lay a counter-hand. But as if responding to all the manual cues in the original, artists gave the angel hands, turning the story into an ambidextrous drama of four hands. Caravaggio's sacrifice of 1603 centers on a drama of hands on the diagonal. Reading upward from the focal point of the son's open mouth (bottom right), we see Abraham's left hand pressing his son's face down on the altar; his right tensed over the knife poised within inches of the jugular; and the two hands of the angel, one restraining the hand that holds the knife and the other pointing to the surrogate ram in the shadows (fig. 1.3).

Rembrandt's sumptuously theatrical Oriental sacrifice, painted in 1635 (nine years before the publication of Bulwer's *Chirologia*), centers on a vertical chain of hands (fig. 1.4). The angel hands at the top (one raised in a gesture of "halt," one gripping Abraham's wrist) lead down to the two hands of Abraham: the hand that loosens its hold on the knife through the pressure of the angel's hand, and the swarthy paw on the lower right-hand side, covering Isaac's face. Like Bulwer

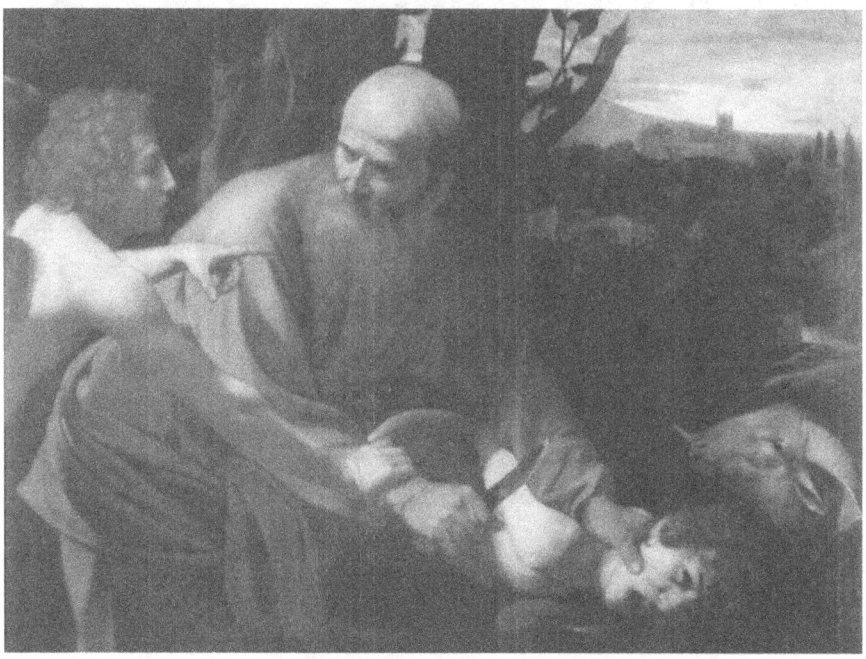

FIGURE 1.3   Caravaggio's 1603 sacrifice of Isaac (Uffizi, Florence).
The drama centers on the diagonal chain of hands (top left to bottom right).

FIGURE 1.4 Rembrandt, *Sacrifice of Isaac*, 1635 (Hermitage, St. Petersburg). The drama centers on a vertical chain of hands and the contact between the angel hand and Abraham's hand, causing the dangerous release of the knife.

and his strange readings of the angel hand, Rembrandt adds his own strange visual glosses to this drama of the hand. First, Abraham has not intentionally dropped the knife. This is an unintentional, even accidental gesture. Second—and far more strikingly—the knife is still hurtling toward the exposed torso of Isaac, threatening collateral damage and warning that the *technically* aborted sacrifice may yet take place.[83]

We cannot read these artistic cross sections of a second sequentially. Our eyes are drawn to all four hands around which competing gestures wrestle and collide. The fatherly hands pressing down on Isaac's face press home the terrifying proximity of aggression and protection, tool and the weapon, breaking and making, the killing of a son, the building of a nation, the splattering of blood and the (pro)creative burst of heavenly stars (Gen. 22.17).

Abraham's hand condenses, in its swarthy fist, all the dense paradoxes of Heidegger's hand. For Heidegger, the "hand exists as hand only where there is disclosure and concealment." The possibility of doing and not doing, and also dissimulating, separates the human hand from the talon, claw or paw. An ambiguity of agency as well as ethical ambiguity are concentrated in Abraham and Heidegger's hand. "Through the hand can occur both prayer and murder, greeting and thanks, oath and signal, and also the 'work' of the hand, the 'hand-work' and the tool. The handshake seals the covenant. The hand brings about the 'work' of destruction."[84] Abraham's handshake with God, so to speak, builds a world by destruction—or a gesture toward destruction. Abraham's hand is the exemplary human hand because its gesture is ethically ambiguous, and because it leaves us fundamentally uncertain about what it is doing. It does something and withdraws, as Abraham is praised for "not withholding" the son.

In the original text the angel (who does not have hands but commands Abraham not to lay a hand) praises Abraham twice for having *not withheld* (Gen. 22.12, 16). It is good that Abraham has let go of his son, released his grip and given him up to God in sacrifice. It is also good that then, in obedience to the second voice, he has released his grip on the knife. What appears as the only glimpse of interiority is, in the original text, something of a tautology. Angels, gods, and readers can deduce that Abraham "fears" God from the fact that he has cut, saddled, carried, walked, built, laid, put out his hand, held, and not withheld. But in not withholding, he has still held onto the son—or at the very least, offered him and snatched him back.

And this is what makes this story so strange and so compelling. What happens is delineated very clearly at the end as a gesture in the sense of a weak act: an act that does not make it to completion. For accuracy, the word *happens* should be placed in the kind of inverted commas that are used to cast doubt on the reality of phenomena, as should "sacrifice," since nothing happens. The event is canceled out, and there is no sacrifice at all. This is deeply confusing. The human sacrifice looked set on course to be a real act, a really real act, the most real kind of act: the kind of act that tries to evoke the guarantee of the real in the body and damage to the body, in the spurt of blood, the touch of cold metal on flesh. But then, having gone to all this trouble (and such trouble, such labor), having gone for the very jugular of the real, the act is commuted at the last minute to a mere gesture. Abraham's hand is stayed by the angel hand, just before contact: "Do not lay a hand." The contrast and the pathos are unbearable. Abraham does nothing in the end. It turns out that this act that was going to go through with it, all the way down to the very depths of the body, does not have to go to the bother of taking place. *It is enough that Abraham has gestured toward sacrifice.*[85] The act that was going to go to the very heart of the matter does not matter. The body slips away from us, just when we were about to grasp it. "The body, bodily, never happens, least of all when it's named and convoked. For us, the body is always sacrificed."[86] We do not touch the body after all.

In the divine director's cut, the act is cut off just before the fatal cut. It is as if someone has taken the typewritten script and penned in an alternative ending, more suitable for Hollywood. An angel or runner comes on to snatch the knife. Maybe for effect the director chooses not to tell the actor so that we can see him really "blink," hear the "stammered tone," and watch the "worried look" that "pass[es] over his brow."[87] Saying "not really, not literally, I will take a substitute," the messenger produces from the wings a fleecy understudy for Isaac which has, we are told, been hiding there all along. This first act of substitution legitimates all those further substitutions—all those further quests for hidden meaning. Anything can happen now. Isaac can be substituted by the ram, and the ram can turn into a lamb who is really a man in sheep's clothing, Christ. Transformed into a frozen, stilted tableau of typology, the text's gestures will be corralled into a very precise verbal utterance, focused purely and exclusively on the gospel. The son carries the wood on his back as Jesus will carry the cross; the ram, morphing conveniently into a lamb, will really shed his blood once he finds his true identity as the crucified Christ.

But the original text performs a far more ambiguous and ambidextrous gesture—and one that opens up into all the ambiguities of gesture. We cannot simply read the deity's or angel's "do not lay a hand" as repudiation or negation. This is a delicately, even precariously, balanced gesture. We need to get the balance just right. But it is so easy to overstep (for the sake of clarity and important alliances between gods, laws, and morality) as Bulwer demonstrates when he overreads the commuting of the act as divine chastisement or even revenge. We have to remember that even as it is canceled and radically altered, Abraham's perfect enactment gets hearty applause, rave divine reviews: "Because you have done this and not withheld your son, your only son, I will surely bless you, etc." "Done" in the modified sense here should really be in inverted commas. "Not withholding is a very different thing to killing a son and burning him whole. The text leaves us with the fundamental aporia of a laudable, perfect act and an act that is all the more (or perhaps just equally) laudable for never having happened. A similar paradox haunts the performance in the Koran. Having seen the act performed in a dream, Ibrahim consults the son: "My son, I see in a dream that I am sacrificing you. What do you think?" As the two begin to enact the dream they are rewarded by the cancellation of this literal enactment. In an ambiguous statement, Ibrahim receives divine approval for "believing the dream." Both the Bible and the Koran present the sacrifice, ambiguously as an iconic act and a ban on acting out.

And Abraham's sacrifice is remembered for precisely this, this gesture toward sacrifice without actually getting there. With Caravaggio and Rembrandt, cultural memory freezes the scene in this moment, *Augenblick*, this split second in which Abraham's hand is poised to strike and has been stopped just after he was prepared to strike. In this split second, these two gestures ("he is about to do it" and "he has just ceased to act") collide. The site of collision dramatizes the split between will and expression, the motion and the act, the inside and the outside. And this split is not a one-off for the crisis scene only. The split between inside and outside is insisted on, awkwardly and relentlessly, in several dramas on the surface of the text. Forced to answer the questions of Isaac and his servants, Abraham seems uncomfortably close to lying or at the very least euphemism. "Stay here with the donkey; the boy and I will go over there; we will worship, and then we will come back to you" (Gen. 22.5). Looking at this scene, we are meant to understand that the obedient acts of these bodies do not externalize the will of god in a way that is decipherable and legible. They do not enact the idea of "visible utterance" that is one of the pipe dreams of "gesture." Looking at his tableau of perfect, acute, intense obedience, we learn that God's will is not quite this, but something else. The two hands, the hands of the angel and the hands of Abraham, coexist rather than cancel one another out. If a gesture can be taken to indicate meaning or intention, then the hands that thrust and push in different directions mystify and complicate God's true desire. The right hand does not know what the left hand is doing, but both hands belong to the same corpus, the same body. The command to kill and the command to stop the killing are part of the same structure of exemplarity and perfection. Or as Hent de Vries comments, reflecting on the ambidextrous signification and ethics of religion (with strong echoes of Heidegger's hand, as ambidextrous site of "prayer and murder . . .

'hand-work' and the 'work' of destruction"), "religion's striving toward perfection (or perfectibility) and its tendency towards perversion (or, more precisely, 'pervertibility'), go hand in hand."[88]

Gesture, Promise, Theater, and Test

The so-called sacrifice of Isaac orbits around those two perennial themes of twentieth-century philosophy: the promise and the hand. God is, like Nietzschean man, a promising animal. He has promised Abraham the land of Canaan and descendants as numerous as sand on the seashore and stars in the sky. The relationship between God and Abraham and his descendants is woven from a complex fabric of promise, credence, obligation, and credit.[89] The story then develops (or is retarded) in such a way as to drive home the difference between a promise and a constative statement. Indeed, the whole of Genesis can be read as a gigantic riff on the precariousness of the promise. As J. L. Austin and Jacques Derrida have taught us, that most classic performative, the promise, is profoundly and insistently vulnerable. Perhaps the one making the promise is not serious. Perhaps he or she might die before the fulfillment of the promise. Or perhaps the one receiving the promise could die, or forget the promise, or be distracted at the moment of its fulfillment, and not see, because looking the other way. Or maybe the one making the promise is not to be trusted, not who she says she is. For these and myriad other reasons there is "an unbelievable, and comical, aspect of every promise."[90]

The only one of these possibilities that the book of Genesis shies away from is the possibility that *God* the promiser might die before the fulfillment of the promise. Genesis pushes the possibility of the death of the recipient of the promise as far as it could possibly go—into the terrain of absurdity in fact. Abraham and Sarah are pushed to the very end of their lives before they get Isaac in the very last moment, their last menopausal gasp or breath. They get so bored and restless waiting that, improvising with the (forced) help of the Egyptian slave woman, Hagar, they make another son: Ishmael. When she finally becomes pregnant, Sarah finds the realization of the promise so absurd that she names her son Isaac, meaning, "He will laugh." Then, as if to belabor the point (and Genesis does belabor the precariousness of the promise to the point of absurdity or laughter) Isaac/laughter is, in a fit of very dark divine humor, placed under the knife.

By launching a divine command against his own promise, by commanding Abraham to kill his one descendant and mutilate forever the promise of descendants, God seems pretty determined to push Abraham out of the safe haven of what Austin calls the "ordinary circumstances," which allow the promise to work.

"When I say 'I promise to,'" writes Austin, "surely the words must be spoken seriously, and so as to be taken seriously? I must not be joking, for example, nor writing a poem."[91] The efficacy of the promise is jeopardized by poetry, joking, and theater. Poetry, joking, and theater can reduce the efficacy of the promise to a mere gesture. A performative utterance will "be in a peculiar way hollow or void" if "introduced in a poem, or spoken in a soliloquy" or "said by an actor on the stage."[92]

The extraordinary conditions of Abraham's sacrifice seem calculated to explicitly raise the possibility that God might not be speaking literally nor seriously. He might be writing something less like scripture (in a fundamentalist sense) and more like a joke, a poem, or a play. How else to read this event that didn't exactly "happen" and that is lauded and applauded for not having happened, even as Abraham is praised for having been prepared to push through the curtain and the skin all the way to a "real" event. Through God's colliding words, the text seems to be telling us to listen carefully and to avoid the most obvious meaning. We must decipher, decode, and tune in to the nature of the speech act so that we can learn to distinguish between the promise and the statement, the act as action and law, and the act as event in a play. The text seems to dramatize the extremes of fundamentalism and fanaticism: the willingness to carry out the will of God to the letter. But then God annuls, or bans, the literal reading. Piety in this case means stopping short of the literal execution. Sacrifice is to be substituted by "sacrifice" as gesture and an act that is not a thing done, but something else.

It seems particularly important to remember, in the context of the revival and reinvention of religious fundamentalism, that a text that thwarts simplistic retrojections of literalism and fundamentalism lies at the origins of the so-called Abrahamic religions. Scripture is *not* simply to be executed or repeated. Even Abraham, the father at the very origin of scripture, does not get to repeat or rehearse the command in any straightforward way. The lesson, if a lesson can be deduced, seems to be that the word or the script must be deciphered and interpreted or deflected differently, even to the point of the reverse of what it seemed to want or say.

Another way of saying this is that the text becomes, very explicitly, an "act," a piece of theater, and a test. "God tested/tempted Abraham," (Gen. 22.1) the text/test declares, opening itself to all the ambiguities of Hebrew *nisah* and *Versuchung* which combine the senses of trial, temptation, and test. (*Versuchung/Versuch* even throws in, for good measure, the modern techniques and trials of *Wissenschaft*, the academic experiment, hypothesis, or test.[93]) "Whence this drive to testing?," asks Avital Ronell in *The Test Drive*. What is the provenance of this need to torture and to test? And whence this relation between testing and the truth of the body: the desire "to push out the truth in the medium of torture or pain?"[94]

In this age of biopolitics, tests proliferate, driven by the quest for the quantification and maximalization of life. Contemporary devices for maximizing life mimic strange old religious structures such as human sacrifice and resurrection. Though they take on new forms and new intensities, late modern tests find ancient precedents in trials of love and faith. As Ronell puts it, "The Almighty Himself has proven time and time again to be addicted to the exigencies of testing."[95] And good old Abraham heads these trials of faith. Ronell, like others, keeps going back to the old patriarch in her quest for the Ur-punkt of the test. "It seems that everything—nature, body, investment, belief—has indeed to be tested, including your love, including your faith."[96] Abraham's sacrifice amplifies life: it substitutes sacrifice as "birth done better" in a world where matriarchs are always barren.[97] A star splatter of descendants bursts from Isaac's body through the knife that is prepared to make the cut in the C-section of faith (Gen. 22.15–17). But at the heart of the test/text is a fundamental paradox. Judged as an act of sacrifice, Abraham's "sacrifice" can surely only get a B or maybe B+, or at a push an A-. And yet, by failing or not perfecting the act, he succeeded and made the grade.

The densely packed paradoxes that I was trying to get at earlier by poking and prodding at that little word *gesture* are dramatically if not flamboyantly staged in the extraordinary conditions of theater and the test. Like gesture, testing and theater trouble self-identity, transparency, legibility, and the orthodoxies of metaphysics. (And they do so very overtly, as in a piece of in-your-face theater, with sequined costumes, strobe lights, dancing girls, and trombones.) As "a mode of questioning, a structure of incessant research—perhaps even a mode of modality of being," testing "scans the walls of experience, measuring, probing, determining the 'what is' of the lived world." But the "very structure of testing tends to overtake the certainty that it establishes when obeying the call of open finitude." Testing reveals an "unpresumed fold in metaphysics," insofar as it "asserts another logic of truth, one that subjects itself to incessant questioning while reserving a frame, a trace, a disclosive moment to which it refers."[98]

Like testing, theater is also a "fold in metaphysics." Theatrical singularity "haunts and taunts the Western dream of self-identity," as Samuel Weber beautifully explains:

> When an event or series of events takes place without reducing the place "taken" to a purely neutral site, then that place reveals itself to be a "stage", and those events are theatrical happenings. As the gerund here suggests . . . such happenings never take place once and for all but are ongoing. This in turn suggests that they can neither be contained within the place where they unfold nor entirely separated from it. They can be said, then, in a quite literal

sense, to come to pass. They take place, which means in a particular place, and yet simultaneously also to pass away—not simply to disappear but to happen somewhere else. Out of the dislocations of its repetitions emerges nothing more or less than the singularity of the theatrical event.[99]

Theatrical space "allows no simple extraterritoriality." "To reside in it is to be most distant from it—from its truth, its reality." From the dreamt-of vantage point of self-identity, the "desire to occupy a place from which one can take everything in, first and foremost visually, but also orally and audibly," theatricality is profoundly suspect. Hence the fundamental allergy between philosophy and theater: "Insofar as one proceeds from a presumption of self-identity and self-presence, all departures from their putative self-enclosure—and theater entails just such a departure—are to be vigilantly controlled, if not condemned."[100]

In a little-known conversation between Jacques Derrida and the experimental French director Daniel Mesguich, published as *The Ephemeral Eternal*, Abraham's sacrifice is taken up as an exemplary case of theater, just as Ronell summons Abraham as the *Urpunkt* of the test.[101] In Christian tradition, Abraham and Isaac play the part of typological trailer or warm-up act to the crucifixion. Mesguich and Derrida's discussion models a very different relation between the sacrifice and Christology. Abraham's sacrifice becomes an instance of experimental, overtly *theatrical* theater which is opposed to a "Christological" theory of theater: the kind of theater that dreams of incarnation and real presence. Written at the same time that Derrida was working on *Donner la mort* (*The Gift of Death*), the conversation foregrounds a dimension of *se donner* that is less to the fore in *Donner la mort*. *Se donner* can also mean "to stage" as in "*Hamlet se donne se soir*" (Hamlet is playing tonight). Derrida's reflections on Abraham's sacrifice and *Hamlet* are influenced by Mesguich's experimental staging of *Hamlet* in 1977. In what Mesguich called a deliberate staging of "the Hamlet effect," the apparition of the ghost became a figure for the spectrality of theater as an ephemeral eternal, on constant replay and delay.[102]

Reflecting on what he calls "the Abraham effect," Mesguich writes: "Tragedy is when the tortured one cries 'No' but the spectators hear the melodious outpouring of the 'No' and applaud. True tragedy has never taken place in the theater. In theater, tragedy is turned into sport or play [*Au théâtre, la tragédie est mise en jeu*]."[103] In a section titled "*Même l'agneau?*" (even the lamb?) he elaborates: "The actor, offered up, is not, however, a Christ, who makes good 'with his body the shortcomings/lapses of the law', written, fulfilled, terminated ["It is finished; *Consummatum est*" (John 19.30)]. In theater, the body is immersed [*immiscer*, "to interfere, meddle with"] in the flaws of writing: for the actor it is not finished, no one dies, it was only for fun [*pour de rire*]; it is necessary to return to the scene, incessantly. . . . The actor is not like an expiatory victim, a scapegoat, but like one who plays with the law, in front of the whole world. One who apes the scapegoat [*singer le bouc*]. In theater, at the end, Isaac, Abraham, and the lamb get up and bow."[104] Note how Mesguich unconsciously incorporates the drama's most dominant, Christian repetitions by making a Christological "lamb" from the ram. As "lamb" of God, the ram does not die (just as Isaac does not really die) but resurrects and lives eternally. It also turns out that he was a man in a sheep's costume all along.

Abraham's sacrifice highlights the fissure between act as law, rule, and script and act as extemporization, transgression, and one-off event. Neither cancels out the other, as with Abraham and the angel's conflicting hands. The actor can never perfectly fulfill and eliminate the barrier of the law, script, or mediation. (This role is reserved for Christ.) Mediating words and a sense of production cling to and subvert any incarnation. And in a sense, this saves the spectator. Any "cry" is always framed by a self-conscious sense of a script that also gives pleasure and buffers the audience, saving them from pain. Even scenes of starkest suffering suffer from an injection of comedy. Theater is like the promise. As there is "an unbelievable, and comical, aspect of every promise,"[105] comedy enters every tragedy through the simple fact of representation as a play.

Again, Abraham's sacrifice becomes the exemplary instance. Comedy creeps in, at the very least in the technical sense, through the resurrections that take place at the end. Theater functions like a *deus ex machina*. The god that is theater can always be relied on to reach out its hand onto the stage (cf. Gen. 22.10) and save the characters at the end. Therefore, theater is a form of salvation, in which "cruelty does not exist."[106] Abraham's sacrifice becomes a figure for the theatrical remission or redemption that turns human sacrifice into "human sacrifice." Having aped the the ram or lamb, the actor gets up from the altar and lives to play or laugh another day.

When we witness an act or act of theater, it seems that, at the same time (a time that disagrees with itself all the time), it is taking place; that it has never taken place; and that any sense of a present moment is subverted by alternative ways of acting this out (those to come and those that have been). "A certain repetition/rehearsal" lies at the heart of the curious time of theater: not as "a representation of a model present elsewhere, of which it would be an image," but rather "repetition haunting any illusion of presence and the unique event."[107] The at least "double-faced" time of theater is at one and the same time [*à la fois*], 'a premiere and a last night [*dernière fois*], of the morning and of the womb' and, at the same time, 'melancholic, autumnal, belonging to the twilight, the eschaton, the grave.'"[108] In a theatrical revelation (*manifestation theatrical*) "instantaneousness unfolds itself, or analyses itself perhaps in two hours or four, it does not matter." In each performance "the repetition that is essential to it vibrates."[109]

There is an unseemly haste about the time of theater, which is borrowed time, outside the normative laws of time: "Everything must be performed very quickly in the theater, the actor is pressed as if he is stealing, as if he is in a situation of transgression and fraud; he is a thief, and this forms part of the time of theater; the category of the furtive or the clandestine signifies that the essential instance of the theater does not allow itself to be integrated into general temporality, it is a thief of time, it is at once a moment of presentation of the law and transgression of the law."[110] Theater is always "serial" even if there is a single production, one night only. Each performance is a "fugue, suite variations, and [a] reprise" for "in each performance all performances sing, those that are past and those that are to come." The curiously syncopated times of the "ephemeral eternal" relate to the question of belief and the event:

> In theater one neither believes nor disbelieves, one neither looks or hears directly; one looks at or listens to the child or the idiot in us who believes. . . . When we go to the theater we are not dupes, we know that it is an illusion or a simulacra. . . . But what is it to believe? This is the question posed, and it is staged or set on fire by the theater [*mise en scene ou en feu par le théâtre*].[111]
>
> The experience of repetition is memory; however, everything seems new, inaugural, beyond anticipation; almost as surprised and surprising as an event. It's the event as repetition that we need to think in theater. How can a present, in its freshness, in its irreplaceable rawness (crudity) of "here and now," how can that be repetition? What would the time of experience and the time of theater have to be for that to be possible?[112]

Theater profoundly disturbs the chimera of experience, the holy grail of the really real. In the fleshy undeniable presence of the crude, raw, here and now, it promises utmost immediacy—or rawness, believability—coupled with the most extreme sense of representation, transformation, production, construction, or repetition. Or as Mesguich puts it, "The only raw/believable thing in the theater is that it is taking place in front of you: everything else is a rehash, warmed over, nothing new. Theater puts on a spectacle that is raw/believable and already cooked."[113] Derrida and Mesguich have in mind far more than a virtuoso performance of wordplay, as they pun on *cru* as "raw, uncooked," and *cru* from *croire*, to "believe."

Abraham's sacrifice graphically foregrounds the strange conditions of theater. It does so almost allegorically, typologically—as if every element of the text were determined to point to the paradoxes of the theater with the same devotion that it once pointed to the passion of Christ. Genesis 22 stages a spectacle, "*cru et déjà cuit.*" As I commented earlier: "This looked set to be a real act, a really real act, the most real kind of act: the kind of act that tries to touch or evoke the guarantee of the real in the body, in the damage to the body, in the spurt of blood, the touch of cold metal on flesh.... But then, having gone to all this trouble (and such trouble, such labor); having gone for the very jugular of the real, the act is converted, at the last minute, to a mere gesture." Like theater, the text/test seems to go for the most extreme collision between the rawest, crudest, most essential, most believable, most tangible—and the most "cooked, transformed, displaced."

The text also plays with the act: act as play and script and act as the most fundamental legal commandment: the law not to murder. It stages an overt trial of believability by opening with a command that subverts the prior promise that Abraham will become a nation through Isaac. Leaving early in the morning (in secret) and then taking a three-day journey condensed into an instant, Abraham seems to embody the concept of clandestine, fraudulent guilty time. In the syncopated time of this piece of biblical theater, three days pass in a moment. Conversely, in the slow-motion extension of the hand to take the knife to slaughter the son (Gen. 22.10), a moment becomes three days. The body of Isaac/the nation (only just born a moment ago and now on the altar) seems to offer itself as a figure for theatrical time, suspended between morning and evening, womb and eschaton or grave. The *first* performance already feels, very explicitly, like a repetition. Following hard on the heels of the expulsion of Hagar and Ishmael in Genesis 21 and rehearsing specific elements of that script, it reads like a variation on the "Almost-Death of the Son: A (Re)Play." There is already at least one Abraham: one who fulfills the script and one who fulfills it by breaking with it; and at least one Isaac, one who dies and one who does not. There is also, even here, at the beginning, another one: a near Isaac or understudy called Ishmael. As Derrida writes, the name of Abraham seems to be inscribed with "serial multiplicity of the 'more than one [*plus d'un*].'"[114]

Even within the biblical corpus and early Christianities and Judaisms, the sacrifice generates more and more anxious repetitions and substitutions; more ways of attempting to making good (once and for all) the difference between sacrifice and a 'sacrifice' that never takes place. As Ronell puts it: "What appears to have been meant to suspend human sacrifice—Isaac reprieved—in fact has introduced a structure that perpetuates sacrifice and substitution. As though the tribes were made ever more to pay the difference, and the sacrifice, once demanded, was reset and futured—tendered, so to speak, as that which was yet to come."[115]

Rehearsing Sacrifice

It is hard to think of a piece of scripture that has produced so many variations—variations that seem to "come to pass," to "take place, which means in a particular place, and yet simultaneously also to pass away."[116] Accidents or deviations have been perceived as sponsored or licensed by the original. The swerve from the original script faithfully follows the divine poetic license to change the scene, play it otherwise, just as God did that first time. Deviation from this particular script has been understood as obedience itself.

Crises follow from the intermixing of obedience and deviation, and the suspension of the literal. It has proved extremely difficult to police the distinction between orthodoxy and heterodoxy, transgression and faith. Many "believers" (as we used to say in the naïve old days before we learned to use more appropriate words such as actors, adherents, or affiliates[117]) have found themselves worrying about how to believe and what to do (or not to do) in order to perform a properly faithful relation to the text. The most pious of interpreters have been torn between the real and the virtual: actual sacrifice, on the very edge of a knife, and sacrifice as a mere act, something staged—and also a stage on the way to a better (nonsacrificial) way.

In his *Abraham sacrifiant* (1550), written as an end-of-term performance for students in Geneva, the Protestant theologian Theodore Beza pushed sacrifice hard toward gesture, in the sense of a trivial, ineffective, and tangential event.[118] The brute fact of sacrifice was compressed into metaphor and vague talk of the Christian as "living sacrifice." Even the sacrifice of the sheep (emphatically not a Christ-lamb) at the end of the story (Gen. 22.13) was pushed aside into an embarrassed marginal stage direction: "*Ici prend le mouton*" (Heere he takes the sheepe). Nor was the anxiety around literal sacrifice exclusively Protestant. (We are often too quick to polarize the Catholic and Protestant, because we like to call on the simple dichotomy of the Catholic and the Protestant to help us believe that we can make clear distinctions between act or rite and text.) In 1539, Franciscan friars and their Nahua collaborators produced an act of theater that came very close to Beza's *Abraham sacrifiant* as they attempted the highly risky act of attempting to stage a Sacrifice of Isaac for the human-sacrificing Mesoamericans in New Spain. Anxious about the danger of indigenous peoples merely aping the biblical/Christian and only making gestures toward Christianity, the play emphasized the literal act of sacrifice, perfect obedience with no space for theater or pretense. But then, embarrassed by the biblical affirmation of literal human sacrifice, the play turned volte-face and drew a firm line between Nahua sacrifice (real, cruel, bloody) and Christian sacrifice (metaphysically transformed, suspended, staged). The sacrifice became nothing more than a minor sideshow in a play that was all about obedience. As in Beza's *Abraham sacrifiant*, Abraham was only allowed to sacrifice a lamb (in fact, a little lamb) offstage.[119]

The strange conditions of the sacrifice of Isaac led the pious and faithful followers and evangelizers of the biblical tradition to *emphasize* the ideas of fiction and theater, making the text unreal, a construction, in order to make it (relatively) safe. This tendency was amplified and effectively canonized in modernity when religious actors and affiliates joined forces with the deists and skeptics (those who presented themselves as having seen through the "acts" and antics of religion) to affirm that text was an act with a tendentious relationship to truth as such. For the so-called deists, "angels, dreams, visions, voices from heaven" and all other special (theatrical) effects were exposed as unreal by the "*moral unfitness* of the action."[120] The immorality of the action proved their theatricality, their separation from truth, reality, and the true God who must be at peace with law and the humane. For Kant, it was clear that Abraham "should have replied to this supposedly divine voice: 'That I ought not to kill my good son is quite certain. But that you, an apparition, are God—of that I am not certain, and never can be, not even if this voice rings down to me from (visible) heaven.'" The command to "butcher and burn" turned the God of the text into an illusion (*Tauschung*) and pushed the text into that ultimate modern category of the virtual: myth.[121] Those religious actors who attempted to save the Bible in and from the force fields of thought that we call Enlightenment, *mirrored* this radical qualification of the text's truth and reality. The origin of the command to sacrifice the son was demoted from God to God as construct: "God" as misheard, as piously projected by Abraham's misunderstanding or his mistaken fervor, or "God" as an effect of context. Because Abraham saw similar practices among the gods of the Canaanites, he mistakenly deduced that his God also wanted human blood—a mistake that his God had to go to some lengths to correct.

With a sleight of hand, the pious reading made the text all about the angel's voice and hand. The divine command to sacrifice, and indeed the majority of the text, became an aberration: a journey on the way to truth through falsehood. The only truth was the negation: "Do not lay a hand." This hand was now seen as scoring out and correcting all the actions up to this point. In this reading the lesson became clearly and unequivocally "No More Sacrifice" or "Sacrifice is Finished" (in the sense of aborted rather than *consummatum est*), or "One Night Only (No Repetition)" or "Don't copy Abraham; don't do this at home." The pious new orthodoxy turned Abraham into a curious kind of example: an example of what should not be done.

There are clear reasons for this act of religion, this act of faith. Like theater, the sacrifice of Isaac has haunted and obsessed readers as "a moment of presentation of the law and transgression of the law."[122] For many premodern interpreters, the text was only and acutely about the theological-political conundrum of the proper relationship between the divine sovereign and the law. The conflict between this test and the divine commandment "Thou shalt not murder" became the stage for a long and convoluted trial of the relative powers and accountabilities of gods and laws—one even staged, at times, in the law courts.[123] On the verdict hinged nothing less than the stability of the world and all its nouns, things, and laws. Wild nominalist and voluntarist theories unleashed the divinity of God to the point where God's sovereign will could transform crimes into virtues and dissolve the stability of nouns and laws. Unsurprisingly, the premodern church tended to favor compromise theologies, which gently forced God to consent, by grace, to subject himself to natural law and the edifices of reason and morality propped up by natural law. Modern thinkers not only amplified this tendency but took it to the point where we could forget that there ever had been any conflict between God and law. This necessarily (and for pressing reasons of safety and morality) turned the command to sacrifice into a *mere gesture*, suspended in the realm of the virtual and the theatrical, disconnected from the will of God and Truth as such.

The example of Abraham's sacrifice demonstrates the paradoxical fortunes of scriptures in the dramas of modernity in the West. Counterintuitively, the pious reading is often the one that qualifies the "voice of God" and turns the text into projection, fantasia, or myth. Good, modern religions are expected to relate to their scriptures in acts of self-conscious reading, with all the distance and particularly historical distance that this implies. In the view of the think-tank the Rand Corporation, conservative Muslims are held back from attaining the status of liberal, democratic religion by "the belief in the divinity of the Quran and a failure to regard it as a historical document" and the "failure to realize that Mohammad is a product of his time."[124] The better, more faithful response is to understand our scriptures as theater. We need to come to the enlightened realization that the scriptural event takes place not in a neutral, eternal, truth but on a historical stage. "To reside in [theater] is to be most distant from it—from its truth, its reality."[125] But these ambiguities can create real problems for those who seek not simply to read but to take the word into their bodies and to enact the texts, in faith.

On September 11, 2001, the Qur'anic version of Ibrahim's sacrifice was transformed into an act that generated spectacular images that seemed to belong less to so-called reality than to Hollywood's special effects.[126] In a theurgical appropriation of the Qur'an, the text was spoken into cupped hands and then rubbed into the bodies of the perpetrators and the tools of what they called the "action." The textual remains of the act in the last documents left by one of the hijackers, Mohamed Atta, carry a strong sense of breaking through into the real, the fundamental. The script for the action contrasted a rudimentary toolkit of bag, cloth, knife, tools, and weapon with the remote-controlled, hands-off technology of the United States.[127]

In 1991 in California, Cristos Valenti attempted his own faithful rehearsal of the test. Carole Delany gives the following account of the actualization of Abraham's sacrifice in the acts of this latter-day "Christ":

> The evening was just passing into darkness, the first stars were becoming visible. Christos Valenti took his youngest child, his most beloved child, with him in his truck. . . . He took her hand and together they walked into the park. It was dark and quiet. She held onto his hand more tightly. "Don't be afraid," he said, trying to allay her fears. "We are going to meet God." "I don't know anyone named God." "You will meet him soon," was the answer, and they walked on in silence. When they arrived at the place God had appointed, her father told her to lie down on the grass. "Start praying the Our Father who art in Heaven," he said as he took the knife and took her life.[128]

Delaney's style is journalistic, like Courtney Bender's. But it is also explicitly literary, as if attempting to create a jarring mix of reality and old biblical theater. The journalistic idiom of "the real" is intruded on by echoes of the old biblical archive. Following too faithfully in the footsteps of the book of Genesis, Cristos and his daughter walk to the "place that was appointed," and "walk together" (twice). His daughter is his "most beloved child." When he arrives back home, with the girl in his arms, his oldest child opens the door to see her "father holding the child, like a pieta."[129] The biblical text is actualized as if in a horrific stagey typology in the actions of this latter-day Cristos/Christ.

Cristos as would-be Abraham had to answer (as Søren Kierkegaard, followed by Jacques Derrida and John Caputo, had predicted) to the psychologists, the criminologists, the journalists, and the police.[130] The acts of 9/11 were widely denounced as a mere nod or gesture to true religion. The atrocity elicited many public statements on behalf of and to religion proper, designed to reassure and at the same time reiterate to religion and its affiliates what true religion ought to be. In one of these addresses, or exhortations, the then Archbishop of Canterbury, Rowan Williams, accused the terrorists of cloaking "organized slaughter" and "suicide" in the "spiritual power of martyrdom."[131] They had gestured to religion, but fallen far short of it, or overshot. The mereness of the mere gesture had to be that of insincerity of hypocrisy or aping (as in "Donald Trump made a gesture toward combating racism by appointing Ben Carson as Secretary of Housing and Urban Development.") They could hardly be accused of the kind of mereness that comes from lack of force, will, or effect. The act was a failed gesture toward true religion because, unlike Abraham/Ibrahim, they had committed a literal act of killing rather than going through the motions of a holy putting to death that did not finally take place.

Rowan Williams denied, as perhaps one must if one is an archbishop, how in the force field what we call religion, and in Abraham's test in particular, "perfectibility and pervertibility go hand in hand."[132] As Hent de Vries comments: "Religious orthodoxies of all stripes seek to interpret the latter possibility or virtuality as external to themselves—and, by extension, as inessential to their theologico-political project. They portray these aberrations as idolatry, blasphemy, apostasy, heresy, scandal or offense."[133] But in the case of Abraham/Ibrahim the clash between truth and heresy becomes particularly intense. According to Williams, and all good modern readers, the blasphemous gesture is the one that takes the text too seriously, too literally. Despite the manual emphasis in the biblical original, we should understand that this is a text for eyes not hands. To read with correct late modern piety (safe piety), one must understand the text was always a mere gesture—never realized, never-to-be-acted-on, unreal. Rubbing the text into real hands and a real knife and fire(arms) and acting it out is a *transgression into literalism*. But this is curious and instructive kind of offense.

Modernities, then, naturalize Abraham's sacrifice as theater—so much so that we automatically think of this as the kind of story that lies furthest from real experience and lived religion—the very textiest of texts. Michael Lambek demonstrates this beautifully in his essay "Provincializing God? Provocations from an Anthropology of Religion," as he falls naturally into a Hollywood-Orientalist rehearsal of the good old text: "Scene 1. A stark rocky desert landscape, 1950s MGM-style. The orb of the sun burns pitilessly from a cloudless sky. Father and son, encumbered in orientalist garb, toil up the mountain. The old man has unruly gray hair, a long tangled beard, and a tragic, determined, almost mad look in his eye."[134]

We could not be further from the genres and codes of realism in Bender's essay "Practicing Religion." Whereas Bender uses stylistic codes that evoke the immediate and (relatively) unmediated, Lambek uses overtly literary and stylized codes that evoke distance: the distance of the profoundly mediated dark old distant scriptures and the self-distancing command of heteronomy and blind belief. In an overtly theatrical whisper of the "ephemeral eternal," the old bearded biblical father speaks in a "gruff voice . . . disappearing in the wind that suddenly whips up, as if across the centuries."¹³⁵ This seems to be, for Lambek, a deliberate gesture. He seeks to put the biblical text in scare quotes and thereby distance himself from its unreality and mark himself as one who does not believe in this provincial script. This relates to the staging of the work of anthropology/religious studies as a labor of representing "religion" as a projection, a scholarly construct, or a sociological or a psychological special effect. But what makes this gesture really interesting is its long history in this particular case. It extends back into the histories of belief and confession. Sixteenth-century Franciscan friars in Meso-america, Theodore of Beza, Immanuel Kant, and the most earnest biblical scholars (among others) all found themselves overtly theatricalizing for reasons of piety, in an attempt to make the example of Abraham relatively safe.

Pious and Impious Play

Given the unanimity between the heterodox and orthodox, distinctions between impiety and piety have to be performed at the level of style. Impiety flashes up, by accident, as much as design. Piety affirms a certain theatricality, in all seriousness. Impiety amplifies and enjoys a sense of mockery and play. The trick for piety is—and maybe always has been—to make this text less than real, but not too much less than real. It must suspend the text in the passing time of theater. But it must not laugh out loud or give in to the full force of demystification. The play must still be tragic, even if comic in the technical sense. Impiety winks with overt markers of theatricality, as in Lambek's performance "1950s MGM style," or the laconic staginess of David Aronson's *Sacrifice of Isaac* (1957; fig. 1.5).

Aronson's painting is one of many compulsive repetitions of the sacrifice as

FIGURE 1.5 David Aronson, *Sacrifice of Isaac* (1957). In this overt performance of the sacrifice of Isaac, all the actors play out the choreographed moves with complete indifference.

theater. In his gorgeously irreverent performance, splendid pageantry seems unable to compensate for the sense of ritual repetition to the point of *ennui*. The sacrifice appears to take place on a eucharistic altar, somewhere between a surgeon's table, an altar, and a stage. A lavishly costumed Abraham (more sumptuously overdone than even Rembrandt's Abraham) prepares, surgeon-like, to make the familiar incision. A bored officiant, like a staff nurse attending at an operation, obligingly holds Isaac's legs. Isaac lounges in complete detachment from his story and from his body, looking like a luxuriating recumbent or a chicken on a platter. The scene evokes Kafka's Abraham-waiter, serving up Isaac on a platter.[136] Overtly aping the scapegoat, this sacrificial victim does not even bother to cry, "No." He knows that he is a participant in *The Sacrifice: A Play*. He knows that the play has already been transformed even at the moment of its first staging, into comedy, resurrection, farce. The salvific "Do not lay a hand" is parodied in the grotesque figure swinging down from the right-hand side of the frame, as on a trapeze. He ticks off naughty Abraham, as if remembering John Bulwer's forgotten interpretation of the meaning of the angel hand as *Castigo*, "I chastise."

Contemporary rehearsals of the sacrifice have pushed well beyond the old Kantian move of turning the God of sacrifice into an illusion. Since this is now standard both for religious actors and those who demystify religious acts, this traditional reading offers little more than the ritualized sensation of a long-assimilated and repeated shock. The most provocative contemporary gestures no longer focus the force of disillusionment on the old biblical God and the sphere of "the Abrahamic." Instead, they allow the critique of the "act" of death to spread beyond the sphere of the religious.

In the Yishuv/Israel, the sacrifice of Isaac, known in Hebrew as the *akedah* or akedat Yizhak (the binding of Isaac) was adopted as a foundation myth for the modern state. God was secularized as the force of necessity, but he did not lose any of his propulsive power. Indeed, the command to sacrifice became more intense, since the commanding force was not (incredibly) god, but, far more credibly, the future, security, Realpolitik, and the state. Almost at the moment of its inception, this grandiose gesture was met with a deflationary theatricality. The founding mythology of sacrifice was attacked as an act that was only for a show, and an act of bad faith." In the controversial performance *Queen of the Bathtub*, master of Israeli meta-theater, Hanoch Levin turned the akedah into something like a vaudeville music review. "Get up missionary, wave the knife as missionary over the son you love," Isaac taunts, while the father retorts, "Very nice Isaac, make it difficult for your unfortunate father, put him in a bad mood, as if he hasn't already got enough on his plate."[137] In his poem "The True Hero of the Sacrifice," Israeli poet Yehuda Amichai put ""the sacrifice"" in quadruple inverted commas, as slick magazine image or consciously posed memorial photograph. The poem predates the selfie but effectively presented a selfie of Isaac with the angel. The so-called sacrifice became a highly theatricalized fashion photo-shoot: a "tanned spoilt youth," an angel, empty chairs long ago vacated by God and Abraham—and the ram, the true victim, differently absent, cut out of the shot.[138] In Amichai's sacrifice, religion and the gods have long since left as inspiration, or target. The absence of the "sacrificed" ram points to all those innocent victims, all that collateral damage, haunting the central tableau.

The improvised scene in Samuel Bak's "Dress Rehearsal" defamiliarizes the akedah to the point of nonrecognition (fig. 1.6). It deflates the once strong act to gesture, with all its impious hints of hypocrisy, irony, and lack of force. The numerous hands in the original biblical script turn into stagehands, rigging up the scene. The actors seem to be making gestures that are at once futile (weak) and guilty, as if impotent but at the same time capable of forcing something strong, irrevocable, prohibited. ("Everything must be performed very quickly in the theater, the actor is pressed as if he is stealing, as if he is in a situation of transgression and fraud."[139]) The hand of the metal-winged angel on the left (let us call him First Angel, as befits his seeming role as self-conscious actor) lacks the firm grip of Rembrandt's or Caravaggio's angel. It has no power to dislodge the sword or scimitar from Abraham's hand.[140] The hand of the Second Angel on Abraham's shoulder *may* be attempting to stop Abraham, but then again it could be the hand of an angelic stagehand or choreographer simply motioning, "Abraham, could you just move a little bit to the right or to the left?" The Third Angel (to the right behind the curtain) may be hooking up the ropes that will winch Isaac to safety at the last moment, in a bathetic deflation of the *deus ex machina*, reduced to a winch and stage mechanics. Alternatively, he may be binding Isaac, trying to stay faithful to the traditional Jewish title for the story: *akedat Yitzhak*, "the binding of Isaac." The whole scene looks like a piece of amateur dramatics, cobbled together in front of crematorium chimney. The gods have long gone. God is not the focus in these Chinese box relationships of credibility, act, incredibility, and "act." One modulation of the unbelievable confronts another. The foreground is humiliated as an obscene theater of signification (like crosses at Auschwitz), an empty gesture, a farce. The ineffective gestures appear as a fake drama, a screen, like the beautification of Theresienstadt for the visit of the International Red Cross. It is as if the painting is screaming to Abraham, as the mother of the seven tortured brothers in the book of Maccabees allegedly screamed to him across the centuries (in so many words): "Your sacrifice was a mere dress rehearsal, but all my sons (and daughters and fathers, mothers, and all my relatives) were actually killed."[141]

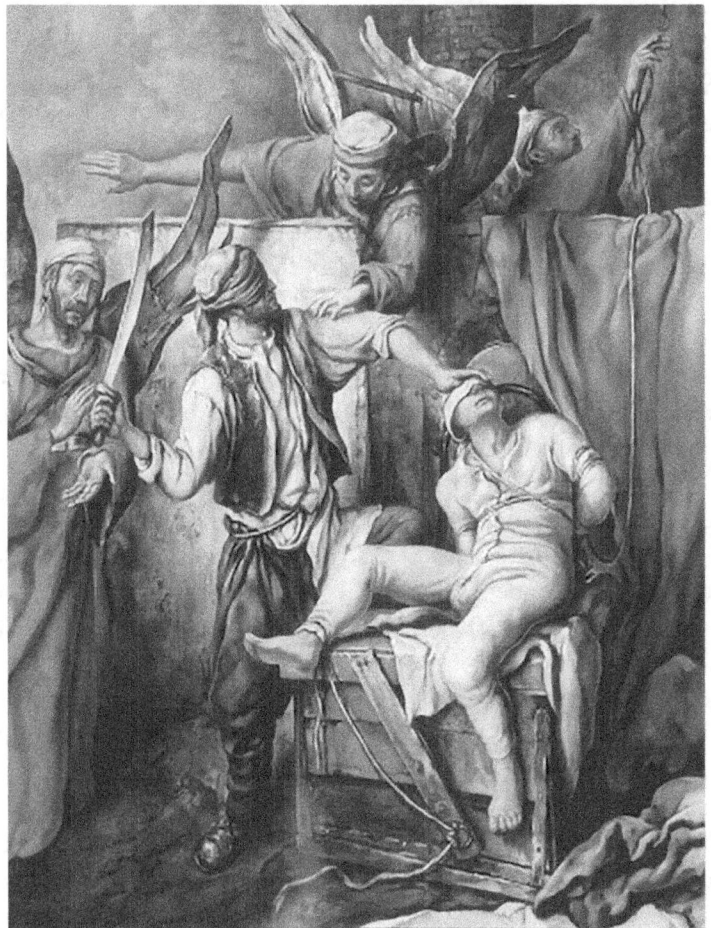

FIGURE 1.6   Samuel Bak, *Dress rehearsal* (1999). Abraham's sacrifice is staged in front of a crematorium chimney, with a very hesitant intervention from the weak angel actor on the left.

In *Fear and Trembling* (1843), Johannes de Silentio, one of the many pseudonyms and puppets of Søren Kierkegaard. attempts a double gesture. He exaggerates the theatrical; and he tries to force the reader out of the merely theatrical, as if attempting to strong-arm the ectoplasmic biblical/religious into the force and flesh of "the real." Saving the good old text from theatrical remoteness, he tries to bring it as close to us and the contemporary as a train from Newark to Philadelphia, or the Bronx—or, in his terms, the Jutland Heath. Struggling to force himself and his contemporaries to "speak humanly about [the sacrifice] as if it happened yesterday" and to overcome the belief that "hundreds, yes even thousands of years [lie] between [us] and the earthquakes of existence," Johannes de Silentio tries to salvage the story from its Hollywood-Orientalist habitat: the fuzzy felt world of the "biblical" and the "beautiful regions of the east."[142] The biblical scene has been so thoroughly theatricalized and demystified that it takes an immense effort to push it out of its red-curtained neverland and enact its "becoming real." The brute fact of the body is appealed to as the guarantor of the tangible, as if the holy grail of the real lay in the touch of skin on skin. Striving to take the "sacrifice" out of the soft cotton wool of inverted commas, Johannes/Søren wants us to feel the impact of an Abraham who really *did* this, or who was absolutely set on the act. The thought of this Abraham becomes a force that "shatters," "paralyzes," and "virtually annihilates" the thinking subject, marking his or her body with the scar of true thinking.[143]

Attempting to save Abraham from his ghost-life as a piece of ectoplasmic nothing, Johannes/Søren tries to turn him into the kind of thought that feels so real, so embodied, that we can feel the pressure of it, as it presses close to us, shocks and thrills us—indeed (almost) kills us. Abraham becomes a set of bodily symptoms, a motion, a sensation. If you really *read* this text (in a mode of reading a long way from sitting in an armchair puffing at one's pipe by the fireplace, or the models of composed engagement with a text assumed by parodies of the readers of scripture), you will feel the frisson of fear and trembling; you will shake with the shudder of thought; your brain will reel; you will be struck blind; you will suffer from congestion of the blood; you will become sleepless; you will feel the heat of perspiration; you will feel all the convulsions (or concussions?) of existence; your intellectual digestive system will be strained to its limits by the gigantic thoughts that you must try to gulp down whole; and you will be paralyzed by the twists of thought that you must put your mental body through like a tightrope dancer or a trampoline artist in a circus.[144] Reading becomes painfully "sonic, tactile, olfactory, gustatory, and kinetic."[145] Indeed the true reader is imagined running to the spiritual chiropractor, ophthalmologist, neurologist, and gastroenterologist, as his or her pain testifies to the intimate relation between testing and the truth of the body, the desire "to push out the truth [or "the real"] in the medium of torture or pain."[146]

Kierkegaard's Abraham causes thought to "break out in the strangest leaps and somersaults" in self-consciously gestural figures of thought.[147] In the *Stemning* or "Attunement" section of *Fear and Trembling*, and in copious notes in Kierkegaard's notebooks, a whole series of Abrahams (and Isaacs and Sarahs) are produced and directed by Søren/Johannes in an insincere gesture toward wrapping up the story once and for all. These include an Abraham who, in order to tear the child away from Sarah, tells her that the one to be sacrificed is but a phantom, a ghost, an illusion, or an actor; an Abraham who kills Isaac because he is deaf to or cannot believe in the second voice; an Abraham who kills Isaac and is given a new Isaac but is not satisfied with the resurrection, replacement, or repetition; and an Abraham who confides in Sarah, "It was a strange business! It is eternally certain that God asked me to sacrifice Isaac. God himself cannot deny that—and yet when I carried it out, it was a mistake on my part and it was not God's will."[148] So many of these compulsive rehearsals of the Abraham drama are overtly theatrical and set on subverting the theater of the biblical. Committed to the first voice, the first draft, one Abraham cannot hear or accept changes to the script. In another version, the *deus ex machina* does not show up. Alternatively, he turns up and no one sees or hears him. In another, a traumatized Abraham worries that his real act has been transformed into theater, and wonders what this means. Alternatively, in another repetition, he is worried that he has not correctly executed, or believed, the divine script. He followed the script to the letter, but then collisions in the script created space for unbelief. (The question posed or set on fire by theater is, "What is it to believe?"[149]) Another Abraham lies, or acts, in front of Sarah, as if determined to draw attention to those awkward lies/euphemisms/hypocrisies/gestures in the biblical original. This Abraham tells his wife that Isaac is a ghost, an actor: not real, never real.

More essential to *Fear and Trembling* than the much-trumpeted conflict between religion and ethics is another tension: the struggle between the act as accomplished action and the act as a piece of theater, or a gesture. It could well prove easier to find our bearings in relation to the difficult tension between religion and ethics, than to work out what kind of act this really is. *Fear and Trembling* has often been misunderstood as a special text for the believers in the special zone of religion: those prepared to vault over the ethical into the leap of faith. Reading this way allows us to lazily take up our positions according to choreographed religious or nonreligious identities. This is deeply ironic, since Kierkegaard/de Silentio tried so hard to close off such facile means of escape. He would be horrified, I suspect, to find his book confined to a special interest sphere of religion. He wants us all to feel (on our skin) what it is like to be alone, in the moment of decision, the wild leap, under the strange command or compulsion, cast out without a script. He wants to feel the sacrifice as if it were that form of theater known as *Posse* or farce. *Posse* is a form of improvisation that resists a cultured audience's desire "to be able to know in advance what is going to happen that evening."[150] It depends on "self-activity and the viewer's improvisation," so that "the particular individuality comes to assert itself in a very individual way and in its enjoyment is emancipated from all aesthetic obligations to admire, to laugh, to be moved, etc. in the traditional way." *Posse*/farce releases us from "a certain restricted earnestness" and the social etiquette of a "proper response." "Seeing a farce can produce the most unpredictable mood, and therefore a person can never be sure whether he has conducted himself in the theater as a worthy member of society who has laughed and cried at the appropriate places."[151]

By liberating, or expelling, us from the security of the kind of response that we can borrow, second-hand, from the person sitting next to us in the stalls, Søren/Johannes's Abraham improvisations put us in the place of Abraham: alone in the absurd, in the singularity of comedy, in the midst of an act that cannot be accommodated in the canons of tragedy. Kierkegaard is at pains to point out that Abraham is not at all like Agamemnon, the tragic figure who can, for all his pain, at least articulate his reasons in the canons of reason and relax into tragedy as an accepted script. Abraham is the singular individual who loves the universal, but who is forced, at this moment, to break absolutely with it. Exiled from "the tragic," from language, and from any kind of universal grammar, the Abraham idiom expresses itself as dark comedy, strange somersaults, weird gestures, play. One of the forms he takes is the petty bourgeois who, despite having no money whatsoever, believes that he will come home and have a nice little bit of roast lamb (hardly an accidental menu). The pathetic figure of the man believing in his roast lamb dinner is an unlikely apparition of the "knight of faith."

Kafka nudges these peculiar Abraham gestures a little further toward the absurd. We can see the Kierkegaardian inspiration behind Kafka's Abraham who rushes to the task with the promptness of a waiter; his Abraham who worries that his weak performance as knight (or his gesture toward performing as a knight) will make him appear more as a bathetic Don Quixote; or his Abraham who hears the voice of God and does not doubt it but does doubt that *he* is the one meant. Kafka's and Kierkegaard's Abrahams are separated only by a slightly different lexis and (perhaps) a different tone of laughter.[152] Kafka's Abraham and Isaac are ridiculous, old, ugly, and dirty, whereas Kierkegaard's are (but not without a note of irony and different inflections) great.[153] But perhaps these are only false and fragile distinctions that we erect in order to reassure us that we can still separate the believers from the nonbelievers, the faithful actors from the players, because we like to believe that readings and performances happen as an effect of an identity that can be declared in advance.[154] Abraham's sacrifice seems designed to throw this distinctly modern belief into doubt. This is such an ambiguously gestural text—sacrificial and anti-sacrificial, reporting a happening, an act, and its transformation—that accidents of heresy and laughter are bound to happen, even (in fact especially) when we are attempting to read in order to save.

Aping Christ

It is one thing for Christian cultures to let these accidents happen around Abraham, who is quite used to his role as foil for Western emancipation and philosophy. It is quite another thing when they come to rest on Christ. But the strong typological connection between Genesis 22 and the Passion and the similar structures shared by these strange texts/acts meant that Jesus could not escape. In a striking reading of the second-century *Apocalypse of Peter*, from Nag Hammadi, Guy Stroumsa shows how one strong reading of the weak gestures in Genesis 22 turned the crucifixion into a play.[155] The logic ran: "Isaac is Jesus, and Isaac does not really die. Jesus, too, then, only aped the lamb." More specifically, Jesus was played by an actor, a stand-in, often named as Simon of Cyrene. The chain of substitutions spilt over from Genesis 22 to the crucifixion. As the understudy lamb stood in for Isaac and in turn was substituted by the Christ lamb in Christian theology, so now Simon stood in for Christ.

FIGURE 1.7   Paul Fryer, *The Privilege of Dominion*, Marylebone Church, London, 2009.

Fittingly, these accidents take place in pseudepigraphic, extracanonical texts that ape the main protagonists of the biblical drama. In the *Apocalypse of Peter*, we get to see Peter watching a show of the crucifixion. He is sitting in the good seats, up in the gods, next to the true Savior, who passes him some popcorn and fizzy pop. Jesus's gift of death is staged (*se donner*). Like Mesguich's *Hamlet*, it is turned into a play-within-a-play-within-a-play. Foregrounding the strange time of theater, we get to watch Christ watching a simultaneous representation of the death of himself. Understandably confused as he sees his theater companion "apparently being seized," down there, down on the stage, Peter asks Jesus what show he is watching. Jesus clarifies that the real Jesus is not down there but up here next to him. The true Jesus is "one above the cross, who is glad and laughing" up here, in the gods. In fact, he is hooting loudly at the absurdity of the very idea that he was that "other person whose feet and hands they are hammering." The true Christ of course has no hands and feet. The dying one is a "physical part," a "substitute," an actor who is aping the lamb.[156] And Christ is really enjoying the spectacle: he has tears in his eyes and is slapping his thighs.

Christ's laughter is produced, Stroumsa argues, from a conflation of textual sources: a combination of the name Isaac ("He laughs"), and Psalm 2.4: "He who sits in the heavens laughs."[157] But Christ's laughter I suspect, bursts out from several sources. It also bursts out from the unbearable tensions between the real and the apparent, and the need for resurrection, including the resurrection of theater. It is generated by the comic structure of the crucifixion and the strange conditions of theater, in which tragedy cannot exist. "It is finished; *Consummatum est*" (John 19.30)]—but Jesus lives on to tell the tale. Looking at the laughing and glad Jesus, while everyone's eyes are on the crucified Jesus, Peter says, "Lord, no one is looking at you. Let us flee this place. For the actor it is not finished, no one dies, it was only for fun (for a laugh/*pour de rire*)."[158]

This performance transforms *The Crucifixion* from a classic of Christian/Western civilization into something more like Kierkegaard's *Posse* or farce. Like *Posse*, it deliberately leaves us confused as to the correct (faithful) response. Peter can look at the person next to him—no less a figure than the savior himself—and get some assurance that he is doing the right thing, responding properly, indeed following God. And surely our role, as audience, is to copy the apostle who takes his cue from God. But even as we follow Peter who is faithfully following the true Jesus, we begin to feel unsure as to whether we have conducted ourselves as "worthy member[s] of society who [have] laughed and cried at the appropriate places."[159] For *imitatio dei* does not usually take the form of laughing at "God" even when, at the same time, we are following God. Just when we are starting to feel a little uncomfortable, on comes the voice of orthodoxy to tell us that we have, in fact, gone wrong. By following this Peter and his laughing Christ we have slipped unwittingly into the heresy known as Docetism. Docetism, like most early Christian heresies, was never a fixed movement or self-identifying group. As Stroumsa puts it, it is "not a fixed set of doctrines, but an attitude."[160] Perhaps it is best described as an attitude of theater. For Docetism, coined from *dokein* ("to seem") was a polemical term used to denounce a ragbag of theologies of *appearance*, including those that denied the reality of Jesus's suffering body (making the body a phantasm), and those that forced a radical separation between a material, embodied Jesus and the spirit Christ.

The strange world of scripture is such that it is hard to know when the gesture of theater is to be embraced, and when it is to be condemned. As I have argued, a certain attitude of theater has become a standard means of saving the biblical in late modernity. In readings of the sacrifice of Isaac by those who regard themselves as the faithful ones, the religious adherents and actors, Abraham errs and the God who commands human sacrifice regularly becomes "God." But gestures toward the theatrical become touchier around the body of Christ. The crime of the Docetists was to spirit the body away. But this erasure of the reality of Jesus's body was an accidental by-product of the faithful attempt to make the Christian God more convincing, and present, in the context of Greco-Roman philosophy where the true god of monotheism had to be firmly separated from anthropomorphism and blood. Theatricality and denial arose from the desire to save God completely from his body, and from a sincere attempt to negotiate the crucifixion's tortuously delicate paradoxes between a death that really happens, and a death that is transformed into something else; between sacrifice and "sacrifice," law and transgression and word and flesh. But this salvific gesture involved a complete sacrifice of sacrifice. And it made the crucifixion a fake act, a mere gesture toward crucifixion: not real, merely a script, a game, a play.

Docetism was so stridently condemned because it was hard to prevent it from happening. The hermeneutic accident known as Docetism was already being countered in the texts that made it into the canon (e.g., 1 John 4.2: "Every spirit that confesses Jesus Christ has come in the flesh is from God, and every spirit that does not confess Jesus is not from God . . . [and] is the spirit of the antichrist"). Sins of Docetism can be found in the gospel of John.[161] Writers who were institutionalized and canonized were clearly troubled by the scandal of the crucifixion and the implied criminalization of Jesus, placed outside the law and all its acts (Galatians; 1 Cor. 1.24). The Gnostics and the orthodox converged in the desire to save Jesus from the darker side of human-animal materiality and the pollution of death and sperm and shit. A Christ who curses and giggles at the site of his own corpse is only an extreme version of this attempt to save Christ, and so ourselves, from the taint of death. Clement of Alexandria and Origen somehow smuggled themselves into the inside edge of orthodoxy even as they maintained that Jesus did not suffer in his divine nature, but only in his human nature—without spiriting the body, completely, away. The Docetists were among those who came before the Christian establishment had institutionalized the proper delicate (almost excruciatingly impossible) balancing act between sacrifice and "sacrifice," word and flesh.

We could regard all these controversies as peculiarities of old theologies, far removed from modern religious studies. And yet, we may have something to learn from them in our own awkward and not yet thoroughly post-Christian negotiations between word and flesh. We have our own shifting parameters of truth. Like the old defenders and creators of orthodoxy, we, too, seek the truth of the body, the experience of the body, the purity of the act, the authenticity of the flesh. We canonize our orthodoxies against the foil of heresies or rejected postures. At this moment in the history of truth, the heresies or rejected postures are those based on orthodoxy, institutions, word, belief, reason, and text. The little word *gesture* prods us and provokes us to think more about this turn to act. It reminds us that acts can be weak, partial, hypocritical, ironic, accidental—and that they mimic, and overlap with, all the sins of text.

Notes

1. On the repression and resurrection of experience, see Martin Jay, *Songs of Experience: Modern American and European Variations on a Universal Theme* (Berkeley: University of California Press, 2005).

2. F. R. Ankersmit, *Sublime Historical Experience* (Stanford, CA: Stanford University Press, 2005), 14.

3. For a more detailed study of how *Bible* operates as a foil (and mirror) for *religion*, see Ward Blanton and Yvonne Sherwood, "Bible/Religion/Critique," in *Religion/Culture/Critique*, ed. Richard King (New York: Columbia University Press, 2014).

4. I am indebted to Ward Blanton for reflections on the austere spiritual exercises of Descartes and Kant.

5. Nancy, *Corpus*, 5.

6. Robert A. Orsi, "The Problem of the Holy," in *The Cambridge Companion to Religious Studies*, ed. Orsi (Cambridge: Cambridge University Press, 2012), 85.

7. Vasaudha Naryanan, "Embodied Cosmologies: Sights of Piety, Sights of Power," *Journal of the American Academy of Religion* 71, no. 3 (2003): 516.

8. Manuel A. Vásquez, *More than Belief: A Materialist Theory of Religion* (Oxford: Oxford University Press, 2011), 5.

9. Orsi begins his analysis of the holy with a quote from Hannah Arendt which, out of context, seems to exhort us to make a relatively simple move to the "ground of

experience" rather than losing ourselves in the esoteric mists of theory: "What is the subject of our thought? Experience! Nothing else! And if we lose the ground of experience we get stuck in all kinds of theories." Orsi, "Problem of the Holy," 84.

10. Vásquez, *More than Belief*, 2.

11. "Globalatinization," or "mondialatinization," is Derrida's term for the hegemonic universalization of the Roman word and concept of religion. See Jacques Derrida and Gianni Vattimo, *Religion* (Stanford, CA: Stanford University Press, 1998).

12. Catherine Bell, "Performance," in *Critical Terms for Religious Studies*, ed. Mark C. Taylor (Chicago: University of Chicago Press, 1998), 205.

13. Courtney Bender, "Practicing Religions," in Orsi, *Cambridge Companion to Religious Studies*, 280.

14. Bell, "Performance," 205.

15. Bender, "Practicing Religions," 276.

16. Bender, 276.

17. Nancy, *Corpus*, 11. See also Nancy, 17: "'Writing' means: not the monstration, the demonstration, of a signification but a gesture toward *touching* upon *sense*. A touching, a tact, like an address."

18. Bender, "Practicing Religions," 277.

19. Orsi, "Problem of the Holy," 87.

20. Orsi, 88.

21. Orsi, 87–88.

22. Orsi, 91.

23. Orsi, 88.

24. Bender, "Practicing Religions," 294.

25. Bender, 277.

26. Derek Attridge, "Introduction: Derrida and the Questioning of Literature," in *Acts of Literature*, ed. Derek Attridge (New York: Routledge, 1992), 2.

27. Bulwer, *Chirologia Or the Naturall Language of the Hand, Composed of the Speaking Motions, and Discoursing Gestures Thereof Whereunto is added Chironomia: Or, the Art of Manuall Rhetorike, Consisting of the Naturall Expressions, digested by Art in the Hand, as the chiefest Instrument of Eloquence, By Historicall Manifestos Exemplified* (London: 1644), "To the Candid and Ingenious Reader," no page numbers.

28. Bulwer, *Chirologia*, Index A1, 154.

29. Ankersmit, *Sublime Historical Experience*, 14.

30. There are in fact two amphitheaters of the body. Bulwer has planned his *Cephalelogia*, which (according to the hierarchies of anatomy and philosophy) should have come out first, since it is above the hand. But as he reports in a belabored jocular quip to his "Heroic Friend" and patron, Edward Goldsmith of Gray's Inn, "it fell out in the contention somewhat as in the case of Tamar's twins, where Zarah put forth his *Hand*, and the midwife said, This is come out First" (Bulwer, *Chirologia*, Dedication "To His Heroic Friend Edward Goldsmith," no page number).

31. Bulwer, *Chirologia*, 2.

32. For two of many accounts of the multiple births of the concept of religion in early modernity see, for example, Brent Noghri, *Before Religion: A History of a Modern Concept* (New Haven, CT: Yale University Press, 2013); and Peter Harrison, *"Religion" and the Religions in the English Enlightenment* (Cambridge: Cambridge University Press, 1990).

33. Bulwer, *Chirologia*, "To the Candid and Ingenious Reader."

34. Bulwer.

35. José de Acosta, *Natural and Moral History of the Indies* [1590], ed. Jane E. Mangan; introduction and commentary by Walter D. Mignolo (Durham, NC: Duke University Press, 2002), 334.

36. Bulwer, *Chirologia*. In an appropriate irony, this universal language of gesture, modeled in the biblical and classical canons of Europe and organized according to the Greco-Roman alphabet, expresses its universality in the biblical idiom of Qoheleth/Ecclesiastes ("under the sun").

37. Fray Juan de Torquemada, *Monarquia Indiana* (Seville: 1615), 15, 13.31, cit. and trans. Marilyn Ekdahl Ravicz in *Early Colonial Drama in Mexico: From Tzompantli to Golgotha* (Washington, DC: Catholic University of America Press, 1970), 31.

38. Christopher Columbus, *The Diaro of Christopher Columbus's First Voyage to America, 1492–1493*, abstracted by Fray Bartolomé de las Casas; transcribed, notes and concordance Oliver Dunn and James E. Kelley Jr. (Norman: University of Oklahoma Press, 1989), 197; entry for December 1492.

39. Bulwer, *Chirologia*, 3.

40. For a discussion of the sleight of hand in the international law of nations, see Sherwood, "Francisco de Vitoria's More Excellent Way: How the Bible of Empire Discovered the Tricks of [the Argument from] Trade," *Biblical Interpretation* 21, no. 2 (2013): 1–61.

41. Bulwer, *Chirologia*, 3.

42. Bulwer, 6–7.

43. Bulwer, 3.

44. Bulwer, 6–7.

45. Bulwer, 7.

46. Bulwer, 145.

47. In fact, to be more precise, Bulwer allows Gestus I, *Supplico* ("to importunate, entreat, request, sue, solicit, beseech, and ask mercy and grace at the hands of others") to shade into Gestus II, *Oro* (Bulwer, *Chirologia*, 11, 14). This seems symptomatic of an early point in the gradual sequestering of the concept of religion, where the theological and the social are still far more open to one another than they would become in late modernity.

48. Bulwer, *Chirologia*, 14.

49. Heidegger, *Parmenides*, 80–81.

50. Heidegger, 80–81.

51. Heidegger, 80–81. This brief discussion runs counter to popularized accounts of Heidegger's hand. Heidegger's hand is often taken to be humanist and anthropocentric in a simple sense. In posthumanist discourse his hand is often dismissed (with a casual wave of the hand) as a consolidated center of action and agency, which gives the human

a standard advantage over the poor "world-poor" animal. This reading forgets that it was Heidegger who gave us the idea of *thrownness*, or *Geworfenheit*, which traumatizes agency and subjects (in all senses). The uniqueness of the human is related to anxiety, the possibility of not-doing, undoing, dispossession, weakness, gesture: "Man does not 'have' hands, but hands hold the essence of man."

52. Moshe Barasch, "Gesture," *New Dictionary of the History of Ideas* (Gale Group: 2005), http://www.encyclopedia.com/topic/Gesture.aspx.

53. Calvin *Institutes*, iv, xviii [1613], 713.

54. Bulwer, *Chironomia* (published as an appendix to *Chirologia*), "Indigitatio, or the Canons of the Fingers," 67.

55. Bulwer, *Chirologia*, 5.

56. Adam Kendon, *Gesture: Visible Action as Utterance* (Cambridge: Cambridge University Press, 2004).

57. Barasch, "Gesture," *New Dictionary of the History of Ideas*.

58. Kendon, *Gesture*, 8. To qualify as gesture in the professional sense, a gesture must be more a case of acting than being acted upon. It must stay close to the sense of agency and self-identity threatened by the very idea of "gesture" in its more radical forms. Laughing and weeping do not qualify as gestures; nor does the reflex action when a doctor hits a hammer against my knee, or the hand I put out to break my fall.

59. Bulwer, *Chirologia*, xxv, 15.

60. Bulwer, 15.

61. The first dictionaries in English were those of Robert Cawdrey (1604) and Thomas Blount (1656). Samuel Johnson's famous dictionary came over a century later in 1755. It would be an interesting project to think further about the conjoined births of dictionaries, religion, and gesture. For accounts of the multiple births of the concept of religion in early modernity, see Noghri, *Before Religion*, and Harrison, *"Religion" and the Religions in the English Enlightenment*.

62. Bulwer, *Chirologia*, 84.

63. Orsi, "Problem of the Holy," 88.

64. For famous descriptions of the hypocrites, see for example Matthew 6 and Matthew 23.

65. Bulwer, *Chirologia*, 20–21.

66. Below I suggest a new twist on the phrase "comparative religion." By comparison and contrast with religions as controlled, scripted, and managed by philologists, professors, and angels, the new religion of religious studies appears as comparatively free and the comparatively real.

67. Orsi, "Everyday Miracles: The Study of Lived Religion," in *Lived Religion in America: Toward a History of Practice*, ed. David Hall (Princeton, NJ: Princeton University Press, 1997), 6.

68. True enough, the professionalized institution of *Bibelwissenschaft* has produced a smooth Bible, compatible with good citizenship. But it has also thrived on ambiguities and problems and produced a smooth (public) Bible by professionalizing these ambiguities

and problems and making them the subject of specialist study. See further, Stephen D. Moore and Yvonne Sherwood, *The Invention of the Biblical Scholar: A Critical Manifesto* (Minneapolis: Fortress, 2011), and Sherwood, *Biblical Blaspheming: Trials of the Sacred for a Secular Age* (Cambridge: Cambridge University Press, 2012), 67–95.

69. Karel van der Toorn, *Scribal Culture and the Making of the Hebrew Bible* (Cambridge, MA: Harvard University Press, 2007), 15.

70. Bender, "Practicing Religions," 276.

71. Elaine Scarry, *The Body in Pain: The Making and Unmaking of the World* (Oxford: Oxford University Press, 1985). The discussion of the materiality of the Hebrew Bible/Old Testament is excellent, but the book suffers from a Platonic/Christian reflex that separates the New Testament from materiality and the wound.

72. Orsi, "Everyday Miracles," 6.

73. See further, Sherwood, *Biblical Blaspheming*, 129–175.

74. The highly versatile principle of accommodation or *sygkatabasis*/condescension was based on the principle: *Scriptura humane loquitur* ("The Scriptures speak the language of man"). Understood as a "loving gesture of divine considerateness" modeled on the incarnation, accommodation presumed that "holy scripture frames itself to our manner of conceiving and speaking." See also Amos Funkenstein, *Theology and the Scientific Imagination from the Middle Ages to the Seventeenth Century* (Princeton, NJ: Princeton University Press, 1989), 213; Robert C. Hill, *Reading the Old Testament in Antioch* (Leiden: Brill, 2005), 85.

75. Bulwer, *Chirologia*, 13.

76. Bulwer, 13.

77. Bulwer, 33, 91.

78. Bulwer, 133.

79. Bulwer, 64.

80. Heidegger, *Parmenides*, 80–81.

81. Scarry, *Body in Pain*, 205.

82. Erich Auerbach, "Odysseus' Scar," in *Mimesis: The Representation of Reality in Western Literature* (Princeton, NJ: Princeton University Press, 1991), 3–23; "Die Narbe des Odysseus," in *Mimesis: Dargestellte Wirklichkeit in der Abendländischen Literatur* (Bern: A. Francke, 1946), 7–30.

83. Frank Kuppner makes the same point in his short story, "A Lesson for Us All," in *In the Beginning There Was Physics* (Edinburgh: Polygon, 1999), 11–14.

84. Heidegger, *Parmenides*, 80–81.

85. Cf. Avital Ronell, *Stupidity* (Champaign: University of Illinois Press: 2003), 309.

86. Nancy, *Corpus*, 5.

87. Bender, "Practicing Religions," 277.

88. Hent de Vries, "Introduction: Before, Around and Beyond the Theologico-Political," in *Political Theologies: Public Religions in a Post-Secular World* (New York: Fordham University Press, 2006), 3.

89. In Jewish tradition, the fact that Abraham "did" this becomes a kind of credit of "akedah-merit." This leads God to act mercifully on occasions when, by implication, he might not have acted mercifully otherwise. While this is not a straightforward transaction, it is hard to show how the akedah does not function, here, as a kind of down payment, giving Abraham's children the inbuilt security of the God (in some sense) in awe and debt. See Sherwood, "Textual Carcasses and Isaac's Scar: What Jewish Interpretation makes of the Violence that Almost Takes Place on Mount Moriah," in *Sanctified Aggression: Legacies of Biblical and Post-Biblical Vocabularies of Violence*, ed. Jonneke Bekkenkamp and Yvonne Sherwood (Edinburgh: T&T Clark/Continuum, 2004), 22–44.

90. Derrida, *Mémoires: For Paul de Man*, trans. Cecile Lindsay, Jonathan Culler, and Eduardo Cadava (New York: Columbia University Press, 1986), 94; see also Derrida, *Specters of Marx* (New York: Routledge, 1994), 7–8.

91. J. L. Austin, *How to Do Things with Words: The William James Lectures Delivered at Harvard University in 1955*, ed. J. O. Urmson and Marina Sbisà (Oxford: Oxford University Press, 1975 [1962]), 9.

92. Austin, *How to Do Things with Words*, 21–22.

93. For a pun on the two senses of testing, see G. Steins, "Die Versuchung Abrahams (Gen. 22–19), Ein neuer Versuch," in *Studies in the Book of Genesis: Literature, Redaction and History*, ed. A. Wénin (Leuven: Peeters, 2001), 509–519.

94. Avital Ronell, *The Test Drive* (Champaign: University of Illinois Press, 2008).

95. Ronell, 6.

96. Ronell, 18.

97. For sacrifice as "birth done better," see Nancy Jay, *Throughout Your Generations Forever* (Chicago: University of Chicago Press, 1992).

98. Ronell, *Test Drive*, 5.

99. Samuel Weber, *Theatricality as Medium* (New York: Fordham University Press, 2004), 7.

100. All citations in this paragraph are from Weber, *Theatricality as Medium*, 7.

101. Daniel Mesguich, *L'éternel éphémère (suivi de 'Le sacrifice' par Jacques Derrida)* (Paris: Éditions Verdier, 2006).

102. In Mesguich's production, the ghost became the play *Hamlet*. The stage contained a small ruined baroque theater, with red velvet curtain and adjoining box seats (the play within the play). When Barnardo, Marcellus, and Horatio saw the Ghost, the curtain of the small stage opened revealing a second performance of Hamlet, several moments ahead of the play on the main stage. Horatio, looking out over the ramparts of Elsinore in the mist and darkness, saw himself, his double or mirror image. Marcellus said: "Brise-toi ma langue, thee off look where, it comes again." With the appearance of the Ghost appeared, language broke down, leaving a ghost text (Shakespeare's English in fractured fragments) on stage. See Judith Gershman, "Daniel Mesguich's 'Shakespeare's Hamlet,'" *Drama Review* 25, no. 2 (Summer 1981): 17–28.

103. Mesguich, *L'éternel éphémère*, 118.

104. Mesguich, 32: "L'acteur, offert, n'est pas un Christ pourtant qui, comblant 'avec son corps les manquements de la loi' écrite, l'accomplit, l'achève enfin, la *termine*. Au théâtre, c'est infiniment provisoirement que le corps s'immisce dans les failles de l'écriture: pour l'acteur *ce n'est pas fini*, personne ne meurt, c'était pour de rire, il va falloir y revenir, incessamment . . . L'acteur non comme victime expiatoire, bouc émissaire, mais comme celui qui joue la victime; qui joue, devant tout le monde, avec la loi. Celui qui singe le bouc. Au théâtre, à la fin, Isaac, Abraham et l'agneau se relèvent et saluent."

105. Derrida, *Mémoires*, 94.

106. Mesguich, *L'éternel éphémère*, 54.

107. Derrida, "Le sacrifice," 150: "L'un des aspects les plus provocants du théâtre de Mesguich, c'est—à contre-courant de la *doxa*—de penser que le théâtre a pour essence une certaine répétition. Non pas la répétition qui prépare la première, mais une répétition qui divise, qui creuse et fait surgir l'unique présent de la première fois. La présentation non pas comme réprésentation d'une modèle présent ailleurs, comme le serait une image, mais la présence une première et unique fois comme répétition."

108. Derrida, 150: "On est souvent tenté de penser le théâtre comme l'art de ce qui, sans doute préparé par les répétitions, n'a proprement lieu qu'une seule fois. Soit en même temps une première et une dernière fois; ce qui lui donne ce double visage à la fois matinal, oriental ou archéologique et automnal, mélancolique, occidental, crépusculaire ou eschatologique."

109. Mesguich, *L'éternel éphémère*, 54; see also Derrida, "Le sacrifice," 151: "Jamais il n'y a théâtre s'il ne se produit qu'une fois. Le théâtre, toujours, se donne en séries—et cela, même si les acteurs ne jouent qu'une seule représentation de la piéce. En chaque représentation vibre sa répétition essentielle. En toute représentation chantent toutes les représentations, ses elles-mêmes passées et à venir. Chacune est fugue, suite et variations, reprise, ligne de fuite devant celle qui la précède, derrière celle qui la suit. Une manifestation théâtrale et une seule—bacchanale, crudité: cruauté—impliquerait la totalité, la plénitude, l'irréversibilité. Une manifestation théâtrale et une seule ne serait pas du théâtre: elle aurait lieu."

110. Derrida, "Le Sacrifice," 152.

111. Derrida, "Le Sacrifice," in Mesguich, *L'éternel éphémère*, 154: "Au théâtre on ne croit ni on ne croit pas, on ne regarde ni on n'écoute jamais directement; on regarde ou on écoute l'enfant ou l'idiot en nous qui croit. . . .Quand nous allons au théâtre nous ne sommes pas dupes, nous savons que c'est une illusion ou un simulacre. . . . Mais qu'est-ce que croire? Voilà la question posée, elle est mise en scène ou en feu par le théâtre." Recall relatedly Derrida's obsessive meditations on Hamlet's encounter with the ghost: "'I am thy Father's Spirit' can only be taken at his word. An essentially blind submission to the secret of his origin: this is a first obedience to the injunction. It will condition all the others. It may always be a case of still someone else. Another can always lie, he can disguise himself as a ghost, another ghost may also be passing himself off as this one. It's always possible." Derrida, *Specters of Marx*, 7.

112. Derrida, "Le sacrifice," 150–151.

113. "La seule chose crue, au théâtre, c'est qu'il a lieu devant vous; tout le reste, c'est du réchauffé [le théâtre] fait un spectacle, cru et déjà cuit." Mesguich, cited in Derrida, "Le sacrifice," 151; translation mine.

114. Derrida, *Abraham, the Other*, 1–2.

115. Avital Ronell, *Stupidity* (Champaign: University of Illinois Press, 2002), 310.

116. Weber, *Theatricality as Medium*, 7.

117. Cf. Bender, "Practicing Religions," 280.

118. C. R. Frankish, ed., Théodore de Bèze, *Abraham Sacrifiant, Tragedie Françoise* (Wakefield, Yorkshire: S. R. Publishers, 1969); Theodore Beza, *A Tragedie of Abrahams Sacrifice*, trans. Arthur Golding and ed. Malcolm W. Wallace (Toronto: University of Toronto Library, 1960). See also Daniel Weidner, "Glaubens-Drama und Theater: Théodore de Bèzes Bibeldrama *Abraham Sacrifiant*," *Germanisch-Romanische Monatsschrift* 58, no. 2 (2008): 127–147.

119. For more detailed discussion of this strange play, see below. The director-angel commands: "Now know that the substitute for your beloved child will be a little lamb you are to make ready. Such is the will of God. Let us be on our way, for I am going to leave you at your home." "The Sacrifice of Isaac," in *Nahuatl Theater Series: Life and Death in Colonial Mexico*, vol. 1, ed. Barry D. Sell and Louise Burkhart (Norman: University of Oklahoma Press, 2004), 161.

120. Thomas Chubb, "Treatise XIX: The Case of Abraham with Regard to His Offering Up Isaac in Sacrifice, Re-examined, In a Letter to a Clergyman," in *A Collection of Tracts on Various Subjects* (London: n.p., 1730), 244.

121. I am here combining Kant's comments on the sacrifice in Immanuel Kant, *The Conflict of the Faculties/Der Streit der Fakultäten*, trans. Mary J. Gregor (Lincoln: University of Nebraska Press, 1979 [1798]), 115; and Kant, *Religion Within the Limits of Reason Alone*, trans. with an introduction by Theodore M. Greene and Hoyt H. Hudson (Chicago: Open Court Publishing, 1934 [1793]), 174.

122. Derrida, "Le Sacrifice," 152.

123. See Sherwood, "The God of Abraham and Exceptional States, or the Early Modern Rise of the Whig/Liberal Bible," *Journal of the American Academy of Religion* 76, no. 2 (2008): 312–343.

124. Saba Mahmood, "Secularism, Hermeneutics, and Empire: The Politics of Islamic Reformation," *Public Culture* 18, no. 2 (Spring 2006): 334. See also Sherwood, *Biblical Blaspheming*, 366–374.

125. Weber, *Theatricality as Medium*, 7.

126. Kanan Makiya and Hassan Mneimneh, "Manual for a 'Raid,'" *New York Review of Books*, January 17, 2002, 19.

127. Malise Ruthven, *A Fury for God: The Islamist Attack on America* (London: Granta, 2002), 37. For further discussion of this act, see Sherwood, "Binding-Unbinding: Precritical 'Critique' in Pre-modern Jewish, Christian and Islamic Responses to the 'Sacrifice' of Abraham/Ibrahim's Son," in Sherwood, *Biblical Blaspheming: Trials of the Sacred for a Secular Age* (Cambridge: Cambridge University Press, 2012), 33–374.

128. Carol Delaney, *Abraham on Trial: The Social Legacy of Biblical Myth* (Princeton, NJ: Princeton University Press, 1998), 35.

129. Delaney, *Abraham on Trial*, 35.

130. Søren Kierkegaard, *Fear and Trembling: Dialectical Lyric by Johannes de Silentio*, trans. and introduction Alastair Hannay (Harmondsworth: Penguin, 1985 [1843]), 59.

131. See www.archbishopofcanterbury.org/sermons_speeches/060709.htm, accessed 10.10.2009. The speech is cited and discussed in Talal Asad, "Reflections on Blasphemy and Secular Criticism," in "Is Critique Secular?," http://townsendcenter.berkeley.edu/swg_crittheory.shtml.

132. Citing Hent de Vries, "Introduction: Before, Around and Beyond the Theologico-Political," in *Political Theologies: Public Religions in a Post-Secular World*, ed. Hent de Vries and Lawrence E. Sullivan (New York: Fordham University Press, 2006), 3.

133. De Vries, "Introduction," 3.

134. Michael Lambek, "Provincialising God? Provocations from an Anthropology of Religion," in *Religion: Beyond a Concept*, ed. Hent de Vries (New York: Fordham University Press, 2008), 125–26.

135. Lambek, 126.

136. Franz Kafka, *Parables and Paradoxes* (New York: Schocken, 1961), 44–45.

137. Hanoch Levin, *Malkat'ambatyah* [Queen of the Bathtub], in *Mah Ikhpat la Tsippor* [What Does it Matter to a Bird?] (Tel Aviv: Publisher, 1987). Moshe Dayan deemed the work an act of secular blasphemy. See also Sherwood, "Abraham in London, Marburg/Istanbul and Israel: Between Theocracy and Democracy, Ancient Text and Modern State," *Biblical Interpretation* 16, no. 2 (2008): 105–153.

138. Yehuda Amichai, "HaGibor Ha Amiti shel HaAkedah" [The true hero of the sacrifice], *She-at Hesed* [The hour of mercy] (Jersualem/Tel Aviv: Publisher, 1983), 21.

139. Derrida, "Le Sacrifice," 152.

140. The painting seems to point to something infidel and other about "our" scriptures. A surprisingly young and *unheimlich* Abraham (*sans* white beard) carries a scimitar.

141. See the story of Hannah and her seven sons, tortured at the beginning of the persecutions by Antiochus IV Epiphanes in 2 Maccabees 7, as expanded in *Yalkut Deut* 26, and *Lamentations Rabbah*. Of course, this is my own improvisation around the script. Hannah actually says, "Go and tell Father Abraham: Let not your heart swell with pride! You built one altar, but I have built seven altars and on them have offered up my seven sons. What is more: Yours was a trial; mine was an accomplished fact!"

142. Søren Kierkegaard/Johannes de Silentio, *Fear and Trembling*, ed. and trans. Alastair Hannay (London: Penguin, 1985), 91; Kierkegaard, *Fear and Trembling and Repetition*, ed. and trans. Howard V. Hong and Edna Hong, in *Kierkegaard's Writings*, vol. 6 (Princeton, NJ: Princeton University Press, 1983), 34–63.

143. Kierkegaard, *Fear and Trembling* (ed. Hannay), 62–63.

144. Kierkegaard, 45, 76, 55, 81, 60, 59, 91, 60, 66.

145. Vásquez, *More than Belief*, 2.

146. Ronell, *Test Drive*, 5.

147. Søren Kierkegaard/Constantin Constantius, *Repetition: An Essay in Experimental Psychology*, trans. Walter Lowrie (Princeton, NJ: Princeton University Press, 1946), 49.

148. For myriad Abrahams and their weak and imperfect gestures toward sacrifice, see the "Attunement/Tuning Up" section in *Fear and Trembling* and *Journals and Papers* (Hongs), 3.3020; *Journals and Papers* (Hongs) 3.3020; *Journals and Papers* (Hongs), 2.2223; *Fear and Trembling* (Hongs), 270–271; and *Fear and Trembling* (Hongs), 268–269.

149. Derrida, "Le Sacrifice," 54.

150. Søren Kierkegaard, *Repetition*, trans. Howard V and Edna H. Hong (Princeton, NJ: Princeton University Press, 1983), 159–160.

151. Kierkegaard, *Repetition*, 160.

152. Franz Kafka, *Parables and Paradoxes* (New York: Schocken, 1961), 44–45.

153. Kierkegaard/de Silentio repeatedly apostrophizes Abraham as "great" but also mocks the assumption that he has somehow (by virtue of his appearance in the Bible) acquired "proprietary rights" to the honorific "great."

154. For discussion of the management of religious gestures through the politics of identity, see Sherwood, "Binding-Unbinding," 366–374.

155. See Guy G. Stroumsa, "Christ's Laughter: Docetic Origins Reconsidered," *Journal of Early Christian Studies* 12, no. 3 (2004): 267–288.

156. This performance of Jesus's death is from the *Apocalypse of Peter* (NHC VII, 3), trans. J. Brashler, in B. Pearson, *Nag Hammadi Codex* VII, *Nag Hammadi and Manichaean Studies* 30 (Leiden: Brill, 1996), 241. A similarly split performance can be found in *The Second Treatise of the Great Seth* (Pearson, Nag Hammadi Codex, 137–138). See Irenaeus, *Adversus Haereses* 1.24.4, trans. Bentley Latyon, in *The Gnostic Scriptures: A New Translation with Annotations and Introductions* (New York: Doubleday, 1987). For discussion, see Stroumsa, "Christ's Laughter."

157. See Stroumsa, "Christ's Laughter."

158. Mesguich, *L'éternel éphémère*, 32: "L'acteur, offert, n'est pas un Christ pourtant qui, comblant "avec son corps les manquements de la loi" écrite, l'accomplit, l'achève enfin, la *termine*. Au théâtre, c'est infiniment provisoirement que le corps s'immisce dans les failles de l'écriture: pour l'acteur *ce n'est pas fini*, personne ne meurt, c'était pour de rire, il va falloir y revenir, incessament. . . . L'acteur non comme victime expiatoire, bouc émissaire, mais comme celui qui joue la victime; qui joue, devant tout le monde, avec la loi. Celui qui singe le bouc. Au théâtre, à la fin, Isaac, Abraham et l'agneau se relèvent et saluent."

159. Kierkegaard, *Repetition*, 160.

160. Stroumsa, "Christ's Laughter," 269.

161. Ernst Käsemann famously described the Christology of John as "naïve Docetism." See Bart D. Ehrman, *The Orthodox Corruption of Scripture: The Effect of Early Christological Controversies on the Effect of the New Testament* (Oxford: Oxford University Press, 1996), 197.

CHAPTER 2

Unpacking "Performance"

Felicity Conditions, Efficacy, and Indexicals in Islamic Actions

John R. Bowen

Most of the time, when we teach about religions, we start from some key ideas—sin, merit, how the world began or why it contains evil. Starting this way makes sense, as it corresponds to the self-understandings many large-scale religions produce: dogma, beliefs, the three jewels of the Buddha. It also helps us sort out why people act the way they do, by figuring out how they see the world. Weber's influence is strong here, in assuming that doctrines produced ideas, emotions, and orientations, and that these in turn led to acts. In anthropology, of course, it was Clifford Geertz who lent broad philosophical backing to what most of us in anthropology did anyway in our ethnography: ask people why they did what they did.[1]

But with this move came another: the assumption that at their core, religions enjoy agreement about symbols, meanings, and key practices. Indeed, it might be reasonable to assume that once a scriptural religion (to delimit the field) is well-established, its practitioners come to accept as settled, as beyond controversy, the practices most central to its observance. How you are to pray, to marry, or to offer a sacrifice would, after all, be clearly enunciated in the core texts, deeply grounded in historical practice, and therefore remain beyond dispute.

But such is far from the case. It is precisely the central practices of a scriptural religion that have led to the most bitter internal disputes—liturgies the basis of schisms, sacrifice the basis of revolutions.[2] They do so, I think, because of the multiple ways in which they are meaningful, which we can usefully sum up in terms of their elements of *performance*.

First, these practices nearly always are said to accomplish something: communion or commemoration, transfer or receipt of merit, communication with a deity, marriage or divorce, or simply one more act of obedience to a rule: pray five times daily, cleanse yourself of pollution. Usually there are rules to let you know when you have been successful at accomplishing this goal; the philosopher and jurist J. L. Austin called these the "felicity conditions" for a successful performance.[3] You perform the hajj if and only if you have done this and that and avoided doing these other things; your Islamic marriage is dissolved (*faskh*) if and only if a duly constituted Islamic authority proclaims it so, and so on. This is the sense in which in Islam you can speak of a *hukm* as the legal consequences of an action: the *hukm* of pronouncing a talak is a divorce, for example. This sense of performance as accomplishing an explicit goal—doing what it is supposed to do—was the central insight of early speech act theory.

But actions do more than that, which brings me to the second element of performance. Some religious acts also diagram a central orientation of the religion, as when the spatial separation of the priest behind a rood screen stood for the unique power of the church to perform sacraments—you were not summoning Christ's body and blood, the priest was doing that—or when the coming together of diverse faithful at Mecca or in a *jemaah* prayer stands for Islam's qualities of egalitarian universalism. We sometimes speak of "iconic" relations of meaning here: a picture or, as I prefer, a diagram. Relationships diagrammed may be spiritual ones, as well, as when the bodily positions assumed during salat are thought to indicate relationships of the worshipper to God. Rites of passage also diagram, by making actions on the ground stand for a passage from one spiritual or normative state to another: we find these aplenty in Islam, from the steps of ablutions to the stages of the hajj. You don't just obey God; you change your state. Here was a major addition to speech act theory, coming in part from the work of C. S. Peirce.[4]

Third, and also drawing from Peirce, acts may index particular socioreligious statuses. To "index" here refers to a relationship of copresence, as when a vestment indicates the priestly status of the wearer, or a particular placement of the hands at salat can indicate the legal tradition or the religious movement with which the worshipper identifies. Much of the communicating we do in life is of this order—as when we indicate our refinement and social capacities through speech registers and knowing asides (think Bourdieu at his best moments of observation) or, with very different signals, our willingness to carry out a physical threat (think Bruce Willis or Clint Eastwood)—without "saying" anything, but by sending the right signals.

A gesture forming part of a religious event can do all these things, as I already have suggested with reference to the salat: through worship, I may accomplish my obligation to God, diagram my submission to His will, and index many things, including: showing my status in the set of regular worshippers when I stand in the first row, showing my status as a hajj by my choice of garments and my affiliation to a particular socioreligious movement by whether I hold my hands crossed or by my side, and "saying something" about my piety by remaining afterward to perform dhikr recitations—which, depending on how I perform them, may also indicate my membership in a particular Sufi order. I will come back to these meanings below.

But why would all this indexing and diagramming and accomplishing make key religious actions into loci of conflict? First, because people agree no more on the key theological issues than they do on the manners of practice and so much of what is disputed theologically concerns performance—what you should do, how you should do it, and what the consequences will be: Should Jews or Hindus sacrifice animals? How does transubstantiation work? What invalidates the salat? Here is where theology is made flesh, or word, depending on how you come out on these issues: where it becomes specific practical imperatives, how to do things in your religion. Second, because much dispute about actions also concerns the legitimacy of the authority involved in them: Who is it who makes Christian communion "work"? Who is it who annuls an Islamic marriage? The legitimacy of one's marriage, one's worship, or one's salvation may depend on the answers to these questions. And because it is greatly important to religious authorities that they be able to control access to the goods of salvation, disagreements about the right way to accomplish these ends is likely to lead to conflict. And third, because these practices are so salient and central, they become excellent theaters for social performance, for commentary on other matters, less narrowly religious than social, political, and cultural.

Salat

Several years ago, I argued that precisely because the form of the salat was so clearly prescribed, its "core," to speak in the anthropology of ritual language of the late 1980s, was not "propositional" but performative: although among the utterances included are affirmations of God's unity, one's own surrender to Him, and so forth, the central criteria for including an act or statement in the ritual is whether or not it corresponds to what Muhammad did when he worshipped, *not* whether it conforms to a set message.[5] One may choose different verses and thereby convey different meanings, but one may not add or subtract formal elements—adding a prostration, hastening the proper time of worship—without incurring charges of illegitimate innovation, *bid'a*.

Because the focus of normative scrutiny is this set of formal elements, "orthopraxy" becomes a minutely observed metric of certain convictions about hadith or about other ritual traditions, or about social affiliations. Some of these convictions or stances have to do with the theory of correct ritual performance itself. In certain times and places, for example, some worshippers choose to say the opening bismillah silently rather than aloud, because they insist on only doing what the Prophet Muhammad did, and they believe that he was not known with certainty to have pronounced the bismillah aloud. Well, fine, but this particular choice of speech style within the worship ritual indexes the general orientation of the worshipper on the question of how to carry out Islamic rituals. Numerous Sunni reform movements have tried to realign Muslims' everyday behavior around a commitment to follow Muhammad's example as attested in reliable or sound hadith and not to follow the teaching of the legal schools, the *madhahib*, unless they are based on such a footing. The mere fact of not saying the bismillah aloud signals one's likely position on a range of ritual-related issues.

In the Dutch East Indies of the 1930s and 1940s, this question—silent or audible bismillah—often became a sensitive matter, along with several other key indices of ritual commitment. Those who argued for the quiet bismillah marshaled their arguments in widely read books and considered the issue to be an example of how so many Muslims were unwilling to know their religion in a satisfactory way. Those who argued for the audible bismillah argued in defense of following a legal school, in this case the Shafi'i school, so as to keep useless and divisive disputation to a minimum. They marshaled their own hadith in their own books on the matter.

Other considerations sometimes entered as well. For example, Gayo villagers in highland Aceh argued that they always must pronounce the words clearly and audible so that God could hear them. In their minds, ritual was mainly about communicating with God. For them, this view also explained why one should engage in chanting after someone's death and why one could speak to the souls of the dead at graves or on other occasions. For them, the audible bismillah indexed a belief that ritual practices were *mainly* about communication rather than *mainly* a mimesis of Muhammad's acts.[6]

In these cases, the debates turn on the rules for correctly performing the salat, in other words, the felicity conditions—whether the right rules are the out-loud ones or the silent ones. But the messages being sent are far broader, about your whole attitude toward the traditions of Islam. These sorts of indexicals we can call "diacritic," for the ways in which they serve to set off one position or group vis-à-vis another.

Some of these diacritic indexicals regard social affiliations. How you hold your hands or move your fingers, for example, does not have intrinsic social meaning but can become diacritics, that is, ways of telling who belongs to one or another social group. Arbitrary with respect to doctrine, such minute differences index social affiliations and thus, once imbued with this meaning, become perceived as highly motivated signs.

For example, in northern Nigeria in the late nineteenth and early twentieth centuries, if you crossed your arms during worship rather than letting them hang at your sides, you marked yourself off as a member of a specific Islamic movement. Which movement depended on where in Nigeria you were worshipping: if you were in Kano, you were proclaiming yourself a member of a Sufi reform movement; if you were in nearby Sokoto, you were "saying" that you were aligned with a messianic movement, the Mahdiyya. Later on, in the city of Ibadan, this same distinction in arm-placement became a signal of either Hausa or Yoruba ethnic identity. The same physical gesture and same kind of meaningfulness (diacritic indexing) yielded completely different social contents.[7]

Ways of organizing the jemaah (the congregational salat) also can send social messages about Islam: in 1950s Aceh, attracting large numbers of worshippers was intended to highlight Islam's universal character and thus its suitability as the basis for a new Acehnese society. By contrast, in a Jakarta worship group practicing in the 1970s, only Muslims deemed to be very pure were admitted to the jemaah. This restriction signaled Islam's capacity to create a pure community and, perhaps eventually, a purer society.[8]

The ways in which specific arrangements of salat can be taken to convey social meaning are almost endless. Often rather strong debates arise about what precisely the social meanings are. For example, what is signified by the separation of men and women in the mosque during jemaah worship? When women are behind men, does it diagram their subordinate status, does it reflect a theory about the unequal distribution of sexual desire (how men and women respond upon seeing the other prostrate), or is the second simply a way to continue the first? If men and women are on different sides of the mosque, is the message different, and to whom?

In these cases, choices about how to worship signal certain stances, whether about the ritual itself or about one's social affiliations. But Muslims sometimes develop ways to avoid doing so, that is, to hold distinct positions on a ritual but to avoid indexing that position. For example, in the Gayo highlands as in many Muslim societies, relatives of a deceased person will gather to chant verses of the

Koran on certain set intervals, often seven and forty or forty-four days after the death. In the village of Isak where I did fieldwork in the 1980s, villagers with very different ideas about the nature of this chanting came together on these occasions and chanted in identical fashion.

But these men and women held a range of distinct ideas about what it is they are doing, and these quite different theories of efficacy, if made public, would lead to heated arguments. For some, recitations automatically relieve the torment inflicted on the deceased, a theory akin to the theory that accompanied the chanting performed after a death in pre-Reformation Europe (the Gregorian chants). Others thought that the chanting did please God, but that He then could exercise discretion in relieving the deceased's suffering or not doing so. Still others thought that God would do nothing in favor of the deceased simply because people were chanting. (These "modernists" also recited the bismillah silently.)

On other occasions people would debate this issue and put forth their hadiths or verses that supported their position. But on these postmortem occasions no commentary was provided, no reason emerged to have to defend one position or another. And nothing about the form or content of the chanting indexed one or another position. There are powerful social and emotional incentives to leave things this way, of course: most people would have found it in very bad taste to engage in open arguments at a funeral.

In recent work in France, I have found a quite different example of indexing a position through commentary about the salat. I have been struck by the force of the position that one should uphold the idea of a legal school or *madhhab*, in this case the Maliki school, because doing so provides a sort of bulwark against the "wind from the East," in other words, Salafi teachings that claim to derive entirely from Koran and hadith. In one Islamic institute I attended, students learn Maliki teachings on how to perform salat in minute details, for example, concerning how much one can turn to avoid another person while praying without invalidating the prayer. No one in the school argues that following these rules for salat gives the worshipper the moral upper hand compared to people who follow other Sunni schools, nor do they say that God has any preference in the matter. Indeed, the position of the institute is that you should learn one *madhhab* well and then you can choose intelligently among different schools' opinions. But the broader message that these teachers hope to send is that learning matters, in this domain as in all others, and that true Islamic learning is rooted in traditional scholarship even if it innovates on the basis of that scholarship. The teacher is indeed "performing the worth of tradition" as he teaches intricacies of worship.

These examples illustrate the social indexical ways in which salat—and even teaching about salat—can be meaningful, but we could also, of course, discuss the broader range of things salat can be said to accomplish above and beyond responding to God's commands. Commentary on the internal states of worshippers may play a key role in evaluating individuals' performances of salat along at least two dimensions. First, inner states may be considered as elements of the felicity conditions for worship. Many Muslims would, citing a hadith to this effect, agree that having the right intent (*niyya*) is necessary for a series of gestures and utterances to count as an act of worship. But one can go further, and some do, to say that focusing on the worship act, bringing to the performance a sense of humility and submission, also are required for a proper act of worship. In Indonesia, "modernist" Muslim movements in the 1930s and 1940s often stressed these points as part of a general argument that Muslims had to take more seriously the core acts of religious practice and leave aside all that pretended to be religion but was in fact not part of Muhammad's legacy.

Furthermore, states of mind can be seen as the outcome of salat performance. Saba Mahmood, in her study of women's devotional practices in contemporary Cairo, stresses that these women see salat and other prayer practices as ways of shaping and refining their inner orientations. For them, the practical imperative of performing salat is to work on their faith.[9] One's state of mind is part of the felicity conditions for God accepting the worship, the point I have been stressing, but it also is the target of salat performance itself. And for that reason, the performance of salat and other prayer actions also may be taken as an index of the worshipper's piety—or perhaps more precisely, of the importance the worshipper places on refining her piety. Here is a case where the theory of efficacy then makes possible an additional social-indexical function: you pray often to raise your piety, and your frequent prayer indicates that your piety is probably increasing.

The general point is hardly specific to Islam, of course, and we can think about a broad range of ways in which Christian exegetes and ordinary people put forward doctrines of signs of salvation, from the successful ascetic Protestant businessmen described by Max Weber, whose work in the world was proof that God must be smiling on them, to the snake-handlers of West Virginia, who, taking a cue from the Gospel of Mark, find injury-free snake-handling to be a sign of possession by the Holy Ghost.

In all these cases, successful performance indexes the appropriate inner state or even the presence of grace in the performer. If successful, these indexing events then can become the basis for making certain social claims—to be a proper imam for a salat jemaah or to be a member of a Puritan church.

Marriage and Divorce

If salat points to the multiple indexical functions of a religious action, issues of marriage and divorce point to the political and legal importance of debates over felicity conditions. These debates arise in response to two related developments: the increasing "étatisation" of Islamic social norms and the increasing demands in Europe and North America to find bridges between Islamic and civil legal processes.

Let me focus on divorce, although marriage is equally critical. In those countries where the state sets conditions for a divorce to take place, an intriguing question arises regarding a man's right to divorce his wife by pronouncing the formula referred to as the *talak*. In a number of countries, Indonesia among them, the law does not challenge the husband's right to divorce through talak but rather sets the conditions under which the husband may carry it out. In these countries, a talak occurs legally only if the husband appears in court and shows good grounds for divorce, and the judge grants permission. An intriguing issue then arises regarding the performativity of a talak: If a husband says the talak at home, has he divorced his wife Islamically? The issue can arise for the courts if he does so and then remarries, and the first or ex-wife challenges the remarriage on grounds that her consent, required for taking a second wife, was not obtained. Such cases do arise, and the question the court must then decide is: Did the "wild" talak, uttered at home, dissolve the first marriage? If a judge takes the view that the state sets its own rules but the husband retains his own Islamic rights as before, then the husband's utterance did indeed dissolve the first marriage and the couple is divorced. Of course, the man may be fined for not appearing in court, but as long as his remarriage was itself carried out according to the law, he is not guilty of improperly taking a second wife. But if the state in effect has defined one's Islamic rights, then the husband's private talak no longer meets the religious felicity conditions any more than it meets the civil law felicity conditions. In that case he never divorced his wife, and so he improperly married the second wife because he never asked permission of his first, still-married, wife.

As it happens, the Indonesian Supreme Court has ruled in both ways on this question, leaving some uncertainty. In Aceh, where I work, judges and ulama are uncertain and divided on the matter. This issue matters well beyond the few cases that make it to court, because it touches the heart of the issue of legitimacy: Can the state, through laws and proclamations, change what counts in the eyes of God? In the language of this volume, are the political and religious gestures that make up the act of divorcing now unified, so that the state performs a political and a religious act at once? Or are they distributed to different actors, so that the husband retains full religious performative capacity regardless of the state's (here, the judge's) actions?[10] The answer to this question matters to religious scholars and judges, because if the answer is the latter, then respected religious scholars retain their capacity to say what counts as proper acts in Islam; no delegation of religious authority has occurred.[11]

This question changes and becomes still more acute for Muslims living in societies without Islamic judges, as in most of Europe and North America. Here the new element regards the plight of wives. In Morocco or Pakistan, or other societies with Islamic courts, a wife may take action to dissolve her marriage in one of a number of ways, principally by persuading her husband to issue a talak, often following a payment from her, or by persuading a judge to dissolve the marriage. Although a judge may decide that a talak has been issued, technically the husband performs it—even in the case of a "delegated talak," whereby the husband states that if he does this or that (failing to support his wife, leaving home for long periods), then a talak automatically occurs. But the judge also may issue an annulment of the marriage, called a *faskh*. The annulment is performed by the judge and so requires that there be judges to do the performing.

But who gets to nominate an Islamic judge? You already see that a question that arises now in Europe could accentuate the ambivalence common to all Islamic societies mentioned above concerning the efficacy of a state in Islamic terms. I recently spoke with the imam of the main mosque in Lyon whose own long experience in Tunisia made it clear to him that he was not a judge and so had no right to issue a divorce. But he was frequently asked to do so, as are many imams in Europe, and he said that there ought to be some sort of properly empowered Islamic tribunal for France or for Europe.

Some Muslim scholars, however, have taken on themselves the authority to dissolve marriages. One finds them throughout Europe and North America, but most strikingly in England. Recently I have been spending time with the Islamic Sharia Council (ISC) in London that alternates its sessions between the Regent's Park Mosque and an office in Leyton, east of London. Despite the concerns fulsomely expressed in English newspapers that England now has "sharia law," nearly all the work of this and other ISCs lies in considering requests by married women to annul their marriage.

The ISC faces two challenges concerning the felicity conditions of its actions. The first comes from some lawyers, so far in Pakistan, who deny that the ISC's scholars are properly empowered and that the divorces ever happened. (The issue is of course hugely complex and potentially ironic if appointment by whoever happens to rule Pakistan is what makes an actor legitimate in God's eyes.) Their position may be consequential, as most women seeking annulments or divorces are from Pakistan and some will seek to remarry there.

The second challenge comes from many in England who do not wish to see any legitimacy attached to something called a sharia council. Their unease is difficult to understand if we look only at what the council's action accomplishes. It does nothing that a civil court could otherwise have done—unlike most arbitration panels, it does not substitute its acts for those of the civil court, since the latter has no jurisdiction in religious law. I think the unease has to do with the indexicality of its actions: the desire of some Muslims to appeal to an ISC indexes the close attachment many have to Islamic norms, and in the eyes of some outside commentators this desire also points to a weak attachment to English society: in today's officialese, not enough "community cohesion." We all know that legal acts "send a message" about society, and it is on these grounds that, for example, in 2008 the prime minister chose to attack the archbishop of Canterbury for the latter's partial support of Islamic mediation, saying that such councils weaken the uniformity of law in Britain.

This example concerns effects and messages attributable to an Islamic body in a secular legal environment. What about the performativity of an English civil tribunal in terms of its Islamic effects? Might a civil marriage also constitute an Islamic one, a *nikah*? Some Muslim scholars argue that it does, or at least that one could consider a civil marriage to constitute an Islamic one, because consent by the two parties is the key felicity condition of both kinds of marriage. Of course, each system also poses other conditions: for example, the bride's guardian must give his consent for the marriage to be Islamically effective. But to facilitate a rapprochement between the two systems, the ISC in London says that it recognizes an element of Hanafi law that if the guardian is absent from the marriage, but he does not invalidate the marriage within a set period of time, then the marriage is valid. Even the Ahlul Hadith secretary of the ISC urges using this Hanafi provision to recognize a civil marriage as already Islamic. Parallel arguments have been put forth in France and elsewhere in Europe by certain Islamic scholars.

Not everyone likes this idea, not because it is technically wrong but because it indexes a certain copresence of Islam and civil law that some dislike. A French Muslim wrote in a long Internet exchange on this issue: "City hall does not validate a marriage! If for you, marrying in front of a guy in a bow tie with the red white and blue flag is more important than [marrying] before God, good for you!"

The war of indexicalities is, if anything, more strongly fought in France than in England. Out of the long war for control of society waged by the Fifth Republic against the church came a series of laws designed to reinforce the capture of religions by the state. For example, the law "diagrams," in the sense explained above, the absolute priority of civil law over religious institutions by prohibiting a religious official from celebrating a marriage before the couple has married legally, at city hall. The law was passed in a period where priests were its intended target, but in 2008 two imams were found guilty of what is a criminal offense, because they had presided over *nikah* rituals, in their mosques, for couples who were not yet legally married. This very recent decision to enforce what had been an unused law came about, not because of the importance of marriage per se, but because it shows that the Constitution stands above the Koran, that Muslims must give priority to law over religion. Temporal precedence diagrams normative priority.

I also think that the many attempts by French officials to prevent Muslim women wearing headscarves from entering various civic places—city halls, school grounds, even the National Assembly—is mainly about indexing the distinction between secular space and religious practices, and stressing the priority of the former. At issue is maintaining the boundary between a sort of secularist sacrality and the profane space of ordinary life by policing those who cross the threshold. This policing—almost always in violation of laws about citizens' and residents' rights to enter all civic spaces—is carried out less because of a general sense that religious signs will pollute these civic spaces than from a desire to send a narrow-band message to Muslims, that they must acknowledge the superiority of the republic.[12]

Across this broad range of acts, religious and political, it should be apparent that (a) performativity is an interpretation of an act potentially carried out by multiple actors, reaching divergent conclusions, and that (b) no single relationship holds between performativity and indexicality. A worshipper may consider his salat to be an ordinary and even mundane performance of his obligations, while someone watching him may focus on certain signals sent about piety, state of mind, and affiliation to one or another socioreligious movement. It is the latter and not the former who is reading indexes off of the act. Men and women chanting after someone's death may have quite distinct ideas about what is accomplished by their acts, none of which are observable: an example of considered, deliberate avoidance of what could have been disruptive indexing. A talak uttered in the wilderness may be heard by God, but people may disagree as to what He thinks about its performativity: a useless attempt to divorce a wife or an effective divorce act unrecognized by the state? A woman wearing a headscarf may do so without thinking much about it, in a fully felt sense of piety and submission to God, or to send a message that "I am a Muslim" to others who might otherwise extend unwanted advances. Those around her might have their own range of readings of what is indexed by her decision to wear the scarf, from all of those above to an assertion of a more pious inner life than those around her or a commitment to political Islam.

What these examples show is that we can draw on Austin's approach to highlight certain modes of meaningfulness of Islamic (and "counter-Islamic") acts but also to understand that studying indexicality, with respect to Islamic or other religious acts, goes well beyond performativity.

Notes

1. Max Weber, *The Protestant Ethic and the Spirit of Capitalism* (New York: Charles Scribner's Sons, 1958); Clifford Geertz, *The Interpretation of Cultures* (New York: Basic Books, 1973).

2. For a slightly different critique of the symbolic approach, see Talal Asad, "The Construction of Religion as an Anthropological Category," in *Genealogies of Religion* (Baltimore, MD: Johns Hopkins University Press, 1993), 27–54.

3. J. L. Austin, *How to Do Things with Words*, 2nd ed. (Oxford: Oxford University Press, 1976).

4. See Michael Silverstein's critique of the Austinian approach to meaning in his "Cultural Prerequisites to Grammatical Analysis," in *Linguistics and Anthropology: Georgetown University Round Table on Languages and Linguistics*, ed. M. Saville-Troike (Washington, DC: Georgetown University Press, 1977), 139–151.

5. For these and the other Indonesian examples mentioned here, see John R. Bowen, "Salat in Indonesia: The Social Meanings of an Islamic Ritual," *Man* 24, no. 4 (1989): 600–619.

6. Bowen, "Salat in Indonesia."

7. See J. N. Paden, *Religion and Political Culture in Kano* (Berkeley: University of California Press, 1973); and A. Cohen, *Custom and Politics in Urban Africa* (Berkeley: University of California Press, 1969).

8. Bowen, "Salat in Indonesia."

9. Saba Mahmood, *Politics of Piety: The Islamic Revival and the Feminist Subject* (Princeton, NJ: Princeton University Press, 2005).

10. On these examples, see John R. Bowen, *Islam, Law and Equality in Indonesia: An Anthropology of Public Reasoning* (Princeton, NJ: Princeton University Press, 2005); and Arskal Salim, *Challenging the Secular State: Islamization of Law in Modern Indonesia* (Honolulu: Hawai'i University Press, 2008).

11. This issue runs throughout the history of state-*ulama* relations in Islamic societies; for the case of Egypt, see Malika Zeghal, *Gardiens de l'islam: Les oulémas d'al-Azhar dans l'Égypte contemporaine* (Paris: Presses de la Fondation Nationale des Sciences Politiques, 1996).

12. On these issues, see John R. Bowen, *Why the French Don't Like Headscarves* (Princeton, NJ: Princeton University Press, 2007).

CHAPTER 3

"Thou Shalt Not Freeze-Frame"
How Not to Misunderstand the Science and Religion Debate

Bruno Latour

I have no authority whatsoever to talk to you about religion and experience because I am neither a predicator, nor a theologian, nor a philosopher of religion—nor even an especially pious person.[1] Fortunately, religion might not be about authority and strength but exploration, hesitation, and weakness. If so, then I should begin by putting myself in a position of most extreme weakness. William James, at the end of his masterpiece, *Varieties of Religious Experience*,[2] says his form of pragmatism possesses a "crass" label, that of pluralism. I should better state at the beginning of this talk that my label—or my stigma?—is even crasser: I have been raised a Catholic; and worse, I cannot even speak to my children of what I am doing at church on Sunday. It is from this very impossibility of speaking to my friends and to my own kin about a religion that matters to me, that I want to start tonight: I want to begin this lecture by this hesitation, this weakness, this stuttering, by this speech impairment. Religion, in my tradition, in my corner of the world, has become impossible to enunciate.[3]

But I don't think I could be allowed to talk only from such a weakened and negative position. I have also a slightly firmer ground that gives me some encouragement in addressing this most difficult topic. If I have dared answering the invitation to speak, it is also because I have been working for many years on offering other interpretations of scientific practice than common ones.[4] It is clear that in an argument on science and religion, any change, however slight, however disputed, in the way science is considered, will have some consequences on the many ways to talk about religion. Truth production in science, religion, law, politics, technology, economics, and so on is what I have been studying over the years in my program to advance toward an anthropology of the modern (or rather nonmodern) world. Systematic comparisons of what I call "regimes of enunciation" is what I am after, and if there is any technical argument in what follows, it is this rather idiosyncratic comparative anthropology from which they will come. In a sort of weak analogy with speech act theory, I have devoted myself to mapping out the "conditions of felicity" of the various activities that, in our cultures, are able to elicit truth.

I have to note at the beginning that I am not trying to make a critique of religion. That truth in question in science, as well as in religion, is not for me in question. Contrary to what some of you who might know my work on science (most probably by hearsay) could be led to believe, I am interested mainly in the practical conditions of truth-telling and *not* in debunking religion after having, so it is said, disputed the claims of science. If it was already necessary to take science seriously without giving it some sort of social explanation, such a stand is even more necessary for religion: debunkers simply would miss the point. Rather, my problem is how to become attuned to the right conditions of felicity of those different types of truth generators.

And now to work. I don't think it is possible to speak of religion without making clear the form of speech that is adjusted to its type of predication. Religion, at least in the tradition I am going to talk from, namely the Christian one, is a way of preaching, of predicating, of enunciating truth in a certain manner—this is why I have to mimic in writing the situation of an oration given from the pulpit. It is literally, technically, theologically a form of news, of "good news," what in Greek was called *evangelios*, what has been translated into English as "gospel." Thus, I am not going to speak of religion in general, as if there existed some universal domain, topic, or problem called "religion" that could allow one to compare divinities, rituals, and beliefs from Papua New Guinea to Mecca, from Easter Island to Vatican City. A person of faith has only one religion, as a child has only one mother. There is no point of view from which one could compare different religions and *still* be talking in the religious fashion. As you see, my purpose is not to talk *about* religion but to talk to you *religiously*, at least religiously enough so that we can begin to analyze the conditions of felicity of such a speech act, by demonstrating in vivo, tonight, in this room what sort of truth condition this speech act requests. Since the topic of this series implies experience, experience is what I want to generate.

Talking of Religion, Talking from Religion

What I am going to argue is that religion—again in the tradition which is mine—does not speak *of* things but *from* things, entities, agencies, situations, substances, relations, experiences, whatever is the word, which are highly sensitive to the ways in which they are talked about. They are, so to speak, manners of speech—John would say Word, Logos, or *Verbum*. Either they transport the spirit from which they talk, and they can be said to be truthful, faithful, proven, experienced, self-verifiable, or they don't reproduce, don't perform, don't transport what they talk from, and immediately, without any inertia, they begin to lie, to fall apart, to stop having any reference, any ground. Either they elicit the spirit they utter and they are true or they don't and they are worse than false, they are simply irrelevant, parasitical.

There is nothing extravagant, spiritual, or mysterious in beginning to describe religious talk in this way. We are used to other, perfectly mundane forms of speech that are evaluated not by their correspondence with any state of affairs either but by the quality of the interaction they generate from the way they are uttered. This experience—and experience is what we wish to share—is common in the domain of "love talk" and, more largely, personal relations. "Do you love me?" is not assessed by the originality of the sentence—none are more banal, trivial, boring, rehashed—but rather by the *transformation* it manifests in the listener, as well as in the speaker. *In*formation talk is one thing, *trans*formation talk is another. When the latter is uttered, something happens. A slight displacement in the normal pace of things. A tiny shift in the passage of time. You have to decide, to get involved: maybe to commit yourselves irreversibly. We are not only undergoing an experience among others but a change in the pulse and tempo of experience: *kairos* is the word the Greeks would have used to designate this new sense of urgency.

Before going back to religious talk, in order to displace our usual ways of framing it, I wish to extract two features from the experience we all have—I hope—in uttering or listening to love-carrying sentences.

The first one is that such sentences are not judged by their *content*, their number of bytes, but by their performative abilities. They are mainly evaluated by only this question: do they produce the thing they talk about, namely, *lovers*? (I am not so much interested here in love as "eros," which often requires little talk, but in love as "agapè," to use the traditional distinction.) In love injunction, attention is redirected not to the content of the message but to the container itself, the person-making. One does not attempt to decrypt it as if it transported a message, but as if it transformed the messengers themselves. And yet, it would be wrong to say that they have no truth-value simply because they possess no informational content. On the contrary, although one could not tick *p*'s and *q*'s to calculate the truth table of those statements, it is a very important matter—one to which we devote many nights and days—to decide whether they are truthful, faithful, deceitful, superficial, or simply obscure and vague. All the more so, because such injunctions are in no way limited to the medium of speech: smiles, sighs, silences, hugs, gestures, gazes, postures, everything can relay the argument—yes, it is an argument and a tightly knit one at that. But it is an odd argument that is largely judged by the *tone* with which it is uttered, its tonality. Love is made of syllogisms whose premises are persons. Are we not ready to give an arm and a leg to be able to detect truth from falsity in this strange talk that transports persons and not information? If there is one involvement in truth detection, in trust building that everyone shares, it is certainly this ability to detect right from wrong love talk. So, one of the conditions of felicity we can readily recognize is that there exist forms of speech—and again it is not just language—that are able to transfer *persons* not information, either because they produce in part personhood, or because new states—"new beginnings," as William James would say—are generated in the persons thus addressed.

The second feature I wish to retain from the specific and totally banal performance of love talk is that it seems to be able to shift the way space is inhabited and time flows. Here, again, the experience is so widespread that we might overlook its decisive originality. Although it is so common, it is not often described, except in a few movies by Ingmar Bergman or in some odd novels, because eros, Hollywood eros, usually occupies the stage so noisily that the subtle dynamic of agapè is rarely noticed. But we can share, I think, enough of the same experience to capitalize on it later for my analysis: what happens to you, would you say, when you are thus addressed by love-talk? Very simply put: you were *far*, you are now *closer*—and lovers seem to have a treasure of private lore to account for the subtle reasons of those shifts from distance to proximity. This radical change concerns not only space, but also time: you just had the feeling of inflexible and fateful destiny, as if a flow from the past to the ever-diminishing present was taking you straight to inertia, boringness, maybe death; and suddenly, a word, an attitude, a query, a posture, *un je ne sais quoi*, and time flows again, as if it were starting from the present and had the capacity to open the future and reinterpret the past: possibility arises, fate is overcome, you breathe, you feel enabled, you hope, you move. In the same way as the word *close* captured the different ways space is now inhabited, it is the word *present* that now seems the best way to capture what happens to you: you are present again and anew to one another. And, of course, you might become absent and far again in a moment—this is why your heart beats so fast, why you are at once so thrilled and so anxious: a word badly uttered, a clumsy gesture, a wrong move and, instantly, the terrible feeling of estrangement and distance, this despondency that comes from the fateful passage of time, all of that boredom falls over you again, intolerable, deadly. You suddenly do not understand what you are doing with one another: unbearable, simply unbearable.

Have I not sketched a very common experience, the one acquired in the love crisis, on both sides of this infinitely small difference between what is close and present and what is far and absent? This difference that is marked so vividly by a nuance, sharp as a knife, both subtle and sturdy: a difference between talking rightly and talking wrongly about what makes us alive to the presence of one another?

If we now take together the two features of love-addressing I have just outlined, we may convince ourselves that there exists a form of speech that is both concerned with the transformation of messengers instead of the transport of information and so sensitive to the tone in which it is uttered that it can abruptly shift, through a decisive crisis, from distance to proximity—and back to estrangement—and from absence to distance and, alas, back again. Of this form of talk, I will say that it "represents" in one of the many literal meanings of the word: it presents anew what it is to be present in what one says. And this form of talk is at once completely common, extremely complex, and not that frequently described in detail.

How to Redirect Attention?

Such is the atmosphere I want to benefit from, in order to start again my predication—since to talk, nay, to preach religion is what I want to attempt, so as to obtain enough common experience that it can be analyzed afterward. I want to use the template of love-addressing so as to rehabilitate ourselves to a form of religious talk which has been lost, unable to represent itself again, to repeat itself because of the shift from religion to belief; more on this later. We now know that the competence we are looking for is common, that it is subtle, that it is not very much described, that it easily appears and disappears, tells the truth and then gives the lie. The conditions of felicity of my own talk are thus clearly outlined: I will fail if I cannot produce, perform, educe what it is about. Either I am able to represent it to you again, that is to present it in its renewed and olden presence, and I speak in truth; or I am not, and although I might have pronounced the same words, it is in vain that I speak, I have lied to you, I am nothing but an empty drum that beats in the void.

Three words are important, then, in respect to my risky contract with you: close, present, and transformation. To give me some chance to succeed in reenacting the right way to say religious things—in the Word tradition I have been raised in—I need to redirect your attention away from topics and domains thought to pertain to religion but which might render you indifferent or hostile to my way of talking. We have to resist two temptations in order for my argument to stand a chance of representing anything—and thus to be truthful. The first temptation would be to abandon the transformation necessary for this speech act to function; the second would be to direct our attention to the far away instead of the close and present.

To put it simply, but I hope not too provocatively: if, when hearing about religion, you direct your attention to the far away, the above, the supernatural, the infinite, the distant, the transcendent, the mysterious, the misty, the sublime, the eternal, chances are that you have not even begun to be sensitive to what religious talk tries to involve you in. Remember, I am using the template of love-addressing, to speak of different sentences with the same spirit, the same regime of enunciation. In the same way as those love-sentences should transform the listeners in being close and present or else are void, the ways of talking religion should bring the listener as well as the speaker to the same closeness and to the same renewed sense of presence—or else they are worse than meaningless. If you are attracted to the distant, by religious matters, to the far away, the mysteriously encrypted, then you are *gone*, you are literally not *with me*, you remain absent-minded. You make a lie of what I am giving you a chance to hear again tonight. Do you understand what I am saying? The way I am saying it? The Word tradition I am setting into motion again?

The first attempt at redirecting your attention is to make you aware of the pitfall of what I call double-click communication. If you use such a benchmark to evaluate the quality of religious talk, it will become exactly as meaningless, empty, boring, and repetitive as misaddressed love talk, and for the same reason: because they carry no messages, but rather a transport and transform the messengers themselves, or fail. And yet, such is exactly the yardstick of double-click communication: it wants us to believe that it is feasible to transport without any deformation whatsoever of some accurate information about states of affairs which are not presently here. In most ordinary cases, what people have in mind when they ask, "Is this true?" or "Does this correspond to a state of affairs?" is just such a double-click gesture allowing immediate access to information: tough luck, because this is also what gives the lie to ways of talking that are dearest to our heart. On the contrary, to disappoint the drive toward double-click, to divert it, to break it, to subvert it, to render it impossible is just what religious talk is after. Speakers of religious talk want to make sure that even the most absentminded, the most distant gazers, are brought back to attention so that they do not waste their time ignoring the call to conversion. To disappoint, first, to disappoint. "What has this generation in requesting a sign? No sign will be given to them!"

Transport of information without deformation is not, *no* it is not one of religious talk's conditions of felicity. When the Virgin hears the angel Gabriel's salutation, she is so utterly transformed, says the venerable story, that she becomes pregnant with the Savior, rendered through her agency present again to the world. Surely this is not a case of double-click communication! However, asking "who was Mary?," checking whether or not she was "really" a Virgin, imagining some pathway to impregnate her with spermatic rays, deciding whether Gabriel is male or female, *these* are double-click questions. They want you to abandon the present time and to direct your attention away from the meaning of the venerable story. These questions are not impious or even irrational; they are simply a category mistake. They are so irrelevant that no one has even to bother answering them. Not because they lead to unfathomable mysteries but because their idiocy makes them generate uninteresting and utterly useless mysteries. They should be broken, interrupted, voided, ridiculed—and I will show later how this interruption has been systematically attempted in one of the Western Christian iconographic traditions. The only way to understand stories such as that of the Annunciation is to *repeat* them, that is to utter again a word which produces into the listener the same *effect*, which impregnates *you*, because it is *you* I am saluting, I am hailing tonight, with the same gift, the same present of renewed presence. Tonight, I am your Gabriel! Or else you do not understand a word of what I am saying—and I am a fraud.

Not an easy task—I will fail, I know, I am bound to fail, I speak against all odds—but my point is different because it is a little more analytical: I want you to realize through which sort of category mistake belief in belief is being generated. Either I repeat the first story because I retell it in the same efficient mode in which it was first told, or I hook up a stupid referential question to a messenger-transfer one and I do more than a crass stupidity: I make the venerable story lie because I have distorted it beyond recognition. Paradoxically, by formatting questions in the procrustean bed of information transfer so as to get at *exactly* what it meant, I would have *deformed* it, transmogrified it into an absurd belief, the sort of belief that weighs religion down and lets it slide toward the refuse heap of past obscurantism. The truth-value of those stories depends on us tonight, exactly as the whole history of two lovers depends on their ability to reenact the injunction to love again in the minute they are reaching for one another in the darker moment of their estrangement: if they fail (present tense), it was in vain (past tense), that they have lived so long together.

Note that I did not speak of those sentences as being either irrational or unreasonable, as if religion had somehow to be protected against an irrelevant extension of rationality. When Ludwig Wittgenstein writes: "I want to say, 'they don't treat this as a matter of reasonability.' Anyone who reads the Epistles will find it said: not only that it is not reasonable, but that it is a folly. Not only it is not reasonable, but it doesn't pretend to be,"[5] he seems to deeply misunderstand what sort of folly the Gospel is writing about. Far from not pretending to be reasonable, it simply applies the same *common* reasoning to a *different* kind of situation: it does not try to reach a distant state of affairs but brings the locutors closer to what they say of one another. To suppose that, in addition to rational knowledge of what is graspable, there exists also some sort of unreasonable and respectable belief of things too far away to be graspable, seems to me a very condescending form of tolerance. I would rather like to say that rationality is never in excess, that science knows no boundary, and that there is absolutely nothing mysterious or even unreasonable in religious talk—except the artificial mysteries generated, as I just said, by asking the wrong questions, in the wrong mode, in the wrong *key*, to perfectly reasonable person-making argumentations. To seize something by talk or to be seized by someone else's talk might be different, but the same basic mental, moral, psychological, and cognitive equipment is necessary for both.

More precisely we should differentiate two forms of mystery: one that refers to the common, complex, subtle ways in which one has to pronounce love talk for it to be efficacious—and it is indeed a mystery of ability, a knack, like good tennis, good poetry, good philosophy, maybe a sort of folly—and another mystery, totally artificial, that is caused by the undue short-circuit of two different regimes of enunciation colliding with one another. The confusion between the two mysteries is what makes the voice of people quiver when they talk of religion, either because they wish to have no mystery at all—good, there is none anyway—or because they believe they are looking at some encrypted message they have to decode through the use of some special and esoteric grid that only initiates know-how as knowledge of how to use. But there is nothing hidden, nothing encrypted, nothing esoteric, nothing odd in religious talk: it is simply difficult to enact, it is simply a little bit subtle, it needs exercise, it requires great care, it might save those who utter it. To confuse talk that transforms messengers with talk that transports messages—cryptic or not—is not a proof of rationality, it is simply an idiocy doubled by an impiety. It is as idiotic as if a lover, asked to repeat whether she loves her partner or not, simply pushed the "play" button of a tape recorder to prove that five years ago she had indeed said "I love you, darling." It might prove something but certainly *not* that she has renewed her pledge to love presently—it is a valid proof, to be sure, a proof that she is an absentminded and probably lunatic woman.

Enough about double-click communication. The two other features—closeness and presence—are much more important for our purpose, because they will lead us to the third term of our lecture series, namely science. It is amazing that most speakers, when they want to show generosity toward religion, have to couch it in terms of its necessary irrationality. I sort of prefer those who, like Pascal Boyer, frankly want to explain—to explain away—religion altogether, by highlighting the brain loci and the survival value of some of its most barbarous oddities.[6] I always feel more at home with purely naturalistic accounts than with this sort of hypocritical tolerance that ghettoizes religion into a form of nonsense specialized in transcendence and "feel good" inner sentiment. Alfred North Whitehead, in my view, had put an end to those who wish religion to "embellish the soul" with pretty furniture.[7] Religion, in the tradition I want to render present again, has nothing to do with subjectivity, nor with transcendence, nor with irrationality, and the last thing it needs is tolerance from open-minded and charitable intellectuals who want to add to the true but dry facts of science, the deep and charming "supplement of soul" provided by quaint religious feelings.

Here, I am afraid I have to disagree with most, if not all, of the former speakers on the science-religion confrontation because they are talking like Camp David diplomats drawing lines with a felt pen over some maps of the Israel/Palestine territories. They all try to settle disputes as if there was one single domain, one single kingdom to share in two or, following the terrifying similarity with the Holy Land, as if two "equally valid claims" had to be established side-by-side, one for the natural, the other for the supernatural. And some speakers, like the most extremist zealots of Jerusalem and Ramallah—the parallel is uncanny—rejecting the efforts of diplomats, want to claim the whole land for themselves, either by driving the obscurantist religious folks to the other side of the Jordan River or, conversely, by drowning the naturalists in the Mediterranean Sea. I find those disputes—whether there is one or two domains, whether it is hegemonic or parallel, whether polemical or peaceful—equally moot for a reason that strikes at the heart of the matter: they all suppose that science and religion have similar but divergent claims to reach and settle a territory, either of this world or of this other world. I believe, on the contrary, that there is no point of contact between the two, no more, let's say than nightingales and frogs have to enter into any sort of direct ecological competition.

I am not saying that science and religion are incommensurable—because one grasps the objective visible world of here and there and the other grasps the invisible subjective or transcendent world of beyond—but rather that even their incommensurability would be a category mistake. The reason is that neither science nor religion fits even this basic picture that would put them face-to-face or enough in relation to be deemed incommensurable! Neither religion nor science are much interested in the visible: it is science that grasps the far and the distant; as to religion, it does not even try to *grasp* anything.

Science and Religion: A Comedy of Errors

My point might appear at first counterintuitive because I wish to draw simultaneously on what I have learned from science studies about scientific practice and what I hope you have experienced here in reframing religious talk with the help of a love argument. Religion does not even try, if you have followed me until now, to reach anything beyond but to represent the presence of that which is called in a certain technical and ritual idiom the "Word incarnate"—that is to say again that it is here, alive, and not dead over there far away. It does not try to designate something but to speak from a new state that it generates by its ways of talking, its manner of speech. Religion, in this tradition, does everything to constantly redirect attention by systematically breaking the will to go away, to ignore, to be indifferent, blasé, bored. Conversely, science has nothing to do with the visible, the direct, the immediate, the tangible, the lived world of common sense, of sturdy "matters of fact." Quite the opposite, as I have shown many times, it builds extraordinarily long, complicated, mediated, indirect, sophisticated paths so as to reach the worlds—like William James I insist on the plural—that are invisible because they are too small, too far, too powerful, too big, too odd, too surprising, too counterintuitive, through concatenations of layered instruments, calculations, models. Only through the laboratory and instrument networks can you obtain those long referential chains that allow you to maximize the two contrary features of mobility (or transport) and immutability (or constant) that both make up information—what I have called immutable mobiles.

And notice here that science in action, science as it is done practically, is even further from double-click communication than religion: distortion, transformation, recoding, modeling, translating, all of these radical mediations are necessary to produce reliable and accurate information. If science was information *without* transformation, as good common sense would like to have it, we would still be in complete obscurity about states of affairs distant from here and now. Double-click communication does even less justice to the transformation of information in scientific networks than to the strange ability of some speech acts to transform the locutors in religion.

What a comedy of errors! When the debate between science and religion is staged, adjectives are almost exactly reversed: it is of science that one should say that it reaches the invisible world of beyond, that she is spiritual, miraculous, soul-fulfilling, uplifting.[8] And it is religion that should be qualified as being local, objective, visible, mundane, unmiraculous, repetitive, obstinate, sturdy.

In the traditional fable of a race between the scientific rabbit and the religious tortoise, two things are totally unrealistic: the rabbit *and* the tortoise. Religion does not even attempt to race to know the beyond but attempts at breaking all habits of thoughts that direct our attention to the far away, to the absent, to the overworld, in order to bring attention back to the incarnate, to the renewed presence of what was before misunderstood, distorted, and deadly, of what is said to be "what was, what is, what shall be," toward those words that carry salvation. Science does not *directly* grasp anything accurately but slowly gains its accuracy, its validity, its truth condition by the long, risky, and painful detour through the mediations of experiments and not experience, laboratories not common sense, theories not visibility, and if she is able to obtain truth it is at the price of mind-boggling transformations from one media into the next. Thus, to even assemble a stage where the deep and serious problem of "the relationship between science and religion" could unfold is already an imposture, not to say a farce that distorts science and religion, religion and science beyond all recognition.

The only protagonist who would dream of the silly idea of staging a race between the rabbit and the tortoise, to put them face-to-face so as to decide afterward who dominates whom—or to invent even more bizarre diplomatic settlements between the two characters—the only Barnum for such a circus is double-click communication. Only he, with this bizarre idea of transportation *without* transformation to reach a faraway state of affairs, could dream of such a confrontation, distorting the careful practice of science, as well as the careful repetition of religious, person-giving talk. Only he can make both science and religion incomprehensible, first by distorting the mediated and indirect access of science to the invisible world through the hard labor of scientists, into a direct, plain, and unproblematic grasp of the visible; and then, in giving the lie to religion by forcing her to abandon her goal of representing anew what it is about and making all of us gaze, absentmindedly toward the invisible world of beyond which she has no equipment nor competence nor authority nor ability to reach—even less to grasp. Yes, what a comedy of errors, a sad comedy, one that has made it almost impossible to embrace rationalism, because it would mean to ignore the workings of science even more than the goals of religion.

Two Ways of Linking Statements to One Another

Those two regimes of invisibility, which have been so distorted by the appeal to the dream of instant and unmediated communication, might be made more demonstrative by appealing to visual documents. My idea is to move the listener from one opposition between science and religion to one between two types of objectivities. The first traditional fight has pitted science, defined as the grasp of the visible, the near, the close, the impersonal, the knowable, against religion, which is supposed to deal with the far, the vague, the mysterious, the personal, the uncertain, and the unknowable.

To this opposition, which is, in my view, an artifact, I want to substitute another opposition between the long and mediated referential chains of science that lead to the distant and the absent and the search for the representation of the close and present in religion. As I have shown elsewhere, science is in no way a form of speech act that tries to bridge the abyss between words and *the* world—in the singular. That would be amounting to the *salto mortale* so ridiculed by James; rather, science as it is practiced, attempts to "deambulate" (James's expression) from one inscription to the next by taking each of them in turn for the matter out of which it extracts a form. "Form" here has to be taken literally, materially: it is the paper in which you place the "matter" of the stage just preceding.

Because an example is always better to render visible the invisible path that science traces through the pluriverse, take the case of Jean Rossier's laboratory in Paris, where they try to gain information on the releasing factors of a single isolated neuron. Obviously, there is no unmediated, direct, unartificial way to render one neuron visible out of the billions that make up the brain's gray matter. So they have to begin with rats, which are first guillotined. Then the brain is extracted and cut (thanks to a microtome) in very fine slices. Then each slice is prepared in such a way that it remains alive for a couple of hours and put under a powerful microscope. And then, on the screen of the television, a microsyringe and a microelectrode are delicately inserted into one of the neurons on which the microscope is able to focus among the millions that are simultaneously firing—and this may fail because focusing on one neuron and bringing the microsyringe in contact with the same neuron to capture the neurotransmitters while recording the electric activity is a feat few people are able to achieve. Then the activity is recorded, the chemical products triggered by the activity are gathered through the pipette, and the result is written into an article that presents synoptically the various inscriptions. I do not want to say anything about neuron firing—no matter how interesting—but to attract your attention to the movement, the jump from one inscription to the next.

It is clear that without the artificiality of the laboratory, none of this path through inscriptions, where each plays the role of matter for the next that put it into a new form, would produce a *visible* phenomenon. Reference is not the gesture of a locutor pointing with a finger to a cat purring on a mat but a much riskier affair and much dirtier business, which connects a published literature, outside the lab, to published literature from the lab, through many intermediations, one of them, of course, being the rats, those unsung heroes of much biology.

The point I want to make is that these referential chains have very interesting contradictory features: they are producing our best source of objectivity and certainty, yet they are artificial, indirect, and multilayered. There is no doubt that the reference is accurate, yet this accuracy is not obtained by any two things mimetically resembling one another but, on the contrary, through the whole chains of artificial and highly skilled *transformations*. As long as the chain obtains these transformations, the truth-value of the whole reference is calculable. But if you isolate one inscription, if you extract one image, if you freeze-frame the continuous path of transformations, then the quality of the reference immediately deteriorates. Isolated, a scientific image has no truth-value, although it might trigger, in the mythical philosophy of science that is being used by most people, a sort of shadow referent that will be taken, by a sort of optical illusion, to be the model of the copy—although it is nothing but the virtual image of an isolated "copy"!

This proves, by the way, that matters of fact—those famous matters of fact that some philosophers assume to be the stuff out of which the visible common-sense world is made—are actually nothing but a misunderstanding of the artificial but productive process of scientific objectivity, which has been derailed by freeze-framing a referential path. There is nothing primitive or primeval in matters of fact; they are not the ground of mere perceptions.[9] It is thus entirely misguiding to try to *add* to the objective matters of fact some sort of subjective state of affairs that, in addition, would occupy the mind of the believers.

Although some of what I say here, much too briefly, might still be controversial, I need to have it taken as an undisputed background, because I want to use it to shed a new light on the religious regime of invisibility. In the same way that there is a misunderstanding on the path traced by the deambulation of scientific mediations, there is, I think, a common misunderstanding on the path traced by religious images.[10] The traditional defense of religious icons in Christianity has been to say that the image is not the object of a "latry" (as in ido*latry*), but of a *duly*, a Greek term that says a worshipper, at the occasion of the copy—whether it be a Virgin, a crucifix, or the statue of a saint—has turned his or her mind to the prototype, the only original worth adoring. This, however, is a weak defense that never convinced the Platonist, the Byzantine, the Lutheran, or the Calvinist iconoclasts—not to mention Mullah Omar when he had the Bāmiyān Buddhas put to the gun.

In effect, the Christian regime of invisibility is as different from this traditional meek defense, as the scientific reference path is from the glorified matters of fact. What imageries have tried to achieve through countless feats of art is exactly the opposite of turning the spectator's eyes to the model far away: on the contrary, incredible pain has been taken to *break* the habitual gaze of the viewer so as to attract his or her attention to the *present* state, the only one which can be said to offer salvation. Everything happens as if painters, carvers, patrons of the works of art had tried to break the images inside so as to render them unfit for normal informative consumption; as if they wanted to begin, to rehearse, to start a rhythm, a movement of conversion that is understood only when the viewer—the pious viewer—takes upon herself to repeat the same tune in the same rhythm and tempo. This is what I call, with my colleague (and cocurator of *Iconoclash*) Joseph Koerner, inner iconoclasm, compared to which the external iconoclasm looks always at least naïve and moot—not to say plain silly.[11]

A few examples will suffice. In the Fra Angelico fresco in San Marco, Florence, the painter has multiplied ways of complicating our direct access to the topic. Not only is the tomb empty—first a great disappointment to the women—but the angel's finger points to an apparition of the resurrected Christ, which is not directly visible to the women because it shines behind them. What can be more disappointing and surprising than the angel's utterances: "He is no longer here, he has risen"? Everything in this fresco is about the emptiness of the usual grasp. However, it is not *about* emptiness, as if one's attention was directed toward nothingness; it is, on the contrary, slowly bringing us back to the presence of presence: but for that we should not look at the painting, and what the painting suggests, but at what is now there, present for us. How can one evangelist and then a painter such as Brother Angelico better render vivid again the redirection of attention: "You look in the wrong place . . . you have misunderstood the scriptures." And in case we are dumb enough to miss the message, a monk placed on the left—the representant of the occupant of the cell—will serve as a *legend* of the whole story in the etymological sense of the word *legend*, that is, he will show us how we should see. What does he see? Nothing at all, there is nothing to see *there*. But you should look *here* through the inward eye of piety to what this fresco is supposed to mean: elsewhere, not in a tomb, not among the dead but among the living.

Ever more bizarre is the case studied by Louis Marin of an annunciation by Piero della Francesca in Perugia.[12] If you reconstruct the picture in virtual reality—and Piero was such a master at this first mathematization of the visual field that it can be done very accurately with a computer—you realize that the angel actually remains invisible to the Virgin! He—or she?—is hidden by the pillar! And with such an artist this cannot be just an oversight. Piero has used the powerful tool of perspective to recode his interpretation of what an invisible angel is, so as to render impossible the banal, usual, trivial *view* that this is a normal messenger meeting the Virgin in the normal space of daily interactions. Again, the idea is to avoid as much as possible the normal transport of messages, even when using the fabulous new space of visibility and calculation invented by quattrocento painters and scientists—this same space that will be put to use so powerfully by science to multiply those immutable mobiles I defined a minute ago. The aim is not to add an invisible world to the visible one but to distort, to render the visible world opaque enough, so that one is not led to misunderstand the scriptures but to reenact them truthfully.

To paint the disappointment of the visible without simply painting another world of the invisible—which would be a contradiction in terms—no painter is more astute than Caravaggio. In his famous rendering of the Emmaus pilgrims who do not understand at first that they have been traveling with the resurrected Savior and recognize him only when he breaks the bread at the inn table, Caravaggio reproduces in the painting this very invisibility, just by a tiny light—a touch of paints—that redirects the attention of the pilgrims when they suddenly realize what they had to see. And, of course, the whole idea to paint such an encounter without adding any supernatural event is to redirect the attention of the viewer of the *painting*, who suddenly realizes that he or she will never see more than those tiny breaks, these paint strokes, and that the reality they have to turn to is not absent in death—as the pilgrims were discussing along the way coming to the inn—but present now in its full *and veiled* presence. The idea is not to turn our gaze away from this world to another world of beyond, but to realize at last, at the occasion of this painting, this miracle of understanding: what is in question in the Scriptures is now realized among the painter, viewers, and patrons, among you: have you not understood the scriptures? He has risen, why do you look far away in death, it is here, it is present anew. "This is why our heart burnt so much while he was talking."

Christian iconography in all its forms has been obsessed by this question of representing anew what it is about and to make visually sure that there is no misunderstanding in the messages transmitted, that it is really a messenger that is transforming what is in question in the speech act—and not a mere message transfer wrongly addressed. In the venerable and somewhat naïve theme of the St. Gregory Mass—banned after the Counter-Reformation—the argument seems much cruder than in Caravaggio, but it is deployed with the same subtle intensity. Pope Gregory is supposed to have suddenly seen, while celebrating the Mass, the host and the wine replaced in three dimensions by the real body of the suffering Christ with all the associated instruments of the Passion. Real presence is here represented yet again and then painted in two dimensions by the artist to commemorate this act of re-understanding by the Pope *realizing*, in every sense of the verb, what the venerable ritual meant.

This rather gory imaging became repulsive to many after the Reformation, but the point I want to make is that each of those pictures, no matter how sophisticated or naïve, canonical or apocryphal, always sends a double injunction: the first one has to do with the theme they illustrate, and most of those images, like the love talk I began with, are repetitive and often boringly so (the resurrection, the Emmaus encounter, the Gregory's Mass), but then they send a second injunction that traverses the boring repetition of the theme and forces us to remember what it is to understand the presence that the message is carrying. This second injunction is equivalent to the tone, to the tonality that we have been made aware of in love-talk: it is not what you say that is original but the movement that renews the presence through the old sayings.

Lovers, religious painters, and their patrons have to be careful to make the usual way of speaking vibrate in a certain way if they want to make sure that the absentminded locutors are not led far away in space and time. This is exactly what happens suddenly to poor Gregory: during the repetition of the ritual, he is suddenly struck by the very speech act of transforming the host unto the body of Christ, by the realization of the words under the shape of a suffering Christ. The mistake would be to think that this is a naïve image that only backward papists could take seriously: quite the opposite, it is a very sophisticated rendering of what it is to become aware again of the real presence of Christ in the Mass. But for that you have to listen to the two injunctions at once. This is not the painting of a miracle, although it is also that: rather this painting also says what it is to understand the word *miracle* literally and not in the habitual, blasé sense of the word—*literal* here meaning not the opposite of spiritual but of ordinary, absentminded, indifferent.

Even an artist so brilliant as Philippe de Champaigne in the middle of the seventeenth century was still making sure that no viewer ignores that repeating the face of Christ—literally printing it on a veil—should *not* be confused with a mere photocopy (fig. 3.1).

This extraordinary meditation on what is to hide and to repeat is revealed by the presence of three different linens: the cloth out of which the canvas is made, doubled by the cloth of a so-called veronica, tripled by another veil, a curtain, this one in trompe l'œil, which could dissimulate the relic with a simple gesture of the hand if one was silly enough to misunderstand its meaning. How magnificent

FIGURE 3.1 Philippe de Champaigne, *La Sainte Face*, ca. 1650.
Courtesy of Royal Pavilion & Museums, Brighton & Hove.

to call *vera icona*, meaning "true image" in Latin, what is exactly a *false* picture thrice veiled: it is so impossible to take it as a photography that, by a miracle of reproduction, a *positive* and not a negative of Christ's face is presented to the viewer—and those artists, printers, engravers knew everything about positive and negative. So again, as in the case of Piero, this cannot be an oversight. But of course, this is a "false positive"—if I can use this metaphor—because the *vera icona*, the true picture, is precisely not a reproduction in the referential meaning of the world but a reproduction in the representational sense of the world: "Beware! Beware! To see the face of Christ is not to look for an original, for a true referential copy that would transport you back to the past, back to Jerusalem, but a mere surface of cracking pigment a millimeter thick that begins to indicate how you yourself, now, in this Port Royal institution, should look at your Savior." Although this face seems to look back at us so plainly, it is even more hidden and veiled than the one that God refused to reveal to Moses. To show *and to hide* is what true reproduction does, on the condition that it should be a false reproduction by the standard of photocopies, printing, and double-click communication. But what is hidden is not a message beneath the first one, an esoteric message disguised in a banal message, but a tone, an injunction for you, the viewer, to redirect your attention and to turn it away from the dead and back to the living.

This is why there is always some uncertainty to be felt when a Christian image has been destroyed or mutilated (fig. 3.2). This pietà was broken to be sure by some fanatic—we do not know if it was during the Reformation or during the Revolution,

FIGURE 3.2   Pietà (fifteenth century).
Courtesy of Musée Anne de Beaujeu in Moulins, Allier, France. Collection Tudot.

as France has no lack of such episodes. But whoever he was, he certainly never realized how ironic it could be to add an *outside* destruction to the *inner* destruction that the statue itself represented so well. What is a pietà, if not the image of the heartbroken Virgin holding on her lap the broken corpse of her Son, who is the broken image of God, his father—although, as the scripture is careful to say, "none of his bones have been broken"? How could you destroy an image that is already that much destroyed? How would you want to eradicate belief in an image that has already disappointed all beliefs to the point that God himself, the God of beyond and above lies here, dead on his mother's lap? Can you go further into the self-critique of all images than what theology explicitly says? Rather, should it not be better to argue that the outside iconoclast does nothing but add a naïve and shallow act of destruction to an extraordinary and deep act of destruction? Who is more naïve, the one who sculpted this pietà of the kenosis of God or the one who believes there are believers naïve enough to grant existence to a mere image instead of turning spontaneously their gaze to the true original God? Who goes further? Probably the one who says there is *no* original.

How to Continue the Movement of Truth-Making Statements?

One way to summarize my point is to say that we have probably been mistaken in defending the images by their appeal to a prototype they simply alluded to, although this is, as I have shown, the traditional defense of images. Iconophily has nothing to do with looking at the prototype, in a sort of Platonician stair-climbing. Rather, iconophily is in *continuing* the process begun by an image, in a prolongation of the flow of images. St. Gregory continues the text of the Eucharist when he sees the Christ in his real and not symbolic flesh, and the painter continues the miracle when he paints the representation in a picture that reminds us of what it is to understand really what this old mysterious text is about; and I, now, today, continue the painter's continuation of the story reinterpreting the text, if, by using slides, arguments, tones of voices, anything, really anything at hand, I make you aware again of what it is to understand those images without searching for a prototype and without distorting them in so many information-transfer vehicles. Iconoclasm or iconolatry, then, is nothing but freeze-framing, interrupting the movement of the image and isolating it out of its flows of renewed images to believe it has a meaning by itself—and because it has none, once isolated it should be destroyed without pity.

By ignoring the *flowing* character of science and religion we have turned the question of their relations into an opposition between knowledge and belief, opposition that we then deem necessary either to overcome, to politely resolve, or to widen violently. What I have argued in this lecture is very different: *belief is a caricature of religion exactly as knowledge is a caricature of science.* Belief is patterned after a false idea of science, as if it was possible to raise the question "Do you believe in God?" along the same pattern as "Do you believe in global warming?" Except that the first question does not possess any of the instruments that would allow the reference to move on, and the second is leading the locutor to a phenomenon even more invisible to the naked eye than that of God, because to reach it we have to travel through satellite imaging, computer simulation, theories of earth atmospheric instability, high-stratosphere chemistry, and so forth. Belief is not a quasi-knowledge question *plus* a leap of faith to reach even *further* away; knowledge is not a quasi-belief question that would be answerable by looking directly at things close at hand.

In religious talk, there is indeed a leap of faith, but this is not an acrobatic *salto mortale* in order to do even better than reference with more daring and risky means, it is a somersault, yes, but one which aims at jumping, dancing toward the present and the close, to redirect attention away from indifference and habituation, to prepare oneself to be seized again by this presence that breaks the usual, habituated passage of time. As to knowledge, it is not a direct grasp of the plain and the visible against all beliefs in authority, but an extraordinarily daring, complex, and intricate confidence in chains of nested transformations of documents that, through many different types of proofs, lead toward new types of visions that force us to break away from the intuitions and prejudices of common sense. Belief is simply immaterial for any religious speech act; knowledge is not an accurate way to characterize scientific activity. We might move forward a bit, if we were calling *faith* the movement that brings us to the close and to the present and retaining the word *belief* for this necessary mixture of confidence and diffidence with which we need to assess all the things we cannot see directly. Then the difference between science and religion would not be found in the different mental competencies brought to bear on two different realms—belief applied to vague spiritual matters, knowledge to directly observable things—but in the *same* broad set of competences applied to *two* chains of mediators going in two *different* directions. The first chain leads toward what is invisible because it is simply too far and too counterintuitive to be directly grasped—namely, science; the second chain, the religious one, also leads to the invisible but what it reaches is not invisible because it would be hidden, encrypted, and far, but simply because it is difficult to renew.

What I mean is that in the cases of both science and religion, freeze-framing, isolating a mediator out of its chains, out of its series, instantly forbids the meaning to be carried in truth. Truth is not to be found in correspondence—either between the word and the world in the case of science or between the original and the copy in the case of religion—but in taking up again the task of *continuing* the flow, of elongating the cascade of mediations one step further. My argument is that, in our present economy of images, we might have made a slight misunderstanding of Moses's Second Commandment and thus lacked respect for mediators. God did not ask us not to make images—what else do we have to produce objectivity, to generate piety?—but he told us not to freeze-frame, not to isolate an image out of the flows that only provide them with their real (their constantly re-realized, re-represented) meaning.

I have most probably failed in extending the flows, the cascade of mediators to you. If so, then I have lied, I have not been talking religiously; I have not been able to preach, but I have simply talked *about* religion, as if there was a domain of specific beliefs one could relate to by some sort of referential grasp. This then would have been a mistake just as great as that of the lover who, when asked "do you love me?" answered, "I have already told you so many years ago, why do you ask again?" Why? Because it is no use having told me so in the past, if you cannot tell me again, now, and make me alive to you again, close and present anew. Why would anyone claim to speak religion, if it is not in order to save me, to convert me, on the spot?

Notes

1. Editor's note: In the spirit of Latour's argument, the essay is presented in the form of a direct verbal address.

2. William James, *The Varieties of Religious Experience* (Harmondsworth, UK: Penguin, 1902).

3. For an extension of this argument and of its practical demonstration, see Bruno Latour, *Jubiler ou les tourments de la parole religieuse* (Paris: Les Empêcheurs de Penser en Rond, 2002). I have circled those questions in Bruno Latour, "How to Be Iconophilic in Art, Science, and Religion?" in *Picturing Science, Producing Art*, ed. C. Jones and P. Galison (London: Routledge, 1998), 418–440; and Bruno Latour, "Thou Shall Not Take the Lord's Name in Vain—Being a Sort of Sermon on the Hesitations of Religious Speech," *Res* 39 (Spring 2002): 215–235. For a general inquiry into the background of the comparison between science and religion, see Bruno Latour and Peter Weibel, eds., *Iconoclash: Beyond the Image Wars in Science, Religion and Art* (Cambridge, MA: MIT Press, 2002).

4. See, for instance, Bruno Latour, *Pandora's Hope: Essays on the Reality of Science Studies* (Cambridge, MA: Harvard University Press, 1999).

5. Cited in Hilary Putnam, "The Depths and Shallows of Experience," in *Science, Religion, and the Human Experience*, ed. James D. Proctor (New York: Oxford University Press, 2005), 82.

6. See Pascal Boyer, "Gods and the Mental Instincts That Create Them," in Proctor, *Science, Religion, and the Human Experience*, 237–259; and Pascal Boyer, *Religion Explained: The Evolutionary Origins of Religious Thought* (New York: Basic Books, 2001). Evolutionary theology shares with the old natural theology of the eighteenth century the admiration for the "marvelous adjustment" of the world. It does not matter much if this leads to an admiration for the wisdom of God or of evolution, because in both cases it is the marvelous fit that generates the impression of providing an explanation. Darwin, of course, would destroy the natural theology of old as well as this other natural theology based on evolution: there is no fit, no sublime adaptation, no marvelous adjustment. But the new natural theologians have not realized that Darwin dismantled their church even faster than the church of their predecessors, whom they despise so much.

7. Alfred North Whitehead, *Religion in the Making* (New York: Fordham University Press, 1926).

8. Under William James's pen, science is a "she"—a nice proof of political correctness before its time.

9. For a much more advanced argument about visualization in science, see Peter Galison, *Image and Logic: A Material Culture of Microphysics* (Chicago: University of Chicago Press, 1997); Carrie Jones and Peter Galison, eds., *Picturing Science, Producing Art* (London: Routledge, 1998); and Latour and Weibel, *Iconoclash*.

10. See the catalog of the exhibition, Latour and Weibel, *Iconoclash*.

11. See Joseph Koerner, "Icon as Iconoclash," in Latour and Weibel, *Iconoclash*, 164–214.

12. Louis Marin, *Opacité de la peinture: Essais sur la représentation* (Paris: Usher, 1989).

CHAPTER 4

Dorsal Monuments

Messiaen, Sellars, and Saint Francis

Sander van Maas

"It was the Office of Corpus Christi. At the end of Mass, at 10:30 precisely, the A flat of the contrabassoon and saxhorn, assisted by the third tam-tam, started to play. Suddenly the immense nave was filled by a vast and overwhelming presence."[1] With these words the French composer Olivier Messiaen described the performance of one of his most powerful works, *Et exspecto resurrectionem mortuorum*. The performance took place at Chartres Cathedral in June 1965 in the presence of its commissioner, André Malraux, the then minister of culture, and the president of the Fifth Republic, Charles de Gaulle. The grand sonic presence produced by the work was much to the composer's liking. Messiaen, who had been known since the 1940s for his *Turangalîla* symphony and other works of grandeur, had been increasingly interested in the production of musical works suggesting *presence*.

As the opening chapters of his *Traité* on "rhythm, color and ornithology" indicate, Messiaen also had a life-long fascination with the subject of time.[2] The chapters are a veritable compendium of ideas on this subject, quoting sources from theology and philosophy to Albert Einstein and H. G. Wells, followed by a similar *tour d'horizon* on the subject of rhythm. Although these chapters contain many leads for the analysis of Messiaen's experiments with time in his music, they do not sufficiently engage in the conceptualization of presence. As the previous example indicates, the production of presence (Gumbrecht) is an important aspect of the way in which these works manifest themselves. Here this is even more the case than in other musical repertoires. Even though it must be maintained with Carl Dahlhaus that all music lives in "aesthetic presence," Messiaen's works specifically address religious modes of time that *restructure* this presence.[3]

This restructuring may be effected in a variety of ways. In this essay I focus on how gestures modulate the temporality of Messiaen's works and on how these modulations of presence change the works' meaning potential.

In order to describe the relation between gesture and time the first section deals with monumentality in Messiaen. The monumental is shown to move across various temporal planes including, in Messiaen's case, the "absolute future" of the Apocalypse. Studying the function of monumentality in his eschatological works—focusing in particular on the tension between presence and futurity—the discussion gradually shifts toward the largest of all Messiaen's works, his opera *Saint François d'Assise* (1983). In this opera, gesture is naturally embodied through its association with the characters. However, their presence on stage is also used by director Peter Sellars as raw material for the creation of a more specific sense of presence. In his Salzburg productions of Messiaen's opera in the 1990s, Sellars experimented with bodily movement and gestures in a manner that anticipates his more recent projects with video artist Bill Viola. These projects highlight a distinctly different approach to presence (topicality, *Erlebnis*) while at the same time converging with Messiaen's ideas insofar as they depend on futurity.

The modulation of presence in this opera also calls for an exploration of death. Being an opera dedicated to the immortalization of a saint, *Saint François* is a story about presence as finitude and about the undoing of finitude in the spirit of the early opera (the example being Monteverdi's *Orfeo*). In the discussion of this undoing of death Messiaen is shown to inscribe his work in a logic of *dorsality*. This term, coined by David Wills, is introduced to describe the turning-toward and turning-away that inform the conversion of the saint. Dorsality also appears to highlight the fact that Messiaen needed to step outside of his religious frame of reference in order to free himself artistically and produce his monumental opera. Being in this sense an heir to the Orphism of the early tradition *Saint François* reveals a *caesura* of religion rather than the affirmation of theological realism that Messiaen intended. In the opera, dorsality is the "master gesture" that coordinates both the production (through conversion, monumentalization, or topicality) and the infinite undoing of presence.

Monuments for the Future

In 1999, some seven years after Olivier Messiaen's death, the French music journalist Claude Samuel published a new, enlarged edition of the book he had coauthored with the composer, *Permanences d'Olivier Messiaen*. The book, which first appeared in 1967 as *Entretiens with Claude Samuel* and had been reissued in an extended version as *Musique et couleur* in 1986, has become a key source for Messiaen's views on a variety of issues. The reedited book features the original chapters of *Musique et couleur* as well as additional material consisting of new chapters, correspondence documenting the making of the 1986 book, and ruminations on the composer by Samuel. In many respects the book is an act of commemoration: it collects and selects the available source materials, it recollects the process of its own making, and it outlines the archive of what has arguably been one of Messiaen's major channels of communication with the world and with history.[4]

In one of the book's new sections, Samuel addresses Messiaen's preferences regarding the music from the nineteenth century. He relates that Messiaen could hardly appreciate the music of Mahler and Bruckner, even though he lamented the eclipse of romanticism generally. For Messiaen, the attractions of the romantic age were among other things the piano repertoire from Chopin to Debussy, the orchestral colors of Berlioz and Wagner, and the French organ tradition of César Franck, Dupré, and Tournemire. Samuel suggests that Messiaen's indebtedness to the nineteenth century is also discernable in the monumental character of many of his works. Indeed, Samuel observes, "one might embark on a reflection on the theme of 'Messiaen and the monumental.'"[5] The monumental in Messiaen, it seems, is as easily detectible as it is difficult to define. For instance, the earliest published organ works testify to an interest in the grand style of Messiaen's late-Romantic French predecessors. *Apparition de l'Église éternelle* from 1932 is a work in which he typically combines grand gesture, dramatic contrasts, and huge sonorities in order to evoke its vision of the eternal church appearing.

However, such features of monumentality as a style only mask its inherently problematic constitution. In his recent work on musical monumentality in the nineteenth century, Alexander Rehding notes that despite many references to monumentality in such widely read authors as Alfred Einstein, Theodor Adorno, and Carl Dahlhaus, a consistent theory of monumentality is still lacking. This is due to the fact that, according to Rehding, monumentality is at once self-evident, superficial, and for many too problematically weighed down by its ideology to be taken as a serious concept.[6] Similar problems emerge on the level of stylistic analysis: in the nineteenth-century musical monumentality lacks coherence as a stylistic concept. In Messiaen, who is perhaps the twentieth-century composer most easily associated with monumentality, this is no less the case. In order to arrive at a full view, the obvious example of *Apparition*—the grand gestures and grand sonic means—should be complemented with works that, despite being on a chamber music scale, are still associated with monumentality. Here the example would be the *Quatuor pour la fin du temps* (1940–41)—a work described as being monumental by Rebecca Rischin in her monograph on the quartet.[7] In Rischin and elsewhere the adverb remains qualified: Is it the work's impact on its war-time contemporaries that makes it monumental in this case rather than its gestures and means?

Although Messiaen's earliest works accidentally tend toward monumentality, the mid-career works are most often thought of as being monumental in a more substantial sense. As Paul Griffiths notes in his slightly different vocabulary, in the 1960s Messiaen, after a period of avant-garde experimentation and birdsong composition, "was left . . . the possibility of immensity."[8] Griffiths appears to be referring not just to the duration or the instrumental size of these works, but to the aesthetic qualities usually associated with the sublime. Griffiths's remark should be understood as saying that the style of the works expresses the greatness typical of the (mathematical) sublime. That is, what it expresses is similar to the experience of something large beyond comparison, such as the Egyptian pyramids or the starry heavens. Indeed, this type of sublimity is a familiar element in many of Messiaen's monumental works from this middle period. The first of these is *Et exspecto resurrectionem mortuorum* for wind ensemble from 1964, written in response to a request from André Malraux to compose a work in commemoration of the victims of the two World Wars. Messiaen accepted the commission but decided to twist the implied temporal orientation of its intention. Rather than emphasizing the loss of life in what would have become Messiaen's requiem he wanted to create a work of hope: a grand affirmation of faith (*credo*, *exspecto*) in the resurrection of the dead.[9] Musically speaking, the work's monumentality is identifiable as (though not reducible to) the use of slow tempo, the monodic phrases, choral-like brass harmonies, low tam-tams that envelope the orchestra, as well as the extraordinarily long pauses between the movements, setting them apart as static blocks of sound.

Et exspecto would be followed by other works displaying a similar monumentality. In a sense, after the mid-1960s Messiaen's work list as such acquired the vertical features of the individual works. As Malcolm Troup observes, "Messiaen began a succession of works which were as vertically conceived and with as little forward movement as any mountain range."[10] The list reads like an array of cathedral columns: the fourteen-part oratorio *La Transfiguration de Notre-Seigneur Jésus-Christ* (1965–69), the nine-part organ cycle *Méditations sur le mystère de la Sainte Trinité* (1969), the ten-part orchestral *Des canyons aux étoiles . . .* (1971–73)—after which came the opera *Saint François d'Assise: Scènes franciscaines* (1975–83), Messiaen's longest organ cycle *Livre du Saint Sacrement* (1984) and the final grand-scale work for orchestra *Éclairs sur l'au-delà . . .* (1987–91). As usual with Messiaen, these works address religious themes with an emphasis on manifestations of God's greatness in nature and in the human soul. The greatness of the subject may explain why Messiaen preferred musical means that would match this greatness analogically. The "immense" musical structures may be regarded as being relative to the listener's scale as God's creation is to human art. In a similar vein, the overwhelming power of synesthetic colors (to which I shall return below) which Messiaen used in *La Transfiguration* and *Saint François* is meant to create a sense of overwhelming in the human spectator. Such analogical expressions of the divine do, however, not entirely explain the need for the monumental in Messiaen. While some of his musical monuments can be said to be immense, in general, the immense does not need to be monumental, and its musical expression need not be monumental either.[11]

The account of monumentality in Messiaen that I propose takes its relation to time as its starting point. The presence of the monumental in Messiaen is remarkable in the first place for the fact that monuments are always grounded in history. They manipulate our sense of time in such a way as to make past events or things or people present. The monument's "presentification" differs from the document's, such as recordings or photographs, for the reason that the monument needs to be erected.[12] Its inauguration requires a public and collective affirmation of the particular rearrangement of time installed by it. Certain events will recede deeper into the past because of the monument, others will be highlighted and apparently closer to—more urgently important to—the historical present. Given Messiaen's interest in rhythm and theories of (musical) time, he might well have been interested in monuments, but he never really expressed himself on this subject. The monumental certainly gripped his imagination at some point in his career, as for instance at the time of writing *Et exspecto* when he is said to have surrounded himself with "simple and strong images" such as "Mexico's step-pyramids, the temples and statues of Ancient Egypt, and Roman and Gothic churches."[13] Other examples include the two *tombeaux* (musical pieces commemorating the deaths of notable individuals) he wrote in the 1930s, the first being the orchestral *Le Tombeau resplendissant* (1931), according to the composer "a kind of Beatitude for those who discover in their faith something more than the illusions of a distant youth," followed four years later by the piano solo work *Pièce pour le tombeau de Paul Dukas*, a *déploration*, or lament, as it were, for his composition teacher who died the same year.[14]

These works neither engage in a representation of the past nor in the organization of a community. They do not portray the deceased in order to save him from oblivion. Furthermore, they do not attempt to capture the past symbolically, in a condensed and poeticized form, as should be expected from monuments. Regarding his commemoration of Dukas, Messiaen emphasized the sheer material quality of his *tombeau* rather than the work of memory that a *tombeau* is usually designed for, as if he wanted to show his teacher that he was capable of creating the monumentality his teacher once taught him. The *Pièce*, Messiaen explains, is "a [composition in the] third mode, first transposition, of which the orange, white and golden brightness perpetually lands on a long E dominant seventh chord. It's static, solemn and unadorned, like an enormous block of stone."[15] As a sign of commemoration, then, it remains rather empty. The sense of impassibility in this music is clearly meant to evoke the transcendent—the things that do not pass—but it does not express a concern over things lost. To the contrary: in his music Messiaen ignores the historical dimension of his subject in order to establish a relationship with the future: The Second Coming and the Last Things. Not only is this the case in *Et exspecto*, but it also shows in the steady evocation of apocalyptic themes in the final movement of other works, such as *La Transfiguration*, *Des canyons*, and *Éclairs*. The thrust of these works—indeed of the whole of Messiaen's corpus—is toward the events described in Saint John's Apocalypse, in particular the unveiling of the divine in dazzling splendor. The monumental, then, appears to be functioning relative to a *future* rather than to a (lost) past. Messiaen's works are monuments for the future. Furthermore, this future is neither today's future—our present future—nor the legion futures belonging to times past but the *absolute future*, which, strictly speaking, will not be a future at all. The monuments of the future proclaim their own end, and they do so with an eternal, monumentalizing gesture.[16]

Because of this eschatological structure the monumental in Messiaen appears even more paradoxical than musical monuments in general already are. Rehding points to the monument's cyclical constitution: the monument is supposed to express the greatness of its subject which at the same time it is expected to constitute. By definition a monument praises that which does not need praise; any act to bestow praise raises the suspicion that greatness is precisely what is lacking in the monuments' referent.[17] In Messiaen's case this paradox reaches utmost intensity because the referent is the divine Absolute. Why should Messiaen put up a monument for that which, or the One who, is beyond all monuments? Does not this gesture bring out the latent vanity of such monumental pretensions? Does monumentality in Messiaen in fact refer to an impossible monument, one that would only thematize, or monumentalize, the impossibility of erecting a monument? If so, why would he use such a mode of expression?

The answer to this question may be found in the particular charm that things impossible had for Messiaen.[18] However, the charm of the impossible monument may also be understood in relation to a particular mode of address found in the Apocalypse. Jean-François Lyotard's phrase "*il n'y aura pas de deuil* [there shall be no mourning]" could serve as an example of this mode. In his analysis of this phrase, Jacques Derrida, to whom this phrase was originally addressed, points to the fact that it is extremely difficult to read.[19] Written as it is by Lyotard but involuntarily paraphrasing the Apocalypse (21:4, "And God shall wipe away all tears from their eyes; and there shall be no more death, neither sorrow, nor crying, neither shall there be any more pain: for the former things are passed away"), it has a spellbinding and undecipherable quality.[20] As Derrida relates, "Today, . . . I still do not know how to read this phrase, which I nevertheless cannot set aside. I cannot stop looking at it. It holds me. It will not let me go, even while it does not need me as addressee or inheritor, even while it is designed to pass right by me more quickly than it is to pass through me."[21] Although Derrida does not use the word in his discussion, the phrase's overall quality may be described as monumental. Whether it is read as a normative ("it must be thus . . .") or as a prescriptive ("it will be thus . . .") utterance, it invariably asserts a sublime and all-encompassing event in a gesture that is at once concise and grand, clear and puzzling.

Even though the assertion is not clearly addressed to any person or group in particular, it grabs anyone who hears or reads it. This experience, however, only leads back to the same unreadable words which, moreover, tend to disperse. "I will thus turn around," Derrida continues, "turn back to these five words whose imbrication simply cannot be linked up, whose chain cannot be moored or fastened onto any constraining context, as if it risked . . . being given over forever to dispersion, dissipation, or even to an undecidability such that the mourning it speaks of immediately turns back to the mute mumbling of those five words."[22] In Messiaen, the monumental risks the dissipation and dispersal described by Derrida because in this case, too, the addressee and the content of the musical assertion remain unclear. What we are left with is the possibility of a return to the very same gestures of grand affirmation, assertion, proclamation, and wait for someone else to rework their relation to the present. For in this present there is the confrontation between the monument and the times in which the monument is read, listened to, supported, or contested. That is, in which an account is given of its presence. The ghostly, spellbinding element in the monument calls for a response by those who know how to relate the monument to the available resources for sense-making at any given time. In the following section I discuss one such response: the production of Messiaen's opera on Saint Francis by the opera director Peter Sellars in the early (and late) 1990s.

In the Beginning Was the Gesture: Peter Sellars's *Saint François*

Given its scale, style, and subject Messiaen's opera *Saint François d'Assise: Scènes franciscaines*, is an outspoken example of monumentalism. Conceived as a *summa* at the time when the composer entered his eighth decade and presenting a compilation of his accomplishments as an artist and believer the opera is an act of virtual self-monumentalization. It comprises eight scenes distributed over three acts and requires some four and a half hours net performance time. The opera tells the story of Francis's inner development from near sainthood toward the state of "super–Saint Francis" or, as Messiaen phrased it, "the infusion of grace in the soul of one of the greatest of all saints."[23] The Franciscan scenes each depict an episode from this development, starting with (the opera character) François and one of his brothers discussing the nature of perfect joy while traveling to a remote monastery. This topic introduces to the opera the complex relation between spiritual fulfillment of divine love and the ugly reality of suffering and evil in the world. Through the series of scenes, François is shown to learn the lessons of self-forgetting love and perfect joy, sharing these lessons with his friars and the birds and earning divine approval through a musically induced glimpse into the heavens, the stigmatization and a deathless death. These events contain the stock elements of opera since its invention in the early seventeenth century: love, death, and power. However, Messiaen also attempted to weave into the opera's fabric some of his fascination for non-Western music theatre. Among these influences he quotes the Japanese Noh theater, which he adored for its extraordinarily long performances, delicate (and often devious) uneventfulness, and great sense of stylization.[24] His opera, too, proceeds by tableaux which, internally, more often than not appear to come to a complete standstill.

When it was finished in 1983, *Saint François* immediately went on stage at the Palais Garnier in Paris. With Messiaen supervising the process, the production closely followed his stage directions as well as his visual ideas, which were inspired by the Franciscan works of Giotto, the depiction of angels with Fra Angelico, and the actual churches and landscapes of Assisi and Umbria.[25] Messiaen envisioned the recreation of the landscapes and scenes described in the Franciscan sources in a more or less historicizing fashion.[26] Seen from a theatrical perspective, however, it is safe to say that Messiaen's staging ideas are often problematically unsophisticated and naïve.[27] At the world premiere, which was directed by Sandro

Sequi, the stage picture was largely colored in earth shades and divided into a number of boxes. According to the critics, these boxes, although invoking the works of Giotto, were used to little theatrical effect. As Klaus Umbach wrote in *Der Spiegel*, "The stage was divided into multiple small viewing boxes. Now the bored eye was struck by a solitary little church just standing there, then a silent cloister came into view, in which nothing happened."[28] By contrast, the musical first performance, after thirty-six orchestral rehearsals, was generally lauded. "The musical performance," John Rockwell wrote in the *New York Times*, "was masterly, and was greeted as such by the audience. Seiji Ozawa maintained remarkable control over his huge forces, which spilled out of the pit onto special platforms and up into the side boxes, and he achieved a telling plasticity of phrasing."[29]

Peter Sellars's production of *Saint François* was staged at the Salzburg Festival in 1992—in the first year of Gérard Mortier's reign as Festival director, succeeding the rather more conservative Herbert von Karajan.[30] This production, too, had the composer involved but it would eventually become a director's opera. Messiaen met Sellars at the initial stages of the production and gave him his blessing, despite the fact that he was shocked to learn that Sellars was intending to put a second angel-dancer on stage. Messiaen died just before the stage rehearsals and would never see the final result. At the premiere the press reactions were mixed, but this time there was a sense of controversy rather than disappointment. Himself being a synesthete, Messiaen's initial ideas about his opera contained many references to the experience of music as color and the suggested use of laser beams for the stigmatization scene, mimicking the rays depicted in Giotto. These ideas had been followed in Paris—the colors of the angels' wings, the use of lasers and luminous stains on the walls—but Sellars lifted the use of light to a new level. The stage picture that he had George Tsypin design included a huge wall of light tubes, and all around, on stage as well as in the air, there were some forty television monitors. Through most of the opera, the monitors showed a sequence of shaky video images shot by Sellars himself: images of cactuses, birds, and out-of-focus flowers. According to the director, the television, as it depicts figures and stories, is for our contemporaries what the stained-glass windows were for the faithful in the thirteenth century.[31] The monitors and neons gave rise to critical reactions decrying the "new age disco" ambience that allegedly reduced the opera to "the death of a saint in the manner of a TV orgy."[32] "The telly is Sellars' tabernacle," Umbach wrote in his more interesting take on the interaction between religion and media technology in this opera, "He has over 40 monitors, perhaps as treasure chests of the modern age, installed on and above the stage in varying arrangements: the television sets are sickbed, catafalque and, how could it be otherwise, crucifix. All the mystic's visions become tele-visions."[33]

At the time of the first Salzburg *Saint François*, Sellars had already gained fame as a director of radical and topical productions of Mozart/Da Ponte operas. These productions in the late 1980s—*Don Giovanni, Così fan tutte,* and *Le nozze di Figaro* were staged at Pepsico's Summerfare at Purchase in 1987 and 1989—by juxtaposing eighteenth-century music and Italian words with late twentieth-century American scenes smacking of popular culture sent a shock through their audiences. Edward Said drew attention to the political implications of Sellars's "topicalizing" of Mozart, arguing for the importance of this approach for raising our social awareness. The operas are made to draw a parallel between the waning of the *ancien régime* and the position of the present-day cultural elite. "Thus *Figaro* is set in Trump tower, in which Count Almaviva is a wealthy but lecherous tenant who employs Figaro and Susanna as driver and maid; *Don Giovanni* is set in a New York ghetto, its hero a black pusher and addict who is seen as parasitical on the 'oppressive class structure that Mozart depicted'; *Così*—the finest of Sellars' productions—is set in Despina's Diner, with its manager, Don Alfonso, a 'Vietnam vet who is having trouble hanging on,' and the two couples portrayed as silly yuppies."[34] Despite his adherence to this approach Said confessed his concern over Sellars's insouciance in matters musical. This insouciance, however, also reveals the real stakes of his stark juxtapositions and topicality. As Said explains, since Wagner music has been regarded as the most important factor in opera—it is principally seen as a musical genre. Sellars, by contrast, "has the idea of treating the work, as a full-scale intellectual, social and aesthetic project, and *not* mainly as a musical one."[35] Sellars and Messiaen, then, seem to work in the opposite direction. While the latter put the orchestra on stage in order to turn into an actor—and thereby increasing the importance of what is heard—Sellars tends to move the operatic center away from the music.

This shift does not mean, however, that Sellars moves the focus toward the visual elements. This is important for understanding the unique strength of Sellars's *Saint François* production. David Littlejohn, discussing the same Mozart productions as Said, argues that Sellars's method amounted to a reworking of ideas from the Russian experimental director Vsevolod Meyerhold whose work he had already staged several times in his student years at Harvard.[36] What is striking about Sellars's productions is the way in which gesture comes to replace musical steering. As the critic Andrew Porter wrote about Sellars's version of Händel's *Giulio Cesare*, "Sellars hears Händel's music kinetically and realizes it in stage movement suggested by its flow, its tensions, its melodies, rhythms, and dynamic shapes. At its best, his 'choreography' is as subtle, musical, and revealing as Balanchine's."[37] Littlejohn describes Sellars's approach as a shift toward a theatrical aesthetics of *gesture*, the idea is "neither *prima la musica* nor *prima le parole*, but—In the beginning was the Gesture."[38] In *Saint François*, too, Sellars relies on the power of gesture. A witness to this fact is the dancing angel, which appears in the Third Scene ("The Kissing of the Leper"). After being miraculously healed by Francis's kiss—himself being at once healed from his fear of ugliness and suffering—this Leper is supposed to make a leap of joy. Instead of the Leper leaping Sellars introduced a second angel, dressed in dark red and wearing wings, to perform a joyful dance.

There is more to Sellars's use of gesture than the obvious use of dance and mime. Its special application becomes clear in what is arguably the most impressive moment in his Messiaen production: the role of the (original) Angel, performed by Dawn Upshaw in both of the 1990s performances. Sellars decided to make the angel appear in ordinary clothes, sneaking into the world of Francis and the Leper without wings or grand gestures ("arrive in a laser show," as the director has it). As Paul Griffiths describes, "Dawn Upshaw, dressed in quiet grey and blessedly wingless, had simply loomed up from behind a bank of the monitors: the supernatural slid into the proceedings without fuss, like an animal into the water, and revealed itself far more persuasively thus than the mauve-draped, polychrome-winged figure of the Paris premiere."[39] The figure of the Angel exemplifies Sellars's tendency to turn religion and spirituality toward the social and political world. Contrasting his position again with Messiaen's, he contends that "Messiaen's opera is not just a form of entertainment; it moves us more profoundly and it offers us much more. The question it raises is not 'what is going to happen now?' but 'what is the meaning for our lives of what is happening now?'"[40] Thus, as a source of inspiration for the Angel he refers to Dorothy Day and the Catholic workers movement rather than to the ethereal world of Fra Angelico. "I think [in this opera] the angel is introduced as a hospital worker. As somebody who's devoting their life working in this hospice for lepers. Volunteer, probably."[41]

In addition, rather than presenting the Angel in such a way that the audience will clearly recognize it as being an angel (in contrast to some of the Friars, who do not, by lack of saintliness), Sellars puts the audience in a position of uncertainty, as though he were asking each one of them: Would you recognize an angel if it came into your life? Although this might also have produced a sermonizing effect, measuring as it were the progression of grace in the soul of the spectator, it reveals the inherent immanence of his spirituality. For Sellars, the divine is in a sense what it had been for his distant predecessors in the ancient Greek theater. In Euripides, whose *Children of Herakles* he staged at the Ruhrtriennale in 2002, the gods are mental forces and motives for action that originate from the realm of human existence rather than transcendent entities who live high on a sacred mountain top or in the heavens. As Sellars argues, explaining the reason for his openly spiritual engagement in the decade since *Saint François*, "it's a very important thing in a theatre to speak of spiritual topics and sacred topics, but not simply with believers, and to ask everybody present to in some way to acknowledge what the nature of their spiritual life really is. Artists—Michelangelo, or a shaman—have always rendered spirituality in a way that goes beyond doctrine."[42]

Then what happens in Sellars's production of Messiaen's monumental opera, of which every fiber seems engaged in making a turn, an *epistrophè*, toward the divine? Is this opera not the very site where all mourning ends because there will no longer be a world to mourn? By overcoming the first death—the death of the soul by kissing the Leper—super-Saint Francis attains the most sacred thing imaginable: a deathless death, a second death which is none because, as Francis has it near the end of the opera, "Blessed are those whom the first death will find submitting to Divine Will: the second death will do him no harm."[43] Sellars, by contrast, appears to produce a movement, a turn, in the opposite direction. He turns the opera—this impossible monument for the future—toward the present. Through this turning he highlights the postmodern dimension in the work of Messiaen. As Griffiths observes, in *Saint François*, "repetition... keeps the music in a continuous present, where time is not long but deep. We are not carried forward, as in most western music, but held stationary. The time is not that of our lives but time that has not been touched yet by human beings, time within which every instant lasts forever. In giving us this time—in presenting us with the fresh present—*Saint François* exceeds the boundaries of its particular denomination. It is about eternity before holiness."[44] This production of the *presence* of a certain (yet to be determined) present should indeed be considered as an *effect* of the opera performance rather than as its (spiritual) raw material. Griffiths quotes repetition as an important factor in the production of this presence effect but Sellars's use of gesture should also be taken into account.

Two aspects stand out here, the first of which may be illustrated with reference to the third scene. In this scene the Angel intervenes in the confrontation between Francis and the Leper. The Angel tries to make the Leper understand that God is greater than the Leper's heart which is petrified because of his anger and hatred toward himself and the world. As can be seen in rehearsal footage in Jean-Pierre Gorin's documentary on the stage production, Sellars carefully instructed Upshaw to create a sense of continuous movement throughout her sneaking appearance in this scene as well as throughout her subsequent address to the Leper.[45] Upshaw repeatedly practices the sweeping movement of washing and comforting the Leper's hand. The continuous movement is about touching, but not *actually*. It is about intensifying presence rather than pointing toward the present. It gestures toward the apex of intensity but never actually turns the *haecceity* of this apex into "human time" (Griffiths). Sellars's present is a thick, haptic, and lyrical present rather than the kenotic present of contemplation—yet it feeds on a minimal distance which should never be allowed to collapse. This sense of distance is symbolized by a staircase on the right-hand side of the stage. From stage level up into the wooden cathedral that Tsypin constructed for the choir, there had been a staircase—but this staircase was never used. Although being a prominent structure it would forever create a sense of anticipation, of openness toward something other than the actual scene that goes on. In a similar way haptic gesture in Sellars is characteristically open: it creates a presence which is shot through with opportunities for new (temporal) connections and affects.

The second aspect of Sellars's use of gesture is related to codified gesture. In the fourth scene ("The Journeying Angel") the Angel reappears knocking at the door of the friars' monastery. It quizzes them about theological issues in order to test their spiritual progress. Jean-Philippe Courtis in his role of Frère Bernard is asked by the Angel (Upshaw) about his feelings about predestination: "hast thou put off the old man, to put on the new and find thy true face"? For this question, Sellars relies on gestures that very effectively enlarge the experiential space.[46] On the first level the logic is arguably didactic. Seeing the gestures and the direction in which the Angel looks—hands and gaze are always firmly in touch with Sellars—facilitates our understanding of the words sung. Here, gestures function within what Patrice Pavis would call a *gestural text*, that is, "connecting isolated gestures into a coherent discourse whose rules and syntax could be 'read.'"[47] On a deeper level, however, the gestures open an affective space which brings out the experiential horizon of what is said. Here, the semantic space is opened by the inherent semiotic instability of the gestural text which, as Pavis notes, cannot be based on a stable catalogue of gestural kernels or *gestèmes*. A notable aspect of the way in which Sellars at once enhances and destroys the meaning potential of gestures is a technique commonly found in both Messiaen and Sellars: slow motion. In Messiaen the use of extremely slow tempo markings goes back to his very first pieces and is often interpreted as an attempt to transcend time.[48] In his staging Sellars obviously had to remain "in sync" with the music but rather than being a mere adjustment to the score his use of slow motion should be also understood as an anticipation of his future collaboration with video artist and old-time friend Bill Viola. In 1995 Viola started to create video works based on scenes from Renaissance paintings in extremely slow motion. The first of such works was *The Greeting*, which may be described as a contemporary interpretation of the sixteenth-century altarpiece *The Visitation* by Jacopo Pontormo. Due to technical restrictions, the original scene, which was filmed at high speed and slowed down, remained without cuts or editing and showcases an extreme continuity of movement.

The effect of *The Greeting* is greatly enhanced by an evocative noise soundtrack. These noises suggest that the slowed-down reality shown in the images originally included significant—and possibly musical—sound. The track highlights the impossibility of slowing down (musical) sounds in the same way as moving images without losing their meaning (and ultimately also their musical nature). In the attempt to produce a strong presence effect, it is arguably important not to allow the moving image to become a still. There must be a minimum sense of movement in order to produce presence. As Messiaen demonstrates, in music, too, it is important not to allow the sounds to gel into motionless, frozen blocks of sound. Even in his most grandiose and extremely long-held block chords ("monumental chords," as Griffiths refers to them in a different context) on the organ, or in the orchestra and choir at the close of *Saint François*, Messiaen makes sure that there is always a ripple effect.[49] This effect allows the overtone structure of the block chord to produce minute frequency movements that hold the attention during the experience of massive and protracted sounds. Presence in a sense needs to be stolen from the present. The examples of Messiaen, Sellars, and Viola, then, suggest that the attempt to produce presence by means of slow motion is a matter of keeping an infinitely small distance to the punctual present. Both haptic gesture and slow-motion gesture involve an economy of absence through which they retain their rootedness in time, in history, and hence in the process of their own absentification.

If Sellars's production of *Saint François* successfully turns Messiaen's impossible monument for the future into a monument for the present—or more precisely a monument for the power of lived experience (*Erlebnis*)—it does so by infinitely paying its debts to this small distance. At once the distance donates presence *and* it takes it away, by suspending the haptic (*noli me tangere*) and by maintaining the temporal flux respectively. Sellars's *Saint François* infuses the monument with a *passion* caused by the realization that a Gertrud Steinian "complete, actual present" and its realization in social structures are perpetually out of reach.[50] It remains a sociopolitical and spiritual utopia. Hence, the answer this production of the opera gives to the question it poses—according to its director: "What is happening now, to us, in our life?"—will inevitably invoke its hoped-for *future* fulfillment. It belies Sellars's affirmation that "the promised redemption . . . is a very present reality. It is around us every day of our life. It is completely accessible to us."[51] His monument for the present holds in reserve, keeping it as it were behind its back, the very same impenetrable assertion that underlies the majority of Messiaen's works—the assertation that "there shall be no mourning."

The Dorsal Turn in Messiaen

If indeed there shall be no mourning, there shall also be no opera. This follows not only from the apocalyptic vision this assertion refers to—the new world will probably lack opera houses—but also from the fact that there is no opera without death. Such is the thesis of Linda Hutcheon and Michael Hutcheon in their *Opera: The Art of Dying*, "Opera is an art form that has proved to be obsessed with death from its birth. Jacopo Peri's early *Euridice* (1600) and Claudio Monteverdi's *La Favola d'Orfeo* (1607) establish a story pattern of love and loss that influences the staged representations of operatic death from the very start."[52] This obsession with mortality, the authors suggest, is both a universal in the history of opera and a source of information about how each historical period and each society has represented their cultural values, beliefs, and customs. The examples of Sellars and Messiaen highlight two late-twentieth-century responses to death that, although being very different in orientation, have a certain negation of finitude in common. The cultural background producing this view of morality is discussed by many authors and, being a widespread cultural phenomenon in the West, need not concern the present discussion.[53] The relation between opera and death, however, is of great importance, for if both Sellars and Messiaen speculate on the absence of death, it must be suspected that, at bottom, their work cannot function as an opera (but perhaps very well as music theater). Still, the evidence discussed above suggests that both Messiaen and Sellars do in fact engage in a confrontation with mortality. Neither the monument for the future nor the monument for the lived present evades the question of human finitude. The aim of this final section is to describe the nature of this confrontation. That is, the aim is to show in what sense *Saint François d'Assise* really is an opera and what this implies for its religious intentions.

When asked about it, Messiaen readily admitted that his opera was not a usual one. Restricting his discussion to its formal aspects, he remarked, "it is obviously not a traditional opera. There's no overture, no interludes between the various scenes, no symphonic numbers that can be played separately, like a hunting tune or a funeral march. Finally, there are neither arias nor vocal ensembles. It is very far from Mozartian or Wagnerian opera. Let's say again, it is a musical spectacle. But I have a chorus, as in *Boris*, as in Japanese No theater, as in ancient Greek drama. A chorus that plays the role of commentator and that, like a sort of divine voice, constantly intervenes."[54] Even though the *Saint François* is more static than many operas that are plot-driven and that rely, as Messiaen critically observes, on tensions produced by murder and adultery, the opera is not entirely un-dramatic. Its key tensions are situated on a different plane—they involve a Christological dimension—but remain essentially within the framework of early Renaissance opera. This may be illustrated by comparing the Saint Francis opera to Monteverdi's *Orfeo*. Like the latter work it tells a story of love—*agapè* this time rather than *eros*—and how it overcomes death. Francis is seen learning the lessons of love in order to be saved from mortality and to be led toward the eternal light. Grace progresses in his soul through a number of challenges that reveal the action of Christ who, descending into the realms of finitude, appears to Francis in disguise.[55] Staring with the ill-tempered doorkeeper in the first scene ("The Cross") these appearances become ever more explicit, the most dramatic one (in a theatrical sense) being the figure of the Leper. According to the Franciscan sources used by Messiaen for this libretto, the latter appeared to Francis in order to lead him toward the faith through visions and acts of compassion.[56] Insofar as his salvation is mediated by the coming of a savior from beyond the realm of suffering and death, Saint Francis's initial position can thus be likened to Eurydice's in Monteverdi. Although its subject matter may be different, Messiaen's work is thematically related to the early models of the genre.

Such connections notwithstanding, the Saint Francis work—this monument for the saint in which Messiaen recognized most of himself—is structured in a way that sets it apart from its early modern ancestors. This structure becomes apparent when the movements of Francis's soul are generalized under the concept of a (re)turn, and more specifically a turning around. Informed as it is by the notion of a return to God the opera stages the conditions for Francis's gradual turn around. In the first scene, Francis and the friar who are refused at the monastery door are turned away and toward recognition of perfect joy. In the Leper scene, Francis, who was initially appalled by the sight of the suffering, turns toward the afflicted man and kisses him. In the sixth scene ("The Preaching to the Birds"), Francis turns toward the birds in order to address them about the heavens, making them in their turn perform a turn around. Finally, in the seventh scene ("The Stigmata"), when Francis receives the stigmata, he is addressed by Christ and engages in mystical conversation. On the musical level the opera puts into practice the rhetorical device of return—equally called *epistrophè*—in a rigorous manner. This is particularly evident in Messiaen's use of leitmotifs which are repeated throughout the opera without significant variation. These motifs include themes (of joy, of decision) that point up and affirm important moments in Francis's process of turning toward God. Insofar as this process involves a turning toward (and facing) the divine light, it not only reveals the darkness of the world but also introduces a choreographic element: the turning emphasizes the role of the back—the reverse side—in the story of divine interpellation (calling out, dorsal turn, address and response).[57] The back is the irreducible place where the shadow of Francis's mortal existence extends when he faces his Creator. It is the place where his mortality and the possibility of his conversion are located.

Regarding this role of the back, Maurice Blanchot noted that human existence is characterized by being turned away from things it cannot freely turn toward. "What is it that stops us from turning whichever way we please? Apparently, it is our limitations: we are limited beings. When we look ahead, we cannot see behind us. When we are here, we cannot be elsewhere. Our boundaries bind us, withhold us, constrain us into being what we are, turned toward ourselves, away from otherness. Our boundaries make of us turned away beings."[58] In essence Messiaen's opera is an experiment in as well as a meditation on the possibilities of human life to take turns—*dorsal* turns—in the space between death and life (and, so the libretto goes, Life itself). The opera's final part is particularly important in this respect. Here, in the eighth scene ("Death and the new Life"), after having received the stigmata, Francis prepares to die for the second time. The audience hears how Saint Francis pays farewell to creation: to the birds, to the friars, and to the music and poetry that had led him toward God (in the second scene, "Lauds," and fifth scene, "The Angel-Musician"). After Frère Léon, whom the audience had come to know as being afraid of death, has reported Francis's death, the stage becomes all dark and the massive final choir begins, in all-out manner supported by the grand orchestra. These overpowering means are mobilized in order to create a final affirmation of the resurrection which Messiaen imagined to be similar in force to a nuclear explosion.[59]

The choir, stating the words in homophonic, granite columns of sound is arguably one of the most exuberant attempts in all of Messiaen's works to create a sublime monument for his faith. The audience is included in this evocation of the Absolute by means of a blinding white light coming from the stage. In the 2008 Amsterdam production of the opera directed by Pierre Audi, a square of very bright light shone straight from the backdrop into the venue producing pitch black shadows that indeed reminded of footage of 1950s above-ground nuclear tests.[60] Messiaen hoped this sonic and visual force would produce in the spectator what he called dazzlement (*éblouissement*): an overwhelming of the senses that would stir the soul to divine experience.[61] Thought as such, and imagined as being a permanent state after resurrection, dazzlement is the final accomplishment of the *epistrophè*. Nevertheless, the question remains if it provides the sense of plenum required of the full turn, the rectilinear, face-to-face alignment with the focal point of all converting.

Arguably it does not. On the contrary, Messiaen's decision to recreate *éblouissement* ultimately deepens the (mortal) darkness from which the opera as a whole appears to emerge.[62] The process of blinding the spectator opens a void that hitherto had not been perceptible. In order to bring this darkness into focus, a brief return to the myth of Orpheus and the modernism of Blanchot is instructive. In the latter's interpretation of the myth, Orpheus made the right decision when he performed the dorsal turn and looked back on his journey from the darkness of the Hades toward the light. Rather than facing this blinding light and regaining the object of his desire, he turned around and lost her—but, in Blanchot's reading, he thereby secured his source of inspiration. Orpheus had to sacrifice both his musical art and the object of his desire in order to attain a supreme freedom. "The moment of inspiration is, for art, the point of maximum insecurity. That is why art tends so often and so violently to resists what inspires it. And why, too, it defends itself by saying to Orpheus: You will have me only if you don't look at *her*. Yet the forbidden gesture is precisely what Orpheus must do so that art may rise above what makes it certain—which can only be done by ignoring art and responding to an urge that emerges from darkness, merges with darkness as with its source."[63] Thus, according to Blanchot, Orpheus had to turn around and look in Eurydice's direction because there was no other way—nor will there ever be another way—in which he could preserve his music and himself as a musician. Ultimately, the source of inspiration for art is not his beloved as such but the sacred darkness from which her shadow emerges and which ensures the freedom of the resulting music. "This sacred darkness contains Eurydice and contains that which, in the song, surpasses the song."[64]

In analogical fashion Messiaen is the one who performs the dorsal turn in *Saint François*. He accompanies with his monumental opera Christ and Francis as they, the one following the other in his footsteps, journey toward the light. In contrast to Christ, who never looks back and who eventually takes the whole of creation with him away from finitude, Messiaen decides to turn around and look in the direction of Francis, the religious figure. His gaze penetrates the sacred darkness and produces the sight of Messiaen's model of the religious life—a life that he, remaining true to his musicianship, never lived. Losing Francis and all that this saint represents in terms of religious life and salvation, he creates *Saint François*, and in doing so preserves both his musical art and the darkness, which represents the infinite freedom of inspiration. In contrast to Orpheus in Monteverdi's *Orfeo*, Messiaen does not accept the solution offered by the *deus ex machina* of Apollo, that is, he does not trade the "real" Francis for the poetical character Francis, whose merits he could then recognize in the stars and the birds and recreate and praise in his songs. On the contrary, the final gesture of his opera, the darkness produced by dazzlement, shows how the poetical fiction of Francis itself, too, is sacrificed and allowed to recede into the sacred darkness beyond dazzlement. Rather than being a monumental affirmation of his faith, it is thus suggested that *Saint François*, through its structure as an artwork, necessarily ruptures the represented religion of devout gestures and faithful intentions. The real message it conveys is that in this opera religion is sacrificed in view of the higher and more ineluctable principle of artistic creation: free inspiration. Regarding this it should be recalled that Messiaen has never wished his work to become inscribed into the (musical) body of the church—not even into the body of the Franciscan order.

Further support for the claim that the true message of *Saint François* is Messiaen's sacrificing of religion comes from the medium in which the work is written.[65] Since its early beginnings opera has been a medium of (and for) the impossible. As suggested by the two extant versions of Monteverdi's *Orfeo* one of the ways in which opera came into its own was by distancing itself from the harsh realities evoked by tragedy.[66] In the first version of the work (1607), which only survives as a libretto, Orpheus leaves his beloved behind in the Hades and, after sinking into despair and renouncing all other women, is devoured by the Bacchae. The second (full) version replaced this ending with the famous *lieto fine* (happy ending) in which Apollo descends from the heavens and offers the consolations of music and poetry in exchange for possession of the beloved. Accepting this offer Orfeo is then taken up into the heavens. This theatrically attractive alternative ending introduced a sense of the impossible (substituting for the tragic real) in opera which has since become a standard element in its vocabulary.[67] In choosing for opera as medium for his religious subject, Messiaen suggests that whatever is represented is inscribed into the realm of the impossible, as if saying, "what we see here is the impossible that we desire and because of its impossibility we need opera to give it material substance." Although intending his work as a form of theological and religious realism, Messiaen nevertheless felt that he needed to inscribe this reality in a medium that has become the preserve of the impossible. As Francis sings in the final scene, "music and poetry have led me to Thee," and it is precisely the precedence of these media—constellated as they are in his opera—that hides behind its back the irreducibility of that which keeps Messiaen's faith alive.

In sum, dorsality is what appears to coordinate the choreography involved in Messiaen's attempt to produce the religious reality of conversion and resurrection as an ineluctable presence in our world. The monumentality of his approach—his gestures, sonic material, and textual and visual references—suggests that this attempt at religious realism is informed by an altogether different turning than is suggested by the opera's narrative. Rather than accomplishing, over the course of multiple hours of performance, gradual turning toward a divine light that would absorb all of the foregoing, the opera suggests that there is no ending to the movement. The turning forever keeps in reserve what it appears to promise; it suspends the opera's ultimate attempt to produce presence. This suspension reflects in the temporal modalities that traverse the work. Regarding the past, the work's monumentality is not designed to mourn or commemorate the historical figure of Francis of Assisi. Regarding the future, its gesture of announcement is crossed out by the impossibility of identifying its temporal correlate—hence its structural resemblance to the phrase "there shall be no mourning." Finally, regarding the present: although the work allows itself to be turned toward the present world (Sellars), this actually reveals its distance with regard to the touchable here and now. The opera wrestles itself loose from time by turning infinitely around—in the manner of the whirling Sufis or Orpheus caught in the moment of his turning (as in Beat Furrer's dystopian music theater work *Begehren*[68])—forever dedicated as it is to the sacred darkness that seals its ineluctable spell.

Notes

The research for this essay was part of the project New Music and the Turn to Religion, funded under the NWO program Future of the Religious Past. It was first presented at the 2008 "Gestures: Religion as Performance" conference. An earlier version was published under the same title in *The Opera Quarterly* 27, no. 4 (Autumn 2011).

    1. Peter Hill and Nigel Simeone, *Messiaen* (New Haven, CT: Yale University Press, 2005), 263.

    2. Olivier Messiaen, *Traité de rythme, de couleur, et d'ornithologie* (Paris: Leduc, 1994–2002), 1:5–68.

    3. Carl Dahlhaus, *The Foundations of Music History* (Cambridge: Cambridge University Press, 1999), 60.

    4. Messiaen's concern for his place in history was remarkable. Beyond the self-definition which is always at stake in the editing of scores, texts, and other works, Messiaen was also acutely aware of the fact that he would occupy a place in *the* history of Western music. In view of this he carefully separated his career and his private life. He has never been very communicative about the genesis of his works either.

    5. Claude Samuel, *Permanences d'Olivier Messiaen: Dialogues et Commentaires* (Arles: Actes Sud, 1999), 9.

    6. Alexander Rehding, *Music and Monumentality: Commemoration and Wonderment in the Nineteenth Century* (Oxford: Oxford University Press, 2009), 3–4.

    7. Rebecca Rischin, *For the End of Time: The Story of the Messiaen Quartet* (Ithaca, NY: Cornell University Press, 2006), 2, 11.

    8. Paul Griffiths, *Modern Music and After: Directions since 1945* (Oxford: Oxford University Press, 1995), 228. See also Malcolm Troup, "Orchestral Music of the 1950s and 1960s," in *The Messiaen Companion*, ed. Peter Hill (London: Faber, 1995), 437.

9. Olivier Messiaen, *Music and Color: Conversations with Claude Samuel* (Portland, OR: Amadeus Press, 1994), 16. Messiaen removed references to the intentions of Malraux's commission from the printed version of the score. See Hill and Simeone, *Messiaen*, 261. Such outspoken negation of death is especially remarkable in Messiaen's case because as a former prisoner of war (1940–41) he must have been acutely aware of wartime suffering.

10. Troup in Hill, *Messiaen Companion*, 437.

11. It requires artistic intervention to evoke the immense in the aesthetic mode of the monumental. Although their modes may occasionally overlap, they should be considered as separate phenomena and accordingly given their own account. Christopher Dingle, discussing the ensemble piece *La Ville d'en-haut* (1987), speaks of the "bite-size monumentalism" of this ten-minute work, suggesting the term *monumentalette* for such petite forms of musical grandeur. Dingle, "Charm and Simplicity: Messiaen's Final Works," in *Tempo*, no. 192 (April 1995): 3.

12. As is made abundantly clear by Alexander Rehding, "Liszt's Musical Monuments," in *19th Century Music* 26, no. 1 (Summer 2002): 52–72. On presentification, see Hans Ulrich Gumbrecht, *The Production of Presence: What Meaning Cannot Convey* (Stanford, CA: Stanford University Press, 2004), 122–123.

13. Olivier Messiaen, "Note the l'auteur," in the score of *Et exspecto resurrectionem mortuorum* (Paris: Leduc, 1966).

14. Messiaen, in Hill and Simeone, *Messiaen*, 39.

15. Messiaen, in Harry Halbreich, *Olivier Messiaen* (Paris: Fayard/Fondation Sacem, 1980), 209.

16. The notion of a monument for the future resonates against certain musical practices during the French Revolution aimed at consolidating the new values. James Johnson, *Listening in Paris: A Cultural History* (Berkeley: University of California Press, 1995), 126. These monuments *for* the future should be clearly distinguished from the future implied by monuments in general, that is, from the trajectory monuments cast into the future described in Rehding, *Music and Monumentality*, 57.

17. Rehding, "Liszt's Musical Monuments," 59.

18. See his remarks on the "charme des impossibilités" in his treatise *Technique de mon langage musical* (1944).

19. Jean-François Lyotard and Sam Francis, *Leçon de ténèbres* (Leuven: Leuven University Press, 2010).

20. See also Rev 7: 17 ("and God shall wipe away all tears from their eyes") used by Messiaen in his final large work, the orchestral *Éclairs sur l'au-delà . . .* (1987–91).

21. Jacques Derrida, *The Work of Mourning* (Chicago: University of Chicago Press, 2001), 220.

22. Derrida, 220.

23. Messiaen, interview in booklet to *Saint François d'Assise*, conducted by Kent Nagano (Deutsche Gramophon, CD, 445 176-2, 1999), 17.

24. Messiaen, *Music and Color*, 223.

25. See Messiaen's stage directions in the score (reprinted in most libretto editions).

26. See the reprinted set design sketches in Catherine Massip, ed., *Portrait(s) d'Olivier Messiaen* (Paris: BNF, 1996), 140–149.

27. Messiaen admitted to being a poor dramatist: "The majority of my predecessors were ... good dramatists, even if they were bad composers. My problem was somewhat the opposite." Messiaen, *Music and Color*, 208.

28. Klaus Umbach, "Vogelpredikt vom Bariton," in *Der Spiegel*, December 5, 1983, 227, 233; my translation. "Die Bühne war mehrfach in kleine Guckkästen unterteilt. Mal stand da verloren ein Kirchlein, das ins gelangweilte Auge sprang, mal öffnete sich ein stiller Klosterhof, in dem sich nichts tat."

29. John Rockwell, "Paris Opera: The Debut of Messiaen's 'François,'" *New York Times*, November 30, 1983.

30. Sellars's version of *Saint François* went on stage again in Salzburg in 1998.

31. Sellars in the documentary *Letter to Peter*, dir. Jean-Pierre Gorin (ORF / Loft / La Sept, 1992). Sellars highlights two motifs for the use of the monitors. First, the idea that television represents the pantheon of contemporary idols in a manner similar to the figures and stories in stained-glass windows. Second, their constant presence on the stage suggests the constant changing of the world we live in. Renewing themselves perpetually the images suggest the idea of predestination. These motifs seem to imply that the irritation the flickering caused in many reviewers may be thought to reflect the dissonance between the secular and the eternal.

32. Klaus Umbach, "Man trägt wieder Kutte," *Der Spiegel*, August 24, 1992, 205. Martin Bernheimer, "Salzburg Diary: The Verdict, Salonen *Ja* Sellars *Nein*," *Los Angeles Times*, August 21, 1992.

33. Umbach, "Man trägt wieder Kutte," 205.

34. Edward W. Said, "Peter Sellars' Mozart," in *Music at the Limits* (New York: Columbia University Press, 2008), 87–88.

35. Said, 89.

36. David Littlejohn, "Reflections on Peter Sellars' Mozart," *Opera Quarterly* 7, no. 2 (1990): 7.

37. Littlejohn, 12.

38. Littlejohn, 31.

39. Paul Griffiths, *The Substance of Things Heard: Writings about Music* (Rochester, NY: University of Rochester Press, 2005), 84. See also, Robert Marx, "A Landscape for a Saint," on HotReview.org (accessed February 2, 2010): "Sellars' controlled use of his cast and design team was the fulfillment of all his stage experience, knowing when to be bold, when to revel in mass effects, and when to sustain intimacy. His refined stage vocabulary of hand and arm gestures was used to great effect. At no point did these characters of the Catholic Church conventionally cross themselves or genuflect. Instead, their choreographed hand movements revealed impulses of the heart and mind—most movingly when the Singing Angel suddenly appeared before a seemingly hopeless Leper and with simple

outstretched arms suggested the peace and salvation of an unquestioned and inevitable world to come."

40. Peter Sellars, "Pierre de touche," in *L'Avant-scène opéra*, hors série, no. 4: "Saint François D'Assise" (Paris: Premières Loges, 1992), 120.

41. Sellars, in Gorin, *Letter to Peter*.

42. Sellars, in "Performance and Ethics: Questions for the 21st Century, Peter Sellars interviewed by Boonie Marranca," *Performing Arts Journal*, no. 79 (2005): 44.

43. Messiaen, libretto of *Saint François d'Assise*, Act 3, Scene 8. See also my comments on this deathless death in "Messiaen's Saintly Naïveté," in *Messiaen the Theologian*, ed. Andrew Shenton (Aldershot: Ashgate, 2010).

44. Griffiths, *Substance of Things Heard*, 89.

45. The relevant clip of this documentary is available on YouTube, http://www.youtube.com/watch?v=eulM3q_NCIU (accessed February 2, 2010). The presence produced here should be distinguished from the presence inherent in gesturality. The latter is described in Patrice Pavis, "Problems of a Semiology of Theatrical Gesture," *Poetics Today* 2, no. 3 (Spring 1981): 71–72.

46. Gorin, *Letter to Peter*; relevant clip available on YouTube, in particular from 1'42," at http://www.youtube.com/watch?v=T6SR94aOkQs&feature=related (accessed February 2, 2010).

47. Pavis, "Problems of a Semiology of Theatrical Gesture," 73.

48. The short organ work *Le banquet céleste* (1926), for instance, unfolds in a tempo marked "Très lent, extatique (lointain, mystérieux)" and no more than 52 bpm.

49. Paul Griffiths, *Olivier Messiaen and the Music of Time* (London: Faber, 1985), 214.

50. Marx, "Landscape for a Saint": "Like a [Gertrud] Stein libretto that explores relationships, not situations, Sellars' staging of *Saint Francois*, unable to rely upon conventional narrative, reveled in a Steinian 'complete, actual present' of simultaneous images and sounds of faith spread across the cathedral, ramp, video monitors and light grid."

51. Sellars, "Pierre de touche," 120.

52. Linda Hutcheon and Michael Hutcheon, *Opera: The Art of Dying* (Cambridge, MA: Harvard University Press, 2004), 8.

53. See the sources quoted in Hutcheon and Hutcheon, *Opera*, 2–7, and studies such as Manuel Castells, *The Rise of the Network Society*, 2nd ed. (Malden, MA: Blackwell, 2008), 481–484; and Sandra M. Gilbert, *Death's Door: Modern Dying and the Ways We Grieve* (New York: Norton, 2006), 103–105.

54. Messiaen, *Music and Color*, 223.

55. On Christian allegorical readings of the Orpheus myth, see Frederick W. Sternfeld, "Orpheus, Ovid, and Opera," *Journal of the Royal Musical Association* 113, no. 2 (1988): 179–180.

56. According to legend, the figure of the leper appeared at least twice to Francis. The first time he did so in a vision when Francis was riding on horseback, the second time in the hospice. See the "Life of Saint Francis," in *Bonavanture* (New York: Paulist Press, 1978), 188–189; and the *Fioretti*, chap. 25. Because the incognito appearances of Christ are

not communicated as such to the opera's audience it may often appear—as indeed has been the case with many critics—as though there is no dramatic unfolding at all. The dramatic encounters pass by unnoticed.

57. On interpellation and dorsality, see David Wills, *Dorsality: Thinking Back Through Technology and Politics* (Minneapolis: University of Minnesota Press, 2008), 34–36.

58. Maurice Blanchot, "Rilke and Death," in *The Sirens' Song: Selected Essays* (Sussex: Harvester Press, 1982), 153.

59. See Robert Fallon, "Birds, Beasts, and Bombs in Messiaen's Cold War Mass," *Journal of Musicology* 26, no. 2 (2009): 175–204.

60. This nuclear history has been the subject of a more recent opera project by Peter Sellars and John Adams, *Doctor Atomic* (2005).

61. See my *The Reinvention of Religious Music: Olivier Messiaen's Breakthrough Toward the Beyond* (New York: Fordham University Press, 2009), 13–36.

62. See also the remarks on evil and naïveté in this opera in my "Messiaen's Saintly Naïveté."

63. Maurice Blanchot, "Orpheus' Gaze," in *Siren's Song*, 180.

64. Blanchot, 181.

65. See also, Philippe Lacoue-Labarthe, "The *Caesura* of Religion," *Opera through Other Eyes*, ed. David Levin (Stanford, CA: Stanford University Press, 1994), 75.

66. Iain Fenlon, "Monteverdi's Mantuan 'Orfeo': Some New Documentation," *Early Music* 12, no. 2 (May 1984): 163–172.

67. Lawrence Kramer, "Two or Three Things I Know About Her," in *Siren Songs: Representations of Gender and Sexuality in Opera*, ed. Mary Ann Smart (Princeton, NJ: Princeton University Press, 2000), 202.

68. Furrer's *Begehren* focuses entirely on Orpheus's looking back. It includes textual fragments from Cesare Pavese, Günther Eich, Ovid, and Virgil. The work was written in 2001 and performed in Graz in 2003; it was released on DVD by Kairos (KAI0012792, 2008).

Part II

Embodiment and Materiality

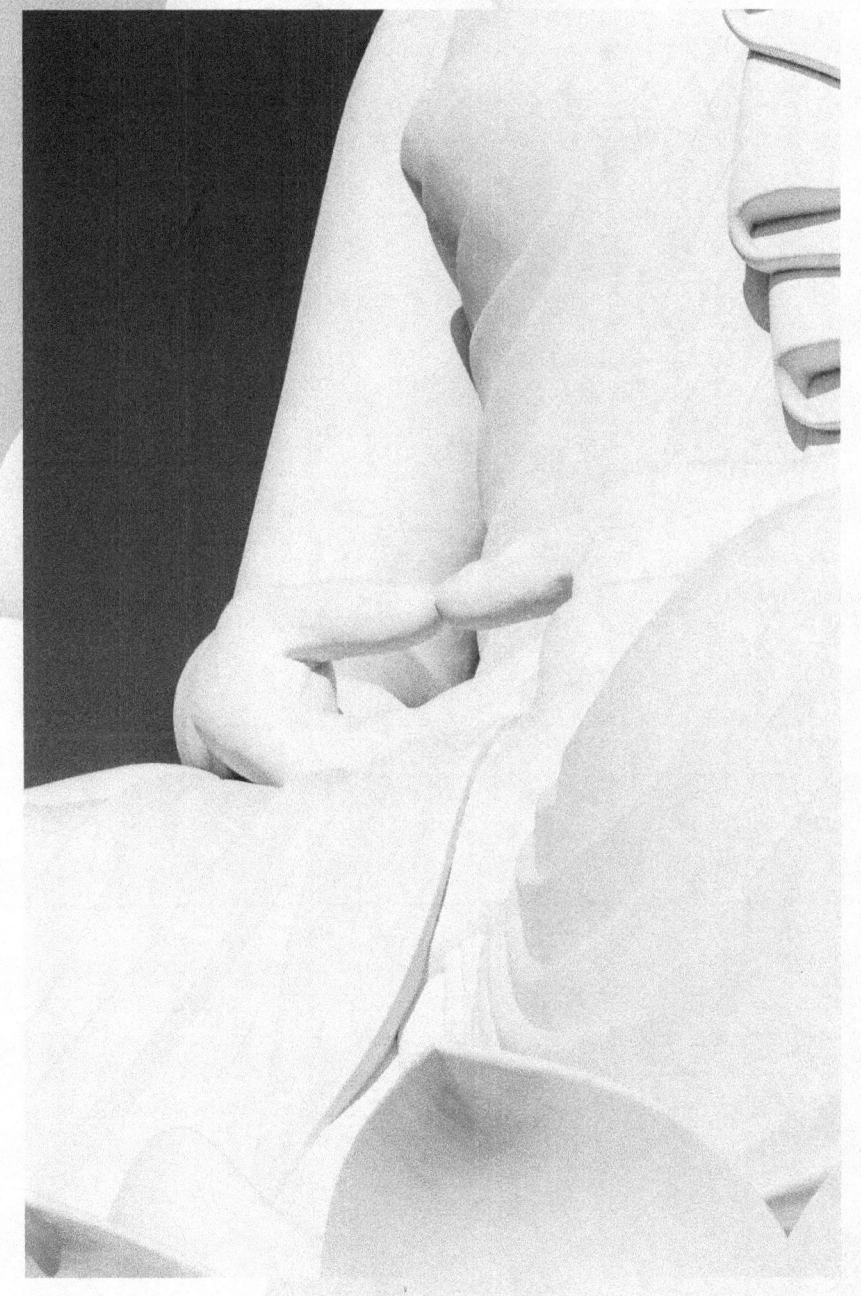

Even when dealing with the spiritual and the otherworldly, religious practices are not just mental or intentional but also material acts, in view of both the actors' embodiment and the materiality of the media or semiotic forms they involve. This materiality, of course, applies to practices in general; but in recent years, Birgit Meyer, among other authors, has emphasized the materiality of religion as well. One of the earlier volumes in this series was devoted to the material in religion; today, there is also a journal, *Material Religion*, specifically devoted to the topic.

The fact that religious practices are performed by embodied actors opens up an array of questions about human agency, in particular in relation to language (and more generally semiotic forms of media), gender, and sexuality. In its materiality, language (whether spoken or written, and whether or not mediated by technological means) shapes religious practice; and conversely, the public use of language may be informed by either a privately formed religious agency or subjectivity or by the exclusion of religion from public debate. In different ways, the contributions in this part show how embodied public action may be used either to reinforce or to contest religiously sanctioned gender norms. As such, these contributions may also enrich and add nuance to the discussions of secularism and religion in the public sphere that form the final part of this volume. (Sexuality and gender also play a crucial role in the transgressive religious acts discussed in part IV.)

Wendy Doniger opens her fascinating "From Kama to Karma" with a discussion of the new forms of puritanism proclaimed, on occasion by violent means, by present-day Hindutva groups. These groups defend both the purity and the puritan character of a Hindu tradition presented as timeless against what they perceive to be a Western or Western-inspired exaggeration of matters sexual in this tradition. Against such claims, Doniger points out that from the earliest sacred texts on, Hinduism has in fact known explicitly erotic religious imagery, from the language of pleasure and fertility that may be found from the *Rig Veda* to the famous sculptures of couples engaged in sexual intercourse that adorn the Khajuraho temples in Madhya Pradesh. Throughout its history, she maintains, Hinduism has known a tension between a worldly path of sensuality, sacrifice, and violence and a spiritual, ascetic, and nonviolent path of renunciation. Doniger illustrates her comments with a discussion of different sexual actors and activities in the *Kamasutra*, which she then contrasts with the modern reception of that work, triggered by Richard Burton's famous but flawed 1883 translation. In the wake of, and in part against, European orientalists who celebrated a (partly invented) sexual freedom they claimed to have found in ancient Hinduism, Indian nationalists (including, most famously, Mahatma Gandhi) developed more puritan forms of Hinduism that were strongly influenced by British Protestantism. Doniger refuses to reject early Hindu sensualism as a mere orientalist projection; nor does she dismiss modern Hindu prudery as a foreign import of either British or Muslim origin. Thus, she reaffirms historically variable and power-saturated forms of local agency both against sweeping postcolonial claims about Western orientalist hegemony and against communitarian claims concerning the integrity of religious traditions.

Ironically, in 2014, Doniger's book, *The Hindus*—which traces the incarnations of Hinduism through the ages with a focus on women, lower-caste believers, animals, and other nondominant actors—was banned by an Indian court on charges of offending Hindu sensibilities. Several Hindutva groups had been actively lobbying for the ban; in her response, "Banned in Bangalore" (*New York Times*, March 5, 2014), Doniger showed herself exhilarated rather than disappointed, because, she wrote, the court case and the controversial ban had led to a countrywide public debate on the limits of both free speech and religious claims.

Judith Butler's "Bodies in Alliance and the Politics of the Street," which develops several ideas from Hannah Arendt, begins with the 2011 demonstrations on Tahrir Square in Cairo, Egypt, against the regime of then President Hosni Mubarak. Butler's discussion elucidates that public bodily action cannot be explained in terms of nor be reduced to the ideality of the public realm; rather, the public is performatively *produced* through bodily and linguistic action. Against Hannah Arendt's influential conception of the public realm as the sole domain of genuinely free action, Butler notes that the ancient Athenian public realm was defined by the exclusion of women, slaves, and foreigners, and as such constituted by a prior operation of power. Hence, she argues, demonstrations like those on Tahrir Square and the Occupy movement involve not only making claims *in* a given public space but also contesting the very publicness *of* that space. This line of argument implies that the secular and heteronormative character of the public sphere rests on a prior power-saturated operation of exclusion. Thus, *pace* Habermas, the public sphere is not an abstract normative domain or ideal but an inherently material space in which irreducibly embodied actors act out irreducibly material practices. However, the exclusion of both religion and sexual orientation from the public sphere as private matters involves not only an act of power; the public assertion of seemingly private matters is also decisive for *how* one enters into the public realm. Demonstrators may not antecedently have a right to gather in public, but they may performatively assert or arrogate such a right by publicly acting and speaking; thus, by the performativity of not only their language but their very bodies, they question the legitimacy of the state. Similar protests in Turkey, Butler argues, included both LGBT activists and Islamists, and thus overcame divisions that in Northern Europe separate feminists, gay rights workers, and freedom of religion movements.

Religion plays an unobtrusive but significant part in Butler's argument, for example, when—following Arendt—she calls the bringing into being of public space by bodily acts a "divine performative allocated to the human form." Further, she suggests that, in chanting *"silmiyya"* ("peacefulness," a term with the same verbal root as *Islam*), the Egyptian demonstrators asserted a nonviolent public religion in the face of the secular state's violence. Finally, Butler presents an important corrective to Giorgio Agamben's notion of the *homo sacer*. Famously, Agamben had linked the ancient Roman notion of the individual who is excluded from the law while simultaneously remaining under the spell of the law to a discussion of the contemporary form of the state of exception as the suspension of the law. Against this conception, Butler emphasizes the political character of this exclusion: she argues that present-day *homines sacres* like stateless people may be deprived of rights, excluded from the political, and reduced to a nonpolitical bare life; but they are still enmeshed in power relations.

Rokus de Groot's "Divine Impersonations," like Doniger's essay, discusses the disciplining powers exercised on bodies in the name of religious morality; but de Groot focuses on contemporary India. In his study of the transgressive features of Hindu devotion, he analyzes divine incarnation or impersonation as a particular kind of religious embodiment, starting with the case of an Indian police inspector with a Bhakti background who one day appeared in a local courtroom cross-dressed as Radha, Lord Krishna's consort. The man's claim to be a divine incarnation, or avatar, was widely contested and dismissed by some as a mere case of sexual perversion or mental illness. Soon, however, it also became politicized, reflecting questions of religion, gender, and national identity. In India, de Groot argues, it is generally quite acceptable for men to take on a female guise in theatrical or literary contexts; but the inspector quoted this form of drag out of context, so to speak, by appearing cross-dressed in court. De Groot calls this tension between bodily sensuality and asceticism in Bhakti faith "embodiment dissonance." Thus, this act of cross-dressing and divine impersonation resonates both with Doniger's work on the ambivalence between sexuality and asceticism— or kama and karma—in Hinduism and with Butler's ideas on drag as iteration. In conclusion, de Groot illustrates how music plays an integral role in the traumatic epiphany of divine embodiment.

In "Islamic Dress and Fashion," Annelies Moors turns to the religious and aesthetic aspects of Islamic dress, in particular headscarves. Moors argues, first, for an approach that systematically combines the study of dress with the study of religion and, second, for a multisensorial approach that involves not only vision but also touch. Her argument that Islamic dress is simultaneously a religious and a sartorial practice takes us beyond the reductionist question of whether headscarves are donned by force or by choice, and beyond an equally reductionist opposition between "purely" Islamic dress—tacitly assumed to be sober—and fashion seen as flashy and, ultimately, non-Islamic; for many Muslim actors, Islamic fashion is not an oxymoron but a field for the presentation of a self that is shaped by aesthetic as much as by religious concerns. In Moors's analysis, the wearing of fashionable dress style need not indicate a lack of concern with religion; in fact, some actors argue that dressing in a pleasant and harmonious way is itself an act that pleases God. Elaborating several points first raised by Saba Mahmood, Moors concludes that in the complex relation between Islam and dress and fashion, beauty may become a kind of visual *da'wa*, or call to Islam.

In "On Spirit Writing," Webb Keane calls attention to the materiality of spoken and written language, and of signs more generally. The relationship between humans and gods and spirits, he argues, is not only power-laden; it is also mediated by the materiality of signs, and in particular by writing. In his earlier work, most notably his *Christian Moderns*, Keane had already called attention to the role of linguistic or semiotic ideologies (i.e., folk beliefs or rationalizations about what words or signs are, and about what they can do) in articulating this materiality. Here, Keane introduces what he calls "spirit writing," for example, writing down a sacred text fragment on a piece of paper, which is then burned; next, the ashes are dissolved in water and imbibed by the believer. This experience of signs is not caused by the actual material or linguistic properties of words, he contends, but mediated by semiotic ideologies, that is, by what people *believe* words can achieve. Writing down divine words renders them more enduring and transportable, in short, more material; the practice of spirit writing aims at achieving the opposite effect: it tries to dematerialize the words materialized in and through writing and to lend them new immaterial or spiritual efficiency, for example, by kissing them or spitting upon them, or by copying or burning them. Such practices of spirit writing may generate religious powers by means of what Keane calls "semiotic transduction," that is, the activity of transforming religious forces from one semiotic domain to another. Although they are shaped by particular, and variable, semiotic ideologies, Keane believes practices of spirit writing may open up the possibility of comparative study of the perceptual experience of (religious) writing, which involves both materialization and dematerialization; they point to general religious problems of materializing spirit in (written) language and of conversely dematerializing words toward the nonphenomenal world of the divine.

CHAPTER 5

From Kama to Karma

The Resurgence of Puritanism in Contemporary India

Wendy Doniger

A pervasive and often violent moral policing has taken over parts of the Indian world today. A typical instance of this occurred in 2007 when Chandramohan Srilamantula, a twenty-three-year-old student of fine arts at the University of Baroda (in Vadodara, Gujarat), mounted an exhibition for other students and staff. He had previously received awards for his work, including the forty-ninth Lalit Kala Akademi National Exhibition award in 2006; later he won first prize in the 2009 Bhopal Biennial. In the 2007 exhibition, one painting depicted a crucified Christ with explicit genitals and a toilet beneath the cross; another, entitled *Durga Mate*, was of a nude woman using a trident (the weapon of the god Shiva) to kill a baby issuing from her womb.

Christian leaders lodged protests against the first painting, and a group of activists from the Vishva Hindu Parashad (VHP, "All-Hindu Council") and the Bharatiya Janata Party (BJP, "National People's Party") vandalized the exhibition and roughed up Chandramohan.[1] They were led by Niraj Jain, who has been known to brandish a revolver and once threw eggs at the Gujarat education minister for including them in school midday meals.[2] The police stood by and then arrested not the vandals but the artist. (He was later released.) When the acting dean of the Faculty of Fine Arts, Shivraj Panikkar, refused to close down the exhibition, the vice chancellor, Manoj Soni, suspended him. Panikkar, stating that he feared for his life, went into hiding. Students and spokespersons of the Indian art community held protests throughout

India, claiming that the closing of the exhibition was a direct assault on the rights of freedom of expression.

In commenting on this event, the well-known editor, columnist, and critic Anil Dharker remarked: "What has made the artists come together in protest is that this attack isn't an isolated one, but one more in a series now increasing in both frequency and wantonness. . . . The Mumbai Police stood by when Shiv Sainiks attacked cinema theatres showing a Deepa Mehta film. Recently, the Mumbai cops did some moral policing of their own, arresting young couples found in 'compromising positions' (police-speak for young men and women having their arms around each other)."[3]

Dharker went on to list several more instances, but even these few are representative of broad patterns of attacks by various Hindutva groups, whose members are known as Hindutvadis. Some Hindutvadis forced Deepa Mehta to leave Varanasi, where she was making a film about the mistreatment of widows in Varanasi *(Water* 2005); on January 30, 2000, "fundamentalist thugs" from the BJP—a coalition of Rashtriya Swayamsevak Sangh (RSS, "National Corps of Volunteers"), VHP, and others, together with Uttar Pradesh government officials—destroyed the film sets and later threatened the cast and crew; on February 6, 2000, the state of Uttar Pradesh ordered a suspension of production, and Mehta finished the film in Sri Lanka.[4] Other BJP groups stopped the screening of films starring actors such as Shahrukh Khan (who had expressed admiration for Pakistani cricketers) and Aamir Khan (who had supported Medha Patkar, a famous woman social activist).[5]

The protest against Chandramohan Srilamantula was one of a number of campaigns against artists and writers who linked Hindu deities with sexuality. In 1996, Hindutvadis began terrorizing M. F. Husain for his paintings of naked Hindu goddesses. In 2006, after death threats and legal cases, the ninety-one-year-old Husain, whom many regard as India's greatest living artist, was forced into exile; he now lives in Dubai. The Mumbai policing of young couples that Dharker mentioned is matched by equally outrageous attacks on young "pub-crawling" Indian women in Mangalore, and by regular efforts to attack stores and restaurants that celebrate Valentine's Day (on the grounds that it is a Western corruption of Indian values). The Hindutvadis often blame Western influence on the people they censor, while, ironically, many of the Hindutvadis' own actions closely resemble censoring frenzies in the United States. But the Indian incidents are better seen as part of a separate logic of Hindu Puritanism, which has a long history of its own.

The Early History of Hindu Eroticism and Asceticism

When a group of students and artists at Baroda University attempted to stage a protest demonstration for Chandramohan at the Faculty of Fine Arts, they organized an exhibition of photographs taken from the explicitly erotic sculptures that adorn the temples at Khajuraho, in Madhya Pradesh.[6] In choosing Khajuraho, they were making an implicit historical statement: the art heritage of India is rich in erotic themes, of which the images on the Khajuraho temples (built between 900 and 1100 CE) are a famous example. What happened to that tradition? How did India get from there to the scandal in Baroda? Erotic religious imagery is as old as Hinduism. The earliest Hindu sacred text, the *Rig Veda* (ca. 1500 BCE), revels in the language of both pleasure and fertility. The Upanishads, which followed a few centuries later, analogized the Vedic oblation of butter into the fire to the act of sexual procreation.[7] The worshipper in a sexual embrace with his wife imagines each part of the act as a part of the ritual of the oblation, while presumably anyone making the offering into the fire could also imagine each action as its sexual parallel. Sensuality continued to keep its foot in the door of the house of religion throughout the history of India.

But the Upanishads also introduced into India the concept of two paths: one, the path of family life, society, and children, the other, the path of renunciation, solitary meditation, and asceticism. And although asceticism always remained alive and well and living in India, householders continued to obey the command to be fruitful and multiply. The tension between the two paths—on one hand, the violent, sacrificial, materialistic, and sensual path of worldliness and, on the other hand, the nonviolent, vegetarian, ascetic, and spiritual path of renunciation—was sometimes expressed as the balance between bourgeois householders and homeless seekers, or between traditions that regarded *karma*—the accumulated record of good and bad deeds—as a good or a bad thing, respectively.

The tension remains in the Tantras, a large body of texts composed between about 650 and 1800 CE that proposed strikingly transgressive ritual actions, violating all the taboos of conventional Hinduism, such as drinking wine and menstrual blood, eating meat, and engaging in sexual activity with forbidden women. These Tantras thus collapsed the Upanishadic metaphor, saying that the ritual sexual act is not just *like* a ritual (as it is in the Upanishads) but *is itself* a ritual, the equivalent of making an offering into the fire. But other Tantras, situated within the anti-erotic tradition of Hinduism, insisted that the ritual instructions were never intended to be followed literally, but were purely symbolic. They argued that "wine" really meant a meditational nectar, that "flesh" meant the tongue of the practitioner, and that the sexual act stood for "the supreme essence."[8] This was a very early form of censorship, and a very mild form, for it merely proposed an alternative, anti-erotic interpretation of the text but did not attempt to muzzle the other, erotic interpretation.

And so the two paths of Tantra, meditation and ritual action, lived side by side, sometimes coexisting in a single worshipper, sometimes within a group—as, for instance, in some texts that say beginners actually do the ritual, while advanced practitioners just meditate. The split-level connotations were present from the start. Given the attention that Indian literary theory pays to double meanings, words, and indeed whole literary works that simultaneously mean two different things,[9] it seems wise to assume that the Tantrics were capable of walking and chewing imaginary gum at the same time.

The erotic tradition continued to thrive in Hinduism. Many poems to gods in the medieval devotional tradition of *bhakti* imagine the god as a lover, often an unfaithful lover, and depict the relationship with all the sensual details of good erotic poetry. The poet Kshetrayya, who may have lived in the mid-seventeenth century and who worshipped a form of the god Krishna, imagined a courtesan speaking to her customer who is both her lover and her god. Kshetrayya's songs survived among courtesans and were performed by male Brahmin dancers who played female roles. His poems treat of such down-to-earth matters as a woman's concern to find a drug or a magic potion to abort the child that she conceived from her lover, the king, the god, and her customer.[10]

The *Kamasutra*

In addition to these religious texts that incorporated eroticism, there were more worldly texts that treated the erotic *tout court*, of which the *Kamasutra*, composed in north India, probably in the third century CE, is the most famous. The two words in its title mean "desire/love/pleasure/sex" (*kama*) and "a treatise" (*sutra*). Virtually nothing is known about the author, Vatsyayana, other than his name and what we learn from this text. There is nothing remotely like it even now, and for its time it was astonishingly sophisticated; it was already well known in India when the Europeans were still swinging in trees, culturally (and sexually) speaking. The *Kamasutra*'s ideas about gender are surprisingly modern, and its stereotypes of feminine and masculine natures are unexpectedly subtle. It also reveals attitudes to women's education and sexual freedom, and views of homosexual acts, that are strikingly more liberal than those of other texts in ancient India—or, in many cases, in contemporary India.

Vatsyayana dismisses with one or two short verses the possibility that the purpose of the sexual act is to produce children; one of the things that make sex for human beings different from sex for animals, he points out, is the fact that human women, unlike animals, have sex even when they are not in their fertile period.[11] Given the enormous emphasis that the traditional texts of Hindu religious law (dharma) place on having sex *only* to produce children, the *Kamasutra*'s attitude here is extraordinary. It is also extraordinary in assuming that women would, and should, know this text:

> A woman should study the Kamasutra and its subsidiary arts before she reaches the prime of her youth, and she should continue when she has been given away, if her husband wishes it. Scholars say: "Since females cannot grasp texts, it is useless to teach women this text." Vatsyayana says: But women understand the practice, and the practice is based on the text. This applies beyond this specific subject of the *Kamasutra*, for throughout the world, in all subjects, there are only a few people who know the text, but the practice is within the range of everyone. And a text, however far removed, is the ultimate source of the practice. "Grammar is a science," people say. Yet the sacrificial priests, who are no grammarians, know how to gloss the words in the sacrificial prayers. "Astronomy is a science," they say. But ordinary people perform the rituals on the days when the skies are auspicious. And people know how to ride horses and elephants without studying the texts about horses and elephants. In the same way, even citizens far away from the king do not step across the moral line that he sets. The case of women learning the *Kamasutra* is like those examples. And there are also women whose understanding has been sharpened by the text: courtesans and the daughters of kings and state ministers.[12]

Vatsyayana is also a strong advocate for women's sexual pleasure. He tells us that a woman who does not experience the pleasures of love may hate her man and leave him for another.[13] If, as the context suggests, this woman is married, the casual manner in which Vatsyayana suggests that she leave her husband is in sharp contrast to the position assumed by the *Laws of Manu*, the most famous of the textbooks of *dharma*, composed a few centuries before the *Kamasutra*: "A virtuous wife should constantly serve her husband like a god, even if he behaves badly, freely indulges his lust, and is devoid of any good qualities."[14] Vatsyayana also presents an argument in favor of female orgasm far more subtle than views that prevailed in Europe until very recently indeed, and certainly worlds above the attitudes of his predecessors, whose cockamamie ideas he quotes. Vatsyayana also knew about the G-spot (named after the German gynecologist Ernst Gräfenberg): "When her eyes roll when she feels him in certain spots, he presses her in just those spots."[15] He also tells the man how to recognize when a woman has reached a climax—or, perhaps, if we assume (as I think we should) that the text is intended for women, too, he is telling the woman how to fake it.[16] And he argues that the woman has seed just like a man and therefore, by implication, contributes an equal portion to the child; that women have orgasms just like men; and in fact that the woman must have an orgasm in order to become pregnant, presumably in order to release her seed. He concludes: "Therefore the woman should be treated in such a way that she achieves her sexual climax first."[17] Here at least, he is on the side of the angels.

Some parts of the book were evidently designed to be used by women. Book three devotes one episode to advice to virgins trying to get husbands,[18] and book four consists of instructions for wives. Book six is said to have been commissioned by the courtesans of Pataliputra, presumably for their own use.[19] The earliest extant commentator, Yashodhara, writing in the thirteenth century, tells us how this happened:

> A Brahmin named Dattaka learned all the arts and sciences in a short time. One day he had the idea of learning the finest ways of the world, best known by courtesans. And so he went to the courtesans every day, and learned so well that they asked *him* to instruct *them*: "Teach us how to give pleasure to men." But another quite plausible story is also widely believed: Dattaka once touched (the god) Shiva with his foot in the course of a festival to bless a pregnant woman, and Shiva cursed him to become a woman; after a while he persuaded Shiva to rescind the curse and let him become a man again, and because of that double knowledge he made the separate book. But if the author of the *Kamasutra* had known that he had such double knowledge, then he would have said, "Dattaka, who knew both flavors, made this book."[20]

It is an inspired move on the part of the commentator to make the author of this text a bisexual like the Greek Teiresias (queen for a day, king for a day), who "tastes both flavors," or, as we would say, swings both ways or bats for both teams. (The Arabic expression is "he eats both pomegranates and figs," and the British, "oysters and snails.") Yet this is also a move that greatly mitigates the strong female agency in the text: where Vatsyayana tells us that women had this text made, the commentator tells us that an extraordinary man knew more about the courtesans' art than they knew themselves. During the millennium that separates the text from the commentary, the control of women by men increased dramatically in India, and this erosion of their status is reflected in the transition from the text's statement that women commissioned the text to the commentary's statement that a man did it better than they could do it.

Most extraordinary is Vatsyayana's attitude to people who engage in homosexual acts. Classical Hinduism is in general significantly silent on the subject of homoeroticism, but Hindu mythology does drop hints from which we can excavate a pretty virulent homophobia. The *dharma* textbooks, too, either ignore or stigmatize homosexual activity. Male homoerotic activity was punished, albeit mildly: a ritual bath or the payment of a small fine was often a sufficient atonement.[21]

The Sanskrit word *kliba* has traditionally been translated as "eunuch" but almost certainly did not mean "eunuch." The political textbook called the *Arthashastra*, on which the *Kamasutra* modeled itself in many ways, uses another term (*varsha-dhara,* "rain-holder," that is, celibate) to designate what may have been eunuchs—that is, men intentionally castrated, particularly in order to serve as guardians in the royal harem.[22] Men were castrated in punishment for various crimes in ancient India (and animals were gelded to control them), but such men were not employed as eunuchs. "*Kliba,*" rather, includes a wide range of meanings under the general rubric of "a man who does not act the way a man should act," a man who fails to be a man, a defective male, a male suffering from distortion and Lacanian lack. It is a catch-all term that traditional Hindus coined to indicate a man who is in their terms sexually dysfunctional (or in ours, sexually challenged), including someone who was sterile, impotent, castrated, a transvestite, a man who had oral sex with other men, who had anal sex, a man with mutilated or defective sexual organs, a hermaphrodite, or, finally, a man who produced only female children. Often, it has the vaguely pejorative force of "wimp" or, more literally, "limp-dick." Thus, when the incarnate god Krishna wishes to stir the martial instincts of the conscience-stricken human hero Arjuna, he says to him, "Stop being a *kliba*!"[23] (A similarly broad definition of sodomy, even broader than the one still on the books in several American states, prevailed during the renaissance, a definition that included masturbating, sex in the wrong orifice, bestiality, and sex between Christian and Jew).[24]

The *Kamasutra* departs from the *dharma* view of homosexuality in significant ways. It does not use the pejorative term *kliba* at all but speaks instead of a "third nature" (*tritiya prakriti*, a term that first appears a few centuries earlier, in the great Sanskrit epic, the *Mahabharata*) or perhaps a "third sexuality" or "third gender" in the sense of sexual behavior:

There are two sorts of third nature, in the form of a woman and in the form of a man. The one in the form of a woman imitates a woman's dress, chatter, grace, emotions, delicacy, timidity, innocence, frailty, and bashfulness. The act that is [generally] done in the sexual organ is done in her mouth, and they call that "oral sex." She gets her sexual pleasure and erotic arousal as well as her livelihood from this, living as a courtesan. That is the person of the third nature in the form of a woman.[25]

The *Kamasutra* says nothing more about this cross-dressing male, with his stereotypical female gender behavior, but it discusses the fellatio technique of the closeted man of the third nature in considerable sensual detail, in the longest consecutive passage in the text describing a physical act, and with what might even be called gusto:

The one in the form of a man, however, conceals her desire when she wants a man and makes her living as a masseur. As she massages the man, she caresses his two thighs with her limbs, as if she were embracing him. Then she becomes more boldly intimate and familiar..., pretending to tease him about how easily he becomes excited and laughing at him. If the man does not urge her on, even when he has given this clear sign and even when it is obvious that he is aroused, she makes advances to him on her own. If the man urges her to go on, she argues with him and only unwillingly continues.[26]

And so forth, and so on. This is a remarkably explicit analysis of the mentality of the closet, the extended double entendre of an act that is cleverly designed to appear sexually innocent to a man who does not want, or does not want to admit that he wants, a homosexual encounter, but is an explicit invitation to a man who is willing to admit his desire for such an encounter. And a massage is a massage in the *Kamasutra:* "Some people think that massaging is also a kind of close embrace, because it involves touching. But Vatsyayana says: No. For a massage takes place at a particular time set aside, has a different use, and is not enjoyed by both partners in the same way."[27] Or is it? Consider this: "But when a woman who is giving the man a massage makes sure he has understood her signals and rests her face on his thighs as if she had no desire but was overcome by sleep, and then kisses his thighs, that is called a kiss 'making advances.'"[28] And this: "'Gooseflesh' is made when nails of medium length are brought close together and moved over the chin, breasts, or lower lip, so lightly that they leave no line but by the mere touch cause the thrill of gooseflesh and make a sound as they strike one another. A man can do this to the woman he wants, in the course of massaging her body."[29]

One passage suggests that some people, cited when Vatsyayana warns the bridegroom not to be too shy with his shy bride, disapprove of men of the third nature: "[Certain scholars] say, 'If the girl sees that the man has not spoken a word for three nights, like a pillar, she will be discouraged and will despise him, as if he were someone of the third nature.'"[30] So judgmentalism appears to creep in after all. But when we look closer, we see that the people who make this judgment are the "scholars" with whom Vatsyayana almost always disagrees, as he does here, for he goes on to remark: "Vatsyayana says: He begins to entice her and win her trust, but he still remains sexually continent. When he entices her, he does not force her in any way, for women are like flowers, and need to be enticed very tenderly. If they are taken by force by men who have not yet won their trust, they become women who hate sex. Therefore, he wins her over with gentle persuasion."[31] This is the sort of man whom the wrong sort of scholar, but not Vatsyayana, might fear that some people might stigmatize as someone of the third nature.

Men of the third nature are always designated by the pronoun *she*, basically because the word *nature* is feminine in Sanskrit (as it, and most abstract nouns, are also in Latin and Greek). Indeed, the idea of a third gender, rather than a binary division, may come from the basic habit of Indo-European languages to assign three genders—neuter as well as masculine and feminine—to all nouns. Yet the very use of the word *third*—which clearly implies a previous *first* and *second*—demonstrates that Vatsyayana is thinking primarily in binary, more precisely dialectic, terms that would have satisfied Hegel or Claude Lévi-Strauss: two opposed terms modified by a third. Vatsyayana actually analogizes men and women to grammatical terms, in the discussion of gender stereotypes, which does not take account of the third nature at all: "By his physical nature, the man is the active agent (the subject) and the young woman is the passive locus (the locative case, in which the action takes place)."[32] (The object is the sexual act.) But there is another, better reason why Vatsyayana uses the female pronoun for a person of the third nature, and that is because of her perceived gender: he lists the third nature among *women* who can be lovers.[33] This use of the pronoun *she* can also be seen as an anticipation of the practices of some cross-dressing gay men of our day. What about homoerotic women? Vatsyayana is unique in the literature of the period in describing lesbian activity. He does this at the beginning of the chapter about the harem, in a brief passage about what he calls "Oriental customs."[34] (The use of the term *Oriental* or *Eastern* for what Vatsyayana regards as a disreputable lesbian practice in what was soon to be a colonized part of the Gupta Empire—indeed, the Eastern part—suggests that "Orientalism" began not with the British but with the Orientals themselves.) These women use dildos, as well as bulbs, roots, or fruits that have the form of the male organ, and statues of men that have distinct sexual characteristics. But they engage in sexual acts with one another only in the absence of men, as we sometimes say of men in prison, or English boys in posh boarding schools, not through the kind of personal choice that drives a man of the third nature: "The women of the harem cannot meet men, because they are carefully guarded; and since they have only one husband shared by many women in common, they are not satisfied. Therefore, they give pleasure to one another with the following techniques."[35] Yashodhara's commentary on this passage makes this explicit, and also helpfully suggests the particular vegetables that one might employ: "By imagining a man, they experience a heightened emotion that gives extreme satisfaction. These things have a form just like the male sexual organ: the bulbs of arrow-root, plantain and so forth; the roots of coconut palms, bread fruit, and so forth; and the fruits of the bottle-gourd, cucumber, and so forth." One can imagine little gardens of plantain and cucumber being cultivated within the inner rooms of the palace, the harem.

The *Kamasutra* makes only one brief reference to women who may have chosen women as sexual partners in preference to men: the text says that a girl may lose her virginity with a girlfriend or a servant girl, and the commentator specifies that "they take her virginity by using a finger."[36] The *dharma* text of Manu says that a woman who corrupts a virgin will be punished by having two of her fingers cut off,[37] a hint of what Manu—like Yashodhara—thinks lesbians do in bed. Vatsyayana never refers to women of this type as people of a "third nature," but the commentator's belief that the children produced when the woman is on top might be "a little boy and little girl with reversed natures" refers to the view that the "reverse" intercourse of parents might wreak embryonic damage,[38] resulting in the reversed gender behavior of the third nature—significantly, for a girl as well as a boy, the female type not spelled out by the text's discussion of the "third nature."

In addition to male and female homosexual acts, a few oblique, passing remarks suggest bisexuality. The female messenger who is sent to praise the man in the presence of the woman he is wooing may have had bisexual behavior in mind when, praising the man's charm, she says, according to the commentator, "He has such luck in love that he was desired even by a man."[39] And two verses describe men who engage in oral sex not by profession, like the men of the "third nature," but out of love.

Even young men, servants who wear polished earrings, indulge in oral sex only with certain men. And, in the same way, certain men-about-town who care for one another's welfare and have established trust do this service for one another.⁴⁰ These men, who seem bound to one another by discriminating affection rather than promiscuous passion, are called "men about town," *nagarakas*, the term used to designate the heterosexual heroes of the *Kamasutra*. In striking contrast with men of the third nature, always designated by the pronoun *she*, these men are described with nouns and pronouns that unambiguously designate males. Perhaps, then, they are bisexuals. The commentator on the *Kamasutra*, as we have seen, even makes Dattaka, the author of the part of the text commissioned by the courtesans, a serial bisexual.⁴¹

Thus, it is possible for us to excavate several alternative sexualities latent in the text's somewhat fuzzy boundaries between homoeroticism and heteroeroticism. But we must admit that we find these alternatives in the Sanskrit original, carrying meanings that have value for us, only by transcending, if not totally disregarding, the original context. Were we to remain within the strict bounds of the historical situation, we could not notice the voices speaking against their moment in history, perhaps even against their author. Only by asking our own questions, which the author may not have considered at all, can we see that his text does contain many answers to them, fortuitously embedded in other questions and answers that were more meaningful to him. This reading suggests various ways in which the *Kamasutra*'s implicit claim to sexual totality might be opened out into a vision of gender infinity.

The *Kamasutra* was a revolutionary document, for women and for people of the "third nature." It exerted a profound influence on subsequent Indian literature, particularly in court life and in the privileged, classless society that it describes at great length. But, at the same time, the *dharma* texts with their deep suspicion of women and eroticism retained their stranglehold on much of Hindu society. And then came the British.

Sir Richard Burton's Version of the *Kamasutra*

The *Kamasutra* plays almost no role at all in the sexual consciousness of contemporary Indians, and one reason for this is that it is known, in both India and Europe, almost entirely through the flawed English translation by Sir Richard Francis Burton, published in 1883. Burton did for the *Kamasutra* what Max Müller did for the *Rig Veda* during this same period; his translation had a profound effect upon literature across Europe and America. Burton's main contribution was the courage and determination to publish the work at all; he was the Larry Flynt of his day. To get around the censorship laws, Burton set up an imaginary publishing house, The Kama Shastra Society of London and Benares, with printers said to be in Benares or Cosmopoli.[42] Even though it was not legally published in England and the United States until 1962, the Burton *Kamasutra*, soon after its publication in 1883, became "one of the most pirated books in the English language," constantly reprinted, often with a new preface to justify the new edition, sometimes without any attribution to Burton.[43] It is free (at first poached from the illegal editions, then long out of copyright) and recognizable as what people think the *Kamasutra* should be. Indeed, it is quite a wonderful text: great fun to read, extraordinarily bold and frank for its time, and in many places a fairly approximate representation of the Sanskrit original. It remains precious, like Edward Fitzgerald's *Rubaiyat*, as a monument of English literature, though not much closer to Vatsyayana than Fitzgerald was to Omar Khayyam. For the Sanskrit text often simply does not say what Burton says it says.

Moreover, it is not even the work of the man who is known as its author, Sir Richard Francis Burton. It was far more the work of Forster Fitzgerald ("Bunny") Arbuthnot, whose name appears on the title page with Burton's only in some editions, though Burton later referred to the *Kamasutra* translation as "Arbuthnot's Vatsyayana."[44] But the translation owed even more to two Indian scholars whose names do not appear on the title page at all: Bhagavanlal Indrajit and Shivaram Parashuram Bhide. There is a pre-postcolonial irony in the fact that Arbuthnot later tried to get the censors off his trail by stating, in 1885, a half-truth that he almost certainly regarded as a lie: that the translation was done entirely by Indian pandits.[45] It really should, therefore, be known as the Indrajit-Bhide-Arbuthnot-Burton translation, but since Burton was by far the most famous member of the team, it has always been called the Burton translation.

In many ways, it should be called the Burton mistranslation. W. H. Auden put it bluntly: "thus, squalid beery Burton stands/for shoddy thinking of all brands."[46] Consider the G-spot. Vatsyayana quotes a predecessor who said, "This is the secret of young women,"[47] and indeed, it remained a secret in Europe. It is not widely recognized that the *Kamasutra* knows this secret, and that is because Burton missed the G-spot. His translation of the relevant passage reads like this: "While a man is doing to the woman what he likes best during congress, he should always make a point of pressing those parts of her body on which she turns her eyes."[48] Where did Burton go wrong? He was following the commentator, who first gives a correct gloss of the crucial verb ("the pleasure of that touch makes her eyes whirl around in a circle") but then goes on to suggest several alternative glosses of that same verb, just as he had told an alternative story about Dattaka and the courtesans: "This remains secret because women do not make it known.

There is some argument about this. Some people say that whatever place the woman *looks at*, either specifically or vaguely, that is the place where he should press her. Others say that, if she looks at many places, he should press her in one place after another. Or, whatever place she looks at very hard is the place where he should press her very hard."[49] By following this part of the commentary, Burton has missed one point of the passage (how to locate the G-spot), and by inserting, gratuitously, the phrase "what he likes best" ("while a man is doing to the woman what he likes best during congress"), he has totally missed the larger point: the importance of learning how to do what the woman likes best. As for Burton's use of the term *congress*, I always wonder, "Where is the Senate, and where is the House of Representatives?"

The Burton translation also robs women of their voices, turning direct quotes into indirect quotes, thus losing the force of the dialogue that animates the work and erasing the vivid presence of the many women who speak in the *Kamasutra*, replacing these voices with reported speech rephrased by a man. Thus, where the text says that, when a man is striking a woman, "She uses words like "Stop!" or "Let me go!" or "Enough!" or "Mother!"[50] Burton translates it like this: "She continually utters words expressive of prohibition, sufficiency, or desire of liberation." Moreover, when the text says that this may happen "When a man [is] in the throes of passion," and "If a man tries to force his kisses and so forth on her," Burton says it happens "when the woman is not accustomed to striking," reversing the genders and reversing the point.[51]

Burton also erodes women's agency by mistranslating or erasing some passages in which women have strong privileges. Take this passage (here translated more or less literally): "Mildly offended by the man's infidelities, she does not accuse him too much, but she scolds him with abusive language when he is alone or among friends. She does not, however, use love-sorcery worked with roots, for, Gonardiya says, 'Nothing destroys trust like that.'"[52]

Burton renders it: "In the event of any misconduct on the part of her husband, she should not blame him excessively, though she be a little displeased. She should not use abusive language toward him, but rebuke him with conciliatory words, whether he be in the company of friends or alone. Moreover, she should not be a scold, for, says Gonardiya, 'There is no cause of dislike on the part of a husband so great as this characteristic in a wife.'"[53]

What is wrong with this picture? In the first place, Burton mistranslated the word for "love-sorcery worked with roots" (*mulakarika*), which he renders as "she should not be a scold" (though elsewhere he correctly translates *mulakarika*). Second, "misconduct" is not so much a mistranslation as an error of judgment, for the word in question (*apacara*) does have the general meaning of "misconduct," but in an erotic context it usually takes on the more specific meaning of "infidelity," a choice that is supported both by the remedy that the text suggests (and rejects)—love-magic—and by the commentator's gloss (*aparadha*). But the most serious problem is the word *not* that Burton gratuitously adds and that negates the wife's right to use abusive language against her straying husband, a denial only somewhat qualified by the added phrase, "rebuke him with conciliatory words." Was this an innocent error or does it reflect a sexist bias? We cannot know.

More significantly, Burton's translation misses the entire point about same-sex eroticism because he renders "third nature" as "eunuch" (the usual mistranslation of *kliba*) throughout. He also leaves out, entirely, the line that includes the "third nature" in the list of women who are sexually available.[54] Why did Burton make such an error? Probably he used the word *eunuch* in its broader sense: to designate not a guardian in the harem but a man who had been castrated for one reason or another. It is possible that Burton confused the men of the third nature with the Hijras, castrated transvestites who function as male prostitutes in India today and are often called "eunuchs."[55] The Hijras do correspond rather closely to the first type of third nature, the cross-dressing female type that is dismissed after just a sentence or two, but not to the second type, the closeted male type, to which Vatsyayana devotes so much attention. Burton had written about the Hijras in the notes to his translation of the *Arabian Nights*, but there is no evidence of their existence at the time of the *Kamasutra*. Why, then, did he not recognize the text's reference to sexually "entire" men who happened to prefer having (oral) sex with other men? Did he read the text as implying that this was the only option available to them due to some sort of genital malfunction? Did he confuse the third sex with *klibas*, the elastic category that includes both castrated men and homosexual men? There is no question about his knowledge of homosexuality, both in the *Arabian Nights* and in the India of his day; he had undertaken a study of male brothels, staffed by "boys and eunuchs," in Karachi in 1845.[56] His famous "Terminal Essay" to the *Arabian Nights*, published in 1885, includes an eighteen-thousand-word essay entitled "Pederasty" (later republished in his collection of essays, *The Erotic Traveller*) that was one of the first serious treatments of the subject in English, though he called it "the vice, the abuse, pathological love" and stated that Hindus held the practice in abhorrence.[57] No, Burton's "eunuchs" are, rather, a matter of "Orientalism": the depiction of "Orientals" as simultaneously oversexed and feminized. The word *eunuch* was bandied about loosely in British writings about the Orient, conveying a vague sense of sexual excess, cruelty, and impotence, and it infected Burton's translation of the *Kamasutra*, too.

Detumescence under the British

Though many of the British in India, particularly at the start, in the eighteenth century, appreciated all forms of Hindu culture, including its eroticism, British scholars of India remained largely ignorant of the *Kamasutra*. (Sir Monier Monier-Williams, who composed, in 1899, the great Sanskrit-English dictionary still used by most scholars, lists Vatsyayana but not the *Kamasutra* as potential sources and seldom, if ever, cites a word from that text in his lexicon.) And the puritanical Protestant ministers who evangelized India after 1813 loathed the eroticism of the temples, the temple dancers, and the amatory excesses of the god Krishna. A Supreme Court ruling from 1862 states that "Krishna . . . the love hero, the husband of 16,000 princesses . . . tinges the whole system (of Hinduism) with the strain of carnal sensualism, of strange, transcendental lewdness."[58] These were, after all, the Victorians, who were not amused by the copulating couples on the walls of the temples of Khajuraho. The officers and missionaries under the British Raj despised all forms of what they regarded as Oriental excess, all those arms, all those heads, all those wives. The fraction of Hinduism that appealed to Protestant, evangelical tastes at all was firmly grounded in the other path of Hinduism, the philosophical, renunciant path.

Scholars have noted a pattern in which colonized people take on the mask that the colonizer creates in the image of the colonized, mimicking the colonizer's perception of the colonized.[59] Many highly placed Hindus so admired their colonizers that, in a kind of colonial and religious Stockholm syndrome, they swallowed the Protestant line themselves, and not only gained a new appreciation of those aspects of Hinduism that the British approved of (the *Gita*, the *Upanishads*), but became ashamed of those aspects that the British scorned (erotic sculptures on temples, temple dancers). Following the British lead, these Hindus largely wrote off the dominant strain of Hinduism that celebrated the passions of the gods.

The highly Anglicized Indian elite developed new forms of Hinduism heavily influenced by British Protestantism. The key figure in this movement was Ram Mohan Roy (1772–1833), whose religion combined monistic elements of Hinduism and Islam (he had studied the Koran as well as the Vedas and the Upanishads) and, later, eighteenth-century Deism (belief in a transcendent Creator God reached through reason), Unitarianism (belief in God's essential oneness), and the ideas of the Freemasons (a secret fraternity that espoused some Deistic concepts). His beliefs were further fueled by his realization that the colonial government viewed Hindu customs alternately with abhorrence (Vedic polytheism) and fascination (Vedantic, or Upanishadic, monism), and by his desire to rebut the scathing critiques of the missionaries. Rammohan Roy formulated a new Hinduism, called the Brahmo Samaj ("Assembly of God"), which extracted the Sufism from Islam, the Vedanta from Hinduism, and Unitarianism from Christianity. He gave educated Hindus a basis on which they could justify their religion to an Indian consciousness increasingly influenced by Western values.

Rammohan Roy's most influential successor was Swami Vivekananda (1862–1902), who carried a form of Neo-Vedanta to America. In 1883 (the same year that Richard Burton published the first English translation of the *Kamasutra*), a Brahmo Samaj leader named Protap Chunder Mozoomdar visited America, initiating the Hindu mission movement there.[60] In 1893, at the World's Parliament of Religions, Vivekananda brought Vedanta to Chicago. Vivekananda's Hinduism jettisoned much of the worldly and erotic path of Hindu polytheism (doctrines, dogmas, rituals, books, oral traditions, and temples) in order to extract a universal essence of "spirituality." He influenced Hindus far beyond the bounds of the Brahmo Samaj, inspiring the form of Neo-Vedanta called Sanatana Dharma (Eternal or Universal Dharma) embraced by many Hindus to this day. Sanatana Dharma is the banner of Hindutva, which presides over the censorship of art, film, literature, and social behavior.

The British, even after 1947, continued to shackle Indian freedom of expression through the Film Censor Board, which, from the early 1950s, implemented a policy basis that had roots among the Raj administrators (who had worried more about sedition than about sex). The Film Censor Board's concern for visual pedagogy, nationalism, and publicity broadcast a shadow that extended over Indian visual arts and literature as well as film.

Hindu attitudes toward sexuality were further confused by the very public, and very contradictory, sexuality of the man who was one of the most important Hindus of the twentieth century, Mahatma Gandhi. Gandhi's insistence on celibacy among his disciples caused difficulty for some of them, as did his habit of sleeping beside girls young enough to be called jailbait in the United States, to test or prove his own celibate control. His practice drew not so much upon the Upanishadic and Vaishnava ascetic traditions, which were the source of many of Gandhi's practices, as upon the hydraulic Tantric techniques of internalizing power, indeed creating quasi-magical powers, by first stirring up the sexual energies and then withholding semen. Gandhi was a one-man model of the perennial Hindu attempt to deal with sexuality by driving with one foot on the accelerator and one foot on the brake.

In the nineteenth and twentieth centuries, liberal Indian intellectuals, who noticed the shift in attitudes to Hinduism's erotic past from appreciation to embarrassment, tended to explain contemporary Hindu prudery in terms of power and patronage from the past. As James McConnachie summarized this attitude, "Erotic literature had been the creation of poets and princes, the argument ran, and as 'lascivious' Hindu despots had given way to 'fanatical' Mughal overlords, the patronage on which erotic literature depended had withered and died."[61] V. S. Naipaul in his *Half a Life* offers his own, rather jaded, version of this accusation: "In our culture there is no seduction. Our marriages are arranged. There is no art of sex. Some of the boys here talk to me of the *Kama Sutra*. Nobody talked about that at home. It was an upper-caste text, but I don't believe my poor father, brahmin though he is, ever looked at a copy. That philosophical-practical way of dealing with sex belongs to our past, and that world was ravaged and destroyed by the Muslims."[62] And then (the twisted, chauvinist argument goes), then came the British missionaries, adding insult to injury. Thus, nationalists blamed India's sexual conservatism on "an unholy combination of imposed Muslim religiosity and imported British 'Victorianism.'"[63]

There is some truth in that general historical argument, but it has three serious flaws. First, as for the Mughals, it ignores the enthusiasm for the erotic arts on the part of such Muslims as the Lodi dynasty in the sixteenth century, who commissioned one of the last great works of Sanskrit eroticism, the *Ananga Ranga*,[64] and the Mughals, who had textbooks of Hindu erotic arts and religious texts translated from Sanskrit to Persian and illustrated with Persian painting techniques. The nationalists dismissed all of this, ungenerously, as "the last, valedictory flourishing of a tragically deracinated tradition." Second, blaming the British for Hindu prudery allows the very real memory of missionary puritanism and the racist snobbery of the Raj club culture to overpower the equally important role of other sorts of Brits in the rediscovery of India's erotic heritage.[65] Most of all, blaming the Muslims and the British ignores the history of native Hindu anti-eroticism. For, as we have seen, India had its own homegrown traditions of prudery in opposition to its own sensuality.

The Fall of Kama and the Rise of Karma

An adolescent girl in Vikram Chandra's story "Kama" says, "Sister Carmina didn't want to tell us. It's the *Kama Sutra*, which she says isn't in the library. But Gisela's parents have a copy which they think is hidden away on the top of their shelf. We looked it up there." And the adult to whom she tells this says, "You put that book back where you found it. And don't read any more."[66] In India today, people will often give a copy of the *Kamasutra* as a wedding present, to demonstrate their open-mindedness and sophistication, but most people will merely sneak a surreptitious look at it in someone else's house.

And on the public scene, "a Hindu-nationalist Health Minister can insist that the 'Indian traditions' of abstinence and fidelity are more effective barriers against HIV than condoms; and . . . the 1860 Penal Code [still in effect] defines all extramarital sex as criminal."[67] These are the Hindus in India but also increasingly in the American diaspora who advocate a sanitized, "spiritual" form of Hinduism (and, in India, a nationalist and anti-Muslim form). For such Hindus, the problem is not (as it was for some liberal Indian intellectuals) how to explain how India lost its appreciation of eroticism but, on the contrary, how to maintain that Hinduism was always the pure-minded, anti-erotic, ascetic tradition that it became, for many upper-class Hindus, in the nineteenth century. One way to make this argument was to swing to the other side of the pendulum and blame the British not for *suppressing* Indian eroticism but for *causing* it. Under Nehru, the Indian government passed a penal code of sexual repression, Article 377, which prohibits "sexual relations against nature with a man, woman, or animal, whether the intercourse is anal or oral." Nehru insisted that "such vices in India were due to Western influence."[68] The irony is that in aping the Muslim and British scorn for Indian sexuality, contemporary Hindus who favor censorship are surrendering their own identity, letting foreign ideas about Hinduism (and Protestant fundamentalist ideas about censorship) triumph over and drive out native Hindu ideas about and pride in their own religion and in the diversity and tolerance that have always characterized the world of the mind in Hinduism. Among the other bad habits they picked up from the West—from seeds sown, perhaps, during colonization but flowering only in the more recent contacts with American imperialism—was the habit of censorship. Never before has the old tension between the erotic and ascetic strains of Hinduism taken the form of one path telling the other path that it has no right to exist.

But the India of the ancient erotic past is not so easily stamped out. Even in the nineteenth century, most Hindus on the path that celebrated the earthier aspects of life did not even know that the Anglophone Hindus regarded them as either beneath contempt or entirely nonexistent. They went on worshipping their gods, singing their songs, telling their stories. And now they live on in "a reported two-thirds of young adults who would have casual, premarital sex before an arranged marriage" and who, since 1991, can buy condoms called *KamaSutra*.[69]

Notes

1. Binoy Valsan, "Baroda Art Student's Work Stirs Up Religious Controversy," *Rediff India Abroad*, May 10, 2007.

2. Anil Dharker, "Beauty and the Beast: Baroda Episode Underscores Threat to Creative Expression," *Mainstream* 45, no. 23 (May 25, 2007).

3. Dharker, "Beauty and the Beast."

4. Richard Philips and Waruna Alahakoon, "Hindu Chauvinists Block Filming of Deepa Mehta's *Water*," World Socialist Web Site, February 12, 2000, http://www.wsws.org/articles/2000/feb2000/film-f12.shtml.

5. Dharker, "Beauty and the Beast."

6. Sandhya Bordewekar, interview with Shivaji K. Panikkar and Chandramohan, *Artindia* 12, no. 3 (2007): 61–67.

7. *Brihadaranyaka Upanishad*, in *Early Upanishads*, ed. and trans. Patrick Olivelle (New York: Oxford University Press, 1998), 6.2.13, 6.4.3.

8. David White, *Kiss of the Yogini: "Tantric Sex" in Its South Asian Contexts* (Chicago: University of Chicago Press, 2003), 220.

9. Yigal Bronner, *Extreme Poetry: The South Asian Movement of Simultaneous Narration* (New York: Columbia University Press, 2010).

10. A. K. Ramanujan, V. Narayana Rao, and David Shulman, *When God Is a Customer* (Berkeley: University of California Press, 1994), 117–118.

11. Vatsyayana, *The Kamasutra of Vatsyayana*, trans. Wendy Doniger and Sudhir Kakar (London and New York: Oxford World Classics, 2002), section 2.2.20.

12. Vatsyayana, 1.3.1–11.

13. Vatsyayana, 3.2.35, 4.2.31–35.

14. Manu, *Laws of Manu*, trans. Wendy Doniger with Brian K. Smith (Harmondsworth: Penguin Classics, 1991), section 5.154.

15. Vatsyayana, *Kamasutra*, 2.8.16.

16. Vatsyayana, 2.8.17.

17. Vatsyayana, 2.1.23–30.

18. Vatsyayana, 3.4.36–47.

19. Vatsyayana, 1.1.11.

20. Vatsyayana, 1.1.11.

21. On the ritual bath, see Manu, *Laws*, 11.174. On the fine, see Kautilya, *Arthashastra*, ed. and trans. R. P. Kangle (Bombay: University of Bombay, 1960), 3.18.4.

22. Kautilya, *Arthashastra*, 1.21.1–2.

23. *Bhagavad Gita*, 2.3.

24. Alan Bray, *Homosexuality in Renaissance England* (New York: Columbia University Press, 1996).

25. Vatsyayana, *Kamasutra*, 2.9.1–5.

26. Vatsyayana, 2.9.6–11.

27. Vatsyayana, 2.2.27–28.

28. Vatsyayana, 2.3.31.

29. Vatsyayana, 2.4.12–13.

30. Vatsyayana, 3.2.3.

31. Vatsyayana, 3.2.4–6.
32. Vatsyayana, 2.1.26.
33. Vatsyayana, 1.5.27.
34. Vatsyayana, 5.6.2–4.
35. Vatsyayana, 5.6.2.
36. Vatsyayana, 7.1.20.
37. Manu, *Laws*, 8.369–370.
38. Vatsyayana, *Kamasutra*, 2.8.41.
39. Vatsyayana, 5.4.15.
40. Vatsyayana, 2.9.35–36.
41. Vatsyayana, 1.1.11.
42. The title page read: "The Kama Sutra of Vatsyayana, Translated from the Sanskrit. In Seven Parts, with Preface, Introduction and Concluding Remarks. Cosmopoli: 1883: for the Kama Shastra Society of London and Benares, and for private circulation only."
43. Fawn M. Brodie, *The Devil Drives: A Life of Sir Richard Burton* (New York: Ballantine, 1967), 358.
44. William G. Archer, "Preface," *Kama Sutra* (London: George Allen and Unwin, 1963).
45. Brodie, *Devil Drives*, 357.
46. W. H. Auden, *Collected Poems* (New York: Random House, 2007), 225.
47. Vatsyayana, *Kamasutra*, 2.8.1.
48. Sir Richard Francis Burton, *The Kama Sutra of Vatsyayana: The Classic Hindu Treatise on Love and Social Conduct* (New York: E. P. Dutton, 1962), 121.
49. Vatsyayana, *Kamasutra*, 2.8.1.
50. Vatsyayana, 2.7.20.
51. Burton, *Kama Sutra*, 117–118.
52. Vatsyayana, *Kamasutra*, 4.1.19–21.
53. Burton, *Kama Sutra*, 160.
54. Vatsyayana, *Kamasutra*, 1.5.27.
55. Serena Nanda, *Neither Man nor Woman: The Hijras of India* (Belmont, CA: Wadsworth, 1990).
56. Archer, "Preface," 17; Brodie, *Devil Drives*, 369.
57. Brodie, *Devil Drives*, 370.
58. Bombay (Presidency). Supreme Court, *Report of the Maharaj Libel Case and of the Bhattia Conspiracy Case* (Bombay: Bombay Gazette Press, 1862), 213.
59. Ashis Nandy, *The Intimate Enemy: Loss and Recovery of Self under Colonialism* (Delhi: Oxford University Press, 1983).
60. Sunrit Mullick, *The First Hindu Mission to America: The Pioneering Visits of Protap Chunder Mozoomdar* (New Delhi: Northern Book Centre, 2010).
61. James McConnachie, *The Book of Love: In Search of the Kamasutra* (London: Atlantic, 2007), 197–198.
62. V. S. Naipaul, *Half a Life* (New York: Vintage Books, 2002), 110.

63. McConnachie, *Book of Love*, 197–198.
64. McConnachie, 55. 57.
65. McConnachie, 197–198.
66. Vikram Chandra, *Love and Longing in Bombay* (Boston, MA: Little, Brown and Company, 1997), 126.
67. McConnachie, *Book of Love*, 228.
68. McConnachie, 209.
69. McConnachie, 229.

CHAPTER 6

Bodies in Alliance and the Politics of the Street

Judith Butler

In the last months there have been, time and again, mass demonstrations on the street, in the square, and though these are very often motivated by different political purposes, something similar happens: bodies congregate, they move and speak together, and they lay claim to a certain space as public space.[1] Now, it would be easier to say that these demonstrations or, indeed, these movements, are characterized by bodies that come together to make a claim in public space, but that formulation presumes that public space is given, that it is already public, and recognized as such. We miss something of the point of public demonstrations, if we fail to see that the very public character of the space is being disputed and even fought over when these crowds gather. Although these movements have depended on the prior existence of pavement, street, and square, and have often enough gathered in squares, like Tahrir, whose political history is potent, it is equally true that the collective actions collect the space itself, gather the pavement, and animate and organize the architecture. As much as we must insist on there being material conditions for public assembly and public speech, we have also to ask how it is that assembly and speech reconfigure the materiality of public space, and produce, or reproduce, the public character of that material environment. And when crowds move outside the square, to the side street or the back alley, to the neighborhoods where streets are not yet paved, then something more happens. At such a moment, politics is no longer defined as the exclusive business of public sphere distinct from a private one, but it crosses that line again and again, bringing attention to the way that politics is already in the home, or on the street, or in the neighborhood, or indeed in those virtual spaces that are unbound by the architecture of the public square. When we think about what it means to assemble in a crowd, a growing crowd, and what it means to move through public space in a way that contests the distinction between public and private, we see some way that bodies in their plurality lay claim to the public, find and produce the public through seizing and reconfiguring the matter of material environments; at the same time, those material environments are part of the action, and they themselves act when they become the support for action. In the same way, when trucks or tanks suddenly become platforms for speakers, then the material environment is actively reconfigured and refunctioned, to use the Brechtian term. And our ideas of action then, need to be rethought. In the first instance, no one mobilizes a claim to move and assemble freely without moving and assembling together with others. In the second instance, the square and the street are not only the material supports for action, but they themselves are part of any theory of public and corporeal action that we might propose. Human action depends upon all sorts of supports—it is always supported action. But in the case of public assemblies, we see quite clearly not only that there is a struggle over what will be public space, but a struggle as well over those basic ways in which we are, as bodies, supported in the world—a struggle against disenfranchisement, effacement, and abandonment.

Of course, this produces a quandary. We cannot act without supports, and yet we must struggle for the supports that allow us to act. Of course, it was the Roman idea of the public square that formed the background for understanding the rights of assembly and free speech, to the deliberate forms of participatory democracy. Hannah Arendt surely had the Roman Republic in mind when she claimed that all political action requires the "space of appearance." She writes, for instance, "the Polis, properly speaking, is not the city-state in its physical location; it is the organization of the people as it arises out of acting and speaking together, and its true space lies between people living together for this purpose, no matter where they happen to be." The "true" space then lies "between the people" which means that as much as any action takes place somewhere located, it also establishes a space that belongs properly to alliance itself. For Arendt, this alliance is not tied to its location. In fact, alliance brings about its own location, highly transposable. She writes, "action and speech create a space between the participants which can find its proper location almost anywhere and anytime."[2] How do we understand this highly transposable conception of political space? Whereas Arendt maintains that politics requires the space of appearance, she also claims that space is precisely what politics brings about: "it is the space of appearance in the widest sense of the word, namely, the space where I appear to others as others appear to me, where men [sic] exist not merely like other living or inanimate things but make their appearance explicitly." Something of what she says here is clearly true. Space and location are created through plural action. And yet, her view suggests that action, in its freedom and its power, has the exclusive power to create location. And such a view forgets or refuses that action is always supported, and that it is invariably bodily, even in its virtual forms. The material supports for action are not only part of action, but they are also what is being fought about, especially in those cases when the political struggle is about food, employment, mobility, and access to institutions. To rethink the space of appearance in order to understand the power and effect of public demonstrations for our time, we will need to understand the bodily dimensions of action, what the body requires, and what the body can do, especially when we must think about bodies together, what holds them there, their conditions of persistence and of power.

This evening I would like to think about this space of appearance and to ask what itinerary must we travel to move from the space of appearance to the contemporary politics of the street? Even as I say this, I cannot hope to gather all the forms of demonstration we have seen, some of which are episodic, some of which are part of ongoing and recurrent social and political movements, and some of which are revolutionary. I hope to think about what might gather these gatherings, these public demonstrations during the winter of 2011 against tyrannical regimes in North Africa and the Middle East, but also against the escalating precarization of working peoples in Europe and in the Southern hemisphere, the struggles for public education throughout the United States and Europe, and those struggles to make the street safe for women, gender, and sexual minorities, including trans people, whose public appearance is too often punishable by legal and illegal violence. Very often the claim that is being made is that the streets must be made safe from the police who are complicit in criminality, especially on those occasions when the police support criminal regimes, or when, for instance, the police commit the very crimes against sexual and gender minorities that they are supposed to stop. Demonstrations are one of the few ways that police power is overcome, especially when they become too large and too mobile to be contained by police power, and when they have the resources to regenerate themselves. Perhaps these are anarchist moments or anarchist passages, when the legitimacy of a regime is called into question, but when no new regime has yet come to take its place. This time of the interval is the time of the popular will, not a single will, not a unitary will, but one that is characterized by an alliance with the performative power to lay claim to the public in a way that is not yet codified into law and that can never be fully codified into law. How do we understand this acting together that opens up time and space outside and against the temporality and established architecture of the regime, one that lays claim to materiality, leans into its supports, draws from its supports, in order to rework their functions? Such an action reconfigures what will be public, and what will be the space of politics.

Arendt's view is confounded by its own gender politics, relying as it does on a distinction between the public and private domain that leaves the sphere of politics to men, and reproductive labor to women. If there is a body in the public sphere, it is masculine and unsupported, presumptively free to create, but not itself created. And the body in the private sphere is female, aging, foreign, or childish, and pre-political. Although she was, as we know from the important work of Adriana Cavarero, a philosopher of natality, Arendt understood this capacity to bring something into being as a function of political speech and action. Indeed, when male citizens enter into the public square to debate questions of justice, revenge, war, and emancipation, they take the illuminated public square for granted as the architecturally bounded theater of their speech. Their speech becomes the paradigmatic form of action, physically cut off from the private domicile, itself shrouded in darkness and reproduced through activities that are not quite action in the proper and public senses. Men make the passage from that private darkness to that public light and once illuminated, they speak, and their speech interrogates the principles of justice it articulates, becoming itself a form of critical inquiry and democratic participation. For Arendt, rethinking this scene within political modernity, their speech is understood as the bodily and linguistic exercise of rights. Bodily and linguistic—how are we to understand these terms and their intertwining here?

For politics to take place, the body must appear. I appear to others, and they appear to me, which means that some space between us allows each to appear. We are not simply visual phenomena for each other—our voices must be registered, and so we must be heard; rather, who we are, bodily, is already a way of being "for" the other, appearing in ways that we cannot see, being a body for another in a way that I cannot be for myself, and so dispossessed, perspectivally, by our very sociality. I must appear to others in ways for which I cannot give an account, and in this way my body establishes a perspective that I cannot inhabit. This is an important point, because it is not the case that the body only establishes my own perspective; it is also that which displaces that perspective and makes that displacement into a necessity. This happens most clearly when we think about bodies that act together. No one body establishes the space of appearance, but this action, this performative exercise happens only "between" bodies, in a space that constitutes the gap between my own body and another's. In this way, my body does not act alone, when it acts politically. Indeed, the action emerged from the "between."

For Arendt, the body is not primarily located in space but, with others, brings about a new space. And the space that is created is precisely between those who act together. The space of appearance is not for her only an architectural given: "the space of appearance comes into being," she writes, "wherever men are together in the manner of speech and action, and therefore predates and precedes all formal constitution of the public realm and the various forms of government, that is, the various forms in which the public realm can be organized."[3] In other words, this space of appearance is not a location that can be separated from the plural action that brings it about. And yet, if we are to accept this view, we have to understand how the plurality that acts is itself constituted. How does a plurality form, and what material supports are necessary for that formation? Who enters this plurality, and who does not, and how are such matters decided? Can anyone and everyone act in such a way that this space is brought about? She makes clear that "this space does not always exist" and acknowledges that in the classical Polis, the slave, the foreigner, and the barbarian were excluded from such a space, which means that they could not become part of a plurality that brought this space into being. This means that part of the population did not appear, did not emerge into the space of appearance. And here we can see that the space of appearance was already divided, already apportioned, if the space of appearance was precisely that which was defined, in part, by their exclusion. This is no small problem since it means that one must already be in the space in order to bring the space of appearance into being—which means that a power operates prior to any performative power exercised by a plurality. Further, in her view, to be deprived of the space of appearance is to be deprived of reality. In other words, we must appear to others in ways that we ourselves cannot know, that we must become available to a perspective that established by a body that is not our own. And if we ask, where do we appear? Or where are we when we appear? It will be over there, between us, in a space that exists only because we are more than one, more than two, plural and embodied. The body, defined politically, is precisely organized by a perspective that is not one's own and is, in that sense, already elsewhere, for another, and so in departure from oneself.

On this account of the body in political space, how do we make sense of those who can never be part of that concerted action, who remain outside the plurality that acts? How do we describe their action and their status as beings disaggregated from the plural; what political language do we have in reserve for describing that exclusion? Are they the de-animated "givens" of political life, mere life or bare life? Are we to say that those who are excluded are simply unreal, or that they have no being at all—the socially dead, the spectral? Do such formulations denote a state of having been made destitute by existing political arrangements, or is this the destitution that is revealed outside the political sphere itself? In other words, are the destitute outside of politics and power, or are they in fact living out a specific form of political destitution? How we answer that question seems important since if we claim that the destitute are outside of the sphere of politics—reduced to depoliticized forms of being—then we implicitly accept that the dominant ways of establishing the political are right. In some ways, this follows from the Arendtian position which adopts the internal point of view of the Greek Polis on what politics should be, who should gain entry into the public square and who should remain in the private sphere. Such a view disregards and devalues those forms of political agency that emerge precisely in those domains deemed pre-political or extra-political. One reason we cannot let the political body that produces such exclusions furnish the conception of politics itself, setting the parameters for what counts as political—is that within the purview established by the Polis those outside its defining plurality are considered as unreal or unrealized and, hence, outside the political as such.

The impetus for Giorgio Agamben's notion of "bare life" derives from this very conception of the polis in Arendt's political philosophy and, I would suggest, runs the risk of this very problem: if we seek to take account of exclusion itself as a political problem, as part of politics itself, then it will not do to say that once excluded, those beings lack appearance or "reality" in political terms, that they have no social or political standing, or are cast out and reduced to mere being (forms of givenness precluded from the sphere of action). Nothing so metaphysically extravagant has to happen if we agree that one reason the sphere of the political cannot be defined by the classic conception of the Polis, is that we are then deprived of having and using a language for those forms of agency and resistance that focus on the politics of exclusion itself or, indeed, against those regimes of power that maintain the stateless and disenfranchised in conditions of destitution. Few matters could be more politically consequential.

Although Agamben borrows from Foucault to articulate a conception of the biopolitical, the thesis of "bare life" remains untouched by that conception. As a result, we cannot within that vocabulary describe the modes of agency and action undertaken by the stateless, the occupied, and the disenfranchised, since even the life stripped of rights is still within the sphere of the political, and is thus not reduced to mere being, but is, more often than not, angered, indignant, rising up and resisting. To be outside established and legitimate political structures is still to be saturated in power relations, and this saturation is the point of departure for a theory of the political that includes dominant and subjugated forms, modes of inclusion and legitimation as well as modes of delegitimation and effacement.

Luckily, I think Arendt does not consistently follow this model from *The Human Condition*, which is why, for instance, in the early 1960s she turns her attention to the fate of refugees and the stateless and comes to assert in that context the right to have rights. The right to have rights is one that depends on no existing particular political organization for its legitimacy. In her words, the right to have rights predates and precedes any political institution that might codify or seek to guarantee that right; at the same time, it is derived from no natural set of laws. The right comes into being when it is exercised, and exercised by those who act in concert, in alliance.

Those who are excluded from existing polities, who belong to no nation-state or other contemporary state formation may be "unreal" only by those who seek to monopolize the terms of reality. And yet even after the public sphere has been defined through their exclusion, they act. Whether abandoned to precarity or left to die through systematic negligence, concerted action still emerges from such sites. And this is what we see, for instance, when undocumented workers amass on the street without the legal right to do so, when populations lay claim to a public square that has belonged to the military, or when the refugees take place in collective uprisings demanding shelter, food, and rights of mobility, when populations amass, without the protection of the law and without permits to demonstrate, to bring down an unjust or criminal regime of law or to protest austerity measures that destroy the possibility of employment and education for many.

Indeed, in the public demonstrations that often follow from acts of public mourning, especially in Syria in recent months where crowds of mourners become targets of military destruction, we can see how the existing public space is seized by those who have no existing right to gather there, and whose lives are exposed to violence and death in the course of gathering as they do. Indeed, it is their right to gather free of intimidation and threat of violence that is systematically attacked by the police or by the army or by mercenaries on hire by both the state and corporate powers. To attack the body is to attack the right itself, since the right is precisely what is exercised by the body on the street. Although the bodies on the street are vocalizing their opposition to the legitimacy of the state, they are also, by virtue of occupying that space, repeating that occupation of space, and persisting in that occupation of space, posing the challenge in corporeal terms, which means that when the body "speaks" politically, it is not only in vocal or written language. The persistence of the body calls that legitimacy into question and does so precisely through a performativity of the body that crosses language without ever quite reducing to language. In other words, it is not that bodily action and gesture have to be translated into language, but that both action and gesture signify and speak, as action and claim, and that the one is not finally extricable from the other. Where the legitimacy of the state is brought into question precisely by that way of appearing in public, the body itself exercises a right that is no right; in other words, it exercises a right that is being actively contested and destroyed by military force, and which, in its resistance to force, articulates its persistence, and its right to persistence. This right is codified nowhere. It is not granted from elsewhere or by existing law, even if it sometimes finds support precisely there. It is, in fact, the right to have rights, not as natural law or metaphysical stipulation, but as the persistence of the body against those forces that seek to monopolize legitimacy. A persistence that requires the mobilization of space, and that cannot happen without a set of material supports mobilized and mobilizing.

Just to be clear: I am not referring to a vitalism or a right to life as such. Rather, I am suggesting that political claims are made by bodies as they appear and act, as they refuse and as they persist under conditions in which that fact alone is taken to be an act of delegitimation of the state. It is not that bodies are simply mute life-forces that counter existing modalities of power. Rather, they are themselves modalities of power, embodied interpretations, engaging in allied action. On one hand, these bodies are productive and performative. On the other hand, they can only persist and act when they are supported, by environments, by nutrition, by work, by modes of sociality and belonging. And when these supports fall away, they are mobilized in another way, seizing upon the supports that exist in order to make a claim that there can be no embodied life without social and institutional support, without ongoing employment, without networks of interdependency and care. They struggle not only for the idea of social support and political enfranchisement, but their struggle takes on a social form of its own. And so, in the most ideal instances, an alliance enacts the social order it seeks to bring about, but when this happens, and it does happen, we have to be mindful of two important caveats. The first is that the alliance is not reducible to individuals, and it is not individuals who act. The second is that action in alliance happens precisely between those who participate, and this is not an ideal or empty space—it is the space of support itself—of durable and livable material environments and of interdependency among living beings. I will move toward this last idea toward the end of my remarks this evening. But let us return to the demonstrations, in their logic and in their instances.

It is not only that many of the massive demonstrations and modes of resistance we have seen in the last months produce a space of appearance, they also seize upon an already established space permeated by existing power, seeking to sever the relation between the public space, the public square, and the existing regime. The limits of the political are exposed, and the link between the theater of legitimacy and public space is severed; that theater is no longer unproblematically housed in public space, since public space now occurs in the midst of another action, one that displaces the power that claims legitimacy precisely by taking over the field of its effects. Simply put, the bodies on the street redeploy the space of appearance in order to contest and negate the existing forms of political legitimacy—and just as they sometimes fill or take over public space, the material history of those structures also work on them, and become part of their very action, remaking a history in the midst of its most concrete and sedimented artifices. These are subjugated and empowered actors who seek to wrest legitimacy from an existing state apparatus that depends upon the public space of appearance for its theatrical self-constitution. In wresting that power, a new space is created, a new "between" of bodies, as it were, that lays claim to existing space through the action of a new alliance, and those bodies are seized and animated by those existing spaces in the very acts by which they reclaim and resignify their meanings.

For this contestation to work, there has to be a hegemonic struggle over what we are calling the space of appearance. Such a struggle intervenes in the spatial organization of power, which includes the allocation and restriction of spatial locations in which and by which any population may appear, which means that there is a spatial restriction on when and how the "popular will" may appear. This view of the spatial restriction and allocation of who may appear, in effect, who may become a subject of appearance, suggests an operation of power that works through both foreclosure and differential allocation. How is such an idea of power, and its corollary idea of politics, to be reconciled with the Arendtian proposition that politics requires not only entering into a space of appearance, but an active participation in the making of the space of appearance itself. And further, I would add, it requires a way of acting in the midst of being formed by that history and its material structures.

One can see the operation of a strong performative in Arendt's work—in acting, we bring the space of politics into being, understood as the space of appearance. It is a divine performative allocated to the human form. But as a result, she cannot account for the ways in which the established architecture and topographies of power act upon us and enter into our very action, sometimes foreclosing our entry into the political sphere or making us differentially apparent within that sphere. And yet, to work within these two forms of power, we have to think about bodies in ways that Arendt does not do, and we have to think about space as acting on us, even as we act within it, or even when sometimes our actions, considered as plural or collective, bring it into being.

If we consider what it is to appear, it follows that we appear to someone, and that our appearance has to be registered by the senses, not only our own, but someone else's, or those of some larger group. For the Arendtian position, it follows that to act and speak politically we must "appear" to one another in some way, that is to say, that to appear is always to appear for another, which means that for the body to exist politically, it has to assume a social dimension—it is comported outside itself and toward others in ways that cannot and do not ratify individualism.

Assuming that we are living and embodied organisms when we speak and act, the organism assumes social and political form in the space of appearance. This does not mean that we overcome or negate some biological status to assume a social one; on the contrary, the organic bodies that we are require a sustaining social world in order to persist. And this means that as biological creatures who seek to persist, we are necessarily dependent on social relations and institutions that address the basic needs for food, shelter, and protection from violence, to name a few. No monadic body simply persists on its own, but if it persists, it is in the context of a sustaining set of relations. If we approach the question of the biopolitical in this way, we can see that the space of appearance does not belong to a sphere of politics separate from a sphere of survival and of need. When the question of the survival not only of individuals, but whole populations, is at issue, then the political issue has to do with whether and how a social and political formation addresses the demand to provide for basic needs such as shelter and food as well as protection against violence. And the question for a critical and contesting politics has to do with how basic goods are distributed, how life itself is allocated, and how the unequal distribution of the value and grievability of life is instituted by targeted warfare as well as systematic forms of exploitation or negligence, which render populations differentially precarious and disposable.

A quite problematic division of labor is at work in Arendt's position, which is why we must rethink her position for our times. If we appear, we must be seen, which means that our bodies must be viewed, and their vocalized sounds must be heard: the body must enter the visual and audible field. But we have to ask why, if this is so, the body is itself divided into the one that appears publicly to speak and act, and another, sexual and laboring, feminine, foreign, and mute, that generally relegated to the private and pre-political sphere. That latter body operates as a precondition for appearance, and so becomes the structuring absence that governs and makes possible the public sphere. If we are living organisms who speak and act, then we are clearly related to a vast continuum or network of living beings; we not only live among them, but our persistence as living organisms depends on that matrix of sustaining interdependent relations. And yet, if our speaking and acting distinguishes us as something separate from that corporeal realm (raised earlier by the question of whether our capacity to think politically depends on one sort of *physei* or another), we have to ask how such a duality between action and body can be preserved if and when the "living" word and "actual" deed—both clearly political—so clearly presuppose the presence and action of a living human body, one whose life is bound up with other living processes. It may be that two senses of the body are at work for Arendt—one that appears in public, and another that is "sequestered" in private—and that the public body is one that makes itself known as the figure of the speaking subject, one whose speech is also action. The private body never appears as such, since it is preoccupied with the repetitive labor of reproducing the material conditions of life. The private body thus conditions the public body, and even though they are the same body, the bifurcation is crucial to maintaining the public and private distinction. Perhaps this is a kind of fantasy that one dimension of bodily life can and must remain out of sight, and yet another, fully distinct, appears in public? But is there no trace of the biological that appears as such, and could we not argue, with Bruno Latour and Isabelle Stengers, that negotiating the sphere of appearance is a biological thing to do, since there is no way of navigating an environment or procuring food without appearing bodily in the world, and there is no escape from the vulnerability and mobility that appearing in the world implies? In other words, is appearance not a necessarily morphological moment where the body appears, and not only in order to speak and act but also to suffer and to move, to engage others' bodies, to negotiate an environment on which one depends? Indeed, the body can appear and signify in ways that contest the way it speaks, or even contest speaking as its paradigmatic instance. Indeed, could we still understand action, gesture, stillness, touch, and moving together, if they were all reducible to the vocalization of thought through speech?

Indeed, this act of public speaking, even within that problematic division of labor, *depends upon* a dimension of bodily life that is given, passive, opaque, and so excluded from the realm of the political. Hence, we can ask, what regulation keeps the given body from spilling over into the active body? Are these two different bodies, and what politics is required to keep them apart? Are these two different dimensions of the same body, or are these, in fact, the effect of a certain regulation of bodily appearance that is actively contested by new social movements, struggles against sexual violence, for reproductive freedom, against precarity, for the freedom of mobility? Here we can see that a certain topographical or even architectural regulation of the body happens at the level of theory. Significantly, it is precisely this operation of power—foreclosure and differential allocation of whether and how the body may appear—which is excluded from Arendt's explicit account of the political. Indeed, her explicit account of the political depends upon that very operation of power that it fails to consider as part of politics itself.

What I accept is the following: Freedom does not come from me or from you; it can and does happen as a relation between us or, indeed, among us. This is not a matter of finding the human dignity within each person, but rather of understanding the human as a relational and social being, one whose action depends upon equality and articulates the principle of equality. Indeed, there is no human on her view if there is no equality. No human can be human alone. And no human can be human without acting in concert with others and on conditions of equality. I would add the following: The claim of equality is not only spoken or written, but is made precisely when bodies appear together or, rather, when, through their action, they bring the space of appearance into being. This space is a feature and effect of action, and it only works, according to Arendt, when relations of equality are maintained.

Of course, there are many reasons to be suspicious of idealized moments, but there are also reasons to be wary of any analysis that is fully guarded against idealization. There are two aspects of the revolutionary demonstrations in Tahrir square that I would like to underscore. The first has to do with the way a certain sociability was established within the square, a division of labor that broke down gender difference, that involved rotating who would speak and who would clean the areas where people slept and ate, developing a work schedule for everyone to maintain the environment and to clean the toilets. In short, what some would call "horizontal relations" among the protestors formed easily and methodically, and quickly it seemed that relations of equality, which included an equal division of labor between the sexes, became part of the very resistance to Mubarak's regime and its entrenched hierarchies, including the extraordinary differentials of wealth between the military and corporate sponsors of the regime and the working people. The social form of the resistance began to incorporate principles of equality that governed not only how and when people spoke and acted for the media and against the regime but how people cared for their various quarters within the square, the beds on pavement, the makeshift medical stations and bathrooms, the places where people ate, and the places where people were exposed to violence from the outside. These actions were all political in the simple sense that they were breaking down a conventional distinction between public and private in order to establish relations of equality; in this sense, they were incorporating into the very social form of resistance the principles for which they were struggling on the street.

Second, when up against violent attacks or extreme threats, many people chanted the word *silmiyya*, which comes from the root verb, *salima*, which means to be safe and sound, unharmed, unimpaired, intact, safe, and secure; but also, to be unobjectionable, blameless, faultless; and yet also, to be certain, established, clearly proven. The term comes from the noun *silm*, which means "peace" but also, interchangeably and significantly, "the religion of Islam." One variant of the term is *hubb as-silm* which is Arabic for "pacifism." Most usually, the chanting of *silmiyya* comes across as a gentle exhortation: "peaceful, peaceful." Although the revolution was for the most part nonviolent, it was not necessarily led by a principled opposition to violence. Rather, the collective chant was a way of encouraging people to resist the mimetic pull of military aggression—and the aggression of the gangs—by keeping in mind the larger goal—radical democratic change. To be swept into a violent exchange of the moment was to lose the patience needed to realize the revolution. What interests me here is the chant, the way in which language worked not to incite an action but to restrain one. A restraint in the name of an emerging community of equals whose primary way of doing politics would not be violence

Of course, Tahrir Square is a place, and we can locate it quite precisely on the map of Cairo. At the same time, we find questions posed throughout the media: will the Palestinians have their Tahrir square? Where is the Tahrir Square in India? To name but a few. It is located, and it is transposable; indeed, it seemed to be transposable from the start, though never completely. And, of course, we cannot think the transposability of those bodies in the square without the media. In some ways, the media images from Tunisia prepared the way for the media events in Tahrir and then those that followed in Yemen, Bahrain, Syria, and Libya, all of which took different trajectories, and take them still. As you know many of the public demonstrations of these last months have not been against military dictatorships or tyrannical regimes. They have also been against the monopoly capitalism, neoliberalism, and the suppression of political rights, and in the name of those who are abandoned by neoliberal reforms that seek to dismantle forms of social democracy and socialism, that eradicate jobs, expose populations to poverty, and undermine the basic right to a public education.

The street scenes become politically potent only when and if we have a visual and audible version of the scene communicated in live time, so that the media does not merely report the scene but is part of the scene and the action; indeed, the media *is* the scene or the space in its extended and replicable visual and audible dimensions. One way of stating this is simply that the media extends the scene visually and audibly and participates in the delimitation and transposability of the scene. Put differently, the media constitutes the scene in a time and place that includes and exceeds its local instantiation. Although the scene is surely and emphatically local, and those who are elsewhere have the sense that they are getting some direct access through the images and sounds they receive. That is true, but they do not know how the editing takes place, which scene conveys and travels, and which scenes remain obdurately outside the frame. When the scene does travel, it is both there *and* here, and if it were not spanning both locations—indeed, multiple locations—it would not be the scene that it is. Its locality is not denied by the fact that the scene is communicated beyond itself, and so constituted in a global media; it depends on that mediation to take place as the event that it is. This means that the local must be recast outside itself in order to be established as local, and this means that it is only through a certain globalizing media that the local can be established, and that something can really happen there. Of course, many things do happen outside the frame of the camera or other digital media devices, and the media can just as easily implement censorship as oppose it. There are many local events that are never recorded and broadcast and some important reasons why. But when the event does travel and manages to summon and sustain global outrage and pressure, which includes the power to stop markets or to sever diplomatic relations, then the local will have to be established time and again in a circuitry that exceeds the local at every instant. And yet, there remains something localized that cannot and does not travel in that way; and the scene could not be the scene if we did not understand that some people are at risk, and the risk is run precisely by those bodies on the street. If they are transported in one way, they are surely left in place in another, holding the camera or the cell phone, face to face with those they oppose, unprotected, injurable, injured, persistent, if not insurgent. It matters that those bodies carry cell phones, relaying messages and images, and when they are attacked, it is more often than not in some relation to the camera or the video recorder. It can be an effort to destroy the camera and its user, or it can be a spectacle of destruction for the camera, a media event produced as a warning or a threat. Or it can be a way to stop any more organizing. Is the action of the body separable from its technology, and how does the technology determine new forms of political action? And when censorship or violence are directed against those bodies, are they not also directed against its access to media, and in order to establish hegemonic control over which images travel and which do not?

Of course, the dominant media is corporately owned, exercising its own kinds of censorship and incitement. And yet, it still seems important to affirm that the freedom of the media to broadcast from these sites is itself an exercise of freedom, and thus a mode of exercising rights, especially when it is rogue media, from the street, evading the censor, where the activation of the instrument is part of the bodily action itself. The media not only reports on social and political movements that are laying claim to freedom and justice in various ways; the media is also exercising one of those freedoms for which the social movement struggles. I do not mean by this claim to suggest that all media is involved in the struggle for political freedom and social justice (we know, of course, that it is not). Of course, it matters which global media does the reporting and how. My point is that sometimes private media devices become global precisely at the moment in which they overcome modes of censorship to report protests and, in that way, become part of the protest itself.

What bodies are doing on the street when they are demonstrating is linked fundamentally to what communication devices and technologies are doing when they "report" on what is happening in the street. These are different actions, but they both require bodily actions. The one exercise of freedom is linked to the other exercise, which means that both are ways of exercising rights, and that jointly they bring a space of appearance into being and secure its transposability. Although some may wager that the exercise of rights now takes place quite at the expense of bodies on the street, that twitter and other virtual technologies have led to a disembodiment of the public sphere, I disagree. The media requires those bodies on the street to have an event, even as the street requires the media to exist in a global arena. But under conditions when those with cameras or Internet capacities are imprisoned or tortured or deported, then the use of the technology effectively implicates the body. Not only must someone's hand tap and send, but someone's body is on the line if that tapping and sending gets traced. In other words, localization is hardly overcome through the use of a media that potentially transmits globally. And if this conjuncture of street and media constitutes a very contemporary version of the public sphere, then bodies on the line have to be thought as both there and here, now and then, transported and stationery, with very different political consequences following from those two modalities of space and time.

It matters that it is public squares that are filled to the brim, that people eat and sleep there, sing and refuse to cede that space, as we saw in Tahrir Square, and continue to see on a daily basis. It matters as well that it is public educational buildings that have been seized in Athens, London, and Berkeley. At Berkeley, buildings were seized and trespassing fines were handed out. In some cases, students were accused of destroying private property. But these very allegations raised the question of whether the university is public or private. The stated aim of the protest—to seize the building and to sequester themselves there—was a way to gain a platform, indeed, a way to secure the material conditions for appearing in public. Such actions generally do not take place when effective platforms are already available. The students there, but also at Goldsmiths College in the UK more recently were seizing buildings as a way to lay claim to buildings that ought properly, now and in the future, to belong to public education. That does not mean that every time these buildings are seized it is justifiable, but let us be alert to what is at stake here: the symbolic meaning of seizing these buildings is that these buildings belong to the public, to public education; it is precisely the access to public education which is being undermined by fee and tuition hikes and budget cuts; we should not be surprised that the protest took the form of seizing the buildings, performatively laying claim to public education, insisting on gaining literal access to the buildings of public education precisely at a moment, historically, when that access is being shut down. In other words, no positive law justifies these actions that oppose the institutionalization of unjust or exclusionary forms of power. Can we say that these actions are nevertheless an exercise of a right and, if so, what kind?

Modes of Alliance and the Police Function

Let me offer you an anecdote to make my point more concrete. Last year, I was asked to visit Turkey on the occasion of the International Conference against Homophobia and Transphobia. This was an especially important event in Ankara, the capital of Turkey, where transgendered people are often served fines for appearing in public, are often beaten, sometimes by the police, and where murders of transgendered women in particular happen nearly once a month in recent years. If I offer you this example of Turkey, it is not to point out that Turkey is "behind"—something that the embassy representative from Denmark was quick to point out to me, and which I refused with equal speed. I assure you that there are equally brutal murders outside of Los Angeles and Detroit, in Wyoming and Louisiana, or even New York. It is rather because what is astonishing about the alliances there is that several feminist organizations have worked with queer, gay/lesbian and transgendered people against police violence, but also against militarism, against nationalism, and against the forms of masculinism by which they are supported. On the street, after the conference, the feminist lined up with the drag queens, the genderqueer with the human rights activists, and the lipstick lesbians with their bisexual and heterosexual friends—the march included secularists and Muslims. They chanted, "we will not be soldiers, and we will not kill." To oppose the police violence against trans people is thus to be openly against military violence and the nationalist escalation of militarism; it is also to be against the military aggression against the Kurds, but also to act in the memory of the Armenian genocide and against the various ways that violence is disavowed by the state and the media. This alliance was compelling for me for all kinds of reasons, but mainly because in most Northern European countries, there are now serious divisions among feminists, queers, lesbian, and gay human rights workers, anti-racist movements, freedom of religion movements, and anti-poverty and anti-war mobilizations. In Lyon, France last year, one of the established feminists had written a book on the "illusion" of transsexuality, and her public lectures had been "zapped" by many trans activists and their queer allies. She defended herself by saying that to call transsexuality psychotic was not the same as pathologizing transsexuality. It is, she said, a descriptive term, and makes no judgment or prescription. Under what conditions can calling a population "psychotic" for the particular embodied life they live not be pathologizing? This feminist called herself a materialist, a radical, but she pitted herself against the transgendered community in order to maintain certain norms of masculinity and femininity as prerequisites to a nonpsychotic life. These are arguments that would be swiftly countered in Istanbul or Johannesburg, and yet, these same feminists seek recourse to a form of universalism that would make France, and their version of French feminism, into the beacon of progressive thought.

Not all French feminists who call themselves universalists would oppose the public rights of transgendered people or contribute to their pathologization. And yet, if the streets are open to transgendered people, they are not open to those who wear signs of their religious belonging openly. Hence, we are left to fathom the many universalist French feminists who call upon the police to arrest, detain, fine, and sometimes deport women wearing the *niqab* or the *burka* in the public sphere in France. What sort of politics is this that recruits the police function of the state to monitor and restrict women from religious minorities in the public sphere? Why would the same universalists (Elisabeth Badinter) openly affirm the rights of transgendered people to freely appear in public while restricting that very right to women who happen to wear religious clothing that offends the sensibilities of die-hard secularists? If the right to appear is to be honored "universally," it would not be able to survive such an obvious and insupportable contradiction.

Perhaps there are modalities of violence that we need to think about in order to understand the police functions in operation here. After all, those who insist that gender must always appear in one way or in one clothed version rather than another, who seek either to criminalize or to pathologize those who live their gender or their sexuality in nonnormative ways, are themselves acting as the police for the sphere of appearance whether or not they belong to any police force. As we know, it is sometimes the police force of the state that does violence to sexual and gendered minorities, and sometimes it is the police who fail to investigate, fail to prosecute as criminal the murder of transgendered women, or fail to prevent violence against transgendered members of the population. If gender or sexual minorities are criminalized or pathologized for how they appear, how they lay claim to public space, the language through which they understand themselves, the means by which they express love or desire, those with whom they openly ally, choose to be near, engage sexually, or how they exercise their bodily freedom, what clothes they wear or fail to wear, then those acts of criminalization are themselves violent; and in that sense, they are also unjust and criminal. In Arendtian terms, we can say that to be precluded from the space of appearance, to be precluded from being part of the plurality that brings the space of appearance into being, is to be deprived of the right to have rights. Plural and public action is the exercise of the right to place and belonging, and this exercise is the means by which the space of appearance is presupposed and brought into being. Let me return to the notion of gender with which I began, both to draw upon Arendt and to resist Arendt. In my view, gender is an exercise of freedom, which is not to say that everything that constitutes gender is freely chosen, but only that even what is considered unfree can and must be claimed and exercised in some way. I have, with this formulation, taken a certain distance from the Arendtian formulation. This exercise of freedom must be accorded the same equal treatment as any other exercise of freedom under the law. And politically, we must call for the expansion of our conceptions of equality to include this form of embodied freedom. What do we mean when we say that sexuality or gender is an exercise of freedom? To repeat: I do not mean to say that all of us choose our gender or our sexuality. We are surely formed by language and culture, by history, by the social struggles in which we participate, by forces both psychological and historical—in interaction, by the way with biological situations that have their own history and efficacy. Indeed, we may well feel that what and how we desire are quite fixed, indelible or irreversible features of who we are. But regardless of whether we understand our gender or our sexuality as chosen or given, we each have a right to claim that gender and to claim that sexuality. And it makes a difference whether we can claim them at all. When we exercise the right to appear as the gender we already are—even when we feel we have no other choice—we are still exercising a certain freedom, but we are also doing something more. When one freely exercises the right to be who one already is, and one asserts a social category for the purposes of describing that mode of being, then one is, in fact, making freedom part of that very social category, discursively changing the very ontology in question. It is not possible to separate the genders that we claim to be and the sexualities that we engage from the right that any of us has to assert those realities in public or in private, or in the many thresholds that exist between the two, freely, that is, without threat of violence. When, long ago, one said that gender is performative, that meant that it is a certain kind of enactment, which means that one is not first one's gender and then one decides how and when to enact it. The enactment is part of its very ontology, is a way of rethinking the ontological mode of gender, and it matters how and when and with what consequences that enactment takes place, because all that changes the very gender that one "is."

To walk on the street without police interference is something other than assembling there en masse. And yet, when a transgendered person walks there, the right that is exercised in a bodily form does not only belong to that one person. There is a group, if not an alliance, walking there, too, whether or not they are seen. Perhaps we can call "performative" both this exercise of gender and the embodied political claim to equal treatment, to be protected from violence, and to be able to move with and within this social category in public space. To walk is to say that this is a public space in which transgendered people walk, that this is a public space where people with various forms of clothing, no matter how they are gendered or what religion they signify, are free to move without threat of violence. But this performativity applies more broadly to the conditions by which any of us emerge as bodily creatures in the world.

How, finally, do we understand this body? Is it a distinctively human body, a gendered body, and is it finally possible to distinguish between that domain of the body that is given and that which is made? If we invest in humans the power to make the body into a political signifier, then do we assume that in becoming political, the body distinguishes itself from its own animality and the sphere of animals? In other words, how do we think this idea of the exercise of freedom and rights within the space of appearance that takes us beyond anthropocentrism? Here again, I think the conception of the living body is key. After all, the life that is worth preserving, even when considered exclusively human, is connected to nonhuman life in essential ways; this follows from the idea of the human animal. Thus, if we are thinking well, and our thinking commits us to the preservation of life in some form, then the life to be preserved takes a bodily form. In turn, this means that the life of the body—its hunger, its need for shelter and protection from violence—would all become major issues of politics. Even the most given or nonchosen features of our lives are not simply given; they are given *in* history and *in* language, in vectors of power that none of us chose. Equally true is that a given property of the body or a set of defining characteristics depend upon the continuing persistence of the body. Those social categories we never chose to traverse this body that is given in some ways rather than in others, and gender, for instance, names that traversal as well as the trajectory of its transformations. In this sense, those most urgent and nonvolitional dimensions of our lives—which include hunger and the need for shelter, medical care, and protection from violence, natural or humanly imposed—are crucial to politics. We cannot presume the enclosed and well-fed space of the Polis where all the material needs are somehow being taken care of elsewhere by beings whose gender, race, or status render them ineligible for public recognition. Rather, we have to not only bring the material urgencies of the body into the square but make those needs central to the demands of politics.

In my view, a different social ontology would have to start from the presumption that there is a shared condition of precarity that situates our political lives. And some of us, as Ruthie Gilmore has made very clear, are disproportionately disposed to injury and early death than others, and racial difference can be tracked precisely through looking at statistics on infant mortality; this means, in brief, that precarity is unequally distributed and that lives are not considered equally grievable or equally valuable. If, as Adriana Cavarero has argued, the exposure of our bodies in public space constitutes us fundamentally and establishes our thinking as social and embodied, vulnerable and passionate, then our thinking gets nowhere without the presupposition of that very corporeal interdependency and entwinement. The body is constituted through perspectives it cannot inhabit; someone else sees our face in a way that none of us can. We are in this way, even as located, always elsewhere, constituted in a sociality that exceeds us. This establishes our exposure and our precarity, the ways in which we depend on political and social institutions to persist.

After all, in Cairo, it was not just that people amassed in the square: they were there; they slept there; they dispensed medicine and food, they assembled and sang, and they spoke. Can we distinguish those vocalizations from the body from those other expressions of material need and urgency? They were, after all, sleeping and eating in the public square, constructing toilets and various systems for sharing the space, and so not only refusing to be privatized (refusing to go or stay home) and not only claiming the public domain for themselves (acting in concert on conditions of equality) but also maintaining themselves as persisting bodies with needs, desires, and requirements. Arendtian and counter-Arendtian, to be sure. Since these bodies who were organizing their most basic needs in public were also petitioning the world to register what was happening there, to make its support known, and in that way to enter into revolutionary action itself. The bodies acted in concert, but they also slept in public, and in both these modalities, they were both vulnerable and demanding, giving political and spatial organization to elementary bodily needs. In this way, they formed themselves into images to be projected to all of who watched, petitioning us to receive and respond, and to enlist media coverage that would refuse to let the event be covered over or to slip away. Sleeping on that pavement was not only a way to lay claim to the public, to contest the legitimacy of the state, but also quite clearly a way to put the body on the line in its insistence, obduracy and precarity, overcoming the distinction between public and private for the time of revolution. In other words, it was only when those needs that are supposed to remain private came out into the day and night of the square, formed into image and discourse for the media, did it finally become possible to extend the space and time of the event with such tenacity to bring the regime down. After all, the cameras never stopped, bodies were there and here, they never stopped speaking, not even in sleep, and therefore could not be silenced, sequestered, or denied—revolution happened because everyone refused to go home, cleaving to the pavement, acting in concert.

Notes

1. These reflections were written in the summer of 2011, in response to the mass demonstrations of the so-called Arab Spring, notably those on Cairo's Tahrir Square. The text was originally a lecture held in Venice, September 7, 2011, in the framework of the series The State of Things, organized by the Office for Contemporary Art Norway (OCA).

2. Hannah Arendt, *The Human Condition* (Chicago: University of Chicago Press, 1958), 198.

3. Arendt, 199.

CHAPTER 7

Divine Impersonations
Transgressive Gestures in Hindu Devotion

Rokus de Groot

In the context of the theme gestures and embodiment, the "gesture of embodiment" itself deserves special attention. In Hinduism, appearances of divine incarnations are not only part of an accepted belief, they also are quite common experiences and expressions among *bhaktas* (devotees). Such an epiphanic event may elicit responsive gestures—even provocative ones—from devotees who have experienced it that involve exceptional behavior derived from shared religious sources. The epiphanic happening may include the activation of various senses and so does the response.

In this essay, I take a closer look at two cases involving allegedly divine visions and auditions as well as the media coverage and public responses they received. I analyze the religio-historical references of the *bhaktas*' gestures within the Indian context, including how they are characterized by the country's media, and discuss the traumatic nature of the epiphanic events involving divine embodiment as well as the seemingly paradoxical combination of sensuality and asceticism in the *bhaktas*' response to them. In closing, I comment on the privileged role of music in both the alleged divine appearance and the *bhaktas*' response to it.

Embodiment and Incarnation:
The Case of Inspector General Panda

In November 2005, Inspector General of Police Devendra Kumar Panda caused an outrage when he appeared at the Lucknow bench of the Allahabad High Court, India, in female attire (fig. 7.1). He insisted to be addressed as Radha, the consort of Lord Krishna (fig. 7.2). Wearing a *sari, mangtika* (female head jewelry), *sindoor* (red powder on the forehead as a sign of the married state), nose ring, anklets, and red lipstick and with his finger- and toenails painted red, the fifty-seven-year-old police officer was dancing and singing devotional songs (*bhajans*) that supposedly had been sung by Radha in her pining for the divine Lover. Eventually, his behavior would result in a call by the national Congress Party upon the government to take action.[1]

When exploring religious gestures and embodiment, one cannot but take a closer look at people's beliefs in divine incarnations, which are indeed "gestures" of embodiment in a quite fundamental sense. The belief in reincarnations of the gods, or avatars, plays a central role in Hindu religion. Krishna, the eighth avatar of Vishnu, is maybe the most beloved among them. Divine incarnations are held to meet and direct the performative needs of the believers.

The gods are also taken to be prime performers themselves. In fact, Hinduism as well as Christianity profess that it was God himself (or the gods themselves) who started the affair of embodiments and gestures in the first place; and they believe that divine presence in human or other form continues to offer guidance up to the present day in the form of model gestures.[2]

In Hinduism, the confrontation with a divine incarnation in visions, dreams, or (the believer's) reality may provoke quite radical gestures from the believer. He or she may act out roles from their favored avatar's life, as handed down in written,

FIGURE 7.1 Inspector General Devendra Kumar Panda took on the manner of what he called "the second Radha." *The Hindu*, November 14, 2005.

oral, iconographic, and now also audio-visual transmissions, especially through the role of the avatar's beloved on earth. Of course, from the viewpoint of the believer, this is not a matter of "acting" but of passionate identification—which is what may have happened in Inspector General Panda's case when he appeared in public as Radha. The reverse may also occur: a man or woman may be so much devoted to an avatar that he or she dresses or behaves like the avatar's beloved in order to elicit his *darshan* (vision of the divine/being seen by the divine). During my fieldwork in India, beginning in 1992, I have encountered quite a few reports, among them several first-hand, of both divine *darshans* and "provocative" behavior of devotees.

According to Hindu belief, human beings themselves are subjected to reincarnation—they are embodiments of *atman* (as *jivas*, or individual souls)—usually in a chain of rebirths that unfolds as a spiritual evolution or devolution. Devotees ardently believe that ultimately, they may be freed from this chain, in *moksha* (liberation: the resolution of *atman* in *paramatman*, supreme soul). In their views, to be granted the *darshan* of an avatar is most auspicious. And identifying with a person from the avatar's life on earth—a beloved or a member of his family— is seen as sanctifying and propitious on the way to be relieved from further embodiments. Legendary persons such as Radha, have acquired a saintly or semi-divine status.

The *cause célèbre* of the Radha enactment by the Lucknow police officer had its origin in 1991, when he got a *darshan* of Krishna. According to him, it was the flute-playing god himself who had called him by the name of his beloved Radha. This radically transformed his life. Since that incident he impersonated the role of Radha in an intense Krishna *bhakti* (devotion). In front of television cameras he declared: "Lord Krishna has himself assigned me the role of Radha, and whatever I am doing is in pursuance of his wishes."[3]

His wife Veena was not at all happy with this course of events, calling him a dramatist. She had him summoned to court in order to exact from him a monthly allowance. She was the first to dismiss his claims about divinity, accusing him of using his Radha-role to enjoy the company of women with whom he, as Radha, could now freely move. In his perception, according to her, they were all "Krishna's gopis," the cowherd girls who according to the *Bhagavata Puranas* were frolicking with the Lord on the banks of the river Yamuna in the land of Braj. Moreover, Veena complained that Mr. Panda had not acted like a husband since his Radha infatuation.[4]

It was not long before similar embodiments made the news. On December 17, 2005, the *Deccan Herald* reported that a Mithilesh Pathak had entered the office of the civil surgeon at Jamshedpur dressed in a brightly colored costume

FIGURE 7.2 *Radha and Krishna Walk in a Flowering Grove*, miniature painting by the Kota Master, ca. 1720. Metropolitan Museum of Art, New York.

with a headdress of peacock feathers and dancing to a tune that only *he* could hear—he claimed to be a reincarnation of Krishna himself. After watching the news, how could the Lord remain deaf to the ardent call of the *bhajan*-singing Lucknow inspector general turned Radha?

Public Responses to Mr. Panda's Behavior

Mr. Panda's Radha embodiment received wide coverage both in newspapers and online, eliciting various reactions from readers. Some considered it a case of personal frustration, an instance of mental illness, an example of gender transgression, or an excuse for cross-dressing. One person, critical of the Indian police force, commented online, "This IPS officer was denied promotion due to which he transformed into Radha."[5] Another commenter, Nettie from Western Australia, joked, "I bet he just can't admit he likes wearing his wife's knickers!"[6] Western commenters obviously did not have the Hindu framework to assess the Radha performance.

Author Akshay Khanna had a different take altogether on the issue of cross-dressing. In her article "Trans-Gender Trauma in the Police Force," she views the case as challenging "the police force, as the seat of power in the masculine domain, of maintaining the patriarchal state" and calls for a fresh approach in gendering that force.[7]

Those who dismissed Mr. Panda's behavior as a case of mental illness strongly recommended that the officer appear before the state medical committee for psychological evaluation. (The person behind the Jamshedpur Krishna reincarnation, too, was pressed to seek medical help.)

Some, however, considered the police officer's conduct from the point of view of religion. Members of the Hare Krishna faith not surprisingly censured Mr. Panda's behavior, as revealed in the following comment—since Hare Krishnas, on the basis of certain scriptures, do not view Krishna as an avatar embodiment but as God Supreme Itself; how could there have been a divine interaction with a police officer?

Hare Krishna!
This Devendra Kumar [Panda] is just another *prakrta sahajiya* [which] means false and material pretenders.
This word can be found in the scriptures and how to detect such person is also mentioned. Lord Krishna is not a mere avatar of Vishnu as some claim. He is the source of all Vishnus and Devas.

This is not our concoction but based on the *sastra* [knowledge deemed unshakable, based on holy scriptures]. In Srimad Bhagavat Gita all the verses mention Krishna as the Original Supreme Personality of Godhead. . . . He is "Adi Devam" the Primeval Lord, "Ajam" the Unborn and "Vibhum" the Greatest."

. . . What to speak of those who think Krishna as a mere mortal. Read Bhagavad Gita as it is and see what Lord Krishna say about Him and those who think Him as a mortal. He is Parabrahman [beyond Brahman, the Creator].

. . . Thank you. Hare Krishna![8]

Another Hindu commenter takes a less orthodox view, mixed with apology and self-defense:

We must not forget one thing here, the person being talked about was at a very senior position in one of the elite services in India, so its bit difficult to believe that he did it for cheap popularity, although only Krisna knows best as far as i think, we shouldnt dismiss it straight away, i know this wont go down well with skeptical people but you never know what all is possible in this world. in the end i would like to state that i am not an ignorant Hindu fundamentalist, i have received best education from top colleges both in India and abroad in engineering and management, thanks.[9]

Journalist Sandhya Jain wrote an interesting editorial in defense of Mr. Panda's performance.[10] Instead of dismissing the officer's female behavior as mere travesty, she referred to a story about Mirabai, a still very popular *bhakti* saint from the sixteenth century. When Mirabai had asked permission to see a famous spiritual teacher in Vrindaban, he declined, stating that he had taken a vow never to look at a woman's face. "Why," Mirabai is reported to have said, "In Vrindaban there is no masculinity except Krishna himself. To God we are all women." Jain argues that for centuries male dancers have dressed as women in Krishna *bhakti*, up to the present-day practice of Vedantam Satyanarayanan Sharma, exponent of female roles in the Kuchipudi tradition. She stresses that the police officer's identification with Radha should be considered as sublime: Radha symbolizes the unification of the deity and the devotee through *bhakti*; she is the embodiment of the body as a temple for the divine. Referring to Jayadeva's *Gita Govinda* (written in the twelfth century), Jain endorses the long-standing belief in Radha's divinity. Officer Panda is worthy of her highest praise: while he is acting out *in public*, Sri Ramakrishna Paramahansa and Sri Aurobindo, who had visions of Divine Mother Kali, renounced the world in ascetism.

Religion and Politics

Jain's take on Mr. Panda's case gets quite interesting when she combines a religious perspective with a nationalist outlook. She calls the Indian media, which ridiculed the Panda case by calling it just a case of travesty, "de-nationalized." According to her, this is also a blatant injustice to Radha: she was so completely devoted to her Lord that she was called in one breath with his name, Radha-Krishna. Moreover, Jain suggests that one of the most famous Krishna *bhaktas* in history, Chaitanya Mahaprabhu (1486–1534), considered Radha his *ishta deva* (personal god) and, by proclaiming his veneration in public dance and song, had resisted strongly the political and cultural oppression by the *nawabs* (Muslim rulers) of his day. One will not miss her support of the police officer's Radha identification as a *politically* significant act.

The whole issue got an even stronger political dimension when the well-known Indian novelist and literary critic Pankaj Mishra transposed the case in the context of globalization through his 2006 article in the *New Statesman*.[11] He professed that India, while "emerging as one of the powers of the twenty-first century . . . will progress on its own terms, reinventing the whole notion of modernity in the process."

Mishra heavily criticized the English language media for rejecting the Radha impersonation as backward and immediately continued with rebuking the media's "repressive demand to behave like a modern, rational country inspired by the West, based on free-market capitalism, a secular state and a nuclear-equipped army." Pointing to the overwhelming majority of India's population which consists of peasants, the working class, and the destitute, he demanded to pay attention to "older, apparently irrational, traditions: asceticism, hedonism and devout religiosity." He stresses, "Almost every day, newspapers report further signs of individual resistance to the homogenizing influence of modernity. The police officer donning the robes of Radha is self-consciously harking back to Wajid Ali Shah, the last ruler of the principality of Awadh, who also dressed up as Radha and whom the British denounced as effeminate before deposing of him in 1856. In his androgynous dress, the police officer is also rejecting the role required of him by a hard, hyper-rational world."[12]

Bhakti

When Mr. Panda enacted Radha, cross-dressing, dancing, and singing like her, he was performing gestures in a very long line of precedents. These are part of the *bhakti* tradition of India. *Bhakti* is usually translated as "devotion" and *bhakta* as "devotee," "lover of God." The terms are derived from the Sanskrit root *bhaj*, "to share." We find the same root in *bhajan*, "devotional song." The aspect of sharing gives *bhakti* a strong performative as well as social base: "it points to the importance of [a personal] relationship—both to God and to human beings—in . . . [a] kind of enthusiastic, often congregational, religion."[13] The enactment of religion includes the identification with famous *bhaktas* from the present and the past, particularly poet-saints, who serve as models and whose *bhajans* are performed. One of these model poet-saints is Mirabai, who was mentioned in the article by Sandhya Jain.

Parita Mukta has pointed out that the *bhakti* communities have strongly transgressive traits: "bhakti has . . . led to a radically different form of community association—one that is not (at least initially) based on social prescriptions of birth, caste status, and defined sexual roles, but one that is based on an active will and a choice of belief." She observes, "bhakti has . . . given rise to religious fervour and passion which, by emphasizing religious experience as the truth, places the conscience of the believer and the spiritual experience of the devotee over and above both the claims of religious authorities and existing social ties."[14]

In Hinduism, compared to Brahminic ritualistic practices, *bhakti* has favored the development of the emotional, aesthetic, physical, and sensory aspects of religion. *Bhakti* is a strong case of the individualization, emotionalization, and deinstitutionalization of religion.

Bhakti may also imply a resacralization of public space, given the one-pointedness of the *bhaktas*, which makes it impossible for them to conceal their state of mind and to differentiate between the private and the public. However, in the Indian middle class, the individualization of *bhakti* has developed at the cost of social embedding, though especially among women there still is a community-building tradition (singing *bhajans* in *kirtan* meetings).[15]

Generally, Hinduism differentiates between devotion to *God without qualities* and to *God with qualities*; the former is called *nirguna bhakti* and the latter *saguna bhakti*. In practice there is nearly always some mixture of the two.

Nirguna bhakti originally does not accept either icon or legend. A connection is made with the ascetics, especially the Nath Yogis. This stance is based upon the principle that God cannot be spoken of or conceptualized. Hawley and Juergensmeyer summarize, "They [*nirguna* Indian devotional saints] insist that God, more than any other reality, exceeds the shapes by means of which human senses interpret the world, and hold therefore that to move in the direction of truth is to leave those senses behind, particularly those that are most successful in convincing us that the world is solid, definite, and real." This concerns taste, touch, but especially sight: "Seeing is an enormous part of believing—particularly in Hinduism, with its powerful iconic thrust." While any objectification is rejected, the conviction is that "the only real access [to the divine] is from the inside, through one's heart and soul."[16] Well-known examples of *nirguna bhakti* include Ravidas, Kabir, and Nanak.

In Mr. Panda's case, we are clearly dealing with *saguna bhakti*. It is typically a tradition of Vishnu devotees, or *Vaishnavas*. Since Vishnu stands for the maintenance of the universe, it is no wonder that especially he has manifested in various *avatar* embodiments. Vaishnavas focus on the Vishnu incarnations Rama or Krishna. Krishna is the playful, amorous one of the two, and Rama the model of righteous behavior.[17]

According to Hawley and Juergensmeyer, *saguna bhaktas* maintain:

> that a central feature of divine grace is God's consent to become available to human perception "with attributes" in this way, not just in temple images but in full self-manifestations that have rescued and inspired history from age to age.... what makes for illusion in this world has less to do with our senses as such than with the uses to which we put them: we construct our fantasies and delusions from the inside out, driven by appetite and desire. Given this derangement of the inner person, in fact, one of the ways in which God acts to restore proportion and direction is to assume a sensory manifestation, particularly one that can be seen and visualized.[18]

A crucial notion here is *darshan*, "sight" or "seeing and being seen." This may refer to temple images but also to divine self-manifestations. Ramakrishna once strikingly said to the Western devotee Sister Nivedita: "You do not yet understand India! We Indians are Man-worshippers after all! Our God is man.... You may always say the Image is God: the error you have to avoid is to think God the Image."[19] Indeed, as Hawley and Juergensmeyer characterize *saguna bhakti*: "God exceeds what humans can imagine, but insofar as the remedying of our error and misery is concerned, *saguna* thinkers find it more important and more remarkable that God meets us in the world we actually inhabit, stretching our sense of what is possible."[20] Famous *saguna bhakti* saints include Surdas, Mirabai, both Krishna *bhaktas*, and Tulsidas, a devotee of Rama.

Mirabai is reported to have considered Krishna as her husband. Even though, according to legend, he appeared to her in an embodied way, he is no earthly spouse. The great suffering of *saguna bhaktas* is that the visions of their Lover are ephemeral. One of the means they employ in their effort to bind the divine Lover, is the gesture of impersonating one of those who are known to have been dear to the avatar during his stay on earth, like Radha to Krishna.[21]

Inspector General Panda's References

Saguna bhakti clearly provided the Mr. Panda with justification for his reenactment of Radha. First, model *bhaktas* have often deemed proper civil behavior as of little importance and have comported themselves in transgressive ways while expressing their only love. Chaitanya, the famous Krishna *bhakta*, has been reported singing and dancing in the street, much to the dismay of respectable Brahmin clerics as well as the ruling Muslim *nawabs*. Mirabai, a Rajasthani princess (fig. 7.3), is said to have caused an outrage among her royal in-laws, by mingling with untouchable *bhaktas* and spiritual tutors as well as by denying her husband his marital rights on the grounds of her being already married (to Krishna). Indeed, the Indian tradition of *bhakti* or devotion is "a force that propels a person beyond the confines of ordinary life."[22]

Second, in the enactment of *bhakti*, the female voice is predominant, and the female embodiment is viewed as favorable. Male *bhakti* poets used the gesture of adopting *stri vachya*,[23] a female *persona*, to express their love for Krishna. A famous example is Surdas, who took the voice of a *gopi*, one of the cowherdesses who played with their paramour Krishna on the banks of the river Yamuna.[24] Also Indian Sufi poets like Amir Khusrau have expressed themselves in a similar way in relation to their *sheikh*.

Third, and related to this, men cross-dress as women, especially in religious theater performances. One modern exponent of this is *kuchipudi* exponent Vedantam Satyanarayanan Sharma. Cross-dressing as a performative mode to identify with the divine Lover goes both ways. Mirabai wrote a poem in which she insists to be dressed like Krishna:

> I lost control of my faculties.
> Let me take flute and staff in hand
> And don a yellow loin-cloth.
> Let me rove about with the herds,
> Clad like a herdsman
> And wearing a peacock-plume crown.[25]

FIGURE 7.3 Mirabai singing to Krishna, with the town of Vrindavan in the background. Painting by the Rajastani artist Indra Sharma (d. 2006). Source: *Hinduism Today*, October–December 2017.

Fourth, *bhakta*s, in their single-minded love, do not accept a duality between the personal and the public.

Fifth, many model *bhaktas* have accepted sacrifice and suffered martyrdom. An example can be found in reports of Mirabai's life. Her Rajput in-laws attempted to poison her in order to put an end to her *bhakti* behavior, which was completely at odds with her royal status.

Sixth, a weak point in Mr. Panda's case seems the lack of support of a *bhakti* community. He typically seems to represent middle class individualistic *bhakti*. Yet we may view the public media as offering new ways of community building. For one thing, the police officer received a newspaper and Internet response from an alleged avatar: the Jamshedpur Krishna. Moreover, his case is one among many publicly reported instances of acting as a divine incarnation's consort.[26]

Indeed, these *bhakti* references have earned Mr. Panda some support in the media. In general, though, his case has been deemed quite problematic. Although it is not exceptional for men to speak in a female voice or don a female guise, for the most part these gestures have been accepted in India in historical portraits of poets and saints or forms of theater. Mr. Panda, however, acted out his Radha-persona in an everyday context, that is: neither as *bhakti* art nor as poetry. This gave rise to antithetical reactions, which reflect the situation of transition in which India finds itself—between cherishing traditional religious beliefs and the dynamics of globalization. While these two tendencies are not necessarily mutually exclusive and indeed quite some elements of Indian provenance have been absorbed in globalization trends, the latter has not yet happened to devotional cross-dressing.

How did Mr. Panda's case end? Did the support of *bhakti* references take the upper hand? The Lucknow police force accused him of breaching the police dress code, and he was strongly recommended to appear before the state medical committee for psychological evaluation. In due course he was forced to take early retirement.

Apparition through Voice

A special case of embodiment is the apparition through voice. A famous example in India can be seen in the life of Indira Devi (1920–98; fig. 7.4). Even though from early childhood she loved fun, clothes, and jewelry, she wanted to become an ascetic. When she eventually did marry, she experienced an aversion to sex. Since her childhood, Indira experienced moments of ecstasy. These were followed by bouts of depression and a strong yearning to resolve a painful sense of separation (*viraha*). During the ecstatic moments she would hear heavenly music, which she called "a Flute Call." In Hindu India the flute is intimately connected with its divine player Krishna.

When Indira was twenty-nine, Mirabai came to her in a vision (*darshan*). Mirabai is the most beloved saint of Krishna *bhakti*. Born a Rajasthani princess, she left the palace in order to dedicate herself to her divine Lover. In India her

FIGURE 7.4   Indira Devi (1920-98).

bhajans are still widely sung across caste, gender, and creed. Through the apparition of Mirabai, during moments of trance, songs would come to Indira. These were in Hindi, that is, in a language different from Indira's mother tongue, Urdu. In her experience she did not hear sounds but experienced vibrations. It was a "trance hearing"; according to Indira, the spirit of Mirabai would take expression through her "I"-function, using her mind and body. On another occasion, Indira said she "remembered" the songs. First texts were given, later melodies as well. She did have visions of Mirabai, a Rajasthani lady, without shadow, with feet not touching the floor.

Indira described her state as a transformation of the soul, in constant remembrance of the Lord, repeating his Name, as if "every pore" of her body had "a tongue." In this way eight hundred songs are reported to have been transmitted. She did not sing them publicly, but only to her guru Dilip Kumar Roy, a Krishna *bhakta* and singer himself. He eventually published them, starting with *Shrutanjali*, that is: "songs heard"—not "composed."[27]

Together with the abundance of impressions of color, shape, and sound that Indira experienced, there is at the same time an aspect of asceticism in her life. Indira herself used the term *weaning*. She once observed, "Sense pleasures gave us little relief from our painful nostalgia.... She [referring to herself in the third person] has heard that heavenly voice which came like a flutelet to her way-lost soul to wean her from her lesser loves, her illusions and desires."[28]

Sensuousness and Asceticism

Krishna *bhakti* poetry and imagery abound in exuberant sensuality and sensuousness of sight and sound and is full of eroticism. Yet this does not necessarily imply hedonistic enjoyment of the physical. On the contrary, we also find an outspoken current of asceticism in *bhakti*. In *nirguna bhakti* the key of asceticism is self-evident, but it may come as a surprise to hear it also in *saguna bhakti*. Yet in our examples, we have seen that the present-day and historical *bhaktas*, who had the conviction of being Krishna's beloved, lose interest in erotic and sexual relationships with mortal bodies. It is as if the *bhakta* does not want to become otherwise engaged and keep the physical body constantly ready for imminent *darshans*.

Ideally, the *bhaktas* go through a process of being weaned away from sensuality and sensuousness in the usual physical sense, while becoming increasingly sensitive to spiritual sensuality. In this context it is relevant to know that Surdas was blind. Nevertheless, his depictions of Krishna "are the most acute in their visual detail."[29]

A differentiation between embodiments is called for here, such as Chauvet's differentiation between cosmic, social, and transcendent bodies.[30] In Indira's case, Hindu body concepts should be studied, like those pertaining to the physical and spiritual planes (including "dream" and "visionary-vibrational-auditory" bodies). Each of these bodies would have its own sensitivity, sensuality, and sensuousness, its own expressions, including its own music.

Confusion and tension may arise easily between these bodies or embodiments, not only to the *bhaktas* but especially to the onlookers. Thus, the Lucknow police assessed Mr. Panda's behavior according to criteria pertaining to the social body, while this may have been irrelevant to the officer himself.

Thus, although we may find extravagant sensuality in, for example, the transcendent body plane, we may encounter asceticism in the physical one. We may meet here, at least in the perception of the observers, what I call *embodiment dissonances*.

The tension between types of body and between sensuality and asceticism in *bhakti* is well illustrated by some of Mirabai's *bhajans*. In one of them she addresses Krishna as a *yogi*, that is as an ascetic, while she presents herself as one, too. This is madness in several respects. A female *yogi* was already an abnormality in her times. But to portray Krishna as an ascetic seems outrageous, given his reputation as a womanizer.[31] Yet the image is apt. For all the eroticism, sensuality, and sensuousness in Mirabai's poetry and for all the stunning descriptions of Krishna's dazzling embodied appearance, they do not concern the plane of the physical in the first place. The impossibility of *bhakti* love's consummation in a human frame is expressed in Mirabai's mad words. In the *bhajan* "Yogi mata ja, mata ja," she uses an image to express this fundamental impossibility. Mirabai asks Krishna to light with his own hand the funeral pyre on which she has laid herself and to smear her ashes on his own body afterward:

> O Jogî, do not depart,
> I pray you, do not depart.
> Behold, I fall at Your feet, Your slave.
> Strange is the path of love and devotion!
> Explain to me its intricacies
> Before You depart.
> I am laying a pyre of fragrant aloe
> And sandalwood.
> Light it with Your own hand
> Before you depart.
> When I am burnt to a heap of ashes,
> Smear them on Your body
> Before You depart.
> Says Mîrâ to her Lord, the courtly Giridhara,
> Let my light dissolve in Your light
> Before You depart.[32]

Again, we hear the combination of a very outspoken sensuality and physicality on one hand and the impossibility to experience it in a physical way on the other hand. The ashes refer to the ways of the ascetics, who wander in places of cremation but first and foremost to the physical body's effacement. This is a truly horrifying example of Brent Plate's notion of haptic religiosity![33]

A key element in the tension of *saguna bhakti* is beauty. Beauty is the primal power of attraction. It is not first and foremost beauty in the aesthetic sense, however. The *bhakta* to whom a divine *darshan* has happened is deeply struck by the complete lack of a sense of distance usually implied in the aesthetic. Beauty is the basic trauma for the Krishna *bhakta*.

Visions as Trauma

In both present-day and historical cases, exceptional performative religious behavior in the public sphere seems to have been engendered by a moment of singularity: the *darshan* of the (embodied) deity. After that epiphanic event, typically a life-long single-mindedness ensues in relation to the particular divine shape. The longing is directed toward renewal of the *darshan* and also, ideally, toward the constant presence of the divine beloved. Ultimately the union with him or dissolution in him is longed for. Singing and dancing and putting on beautiful dresses, jewelry, and make-up is intended to move the deity to perceptual manifestation. However, though the *darshan* seemed to involve a physical presence through embodiment, this turns out to be an illusion. The *viraha* (longing in separation) cannot be resolved in permanent *milan* (union), neither physically nor psychologically. That is the root of the dissonance I mentioned earlier.

Apparently, incisive moments of *darshan* work like traumas. The *bhakta* cannot possibly handle the beauty of the vision. A moment ago, I suggested that the *bhakta* seeks to repeat the event. But maybe, like in a trauma, he or she seeks to avoid it as well. Perhaps the emphasis on the aesthetic beauty of reenactment works as an addiction in order to avoid the trauma of the *darshan* occurring again.

It would seem that the embodiment of the gods in *saguna bhakti* is of great help for human beings to relate to the divine. Human agency in interacting with the deity appears to be possible. However, in experience the opposite is true. Often the legends about the gods as well as the stories by witnesses of their *darshan* give testimony of their elusive, unpredictable, often outrageous, and even treacherous behavior. Tulsidas was reportedly granted several visions of Rama. But he happened to miss them: it all passed too fast, or he was not able to make them out among other simultaneous impressions.

This is how Hawley and Juergensmeyer describe the *saguna bhakti* perspective: "To the mystery of God's manifestations, *bhakti* is the only adequate response. [Yet] to understand God from the point of view of his formlessness—the *nirguna* side—is far easier than trying to comprehend what the *saguna* side [with qualities, like in embodiment] can mean. [Since] the confusing presence of God turns things inside out and upside down."[34]

Music and *Bhakti*

It is striking that music plays a very important role in *bhakti*, especially in the devotion to Krishna. It is music as we know it, whether performed during gatherings of *bhaktas* (*bhajans* in *kirtan*), sung in personal devotional practice, or played back in the public space all over India.

There is also music that *provokes bhakti*, music believed to be played by Krishna himself, the divine Flutist. It is allegedly heard by some and pined for by innumerable others in India.

Music is well apt to serve *saguna bhakti*, devotion to the divine "with qualities." It makes possible devotional expression in sound with intense emotionality, praising the dazzling appearance of the divine Lover, elaborating on the qualities of love longing of the devotee in separation as a response to godly *saguna*. *Bhakti* music serves religious reenactment, often by taking the female voice of God's beloved. Indeed, the poetry typically is conceived from the experiential point of a female subject—whether handed down from female poet-saints such as Mirabai or male ones such as Surdas—and is sung passionately by women and men alike. It may happen that a process arises, experienced by the participants as "merging." I have met singers who do believe that, while singing *bhajans*, they unite with their great model poet-saints, such as Mirabai. Indeed, this is going to the root of the terms *bhakti* and *bhajan*—"sharing."

The devotional reenactment and sharing through music are generally more readily accepted in present-day India in everyday life context than reenactment through cross-dressing, which sent Inspector General of Police Devendra Kumar Panda to early retirement.

Moreover, music seems to share some of the ephemeral sensuousness and sensuality as well as the illusiveness of divine *darshans*. A *darshan* is experienced by devotees as traumatically sensuous and sensual, which may wean them from—or, as a reaction, throw themselves into—more common forms of sensuality and may lead them to asceticism in relation to the physical planes of embodiment in order to surrender to what they perceive as divine sensuous splendor. It is intriguing that music combines:

> strong psycho-physiological experiences (being—literally—moved by music on various planes, in various degrees of subtlety),

the semblance of embodiment (the voice as an individuality going through physical and emotional processes),

sensuousness and sensuality (the splendor of vocal unfolding and the overtone-rich instrumentality), and

a degree of ascetism (touch of the skin, including the eardrums, through air vibrations, not through direct bodily contact; leaving particularly the senses behind "that are most successful in convincing us that the world is solid, definite"; all this happening through the modeling of sound by means of highly formalized patterns).

This may well contribute to the privileged position of music in Hinduism, enabling the experience of the paradoxical weaning play by the Divine Seducer *par excellence*.

Notes

The research on which this essay is based was part of the project New Music and the Turn to Religion, funded under the Future of the Religious Past program.

1 See "Senior Cop Turns into 'Doosri Radha,'" *Hindu*, November 14, 2005; the incident made headlines across the Internet and discussions continue to this day. See also, "Swati with IG D K Panda (Doosri Radha)," on YouTube, featuring the Mr. Panda himself, dressed as Radha, eyes modestly cast-down; the video ends with "Radha" singing and dancing.

2. Some Sufi traditions practice the veneration of the physical remains of their saints in Indian and Pakistani *dargah*s (tombs); see R. de Groot, "Music, Religion, and Power: Qawwali as Empowering Disempowerment," in *Powers, Religion as a Social and Spiritual Force*, ed. M. B. ter Borg and J. W. van Henten (New York: Fordham University Press, 2010), 243–264.

3. "Police Officer Declares Himself Hindu Deity," Museum of Hoaxes, November 13, 2005, www.museumofhoaxes.com/hoax/weblog/comments/3764/.

4. "Police Officer Declares Himself Hindu Deity."

5. "Bol Radha Bol," a page dedicated to Mr. Panda, www.dial100dotcom.worldbreak.com/about.html.

6. "Police Officer Declares Himself Hindu Deity."

7. Akshay Khanna, "Trans-Gender Trauma in the Police Force," Women's Feature Service, December 11, 2005, www.boloji.com/wfs5/wfs506.htm.

8. "Police Officer Declares Himself Hindu Deity," comment by Svarat Dasa, Malaysia, November 17, 2005; spelling not corrected.

9. "Police Officer Declares Himself Hindu Deity," comment by Abhishek, UK, July 27, 2006; spelling not corrected.

10. Sandhya Jain, "Don't Demean Divine Radha," *Pioneer*, November 29, 2005.

11. Pankaj Mishra, "A New Sort of Superpower," *New Statesman*, January 30, 2006. Mishra is widely credited with discovering Arundhati Roy. His own international breakthrough novel, *The Romantics*, was published in 1999. Mishra's more recent work includes *An End to Suffering: The Buddha in the World* (2004) and *Temptations of the West: How to Be Modern in India, Pakistan, Tibet, and Beyond* (2006).

12. Mishra, "New Sort of Superpower." Note that Awadh is present-day Lucknow, the domicile of officer Panda; it is noteworthy that reference is made here to a Muslim ruler as a Radha impersonator.

13. John Stratton Hawley and Mark Juergensmeyer, *Songs of the Saints of India* (New York: Oxford University Press, 1988), 4.

14. Parita Mukta, *Upholding the Common Life: The Community of Mirabai* (Delhi: Oxford University Press, 1997), 39 and 38.

15. See in particular Mukta.

16. Hawley and Juergensmeyer, *Songs of the Saints of India*, 91.

17. Hawley and Juergensmeyer, 93.

18. Hawley and Juergensmeyer, 92.

19. Sister Nivedita, *My Master as I Saw Him* (Calcutta: Udbodhan Office, 1987), quoted in Dilip Kumar Roy and Indira Devi, *Pilgrims of the Stars: Autobiography of Two Yogis* (Mumbai: BharatiyaVidya Bhavan, 2002), 135.

20. Hawley and Juergensmeyer, *Songs of the Saints of India*, 92.

21. On Mirabai, see also Rokus de Groot, "The Reception in the Netherlands of an Indian Singing Saint: Meerabai in Film, in Translation and in Concert," *Tijdschrift van de Koninklijke Vereniging voor Nederlandse Muziekgeschiedenis* 56, no. 1 (2006): 25–65.

22. Hawley and Juergensmeyer, *Songs of the Saints of India*, 133.

23. See Mukta, *Upholding the Common Life*, 87. A similar poetic gesture is found in West-European mystical poetry, especially poems based on the biblical *Song of Songs*.

24. Even Kabir, for whom God without attributes (*nirguna*) is key to his poetry, sometimes expresses himself as one "longing for God as a woman might long for her lost lover." Hawley and Juergensmeyer, *Songs of the Saints of India*, 93.

25. A. J. Alston, ed. and trans., *The Devotional Poems of Mîrâbâî* (Delhi: Motilal Banarsidass, 1980), Poem 184, 110–111.

26. In November 1998, Snehlata Rajput, a forty-five-year-old physiotherapist, was married to Krishna by a priest in Kanpur—that is, to Krishna's portrait. As a fifteen-year-old girl, she had fallen in love with Krishna after having received visions. For the marriage she had bought silk saris and gold jewelry. Through Hare Krishna devotees participating in the marriage ceremony, she received silk cloths. Snehlata even purchased a new bed and linen. Several times she had declined a marriage proposal of mortal men. *Trouw*, November 30, 1998 (Dutch newspaper, quoting Associated Press).

27. Dilip Kumar Roy and Indira Devi, *Pilgrims of the Stars*, part 2.

28. Roy and Devi, *Pilgrims of the Stars*, 301.

29. Hawley and Juergensmeyer, *Songs of the Saints of India*, 94.

30. Louis-Marie Chauvet, *Du symbolique au symbole: Essai sur les Sacrements* (Paris: Cerf 1979), translated into English by Patrick Madigan and Madeleine Beaumont as *Symbol and Sacrament: A Sacramental Reinterpretation of Christian Existence* (Collegeville, Minnesota: The Liturgical Press, 1995); and *Symbole et sacrement: Une relecture sacramentelle de l'existence chrétienne* (Paris: Cerf 1988).

31. Hawley and Juergensmeyer, *Songs of the Saints of India*, 132–133.

32. A. J. Alston, ed. and trans., *The Devotional Poems of Mîrâbâî* (Delhi: Motilal Banarsidass, 1980), Poem 46, 53.

33. S. Brent Plate, ed., *Religion, Art, and Visual Culture* (New York: Palgrave Macmillan, 2002).

34. Hawley and Juergensmeyer, *Songs of the Saints of India*, 153.

CHAPTER 8

Islamic Dress and Fashion
A Religious and a Sartorial Practice Revisited

Annelies Moors

In the course of the last two decades an enormous variety of recognizably Islamic styles of dress has appeared on the streets of Muslim majority countries as well as in settings where Muslims constitute a minority, varying from colorful outfits put together by layering highly fashionable items to full-length overcoats in solid colors or black *abayas* in various shapes and qualities.[1] Shop windows, not only in the popular sections of big cities and smaller towns but also those of more upscale fashion houses in places such as London or Dubai, display a wide array of styles of Islamic dress. These outfits are also presented on the catwalks of the spectacular fashion shows held in the luxury hotels of major cities in the Gulf and Southeast Asia as well as in Muslim lifestyle magazines published not only in North America and the United Kingdom but also in Indonesia and the Middle East.[2] All kinds of styles of Islamic dress have also gained a strong online global presence, in the social media and on the Internet more generally.[3] As many of these outfits are highly fashionable, it does not come as a surprise that "Islamic fashion" has become a well-established, if not uncontested, short-hand term. Still, more sober and simple Islamic styles worn by those who obviously keep their distance from the world of fashion also have a measure of public presence, even if less widespread than the highly fashionable ones.[4]

Engaging with this wide-ranging presence of more and less fashionable Islamic styles, the central question of this contribution is how wearing Islamic dress works simultaneously as a sartorial and, in the eyes of at least some, a religious practice. In this essay,

I aim to understand how people do religion by wearing particular kinds of dress while simultaneously recognizing that religious considerations never fully determine the kind of outfits people opt for. I start with a brief note on the need to go beyond a visual analysis and to include people's own perspectives on how they put together an outfit. Next, I point to the need for a double move, that is to include dress in religious studies and religion in the study of dress in order to better grasp the religion-dress nexus. This is followed by a brief analysis of the emergence of fashionable styles of Islamic dress, as what people wear is always structured, albeit in different and often ambiguous ways, in relation to the world of fashion. In the last section, revisiting the relation between appearance and religiosity, I further investigate how covering and uncovering, wearing more and less fashionable styles of dress, may work to shape and publicly present a particular religious self. In doing so, I argue for the need to focus on context to better understand how people do religion through dress.[5]

A Note on Method: Beyond Visuality and Observation

Wearing Islamic styles of dress is, like all sartorial practices, polysemic and ambiguous. This contribution started with a brief sketch drawing on a visual register. While recognizing that acts are not necessarily rational and that a practice approach includes everyday acts that are more habitual than conscious, more matter-of-fact than well thought out, it is equally true that researchers cannot simply read the meanings of such acts through observation. Ethnographic fieldwork has always also included making an effort to gain insight in how people themselves understand the practices they engage in.[6] In order to better understand sartorial practices, in particular the motivations and intentions of those opting for such styles, informal conversations and a topical life-story method that focuses on the religion-dress nexus are particularly helpful.[7] Only then is it possible to understand whether a particular style of appearing in public is, for instance, an intentional religious practice, a response to peer pressure, or a failure to live up to one's own standards of religiosity.

There are also other reasons why a "snapshot" approach with its strong visual register is problematic. Whereas we can discern a diversity of sartorial styles, this diversity may easily slip into categorizations of people on the basis of their appearance. It tends to assume a more or less stable relation between person and sartorial style. In some cases, this may indeed be what is at stake. At the same time, it is important to recognize that there are not only differences between individuals but that one and the same individual may wear different styles of

Islamic dress, depending on the particular context she is operating in. Moreover, a topical life-story approach also helps us to understand how wearing a particular outfit fits into the life trajectories of individuals. The very same colorful yet covered outfit may for one person be the first step to wearing more covered styles of dress, but for someone else it may be a move toward less strict and sober forms of covering.[8]

An approach that focuses on visuality also overlooks how wearing clothing is a *multisensorial* experience that does not only appeal to the distant sense of vision (even if highlighted in Islamic discourse) but also to the proximate sense of touch. Attention to women's talk about dress reveals the extent to which the selection of what to wear also engages with the haptic or tactile qualities of particular fibers and fabrics.[9] Moreover, as the relatively new field of wardrobe studies indicates, whether people keep and wear certain items of dress is not necessarily motivated by ethics or aesthetics but includes the ways in which women acquire particular items of dress as gifts, embodying the relation with the giver, as souvenirs, or for specific events, producing particular attachments and feelings related to the social life of these items of dress.

Wearing Islamic Dress: A Religious Practice and Beyond

How does clothing relate to religion? In religious studies the focus has not only been more on religious doctrine and institutions than on the everyday practices of lay people, but the mundane topic of dress and fashion poses particular problems. With the definition of religion strongly influenced by a modern, largely Protestant perspective, many would consider dressing styles as far too much concerned with appearances, exteriority, and the superficial to be considered worthy of the label religious, which they would reserve for interior states of being, for belief and faith.[10] Moreover, it is not simply such a Protestant take on religion that is at stake. Interior feelings and convictions (matters of content) always need to take on a particular form in order to be present in the world, such as through the material presence of words or bodies.[11]

If a focus on dress needs to be included in religious studies, it has been convincingly argued that religion may need to be taken more seriously in the study of dress. In her *Politics of Piety*,[12] Saba Mahmood has argued that writings about veiling have often employed an instrumentalist perspective, analyzing it as a means for women to acquire greater freedom of movement or as a form of identity politics or sign of allegiance to Islamist movements.[13] Arguing against the Orientalist trope of Muslim women's subordination, these authors analyze veiling as a form of resistance to domination. Based on her research with pious women engaged in the mosque movement in Cairo, Mahmood argues that it is also important to entertain the possibility that veiling may be a religious practice, as this is what the women concerned highlighted. Taking a critical stance vis-à-vis the assumption that humans have an innate desire for freedom defined in terms of individual autonomy, she considers the ethical practices of these women as a form of willed submission and hence of agentic power.[14]

Analyzing how religious dress works, also invites revisiting the relation between sartorial practices and interior states of being. Rather than considering wearing covered dress as an expression of a preexisting inner state of being, Mahmood points out that for the women of the mosque movement outward behavior and bodily acts were crucial means by which to realize or bring about a desired inner state of being, for it is through the repeated performance of such practices that a virtuous self is produced.[15] Such an emphasis on the performative power of dress tallies with much of recent anthropological work on dress, which does not consider sartorial practices simply as a form of representation but rather recognizes how these practices actively contribute to the process of subject-making.[16] Such an approach then shifts the debate from whether dress conceals or reveals inner states of being toward a focus on how sartorial practices are part and parcel of the production of subjectivity.[17]

Whereas women may wear Islamic styles of dress for religious reasons,[18] it is also evident that their religious convictions do not fully determine what they wear. Even if Islamic lines of argumentation are used to argue against wearing particular cuts (insufficiently covering or too revealing of the body shape), materials (too transparent), and designs (images of living creatures), Islamic rulings do not prescribe the specific shapes items should have nor the texture and quality of the fabric, its colors, patterns, or texture. Attention needs to be paid to the multiple forms wearing covered dress may take. Getting dressed is an everyday corporeal practice that relates to the multiple subject positions a person inhabits and includes aesthetic and stylistic choices which may accentuate or reinforce religious concerns or sit in tension with them. How people position themselves in the field of dress is always informed by multiple processes of subjectivation, that produce not only religious subjects, but subjects who are simultaneously co-constituted through other axes of differentiation. The outfits they wear, be it the more sober or the more fashionable styles, refer not only to religiosity but also, for instance, to class and generation, to ethnic and national belonging, and to membership of particular taste in communities that may favor an urban, trendy, sporty, elegant, or feminine look.[19]

When we do not only focus on the act of covering but also on the numerous shapes this may take, we need to engage with the spread of more (and less) fashionable styles of Islamic dress. In the contemporary world, what people wear is strongly influenced by trends in the world of fashion. Even those who purposely distance themselves from fashion wear clothes that represent a reaction against what is in fashion.[20] Bringing fashion into the equation also provides yet another take on women's agency and subjectivity. As mentioned previously, veiling has often been framed in terms of resistance to domination in reaction to the hegemonic discourse about Muslim women's subordination. Something similar is at stake in debates about Islamic fashion. Whereas many have pointed to "the tyranny of fashion," in the specific case of Muslim women, wearing Islamic fashion has often been celebrated as a liberating practice. Such a perspective on fashion stands in a tense relation to fashion theorists' work about how fashion works. Simmel already argued that fashion involves not only individualizing but also conformist impulses that homogenize and work as a disciplinary force.[21] More recently, Finkelstein argued that fashion may better be understood in terms of subjectivation than in terms of individual autonomy or freedom of expression, as in the case of fashion, individualizing involves distinction, but within the boundaries of a shared code, a restricted aesthetics.[22] Even emerging street styles and their improvisational aesthetic tend to soon become mainstreamed through the force of fashion and fashion media.

Secular Outfits, Islamic Dress, and Islamic Fashion

Whereas it is true that for some Muslims the notion of Islamic fashion is an oxymoron, many others are actively engaged in producing, propagating, circulating, and wearing highly fashionable styles of Islamic dress. Such a widespread public presence of Islamic fashion on a global scale is yet another strong indication that the secularization thesis, in as far as it refers to the relegation of religion to the private sphere, has not materialized. It is true that in the course of the twentieth century in many Muslim majority countries elements of a Western lifestyle including European styles of dress had been adopted, especially among the middle and upper classes. However, it is equally true that large sections of the population opted for styles of dress that they themselves considered within the boundaries of what would be religiously acceptable.

Moreover, the 1970s and 1980s saw the ascendency of an Islamic revival movement that encouraged a growing number of women who previously would have opted for Western styles of dress to adopt recognizably Islamic, covered styles of dress.²³ Authors sometimes referred to this trend as "the new veiling" to underline that it entailed a new style of covered dress that was worn by young, well-educated women, who used a strongly reflexive language when explaining why they adopted such a style of dress.²⁴ For some this "new veiling" expressed and embodied their affinity to Islamist movements critical of Western domination and local authoritarian regimes in countries such as Egypt, Turkey, Lebanon, or Indonesia.²⁵ For others wearing new covered styles of dress was part of a broader piety movement that had emerged in response to the increased secularization of everyday life.²⁶

This "new veiling" initially entailed a move toward a relatively uniform, simple, and austere style, which many hoped would do away with the sartorial distinctions between the wealthy and the poor.²⁷ In countries such as Turkey and Egypt, women often wore full-length and loose overcoats in combination with large headscarves that covered all the hair as well as the chest and upper part of the back. Such styles also spread to Muslim communities elsewhere. By the 1990s, however, more fashionable styles of Islamic dress began to appear in Muslim majority countries such as Turkey, giving rise to what has become known as "Islamic fashion."²⁸ In part this shift from dress to fashion reflected a shift within the Islamic revival movement from a radical and anti-consumerist position toward a more individualized reformist stance with identities increasingly produced through consumption.²⁹ It engendered a greater heterogeneity of Islamic styles of dress that included fashions that were attractive and appealing to younger, more affluent Islamic women.³⁰ In some locations, such as Southern Beirut, where a new generation that had grown up in an Islamic environment was coming of age, the turn to Islamic fashion was part of the spread of Islamically licit forms of consumption and entertainment.³¹ The move toward trendy, fashionable, yet recognizably Islamic dress was also discernible in settings where all-covering outerwear had been the norm, such as North Yemen, Saudi Arabia, and the Gulf States. In such locations, the increased commoditization of dress and the turn to consumer culture stimulated more rapid changes in styles of outerwear.³² These were also purchased by migrants, students, and visitors from other parts of the world who integrated them into their wardrobes in their home countries.³³

Whereas some designers and entrepreneurs cater specifically to the Islamic fashion sector, young Muslim women in settings where Muslims are a national minority, especially in Europe, also frequent the same shops—high street brands such as H&M and Top Shop—as do other young women of their peer group and generation. Through layering and combining items of dress that are not specifically designed for Muslims, they put together outfits that look both up-to-date and

Islamic and that signal their engagement with both fashion and faith. By combining elements of existing styles to produce new meanings, they exercise their skill as *bricoleuses* and simultaneously align themselves with the improvisational aesthetics characteristic of contemporary street styles more generally. In doing so, these young Muslim women create a presence that has the potential to destabilize some of the long-established perceptions of Muslim women. Wearing such highly fashionable styles works well against the image of Muslim women as dull, downtrodden, oppressed, and out of sync with modernity. Precisely because the corporeal aesthetics of fashion have historically been so strongly linked to modernity, they become a convenient means by which women are able to distance themselves from the common stereotypical images of Muslim women.

Appearance and Religiosity Revisited

The emergence of the fashion system has made it difficult to remain outside the world of fashion. Even those who purposely distance themselves from fashion wear clothes that represent a reaction against what is in fashion. Yet as those engaging in wardrobe research have pointed out, women also own and wear items of dress that are selected for other reasons than being fashionable, such as the particular feel of an item or the memories it incorporates. This is equally the case for those wearing secular styles of dress and for those who opt for recognizably Islamic styles. Headscarves, for instance, are highly mobile commodities that are easily acquired but hard to discard especially when they are received as gifts or bought as souvenirs, that is, are linked to particular people, places, and events. They are often turned into collections that may be considered as the materialization of the relations of the wearer with those who have "contributed to the collection." In other words, a woman's attachment to particular headscarves goes beyond aesthetic styles.[34]

Returning to the question how wearing Islamic dress works as both a sartorial and a religious practice, or how people do religion through dress, the argument is that the kinds of covered dress that women wear and the ways in which they live Islam mutually constitute each other. This takes us beyond the work of Mahmood, as it does not only consider strict forms of covering, but also uncovering or donning fashionable styles as related to particular forms of religiosity and means to produce and express particular subjectivities.[35]

Particular ideas about covering in some cases intersect with particular strands of Islam. For instance, whereas Salafi-oriented women tend to wear loose and strictly covering styles of dress, Alevi women in Turkey generally do not wear such forms of covered dress. Practitioners of these different strands of Islam conceptualize the relation between religion and dress in divergent ways. Whereas for the former, wearing strictly covered styles of dress is a religious virtue, for the latter external appearances are largely irrelevant for doing religion, which implied that they adopted less Islamically marked styles. In other words, some Muslims also share a concept of religion that foregrounds faith and perceive religiosity as an inner quality that does not require the adoption of covered dress. This then implies that also in this latter case, when noncovering styles are adopted, this may be seen within the framework of particular forms of religiosity. Moreover, the women who highly value strict covering, point out that adopting such styles only works as a God-pleasing act if it is done with the right intention, that is as a conscious, willed act and not for instrumental reasons, under pressure, or simply to fit in.[36]

It is, however, not only when people adhere to such different strands of Islam, that less covering implies a different way of doing religion rather than a disengagement from religion. Another example comes from research in Sana'a, Yemen. Whereas the majority of San'ani women wear a face-veil, since the later 1970s a small yet growing number of women has refrained from doing so. These women would, however, not consider themselves as less concerned with religion. On the contrary, they have argued that according to Islam women do not need to cover their face and hands and that, covering the face is only a San'ani cultural tradition. Hence, they called their style of dress *hijab islami*, the Islamic hijab. Moreover, women who conventionally would cover their face in Sana'a, also use religious arguments to explain why they may take off their face-veil once they travel to countries where wearing it is considered a strongly transgressive practice. In their opinion, wearing a face-veil in Europe goes against the Islamic principle that points to the need to avoid attracting men's gazes. If in Sana'a face-veiling is a majority practice and hence does not draw the attention of others, in Europe the opposite is the case.

In a similar vein, wearing more fashionable styles has also often been taken as an indication of wearers' lesser concern with religion. A strong objection against such a point of view is that it is not necessarily a relative disinterest in religion but rather that such a "seduction by fashion" may point to a failure to live up to one's religious standards. More generally, some would consider the shift to increasingly fashionable styles of Islamic dress as an example of a more general societal shift away from communities of conviction to communities of style.[37] However, it is evident that, as at least some of the women involved have pointed out, appearing well groomed, neat, and presenting a pleasant and harmonious look can be considered an act that pleases God.[38] This theological take on Islamic fashion is further heightened by the idea that wearing aesthetically pleasing forms of Islamic dress can act as a form of *da'wa*, inviting others toward the faith.[39] Islamic fashion with its emphasis on combining Islam with beauty may work as a means to persuade others of the beauty of modesty, while wearing pleasant-looking styles of Islamic dress that fit in with current fashion may produce a positive image of Islam in an Islam-hostile environment.[40] Here Islamic virtue is seen not as external to fashion but potentially integral to it, thereby making the creation and wearing of fashionable styles a form and extension of religious action.

Next to such a more nuanced perspective on the relations between religion and dress—which also allows for religiosity to be expressed and performed through those engaged in less strict and sober forms of covering—the other main argument is that styles of dress are never fully determined by religious considerations.[41] As individuals position themselves simultaneously along different axes of differentiation that co-constitute each other, the outfits they choose—within the range of dress they find acceptable—are also inflected by, for instance, class and generation. The main point is, however, not only that sartorial practices are influenced by other identities and belongings but also that one and the same person may opt to wear different Islamic styles depending on the particular context they are operating in.

Recognizing the multiple positions individuals may take up with respect to Islamic dress also underwrites that it is not possible to slot people into communities of style, as they may adopt a variety of styles depending on the occasion. Some well-educated professional women in Sana'a, for instance, wear very different styles of covered dress depending on the kinds of activities they are engaged in. They may, for instance, wear a full-length pastel-colored overcoat with a large square headscarf in matching colors, when they go to teach or attend university classes. The very same women may change their outfits when they go shopping in the central market area, as in such a setting they prefer to appear in the more anonymous, long, black, abaya-like outfits with black rectangular veils combined with a face-veil. Whereas at the university they feel the desire to present their individuality to others, in the market they like to easily blend in and remain anonymous, as this makes it easier to bargain with the shopkeepers. In a similar vein, Turkish-Dutch women in the Netherlands who are professionally employed are often careful to adopt a style of covered dress that fits in with their work environment, and that is not too markedly Turkish. However, when they attend events organized by the ethnic-religious community they are affiliated with, they make sure to wear an outfit that indicates their closeness to the community, for instance, by tying their headscarf "in the style of the community."[42]

The meaning of outfits may also differ substantially depending on the context one operates in. Some young Turkish-Dutch women have adopted simple monochrome rectangular shawls which they wrap closely around the face. Such shawls are popular among a wide range of Muslim women in the Netherlands and beyond, in particular among Moroccan-Dutch women, but also with those of other ethnic backgrounds and converts. This particular style of headscarf—in terms of shape, texture, fabrics, color, and shine—stands in sharp contrast to the colorful, patterned, shiny satin scarves that many Turkish-Dutch women wear, folded in such a way that it does not show the hair yet stands away a bit from the face, especially on the top. It is precisely because the former style is seen as less strongly ethnically marked, that also some Turkish-Dutch women have started to adopt it in settings where they mingle with those of other ethnic backgrounds. Yet when these women wear the very same shawls in Istanbul, they run the risk of being ostracized for their distinctively unfashionable look, as, in the words of their critics such a style resembles that of "their great-grandmothers."[43] A last example of the very different ways in which a particular style may be interpreted is what some San'ani women experienced who went to study in Cairo in the late 1970s and 1980s. Traveling abroad to Egypt, they had adopted the full-length coats in muted colors that a few women had started to wear in Sana'a (the very same ones who did not adopt the face-veil). In Sana'a, such a style was seen as quintessentially modern and an indication of a more liberal reformist religiosity. An additional reason to wear such an outfit in Egypt was that the more conventional long, flowing black outfits that were commonly worn in Sana'a looked far too similar to the black, loose over-garments that women from the poor sections of Cairo would be seen wearing. However, at that time wearing such full-length coats in Egypt was not linked to a more liberal form of Islam but considered as a sign of affiliation to Islamist movements. In other words, a focus on visuality and observation enables the production of a vivid description of the varieties of Islamic dress present in the public. It does, however, only provide limited insights in how dress relates to how women live religion. This then also points to the problem of how particular styles of dress and the intentions of the women adopting such styles are interpreted by the public.

Notes

1. Annelies Moors and Emma Tarlo, "Introduction: Islamic Fashion and Anti-Fashion: New Perspectives from Europe and North America," in *Islamic Fashion and*

Anti-Fashion. New Perspectives from Europe and North America, ed. Emma Tarlo and Annelies Moors (London: Bloomington, 2013), 1–30; Özlem Sandıkçı and Güliz Ger, "Veiling in Style: How Does a Stigmatized Practice Become Fashionable," *Journal of Consumer Research* 37 (2010): 15–36; and Emma Tarlo, *Visibly Muslim: Integrating Fashion, Politics and Faith* (London: Berg Publishers, 2010).

2. Reina Lewis, "Marketing Muslim Lifestyle: A New Media Genre," *Journal of Middle East Women's Studies* 6, no. 3 (2010): 58–90.

3. H. Akou, "Building a New 'World Fashion': Islamic Dress in the Twenty-first Century," *Fashion Theory* 11, no. 4 (2007): 403–421; Tarlo, *Visibly Muslim*; Annelies Moors, "'Discover the Beauty of Modesty': Islamic Fashion Online," in *Modest Fashion: Styling Bodies, Mediating Faith*, ed. Reina Lewis (London: I. B. Tauris, 2013), 17–40.

4. Annelies Moors, "Fashion and Its Discontents: The Aesthetics of Covering in the Netherlands," in Tarlo and Moors, *Islamic Fashion and Anti-Fashion*, 241–260.

5. This contribution focuses on the public dressing styles of Muslim women. Public refers here to all settings where non-*mahram* men may be present. When I refer to the relevance of context, this goes beyond the presence or absence of non-*mahram* men.

6. Johannes Fabian, *Time and the Other: How Anthropology Makes It Object* (New York: Columbia University Press, 1983).

7. For a topical life-story method, see Daniel Bertaux, *Biography and Society: The Life History Approach in the Social Sciences* (Beverly Hills, CA: Sage Publications, 1981). In spite of the problems of the difference between saying and doing and the ways in which stories about the past are influenced by positions in the present, topical life-stories nonetheless are helpful to better understand how those involved present their actions.

8. Annelies Moors, "'Islamic Fashion' in Europe: Religious Conviction, Aesthetic Style, and Creative Consumption," *Encounters* 1, no. 1 (2009), 175–201.

9. Emma Tarlo, "Islamic Cosmopolitanism: The Sartorial Biographies of Three Muslim Women in London," *Fashion Theory* 11, nos. 2–3 (2007): 143–172; Arzu Ünal and Annelies Moors, "Formats, Fabrics, and Fashions: Muslim Headscarves Revisited," *Material Religion* 8, no. 3 (2012): 308–329.

10. Talal Asad, *Genealogies of Religion: Discipline and Power in Christianity and Islam* (Baltimore, MD: Johns Hopkins University Press, 1993).

11. Birgit Meyer and Dick Houtman, "Introduction: Material Religion—How Things Matter," in *Things: Religion and the Question of Materiality*, ed. D. Houtman and B. Meyer (New York: Fordham University Press, 2012).

12. Saba Mahmood, *Politics of Piety: The Islamic Revival and the Feminist Subject* (Princeton, NJ: Princeton University Press, 2005).

13. For the freedom of movement argument, see, for example, Arlene McLeod, *Accommodating Protest: Working Women, the New Veiling, and Changes in Cairo* (New York: Columbia University Press, 1991). For identity politics, Leila Ahmed, *Women and Gender in Islam: Historical Roots of a Modern Debate* (New Haven, CT: Yale University Press, 1992); Fadwa El-Guindi, "Veiling Infitah with Muslim Ethic: Egypt's Contemporary

Islamic Movement," *Social Problems* 28, no. 4 (1981): 465–485; Nilüfer Göle, *The Forbidden Modern: Civilization and Veiling* (Ann Arbor: University of Michigan Press, 1996); Yael Navaro-Yashin, "The Market for Identities: Secularism, Islamism, Commodities," in *Fragments of Culture: The Everyday of Modern Turkey*, ed. D. Kandiyoti and A. Saktanber (New Brunswick, NJ: Rutgers University Press, 2002).

14. Mahmood, *Politics of Piety*, 17, 28.
15. Mahmood, 158; see also Ünal, "Wardrobes of Turkish-Dutch Women."
16. Tarlo, *Visibly Muslim*; Miller, *Stuff*.
17. Moors and Tarlo, "Introduction: Islamic Fashion and Anti-Fashion."
18. The argument is not that wearing recognizably Islamic styles of dress is necessarily religiously motivated. It is entirely possible that Muslims also may wear such styles for instrumental reasons. In a similar vein, Muslims do not necessarily wear covered dress as a technique of the self; some also do so to express a particular identity or inner state of being (see also Mahmood, *Politics of Piety*). It is, however, important to recognize that wearing particular forms of dress may be a religious practice that functions as a technique of the self.
19. Tarlo, *Visibly Muslim*; Annelies Moors, "'Islamic Fashion' in Europe: Religious Conviction, Aesthetic Style, and Creative Consumption," *Encounters* 1, no. 1 (2009): 175–201.
20. Elizabeth Wilson, *Adorned in Dreams: Fashion and Modernity* (London: Virago Press, 1985).
21. Georg Simmel, *On Individuality and Social Forms: Selected Writings*, ed. Donald N. Levine (Chicago: University of Chicago Press, 1971 [1904]).
22. Joanne Finkelstein, "Chic Theory," *Australian Humanities Review*, no. 5 (2007): 6, http://australianhumanitiesreview.org/1997/03/01/chic-theory/.
23. Fadwa El-Guindi, "Veiling Infitah with Muslim Ethic: Egypt's Contemporary Islamic Movement," *Social Problems* 28, no. 4 (1981): 465–485; and Nilüfer Göle, *The Forbidden Modern: Civilization and Veiling* (Ann Arbor: University of Michigan Press, 1996).
24. McLeod, *Accommodating Protest*.
25. On Egypt, see Fadwa El-Guindi, *Veil: Modesty, Privacy and Resistance* (London: Berg Publishers, 1999); on Turkey: Göle, *The Forbidden Modern*; on Lebanon: Lara Deeb, *An Enchanted Modern: Gender and Public Piety in Shi'i Lebanon* (Princeton, NJ: Princeton University Press, 2006); on Indonesia: Brenner, "Reconstructing Self and Society, 673–697.
26. Notably Mahmood, *Politics of Piety*.
27. Yael Navaro-Yashin, "The Market for Identities: Secularism, Islamism, Commodities," in *Fragments of Culture: The Everyday of Modern Turkey*, ed. D. Kandiyoti and A. Saktanber (New Brunswick, NJ: Rutgers University Press, 2002); Sandıkçı and Ger, "Veiling in Style," 15–36.
28. However, fashionable styles of Islamic dress have a far longer history. As Ünal has indicated ("Wardrobes of Turkish-Dutch Women"), the various items that make up a "covered dress wardrobe" (all-covering outerwear, headscarves, long skirts, and

trousers) all have a genealogy in which at least since the late nineteenth century, fashion also plays a role.

29. Navaro-Yashin, "Market for Identities."

30. Barış Kılıçbay and Mutlu Binark, "Consumer Culture, Islam, and the Politics of Lifestyle: Fashion for Veiling in Contemporary Turkey," *European Journal of Communication* 17, no. 4 (2002): 495–511; Özlem Sandıkçı and Güliz Ger, "Constructing and Representing the Islamic Consumer in Turkey," 189–210; Sandıkçı and Ger "Veiling in Style"; and Mona Abaza, "Shifting Landscapes of Fashion in Contemporary Egypt," *Fashion Theory* 11, nos. 2–3 (2007): 281–299.

31. Lara Deeb and Mona Harb, "Sanctioned Pleasures: Youth, Piety, and Leisure in Beirut," *Middle East Report* 245 (2007): 12–19.

32. Annelies Moors, "Fashionable Muslims: Notions of Self, Religion, and Society in San'a," *Fashion Theory* 11, nos. 2–3 (2007): 319–347; Noor Al-Qasimi, "Immodest Modesty: Accommodating Dissent and the 'abaya-as-fashion' in the Arab Gulf States," *Journal of Middle East Women's Studies* 6, no. 1 (2010): 46–74; Christina Lindholm, "Invisible No More: The Embellished Abaya in Qatar," Textile Society of America Symposium Proceedings (Lincoln: University of Nebraska Press, 2010), http://digitalcommons.unl.edu/cgi/viewcontent.cgi?article=1033&context=tsaconf.

33. Caroline Osella and Filippo Osella, "Muslim Style in South-India," *Fashion Theory* 11, nos. 2–3 (2007): 233–52.

34. Ünal and Moors, "Formats, Fabrics and Fashions."

35. Religious arguments for uncovering, concerning the case of Muslim women in Belgium, are also presented in Nadia Fadil, "Not-/Unveiling as an Ethical Practice," *Feminist Review* 98, no. 1 (2011): 83–109.

36. This tallies closely with broader academic debates on the question how far external appearances can be read as indicators of interior states of being, with many recognizing that outward appearances may reveal as well as conceal inner states of being. On one hand, in everyday interactions people tend to assume that it is possible to read appearances and to know the interior self and inner character from external signs; see Finkelstein, "Chic Theory." On the other hand, at least from the nineteenth century on, there has also been a growing suspicion that appearances are constructed, and hence cannot be trusted as "authentic"; see Joanne Entwistle, *The Fashioned Body: Fashion, Dress, and Modern Social Theory* (Cambridge: Polity Press, 2000), 123. Dress, then, has the potential to both reveal and conceal.

37. Michel Maffesoli, *The Time of the Tribes: The Decline of Individualism in Mass Society* (London: Sage, 1996).

38. Özlem Sandıkçı and Güliz Ger, "Aesthetics, Ethics, and Politics of the Turkish Headscarf," in *Clothing as Material Culture*, ed. S. Kuechler and D. Miller (London: Berg Publishers, 2005); Ünal, "Wardrobes of Turkish-Dutch Women."

39. Yasmin Moll, "Islamic Televangelism: Religion, Media, and Visuality in Contemporary Egypt," *Arab Media and Society* 10 (2010), https://www.arabmediasociety.com/islamic-televangelism-religion-media-and-visuality-in-contemporary-egypt/.

40. Jeannette Jouili, "Negotiation Secular Boundaries: Pious Micro-Practices of Muslim Women in French and German Public Spheres," *Social Anthropology* 17, no. 4 (2009): 455–470; Tarlo, *Visibly Muslim*.

41. Moors and Tarlo, "Introduction: Islamic Fashion and Anti-Fashion"; Ünal, "Wardrobes of Turkish-Dutch Women."

42. Ünal, "Wardrobes of Turkish-Dutch Women"; Ünal and Moors, "Formats, Fabrics, and Fashions."

43. Ünal, "Wardrobes of Turkish-Dutch Women."

CHAPTER 9

On Spirit Writing

Materialities of Language and the Religious Work of Transduction

Webb Keane

This is a speculative essay in comparative possibilities. It looks at some widely separated religious contexts in which a power-laden relationship across ontological difference—for instance, between living humans and a world of gods or spirits—is mediated by operations on the materiality of the written sign. These operations typically result in either materializing something immaterial or dematerializing something material. But they may also involve other activities that take advantage of specific physical properties of the written word such as being persistent, transportable, perishable, alienable, and so forth. Once divine words are rendered into script, they possess a distinctively material quality and form. They appear on some physical medium, and so are both durable and potentially destructible. Anything that can happen to another artifact can happen to them. The practices I dub "spirit writing" subject the written word to radical transformation, taking advantage of its very materiality in order to dematerialize it, even if only in order to be rematerialized in yet some other form (such as a person's body). Many such practices seek to generate or control religious powers by means of transduction across semiotic modalities, material activities that help render experience-transcending forces realistic or at least readily imaginable.

Across a wide range of contexts, people respond to various possibilities and powers that the materiality of writing can seem to suggest.[1] These responses are hardly confined to exotic curiosities. Take, for example, the "Good Riddance Day" staged in New York City at the end of 2007. An industrial-size paper shredder had been brought to Times Square "to give people an opportunity to get rid of their most unpleasant reminders" of the year.[2] As people crowded to the spot, they showed how inventively one might take up the invitation offered by a large mechanical device, bringing all sorts of physical tokens of otherwise immaterial memories they wanted to dispose of. The reminders included failed exam scores, mortgages, evidence of broken engagements, and other forms of paper documentation. Reducing potent words to illegible matter, their bearers took advantage of their ability to act upon material stuff in order to enact a hoped-for transformation of thought and feeling. Thus, the very physicality of writing and its media seems to have prompted ordinary New Yorkers to spontaneously reinvent, in rudimentary form and no doubt with some self-mockery, an aspect of ritual—one they may not have imagined before (and one that, once invented, may or may not take on an explicitly "religious" character)—that belongs, at the margins, to a large and highly diverse family of practices I will call, for economy's sake, "spirit writing."

In this essay I look at some widely separated religious contexts in which a power-laden relationship across ontological difference—for instance, between living humans and a world of gods or spirits—is mediated by operations on the materiality of the written sign.[3] These operations typically result in either materializing something immaterial or dematerializing something material. But they may also involve other activities that take advantage of specific physical properties of the written word such as being persistent, portable, perishable, alienable, and so forth. Once divine words are rendered into script, they possess a distinctively material quality and form. They appear on some physical medium, and so are both durable and potentially destructible. Anything that can happen to another artifact can happen to them: they can be transported, hidden, revealed, embraced, kissed, spat upon, burned, decorated, copied, ingested—the possibilities are, in principle, without limit.

Many of these practices subject the written word to radical transformation, taking advantage of its very materiality (the fact of being soluble ink or flammable paper, for instance) in order to dematerialize it, even if only in order to be rematerialized in yet some other form (such as inscription on or ingestion within a person's body). I argue that such practices often seek to generate religious powers by means of what might be called "transduction" across semiotic modalities.[4] Consider how a turbine works. It transforms the movement of water into the quite different motion of a mechanical device in order to generate power. The water in motion becomes electrical energy. By analogy, semiotic transduction aims to tap into the power that can be obtained by the very act of transforming something from one semiotic modality to another. Although it is probably true that in most cases the divine *source* of the words is considered by practitioners to be the ultimate source of power, this alone does not explain the practice. Rather, the ability of humans to gain access to that divine power depends on the act of transformation. It seems these practices develop a notion that the very capacity to alter or move among semiotic modalities is itself a source of efficacy. I propose that such practices of "spirit writing" are evidence that the perceptual experience of writing offers some very general features. That is, for all their cultural and historical specificity, practices of materialization and dematerialization draw on ubiquitous properties of writing. These properties are thematized in the practices of transduction. Going against the particularizing trend of much humanistic research, I want to suggest that these practices may open up possible avenues for ethnographic and historical comparison. Comparative endeavors in anthropology and history have long been out of favor, mostly for good reason,[5] but their rejection has come at a steep cost. This essay, in a frankly speculative spirit, aims to suggest one opening toward the reinvention of the comparative imagination in these fields.

I hasten to add, however, that this does not mean we should leap to any strong universalistic claims about religion, language, or writing. If writing offers affordances of which people *might* take advantage, it does not determine or require that they *do* so.[6] Local linguistic and semiotic ideologies are crucial preconditions for any practice of transduction. More generally, of course, any given ethnographic analysis will, in the final instance, depend on a grasp of the particularities of social context, the interpretative frames of culture, the pressures of politics, and contingencies of events. To say this, however, verges on mere truism for contemporary sociocultural anthropology and allied disciplines. Taking it to be axiomatic that context is everything, anthropologists sometimes forget to ask what can count as context. The affordances sketched out here can be understood as aspects of context as much as any culturally, sociologically, or politically specific circumstance. Indeed, one might argue that even the ubiquitous, transcontextual aspects of writing are themselves conditions of possibility for the kinds of historical difference on which anthropology has tended to dwell. One reason has to do with the inherent historicity that is implicit in the very materiality—and thus sociality—of religious practice, and the semiotic ideologies it presupposes.[7] But I cannot fully develop that claim within the limits of this essay.

Inscription in the Body

In its materiality, writing shares some features with *any* physical entity that might be taken as a sign. Certain basic themes of spirit writing are apparent, for instance, in nonliterate divination. Haruspicy, or entrails divination, was commonplace on Sumba, in eastern Indonesia, at the end of the twentieth century. (It is noteworthy that Sumbanese sometimes called haruspicy "our writing," comparable to the writing systems possessed by the Javanese, Balinese, Arabs, and the former colonizers, the Dutch, and closely associated with their political, economic, and cultural power.[8]) In Sumba, the living interacted with ancestral spirits by means of spoken words. Spirits were not represented in iconic form; nor did people have clear ideas about where the spirits might be located. Verbal interaction with spirits imposed a material requirement that it be accompanied by the sacrifice of an animal, such as a chicken or pig. Speech was conveyed to the animal, whose demise enabled it to carry words to the dead. But the dead are located somewhere beyond the realm of human sensual experience. The diviner thus faced a common religious problem, namely how do those who exist beyond our perceptions, those whom we cannot see, hear, smell, or feel, respond to us?[9] In Sumba, the conventional solution was to open up the dead animal after the sacrifice and seek out signs in its intestines or liver.

The marks on entrails are *visible* answers to *spoken* questions. One of their fundamental properties is that they cross semiotic modalities. They reply to speech in a medium other than speech. In the process, they also respond to denotational language with indexical (and sometimes iconic) signs.[10] Thus a shift of medium can alter pragmatic functions and the relative weighting of semiotic characteristics, a shift to which the multiple relations among linguistic form, semantics, and pragmatics readily lend themselves. What is crucial here is that this relationship of semiotic difference between query and reply is paralleled by that between the ontological planes in which the agents are situated. The marks on entrails are physical signs that arrive from a nonphysical world that otherwise remains invisible and silent. Their very character as signs embodies the ontological problem to which they are posed, for at the start of the ritual it is never certain whether the spirits are present. Entrails reading is a response to the problem of interaction with nonmanifest others. The spirits enter the perceptual world via the hidden interior of the body—in this case, that of the sacrificial animal. The act of opening that body and reading its entrails draws attention to the very invisibility of the sources of those marks.

The scenario staged by entrails reading shows some basic problems to which spirit writing is often meant as a solution: how does one cope in practical terms with an invisible and silent world, and what can one hope to gain from doing so?[11] This is the practical expression of an ontological dilemma. To the extent that living humans seek out relations with an invisible and silent world, then they will tend to encounter difficulties centering on their own materiality as well as that of the world they perceive and the media for action that are available to them.

The study of religion has two traditional approaches to such problems.[12] One starts from what we might (in shorthand) call a religious perspective; the other does not, but they are symmetrical. If, on one hand, we begin by taking the existence of some realm beyond immediate sense perception as given, then the question will take the form "How does that world reach us? How can we reach it?" If, on the other hand, we start from the position (again in shorthand) of an outsider to the religious perspective, that sensual perceptions of a material world are the given, then the question can be formulated as "What perceptions will count as signs of something beyond? How do material practices make the invisible world a presupposable ground for what practitioners perceive? How do people produce the immaterial using the material means available to them?" Although I will start from the latter perspective, it is important to bear in mind its logical relationship to the former. And spirit writing can work in both directions, as noted earlier: in some cases materializing the immaterial, in others dematerializing the material.

The reading of entrails gives a practical means of coping with the uncertainties implied by the questions "Are you there, spirits? Can you hear me? Can I hear you?" and draws its force in part from the capacity to transform one semiotic modality, speech, into another, physical marks. The reading of entrails displays a logic that is parallel to one of the ways in which script can manifest spirit. Both practices seem to treat writing as a means of bringing something into the empirical realm through a process of externalization.

Balinese practices offer another example of how one might see writing as the externalization of something that otherwise remains inside the body and inaccessible to the senses, albeit one developed with reference to a semiotic ideology quite different from those prevailing on Sumba. Reversing the premise of much modern linguistics, that speech ontogenically precedes writing, Balinese traditionally considered letters to be contained within the body and to be written on the tongue; speech is a subsequent and derivative manifestation of this prior writing. Thus "sacred syllables uttered by the priest ... [are] a vehicle of power and they can affect the outer world because they are a distillation of the written language within the body, a literal exhalation or ex-pression (forcing out) of inner power toward some external goal."[13] This example reveals several common features of spirit writing. First, it portrays writing as emerging from an enclosed and therefore invisible interior space. This seems to be one way of making sense, in concrete terms, of the relationship between nonmanifest and manifest worlds; or to put it another way, it seems to find in perception a correlative to an imperceptible realm. Second, the Balinese seem to be thinking of language at least as much in terms of the materiality of the body as in terms of mind.[14] Third, the Balinese case portrays the externalization of that which is hidden, or control over that possibility, as being an exercise of power.[15] I will return to these points later. Here, however, I want to elaborate a second aspect of the question. For if writing is one instance of the very general problem of materiality for religion, it is also something more specific: an instance of problems concerning language.

Logos and Transcendence

In 726 CE, the Byzantine emperor Leo III banned the worship of icons and initiated a period of iconoclasm in the Christian Orthodox Church. The politics and theology of this ban are beyond the scope of this essay.[16] It is relevant to reflect, however, on the basic logic that it carried out. The ban on worshipping visual images, mere physical objects, derives to an important degree from the core concept of divine transcendence.[17] Whatever else iconoclasm does, it works to sharpen the distinction between spirit and that which can be manifested to the senses. This distinction marks precisely the gap that spirit writing is meant to bridge. In response to the ban, St. John of Damascus wrote a treatise in defense of the veneration of divine images.[18] Among other things, it was a defense of materiality itself. Identifying the iconoclast's sharp opposition between spirit and matter with that between good and evil, he admonished the reader, "Do not despise matter, for it is not despicable. Nothing is that which God has made. This is the Manichean heresy."[19] St. John of Damascus's argument rests on one of the distinctive features of Christian theology, the doctrine of incarnation. As he put it, this doctrine holds that God, being aware of human limitations, condescended to become flesh in the form of Jesus. But if the doctrine is about materiality and morality, it can also take a distinctly linguistic turn. In the words of the Apostle John, "the Word became flesh and made his dwelling among us."[20] So although St. John of Damascus was primarily interested in visual representations, to substantiate his thesis he also drew on ideas about the experience of language: "Just as the Word made flesh remained the Word, so flesh became the Word remaining flesh, becoming, rather, one with the Word through union. Therefore, I venture to draw an image of the invisible God, not as invisible but as having become visible for our sakes through flesh and blood. I do not draw an image of the immortal Godhead. I paint the visible flesh of God, for it is impossible to represent a spirit, how much more God who gives breath to the spirit."[21]

By "Word," St. John of Damascus was referring to *Logos*, which is certainly not strictly linguistic.[22] To reduce some complex theological discussions to rudimentary form, references to Logos and other linguistic terms often arose in Christian traditions as a way of understanding the relationship between divinity and incarnation. In Augustinian thinking, for example, references to language developed the idea that as inner thought is to outer utterance, so God is to the incarnation. The Augustinian analogy draws on a particular understanding of the language. In this particular linguistic ideology, language has a dual character, existing as both immaterial inner thought and material outer expression.[23]

Without conflating Augustine's view with that of St. John of Damascus, the former does suggest a way to understand the latter's invocation of language in a defense of icons. As outer expression, St. John of Damascus's portrayal of language seems to treat it as being like other physical substances in certain key respects. We might surmise that the analogy depends on the fact that speech has form (phonological, morphological, and syntactic) and substance (sound), in addition to semantic and pragmatic functions. I suggest that writing pushes this materiality still further, giving it orthographic form and, if we include the writing medium and surface on which it depends, other physical properties as well. Like other artifacts, the written word has special characteristics that distinguish it from speech, being, for instance, portable, durable, and destructible. The concept of Logos can be seen as one way of responding to a widespread (but not universal) religious problem of grasping the relationship between the immanent world of familiar sense perceptions and the transcendent world of divinity. It deals with this potentially abstruse conceptual and practical problem by drawing on a more familiar intuition (again, not necessarily universal) that language can take the form both of inner thought and outer substance.

It is important to stress that even where this intuition *is* found, it need not necessarily be of great local interest or require any particular treatment. Relations between inner and outer, materiality and immateriality are problems only as they come to be thematized in specific semiotic ideologies, given certain political, religious, or other historically specific circumstances.[24] At the time St. John of Damascus was writing, for instance, the theological requirements of Christian orthodoxy meant that the separation of spirit and matter also required constant vigilance against idolatry. Therefore, at risk of falling into the Manichaeism he eschewed, even while defending materiality against any dichotomous association with evil, St. John of Damascus still had to mark that boundary, and so he wrote: "I do not worship matter, I worship the God of matter, who became matter for my sake, and deigned to inhabit matter, who worked out my salvation through matter."[25] But as suggested by the several bouts of iconoclasm that have recurred across Christian history, if spirit means transcendence, then materialization and people's responses to the perception of things constantly threaten to become problems. People must learn to look beyond the material sign to a source in a realm that lies outside the senses. Image and word must be treated as pointing to something other than themselves. The theologically motivated need to distinguish between sign and signified underwrites a semiotic ideology, largely implicit in practices (albeit in this case also grounded in explicit theological teachings, or the worries about mediation they induce).[26] Writing lends itself to appropriation within activities that deal with the invisible world by virtue of the way in which it lends to language some of the properties common to physical artifacts.

For all its specificity, however, the Christian doctrine of incarnation bears on a general problem faced by those who want to deal with a spirit world (*if* they conceive of that world as lying beyond the senses—which, of course, is not always the case): in just what way can any being that transcends the material world actually be available to perception? The idea of Logos is a highly abstract answer to this question, albeit one that makes use of an analogy based in ordinary linguistic habits. But there are many ways to answer this question not in theory but in practice.

The three examples I have introduced so far—the shredding of documents, the reading of entrails, and the rhetorical identification of language and icons—illustrate a nested set of problems to which spirit writing can be one response. First is the very general religious problem of the materialization of spirit. It is a problem that a wide range of practices, such as linguistic expression, images, altars, and relics, are meant to address. Within this larger religious problem, we can identify a more specific problem, the materialization of spirit in language. Practices that deal with this problem include the use of scriptures, prayers, mantras, sermons, hymns, and so forth. More specific yet is the problem of the materialization of spirit in language in script. Here we encounter practices such as tattooing, the use of amulets, writing-based divination, ingestion of script in the form of potions, the production of obscure or biomorphic calligraphy, monumental inscription, prayer flags and wheels, physical manipulation of sacred texts, and many other practices that treat writing as a material substance with a specific form. The shredding of documents in New York shows how operations on writing can partake of the more common intuition that what happens physically to signs can affect those things of which they are signs. The reading of entrails exemplifies how writing and other semiotic marks can serve as vehicles of communication between the world of the senses and one that is supposed to lie beyond it. The doctrine of Logos exemplifies how script can help make immaterial spirit material, and thus make it present for those for whom it might otherwise be absent.

But the practices of spirit writing to which I now turn serve functions beyond those of communicating (and, by implication, of reference and denotation) and making present. They draw on the fact that any materialization must have a form; and any form opens up more than one possible meaning or use.

Materializing and Dematerializing the Word

I am suggesting that spirit writing takes up certain affordances that are latent in certain properties of language and writing wherever they occur. But any given development of an affordance depends on the nature of people's experiences of language and writing. Such experiences are not direct reflections of linguistic and material properties, but are mediated by particular linguistic and, more generally, semiotic ideologies.[27] As I have noted, for the many traditions of semiotic ideology that do not share, say, the Saussurean doctrine of the arbitrariness of the sign, or related assumptions in contemporary academic theories of language, the forms of writing can be significant in nonaccidental, ways. For instance, writing can be iconic, that is, the very shape of script can itself manifest divine immanence through resemblance. Thus, in some Islamic mystical teachings:

> The letters themselves form an important part of the symbolical language in mystical and profane poetry and prose, some of them being charged with high religious qualities. *Alif*, the first letter, a straight line, numerical value I, is the chiffre for the graceful slim stature of the beloved, but at the same time, and much more, the symbol of Allah, the One God, free from every worldly quality, the Absolute Unity. . . . In poetry, *mim* is the symbol of the small, dot-like mouth of the beloved. . . . Many letters . . . have been compared to the curls or tresses of the beloved.[28]

This doctrine seems to crystallize a widespread notion, that the formal properties of writing are neither accidental nor merely conventional.

If, by contrast, language is viewed (within the terms of a given semiotic ideology) as an arbitrary sign and writing as a second-order arbitrary sign of that sign, then it makes sense to focus on spoken language as ontogenically and logically prior to writing. In that case, linguistic form should not be taken to be meaningful in itself. One should not make anything of apparent iconicity: for instance, the apparent resemblance between the letter *o* and an open mouth—one might notice the resemblance but not find it a plausible candidate for an efficacious practice. Here iconicity of visual form is an affordance that is not taken up in principle.

But if, conversely, language is a divine emanation, then in itself it is *already* a divine presence, and its form is part of that presence. This is one reason given in the Islamic tradition for the untranslatability of the Koran. Having been transmitted orally by the angel Gabriel, the text was first received by the Prophet as certain sounds. Those sounds are an inalienable part of the sacred text that was transmitted. Moreover, since translation is a function of linguistic diversity, to translate the sacred text would implicate it in human differences and the potential for conflict; it is only as a unitary Arabic text that the Koran remains stable as a text that is identical in all possible circumstances.[29] And in addition, if language is an aspect of divine presence, then this might also apply to its visible embodiment as script. A version of this notion is found in the Balinese idea that letters are found in the body and emerge as sound. In this view, spoken sound is derivative of a prior script.

Once attention is drawn to the potential significance of the written form, then script can be manipulated to take advantage of it. In Java, as in many other Islamic societies in which iconographic production is constrained, scribes have developed calligraphic techniques for depicting birds and other animals composed out of letters. In such cases, the script is usually not meant to be read. What is important is to perceive that the visual image of the animal consists of words. The viewer might not understand them but knows they are there. The result is an allegory of divine immanence in creation.[30] This strategy of dealing with the more general problem of immanence and transcendence makes use of the dual character of language as both form and semantic content. Something similar may motivate a very common practice in both Arabic and Chinese writing traditions: the calligraphic production of abstract designs so complex that the result is illegible.[31] Presumably such practices are playing with the aesthetic possibilities of script as a graphic system. But they also seem to imply some notion that even illegible words still maintain a degree of power or efficacy, beyond any merely communicative or archival function. That is, they are versions of the focus on a religious problem of presence.

A common kind of spirit writing that responds to the problem of the presence of spirits or divinity is the amulet or talisman.[32] The Jewish *mezuzah* is one version of an amulet and can be used to demonstrate some of their general features. The *mezuzah* is a small cylindrical container into which a scrolled parchment is inserted. Written on the parchment is the statement of faith (the Shema). In accordance with scriptural directive, the *mezuzah* is posted on the doorframe. Once posted, the contents of the *mezuzah* are no longer visible, and the words—which are, after all, semantically transparent, and, in another context, entirely legible—will never be read. According to one semipopular source, "In Hebrew, the word for human dwelling is *dirah*, while the word for animal dwelling is *dir*. The difference between these two words is the letter *hey*—signifying the Name of God. The presence of God in one's home is what distinguishes us as uniquely human."[33] This source adds that most *mitzvot* (acts that fulfill a divine commandment) have the power to protect while the actors are actively engaged in performing them, but the *mezuzah* is unique because it protects them even as they sleep. What the commentary emphasizes are two characteristic features of the amulet as a medium for establishing divine presence. One is that by treating writing as a physical object, the amulet stabilizes divine language in a way that markedly contrasts to the evanescence of the speech event. The presence of the object itself indexically presupposes the (more or less) permanent presence of that language. If that language is in turn indexically linked to its divine sources, the result is a mode of presence that is at least potentially the vehicle for enduring agency. (Of course, this agency depends on additional, more culturally and theologically specific ideas about the powers of language beyond those about writing itself, but that response to writing is a crucial element this tradition shares with others.)

Consider now another kind of spirit writing. Both Jewish and Muslim popular traditions include techniques for ingesting texts. One method is to write a scriptural passage on a piece of paper, burn it, and dissolve the ashes in a liquid to produce a potion that will then be ingested. Others consist of infusing a liquid with a written text. For example, one may write a passage on the interior surface of a bowl or on a flat board, using water-soluble ink, then, filling the bowl or washing off the board with water, use the resulting solution as a potion. For the Berti of Sudan,

> The highest form of the possession of the Koran is its commitment to memory, which amounts to its internalization in the head, the superior part of the body, whence it can be instantly reproduced by recitation. But the Koran can also be internalized in the body by being drunk. Although drinking the Koran is seen as being far less effective than memorizing it, it is superior to carrying it on the body through the use of amulets. A major disadvantage of amulets is that they are liable to be lost, left behind or rendered ineffective by exposure to ritual pollution.[34]

Note a formal parallel to the logic of entrails reading. Both techniques work with the movement between the exterior and interior of the body in order to manipulate relations between visible and invisible orders of reality. In the Berti case, mental and corporal internalization seem to be similar, if unequal, processes.

Like the amulet, these techniques can be understood as a means of taking advantage of certain features of writing in order to deal with the problem of presence posed by an ontological gap. Of course, writing alone is not sufficient to generate such practices. They also depend on semiotic ideologies concerning both the efficacy of divine speech acts and the capacity of the written word to retain that efficacy. Thus, according to the Berti, "God himself created things by uttering 'words.' The belief is clearly Koranic, as can be attested to by a few verses which are often used in erasure [and text ingestion]: . . . 'when He decrees a thing, He says concerning it: Be, and it is.'"[35] But the important point is that practices give doctrines the sense of immediate reality, and expose them to further, nondoctrinal, potentially open-ended, possibilities derived from people's encounters with writing.

These ingestion techniques and text-bearing amulets depend on the prior existence of scripture and thus build in a basic premise of certain religious traditions that a principal means by which divinity manifests itself to humans is through words. To be sure, divinity may also appear in the form of rituals, relics, prophets, saints, miracles, icons, visions, holy places, laws, prohibitions, spirit possession, and so forth. But many scriptural traditions emphasize scripture and liturgy as people's primary, most regularly available, and most controllable access to divinity for ordinary persons, even if they cannot read the text. In the Islamic case, the source of the scripture itself is revealing.[36] The angel Gabriel spoke to the Prophet Muhammad. The primary link between the phenomenal world of the scripture reader and the nonphenomenal world of the divine is the aural transmission of words. But, importantly, Muhammad himself was illiterate. He memorized the text and in turn transmitted it by reciting the words to scribes. In contrast to, say, bardic traditions of oral transmission, the role of the scribes in this tradition seems to make salient a certain characteristic of the spoken word: that it is evanescent, at least in its most immediately perceptible character, as sound.

Writing and Semiotic Transduction

If an amulet or a stone inscription seems to draw upon the materiality of writing in order to foreground permanence, ingestion works with certain other latent possibilities one might find within the material substance of writing. What comes to the fore is the potency that derives from the very capacity to transform the word from one semiotic modality to another. This is not a simple matter of translation, transformation, or metamorphosis. As I have suggested, a better term might be transduction: the act of transforming something across semiotic modalities in order to produce or otherwise have effects on power.

Semiotic transduction focuses on movement, from invisible to visible, from immaterial to material, and from intelligible to sensible (or, in each pair, the reverse).[37] It may be an especially appropriate means of drawing power from a spirit or divine source because of the ways in which this movement can manifest the relations between worlds nonphenomenal and phenomenal. The practices of transduction I have touched on here each, in some way, seem to imply an analogy: as thought is to speech is to writing, so the unknowable realm of the spirit is to knowledge about the realm of spirit (e.g., as given in scripture) is to practical relations with spirit. In short, these uses of writing are responses to the problem of presence in the active mode of semiotic transduction, taken as a means of generating power.

The idea of transduction is not, of course, something that is necessarily explicit. There may be no doctrine to justify it. Rather, it often seems to be one possible intuitive response to writing and its relation to sound and thought, manifested in the kinds of practices I have called spirit writing. Again, I want to stress that this does not imply any universal claim about writing or the conclusions people will draw from it. But it is important to consider how the aural and visual materiality of language, in its spoken and written forms, and the potential contrast between materialized language and inner speech, do make certain responses possible. Those responses to writing are in turn *available* for appropriation, given certain historical conditions and specific kinds of problems. Thus St. John of Damascus's invocation of the image of Logos, whatever else it involved historically and theologically, at a certain level was making use of a felt distinction between inner speech and outer expression in order to convey the relationship between materiality and divinity. The text-bearing amulet, whatever the particular social and cultural context in which it emerges, draws on people's encounters with written texts in order to cope with the practical demand for portable, enduring, and physically intimate access to divine power.

To the extent that language has a material dimension, it necessarily has form (phonological, sonic, morphological, calligraphic, etc.). And however much people may be inattentive to or even unaware of those forms in the more or less automatic habits of ordinary language use, under some circumstances and in some practices the materiality of language may become salient to their awareness. Roman Jakobson observed something like this long ago, in his analysis of poetics.[38] The concrete forms language takes can become practical and conceptual affordances or provocations that (under certain circumstances and given certain problems or aspirations) people can take up. They may do so through a material practice, such as turning speech into writing, putting writing into a container to serve as an amulet, or burning or swallowing it. This seems to be what happened in New York in 2007: people invented new practices that seem to respond to the ubiquitous experience of documentation in contemporary life, the tactile properties of paper and, I imagine, the violence of the shredding action itself.[39]

Moreover, in reflecting on their experience of forms, and the practices they involve, people may develop new ideas. In some cases, the very idea of spirit may be a backformation, a reaction to the recalcitrant palpability of things, or a trope on their potential for being rendered impalpable. However, nothing necessitates such reactions. The experience of writing will only become salient and only suggest possible actions under certain social conditions and historical circumstances, given certain expectations, puzzles, or needs. For example, the concept of Logos might not have suggested itself, or at least seemed an especially useful image, had early Christianity not had to distinguish itself against Manichaeism or idol worship. The shredder would not have invited the destruction of memories were New Yorkers not thoroughly habituated to identify themselves with bureaucratic and other written documents.

There is in principle no limit to which aspects of writing people might respond to or take advantage of. To repeat, nothing about writing will determine that it be the basis for any particular practice. Also, the very same practices may, depending on the context, bring into salience different dimensions of writing. Burning, for example, might be a means of reducing writing to invisibility (as in everyday Chinese ritual paper burning) or as a step toward ingestion (as described earlier), or it may be a vehicle for the production of light, smoke, or smells. Also, writing does not inherently have any specific effects. It may, for example, allow a certain degree of either alienation (words written by unknown authors in unintelligible languages) or intimacy (words tattooed on the skin, worn as an amulet, ingested as a potion).

Writing has the potential of bringing into play a potentially indefinite number of contrasts. Here are just a few examples: origin/stasis/dispersal; or alienable/inalienable; or sound/sight/touch/smell; or author/scribe/reader; or agent/patient; or content/form; or hidden/revealed. Any one of these sets of contrasts (and they need not take binary form) has the potential to serve a practice mediating relations between distinct ontological domains or characters. Although these different dimensions of writing will coexist, in any given historical context any actual practice will make use of or bring into salience only a few of them.[40] The practice may focus, for example, on iconicity (letters may take their efficacy from a purported resemblance to body parts), detachability (writing may be separated from its owner or author), circulability (the evangelical pamphlet—like a letter in a bottle cast out to sea—may fetch up in an unknown destination), or durability (a text hidden away for some future discoverer like a time capsule). But over historical time, one may switch from a focus on one aspect to another; as long as the properties coexist, that possibility remains, and may be realized in some future historical context. Thus, the sonic form of ritual performance may give rise to illuminated manuscript—or to art music in a concert hall.

Different actions entail different roles for the body: for instance, script is the trace of the motion of the hand, recitation transforms script into voiced sound, tattooing turns the skin into a linguistic medium. All of these can help produce a perceptual contrast to the efforts of trying to make sense of another person's words or to the silent verbalizations of one's own inner thoughts. Different actions give rise to distinct kinds of social roles for the actors: for example, the author of words may be different from their scribe, who may differ from the person who reads those words out loud or another who interprets them.[41] These roles differ in turn from that of the person who sets the writing into an amulet, and in turn from the person who eventually wears the amulet. We can see multiple planes along which comparisons might be possible and along which the very same traditions may undergo transformation over the course of their histories. A form of writing that originated, perhaps, as a technology to aid the memory of a reciter might, in time, enter into technologies of social transmission and spatial circulation. Once materialized, those words are subject to any of the actions to which any material artifact is prone: the Torah may derive its sacred power from the divine source of the words and their pedagogic efficacy, but the scroll itself is also, potentially, something that can be decorated, shrouded, displayed, carried in procession, and kissed.

The Religious Work of Transduction

If we treat haruspicy as a quasi-reading practice at the limit, we can see that it treats question and answer as operating in distinct media, whose differences of semiotic modality are functions of the ontological characters of their respective authors. In other kinds of spirit writing, distinctions among media seem to center more on differences among agentive capacities of different participants. Prayer wheels, the *mezuzah*, or a scroll hidden inside the figurine of a god all derive their efficacy from aspects of language that are notably not due to the voice and take advantage of the capacity of written language to function in the absence of an author or speaker. Part of the appeal of the pronounced separation of voice and language in such instances seems to lie in the notion that the written words continue to function even when the human agent is not engaged in activity. The emphasis may be on extending the human's agency, or conversely (where, for instance, local emphasis is on the fallibility of human agency), obviating it.

Some practices of spirit writing may value voice over writing, and others value writing over voice; nothing about speech or writing dictates that one or the other should be accorded the higher place or greater power. Nor do formal theologies necessarily state explicitly what their relations should be. As is well known, Derrida builds his critique of a certain metaphysical tradition on the way it takes the voice to manifest the authenticating presence of the speaking subject.[42] By contrast, some kinds of spirit writing may take their guarantees precisely from the absence of the speaker. For example, in what we might call the Ozymandias effect, script that seems to have come from a now vanished and forgotten author may bear extra authority by virtue of that separation between unknown origin (in this respect, similar to an imperceptible otherworld) and ourselves. Its power lies not, or not solely, in what it says denotationally, but in the very fact that it addresses us from a lost world. The absence of the author makes the text an indexical icon of the gap across which it speaks to us, providing direct evidence of the power of the text over time, and offering a palpable image of our distance from its sources in the past. By operating on this absence, transduction can bring it into salience. Or, viewing the material durability of script from another angle, the authority of a scripture may derive from its apparent permanence, and thus its ability to speak to an indefinitely distant future audience. Here the text may be iconic of power over time itself, by virtue of its apparent ability to enter into communication with eternity.

Again, the fact that no one can see the writing in an amulet may be an important source of its intuitive power. One may know the writing is there, but it is invisible. In this respect, the persistence of its effectiveness under conditions of invisibility makes it like a certain kind of divine being (and, perhaps, brings into salience a palpable distinction between knowledge and sense perception that may give extra weight to a theological assertion: for instance, if the latter makes knowledge claims about that which lies beyond physical experience). If one takes the power of the amulet to be independent of form, meaning, or communicative function, one may also intuit another parallel to the spirit world: it functions *in itself*, just by virtue of being there, rather than by virtue of some effective mechanism.

Ideas like this could, of course, simply be matters of doctrinal teaching. But what is important about focusing on the practice rather than the belief is that it suggests how the belief comes to seem especially plausible because it seems to arise directly from concrete experiences. In this way, aspects of experience that are potentially available to any cultural tradition at all can, in concrete circumstances, become affordances that support or serve very specific ideas, problems, or needs. Each of the examples I have touched on here suggests, albeit only in sketchy form, how the palpability of writing can enter into practical responses to certain problems posed by immateriality. Through their attempts to overcome the perceived gap between practitioners and the divine or spirit world, the resulting practices help give a sensuous and shareable reality to the silence of a spirit world that might otherwise remain only a private intuition (such as being subjectively affected by a divine or ghostly presence) or a propositional formulation (such as a creed).

The three-step movement from mental to spoken to written word, or vice versa, can be one way of perceiving relations between the spirit world and humans. Transductions among different semiotic modalities are practical analogues for relations between phenomenal and nonphenomenal worlds. But they are not merely representations. They derive their efficacy, in part, from their manifest manipulation of the relationship between two domains by operating within the world of perception. Spirit writing can emphasize this sense of movement across semiotic modalities and endow those relations with a heightened sense of reality. By focusing on the materiality of script and sharpening its separation from either sense or sound, spirit writing can thereby also sharpen the intuition that an ability to effect a transformation from one to the other requires power or is itself power-generating. This is the religious work of semiotic transduction.

The Possibilities of Comparison

Again, I must emphasize that writing only offers raw materials that need not be taken up in any particular way or be taken up at all. Whether they are noticed, and whether, being noticed, they are seen to be interesting or provocative, and if so, exactly how they are taken up in practice are functions of semiotic ideologies, arising within larger representational economies and thereby have an irreducibly historical nature. It is these contexts that help establish degrees of plausibility (e.g., why it should seem reasonable that drinking the word might be efficacious or that one's fate may be tied to bureaucratic documents) and the relative salience of certain conceptual challenges (as with the need to resist the temptations of Manichaeism) or pragmatic problems (such as a conviction that divine presence is inherently uncertain). But affordances may play a more dialectical role in the ways in which they are taken up, not simply allowing themselves to be used in order to deal with existing problems, but even inviting new ways of thinking about them and presenting new problems in turn. Presumably Sumbanese have not thought since time immemorial that the divinatory marks on chicken entrails are like writing. Once they *are* recognized as like writing, however, the possibility that they form an alternative to scripture may be subject to further elaboration. But to point out the obvious role of historical context should not lead to the conclusion that spirit writing is invented from scratch in each cultural world, nor that each case can *only* be understood in its specificity—that the incommensurability of contexts means comparison can only be misleading. The conjunctions brought into this brief essay should allow us to ask, what is it about writing that allows for the recurrence of similar practices, either because of their ready adoption or because of their reinvention? To ask this question can be an opening to comparison, by way of a focus on the materiality of language and people's encounters with it. Among other things, asking this question may help us notice cases like Sherlock Holmes's famous "dog that did not bark in the night": that is, to look more closely into circumstances where a possible experience is denied or an affordance not taken up where it might have been. The suppression of possibilities is quite different from their mere absence. We might surmise, for instance, that there is some aspect of their experiences of material things that iconoclasts and iconodules *share* such that they develop very strong but opposing positions; and, further, that what they share distinguishes both iconoclasts and iconodules from others who are simply indifferent to the power of icons altogether. To attend to their common encounter with objects may—at least in some key respects—be more revealing than treating iconoclasts, iconodules, and the indifferent as simply creating distinct and unrelated interpretations of the icon.

Moreover, for a given particular practice, those aspects of writing that it takes up and develops can be *recognizable* from afar. It is important to stress that this recognizability across contexts itself has historical consequences. Comparison is not only a scholarly device; it may be even more compelling for practitioners whose primary aims are not academic or analytical. After all, religious history is not just a story of revelations, inventions, or developments within isolated traditions; it is also one of constant encounters between traditions, involving imitations, inversions, prohibitions, and refusals. All of these encounters depend on people's capacity to see something they might make sense of, or find compelling or even repugnant, in what strangers are doing. Neither the Sumbanese diviner nor the Berti healer would find the activities of New Yorkers on Good Riddance Day utterly alien. It is precisely this recognizability that helps explain the vigilance with which certain traditions must guard against fetishism—a vigilance, after all, which implicitly acknowledges that material things manifest an appeal to which one might otherwise succumb.[43] Anthropologists and historians may rightly be wary of the political and epistemological risks that comparison poses. But people of all sorts are comparing all the time, and it behooves us to take seriously not just their desire to find something recognizable in alien practices but also the conditions that make that recognition possible.

Notes

1. This is a subset of the even broader topic, people's inventive appropriations of the materiality of language. This materiality includes phonological and other formal features of speech and is taken up by everything from puns and poetry to political book burning. For an overview of the topic in religious contexts, see Ward Keane, "Religious language," *Annual Review of Anthropology* 26 (1997): 47–71.

2. Rich Schapiro, "Times Square Shredder Gets Rid of Bad Memories on Good Riddance Day," *New York Daily News*, December 29, 2007.

3. The history of texts, literacies, and reading practices is, of course, inseparable from political power. Some of the key studies are Richard Bauman and Charles L. Briggs, *Voices of Modernity: Language Ideologies and the Politics of Inequality* (Cambridge: Cambridge University Press, 2003); James Collins and Richard K. Blot, *Literacy and Literacies: Texts, Power, and Identity* (Cambridge: Cambridge University Press, 2003); Carlo Ginzburg, *The Cheese and the Worms: The Cosmos of a Sixteenth-Century Miller* (Baltimore, MD: Johns Hopkins University Press, 1980); Francis Cody, "Inscribing Subjects to Citizenship: Petitions, Literacy Activism, and the Performativity of Signature in Rural Tamil India," *Cultural Anthropology* 24 (2009): 347–380. Ginzburg offers a classic case of reading against domination; Cody provides an insightful account of the power relations surrounding the signature. But since their connections are neither straightforward nor, I think, determinative, for purposes of this brief essay they are kept analytically distinct. I will also have to bracket the topic of reading practices (see also note 23).

4. I owe this image to Michael Silverstein, "Translation, Transduction, Transformation: Skating 'glissando' on Thin Semiotic Ice," in *Translating Cultures: Perspectives on Translation and Anthropology*, ed. P. G. Rubel and A. Rosman (Oxford: Berg, 2003). There, however, the concept is used with reference to the more specific topic of translation between languages rather than the movement along the whole range of semiotic modalities that I am interested in here. Silverstein's central concern, in that essay, is with the reconstruction of pragmatically analogous indexical presuppositions and entailments across different linguistic systems. Although indexical constancy across contexts plays a role in my account of transduction as well, here I chose to emphasize shifts in the materializations that semiotic forms may take and the consequences of those differences—which may include shifts in emphasis between denotation, indexicality, and iconicity. For another use of the term *transduction*, in science and technology studies, with an emphasis on emergence, see Adrian Mackenzie, *Transductions: Bodies and Machines at Speed* (London: Continuum, 2002).

5. See Ward Keane, "Self-interpretation, Agency, and the Objects of Anthropology: Reflections on a Genealogy," *Comparative Studies in Society and History* 45 (2003): 222–248.

6. The concept of affordance was introduced in James J. Gibson, "The Theory of Affordances," in *Perceiving, Acting, and Knowing: Toward an Ecological Psychology*, ed. R. Shaw and J. Bransford (Hillsdale, NJ: Lawrence Erlbaum, 1977).

7. There is a vast literature on the difficulty, impossibility, or political risks of defining religion across contexts. My treatment here is limited, and based on an earlier attempt to bring the analysis of materiality to bear more directly on the question, see Ward Keane, "Evidence of the Senses and the Materiality of Religion," *Journal of the Royal Anthropological Institute* (N.S.), special issue, The Objects of Evidence: Anthropological Approaches to the Production of Knowledge, ed. Matthew Engelke (2008): S110–127.

8. Divination seems to invite comparison to writing in very different contexts; parallel claims are made by Afro-Caribbean practitioners, for example (S. Palmié, pers. comm.). For the relation of bone oracles to the origins of writing in China, see Min Li, "Conquest, Concord, and Consumption: Becoming Shang in Eastern China" (PhD dissertation, University of Michigan, 2008) and Adam Daniel Smith, "Writing at Anyang: The Role of the Divination Record in the Emergence of Chinese Literacy" (PhD dissertation, University of California, Los Angeles, 2008).

9. A good account of Sumbanese haruspicy is provided in Joel C. Kuipers, *Power in Performance: The Creation of Textual Authority in Weyewa Ritual Speech* (Philadelphia: University of Pennsylvania Press, 1990).

10. I am grateful to an anonymous reviewer of this article for stressing this point. Indexicality refers to signs insofar as they are directly affected by their objects: for example, by causality (smoke indexes fire) or proximity (the exit sign indexes the door out). The concept of indexicality is useful for, among other things, situating signs in a world of space and time and drawing attention to the role of inference—in contrast, say, to preexisting conventions and rules for interpretation, a point emphasized in Alfred Gell, *Art and Agency: An Anthropological Approach* (Oxford: Clarendon Press, 1998). For a thoroughgoing development of indexicality for social analysis, see Michael Silverstein, "Indexical Order and the Dialectics of Sociolinguistic Life," *Language and Communication* 23, no. 3 (2003): 193–229. Iconicity refers to the way in which a sign is linked to its object by resemblance: for example, as in diagrams or onomatopoeic sounds.

11. Ward Keane, *Christian Moderns: Freedom and Fetish in the Mission Encounter* (Berkeley: University of California Press, 2007).

12. Keane, "Evidence of the Senses."

13. Mary Zurbuchen, *The Language of Balinese Shadow Theater* (Princeton, NJ: University Press, 2000), 96; see also Raechelle Rubinstein, *Beyond the Realm of the Senses: The Balinese Ritual of Kekawin Composition* (Leiden: KITLV, 2000).

14. For the cultural elaboration and political implications of the idea that a person's thoughts are hidden inside the body, see the essays in Alan Rumsey and Joel Robbins,

eds., "Anthropology and the Opacity of Other Minds," Social Thought and Commentary Special Section, *Anthropological Quarterly* 81 (2008), 407–494.

15. Cf. Margaret J. Wiener, *Visible and Invisible Realms: Power, Magic, and Colonial Conquest in Bali* (Chicago: University Press, 1995).

16. See Andrew Louth, *Greek East and Latin West: The Church AD 681–1071* (New York: St. Vladimir's Seminary Press, 2007).

17. Hans Belting, *Likeness and Presence: A History of the Image before the Era of Art.* (Chicago: University Press, 1994).

18. Andrew Louth, *St. John Damascene: Tradition and Originality in Byzantine Theology* (Oxford: University Press, 2002).

19. St. John of Damascus, *On the Divine Images: Three Apologies Against Those Who Attack the Divine Images*, trans. D. Anderson (Crestwood, NY: St. Vladimir's Seminary Press, 1994), 17.

20. John 1:14.

21. John of Damascus, *On the Divine Images*, 4–5.

22. Elsewhere he writes about the ordinary experiences of speech quite directly to talk about access to spirit: "Just as we hear with our bodily ears audible words and understand something spiritual, so through bodily sight we come to spiritual contemplation" (quoted in Louth, *St. John Damascene*, 207).

23. Augustine famously registered his surprise on first encountering silent reading, a reminder of the historicity of any phenomenology of the written word. See St. Augustine, *The Confessions of Saint Augustine* (New York: Modern Library, 1999); and Brian Stock, *Augustine the Reader: Meditation, Self-Knowledge, and the Ethics of Interpretation* (Cambridge, MA: Harvard University Press, 1998). More generally, it has been argued that the experience of inner speech was transformed by the advent of widespread literacy and, eventually, of silent reading. See, for example, Jonathan Boyarin, ed., *The Ethnography of Reading* (Berkeley: University of California Press, 1993); David R. Olson, *The World on Paper: The Conceptual and Cognitive Implications of Writing and Reading* (Cambridge: Cambridge University Press, 1994); and Michael Silverstein and Greg Urban, eds., *Natural Histories of Discourse* (Chicago: University Press, 1996). For the classic general arguments about the consequences of literacy, see Jack Goody, *The Domestication of the Savage Mind* (Cambridge: Cambridge University Press, 1977); and Walter J. Ong, *Orality and Literacy: The Technologizing of the Word* (London: Methuen, 1982). For all the importance of reading in scriptural traditions, given a strong emphasis on divine transcendence, it can also raise serious worries about mediation. The limit case is perhaps that of the Friday Masowe Apostolics of Zimbabwe, who refuse to use the Bible precisely because of the way its mediating role seems to place it between the faithful and direct contact with God; see Matthew Eric Engelke, *A Problem of Presence: Beyond Scripture in an African Church* (Berkeley: University of California Press, 2007). Much of the discussion of reading centers on the cognitive capacities of readers, the referential and denotational functions of language, or problems in the storage and transmission of information. Although these are certainly not irrelevant

to the discussion here, they open out onto so many additional directions of inquiry that I have chosen to bracket them for the purposes of this essay.

24. Keane, *Christian Moderns*; see also Patrick Eisenlohr, "Technologies of the Spirit: Devotional Islam, Sound Reproduction and the Dialectics of Mediation and Immediacy in Mauritius," *Anthropological Theory* 9, no. 3 (2009): 273–296.

25. John of Damascus, *On the Divine Images*, 15–16.

26. On this issue, see Eisenlohr, "Technologies of the spirit."

27. For foundational readings in language ideology, see Paul V. Kroskrity, ed., *Regimes of Language: Ideologies, Polities, and Identities* (Santa Fe, NM: School of American Research Press, 2000); and Bambi B. Schieffelin, Kathryn Woolard, and Paul V. Kroskrity, eds., *Language Ideologies: Practice and Theory* (Oxford: University Press, 1998).

28. Annemarie Schimmel, *Islamic Calligraphy* (Leiden: Brill, 1970), 12–13; see also Annemarie Schimmel, *Deciphering the Signs of God: A Phenomenological Approach to Islam* (Edinburgh: University Press, 1994).

29. Brinkley Messick, *The Calligraphic State: Textual Domination and History in a Muslim Society* (Berkeley: University of California Press, 1993).

30. Timothy E. Behrend, "Textual Gateways: The Javanese Manuscript Tradition," in *Illuminations: The Writing Traditions of Indonesia*, ed. Ann Kumar and John H. McGlynn (New York: Weatherhill, 1996), 198.

31. James Robson, "Signs of Power: Talismanic Writing in Chinese Buddhism," *History of Religions* 48, no. 2 (2008): 130–169; Schimmel, *Islamic Calligraphy*.

32. See, for example, Don C. Skemer, *Binding Words: Textual Amulets in the Middle Ages* (University Park: Pennsylvania State University, 2006).

33. Rabbi Shraga Simmons, "Mezuzah: The Inside Story," *Aish HaTorah*, August 3, 2002, https://www.aish.com/jl/m/mm/48948731.html.

34. A. O. El-Tom, "Drinking the Koran: The Meaning of Koranic Verses in Berti Erasure," *Africa* 55, no. 4 (1985): 416.

35. El-Tom, 417.

36. William A. Graham, *Divine Word and Prophetic Word in Early Islam: A Reconsideration of the Sources with Special Reference to the Divine Saying or Hadîth Qudsî* (The Hague: Mouton, 1977); Fazlur Rahman, *Major Themes of the Qur'an* (Minneapolis: Bibliotheca Islamica, 1994).

37. One might also include here movement across social and geographical space, a crucial conceptual as well as practical feature of evangelical religion. In addition to the shift in semiotic weight from the denotational to indexical or iconic noted earlier, see, for example, Simon Coleman, *The Globalisation of Charismatic Christianity: Spreading the Gospel of Prosperity* (Cambridge: University Press, 2000); Nicholas Harkness, "Words in Motion and the Semiotics of the Unseen in Two Korean Churches," *Language and Communication* 30, no. 2 (2010): 139–158; and Joel Robbins, "On Reading 'World News': Apocalyptic Narrative, Negative Nationalism, and Transnational Christianity in a Papua New Guinea Society," *Social Analysis* 42, no. 2 (1998): 103–130.

38. Roman Jakobson, "Closing Statement: Linguistics and Poetics," in *Style in Language*, ed. T. Sebeok (Cambridge, MA: MIT Press, 1960).

39. For an especially insightful discussion of the role played by the sheer materiality of documents in the functioning of an urban bureaucracy, see Matthew S. Hull, *Government of Paper: Materiality and Urban Bureaucracy in Pakistan* (Berkeley: University of California Press, 2012).

40. Ward Keane, "Self-interpretation," 222–248.

41. Erving Goffman, "Footing," in *Forms of Talk* (Philadelphia: University of Pennsylvania Press, 1981).

42. Jacques Derrida, *Of Grammatology* (Baltimore, MD: Johns Hopkins University Press, 1976).

43. Keane, *Christian Moderns*; William Pietz, "The Problem of the Fetish, I," *RES: Anthropology and Aesthetics*, no. 9 (1985): 5–17.

Part III

Everyday Religion

Ever since William James, if not much earlier, religion has widely been seen or defined as dealing with the extraordinary, the non-mundane, and the superhuman; yet many, if not most, religious practices occur in everyday settings that are dominated by practical, not to say banal, demands. One of the significant developments in recent studies of religion has been the turn toward "lived religion" which occurs precisely in such everyday settings. The different contributions to this section reflect this reorientation, thus also inviting us to think anew the relation between the sacred and the profane among other binaries.

The experience of the everyday is not a primitive or given. In his *Sources of the Self*, already discussed in the introduction, Charles Taylor argues that Western secular modernity is marked by a novel "affirmation of ordinary life," that is, of everyday concerns with economic and sexual production and reproduction, as opposed to the Aristotelian "good life" of *theôria*, or contemplation. He sees this affirmation of the ordinary life as foreshadowed if not initiated by the down-to-earth spirituality of the Reformation. Thus, everyday life appears to be a historically variable notion that became especially prominent and was accordingly rearticulated in the early modern age. More recently, it has been shaped and reshaped not only by religion but also by such distinctly modern phenomena as the nation-state, romantic love, and economic life. The contributions to this section may be said to extend Taylor's argument by exploring the religious everyday in non-Western settings, in particular, Bolivia, Egypt, and Turkey.

In "The Quotidian Turn," the theoretical discussion that opens this section, Thomas Tweed traces how in recent decades, the categories of everyday life and lived religion have helped to redirect attention to the embodied practices and material culture of ordinary—or rather, lay, lower-class, or subaltern—actors, beyond the threshold of worship spaces. He then proceeds to discuss some conceptual and theoretical problems of this "quotidian turn," as he calls it. In particular, he points out the seemingly paradoxical juxtaposition of the religious—which is often seen as by definition dealing with the supernatural, ecstatic, and extraordinary—and the ordinary, mundane, and natural aspects of everyday life. One can try to resolve this tension, he argues, and thus overcome the binary of the ordinary and the extraordinary (and indeed of the religious and the secular), by redefining religion, with Robert Orsi, as the "practice of making the invisible visible," and of introducing "everyday miracles," that is, introducing the ecstatic in the mundane. Thus, the study of religion should also aim at "trying to hold together what languages pull apart."

Tweed then discusses the possibilities of going beyond this quotidian turn, that is, of overcoming the new presuppositions and limitations it introduces, by theorizing the *dynamic* between the religious and the everyday. Tweed concludes by developing three alternative—and in part overlapping—pairs of concepts: presence/absence, flows/channels, and crossing/dwelling. Partly because of the kinetic imagery they imply, he argues, these pairs avoid the conceptual difficulties of the everyday, in particular the misleading suggestion that it is static and in essence unchanging.

In "Rhythms of Roots," a case study of contemporary Bolivian rituals, Sanne Derks, Catrien Notermans, and Willy Jansen describe how religious practices—in this case, pilgrimages—may involve competing and contested meanings and may have performative effects that go far beyond the religious. They do so by teasing out the political meanings of inclusion and exclusion as well as of empowerment and marginalization implied in the *Entrada Folklórica*, the dance processions of the yearly pilgrimage to the Virgin of Urkupiña in Bolivia. Recently, the state has declared the festivities to be part of Bolivian cultural patrimony; by thus including the procession in its nation-building efforts, it increased both its own prestige and the social status of the participants. In the late twentieth century, however, a distinct procession, the *Entrada Autóctona*, was instituted with the aim of "recovering indigenous values" meant to empower marginalized peoples; as such, it emphasizes differences between ethnic groups rather than a shared national identity. Thus, the participants in these processions not only enact a religious ritual but also perform national and ethnic identities.

Umut Azak's "State Rituals in Turkey" suggests how also the everyday experience of religion may be shaped by the environment of the secular nation-state. Like the preceding contribution, it focuses on the everyday but hardly on the subaltern; rather, it discusses how Kemalist elites in the Turkish state apparatus and civil society appropriated and sacralized secular nationalist symbols. Although ostensibly staunchly secular, the early Kemalist elites in republican Turkey introduced various state rituals that aimed at sacralizing secular nationalism. This involved the reframing of religious notions such as *gazi* ("warrior for the faith") as secular nationalistic concepts (thus, the term was applied to Mustafa Kemal as a hero of national liberation) as well as the creation of national martyrs for secularism such as Mustafa Fehmi Kubilay, who was murdered by religious activists in 1930. Thus, Azak argues, the early Kemalists imposed a "political religion centered on a cult of the leader." In the 1990s, Azak's argument continues, this authoritarian and state-organized "political religion" was transformed into a more democratic "civil religion," when civil society organizations of students and retired officers appropriated these state rituals against what they perceived as the renewed or continuing threat of religious fanaticism against the secular state.

The Turkish glorification of national heroes and martyrs illustrates not only the secularization of religious notions but also the sacralization of secular nationalism; as such, Azak argues, it shows the importance of emotions in nationalism as a secular religion. Further reflections on the social constructions of both religious and secular emotions and on the interaction between religion and—presumably secular—nationalist politics can also be found in other contributions to this volume, notably those by Korte, de Koning, and Kanie.

"There is too much Islam in the anthropology of Islam," Samuli Schielke provocatively opens his "Second Thoughts About the Anthropology of Islam," the final contribution to this part. Basing his arguments on his fieldwork in Egypt, Schielke turns against the overattention for the religious in the study of the everyday lives of believers. In particular, he criticizes Talal Asad's influential 1986 proposal to treat Islam as an overarching "discursive tradition" that shapes Muslims' affects, emotions, and attempts to live pious lives. Asad's account, Schielke argues, has led to an anomalous focus in anthropological research on the question of what Islam *is* rather than what Muslims *do*; moreover, it fails to do justice to the ambivalence, inconsistency, and openness of people's everyday religious and moral practices. A more systematic attention to the mundane might help to shift anthropologists' concerns: everyday practices and existential and pragmatic concerns, he argues, are embedded in but not reducible to traditions, discourses, and powers. Instead, he proposes to treat Islam as an inherently ambiguous "grand scheme" that is seen as external and superior to the everyday lives it informs, shapes, and organizes; as such, it stands alongside other schemes, like romantic love, wealth, education, and Arab nationalist politics. Although Schielke's argument focuses on the anthropology of Islam, it rejects Islamic exceptionalism; hence, it has substantial implications not only for the anthropology of religion more generally but also for both genealogical critiques of secular liberalism and the communitarian representation of religions as moral or discursive traditions and the legitimacy of their public appearance.

CHAPTER 10

The Quotidian Turn

Interpretive Categories and Scholarly Trajectories

Thomas A. Tweed

All scholars in the human sciences use interpretive categories. Those theoretical tools may be employed to make empirical claims that can be confirmed or disputed, but the categories themselves are not true or false. They are more or less adequate for the researcher's purposes. In other words, we assess those categories by appealing to pragmatic criteria.[1] Focusing on the conceptual implications and practical effects of scholars' linguistic usage, I discuss a cluster of related categories, especially *everyday life*, and assess their utility for the study of religion. All categories—the terms and phrases used to guide research—afford a particular angle of vision. In turn, they all have blind spots. In some ways, the history of the study of religion—and all fields and subfields—has been a process of ceaseless change as one perspective replaces another, as scholars claim that the prevailing category—the orienting metaphor, key noun, or favored phrase—obscures something we should notice. That realization prompts a search for another interpretive term that promises to illumine what has been obscured.

As early as the first decade of the twentieth century and increasingly after the 1960s, scholars in the humanities, arts, and social sciences turned to the phrase *everyday life*—and related categories such as *everyday religion* and *lived religion*—to illumine what had been obscured. Religion's interpreters in multiple disciplines used the adjective *everyday* to redirect attention to the embodied practices and material culture of ordinary people beyond the threshold of worship spaces. That redirection, which I call the *quotidian turn*, provided a much-needed corrective; however, I suggest, it was not without its methodological implications and conceptual problems.

The Quotidian Turn:
Toward a History of Converging Interpretive Trajectories

Those who chart the history of the humanities, arts, and social sciences delight in naming the twists and turns in theory and method. For example, we are told that there was a linguistic turn, a poststructuralist turn, and a spatial turn during the second half of the twentieth century. From one point of view, this is silly. The appeal to a single phrase to describe the complex and distinct approaches of many scholars in different disciplines and diverse nations is doomed to fail. Such attempts overstate the novelty and scope of the interpretive shift, and no label is elastic enough to contain all the subtle but significant variations. If we acknowledge the limitations of this scholarly practice, however, the impulse to label academic trends sometimes can be useful. At its best, it can illumine patterns that we otherwise might have overlooked or underemphasized.

With some trepidation, then, I want to propose just such a flawed label: I suggest that it might be helpful to talk about a quotidian turn in the study of religion—and, more broadly, in the study of history, society, and culture. I cannot offer a full account of these parallel—and sometimes intersecting—interpretive trajectories, but it might help to note that this altered focus appeared (or, in some places, accelerated) during and after the 1960s, especially but not only among speakers of English, French, and German in Europe, South Asia, and North America. Its starting point and defining commitments varied by disciplinary affiliation, research topic, and cultural setting. For example, the German *Alltagsgeschichte* of the 1970s and the South Asian Subaltern Studies Group of the 1980s were very different, even if they shared a concern to attend to ordinary people and everyday life.[2] The categories that these diverse scholars employed also diverged depending on whether they most wanted to illumine ignored places, practices, or people.

Since I will say more later about everyday life, consider just a few examples about the impulse to highlight ordinary people. In the 1950s and early 1960s, the work of the British Marxist historians is noteworthy, and none of them had more influence than E. P. Thompson and his *The Making of the English Working Class* (1963).[3] The *Annales* school in the Francophone world and, later, the "new social history" in the Anglophone world aimed to discern the long-term historical patterns and the local variations in the daily life of non-elites, and greater attention to class, race, and gender multiplied the characters in scholars' narratives about the present and the past.[4] The result was a shift in focus: for example, in the United States the number of doctoral dissertations in social history quadrupled between 1958 and 1978.[5] Starting in the 1970s and increasingly after the 1980s, historians also paid more attention to indigenous peoples, who had suffered a second (representational) colonization as the previous scholarship had imagined the landscape as an unpopulated wilderness before colonizers planted their flags. Folklorists in Scandinavia and the North Atlantic World studied "vernacular creativity" embedded in local settings,[6] and geographers in Germany and the United States turned their attention to the interpretation of "ordinary landscapes."[7] Reception theory altered the scholarly viewpoint, and literary critics, theater scholars, and art historians asked how ordinary people cocreated the plural meanings of artistic productions[8]—or how they created their own "outsider" or "folk" art—even if some complained about the emerging "anti-elitist bias."[9] In British cultural studies, media studies, and other fields, the analysis of popular culture emerged as an alternative to the prevailing focus on the cultural production and aesthetic taste of elites.[10]

As with Thompson's influential book, some of that scholarly work on both sides of the Atlantic focused on class as a category of analysis and drew inspiration from Karl Marx or Antonio Gramsci,[11] as did scholarship in and about Latin America and South Asia. Starting with the first volume of the Subaltern Studies Group's multivolume series in 1982, scholars writing from and about South Asia, especially India, adopted a term that had a long history but had been reintroduced by Gramsci: they announced their concern to "rectify the elitist bias" and reconsider "the subaltern," those of subordinate rank, "whether this is expressed in terms of class, caste, age, gender, and office, or in any other way."[12] The term *subaltern* circulated in different parts of the world among proponents of postcolonial studies from different disciplines. The Brazilian anthropologist Darcy Ribeiro had used Gramsci's notion of "subalternity" earlier, in his analysis of indigenous peoples;[13] and some scholars writing from and about that region have acknowledged their debts, including those who founded the Latin America Subaltern Studies Group in 1993.[14]

Other Latin Americanists have been more ambivalent. The literary scholar and postcolonial theorist Walter Mignolo, for example, expressed appreciation for Subaltern Studies but preferred slightly different categories—Michel Foucault's "subjugated knowledges" and Ribeiro's "subaltern knowledges"—because Guha and other South Asia specialists marked "the eighteenth century and the Enlightenment as the chronological frontier of modernity" while the sixteenth century and "the colonial legacies of the Spanish and Portuguese empires in the Americas" are the appropriate starting point for specialists of Latin America.[15] Other scholars of Latin America, including historian William B. Taylor, found Ruha's approach to Subaltern Studies "good to think with . . . since the 1980s," but argued that its sharp distinctions (between "the people"/"the elites" as well as "resistance"/"accommodation") did not provide "a model for understanding the complexities of Spanish American colonialism, at least in Mexico."[16]

Taylor, who attended to religion, also criticized subaltern studies scholars for leaving "aside the religious faith—beliefs and practices—of peasant actors either as false consciousness or beside the point of their politics."[17] Like Taylor, a number of scholars who embraced the quotidian turn strove to take religion seriously, although their terminology varied depending on whether they wanted to emphasize the spaces, participants, or actions that had been obscured in the scholarship. For example, since the 1970s many historians and social scientists in Europe and in the Americas have studied "local religion" or "popular religion."[18] And Gabriel Le Bras influenced a generation of postwar French sociologists to study what he called "lived religion" (*la religion veçue*), which meant mostly the piety of the laity.[19]

Some interpreters in Europe, Latin America, and North America have directly or indirectly aligned themselves with the French sociology of "lived religion." Most of them continued Le Bras's original emphasis on non-elites, although they understood the adjective *lived* as an answer to the question of *how* religion is practiced more than as a response to the question of *who* is practicing it. Among the category's advocates were the contributors to historian David Hall's *Lived Religion in America* (1997), including the French sociologist Danièle Hervieu-Leger and American religious studies scholar Robert Orsi. Since 1997, other interpreters have used the category.[20] Timothy Matovina employed it in a study of Latino Catholics in Texas, and Jennifer Hughes did the same in her study of Mexican Catholicism.[21] Historian Diane Winston and her collaborators studied "television and lived religion," and US sociologist Meredith McGuire analyzed *Lived Religion: Faith and Practice in Everyday Life*.[22] As with McGuire, some European social scientists also referred to the ways that lived religion is practiced in daily life or everyday life, as with Sanne Derks's ethnography of a Bolivian pilgrimage site and as with other volumes on contemporary practices.[23]

Whichever adjective scholars chose—local, popular, or lived—many also appealed to phrases like *ordinary people* and *everyday life* in their analyses of religion. And, as I will show, some scholars even have talked about everyday religion. Keeping these related but distinct scholarly trajectories in mind—especially the intersections with the study of lived religion—I now want to consider one of the central phrases in the analytic vocabulary of what I am calling the quotidian turn: *everyday life*.

Everyday Life: Toward a History of Usage

Before assessing the phrase's accomplishments and limitations, it might help to give a few instances—though not a full historical account—of how scholars have employed it in cultural analysis. A preliminary survey of usage in publications suggests that the English adjective *everyday*—and the rough equivalents in German (*alltäglich*) and French (*quotidienne*)—appeared more frequently in books during the twentieth century, with variations across those languages but with a steady upward trend since 1920 and a precipitous spike after 1980.[24] Various kinds of texts—including fiction—included the term, but especially since the mid-twentieth century social scientists and historians writing in several European languages—and not only German, French, and English—have appealed to notions of everyday life and related categories to signal their intent to broaden the analytical scope of their studies of selves, societies, and the sacred.

Classic religion theorists, such as the psychologist Sigmund Freud and the sociologist Max Weber, used the phrase, even if it was not the focus of their work. In *The Psychopathology of Everyday Life* (1904), Freud redirected the clinician's gaze from the couch to the street and the home as he analyzed how "unconscious psychological processes" drive ordinary people's behavior in daily life, including by excavating the "concealed meanings" of slips of the tongue and erroneous actions as well as common experiences such as *déjà vu* and "foreboding."[25] In that work, Freud confessed that he had those unusual experiences but dismissed them as "superstitions," since "I belong to that class of unworthy individuals before whom the spirits cease their activities and the supernatural disappears, so that I have never been in a position to experience anything that would stimulate belief in the miraculous."[26] Weber admitted he too was "religiously unmusical," but in his *Sociology of Religion* (1920) he was more sympathetic—and more suggestive—than Freud. He not only discussed everyday life and the everyday world but even introduced a category, an "ideal type," that marked off a distinct kind of piety, *Alltagsreligion*, a term that has been translated as the "workaday mass religion" or, better, the "religion of everyday life."[27]

Appeals to *everyday life* appeared in social scientific and historical publications in other European languages, including Norwegian (*hverdagsliv*) and Dutch (*het dagelijks leven*).[28] And a tradition of "everyday life sociology" developed among

Anglophone and Germanophone scholars after World War II.[29] It was an emphasis prompted in part by the Canadian Erving Goffman's 1959 dramaturgical account of *The Presentation of Self in Everyday Life*, and by Austrian-American Peter Berger and Slovenian-German Thomas Luckmann, sociologists who were influenced by Weber and Alfred Schutz and who in 1966 coauthored a widely read phenomenological analysis of "the foundations of knowledge in everyday life."[30] Berger also analyzed religion in "everyday life" in *The Sacred Canopy*;[31] and, as the British social scientist Grace Davie has pointed out, the study of "the everyday" (which includes diet, sexuality, gender, healing, and the lifecycle) had become a predominant "theme" in the qualitative sociology of religion on both sides of the Atlantic by the late 1990s.[32] Of course, anthropologists had been concerned with non-elites and daily life for a long time; and Victor Tuner, Clifford Geertz, and others exerted influence on diverse fields, prompting a "cultural turn" among historians during the 1970s and 1980s and an "ethnographic turn" among religious studies specialists during the 1980s and 1990s.[33] Further, some cultural anthropologists explicitly used the phrase *everyday life*.[34] More recently, European and North American sociologists, anthropologists, and historians of religion have employed variants of Weber's phrase, "everyday religion," including Nancy Ammerman, Grace Davie, Enzo Pace, Martin Riesebrodt, Marja-Liisa Keinänen, and Samuli Schielke.[35]

As I have noted, several generations of French social historians associated with the Annales school also probed the "collective mentality" of ordinary people and the long-term trajectory of everyday life; and sociologist Marcel Mauss, who discussed *la vie quotidienne* in his important study of "bodily techniques" in 1935, and Henri Lefebvre, who published *Critique de la vie quotidienne* in 1947, had enormous influence on subsequent transnational conversations.[36] Among Francophone scholars, the continuing impact of Mauss and Lefebvre, including the latter's Marxist analysis of "perceived, conceived, and lived spaces,"[37] shaped some of the most widely read French social theorists of the next generation, including Michel Foucault, Pierre Bourdieu, and Michel de Certeau. In *The Practice of Everyday Life* (1974), for instance, de Certeau provided a model of how to analyze "everyday practices" while accounting for both the micropolitical agency of the individual and the constraining power of social structures.

Assessing the Quotidian Turn: Everyday as Interpretive Category

As I turn to the task of evaluating the utility of the phrase *everyday life*—and related categories such as *everyday religion* and *lived religion*—I should emphasize that I am sympathetic to these interpretive traditions. In fact, many scholars have understood my work, especially my study of Cuban Catholic piety, as aligned with these methodological impulses.[38] They're right to note the parallels. Further, my theory of religion attends to the body and the home and resonates with many of the themes announced by interpreters who have been associated with these scholarly lineages, including Weber, Schutz, Mauss, Lefebvre, Bourdieu, and de Certeau.[39] My earlier emphasis on "embodied practices," "ordinary devotees," and "social space" owes much to those European theorists, so does my more recent analysis of what I called "vernacular intellectualism."[40] In short, I think there is much to celebrate about these cross-disciplinary traditions of social analysis and historical investigation. Most important, religion specialists—and their colleagues in allied disciplines—have helpfully shifted attention from "religion as prescribed" to "religion as practiced,"[41] from the organized religious rites and the systematized theological beliefs of elites in dominant religious institutions to the practices, artifacts, and environments of ordinary devotees in daily life, including in times and places that might be deemed secular. That redirecting of scholarly attention is a praiseworthy accomplishment, on both epistemological and moral grounds: it has provided a basis for more textured and more inclusive interpretations.

However, the phrase *everyday life* presents some challenges when applied to the study of religion. The focus on everyday life entails methodological challenges: finding relevant sources and employing appropriate approaches. Of course, every approach has its distinctive methodological challenges, and those who analyze contemporary everyday practices have it somewhat easier, since they can encounter human subjects and use participant observation, taped interviews, telephone surveys, focus groups, or oral history, though none of those methods are without flaws. Those engaged in the historical analysis of the religious practices of women, children, migrants, Indigenous people, slaves, the working class, and the socially marginalized face especially vexing questions about how to recover the past. There are some available strategies. We can incorporate disciplinary practices from archaeology, geography, and history, for example, and we can draw on multiple sources. Historians can seek textual sources, like letters, wills, congregational records, court cases, and diaries. Usually, however, we are left to reconstruct practices from other, more mute and opaque sources such as population records, excavated fragments, historical maps, chiseled inscriptions, domestic artifacts, and vernacular architecture—or the tools of so-called ethnohistory, which presupposes a continuity between contemporary and past practices.

Shifting from methodological to theoretical issues, I want to concentrate on some conceptual tensions that arise when we appeal to the study of (to use Weber's phrase) "the religion of everyday life."

First, a conceptual confusion—or, at best, a productive paradox—enters as we strain to conjoin *religion*, which usually refers to the extraordinary, and the *everyday*, which usually refers to the ordinary. A distinction, which amounts to an implied opposition, surfaces as soon as we begin to ask: *When* is the everyday? And *where* is the everyday? Usage in English, French, and German (and other European languages too) suggests the word *everyday* is, in part, a temporal and spatial designation. It refers to the days of the week not reserved for regular, institutionally prescribed worship—"not Sunday," as the *Oxford English Dictionary* puts it. In the pluralistic context of late modernity, the day set aside might be Friday, Saturday, or Sunday—or another day. As the historic significance of the related phrase *ordinary time* signals, the everyday also is imagined in opposition to the liturgical seasons—for many Christians that means Advent, Christmas, Lent, or Easter. So, in terms of time, the everyday (*der Alltag* or *la vie quotidienne*) refers to profane time, moments *not* set apart. It is a spatial indicator too, gesturing beyond the threshold of institutionally sanctioned worship sites (churches, temples, or mosques), outside places where ritual specialists preside at regular and prescribed rites. The everyday, which begins with the body, happens in intimate domestic spaces and the built environment beyond the home, including the street, the park, the factory, the market, the courtroom, the school, the theater, the athletic stadium, the hospital—and since the transportation and communication technologies of late modernity extend and transform space—also the airport and the Internet.[42]

We arrive at similar conclusions if we ask *what* the everyday is and not just about its duration or location. Both vernacular usage and scholarly practice suggest that the everyday refers to the usual, the mundane, the natural, or the routine. It is the quotidian. In turn, the everyday's implied or stated opposite is that which disrupts, suspends, or stands out from the quotidian—the unusual, the exceptional, the supernatural, the special.[43] It is the ecstatic. Berger referred to it as "the experience of 'ecstasy' (in the literal sense of *ek-stasis*—standing or stepping outside reality as commonly defined . . . the world of everyday life)."[44] Not all disruptions, or modes of standing out from the everyday, are religious, as Berger, Weber, and others have pointed out: not only sex and music but also dreams, drama, ritual, dance, and drugs can transport individuals and groups beyond the routine.[45] As one social scientist has argued, societies take shape not only as social groups struggle for power over the means of production and consumption but also as varied institutions battle for control of "the means of ecstatic expression."[46] Churches, temples, and mosques, then, can be understood as one of many "institutions of ecstasy" competing in late-modern societies, performing important functions, even if religious traditions' "chains of memory" have been weakened or broken in secularizing Western Europe.[47]

Many classic and contemporary interpreters of religion have mapped the boundaries of what I am calling the quotidian and the ecstatic. In different ways, Freud, Weber, and William James did so; and since Émile Durkheim defined the sacred as "things set apart," several traditions of the sociological, anthropological, and phenomenological study of religion have assumed that their proper subject matter was the times and spaces that devotees marked as distinct from the mundane.[48] More recently, in her *Religious Experience Reconsidered*, Ann Taves continued and refined this Durkheimian lineage by suggesting that our central task is to analyze how ordinary people and scholarly interpreters deem some things "special," either because they are "ideal" or "anomalous."[49] Many other contemporary scholars of religion have worked from similar assumptions: for example, Michel Despland proposed that we understand the "supernatural" as occurrences and beings that "impinge upon one's everyday experience," and Paul Courtright suggested that religion's objects "lie outside the realm of the everyday objects in time and space."[50]

It is this implied binary—between the ecstatic and the quotidian—that presents the first challenge for those whose stated aim is to analyze "everyday religion" and, thereby, to locate the one in the other, as the British scholar Kim Knott tried to do in her 2005 volume on religion and space: "my original intention in this project," she tells the reader, "was to find a way of locating religion in everyday spaces."[51] But here a problem presents itself for Knott and all of us: if we insist on distinguishing too sharply between the ordinary and the extraordinary, then it is not clear how we might meaningfully talk about religion's expression in everyday time and space, since what is set apart as special appears wholly discontinuous with the quotidian. As one specialist in method and theory has pointed out, "religion becomes an unintelligible activity when we divorce it from ordinary life."[52] However, if we try to avoid that problem by blurring the boundaries between the ordinary and the extraordinary—as with historians of ancient peoples who claim religion was "embedded" in culture, for example[53]—then we risk creating a meaningless and useless category that fails to distinguish what is *not* religious.

Furthermore, I suggest, the tension is not eased by eschewing definitions of religion altogether—or postponing the task indefinitely on empiricist grounds—since scholars inevitably assume, imply, or employ a more or less self-consciously crafted definition in their analysis. Knott, who resists defining the term *religion*, offers a sophisticated, Lefebvre-inspired methodological proposal about "spatial analysis";[54] and she recognizes this categorical problem, as do many other scholars who appeal to the notion of the everyday, including Orsi and the sociologist Nancy Ammerman. "Everyday religion," Ammerman suggests, has to do "with the mundane routines" as well as "the crisis and special events that punctuate those routines."[55] Ammerman does not define or theorize that which "punctuates" the mundane, however. She and her fellow contributors take the approach advocated by Taves and others.[56] They do not stipulatively define the noun in their key phrase, *religion*, as I would do, but instead "ask what makes some social events and individual actions religious in the minds of the actors."[57] But what if the interpreter concludes that some or all of the features of religion are expressed but the actors themselves do not accept the label "religious"—as with twelve-step programs such as Alcoholics Anonymous, for example? Ammerman does not address that issue but she does acknowledge that the phrase *everyday religion* raises a series of "nagging questions," including some about the ordinary and the extraordinary: "When and where do we find experiences that participants define as religious or spiritual? Where do we see symbols and assumptions that have spiritual dimensions, even if they are not overtly defined as such?"[58] Orsi, to mention another sophisticated and influential scholar, also sees the conundrum as he describes religion in the mundane. "Religion," he suggests, "is the practice of making the invisible visible ... present to the senses in the circumstances of *everyday life*."[59] To surface the tension embedded in the categorical binaries, Orsi entitled his contribution to *Lived Religion in America*, "Everyday Miracles." That is a wonderfully evocative phrase, and I support the implied aim to acknowledge and confront the challenge.[60] Yet as that theoretically agile scholar knows well, that phrase does not by itself fully resolve the persistent problem of finding ways to talk about the ecstatic in the quotidian. I realize that those with a principled suspicion of theory will disagree—and some scholars in this interpretive tradition seem to urge us to resist the impulse to elevate our gaze above the empirical particulars[61]—but I would prefer to theorize more systematically the everyday—and its implied opposite—and to ponder a bit more the other key terms in Orsi's definition: *practice*, *making*, and *invisible*. Even then, however, our category (*everyday life*) and the meanings embedded in use still might present conceptual difficulties. In other words, even the most sophisticated scholars of religion who employ the phrase *everyday life*—and Orsi, Knott, and Ammerman are among the most subtle and persuasive—continue to confront the problem of how to overcome the implied binary between the ordinary and the extraordinary, the secular and the religious. It is not their problem alone, of course; all of us who use the phrase inherit it.

A second and related conceptual problem arises when we declare our intention to focus on everyday life: a number of *other* implied distinctions form as concomitants of vernacular usage and scholarly practice, whether we intend to invoke those oppositions or not. The redirected focus corrects for earlier academic blind spots; but the appeal to everyday, popular, or lived religion also wittingly or unwittingly replicates binary pairs and implies value hierarchies, usually privileging one element of the pair as the analysis reverses earlier interpretive patterns. Those interpretive patterns have varied across national borders; yet the felt need to attend to religion in everyday life emerged in most places because the scholarship had obscured what non-elites did at routine times and in mundane spaces. Between the 1880s and the 1920s, and even into the 1960s, religion scholars focused on the collective symbols, rituals, and myths of so-called "primitive peoples," who did not resemble either the positioned Western interpreter or his (and, rarely, her) imagined audience, while many others presupposed that religion was about beliefs, elites, institutions, sacred texts, organized rituals, consecrated spaces, and the public realm. The use of the category *everyday life* signaled the interpreter's opposition to the prevailing focus and usually announced increased attention to one element in each binary. There has been enormous variation among proponents of these transnational and multidisciplinary interpretive lineages—for example, about whether to emphasize power more than meaning, biological constraints more than cultural forces, and social structures more than individual agency—but many have assumed, implied, or argued that everyday religion is more about the body than the mind, about practices and artifacts more than beliefs and values, about ordinary people more than institutional elites, the private sphere more than the public arena, more about the weekday than Sunday.

After the Quotidian Turn: What Next?

I have provided two proposals. The first concerns how to narrate the recent history of the study of religion: the label *quotidian turn*, I have suggested, might be useful for thinking about one cluster of approaches since the 1960s. The second proposal concerns how we might evaluate that methodological shift: I noted that the scholars associated with the quotidian turn accomplished an important corrective by redirecting the focus to ordinary people and everyday life, but their guiding categories, including the modifier *everyday*, created conceptual tensions and categorical binaries—and, despite scholars' best intentions, sometimes led to one-sided interpretations. The first proposal, which is rather ambitious, surely needs refinement. After all, the proposed label brings together many interpretive traditions from varied social contexts. I have either forced things into the box or not made the box large enough. Probably both. But we cannot decide its utility in advance. Time will tell if the label *quotidian turn* proves helpful to those who want to chart the twists and turns in the history of the study of religion. If not, other labels should frame the historical analysis.

As for the second proposal, about the quotidian turn's limitations, I can imagine several responses. Two of them can be stated simply—and set aside as not requiring much more reflection. You might respond by saying that you never much cared for the approaches I classify as aligned with the quotidian turn, perhaps because your own research focus—for example, canonical texts, intellectual history, or institutional leaders—seems to rest on different assumptions and to enact different values, while it also requires different sources and methods. You might be indifferent to the alleged methodological challenges and conceptual difficulties or have only mild interest in accumulating more reasons to reject approaches that you already were spending little time considering. Or, to mention a second possible response, you might be a vigorous advocate of the use of *everyday religion* or *lived religion* as a guiding category and remain unpersuaded by my analysis of the implied oppositions and untroubled by my claims about one-sided interpretations. In both of these imagined responses—unqualified rejection or unqualified affirmation—there does not seem to be much more to say. We can simply agree to disagree and let many flowers bloom.

However, if you think my analysis of the accomplishments and limitations of the quotidian turn raises some issues worth pondering more, then the dangling question is simple: What should we do next? I see two main alternatives.

Scholars might continue to employ the quotidian turn's guiding categories, while trying to confront and minimize the difficulties I identify. Critics might point out that use of the word *everyday* (as well as of the adjectives *lived* and *popular*) encourages one-sided interpretations—for example, by minimizing elites' prescriptive beliefs and ecclesiastical institutions' public power—but some scholars of the everyday have recognized the possible distortions these binaries can introduce. Ammerman, for example, acknowledges that "to start with the everyday is to privilege the experience of non-experts," but "that does not mean that 'official' ideas are never important." She continues, "Similarly, everyday implies activity that happens outside organized religious events and institutions, but that does not mean that we discount the influence of those institutions wield or that we neglect what happens within organized religion 'every day.'" Further, "everyday religion may happen in both private and public life, among privileged and non-privileged people."[62] Orsi uses the related category, *lived religion*, but offers a similar caution: "The study of lived religion directs attention to institutions *and* persons, texts *and* rituals, practice *and* theology, things *and* ideas—all as media of making and unmaking worlds."[63]

Those who want to continue and refine this interpretive tradition might begin their reflection with these useful cautions by Ammerman and Orsi, but others will have their own thoughts about how to deal with the issues I have raised. As a sympathetic conversation partner, I want to make three modest suggestions.

First, it might help to theorize more fully each of the key terms—the *everyday* and the *religious*—and, most important, the dynamic relation between the two. If you cannot imagine a conceptual problem in relating the quotidian and the ecstatic, then that means you probably are *presupposing* a framework—a sacramental theology or a phenomenological perspective, to mention two of many possibilities—that provides an idiom for theorizing their interrelation. If so, it would help to surface those presuppositions. If you insist that you have no presuppositions, we again reach a point where there is not much more to say, since I think presuppositions are inevitable. However, if you are cautious because much of what has passed as theory rests on claims that go beyond the evidence—the assertion that "religion" or "secularity" is the same in all times and places—then there is much more to say. I understand the principled resistance to this sort of theorizing, but I think there are ways to clarify lexical usage and refine scholarly practice without making the contestable empirical claim that the interpreter's categories, including *religion*, are "universal."[64] A bit more theorizing and a few more stipulative definitions—those that stipulate a term's meaning for a particular project—might help with the conceptual problems I have identified. That might nudge us toward accounts that bridge the implied binaries more fully.[65]

Second, as you theorize those key terms—the *religious* and the *everyday*—you might develop a continuum or spectrum model. You might suggest that we should talk about *more or less*, not *either or*. Following the lead of Taves, Knott, and others, you might classify diverse spaces and times—and practices, experiences, narratives, and artifacts—on a continuum between two conceptual poles and understand the scholar's task as analyzing how the things you are studying are deemed more or less "special," "singular," "sacred," or "set apart" by scholars or devotees.[66] I have conditionally endorsed this approach,[67] since it sometimes can be very useful to talk about practices as more or less religious, or quasi-religious. However, that continuum model cannot work if scholars resist the task of defining its conceptual poles—the *everyday* and the *religious*—for how would we know where to classify a practice along the spectrum if we do not know what those categories mean?

Finally, some minor terminological revisions could help. For example, those who want to retain the emphasis on the everyday might distinguish *religion every day* (self-identified devotees' daily practices within or beyond ecclesiastical boundaries as part of the prescribed conduct of the faith) and *everyday religion* (practices conducted by different people, including the avowedly ambivalent and agnostic, in diverse spaces outside churches, temples, and mosques). Taking the lead from Orsi, it also might help to create compound categories that combine both terms of the polarizing binaries, since categories can redirect attention in useful ways, just as the phrase *everyday life* originally shifted the focus to that which had been excluded in earlier studies. In this case, however, those new compound categories and hyphenated phrases might signal an attempt to hold together what language tries to pull apart. Scholars thereby might anticipate objections about one-sidedness and encourage investigators to consider the full complexity of religious life. In my theory of religion, for example, I argued that religions are "confluences of organic-cultural flows," so I could conjoin the biological and the cultural, body and mind, and name the site where embodied brains meet coded cultures. In a similar way, for the study of the everyday, those sympathetic to the study of everyday religion or lived religion might consider the potential uses of compound nouns and hyphenated categories like Orsi's *everyday miracles*. It might make scholars slightly less likely to focus exclusively on one side of the binary at the expense of the other. It might remind interpreters to attend fully to the routine as well to that which breaks it.

A second alternative response—and the one I favor—is to maintain the concern to attend to ordinary people and everyday life but use different orienting categories, theoretical frameworks, and methodological principles.

Using alternative categories that do not directly mention ordinary people and everyday life actually can allow the interpreter to attend to both, and with fewer difficulties. Let me just mention three terminological alternatives that might be more useful: presence/absence; flows/channels; and crossing/dwelling.

I have used all three in my own work, but other scholars have made a good case for *presence/absence* as analytic categories. In a suggestive but overlooked essay from the 1970s, the historian of religion Charles Long dealt with the exclusion of African Americans by talking about who is "visible" and "invisible" in history and in our historical accounts,[68] and Orsi, whose work has focused on Catholics, has persuasively suggested that the theme of "presence is central to the study of lived Catholic practice—the study of Catholicism in everyday life is about the mutual engagement of men, women, children, and holy figures present to each other."[69] Extending the insights of Long and Orsi, I used *presence*—and also *absence*—in a recent historical study of a Marian shrine.[70] That strategy had advantages, even if it had its limitations too. As I delineated corporeal and incorporeal presence, I was able to talk about the ways devotees understood suprahuman beings—God, Mary, and the saints—as present in their lives, so it was helpful for writing *religious* history. More important, I think that theme—and my consideration of ten factors in the interpretation of architecture, including the makers, donors, and users of the space[71]—allowed me to avoid overemphasis on one element in the usual binaries. For example, I could talk about the bishops and architects who planned the building and the lay devotees and women religious who used it. I could note the role of theological beliefs about the church, the saints, and the modern world as well practices such as donation, prayer, and pilgrimage. The theme of *presence* allowed me to document those who traveled there—and those who had an incorporeal presence through mailed donations and devotional letters. And, most important for preserving the originating motives of the quotidian turn, that strategy allowed me to attend to the presence of a wide range of devotees—including women, children, immigrants, Amerindians, and the poor—and to take note of who was absent because of racism, including African Americans.

The theme of presence, as I understand it, is a spatial trope related to other interpretive categories that can reduce—though never eliminate—the conceptual and practical difficulties. Presence can be understood as a form of dwelling. Religions, I have argued, position devotees in four chronotopes or time-spaces: the body, the home, the homeland, and the cosmos.[72] This approach considers varying social spaces, from the intimate, routine, and profane to the formal, grand, and consecrated. In particular, by attending to the body and the home, a wider range of characters enter our narratives of religious life. An interpretive space opens, for example, for analyzing both the elites' prescriptions about embodiment and family as well as how those prescriptions are enacted, revised, and resisted in vernacular practice.

The theme of *dwelling*, in my account, is always related to another theme, *crossing*; and I have used that spatial trope—as well as the aquatic metaphor of *flow*—to propose a kinetic theoretical framework and a set of methodological principles. Religion is as much about crossing, or moving across space, as it is about dwelling, or finding one's place. I have suggested that "religions enable and constrain *terrestrial crossings*, as devotees traverse natural terrain and social space beyond the home and across the homeland; *corporeal crossings*, as the religious fix their attention on the limits of embodied existence; and *cosmic crossings*, as the pious imagine and cross the ultimate horizon of human life."[73] Despite the richness of many studies of everyday religion and lived religion, most interpreters presuppose a theory of culture and religion that is still too static, imagining a religious world filled by stable objects that exist independently of substantial selves. Their presumed framework does not account for the dynamism of religious life, and the concomitant scholarly usage inclines the interpreter to unwittingly harden the categorical distinctions into conceptual oppositions that can lead to one-sided accounts. It might help, I think, to put the everyday—and the ecstatic—in motion, to employ a relational and kinetic view of religion and its wider cultural context.[74] The scheme I have proposed certainly still makes distinctions—*dwelling* and *crossing*—yet, although I cannot fully substantiate this point here, those distinctions do not set up the conceptual problems I have identified with the quotidian turn's lexicon: the problem of how to talk about, for example, both ordinary people and elites, everyday spaces and consecrated sites, beliefs and practices, or the quotidian and the ecstatic. It reduces the conceptual problems by sidestepping them. It shifts the idiom—and the implied framework and methodology. Using *crossing* as an analytic category, as I did in *America's Church*, allows for attention to both sides of those usual binary pairs, as the interpreter traces the movements to and from the shrine and attends to all the people, things, and practices that crossed the building's threshold.

To put the quotidian and the ecstatic in motion, we also might employ aquatic metaphors, as the anthropologist Arjun Appadurai did in his analysis of cultural flows and I have done in my theory of religious flows and in my recent methodological proposals.[75] In that idiom, which reflects a more processive theoretical framework, the "mutual inter-causality" of the biological and the cultural can be imagined in terms of confluences, and politics, society, and economy can be understood as converging streams that impact religions as they emerge from the swirl of transfluvial currents.[76] So the institutional channels of the quotidian—political organizations, social relations, and economic forces—transform the more or less ecstatic spaces, which become sites where power is negotiated as meaning is made. The kinetic and interrelated spaces and times of the ecstatic, or that which stands out from the quotidian, are produced from the swirl of transfluvial currents and, in turn, exert causal influence as they mix with other currents along the way. In this kinetic account, with its emphasis on transfluence, many of the unintended binaries that form when scholars appeal to religion in everyday life are lost in the swirling flows. We certainly can still distinguish bodies and minds, elites and laity, beliefs and practices, churches and the myriad spaces beyond their threshold, Sunday morning and the rest of the time. The categorical distinctions seem less fixed and final, however.

This theoretical framework is more than a metaphor in search of a method, even if I have only gestured toward a fuller methodological proposal here. Most important, this framework affords a vantage from which we can honor the originating concerns of the quotidian turn—to attend to ordinary people and everyday life—while offering a richer account of the kinetics of religious practice that bridges categorical binaries and expands our narratives' characters and settings. It can help us analyze ordinary people *and* institutional elites in ecclesiastical *and* mundane spaces.[77]

My approach is not without its limitations, and its guiding theoretical picture is not the only way to preserve the quotidian turn's insights. Readers might find better ways to proceed. Further, those who are already convinced that we need a kinetic theory might prefer alternative categories that aim for similar ends. My framework relies on aquatic tropes about *flows* and spatial images about *crossing*, but other root metaphors can do helpful interpretive work too, including *routes* (Clifford), *networks* (Vásquez), and *movements* (Tsing).[78] My goal is not to champion a framework or a category as the only one. That would be odd and inconsistent with my pragmatic approach, which suggests all frameworks and categories are only more or less useful for a scholar's particular purposes. They all have "blind spots."[79] Mine too. But I thought it would help to illustrate what I had in mind by making a few tentative suggestions, if only to generate counterproposals. My primary concerns are modest: to suggest a label for one interpretive pattern and prompt more thinking about how to assess it. Whether or not you find my alternative categories promising, I hope we can have a more robust and sustained conversation about the history, uses, and limits of the scholarly trajectories that have highlighted ordinary people and everyday life. Perhaps we can self-consciously evaluate those and other analytic categories, acknowledging their accomplishments and limitations, and, most of all, trying to hold together what language pulls apart, including but not only the quotidian and the ecstatic.

Notes

This is a revised version of a lecture I gave at "The Future of the Religious Past" conference in Amsterdam in 2011 and then published as "After the Quotidian Turn: Interpretive Categories and Scholarly Trajectories in the Study of Religion Since the 1960s," *The Journal of Religion* 95.3 (2015): 361–85. It appears here in modified form with the permission of the University of Chicago. The history of the study of religion and everyday life is a vast subject, and I relied on many colleagues in many academic institutions for advice. I thank some of them in the notes below, but I also should signal my gratitude to others, including Gregory Alles, Janet Hoskins, Jillian Owens, Sherri Sheu, Christian Smith, Michael Stausberg, William Taylor, Ann Taves, and James Turner.

1. I have addressed this issue in many works. I have proposed criteria for the use and evaluation of Weberian ideal types in *The American Encounter with Buddhism, 1844–1912* (Chapel Hill: University of North Carolina Press, 2000), 49–50, and have assessed the guiding categories in the study of US religion and Buddhism in both *Our Lady of the Exile: Diasporic Religion at a Cuban Catholic Shrine in Miami* (New York: Oxford

University Press, 1997), 135–138, and "Theory and Method in the Study of Buddhism: Toward 'Translocative' Analysis," *Journal of Global Buddhism* 12 (2011): 17–32. I laid out my pragmatic approach most fully—and discussed the assessment of categories, definitions, and theories—in my theory of religion. Thomas A. Tweed, *Crossing and Dwelling: A Theory of Religion* (Cambridge, MA: Harvard University Press, 2006), 16–20, 30–31, 165–167, 246–247.

2. Peter Lambert and Phillip Schofield, *Making History: An Introduction to the History and Practices of a Discipline* (New York: Routledge, 2004), 87, 170; David Ludden, "A Brief History of Subalternity," in *Reading Subaltern Studies: Critical History, Contested Meaning, and the Globalization of South Asia*, ed. David Ludden (Delhi: Permanent Black, 2001), 1–39.

3. E. P. Thompson, *The Making of the English Working Class* (London: V. Gollancz, 1963).

4. Lambert and Schofield, *Making History*, 87, 170; Ludden, "A Brief History of Subalternity," 1–39; Guy Bourdé and Hervé Martin, *Les écoles historiques* (Paris: Editions du Seuil, 1983); and Fernand Braudel, *La Méditerranée et le monde Méditerranéen à l'époque de Philippe II* (Paris: Colin, 1949).

5. Robert Darnton, "Intellectual and Cultural History," in *The Past Before Us: Contemporary Historical Writing in the United States*, ed. Michael Kammen (Ithaca, NY: Cornell University Press, 1980); and Lynn Hunt, ed., *The New Cultural History* (Berkeley: University of California Press, 1989), 1.

6. Leonard Norman Primiano, "Vernacular Religion and the Search for Method in Religious Folklore," *Western Folklore* 54, no. 1 (January 1996): 37–56; Marion Bowman, "Vernacular Religion and Nature: The 'Bible of the Folk' Tradition in Newfoundland," *Folklore* 114, no. 3 (December 2003): 285–295; Marion Bowman and Ülo Valk, eds. *Vernacular Religion in Everyday Life: Expressions of Belief* (Sheffield, UK: Equinox, 2012).

7. R. J. Johnston, Derek Gregory, Geraldine Pratt, and Michael Watts, eds., *Dictionary of Human Geography*, 4th ed. (Malden, MA: Blackwell, 2000), 429–432; D. W. Meinig, ed., *The Interpretation of Ordinary Landscapes: Geographical Essays* (New York: Oxford University Press, 1979); John R. Stilgoe, *Common Landscape of America, 1580–1845* (New Haven, CT: Yale University Press, 1982); and Henry Glassie, *Pattern in the Material Folk Culture of the Eastern United States* (Philadelphia: University of Pennsylvania Press, 1969).

8. David Freedberg, *The Power of Images: Studies in the History and Theory of Response* (Chicago: University of Chicago Press, 1989); Philip Smith and Alexander Riley, *Cultural Theory: An Introduction*, 2nd ed. (Malden, MA: Blackwell, 2009), 158–175.

9. Ernst Gombrich, review of David Freedberg, *The Power of Images: Studies in the History and Theory of Response. New York Review of Books* 15 (1990), 6.

10. Smith and Riley, *Cultural Theory*, 144–157.

11. For example, Eric R. Wolf, *Europe and the People without History* (Berkeley: University of California Press, 1982).

12. Ranajit Guha, ed., *Subaltern Studies I: Writings on South Asian History and Society* (Delhi: Oxford University Press, 1982), vii; and Partha Chatterjee, "After Subaltern Studies," *Economic and Political Weekly*, September 1, 2012, 44–49.

13. Darcy Ribeiro, *Las Américas y la civilización: Proceso de formación y causas del desarrollo desigual de los pueblos Americanos*. (Caracas: Biblioteca Ayacucho, 1968), 13.

14. Latin America Subaltern Studies Group, "Founding Statement," *Boundary 2* 20, no. 3 (1993): 110–121.

15. Walter D. Mignolo, *Local Histories/Global Designs: Coloniality, Subaltern Knowledges, and Border Thinking* (Princeton, NJ: Princeton University Press, 2000), 18–21.

16. William Taylor, *Shrines and Miraculous Images: Religious Life in Mexico before the Reforma* (Albuquerque: University of New Mexico Press, 2010), 89.

17. Taylor, 89.

18. For example, William A. Christian, *Local Religion in Sixteenth-Century Spain* (Princeton, NJ: Princeton University Press, 1981); Daniel L. Overmyer, *Local Religion in North China in the Twentieth Century: The Structure and Organization of Community* (Leiden: Brill, 2009). Ellen Badone, *Religious Orthodoxy and Popular Faith in European Society* (Princeton, NJ: Princeton University Press, 1990); Daniel H. Levine, *Popular Voices in Latin American Catholicism* (Princeton, NJ: Princeton University Press, 1992).

19. Grace Davie, "Sociology of Religion," in *Encyclopedia of Religion and Society*, ed. William H. Swatos Jr. (Walnut Creek, CA: AltaMira Press, 1998); Danièle Hervieu-Léger, "What Scripture Tells Me: Spontaneity and Regulation within the Catholic Charismatic Renewal," in *Lived Religion in America*, ed. David D. Hall (Princeton, NJ: Princeton University Press, 1997), 22–40.

20. Manuel Vásquez, *More Than Belief: A Materialist Theory of Religion* (New York: Oxford University Press, 2011), 252–255.

21. Timothy Matovina, *Guadalupe and Her Faithful: Latino Catholics in San Antonio, from Colonial Origins to the Present* (Baltimore, MD: Johns Hopkins University Press, 2005); and Jennifer Scheper Hughes, *Biography of a Mexican Crucifix: Lived Religion and Local Faith from the Conquest to the Present* (New York: Oxford University Press, 2010).

22. Diane Winston, ed., *Small Screen, Big Picture: Television and Lived Religion* (Waco, TX: Baylor University Press, 2009); Meredith McGuire, *Lived Religion: Faith and Practice in Everyday Life* (New York: Oxford University Press, 2008). Another coedited volume uses a related term, *practice*, but approvingly cites David Hall's *Lived Religion* in the introduction. It also was coedited by Leigh Schmidt, one of the contributors to Hall's 1997 book, and it appeared in the "Lived Religions" series edited by Hall and Robert Orsi. See Laurie F. Maffly-Kipp, Leigh E. Schmidt, and Mark Valeri, eds., *Practicing Protestants: Histories of Christian Life in America, 1630–1965* (Baltimore, MD: Johns Hopkins University Press, 2006).

23. Sanne Derks, *Power and Pilgrimage: Dealing with Class, Gender, and Ethnic Inequality at a Bolivian Marian Shrine* (Berlin: Lit Verlag, 2011), 27, 171; Anna-Karina Hermkens, Willy Jansen, and Catrien Notermans, eds., *Moved by Mary: The Power of*

Pilgrimage in the Modern World (London: Ashgate, 2009); and Heinz Streib, Astrid Dinter, and Kerstin Söderblom, eds., *Lived Religion: Conceptual, Empirical and Practical-Theological Approaches: Essays in Honor of Hans-Günter Heimbrock* (Leiden: Brill, 2008). The anthropologist Sanne Derks confirmed my understanding of the intersections between the categories of *everyday life* and *lived religion*. As far as I can tell, Dutch, Swedish, and German anthropologists and religion scholars seem to have led the way in the adoption of the term *lived religion*, a phrase that Derks has translated into Dutch as *"geleefde religie."* Sanne Derks, in an email to the author, March 2, 2012.

24. This claim is based on extensive searches of several terms (and related phrases) in English, French, and German in online library catalogs in North America and Europe, including Harvard University's collections. To test my preliminary results about the history of usage, I also consulted Google Books' N-gram Viewer, an interactive online "culturomics" project based at Google and Harvard University that uses the millions of publications in Google Books and allows researchers to chart the changes in frequency of usage of a term or phrase. See Jean-Baptiste Michel, Yuan Kui Shen, Aviva Presser Aiden, Adrian Veres, Matthew K. Gray, William Brockman, and the Google Books Team: Joseph P. Pickett, Dale Hoiberg, Dan Clancy, Peter Norvig, Jon Orwant, Steven Pinker, Martin A. Nowak, and Erez Lieberman Aiden, "Quantitative Analysis of Culture Using Millions of Digitized Books," *Science*, December 16, 2010. This quantitative method has multiple flaws, of course; it makes no distinctions among types of publications, the context of usage, or the reception among readers—to mention only a few limitations—but it provides noteworthy supplemental evidence about the history of usage.

25. Sigmund Freud, *The Psychopathology of Everyday Life* (New York: Macmillan, 1915), 277–338.

26. Freud, 312–313.

27. Max Weber, *The Sociology of Religion* (Boston, MA: Beacon Press. 1993), 152, 159, 21, 24.

28. For a Norwegian social scientist's use of *hverdagsliv* or everyday life, see Marianne Gullestad, *Kultur og hverdagsliv: på sporet av det moderne Norge* (Oslo: Universitetsforlaget, 1989). For a recent Norwegian work that uses a related phrase, see Şükrü Bilgiç's *Hovedfaktorer i integrering: religion, kultur, økonomi og dagligliv* (Oslo: Kulturbro, 2008), the title of which might be translated as "Main Factors in Integration: Religion, Culture, Economy, and Daily Life." For a recent work in Dutch, see Marjo Buitelaar, *Islam en het dagelijks leven: religie en cultuur onder Marokkanen* ["Islam and everyday life: Religion and culture among Moroccans"] (Amsterdam: Atlas, 2006). I am grateful to Ingvild Gilhus, Lisbeth Mikaelsson, and Einar Thomassen of the University of Bergen for helping me understand the subtle differences in the related Norwegian phrases used in scholarship. On the Dutch phrases, I am indebted to several Dutch scholars, including Anne-Marie Korte and Sanne Derks. Derks has suggested that the best variants in Dutch are *het alledaagse leven* or *het leven van alledag*.

29. Patricia A. Adler, Peter Adler, and Andrea Fontana, "Everyday Life Sociology," *Annual Review of Sociology* 13 (1987): 217–235.

30. Erving Goffman, *The Presentation of Self in Everyday Life* (New York: Anchor, 1959); and Peter L. Berger and Thomas Luckman, *The Social Construction of Reality: A Treatise in the Sociology of Knowledge* (Garden City, NY: Anchor, 1967), 19–46.

31. Peter Berger, *The Sacred Canopy: Elements of a Sociological Theory of Religion* (Garden City, NY: Anchor, 1967), 41–43.

32. Davie, "Sociology of Religion"; Grace Davie, *The Sociology of Religion* (London: Sage, 2007), 224–244; and Stephen Hunt, *Religion and Everyday Life* (London: Routledge, 2005). Quantitative sociologists, who used numerical data about representative samples, hoped to discern the attitudes of a cross-section of society about all sorts of topics, from the mundane to the transcendent, even though they did not appeal explicitly to categories like "everyday life" as often as their qualitatively inclined colleagues. My account here focuses on the qualitative social sciences, but it might be helpful to incorporate quantitative approaches into my historical narrative of the human sciences.

33. Hunt, *New Cultural History*. Thomas A. Tweed, "Between the Living and the Dead: Fieldwork, History, and the Interpreter's Position," in *Personal Knowledge and Beyond: Reshaping the Ethnography of Religion*, ed. James V. Spickard, J. Shawn Landres, and Meredith B. McGuire (New York: New York University Press, 2002), 63–74; and Vásquez, *More Than Belief*, 231–239.

34. See, for example, James Clifford, *Routes: Travel and Translation in the Late Twentieth Century* (Cambridge, MA: Harvard University Press, 1997), 36; Eric Venbrux, *Ongelooflijk!: Religieus handelen, verhalen en vormgeven in het dagelijks leven* (Nijmegen: Radboud Universiteit Nijmegen, 2007); Derks, *Power and Pilgrimage*, 171; and Samuli Schielke and Liza Debevec, eds., *Ordinary Lives and Grand Schemes: An Anthropology of Everyday Religion* (New York and Oxford: Berghahn, 2012).

35. Nancy T. Ammerman, ed., *Everyday Religion: Observing Modern Religious Lives* (New York: Oxford University Press, 2007); Martin Riesebrodt, *The Promise of Salvation: A Theory of Religion* (Chicago: University of Chicago Press, 2010), 92; Marja-Liisa Keinänen, ed., *Perspectives on Women's Everyday Religion* (Stockholm: Stockholm University, 2010); and Schielke and Debevec, *Ordinary Lives and Grand Schemes*.

36. Marcel Mauss, "Body Techniques," in Mauss, *Sociology and Psychology: Essays* (London: Routledge and Kegan Paul, 1979), 105; and Henri Lefebvre, *Critique de la vie quotidienne* (Paris: Grasset, 1947).

37. Henri Lefebvre, *The Production of Space* (Malden, MA: Blackwell, 1991), 36–41.

38. See, for example, Ammerman, *Everyday Religion*, 111, 192; Meredith McGuire, *Lived Religion: Faith and Practice in Everyday Life* (New York: Oxford University Press, 2008), 188, 217; Matovina, *Guadalupe and Her Faithful*, 182; Derks, *Power and Pilgrimage*, 171; and Hughes, *Biography of a Mexican Crucifix*, 15.

39. Thomas A. Tweed, *Crossing and Dwelling: A Theory of Religion* (Cambridge, MA: Harvard University Press, 2006).

40. Tweed, *Our Lady of the Exile*; Thomas A. Tweed, "Toward the Study of Vernacular Intellectualism," *Contemporary Buddhism: An Interdisciplinary Journal* 11, no. 2 (2010): 281–286.

41. William A. Christian, *Local Religion in Sixteenth-Century Spain* (Princeton, NJ: Princeton University Press, 1981), 178.

42. Marc Augé, *Non-places: Introduction to Anthropology of Supermodernity* (London: Verso, 1995); and Manuel Castells, *The Rise of Network Society*, 2nd ed. (Malden, MA: Blackwell, 2000).

43. Speaking of antonyms, one conceptual difficulty with the phrase *lived religion* appears. What is its opposite? Surely, it is not *dead* religion. Is it something only thought but not enacted? For most users of the phrase, I think, its implied or stated opposite is religion as prescribed by institutional elites' doctrinal creeds, moral codes, or ritual guidelines. So, to return to the affirmative claim again, the category refers to religion as it is practiced in everyday life. If I am right that interpreters often intend an indirect gesture to everyday life, then the same oppositions I am identifying apply for this term too.

44. Berger, *Sacred Canopy*, 43.

45. See Abraham Maslow, *The Farther Reaches of Human Nature* (New York: Viking, 1971), 101; and Victor Turner, *The Ritual Process: Structure and Anti-Structure* (Ithaca, NY: Cornell University Press, 1969), 94–165.

46. Philip H. Ennis, "Ecstasy and Everyday Life," *Journal for the Scientific Study of Religion* 6, no. 1 (1967): 47.

47. Ennis, "Ecstasy and Everyday Life," 44; Danièle Hervieu-Léger, *La religion pour mémoire* (Paris: Éditions du Cerf, 1993).

48. William James, *The Varieties of Religious Experience* (New York: Penguin, 1982), 379–429; and Émile Durkheim, *The Elementary Forms of Religious Life* (New York: Free Press, 1995), 44.

49. Ann Taves, *Religious Experience Reconsidered: A Building-Block Approach to the Study of Religion and Other Special Things* (Princeton, NJ: Princeton University Press, 2009), 36.

50. Victor Turner's analysis, I should remind readers here, relied on the opposition between *structure* and *anti-structure*, between everyday social relations and the feeling of *communitas* generated by the *liminal* stage of the ritual process (Turner, *Ritual Process*, 94–130). Even contemporary interpreters of religion with a very different theoretical orientation, like the Slovenian philosopher and cultural critic Slavoj Žižek, presuppose an opposition between the ecstatic and the quotidian: "However, is it not that ALL religion, ALL experience of the sacred, involves—or, rather, simply IS—an 'unplugging' from the daily routine? Is this 'unplugging' not simply the name for the basic ECSTATIC experience of entering the domain in which everyday rules are suspended, the domain of the sacred TRANSGRESSION?" Slavoj Žižek, *On Belief: Thinking in Action* (London: Routledge, 2001), 110.

51. Kim Knott, *The Location of Religion: A Spatial Analysis* (London: Equinox, 2005), 229.

52. Matthew Day, "Exotic Experience and Ordinary Life," in *Contemporary Theories of Religion: A Critical Companion*, ed. Michael Stausberg (London: Routledge, 2009), 127.

53. Brent Nongbri, "Dislodging 'Embedded' Religion: A Brief Note on a Scholarly Trope," *Numen* 55 (2008), 440–460.

54. Knott, *Location of Religion*, 81, 124–130.

55. Ammerman, *Everyday Religion*, 5.

56. Taves, *Religious Experience Reconsidered*; See also Courtney Bender, *The New Metaphysicals: Spirituality and the American Religious Imagination* (Chicago: University of Chicago Press, 2010); and Courtney Bender and Ann Taves, eds., *What Matters? Ethnographies of Value in a Not So Secular Age* (New York: Columbia University Press, 2012).

57. Ammerman, *Everyday Religion*, 5.

58. Ammerman, 5.

59. Robert A. Orsi, *Between Heaven and Earth: The Religious Worlds People Make and the Scholars Who Study Them* (Princeton, NJ: Princeton University Press, 2005), 73; italics mine. In his later work, Orsi continued to refer to the noun *religions* and the adjective *lived*, as in his introduction to an edited volume on religious studies: "Religions are lived, and it is in their living, in the full and tragic necessity of people's circumstances, that we encounter them, study and write about them, and compare them, in the full and tragic necessity of our circumstances." Robert A. Orsi, *The Cambridge Companion to Religious Studies* (New York: Cambridge University Press), 13. "Everyday life" did not appear in that poetic passage, though "people's circumstances" does some of the same conceptual labor, and Orsi used related phrases, "everyday experience," in his own chapter on "The Problem of the Holy" (85). That contribution considered "the prospect of restoring some version of it to our critical lexicon" (104). The "empirical warrant" for continued interest in the term *holy*, Orsi proposed, is vernacular usage: "people all over the world and in different historical periods" have turned to it when they have "experienced something out of the ordinary." (86). This interesting suggestion merits further reflection; but, unless I have missed something, it does not signal a dramatic shift in his thinking. Orsi continues to distinguish the ordinary (the everyday) and the "out of the ordinary" (the holy).

60. Robert A. Orsi, "Everyday Miracles: The Study of Lived Religion," in Hall, *Lived Religion in America* (Princeton, NJ: Princeton University Press, 1997), 3–21.

61. Aaron Hughes, "Boundary Maintenance: Religions as Organic-Cultural Flows: On Thomas Tweed," in *Contemporary Theories of Religion: A Critical Companion*, ed. Michael Stausberg (London: Routledge, 2009), 220–222.

62. Ammerman, *Everyday Religion*, 5.

63. Robert A. Orsi, "Introduction to the Second Edition," in Orsi, *The Madonna of 115th Street: Faith and Community in Italian Harlem, 1880–1950* (New Haven, CT: Yale University Press, 2002), xix.

64. Tweed, *Crossing and Dwelling*, 36–37, 40–41, 55, 78.

65. Orsi seems to agree with my suggestion here: "Religion comes into being in ongoing, dynamic relationship with the realities of everyday life." Orsi, "Everyday Miracles," 7.

66. Knott, *Location of Religion*, 61; Taves, *Religious Experience Reconsidered*, 28–35.

67. Thomas A. Tweed, "Space," "Key Words in Material Religion," special issue, *Material Religion: The Journal of Objects, Art, and Belief* 7, no. 1 (2011): 119–120.

68. Charles H. Long, "Civil Rights—Civil Religion: Visible People and Invisible Religion," in *American Civil Religion*, ed. Russell E. Richey and Donald G. Jones (New York: Harper and Row, 1974), 211–220.

69. Orsi, *Between Heaven and Earth*, 73.

70. Thomas A. Tweed, *America's Church: The National Shrine and Catholic Presence in the Nation's Capital* (New York: Oxford University Press, 2011).

71. Tweed, 16–19, 241–245.

72. Tweed, *Crossing and Dwelling*, 97–122.

73. Tweed, 123, 124–156.

74. Tweed, *Crossing and Dwelling*.

75. Arjun Appadurai, *Modernity At Large: Cultural Dimensions of Globalization* (Minneapolis: University of Minnesota Press, 1996); Tweed, *Crossing and Dwelling*, 59–69; Thomas A. Tweed, "Theory and Method in the Study of Buddhism: Toward 'Translocative' Analysis," *Journal of Global Buddhism* 12 (2011): 17–32; Tweed, "Following the Flows: Diversity, Santa Fe, and Method in Religious Studies," in *Understanding Religious Pluralism: Perspectives from Theology and Religious Studies*, ed. Peter Phan and Jonathan Ray (Eugene, OR: Pickwick Publications, 2014).

76. Tweed, *Crossing and Dwelling*, 60.

77. Some other scholars sympathetic to the quotidian turn also have argued for more inclusive accounts. For example, William Taylor endorsed a "synoptic approach" to the study of Indians under colonial rule in Mexico, which meant for him "keeping in mind and under study as many of the actors, dimensions, and primary sources of an episode or structure as I can manage, without claiming there will be a sum total." William Taylor, *Shrines and Miraculous Images: Religious Life in Mexico before the Reformation* (Albuquerque: University of New Mexico Press, 2010), 2, 90.

78. Clifford, *Routes: Travel and Translation in the Late Twentieth Century*; Vásquez, *More Than Belief*; Anna Tsing, "Conclusion: The Global Situation," in *The Anthropology of Globalization: A Reader*, ed. Jonathan Xavier Inda and Renato Rosaldo (Malden, MA: Blackwell, 2002).

79. Tweed, *Crossing and Dwelling*, 14–15, 21–22, 60–61, 171–178.

CHAPTER 11

Rhythms of Roots

Identity Politics in Religious Dance Processions in Bolivia

Sanne Derks, Catrien Notermans, and Willy Jansen

> The most intense moment is when we arrive at the church, after all those long and exhausting hours of dancing. There, in front of Mary's statue, that has been placed outside, a large crowd has gathered to welcome us and it is the ultimate time that we display our indigenous roots. The energy is tremendous, as it marks the end of the route. It evokes a feeling of victory: We made it together! We save one of our most wild and beautiful steps for this moment, and I love this part the most, as everyone gives everything, completely! We are proud of our culture; therefore, we dance the Tinku San Simon.
>
> —Judy, Tinku dance group member

Judy is a twenty-four-year-old member of the Tinku dance group San Simon from the city of Cochabamba. The dance is staged at the *Entrada Folkórica*, a religious dance procession performed during the yearly pilgrimage to the Virgin of Urkupiña in Quillacollo, Bolivia. The fiesta takes place yearly from August 13 to 16 to celebrate St. Mary's Assumption. During the festival hundreds of thousands of devotees from all over Bolivia and beyond come to this indigenous market town, especially famous as a Marian pilgrimage site. The Virgin of Urkupiña is known for her powerful help in economic and material issues.[1] One of the ways in which people venerate her is by dancing in the processions; in exchange for their promise to dance, people expect Mary's help and protection. Yearly, more than fifteen thousand pilgrims, from more than sixty fraternities, dance through the streets of Quillacollo. They follow each other along a four-kilometer-long trajectory that ends at the church that hosts the image of the Virgin of Urkupiña. Both pilgrims and tourists come to see the dancers who, stirred up by the brass bands, entertain the audience with their well-orchestrated choreographies, brightly colored carnivalesque clothing, and extravagant decorations. Although entertainment and religious devotion are central elements of the dance processions, we will show how these intersect with the political meanings of the performances, inspired by Judy's statement that indigenous roots and cultural pride are displayed in these religious events. We will ask how ethnicity is constructed in the dance processions and what power politics influence the centrality and marginality of certain dance groups.

When studying the processions, one becomes easily overwhelmed by the festive and energetic atmosphere, and the sensory impact of the experience. The combination of movement, singing, colors, music, and drinking makes it very tempting to analyze the dance processions in terms of what the pilgrimage scholars Victor and Edith Turner have called "communitas": an egalitarian state of spontaneous bonding in which social boundaries are dissolved.[2] Although the classical approach to communitas focuses on processes of inclusion, communitas may also be used for exclusion and reinforcing boundaries between groups.[3] In line with Jansen and Notermans' work on Marian pilgrimage,[4] we assume that "differences between the more powerful and the less powerful at pilgrimage sites must be taken into account to analyze the different ways in which Marian devotion is at stake in power conflicts and situations of social inequality at a larger scale."[5] By broadening our study of pilgrimage from the classical focus on communitas to politicized movements of demarcation, we do not take religion as an isolated realm of human activity but connect it to the wider social and political context. We believe that one has to look beyond the boundaries of what officially belongs to a particular pilgrimage in order to understand what power issues are involved in the performance of ethnicity at the pilgrimage site.[6]

Our study is based on a conceptual and analytical framework developed in a comparative study of pilgrimage set up by Jansen and Notermans, and the data gathered by Derks during eighteen months of fieldwork between 2005 and 2010 in Bolivia. Different methods were used, including participant observation and informal conversations, semi-structured interviewing, ethnographic interviewing, the collection of life histories, surveys and the recording of video material. In order to answer our question how ethnicity is constructed in the dance processions and what power politics influence the centrality and marginality of certain dance groups, we will first briefly look at the history of the site and compare the Entrada Folklórica with the *Entrada Autóctona*, a dance procession held the day before.

Then, we will show how ethnicity is performed in both dance processions. Although the dancers in both processions move on the rhythms of their roots and celebrate their indigenous culture, the comparison will show that they differ considerably in wealth, prestige, and political influence. Curious about the apparent distinction between the two performances, we focus on the political meanings of each procession and how both inclusion and exclusion, empowerment and marginalization, take place in the performances. After dealing with identity constructions at the local level of the dance processions, we will turn to the national and global level in order to show how these levels are interconnected and how during the pilgrimage both Mary and Bolivian culture are celebrated, although from different perspectives and power positions.

The Dance Processions for the Virgin of Urkupiña

The legend of the Virgin of Urkupiña traces back to the eighteenth century, when during the Spanish Conquest the Virgin is said to have appeared to a little Quechua shepherd girl at the outskirts of Cota Hill, near the indigenous market town of Quillacollo in Cochabamba.[7] Until the 1950s the fiesta of Urkupiña was mostly celebrated by indigenous Quechua people from the mountain villages around Quillacollo who saw in Mary an embodiment of Pachamama ("Mother Earth," the most important indigenous deity). Quechuas came with their music and dances to Quillacollo to venerate their goddess of fertility. From the 1950s, Quillacollo's inhabitants, mostly merchants of mixed Spanish descent, became interested in the fiesta and started to organize it by founding dance fraternities and arranging formal processions.[8] Since the 1970s the fiesta has begun to attract pilgrims from outside Quillacollo as well and has expanded into a fiesta of national and even international fame.[9]

During the Entrada Folklórica on August 14 and 15, several dances are performed, representing rituals and events of Andean cosmology and history. All dances can be distinguished by their different costumes, characteristic music, and dance styles. Since 1999, an Entrada Autóctona has been organized, which is held on August 13, the day before the Entrada Folklórica. The Entrada Autóctona aims to "rediscover the fiesta of Urkupiña in its origin," that is, to give space to the indigenous communities to perform their dances and show the variety in their cultures.[10] The fact that a distinction is made between the two processions made us curious about the political meanings of each and the creation of an opposition between them.

Entrada Folklórica

In the big national Entrada Folklórica of Urkupiña—like in the parades of the Carnival in Oruro and *Fiesta del Gran Poder* in La Paz—not only local groups perform but fraternities from all over the country are brought together. Most groups are from the urban areas such as Cochabamba, Quillacollo, or La Paz and are often based on a certain profession, for instance, truck, bus, or taxi drivers who may dance the *Morenada* or *Diablada* or students who perform the Tinku or *Caporales*. These nationally renowned dance parades can last for a full twenty-four-hour day, and the dancers perform on two successive days. Over the past decades the national parades have increased the number of groups performing and the numbers of dancers and visitors. According to the local newspaper *Los Tiempos*, in 1977, the total number of dancers who participated in the Entrada Folklórica of Urkupiña was two thousand, divided into approximately twenty dance groups. In 2005 more than ten thousand dancers from fifty-six dance groups participated. In 2008 the newspaper reported fifteen thousand dancers and sixty groups.

The cost of participating in a dance group varies greatly and can be high. For the Tinku dance, performed by students, the costumes are relatively cheap, costing around 200 BOB (20 euros), whereas the impressive hand-made costumes and masks of the Diablada (the devils dance) and Morenada (slavery dance) can rise to over 350 euros. As a result, these dances have become associated with status. Some people save money the whole year to be able to join a dance fraternity. Most fraternities also ask for a membership fee and a contribution to pay the brass band. In addition, each fraternity has to pay a registration fee to the Asociación de los Conjuntos Folklóricos Virgen de Urkupiña in order to participate in the Entrada. This association takes care of the dancers' interests and is responsible for the organization of the Entrada Folklórica. To guarantee the variety of dances, it has made the rule that a maximum of eight fraternities of the same dance is allowed to participate.

Entrada Autóctona

Since 1999, an Entrada Autóctona has been organized because participation in the Entrada Folklórica had become such a costly affair that poor people remained excluded. The Entrada Autóctona takes place prior to the official Entrada of Urkupiña and includes the marginalized indigenous people: farmers and craftsmen rather than students and urban skilled workers. The introduction of an Entrada

Autóctona has been derived from the Carnival in Oruro, in which, since 1995, a dance parade is performed by indigenous groups from the tiny villages and communities around Oruro. In 1999, the *Casa de la Cultura* in Quillacollo and a group of journalists took the initiative to organize a special Entrada for the indigenous groups, with the aim "to rediscover the indigenous values."

In the Entrada Autóctona the groups do not have to pay money to take part in the procession. Participants mostly come from tiny indigenous villages around Quillacollo to perform their dances. The dance groups, each consisting of around twenty dancers, are usually smaller than the groups of the Entrada Folklórica. The procession takes far less time than the Folklórica. In about six hours all groups pass through the streets of Quillacollo. Rather than fifteen thousand participants, less than a thousand dancers divided over thirty-eight small groups take part.[11]

The dances of the Entrada Autóctona are not accompanied by a brass band, but their music is performed on "authentic" instruments, such as *charangos*, wooden flutes, or pan flutes. As the dancers make their own music, their choreographies are less complex than those in the Entrada Folklórica. In addition, there are no representations of devils, slave drivers, or other spectacular figures, and the costumes of the dancers are more modest. Most groups wear hats and ponchos that serve as markers to indicate the ethnic origin of the dance or dancers. Often the dances are named after the instruments used for accompaniment or their rhythms, for example, the *Sicuriada* refers to the *sicu*, or large pan flute.

The organizers of the Entrada Autóctona want to make known that the original instruments, rhythms, and dances are related to Andean rites. Therefore, the Autóctona starts in the morning with an Andean mass at the beginning of the route in which a collective offer ritual, or *k'oa*, is performed in the presence of the organizers, the dancers, and any visitors who want to attend. The *k'oa* is a ritual usually carried out for Pachamama, to ask for her help in fertility issues. Especially the indigenous dancers from the highlands emphasize they venerate Pachamama in their dances. In 2007, the *k'oa* was performed at the square in front of the church, but no church authorities were present. Although for the indigenous people Pachamama is similar to Mother Mary, church authorities see them as different and value them differently.

The route of the Entrada Autóctona is about half the length of that of the Entrada Folklórica and takes the opposite direction, rather than ending at the church it departs from the church. The performance is less spectacular, and the groups do not follow each other in well-organized continuity; there are many breaks and long interruptions. A visitor recounted: "I would like to watch their dances, but I left, because it takes too much time before the next group passes by. I decided to walk the route in the opposite direction, so I could see a bit." As a result, there is a much smaller audience in the street than can be observed during the Entrada Folklórica, nor is there the level of interaction between dancers and public. There is far less clapping, whistling, and yelling to encourage the dancers, fewer offers of refreshments, *chicha*, or beer, and fewer tourists taking pictures. At the end of the day, when the Entrada Autóctona has finished, tribunes are constructed everywhere for the much more popular Entrada Folklórica the next day.

The Performance of Ethnicity

In both dance processions for the Virgin of Urkupiña people express ethnic identities. Dance as an embodied tool for collective identity construction can be seen as a political act through which people transmit who they are, where they come from, and to what community they belong.[12] Mendoza even stated that folkloric music and dance performance in the Andes are among the most dynamic and creative realms in which people shape ethnic distinctions and identities.[13] In the pre-Columbian Andean world, dancing was part of the worship of Andean deities. Spanish missionaries also used the religious dances in order to evangelize the indigenous people by expressing the Catholic doctrine in dance. Religious dancing, therefore, became a performance that was associated with Catholicism. During the colonization, however, dance could also function as a form of resistance for the Andean people, as Poole points out: "Pilgrimage dances were exploited as a means of expressing indigenous identity and non-submission to the foreign culture which Christianity ostensibly represented."[14] Historically, in the pilgrimage dance processions, religion and ethnicity came together.

Over the past decades there seems to be a renewed interest in Bolivian folklore and the transmission of culture in dance. The number of folkloric events, such as dance processions at Catholic feasts or festivals organized to display the variety of Bolivia's dances, has increased. More and more dance groups are founded, and their membership is also increasing. This change is linked to a revaluation of ethnic identity and "traditional customs."[15] According to Gilberto Pauwels, a Belgian missionary and anthropologist living in Bolivia for the past thirty years, the renewed interest has to do with the revival of Andean awareness because the year 1992 was a milestone in Bolivian history, five hundred years after the Spanish *Conquista* of Latin America.[16]

In 2001, the famous procession for the Virgin of Socavón, the Carnival of Oruro, was declared a Masterpiece of the Oral and Intangible Heritage by UNESCO. As Goldstein describes, this distinction is an important event with a collective national identity–building function.[17] He also notes that other places in the country that celebrate a folkloric dance festival can transform their marginal barrio into a location of national folkloric significance, thereby contesting their own political, social, and economic marginalization from Bolivian national life.[18] In Quillacollo, an indigenous migrant town in the shadow of the more cosmopolitan city of Cochabamba, the dance processions have grown into one of the most important to the nation. In 1998, the Virgin of Urkupiña was declared Patroness of National Integration.[19] In October 2003, the Act 2536 declared the festivities of the Virgin of Urkupiña to be part of Bolivian cultural patrimony, in order "to preserve the traditions and customs of the religious festivity of Our Lady of Urkupiña, to protect folkloric and authentic expressions during the celebration and to preserve the religious spirit that is part of the festivity of the Virgin of Urkupiña."[20]

By declaring the Entrada Folklórica to be part of the cultural patrimony, high status is accorded to it. As Goldstein notes: "in becoming folklore, supposedly rural cultural practices are urbanized, while continuing to stand for the countryside that is said to have produced them."[21] In the organized Entrada Folklórica, the *mestizos* from the Bolivian cities have replaced the indigenous dancers who were the protagonists of the fiesta until the 1950s. Paradoxically, it is the *mestizo* dances that are labeled cultural patrimony, as their dances include elements that embody indigenous identity, albeit in a stylized manner.[22] In addition, their dances usually do not represent those of the Quechuas, Aymaras, or other indigenous groups, but refer more generally to cultural events in a collective past.

The majority of participants of both Entradas stated in the survey held for this research that they dance in order "to demonstrate their culture." Out of sixty-two respondents thirty-nine persons mentioned they dance because "[they] are proud of [their] indigenous roots" or "to show [their] connection to [their] ancestors." Because people display their indigenous roots and culture in the dance parades, these can be seen as "festivals of belonging."[23] The rapidly increasing mobility of people, on both a national and a transnational scale, has generated the wider context for people's preoccupation with belonging.[24] The religious dance processions confirm that religion, and Marian devotion in particular, can be a powerful practice of place- and homemaking.[25] People's roots and ethnicities are on display to be received and recognized by Mary and by the audience.

Although both the Autóctonas and Folklóricas confirm that indigenousness is being revalued in the public discourse, the way in which they express their indigenousness is different. Ethnicity is differently expressed in the Entrada Autóctona and the Entrada Folklórica, the last being much more powerful than the first one. While in the Entrada Autóctona, present-day regional identity is expressed in clothing, music, and the dances—with hats, ponchos, and traditional musical instruments as markers of the dancers' origin—in the Entrada Folklórica a national identity is expressed that simultaneously builds on and venerates regional traditions and distances from them by making it a celebration of the reinvented past. While the Entrada Autóctona aims to show the actual differences between ethnic groups and communities in Bolivia, the Entrada Folklórica aims to express an overarching national identity in which the roots lie in a common indigenous past. Ethnic distinctions, then, do not play a major role, people claim a collective identity on the basis of cultural heritage and "being Bolivian."

As the two performances of ethnicity are not equal in performance either, people at the local level discuss and evaluate the two processions. The Folklórica is regularly criticized for representing a distorted vision of ethnic culture by performing too complicated choreographies or by wearing stylized clothes that have never been used in history. The participants of the Autóctona claim to express greater authenticity in their dances than is to be found in those of the Folklórica. Sometimes the spectacular aspects of the performance in the Folklórica are viewed as contradictory to authentic representations as the aesthetics of spectacle are regarded as distorting the authentic representations carried out in the dance. For example, a female visitor in her forties told Derks (August 14, 2005): "I don't like the Entrada Folklórica anymore. It is not original anymore, as you see these dances everywhere in Bolivia. It gets boring after a while. They just want to make a spectacle, a show. The skirts are getting shorter, and it won't take long before it transforms into the Carnival of Rio." Also, one of the organizers of the Entrada Autóctona comments on the folkloric counter-procession by saying that the latter "is only a show, a choreography to show to your friends," while the Entrada Autóctona "shows the variety of cultures that are part of Bolivia. It is authentic, whereas the Folklórica is not authentic." In general, the Entrada Folklórica is associated with spectacle, as show elements play a large part in it. The dances become more stylized every year, the dance figures are mostly carried out correctly synchronized, and the suits, hats, and masks become more sophisticated, with ever more glitter, fringes, embroidery, and details. The performance is made even more spectacular by fireworks and colored smoke during the dancing. In comparison, although all autochthonous dances are different in that they play different music, wear different ponchos, and make different movements, visitors often say that they see less variety in these dances than in those of the Folklórica.

The differences in the construction of ethnicity in the dance processions also express social inequality. The Entrada Autóctona is marginalized, when compared to the Entrada Folklórica, by the organizers, the onlookers, the church, and the local politicians alike. For example, in promotional leaflets it is announced that the fiesta of Urkupiña starts on August 14, whereas the Entrada Autóctona is held on August 13. In the eyes of the organizers of the fiesta, the Entrada Autóctona does not count as the beginning of the fiesta and is ignored as part of the celebrations. When people were asked about this striking fact, many answered: "That is because the *campesinos* do not dance for the Virgin Mary but for Pachamama," ignoring the fact that they see the Virgin Mary as Pachamama. Moreover, the dancers of the Folklórica do not always dance for the Virgin Mary either but rather for their own amusement.

The priests too did not display a welcoming and open attitude toward the dancers of the Autóctona. One priest who commented on the opening ceremony of the Entrada Autóctona said: "The Entrada Autóctona is an event that is not organized in accordance with the church. We allow them to perform the ritual in front of the church, and we hope that it also gives a moment to reflect on the devotion to the Virgin of Urkupiña. Before, the route started at the Calvary Hill and ended at the church. We changed it, as at the end of the route everybody arrived at the church completely drunk."[26]

The reason given for changing the route is the inebriation of the *campesinos* at the end of it. At the Folklórica, however, there is also a high consumption of alcohol. In 2007, the priest of Quillacollo approached especially the fraternities with many young members, such as Tinkus, and invited them to assist in a mass during the fifteen days of prayer prior to the actual fiesta. After the mass he distributed little promise-cards that the dancers could fill in to promise Mary neither to drink alcohol nor to take drugs during the entire route. Yet, the church's disapproval of drink and drugs is not seen as a sufficient reason to change the route of the Entrada Folklórica. The measure therefore denigrates the Entrada Autóctona by classifying the participants as more likely to be drunkards than the participants in the Entrada Folklórica, and the event as being of lesser religious importance, with no explicit blessing by the priest.

During the Entrada Folklórica Mary's icon is placed outside the church, so the dancers can make their promises and pray when passing the central object of their devotion, but during the Entrada Autóctona she is kept inside the church, which decreases the significance of the relation of the dancers to their devoted saint. Only in 1999, for one day, the Virgin Mary was dressed in indigenous clothing and placed outside the church. Although the organizers of the Autóctona have asked the church to dress Mary in indigenous clothes again, the church has resisted to do so since. According to one of the priests, this is because: "We do not want to give the impression that the Virgin of Urkupiña is only for the indigenous people. She is for all Bolivians, regardless of their ethnic backgrounds. We prefer to dress her in neutral clothes, so she won't exclude anybody."[27] Interestingly, by refusing to dress her in indigenous clothing for a single day each year, the church excludes the indigenous population, under the pretense of equality.

The Entrada Autóctona is far less frequented than the Entrada Folklórica. The few visitors who watch this procession stand in stark contrast to the massive numbers of spectators who come to see the dances of the Entrada Folklórica. On August 14 and 15, tribunes, built for the thousands of spectators who come to Quillacollo, line the streets along the route of the Entrada Folklórica. On these days traveling to another part of town is hardly possible, as there are only a few opportunities to leave the tribunes and cross the streets. Police and military are everywhere to protect the audience and guide the dancers through the crowd.

During the Entrada Folklórica a balcony is installed for the mayor and other notables in front of the city hall. Although the route of the Entrada Autóctona also passes the city hall, the political authorities are ostensibly absent. Even more flagrantly, in the year 2007, they scheduled a visit of President Evo Morales to the city hall on the day of the Entrada Autóctona. For some participants, the presidents' visit seemed an honor to the indigenous dancers. A male dancer in his forties of the dance *Phuijay* said: "I hope we will pass the city hall exactly when he arrives. He played an important role in the recent process of revalorization of indigenousness. He can be proud of Quillacollo today, as we have our biggest annual show of indigenous groups."[28] However, Morales did not come to watch the indigenous dancers, and the overlap of the president's visit with the dance procession drew people's attention away from the dance processions. A large crowd gathered in front of the town hall to catch a glimpse of the president and blocked the road for the dancers. One of the dance groups was obliged to take a long pause as they could no longer continue their dance in the street. One dancer complained: "I thought Evo came for us, but he seems not to bother. If he is not interested, could he not come another day? Now the road is blocked and also all journalists and people from the press are gone to take pictures of Evo."[29] The scant interest of the political authorities for the indigenous processions shows once again that the Autóctona is regarded as marginal, having little importance. Even Evo Morales, who exploits his indigenous origin politically, was not interested in the indigenous dance procession.

To make the dance procession into a powerful event, the dancers have to have an audience to whom their message can be conveyed and with whom they share a feeling of communitas.[30] As Judy, the twenty-four-year-old Tinku dancer, said: "It is fantastic to be in such a big group of people moving back and forth to the same rhythm and totally synchronized. The band plays all these tunes with this simple rhythm of the Tinku. And when the audience starts screaming, clapping, and whistling, we dance more and more wildly! It is impossible to describe what I feel at these moments!"

The repetitive movement, the musical beat, the colors of the dresses and other sensory aspects of the performance, as well as the existence of an audience that confirms and supports the performance, call upon profound feelings of joy, happiness, and belonging. The strength of religion is the capacity to evoke a holistic sensorial experience, shared among a broader community; with this capacity, religious experiences can evoke a feeling of authentic belonging in the midst of a world that seems to be fragmenting.[31] Being part of the same dance group causes people to relate to each other, because they have something in common. Class or ethnic differences do not play a role between the members, at least during the performance. We must remark that the social boundaries are dissolved only for the members who are in any way included in the group. The poor *campesinos* are still excluded from the group because they cannot pay the registration fees nor afford the costume with all its adornments.

The experience of communitas is not restricted to the Entrada Folklórica. Bonding between dancers also happens in the Entrada Autóctona. However, to a certain extent, they communicate these feelings differently. In the Folklórica the bonding element is often narrated in terms of being part of the same spectacle, making a show together, and performing in front of an audience. The members of the Autóctona emphasize the experience of communitas more in terms of belonging to a regional or local identity. For example, a man from a small group from a community up in the mountains, six hours by truck from Quillacollo, stated: "We all live in this town. Some work in agriculture, others in transportation and one is a lawyer even. But today we are all equal, because we belong to the same village."

While differences between members of one and the same Entrada or a group within an Entrada are temporarily dissolved by the experience of communitas, at the same time the differences between the different groups and Entradas are reinforced by the same concept of communitas. After all, the strong feelings of group unity and belonging that are built up in the dance groups separately also function to mark the boundaries of the group. As such, it reinforces processes of inclusion and exclusion.

Folklore, Autochthony, and State Politics

To understand what is politically at stake in the two dance processions, we want to focus not only at what happens within but also outside the performances. Processes of inclusion and exclusion seem to reach further than the level of the yearly pilgrimage. Therefore, it is necessary to look more thoroughly at the labels of the two processions and how these relate to state politics. While the rich and spectacular movement is named Folklórica, the marginalized movement is named Autóctona. Although both labels seem to refer to more or less the same phenomenon, to "traditional" beliefs and practices of indigenous people inhabiting a specific location, the labels seem to have different political meanings.

Folklore is mainly about art performances like dance, music, storytelling, and theater, alludes to traditions passed on between generations and is part of the culture of common people rather than that of elites.[32] Folkloric art performances are often meant to celebrate and teach an audience (tourists, outsiders) about people's cultural history. Websites informing visitors about tourism in Bolivia mention the festival of Urkupiña as one of the top ten folkloric feasts of the country.[33] This touristic orientation indicates that the folkloric procession is globally and not locally focused and aims to attract an audience of people from all over the world. By attracting a touristic audience, one also aims to make a profit out of the performances. Moreover, it refers to the past, the former populations rather than the present ones. In Latin America in particular, the term simultaneously refers to the cultural practices of the indigenous peasant communities of the countryside, and to those of the nation in which these people occupy the lowest position in the socioeconomic hierarchy.[34] Accordingly, in Bolivia, folklore is seen as "something profoundly traditional while simultaneously representing the modern nation."[35]

Autochthony, by contrast, is a much more politicized notion. It is about a return of the local in highly different parts of the globalizing world. Autochthony appeals to a primal form of belonging based on a special tie to the soil.[36] Not only decolonialization in Latin America but also democratization and decentralization in Africa, increasing immigration in Western Europe or a global concern over the loss of "indigenous people" and "disappearing cultures" in South East Asia incite the emergence of autochthony movements.[37] The notion of autochthony is used in two ways: by subdominant groups in marginal areas whose way of life is threatened by dominant groups and who reclaim their position of being born from the soil; and by majority groups who defend their position in the name of their "autochthony" through which they claim a national belonging rather than a local belonging.[38] In West Africa (for example, Cameroon, Ivory Coast) and Western Europe (The Netherlands, Flanders) the term *autochthonous* is commonly claimed by well-established groups who are in control of the state and wield the term against immigrants who are still seen as foreigners.[39] In Bolivia, the situation seems to be slightly different.

Evo Morales—an Aymara Indian and Bolivia's first indigenous president, elected in December 2005 and reelected in December 2009—stresses the notion of autochthony and the "return to the soil" to defend and empower the marginalized indigenous population, against outside (that is, non-Indian) and oppressing powers like colonialism, capitalism, and neoliberalism.[40] The indigenous people of Bolivia hold a majority of 55 percent of the population, whereas mestizos compose 30 percent and people of European origins represent 15 percent of the population. For centuries, the indigenous people were banished to the margins of society and felt oppressed, discriminated, and cut off from political power. Morales stresses the importance of ethnicity in Bolivia's make-up, redefining Bolivia as a multiethnic and pluricultural nation. Since Morales's election in 2005, Bolivia has been renamed the Plurinational State of Bolivia in recognition of the diverse indigenous groups that inhabit the country.

In defense of the impoverished autochthonous populations, Morales particularly fights against the neoliberal reforms that have characterized Bolivian politics since 1985.[41] After a socialist period, in which Bolivians had become used to state control and protection, state intervention became minimized, companies were privatized, and the economy was left to the free market. The Bolivian state had complied with the demands of foreign nations (especially the United States), to provide a more favorable climate for multinational investment. Neoliberalism, however, resulted in foreign exploitation of Bolivia's natural resources (silver, tin, lithium, gas, the rainforest) and a worsening poverty for the majority of the national population.[42] Morales wants to reinstall state control over key economic sectors to grant greater autonomy for indigenous communities and to protect indigenous rights. He has also taken on an outspoken role in international climate negotiations, arguing from an indigenous perspective for greater respect for "Mother Earth." Herewith his autochthony claim is directly related to a return to the soil, albeit with a spiritual dimension. Indian spirituality has even become the stage of his own public performances: before his formal inauguration in January 2010, he took part in a traditional Andean ceremony at the ancient site of Tiwanaku that is still regarded as a sacred site by many of Bolivia's indigenous people. An Aymara priest was in charge of the rituals. Dressed in a white tunic with traditional motifs symbolizing prosperity, wisdom, and success, Morales, as a spiritual leader, addressed thousands of supporters and made offerings to Pachamama.

Morales' political attitude shows that "trajectories of nation-building are still very important for understanding present-day expressions of autochthony and belonging."[43] In reaction to foreign exploitation of Bolivia's land and populations,

Morales makes the autochthony claim to defend and empower indigenous populations. Doing this, he aims to build a plurinational state in which all ethnic groups are represented, which, on the local level, corresponds with the performance of the Entrada Folklórica. In this dance performance the idea of national unity and communitas is expressed, bringing people from different ethnic backgrounds harmoniously together. This claim of autochthony obviously is a claim of high classes as it is made by the president, migrants, urban elites, and the wealthy dancers of the Entrada Folklórica. For them it is important to take a stand to the powerful outside world by coming out with an Indian nation that can compete against political powers outside Bolivia. Morales evidently is more sympathetic toward empowering the nation by publicizing the idea of national unity expressed by the Entrada Folklórica than empowering marginal local Indian groups and recognizing the internal differences, expressed by the Entrada Autóctona. He neglected and even obstructed the Entrada Autóctona that showed the variety of indigenous cultures and herewith challenged the idea of one powerful nation. The two dance processions held during the yearly pilgrimage to the Virgin of Urkupiña thus reflect what happens at a larger scale in Bolivian national politics: repression of small indigenous groups claiming autochthony, despite a national ideology of autochthony that has become the language of protests over resources and the defense of the nation against the forces of globalization.

Morales's support of the powerful Entrada Folklórica is not different from the state support of folkloric dance performances in other countries and herewith part of a wider global process of local identity constructions.[44] For example, the national dance of Sri Lanka, the Kandyan dance, is identified with the majority Sinhala ethnic group and heavily supported and adopted by the state as a symbol of Sinhalese national identity and culture in the postindependence period.[45] Still other countries rely on live dance performances by touring companies that advertise national identities and seek to secure international prestige, such as Les Ballets Africains of Guinea and Senegal, Folklórico de Mexico, and Moisiev Russian Dance Company.[46] The state uses the dances to promote culture and national identity. By recognizing the aspect of "dancing the nation" one can understand why the Entrada Folklórica has become successful and powerful and able to marginalize other dancing groups. Although the Entrada Autóctona empowers marginal indigenous village people at the local level, as it enables them to express their religious and ethnic identity, it does not correspond to Morales's political message of national unity and therefore lacks the financial support and the prestige to become as powerful as the other dance procession.

Conclusions

The main question of our essay was how ethnicity is constructed in the dance processions, and how issues of power, marginality, and social inequality in the processions are related to a larger context. We analyzed the differences between the Entrada Autóctona and the Entrada Folklórica and linked the power differences we found at the local level to power politics at a national and global level as we believe that Marian pilgrimage may reveal power conflicts and situations of social inequality at a larger scale.[47] We did not take the yearly pilgrimage to the Virgin of Urkupiña as an isolated realm of human activity but connected it to the wider social and political context in order to understand the power issues that are involved in the performance of ethnicity at the pilgrimage site.

We demonstrated that two different identities are constructed in the dance performances. In the folkloric procession ethnic identity is reclaimed and transformed into an overarching Bolivian indigenous past, whereas in the Autóctona ethnic identity is claimed in the present by presenting the variety of music, dances, and clothing of different regional ethnic groups. Not only differences are expressed but also inequalities. The Autóctona is relegated to a position that calls upon fewer emotions, as there is less spectacle and audience, and it suffers greater disapproval from the church authorities and is neglected by state representatives. On the other hand, by parading indigenous dances in the Autóctona, indigenous culture is also revalued in the public sphere. The marginalized actors that have been left out of the fiesta for years now participate actively in the pilgrimage and make themselves visible and valuable. It is a paradox that the Autóctona, the dance parade that is most autochthonous in following the rhythms of one's roots, is marginalized for not being as spectacular and spiritual as the Folklórica in this ritual celebration of autochthony.

The spectacle and emotions raised by rhythms of the dance reinforce the experience of group identity for each dance group and each Entrada. They call upon feelings of belonging and community, in Turner's term, communitas. The sensory aspects of performance, the collective bodily movement, and the social contract that is established with the audience all play a role. The rhythms confirm their roots. In this sense, this study underscores Turner's theory on the experience of communitas in pilgrimage. At the same time, it demonstrates Eade and Sallnow's criticism that pilgrimage is also marked by competing and contested meanings, in this case of underlying ethnicity and autochthony.[48] Actually, communitas creates these competing differences between the two dance processions, as it creates processes of inclusion and exclusion.

To understand the power politics at stake in the religious dance processions, we focused on the political implications of the meaning of autochthony and found that this notion is best characterized as a "multilayered political discussion."[49] While at the state level dominant groups claim autochthony to empower indigenous groups and to resist foreign, exploitative forces with a strong national identity, at the local level, subdominant groups also claim autochthony to resist these dominant and wealthy elites who try to impose a transethnic national citizenship as an ultimate identity, emphasizing the similarities rather than the differences between them. The apparent "cacophony of autochthony" is the result of different narratives at different levels.[50] The autochthony claim has to be considered at all levels in order to understand the opposition between the dance performances in the pilgrimage to the Virgin of Urkupiña in Quillacollo. By dancing for the Virgin different groups articulate their struggles over local belonging that are closely intertwined with the desire to be recognized as national and global citizens.

Notes

We wish to thank NWO for the funding of the Power of Marian Pilgrimage program, of which this study on Bolivian pilgrimage was part.

1. Sanne Derks, *Power and Pilgrimage: Dealing with Class, Gender, and Ethnic Inequality at a Bolivian Marian Shrine* (Münster: Litt Verlag, 2009); Sanne Derks, Willy Jansen, and Catrien Notermans, "Miniatures and Stones in the Spiritual Economy of the Virgin of Urkupiña in Bolivia," in *Things: Religion and the Question of Materiality*, ed. D. Houtman and B. Meyer (New York: Fordham University Press, 2012), 198–211.

2. Victor Turner and Edith Turner, *Image and Pilgrimage in Christian Culture: Anthropological Perspectives* (Oxford: Blackwell, 1978).

3. Anna Gavanas, "Grasping Communitas," *Ethnos* 73, no. 1 (2008): 128.

4. Willy Jansen and Catrien Notermans, *Gender, Nation, and Religion in European Pilgrimage* (Farnham/Burlington: Ashgate, 2012); Willy Jansen, "Old Routes, New Journeys: Reshaping Gender, Nation, and Religion in European Pilgrimage," in Jansen and Notermans, *Gender Nation*, 1–18; Willy Jansen and Catrien Notermans, "From Vision to Cult Site: A Comparative Perspective," *Archives de Sciences Sociales des Religions* 151 (2010): 71-90; Catrien Notermans, "Loss and Healing: A Marian Pilgrimage in Secular Dutch Society," *Ethnology* 46, no. 3 (2007): 217-233; Catrien Notermans, "Local and Global Icons of Mary: An Ethnographic Study of a Powerful Symbol." *Anthropos* 103, no. 2 (2008): 471-481; Catrien Notermans, "The Power of the Less Powerful: Making Memory on a Pilgrimage to Lourdes," in *Powers: Religion as a Social and Spiritual Force*, ed. Meerten ter Borg and Jan Willem van Henten (New Yok: Fordham University Press, 2010), 181–193;

Catrien Notermans and Willy Jansen, "Ex-votos in Lourdes: Contested Materiality of Miraculous Healings," *Material Religion* 7, no. 2 (2011): 168–193.

5. Anna-Karina Hermkens, Willy Jansen, and Catrien Notermans, eds., *Moved by Mary: The Power of Pilgrimage in the Modern World* (Farnham, UK: Ashgate, 2009), 4.

6. See Simon Coleman, "Do You Believe in Pilgrimage? Communitas, Contestation and Beyond," *Anthropological Theory* 2, no. 3 (2002): 355–368; Simon Coleman and John Eade, eds., *Reframing Pilgrimage: Cultures in Motion* (London: Routledge, 2004).

7. Nestor Taboada Teran, *Urqupiña por Siempre* (Cochabamba: Editora H&P, 1999); Francisko Cano Galvarro, "Su Aparición y sus Misterios," in *Historia del Milagro: Antología de Urqupiña*, ed. Walter G. Valdivia and Mérida Wilson (Cochabamba: Los Tiempos, 2001), 138–145.

8. W. C. Sanchez, "La fiesta en la Entrada de Urqupiña: Música, Identidad y Conflicto Social Alrededor de una Virgen," *Reunión Anual de Etnología* 2 (1992): 141–165.

9. Juan Mendoza Flores, "La Tradicional Entrada Folklórica de Urkupiña," *Taquipacha* 1, no. 1 (1996): 31–45.

10. William Brun, *Urqupiña de Antaño 2007: Convocatoria* (Quillacollo: Fundación Autóctona Urkupiña, 2007).

11. Los Tiempos, "Quillacollo Alista Semana de Folclore, Fe y Riesgo," *Los Tiempos*, August 14, 2008.

12. Hui Wilcox, "Movement in Spaces of Liminality: Chinese Dance and Immigrants' Identities," *Ethnic and Racial Studies* 34, no. 2 (2011): 329.

13. Zoila Mendoza, "Defining Folklore: Mestizo and Indigenous Identities on the Move," *Bulletin of Latin American Research* 17, no. 2 (1998): 165.

14. Deborah Poole, "Rituals of Movement, Rites of Transformation: Pilgrimage and Dance in the Highlands of Cuzco, Peru," in *Pilgrimage in Latin America*, ed. Ross Crumrine and Alan Morinis (New York: Greenwood Press, 1991), 309.

15. See, for example, Stuart Rockefeller, "There Is a Culture Here: Spectacle and the Inculcation of Folklore in Highland Bolivia," *Journal of Latin American Anthropology* 3, no. 2 (1999): 119; Daan Janssens, "De Cosmovisión van de Aymara's: Analyse van hun Kosmocentrische Ecologische visie" (MA thesis, Department of Cultural Anthropology, Catholic University Leuven, 2001), 11.

16. Pauwels in an interview with Derks, August 2, 2005.

17. Daniel Goldstein, *The Spectacular City: Violence and Performance in Urban Bolivia* (Durham, NC: Duke University Press, 2004), 135.

18. Goldstein, 137.

19. Virginie Baby-Collin and Susana Sassone, "Mondialisation de la Virgen de Urkupiña? Religiosité, fêtes populaires et territoires urbains des migrants boliviens, de Buenos Aires à Madrid," *Autrepart* 4, no. 56 (2010): 111.

20. Reglamento de La Ley "No 2536 Declaracion de Patrimonio Cultural de Bolivia a la Festividad Religiosa de la Virgen Nuestra Señora deUrqupiña," unpublished manuscript, Quillacollo, 2003.

21. Goldstein, *Spectacular City*, 175.

22. See, for example, Zoila Mendoza, "Genuine but Marginal: Exploring and Reworking Social Contradictions through Ritual Dance Performance," *Journal of Latin American Anthropology* 3, no. 2 (1999): 91.

23. Peter Geschiere, *The Perils of Belonging: Autochthony, Citizenship, and Exclusion in Africa and Europe* (Chicago: University of Chicago Press, 2009), 33.

24. Geschiere, 17.

25. Thomas A. Tweed, *Crossing and Dwelling: A Theory of Religion* (Cambridge, MA: Harvard University Press, 2006); Notermans, "Local and Global Icons of Mary"; Jansen and Notermans, *Gender, Nation and Religion in European Pilgrimage*.

26. Interview with Derks, August 10, 2005.

27. Interview with Derks, August 10, 2005.

28. Interview with Derks, August 13, 2007.

29. Interview with Derks, August 13, 2007.

30. Turner and Turner, *Image and Pilgrimage*, 250.

31. Birgit Meyer, "Religious Sensations: Why Media, Aesthetics, and Power Matter in the Study of Contemporary Religion," in *Religion: Beyond a Concept*, ed. Hent de Vries (New York: Fordham University Press, 2008), 704–723.

32. Martha Sims and Martine Stephens, *Living Folklore: An Introduction to the Study of People and Their Traditions* (Logan: Utah State University Press, 2005).

33. "Fun-Filled Festivals in Bolivia," Bolivian Life, accessed February 4, 2021, https://www.bolivianlife.com/top-10-festivals-in-bolivia/.

34. Daniel Goldstein, "Performing National Culture in a Bolivian Migrant Community," *Ethnology* 37, no. 2 (1998): 119.

35. Goldstein, 119.

36. Geschiere, *Perils of Belonging*, 2.

37. On increasing immigration in Western Europe, see Geschiere, 2; on concerns in Southeast Asia, see Tania Murray Li, "Articulating Indigenous Identity in Indonesia: Resource Politics and the Tribal Slot," *Comparative Studies in Society and History* 42, no. 1 (2000): 149–179.

38. Geschiere, *Perils of Belonging*, 6.

39. Geschiere, *Perils of Belonging*.

40. Derks, *Power and Pilgrimage*; Edwin Koopman, "Kritiek op de Goede Indiaan," *Trouw*, September 27, 2008. The paper was written when Evo Morales was still in office as president. He resigned in 2019.

41. Derks, *Power and Pilgrimage*, 69.

42. Daniel Goldstein, "Flexible Justice: Neoliberal Violence and 'Self-Help' Security in Bolivia," *Critique of Anthropology* 25, no. 4 (2005), 390; Benjamin Kohl, "Stabilizing Neoliberalism in Bolivia: Popular Participation and Privatization," *Political Geography* 21 (2002): 449–472.

43. Geschiere, *Perils of Belonging*, 171.

44. See also Susan Anita Reed, *Dance and the Nation: Performance, Ritual, and Politics in Sri Lanka* (Madison: University of Wisconsin Press, 2009); Elke Kaschl, *Dance and Authenticity in Israel and Palestine: Performing the Nation* (Leiden: Brill, 2003); and Yvonne Daniel, "Tourism Dance Performances: Authenticity and Creativity," *Annals of Tourism Research* 23, no. 4 (1996): 780–797.

45. Reed, *Dance and the Nation*, 780–797.

46. Daniel, "Tourism Dance Performances," 781.

47. Hermkens, Jansen, and Notermans, *Moved by Mary*, 4.

48. John Eade and Michael Sallnow, *Contesting the Sacred: The Anthropology of Christian Pilgrimage* (Champaign: University of Illinois Press, 1991).

49. Kristin Norget, "A Cacophony of Autochthony: Representing Indigeneity in Oaxacan Popular Mobilization," *Journal of Latin American and Caribbean Anthropology* 15, no. 1 (2010): 135.

50. Norget, "Cacophony of Autochthony," 135.

CHAPTER 12

State Rituals in Turkey

Commemorating the Gazi and Kubilay the Martyr

Umut Azak

This essay explores the evolution of state rituals in Turkey that emerged as practices for sacralizing secular republican nationalism. The sacralization is the foremost aspect of all political religions aiming to make the individual/citizen identify with the state.[1] In the case of Turkey, Kemalism can be seen as the political religion of the republican single-party elite, which monopolized political power from 1923 to 1946.[2] The sacralization of Kemalist values and principles was meant to "develop a system of political legitimacy and to aid in mobilizing the community for secular ends."[3] The regime's radical secularization of political, legal, and cultural spheres and the adoption of a new vision of history, which stressed the break with the pre-republican past, were protected and transmitted by the centralized state education and the army. These two institutions aimed to inculcate in citizens the values of the secular nation-state as sacred—read: unquestionable—values.

What follows is a brief account on the emergence and the transformation of state rituals throughout the republican era. The following sections will focus on the commemorational visits to the mausoleum of Mustafa Kemal Atatürk and to the monument of Kubilay the Martyr, an iconic figure of the early republican period, as two parallel rituals of Kemalist secularism. Comparing these two commemorative rituals, the chapter will analyze the changing meanings attached to these rituals by those who perform them. I shall trace in both cases how official rituals have been transformed into voluntary ritual acts co-organized by nongovernmental organizations and citizens with an even stronger loyalty to Kemalist secularism in the context of the increasing influence of political Islam and its electoral successes from the 1990s onward.

Kemalist Rituals and the Cult of the Leader

Kemalism conveyed its sacred values and mobilized masses through its rituals. Its ritualization has been a process instigated and directed from above in a similar manner to that of the Soviet socialism.[4] As a political religion, Kemalism's specific rituals centered on the cult of the leader. Mustafa Kemal—who adopted the surname of Atatürk, "the father of Turks," in 1934—has been at the center of the republican *iconography* and personified the national ideal of Westernization, or modernization.[5] It was significant that Atatürk was also referred to as *Gazi* (Ar. *ghāzī*), a term that is "used in Islam for someone who has scored an impressive success on the battlefield."[6] The use of the term *Gazi* shows that in their attempt to gain the consent of the masses, the Kemalist elite did not refrain from using terms from the vocabulary of Islam, while reframing them as secular concepts. This was also the case in the appropriation of the Islamic concept of martyr (*şehit*) by the new nation-state. The martyrology of Kemalism aimed at inculcating in citizens that the only ideal to die for was the independence and the progress of the nation.

In Turkey, however, the cult of the Gazi never had to compete with the veneration of anonymous martyrs as is the case in many nations that enshrined their martyrs in tombs of the unknown soldier that subsequently became sites for national ceremonies. Austrian and Italian sculptors were commissioned to construct several monuments in honor of Atatürk in the early republican period, whereas only two monuments were erected to commemorate martyred soldiers.[7] Until 1953, the year the Atatürk mausoleum opened to the public, the main venue for national ceremonies was the Republic Monument at *Ulus* (Nation) Square in Ankara, with its statue of Atatürk on horseback.[8]

State rituals in the form of commemoration ceremonies and national holidays which are jointly celebrated on a regular basis to mark specific dates or events are crucial for the institutionalization of political religions.[9] In the Turkish context too, such ritualized acts of commemorations have taken place around monuments and statues that are material and visual signifiers of official ideology.[10] As stated by Öztürkmen, "the models of celebrations had their roots in late Ottoman secular holidays, such as the Young Turks' *Hürriyet Bayramı* [Freedom Holiday], and these, in turn, were borrowed from European (mostly French) forms of national celebrations."[11] The invented national holidays included Republic Day (October 29) and Victory Day (August 30) which were officially inaugurated in 1925 and

1926, respectively, followed, in 1935, by National Sovereignty and Children's Day (April 23), New Year Holiday (January 1), Spring Holiday (May 1),[12] and, in 1938, Youth and Sports Day (May 19). Another important national day would be Atatürk Commemoration Day (November 10) following his death in November 1938.[13]

The celebration of the tenth anniversary of the republic in 1933 gave the republican state the most important occasion for institutionalizing the state rituals in order to mobilize people for the republican regime. An official organizing committee had prepared a program for the celebration that had to be followed in every single village throughout the country.[14] The mass recital of national marches, as important tools of social mobilization, was part of this program. The most famous of these marches, the Tenth Year March (*Onuncu Yıl Marşı*), was composed by Cemal Reşit Rey. Its lyrics, written by the poets Faruk Nafiz Çamlıbel and Behçet Kemal Çağlar, reflected the nationalist pride of creating a nation of "fifteen million youth in ten years," "of building railroads all over the country," and "of creating an integrated mass devoid of privileges and classes . . . under the leadership of the commander-in-chief respected by the world."[15]

These were also the days when the cult of the national leader was created. In 1933, the erection of statues of Mustafa Kemal in the city centers throughout the country was sped up so that the tenth anniversary celebrations could take place in front of them.[16] On the days of celebration, wreaths were placed in front of these statues, which were usually erected in the central square named Republican Square. National holidays became occasions for celebrating Atatürk as the savior of the nation who was perceived as if he was still alive.[17]

In the wake of World War II, Turkey replaced the one-party rule with a multiparty system. The personality cult of Atatürk developed even further during the multiparty period, however. On July 25, 1951, a "Protection of Atatürk" Law ("Atatürk'ü Koruma" Kanunu, no: 5816) was passed in the assembly to protect his memory from insults (with a penalty of up to three years' imprisonment) and to punish those who damaged his statues, busts, and monuments (with a penalty of up to five years' imprisonment).[18] This law was in fact a measure against the disciples of an illegal Sufi order (*Ticaniye*), who had smashed statues of Atatürk in different parts of the country in protest of what they considered idolatry. That year, the construction of Atatürk's mausoleum was sped up, and in 1953 the embalmed body of Atatürk, who was declared by the party-government the "immortal" and "eternal leader" of the nation, was transferred from his temporary tomb in the museum of ethnography to the new monument,[19] which since "has represented the Turkish nation in the name and person of Atatürk."[20] Located on top of a hill, the mausoleum was built in the shape of a classical Greek temple and takes up an area of 15,000 square meters. Inspired by the ancient Anatolian civilizations of Hittites and in line with the official Turkish history thesis of the 1930s which claims a continuity between these civilizations and the Turkish nation, the mausoleum incorporates no Islamic references in its architecture and design. It quickly became the main location of official commemorations and state rituals, "the nationalist substitute for a space of religious ritual, prayer, and spirituality" (fig. 12.1).[21] Today, the monument still dominates the capital city of Ankara like

FIGURE 12.1 "Dear Atatürk": A prayer-like vow from Turkish youth proclaiming their readiness to protect and defend Turkish independence and the republic. In the background the Atatürk mausoleum. Poster by Kazım Özcan. Courtesy of National Library of Turkey, Ankara, ATA AFİŞ 98.

a pantheon and "serves as a symbol in the service of the creation of a collective memory and a collective identity."[22]

As time passed, the enthusiasm of the early celebrations under the republic's founding fathers gave way to ceremonial formality under the succeeding generations. Celebrations of national days have proceeded in a quasi-religious mood of high seriousness together with military discipline. In parades and ceremonies, the military has been given the primary position.[23] This formalism, which included poetry recitation, stadium performances, and an authoritarian organizational style, has had a rather alienating effect on individuals who were born during the multiparty period.[24] In the 1990s, however, the new political context led to the regeneration of these celebrations as enthusiastic masses participated in public events.

The new enthusiasm was due to a renewed Kemalist civil activism, which escalated after 1994 when the Islamist Welfare Party won in major cities in the municipal elections.[25] The increasing political popularity of the Islamist party led Kemalist nongovernmental organizations such as the Kemalist Thought Society (Atatürkçü Düşünce Derneği, ADD) and the Society for Supporting Contemporary Life (Çağdaş Yaşamı Destekleme Derneği, ÇYDD) to mobilize masses for protecting secularist values against the rising Islamism. These organizations, as well as the national daily newspaper *Cumhuriyet*, reproduced the Kemalist discourse at the level of civil society by reviving its iconography and transforming the mausoleum of Atatürk in Ankara into a "pilgrimage site" for the Kemalist activists all over the country who rush into the monument on major national days.[26]

What characterized these Kemalist civil society organizations and media such as the national daily *Cumhuriyet* has been the postulate that the army is the ultimate guardian of the secularist regime. The Turkish military, which had favored the ideology of the "Turkish-Islamic synthesis" against the threat of extreme left- and right-wing ideologies in the years after the coup of 1980, reviewed its guiding principles and from the mid-1990s onward again identified Islamism as the most important threat to national security. The defense of Turkey's secularism now became a major security issue for the army.[27] On February 28, 1997, the army intervened in the political process and forced the government to take specific measures to protect the secularist regime (and ultimately to resign).

The new Kemalist civil society activism backed by the secularist mainstream media, the army, and the higher echelons of the civil bureaucracy regenerated state rituals such as commemoration ceremonies held at national monuments as emotional manifestations of allegiance to secularism.[28] As the perceived threat of

Islamism increased, the mass celebrations of national holidays began to symbolize support for republican secularism in opposition to Islamism. For instance, the Republic Day on October 29, 1994, and later the special commemorations of the seventy-fifth anniversary of the republic in 1998 were celebrated by thousands of people in city squares of big towns instead of stadiums, with concerts of pop music stars instead of parades of students. State rituals were reframed as "people's holidays," "orchestrated by civil society," and mediated to the larger public by secular mainstream TV channels.[29] As argued by Özyürek, the organizers of such celebrations emphasized three concepts: "mass participation (*kitlesel katılım*), spontaneity (*spontanlık*), and enthusiasm (*coşku*)."[30] In the context of this new conceptualization of state rituals, the Atatürk mausoleum, too, has gained in symbolic importance since the mid-1990s.

The Mausoleum of Atatürk (Anıtkabir) as a Ritual Site

In his analysis of official visits to the mausoleum, Michael Meeker points at the continuity with the "Council of Victory" assemblies at the Topkapı Palace during the Ottoman Empire, where "thousands of the highest military and administrative officials assembled . . . to manifest their personhood before the eyes and ears of the sultan."[31] However, the mausoleum is not merely a site for, in the words of Meeker, "interpersonal exchange between citizen and the founder."[32] Nor is it a mere shrine as suggested by Yael Navaro-Yashin who compared the visits to the mausoleum to those to "a Sheikh's tomb as an expression of ongoing devotion and a desire for favors and support."[33] It is important to stress the continuity between the ritual practices at the mausoleum and earlier official or religious rituals while taking into account the difference of these rituals and the current meanings attached to them by those who perform them.

After the mid-1990s, state rituals at the mausoleum have been transformed into spontaneous and emotional manifestations against the Islamist movement and, from 2002 onward, against the government of the AKP (Justice and Development Party) whose cadres began their political career in the ranks of the Islamist Welfare Party. The monument had some 3.5 million visitors in 2005; 8 million in 2006; and 12 million in 2007, when the AKP's presidential candidate, Abdullah Gül, whose wife wore the Islamic headscarf, was elected as the eleventh president of the republic despite secularist mass rallies and the military's threats against his candidacy.[34] At the mausoleum, secularist citizens of all professions, including university professors and top judges, join forces with the top commanders of the army to protect the secular regime and "complain" to Atatürk about the current state of affairs. The rituals at the mausoleum include not only the laying of wreaths in front of Atatürk's sarcophagus but also writing in the visitors' book, addressing the text to Atatürk as if he were still alive.[35]

The monumentality of the mausoleum and the ceremonial practices performed there reproduce the "grandeur of the state" and encourage visitors to identify with the state-nation. In that sense commemorative rituals at the mausoleum function as a "state-reinforcing" tool.[36] This tool is not only used by the state but also by non-state actors who are in need of a "civil religion" that provides psychological strength against the perceived threat of social movements that derive their force from Islamic solidarity.[37] The necessary emotional strength is provided by a new nationalist discourse named "neo-Kemalism," or "*ulusalcılık*" (as opposed to the term "*milliyetçilik*," which is appropriated by right-wing Islamic nationalism). The emotional dimension of secularism was strengthened by this nationalist discourse which constructed a continuity between martyred ancestors who fought imperialist Western powers and the current secularist struggle against the Islamists who are allegedly collaborators of new "imperialists," that is the United States of America.[38] As a matter of fact, at the mausoleum, secularist activists frame their struggle against Islamists as the continuation of the struggle their ancestors fought for the country's independence under the leadership of Atatürk.[39]

Mausoleum visitors, mostly mobilized by neo-Kemalist nationalism, define their presence as a secular but "holy" or "sacred" (*kutsal*) action, but they would reject framing their action as "asking for favors from the spirit of Atatürk," or "visiting a tomb" (*türbe*) as this would be against their Kemalist conviction about the "backwardness" of Islamic visits to popular shrines and tombs as pilgrimage sites. Theirs is a rather conscious act for sacralizing the memory of Atatürk even further. Their voluntary reproduction of the rituals around the cult of Atatürk is an attempt to fill the ideological vacuum vis-à-vis the popular and powerful discourse of Islamic nationalism. Kemalist activists at the mausoleum try to transform what was once political religion imposed by the authoritarian state into a "civil religion" in congruity with a democratic society.

George Mosse's emphasis on the importance of emotion in the emergence and success of nationalist politics as a secular religion in nineteenth-century Germany helps explain the revival of Kemalism as civil religion.[40] In the Turkish context, as explored by Yazıcı, an increased interest in the 1990s in the War of National Liberation and the early years of the republic "has been accompanied by a claim of bringing to light the personal and emotional aspects of the past and going against the dictates of what is referred to as official history."[41] This stress on the emotional and human side of the past enabled secularist officials and activists to reframe Kemalism as a movement from below.[42] The popularity of books that describe the "heroic" defense of Turks against the "imperialist" powers during the Independence War, "glorifying heroism and sacrifice for the motherland, and highlighting the 'golden' past of Turkey," coincided with this obsession with emotions.[43] This popular interest was also nourished by the mausoleum, upon the initiative of the army unit administering the monument site. A "War of Independence" section was added in 2002 to the Atatürk museum at the monument site which exhibited Atatürk's personal belongings and presents given to him by foreign statesmen since its inauguration in 1960. The new section included objects and gigantic oil-painted panoramas reanimating the battlefields and the events of the period with a three-dimensional impact, aiming to reflect "the hardship on the way toward the Republic of Turkey . . . to visitors."[44]

Consequently, the iconography of Kemalism in recent years included not only the figure of Atatürk but also martyrs whose memory invoked emotions and made the national history closer to the level of ordinary people who were expected to make the same sacrifices if necessary. However, the most important figure in the Kemalist martyrology is not an anonymous soldier who died fighting the enemy, but a known person who died fighting the internal enemy in the seventh year of the republic. He is Mustafa Fehmi Kubilay, a schoolteacher and reserve officer who was beheaded in a local Islamic rebellion against the secular republic in 1930. Named as "the Martyr of the Revolution," Kubilay has been the symbol of the continuous struggle against Islamic fanaticism. Especially from 1997 onward, the commemoration ceremonies at the Kubilay monument located on a hill in Menemen, the town where the rebellion took place, have been revived and brought again to the national agenda by Kemalist associations, the army and the media, as a way to express and restore citizens' dedication to Kemalist secularism.

Commemorating the Martyr Kubilay

On the December 23, 1930, a small group of rebels, turbaned and in Islamic attire, carrying green banners and other Islamic symbols, marched toward the governor's office in Menemen, a town some thirty kilometers from Izmir in western Turkey, and declared war on the "infidel" Republic of Turkey. They were led by a certain Dervish Mehmet, who allegedly had proclaimed himself to be the Mehdi (Messiah) and restorer of the Shariah.[45] A young schoolteacher and reserve officer named Kubilay, who happened to witness the scene, attempted to intervene and stop the rebels, even though he was unarmed. The rebels shot and then beheaded him, placed his severed head on top of their green banner, and carried it around as proof of their victorious challenge of the secular republic. The crowd that had gathered around Dervish Mehmet watched and even applauded his action. It was only after the arrival of military reinforcements that the rebels could be stopped. During the skirmish, Dervish Mehmet and two other rebels were shot dead, the other three were arrested (fig. 12.2).

The event, even though suppressed within a few hours, was immediately framed by the government as a major "reactionary movement/rebellion" (*irticâî hareket* or *gerici ayaklanma*) against the Turkish revolution. Official history textbooks as well as scholarly works referred to the incident as the most important reactionary movement against the Kemalist single-party regime and its secularist reforms.[46] In addition to Kubilay, two village guards, Hasan and Şevki, were also killed while trying to stop the rebels. However, not the martyrdom of these village guards but that of Kubilay, a teacher and an officer, has been central to the nationalist narratives of the rebellion. Kubilay's death, which could have also been interpreted as the result of a courageous, albeit naïve, act without precaution — as he was unarmed — was framed instead as "martyrdom," or as honorable "altruistic self-sacrifice" for the sake of protecting the republic against its enemies.

FIGURE 12.2   Some "reactionaries" arrested after the killing of Kubilay.
Source: Belgelerle Gercek Tarih, belgelerlegercektarih.com.

Other national movements have realized the potential of such cases of secular martyrdom for defining the national struggle as noble and sacred, and for mobilizing broad support. Jeffrey Sluka's observations on the "transformative quality of political martyrdom" in the case of the Irish national struggle are pertinent: "Through altruistic self-sacrifice, martyrs gather attention and arouse popular revulsion and moral indignation, which represents a form of capital which political activists seek to transform through ritual into 'mass mobilization' of popular support and action which will sweep them to victory. Through martyrdom, tactical defeats (deaths) may be turned to strategic advantage; they can be transformed into a resource, a form of symbolic power or political capital, which can be used by those who survive to continue the struggle."[47]

A similar transformation of defeat/death to symbolic power also took place in the case of the Menemen Incident. The Kemalist elite used their defeat in Menemen and turned it into a strategic advantage by framing Kubilay as a heroic victim, a source of inspiration for continuing the struggle against the enemies of the republic. As a matter of fact, Mustafa Kemal's message to the Chief of the General Staff Fevzi Çakmak, which was published on December 28 in all major newspapers, framed Kubilay's martyrdom as a regeneration, rather than a loss: "Kubilay's pure blood will refresh and strengthen the vitality of the republic."[48]

Mustafa Fehmi Kubilay, as a nationalist and idealist young teacher committed to the Kemalist revolution and its reforms, was an ideal person for representing the young republic. Kubilay's murder was perceived by the republican state as an attack against the two most important institutions of the state: the army and the school. He symbolized the ideal of the new Turkey which would be realized despite and under the pressure of the recent Islamic past. His death came to be seen as a heroic act because of his courage to oppose the "reactionaries" all alone and unarmed. The "martyrdom" of Kubilay proved in the eyes of the Kemalist elite the cruelty and vandalism of the enemy who abused and manipulated religious feelings of ignorant masses.

The political elite interpreted the violent murder of Kubilay as proof that reforms such as the abolition of Sufi orders had not led to the disappearance of the latter and that secularization had not taken root.[49] In order to reassert allegiance to the secular state, they gave an extraordinary importance to the incident and transformed it into a myth. The creation of this myth was as a part of the political elite's struggle to establish the hegemony of the Kemalist ideology as a substitute to rival old allegiances to Islam and the Ottoman order.[50] The Menemen Incident has since been officially commemorated every year in Menemen, and it has been made a part of the national memory via official history textbooks narrating the martyrdom of Kubilay for later generations. Official commemorations of this beheaded officer became symbolic assertions of the nation's commitment to protect the republican regime and its secularist principle. In short, the Menemen Incident was used "instrumentally" by the political elite, who institutionalized its commemoration and made its hero, Kubilay, part of the Kemalist "iconography."[51] Throughout the years, hundreds of poems, leaflets, and issues of magazines were dedicated to the memory of Kubilay, the victim/hero of the revolution.[52] Moreover, a ceremony began to be held in Menemen every year on December 23 to commemorate Kubilay, "martyr of the revolution," a victim of "reactionaries," the enemies of the revolution.

A ceremony that was organized by the Türk Ocakları (Turkish Hearths)—the nation-wide social and cultural organizations that were used to spread nationalism and secularism in the country—in Ankara on January 2, 1931 was particularly emotional. Hamdullah Suphi (1885–1966), the president of the Türk Ocakları, presented the event in his speech as the latest example of the fight between the old religious schools (*medrese*) and the new secular schools (*mektep*) and declared Kubilay to be the latest of "the martyrs who had struggled for renewal and freedom over the past 150 years."[53] Hamdullah Suphi's speech framed the Menemen Incident as the crystallization of the struggle for "civilization," that is, modernization, which dated back to the pre-republican period. Interestingly, by tracing the cause of secularism back to the Ottoman period and pointing at a continuity with it, Hamdullah Suphi's speech contradicted the official discourse of the republican break with the recent past. However, his portrayal of those who fight for the cause of modernization as "martyrs" was something new and attractive for the republican elite. This use of the term *martyrdom* reflected the conversion of this Islamic concept into a secular one in the context of the new secular nation-state. "Martyrdom" in this new discourse stood not for the sake of the Islamic faith but for the struggle for modernity against the Islamic past.

However, official commemoration ceremonies held at the monument site have also evolved throughout the republican period, as can be seen in the coverage of the "Kubilay the Martyr Days" from the 1930s onward by the Istanbul-based daily *Cumhuriyet* (Republic), which had played a crucial role in the institutionalization of these commemorations. What follows is a summary of this evolution of the meaning attributed to this commemorative ritual.

In the period after the Menemen Incident, the Kemalist elite were determined to keep the memory of Kubilay alive. In 1931, the *Cumhuriyet* initiated a campaign for the building of a Kubilay monument in Menemen.[54] The proposal was accepted by the government and a bank account was opened for collecting people's contributions for the project. The monument was designed and created by the sculptor Ratip Aşir Acudoğlu (1898–1957) who preferred to erect the monument in a spot that overlooked the town and from where it could be seen even from İzmir if lighted.[55] The foundation of the monument was laid on the tenth anniversary of the republic on October 23, 1933, after a ceremony led by the provincial party leaders of İzmir who stated that "the monument was to be the Ka'ba of the revolution for Turks and the republic."[56] The monument was dedicated to the memory of the "martyrs" of the incident. This was exceptional, because at least during the lifetime of Atatürk, until 1938, Kubilay and the two guards were the only persons, besides Atatürk himself, in whose name a monumental statue was erected.[57] This monument was the earliest of the three monuments in the country that used an allegorical narrative. The bronze statue of a nude muscular figure of a young man holding a spear symbolized the Turkish youth's dedication to protect the republic.[58] The following statement was engraved on the supporting stone of the monument: "*İnandılar, döğüştüler, öldüler, bıraktıkları emanetin bekçisiyiz*" (They believed, fought, and died; we are the guardians of the trust they left behind). During the official inauguration of the monument on December 26, 1934, emotional ceremonies were held while twenty thousand people gathered in Menemen and listened to a speech given by General Secretary of the Republican People's Party (CHP) Recep Peker.[59]

Kubilay the Martyr was commemorated in the following years as well; however, it was as late as in 1952 that the ceremonies in Menemen would be reported again on the front page of *Cumhuriyet*.[60] In fact, Kubilay was commemorated with greater enthusiasm in times of national crisis. As political philosopher John Keane has noted, "Crisis periods ... prompt awareness of the crucial political importance of the past for the present. As a rule, crises are times during which the living do battle for the hearts, minds and souls of the dead."[61] Similarly, the memory of the Menemen Incident was invoked in those years when social and political developments led to an increase in the perceived threat of religious "reaction."

The revival of Kubilay the Martyr in 1952 coincided with a change in the Kemalist discourse. After the replacement of the CHP by the democratically elected government of the Democratic Party in May 1950, the government was no longer identified with Kemalist secularism by those who claimed it. Kemalist intellectuals and politicians who, despite their identification with the foundational ideology of the republic, began to perceive themselves as "oppressed" and lacking in power due to the supposed abuse of democracy.[62] This discourse of victimization has been a permanent characteristic of Kemalism ever since.

In 1952, the theme of victimization was strengthened by an assassination attempt against the liberal, secularist journalist Ahmet Emin Yalman (1888–1972), owner and editor of the Istanbul daily paper *Vatan* (Fatherland). Kemalist intellectuals, who were either loyal to the CHP or cautious supporters of the Democratic Party, drew parallels between the Menemen Incident, that is, the violent reactionary event of 1930, and this attack in 1952 instigated by the emergent discourse of conservative nationalism, which amalgamated anti-Westernism, anti-cosmopolitanism, anti-Semitism, and anti-communism. The public debate triggered by the attack at Yalman reflected a continuity in the rhetorical use of the concept of reaction by the Kemalist intellectual and political elite who depicted the new reactionaries as Dervish Mehmets. In the commemorational ceremonies in Menemen and Izmir, where local university students (İzmir Yüksek Tahsil Gençliği) and teachers (Teachers' Association of İzmir/İzmir Öğretmen Derneği) were present, the national martyr Kubilay was referred to as the last victim of "black reaction" and fanaticism, and recent reactionary movements were damned. For instance, the speech by the president of the students' association for the ceremony in the İzmir People's House accused the Islamic press of pursuing the same aim as the fanatics who had beheaded Kubilay twenty-two years ago:

> There are today those who want to destroy the same ideal, as there were in the past those who did not recognize Kubilay's right to live. Yesterday, there were those who cut Kubilay's head off; today there are those who say, "I would hang a Kemalist at every tree in the country if it were possible." They also express these ideas in practice on every occasion. Yesterday, there were those bigots who were stomping around the corpse of Kubilay; today there are alleged scholars and gurus who practice partisanship of ideas, newspapers, and magazines.[63]

The revived spirit of Kemalism among students and teachers did not find broad popular support. According to the report in the daily *Hürriyet* the fact that local people of Menemen had not participated in the ceremony had caused sorrow and given rise to gossip (fig. 12.3).[64] As in the early 1930s, the townspeople of Menemen were probably disturbed by the identification of their town with fanatical and reactionary Islam even twenty-two years after the event. The sorrow that *Hürriyet* reported concerning the absence of the local people in commemoration ceremonies in Menemen was felt by journalists and members of student organizations who perceived themselves as the guardians of secularism.

The following "crisis" which invoked the memory of Kubilay took place in 1969 after violent attacks by anti-communist groups on leftist student groups and organizations who had organized a demonstration in Taksim Square in Istanbul against the US Sixth Fleet that was visiting Turkey and against the imperialism it represented. The infamous Bloody Sunday of February 16, 1969, when two people

FIGURE 12.3 Commemoration at the Kubilay monument in Menemen, *Hürriyet*, December 25, 1952.

from the communist side were killed, was only the beginning of a decade of left-right political conflicts in Turkey.[65] It was against such a backdrop that the annual commemoration ceremony in Menemen was reported again on the front page of *Cumhuriyet* newspaper in December 1969. This time, Kubilay was depicted as the forerunner of contemporary communist revolutionary youth. In Menemen, the usual participants of the ceremony (students from the primary and secondary schools, the gendarmerie, and the district governor of Menemen) were joined by groups of university students from İzmir. Moreover, in this year's ceremony the only speaker was the president of the leftist Revolutionary Youth Organization (*Dev-Genç*), Atilla Sarp. In his speech, Sarp said in a way similar to that of *Cumhuriyet* writers that "after thirty years, the *same persons* staged new Kubilay incidents," and that "revolutionary youths were killed by fanatical reactionaries who were not considered important by the government."[66] Similarly, a cartoon by Ali Ulvi that depicted Kubilay and the murdered youth of 1969 on the clouds, reflected the spirit of the time: Kubilay says that he had thought of himself as "the last one" but now he realized that he was "the beginning."[67]

In short, a direct continuity was assumed between Kubilay, who was killed by the "reactionaries" of 1930, and the left-wing students of 1969, who were murdered by the religious and ultranationalist anti-communist groups. The depiction of the latter as "new reactionaries" and the appropriation of Kubilay as a symbol of the "progressive" leftist youth crystallized the ideological alliance of socialism and Kemalism in the 1960s up until the 1980 military intervention, which ended all left-wing activism. In 1970, some student organizations could even send a telegram to the mayor of Menemen, requesting the town to be renamed "Kubilay."[68] In the mid-1970s, commemoration ceremonies in Menemen were still attended by the representatives of youth organizations and "revolutionary institutions." However, these had only a marginal impact on the public in general. During the commemoration ceremony in Menemen in 1978, the president of the Youth Branch of the CHP in Menemen criticized the neglect of Kubilay's memory for many years because of the "reactionary" governments: "Reactionary and dark forces which have been in power for many years wanted to make our people forget Kubilay and Atatürk's reforms."[69]

The last revival of the icon of Kubilay the Martyr occurred as late as the mid-1990s, when the electoral successes of the Islamist Welfare Party rekindled Kemalist fears of a "reactionary" Islam. The visits to the Kubilay monument began to gain a new meaning in parallel with the increasing popularity of the mausoleum in Ankara. The figure of Kubilay fit very well the increasing sense of victimhood among the supporters of Kemalist secularism in a context where several prominent secularist intellectuals were assassinated. These murders remain unresolved to this day, causing further distrust among Kemalists vis-à-vis the consecutive governments. There was no uncertainty about the identity of the mob that in 1993 attacked and firebombed a hotel in Sivas in which an Alevi cultural festival took place, resulting in the death of more than thirty intellectuals and artists. Alevis are a heterodox religious minority, traditionally strongly supportive of Kemalism, and the attackers were conservative Muslims.[70] These events created an atmosphere in which the Kemalist fear of an aggressive, fanatical Islamism crystallized. Kemalist intellectuals and Alevi community leaders developed a victim mentality that was combined with an increased awareness of the need to "fight for survival" against Islamists.

Their sense of victimization and failure grew even stronger after the electoral successes of the Islamist Welfare Party in both the 1994 municipal elections and 1996 general elections, a process that would end in the closure of the party under the pressure of the military backed by Kemalist civil activism. It is in the same context of Kemalist revival that the icon of Kubilay was rediscovered and the Kubilay monument in Menemen was deliberately developed as a second pilgrimage site of Kemalism. There were considerable efforts to mobilize citizens' participations in these ceremonies as a sign of dedication to Kemalist secularism. The ceremonies were also occasions at which the army generals asserted themselves as the ultimate guardians of the secularist order, as opposed to the ruling government. From 1995 onward, the words spoken by the chief of the general staff at the Kubilay monument have always made the front page of *Cumhuriyet*. On December 23, 1995, the headline said succinctly: "The Army Stands Face to Face with Reaction" (*Ordu Gericiliğin Karşısındadır*). This was just before the general elections on December 25, in which the Welfare Party was to win 21 percent of the votes. Faced with the electoral success of the Islamist Welfare Party, Kemalist secularism began to be framed as a heritage to be protected even at the expense of democracy. Hence, the army's task as the sole protector of the secularist regime began to be emphasized on every occasion by *Cumhuriyet* writers and Kemalist organizations as well as the army itself. The authoritarian methods implemented by the one-party regime after the Menemen Incident of 1930 were an important source of inspiration for the army and its supporters in the 1990s.

In 1997, the year of the "soft coup" against the governing coalition of the (Islamist) Welfare Party and the conservative True Path Party, *Cumhuriyet* paid enormous attention to the ceremony in Menemen. On December 24, the headline "Contemporary Turkey has not forgotten Kubilay" accompanied the picture of the Kubilay monument surrounded by soldiers participating in the ceremony. This year, it was not only the army but also higher civilian representatives of the state who sent messages to the ceremony in Menemen, including President Süleyman Demirel and Prime Minister Mesut Yılmaz. Moreover, civil and military officials attending the ceremony were of much higher ranks compared to previous years. Among the participants in the ceremony were the commander of the Aegean Section of the Army, the governor of İzmir, the chief of police in İzmir as well as members of the Kemalist Thought Society (Atatürkçü Düşünce Derneği, ADD) in the region. The latter had organized a "Kubilay March" and a panel titled "Atatürk and Kubilay" in Menemen. During the ceremonies and the march, slogans were shouted: "Turkey is secular and will remain secular!" "Damn the Sharia, long live enlightened (*aydınlık*) Turkey!"[71] A routine state ritual was transformed that year into a rally for secularism protesting the political rise of the Islamist movement. One year later, on December 23, 1998, in the middle of the search for a new government to take over Turkey's administration, Chief of Staff General Hüseyin Kıvrıkoğlu asserted the Army's determination to prevent anti-secularist movements from undermining the constitutional order and underlined that the armed forces were "stronger than ever" to protect the republic and Atatürk's principles. Likewise, citizens who participated in the commemoration ceremony in Menemen again shouted Army-friendly slogans such as "Atatürk's Army will be the horror of the fanatics," "Here is the fortress of revolutions/reforms," "Army and nation stand hand in hand, for a fully independent Turkey," and "Turkey is and will remain secular."[72] As reflected in these slogans, the ceremony in Menemen became a platform for the Army to perform its steadfastness in defending secularism. The revival of the commemoration ceremonies in Menemen was, according to the Army, crucial in assuring the young generations' allegiance to the republican regime and Kemalist principles and reforms.[73]

In 1999, the sixty-ninth anniversary of the Menemen Incident was commemorated by members of the Army and the leaders of civil and official organizations including the chair of the CHP, the governor of İzmir and the mayor of the İzmir metropolitan municipality. This year, a special train service named "Kubilay Express" carried more than 1,500 people from İzmir to Menemen. The train service revived a practice that had been initiated by the government in the 1930s in order to increase the participation of the people from the nearby cities of İzmir and Manisa in the ceremony.[74] The Army again gave great importance to the anniversary of the Menemen Incident, being represented by the commander of the Army of the Aegean. Besides, that year, because of the assassination of *Cumhuriyet* columnist Ahmet Taner Kışlalı in October 1999, the İzmir branch of the Kemalist Thought Society organized a panel titled "Martyrs of Revolution from Kubilay to Kışlalı." Moreover, as was reported by *Cumhuriyet*, "participants of the ceremony in Menemen carried the photos of intellectuals such as Bahriye Üçok and Muammer Aksoy, who were believed to be murdered because they had defended republican values" and "shouted the slogan 'We all are Kubilays' as a response to Islamists." The memory of Kubilay's "martyrdom" provided these Kemalist civil activists with inspiration and strength for resisting Islamism.[75]

The army-sponsored awakening of the icon of Kubilay continued at an increasing pace and with even greater enthusiasm of thousands of participants.

The organizers kept further elaborating the procedures of the pilgrimage. Since 2005, the commemoration ceremony has been preceded by a procession toward the monument site (figs. 12.4 and 12.5). This march is organized by the municipality in cooperation with the Society of Kemalist Thought and is called a "rally for secularism." During this rally up the hill where the monument is located, flags and banners in support of secularism are carried by participant organizations. However, only Turkish flags and the pictures of Kubilay and Atatürk are allowed at the site of the monument, which is under the control of the army.[76]

During the ceremony at the monument site, official guests who notified their participation to the garrison in Menemen beforehand sit in their reserved places, while ordinary people stand around the monument. The ceremony includes routine state rituals, such as the placing of wreaths in front of the monument, one minute silence followed by shootings of the guard of honor for paying homage to the memory of Kubilay and the two village guards, and the singing of the national anthem. These are followed by formulaic speeches by the mayor, heads of state institutions, one junior officer, and a poem recited by a student. The reading of Atatürk's "Speech to the Youth" is followed by the collective recitation of the

FIGURE 12.4   Portrait of Kubilay in front of the monument, 2005 commemoration.
Photo by Umut Azak.

FIGURE 12.5   "The Republic of Turkey cannot be a country of shaykhs, dervishes and disciples": banner carried in the 2005 commemoration of Kubilay. Photo by Umut Azak.

speech "The Youth's Reply to Atatürk," which is a declaration of acceptance of the duty to protect the republic assigned to the youth by Atatürk. The speeches are often interrupted by applause of the audience and their slogans in support of secularism. "Turkey is secular and will remain secular!"

Kemalist civil society organizations, associations of retired officers, and university students from the nearby towns who participate in this ceremony at the Kubilay monument in Menemen appropriate this state ritual as a political statement against Islamism. By their voluntary participation in this commemoration ceremony, they strive for a "re-enchantment" of secularism by reviving Kemalist martyrology. While identifying themselves with the army, they refashion Kemalism as a "civil" and popular movement. However, in sharp contrast to their discourse on civil democratic activism, these "civil" Kemalists have not come to terms with the military and antidemocratic measures for limiting the influence of Islamism. As a matter of fact, the most important and paradoxical consequence of the centrality of the theme of martyrdom of Kubilay is that the victimization justified authoritarian and antidemocratic measures against Islamists.

The commemoration of the Menemen Incident was used to stress the early Kemalist state's "efficient use" of authoritarian measures against the rebels. As pointed out by Hamit Bozarslan, the Menemen Incident has been, more than any other act of opposition against the Kemalist regime, an iconic event in the Kemalist memory; it was used to legitimate and justify the authoritarianism and violence of the early republican single-party state in the 1930s.[77] The official history textbooks, unsurprisingly, remain silent on the waves of repression for which the Menemen "rebellion" of 1930 provided the justification. Like the rites of commemoration discussed here, they focus exclusively on the figure of Kubilay as a symbol of the Kemalist commitment to protect the secular regime at all costs.[78]

The state rituals focusing on the figures of Atatürk and Kubilay demonstrate how crucial politics of memory have been for the survival of Kemalist secularism, an ideology that was shaped in the 1920s and 1930s and continues to reverberate throughout the remainder of the twentieth century and well into the twenty-first. In tracing the transformation of state rituals in the commemorative sites dedicated to these two historical icons, I have attempted to show how rituals invented by an authoritarian state may persist and even gain a degree of popular endorsement if they prove adaptable to changing historical and political contexts. The iconography of Kemalist secularism has been sustained through the use of state rituals by secular-minded citizens and political groups who identified strongly with the secular (as well as, often, antidemocratic) values of Kemalism as opposed to all manifestations of political Islam.

Notes

1. David Apter, "Political Religions in the New Nations," in *Old Societies and New States: The Quest for Modernity in Asia and Africa*, ed. Clifford Geertz (New York: Free Press, 1963), 61. For a survey on the concept of political religion, see Emilio Gentile, "Political Religion: A Concept and Its Critics: A Critical Survey," *Totalitarian Movements and Political Religions* 6, no. 1 (2005): 19–32.

2. Kemalism was formulated in the early 1930s as a set of principles enshrined in the program of the Republican People's Party, which appropriated the ideas of its founder and the first president of the republic, Mustafa Kemal (Atatürk, 1881–1938), as its institutional ideology. See Taha Parla, *Türkiye'de Siyasal Kültürün Resmî Kaynakları. 3, Kemalist Tek-Parti İdeolojisi ve CHP'nin Altı Ok'u* [The official sources of political culture in Turkey, 3: The Kemalist single-party ideology and the six arrows of the Republican People's Party] (İstanbul: İletişim, 1992), 22.

3. Apter, "Political Religions," 77.

4. Christel Lane, *The Rites of Rulers: Ritual in Industrial Society: The Soviet Case* (Cambridge: Cambridge University Press, 1981), 45.

5. Günter Seufert and Petra Weyland, "National Events and the Struggle for Fixing of Meaning: A Comparison of the Symbolic Dimensions of the Funeral Services for Atatürk and Özal," *New Perspectives on Turkey* 11 (Fall 1994): 80–81; Aslı Daldal, "Mustafa Kemal kültünün toplumsal ve ruhbilimsel temelleri üzerine ön çalışma" [A preliminary essay on the social and psychological foundations of the cult of Mustafa Kemal], *Birikim*, nos. 105–106 (Ocak-Şubat 1998): 36–49; Hasan Ünder, "Atatürk İmgesinin Siyasal Yaşamdaki Rolü" [The role of Atatürk's image in political life], in *Modern Türkiye'de Siyasi Düşünce: Kemalizm*, vol. 2, ed. Tanıl Bora and Murat Gültekingil (Istanbul: İletişim, 2001), 138–155; Yael Navaro-Yashin, *Faces of the State: Secularism and Public Life in Turkey* (Princeton, NJ: Princeton University Press, 2002), 187–203; Erik Jan Zürcher, "Atatürk İmgeleri" [Images of Atatürk], in *Savaş, Devrim ve Uluslaşma: Türkiye Tarihinde Geçiş Dönemi (1908-1928)* (İstanbul: İstanbul Bilgi Üniversitesi Yayınları, 2005), 253–264; Esra Özyürek, *Nostalgia for the Modern: State Secularism and Everyday Politics in Turkey* (Durham, NC: Duke University Press, 2006), 93–124; Nazlı Ökten, "An Endless Death and an Eternal Mourning: November 10 in Turkey," in *The Politics of Public Memory in Turkey*, ed. Esra Özyürek (Syracuse, NY: Syracuse University Press, 2007), 95–113.

6. Şerif Mardin, *Religion and Social Change in Modern Turkey: The Case of Bediüzzaman Said Nursi* (Albany: State University of New York Press, 1989), 3–4.

7. Klaus Kreiser, "Public Monuments in Turkey and Egypt, 1840–1916," *Muqarnas* 14 (1997), 113; and Faik Gür, "Atatürk Heykelleri ve Türkiye'de Resmî Tarihin Görselleşmesi" [Ataturk statues and the visual representation of official history in Turke], *Toplum ve Bilim*, no. 90 (2001): 147–166.

8. Aygen Erdentuğ and Berrak Burçak, "Political Tuning in Ankara, a Capital, as Reflected in Its Urban Symbols and Images," *International Journal of Urban and Regional Research* 22, no. 4 (1998): 593; Aylin Tekiner, *Atatürk Heykelleri: Kült, Estetik, Siyaset* [Ataturk statues: Cult, aesthetics, politics] (İstanbul: İletişim, 2010), 87–97.

9. Apter, "Political Religions," 98; Paul Connerton, *How Societies Remember* (Cambridge: Cambridge University Press, 1989), 41–48.

10. Mimar Türkkahraman, *Türkiye'de Siyasal Sosyalleşme ve Siyasal Sembolizm* [Political socialization and political symbolism in Turkey] (İstanbul: Birey, 2000), 201-249; İlker Çayla, "Kamusal bir din yaratmak. Milliyetçilik: simgeleri ve torenleri" [Creating a public religion: Nationalism—its symbols and rituals], in *Resmi Tarih Tartışmaları* [Debates on official history], vol. 1, ed. Fikret Başkaya (Ankara: Türkiye ve Orta-Doğu Forumu Vakfı Özgür Üniversite Kitaplığı, 2005), 85–136.

11. Arzu Öztürkmen, "Celebrating National Holidays in Turkey: History and Memory," *New Perspectives on Turkey* 25 (Fall 2001): 50.

12. The republican state's secularism resulted in a neglect of religious holidays. For instance, in the 1930s, the official newspaper, *Hakimiyet-i Milliye*, devoted more space to national days and even New Year's celebrations than to the religious feast ending the

fasting month of Ramadan. Sevgi Adak Turan, "Formation of Authoritarian Secularism in Turkey: Ramadans in the Early Republican Era (1923–1938)" (MA thesis, Istanbul, Sabancı University, 2004), 103.

13. Türkkahraman, *Siyasal Sembolizm*, 203.

14. Çayla, "Kamusal bir din," 96–98. The elite's will to mobilize the people on this day was reflected in their plan of establishing "people's pulpits" (*halk kürsüleri*) in order to allow citizens "to express their enthusiasm, indebtedness and the gratitude felt and kept in hearts and minds toward the revolution, the regime, the *Gazi* and the elders" (101).

15. Çayla, 112–113. This march was to be revived in the 1990s out of nostalgia for the enthusiastic spirit of the early republican period. Özyürek, *Nostalgia for the Modern*, 126.

16. Çayla, 106.

17. Öztürkmen, "National holidays," 68–69.

18. Binnaz Toprak, *Islam and Political Development in Turkey* (Leiden: Brill, 1981), 83.

19. Vamık D. Volkan and Norman Itzkowitz, *The Immortal Atatürk: A Psychobiography* (Chicago: University of Chicago Press, 1984), 345–348; Ökten, "An Endless Death"; and Samuel Christopher Wilson, *Beyond Anitkabir: The Funerary Architecture of Atatürk—The Construction and Maintenance of National Memory* (Aldershot, UK: Ashgate, 2013).

20. Nurettin Can Gülekli, *Anıtkabir Rehberi* [Guide to the tomb monument] (Ankara: TTK, 1973), 30.

21. Sibel Bozdoğan, *Modernism and Nation Building: Turkish Architectural Culture in the Early Republic* (Seattle: University of Washington Press, 2001), 286; Alev Çınar, *Modernity, Islam, and Secularism in Turkey: Bodies, Places, and Time* (Minneapolis: University of Minnesota Press, 2005), 109.

22. Seufert and Weyland, "National Events," 80; Çınar, *Modernity, Islam, and Secularism*, 100, 107–109.

23. Çayla, "Kamusal bir din," 119. In the period following the military coup of 1980, the military was given an even more prominent position in the ceremony (132).

24. Öztürkmen, "National holidays," 51.

25. The Welfare Party (Refah Partisi, or RP) won by a large margin in the municipal elections in 1994, capturing over two hundred mayoralties, including those of Istanbul and Ankara. The Welfare Party rose to power in 1996 as the senior partner of a coalition government formed by the center-conservative True Path Party (Doğru Yol Partisi). The next year, in June 1997, the RP-DYP coalition collapsed under the pressure of the army, which was convinced that the secularist regime was under threat.

26. Necmi Erdoğan. "Kemalist Non-governmental Organizations: Troubled elite in Defence of a Sacred Heritage," in *Civil Society in the Grip of Nationalism: Studies on Political Culture in Contemporary Turkey*, ed. Stéfane Yerasimos et al. (Istanbul: Orient-Institut and Institut Français d'Etudes Anatoliénnes, 2000), 251–282; Navaro-Yashin, *Faces of the State*, 187–203.

27. On April 29, 1997, the directorate of the general staff gave a press conference announcing its analysis and strategy. The main stress was on the reemergence of the "internal threat," that is, "reaction," as in the early republican period. The army made it

clear that it would resort to violence if its responsibility of safeguarding the secular order made this necessary. See Hikmet Çiçek, ed., *İrticaya Karşı Genelkurmay Belgeleri* [Documents of the general staff: Against reaction] (İstanbul: Kayak, 1997), 10–11. Again in the first week of September 1997, General Özkasnak, the secretary general of the General Staff, declared that "senior commanders were ready to follow the path of Atatürk" and stressed "the need for implementation of the methods used by Atatürk in the 1930s to suppress rebellions in order to protect the secular order." *Turkish Probe*, no. 244 (September 12, 1997).

28. Erdoğan. "Kemalist Non-governmental Organizations"; Navaro-Yashin, *Faces of the State*; and Özyürek, *Nostalgia for the Modern*.

29. Navaro-Yashin, *Faces of the State*, 146–152; Öztürkmen, "National holidays," 47; and Özyürek, *Nostalgia for the Modern*, 133–136.

30. Özyürek, *Nostalgia for the Modern*, 37.

31. Michael E. Meeker, "Once There Was, Once There Wasn't: National Monuments and Interpersonal Exchange," in *Rethinking Modernity and National Identity in Turkey*, ed. Sibel Bozdoğan and Reşat Kasaba (Seattle: University of Washington Press, 1997), 163.

32. Meeker, "Once There Was," 170–171.

33. Navaro-Yashin, *Faces of the State*, 191; also see Martin van Bruinessen, "State Rituals and Their Surrogates: Responses to Islam in Turkey, Iran, and the Netherlands," paper presented at the conference "Future of the Religious Past: Powers," Amsterdam, June 2006.

34. The number of visitors was never that high again and declined to around 3.5 million in 2011, 3 million in 2012, and close to 5 million in 2013. These and other monthly visitors since 2005 were listed on the website of the Turkish general staff on the mausoleum, http://www.tsk.mil.tr/anitkabir/guncel/faaliyetler/ziyaretcisayilari.html (discontinued). According to a press report of the general staff, the number of visitors was 5 million in 2005, 4.6 million in 2016, and 6 million in 2017. "TSK, Anıtkabir ziyaretçi sayısını açıkladı . . . 11 ayda müthiş rakam", daily *Hürriyet*, December 1, 2017, http://www.hurriyet.com.tr/gundem/tsk-anitkabir-ziyaretci-sayisini-acikladi-11-ayda-muthis-rakam-40664566.

35. "Anıtkabir defterleri," in Faruk Bildirici, *Anıtkabir Racon Zambak. Anadolu İnsan Bahçesi* (İstanbul: Doğan Kitapçılık, 2001), 93–117.

36. Michael Mann, *The Sources of Social Power*, vol. 2, *The Rise of Classes and Nation-States, 1760—1914* (Cambridge: Cambridge University Press, 1993).

37. The term *civil religion*, first introduced by Rousseau, refers here to what is described by Coleman as "a set of beliefs, rites and symbols which relates a man's role as citizen and his society's place in space, time, and history to the conditions of ultimate existence and meaning." J. A Coleman, "Civil Religion," *Sociological Quarterly* 31 (1974): 70.

38. Doğan Gürpınar, *Ulusalcılık—İdeolojik Önderlik ve Takipçileri* [Nationalism: Its ideological leadership and their followers] (İstanbul: Kitap Yayınevi, 2011).

39. Berna Yazıcı, "'Discovering Our Past': Are 'We' Breaking Taboos? Reconstructing Atatürkism and the Past in Contemporary Turkey," *New Perspectives on Turkey* 25, no. 1 (Fall 2001): 3–4.

40. "Nationalism proved most successful in creating the new politics in part because it was based on emotion." George L. Mosse, *The Nationalization of the Masses: Political Symbolism and Mass Movements in Germany from the Napoleonic Wars through the Third Reich* (New York: Howard Fertig, 1975), 16.

41. Mosse, 10.

42. Mosse, 15; Navaro-Yashin, *Faces of the State*, 144.

43. Lerna K. Yarık, "'Those Crazy Turks' That Got Caught in the 'Metal Storm': Nationalism in Turkey's Best Seller Lists", working paper, Mediterranean Programme Series 2008/04 (Florence: European University Institute, Robert Schuman Centre for Advanced Studies, 2008), http://hdl.handle.net/1814/8002.

44. T. C. Genelkurmay Başkanlığı, *Atatürk and the War of Independence Museum* (n.p., n.d.), 43.

45. *Mehdî*, (Mahdî), is the name given in the Islamic belief to the messianic figure who, as "the restorer of religion and justice," "will rule before the end of the world." W. Madelung, "Al-Mahdî," *Encyclopaedia of Islam*, 2nd ed. (Leiden: Brill, 2003).

46. The official Kemalist account of the incident has been reiterated by most of the Turkish historians and political scientists. Amateur historians and journalists, too, have remained within the framework of official Kemalist historiography. See for example, Mustafa Baydar, *Kubilây*, Türk Kahramanları Serisi 20 (Istanbul: Üstünel Yayınevi, 1954); Kemal Üstün, *Devrim Şehidi Öğretmen Kubilay: 60.yıl (1930–1990)*, 4th ed. (Istanbul: Çağdaş, 1990); and Hikmet Çetinkaya, *Kubilay Olayı ve Tarikat Kampları*, 3rd ed. (Istanbul: Çağdaş, 1995).

47. Jeffrey A. Sluka, "From Graves to Nations: Political Martyrdom and Irish Nationalism," in *Martyrdom and Political Resistance: Essays from Asia and Europe*, ed. Joyce Pettigrew (Amsterdam: VU University Press, 1996), 39.

48. The message was published on the front page of newspapers on December 28, 1930.

49. Feroz Ahmad, *The Making of Modern Turkey* (London: Routledge, 1993), 61; Ayşe Kadıoğlu, "The paradox of Turkish Nationalism and the Construction of Official Identity," *Middle Eastern Studies* 32, no. 2 (1996): 187.

50. Ahmad, 61.

51. Ertan Aydın, "The Peculiarities of Turkish Revolutionary Ideology in the 1930s: The Ülkü Version of Kemalism, 1933–1936," (PhD thesis, Ankara: Bilkent University, 2003), 82. Aydın shows in his study on the official publication of the People's Houses, the cultural organization of the one-party regime, that the regime in fact aimed to create a "revolutionary religion" and "to convert people from their traditional religious ties to the new revolutionary faith" (263).

52. Two early examples of the mythicization of Kubilay are: Kan Demir, *Şehit Kubilay* [Kubilay the Martyr] (n.d., n.p.), and a chapter in Enver Behnan [Şapolyo], *İnkılâp Ötkünçleri* [Stories of revolution] (Istanbul: Devlet Matbaası, 1934), 95–100.

53. Speech reported in *Resimli Şark*, Yıl: 1, Sayı: 2 (February 1931), 4–8.

54. *Cumhuriyet*, December 25, 1931.

55. Nihal Gonca, "Cumhuriyet'in İlk Yıllarında Menemen Kazası (1923–1933)" [The District of Menemen in the first years of the republic (1923–1933)] (MA thesis, Celal Bayar Üniversitesi, 2005), 98.

56. Gonca, "Cumhuriyet'in İlk Yıllarında Menemen," 99. The Ka'ba is the large black cube in Mecca to which all Muslims turn in worship.

57. Gür, "Atatürk heykelleri," 152–153.

58. Others included the *Güven Anıtı* (Trust monument, dated 1935) in Ankara and the *Zafer* (Victory) monument (1936) in Afyon. Kıvanç Osma, *Cumhuriyet Dönemi Anıt Heykelleri (1923–1946)* (Ankara: Atatürk Kültür, Dil ve Tarih Yüksek Kurumu, Atatürk Araştırma Merkezi, 2003), 143, 83–86. All of these monuments used naked and muscular male figures as metaphors for those who guard the nation from its enemies. See also Gür, "Atatürk heykelleri," 163.

59. *Cumhuriyet*, December 26–27, 1934; Gonca, "Cumhuriyet'in İlk Yıllarında Menemen," 99–100.

60. On December 24, 1952, *Cumhuriyet*'s headline read "Türk gençliğinin inkılâplara bağlılığı: Kubilay'ı anmak için Menemen'de ve şehrimizde (İzmir'de) yapılan törenler çok heyecanlı oldu" [Turkish youth's loyalty to the Kemalist reforms: the ceremonies in commemoration of Kubilay in Menemen and our city (Izmir) were very emotional].

61. Quoted in Wilson, *Beyond Anıtkabir*, 173.

62. Erdoğan, "Kemalist Non-governmental Organizations."

63. Reported in *Cumhuriyet*, December 24, 1952; and *Hürriyet*, December 24, 1952.

64. "Kubilay'ı Anma Merasimi" [Kubilay commemoration ceremonies], *Hürriyet*, December 25, 1952.

65. Selman Çelik, "Taksim Square: A Spatial Centre of the Political Conflicts in Turkey," paper presented at Goldsmiths College, University of London, April 24, 2013.

66. *Cumhuriyet*, December 24, 1969.

67. Ali Ulvi, "Kubilay—Ben kendimi son sanıyordum. Meğer başlangıçmışım" [Kubilay—I thought I was the end . . . but then it appeared I was the beginning], *Cumhuriyet*, December 27, 1969.

68. *Cumhuriyet*, December 24, 1970.

69. *Cumhuriyet*, December 23, 1978.

70. The Alevi festival was organized in Sivas on July 2, 1993, in honor of the sixteenth century Alevi poet Pir Sultan Abdal, who was adopted as a symbol by the Left. The attackers were especially angered by the presence of the leftist author Aziz Nesin, who had announced that he would publish a translation of Salman Rushdie's *Satanic Verses*.

71. In Turkish, as reported in *Cumhuriyet*: "*Türkiye laiktir, laik kalacak!*," "*Kahrolsun şeriat, yaşasın aydınlık Türkiye!*"

72. In Turkish: "*İşte burası, devrimlerin kalesi*," "*Atatürk'ün ordusu yobazların korkusu*," "*Ordu millet el ele, tam bağımsız Türkiye*," "*İşte burası devrimlerin kalesi*," "*Türkiye laiktir laik kalacak*."

73. Genelkurmay ATAŞE AREM Başkanlığı, "Menemen olayındaki gerçekler" ["Facts about the Menemen Incident"], statement no. 1776 from the directorate of the general staff, issued on December 22, 2002.

74. In 1940, to secure larger popular participation, the party-government had decided to commemorate Kubilay not on the usual date of December 23 but on April 14. This spring day (and Sunday) was chosen for the departure of the trains from İzmir and Manisa with special discount prices in order to attract citizens to the annual ceremony in Menemen.

75. Academics and journalists such as Muammer Aksoy, a professor of law, the chairmen of the Turkish Law Association and the Kemalist Thought Society; Turan Dursun, an atheist writer critical of Islamic sources; Bahriye Üçok, a former senator, member of parliament, and former dean of the Faculty of Theology at the Ankara University, all three killed in 1990, as well as *Cumhuriyet* columnists, Uğur Mumcu (d. 1993) and Ahmet Taner Kışlalı (d. 1999) who were assassinated by unknown perpetrators—all were referred to as the new "martyrs of secularism."

76. As Günter Seufert points out, the flag in Turkey has a "a sacred aura" with its red color symbolizing for many "independence achieved through martyrdom." The sacred aura of the flag has been combined in recent years with a fetishistic use of it. In the mass rallies such as in Menemen or at the Mausoleum in Ankara, the flag is carried as a symbol of loyalty to the secular republic. See Günter Seufert, "The Sacred Aura of the Turkish Flag," *New Perspectives on Turkey* 16 (Spring 1994): 55.

77. Hamit Bozarslan, "Messianisme et mouvement social: l'événément de Menemen en Turquie (Décembre 1930)," *C.E.M.O.T.I.* 11 (January 1991): 84.

78. Nilay Eyrice, "Tarih eğitiminde yerellik: 1922–1950 döneminde Menemen kazası" [The local in history education: the town of Menemen in the period 1922–1950] (MA thesis, Dokuz Eylül Üniversitesi, Izmir, 2005), 22.

CHAPTER 13

Second Thoughts About the Anthropology of Islam

Samuli Schielke

Islam has become a central topic for the anthropological study of people, societies, traditions, and concepts that in one way or another can be called Muslim. Studies of political movements, education, morality, migration, and diaspora and many other issues have become increasingly embedded in a paradigm of Islamic-ness, with the titles of publications over and again referring to "The role of Islam in . . . ," "Muslims in . . . ," "Islam and . . . ," and so on. Given the indeed great significance of Islam in the lives of a great number of people around the world, this is not entirely past the point. We are well advised to take religion seriously and to avoid the pitfalls involved in reducing religious pursuits to economic or political ones.[1] There is a problem of focus, however. This essay has grown out of a sense that the ways in which some recent influential anthropological research has taken "Islam" as the Archimedean point to study the lives of people who adhere to the message of Muhammad privileges a conceptual engagement with the Islamic-ness of its subjects in a way that needs to be balanced. To put it more provocatively, there is too much Islam in the anthropology of Islam.

This requires some explanation. Too much Islam in what respect? Isn't the anthropology of Islam, after all, about Islam? I think that this seemingly straightforward assumption may actually be part of the problem. To explain what I mean, I will try to briefly point out two peculiarities that characterize many anthropologies of Islam.

First, ethnographies about the religious lives of Muslims often privilege people who consciously present themselves as pious, committed Muslims and participate in the activities of religious groups and organizations—in other words, people who share a sense of activist commitment. This is not to say that it is not important to look at dedicated activists. It certainly is. But most people are not dedicated activists. Focusing on the very pious in moments when they are being very pious (in mosque study groups, for example) risks taking those moments when people talk about religion as religious persons—at different times, they can talk about very different things and enact rather different sides of their personality—as the paradigmatic ones and thus unwittingly reproducing the particular ideological aspiration of Islamist and Islamic revivalist movements: the privileging of Islam as the supreme guideline of all fields of life.

It is evident that in many places, definitely so in Egypt where I have conducted my fieldwork, adherence to Islam really is very important for people, and has become more so in the past couple of decades. This is something that has to be recognized and accounted for. But in many ethnographies of Muslims' lives there has emerged a more far-reaching way to a priori privilege the Muslim-ness of the people involved and the Islamic-ness of the projects they pursue. This, then, is the first part of an explanation: There is too much Islam in the anthropology of Islam in the sense of a lack of balance between the emphasis on religious commitment and a not always sufficient account of the lives of which it is a part.

Second, there is a peculiar preoccupation with the question as to what Islam is. In recent years, many of my colleagues have been highlighting that they study Islam as a discursive tradition. As a PhD student, this was one of the first things I learned in the staff seminars of our institute. Meanwhile, I have come to find it rather peculiar that people find it necessary in the first place to state what they think Islam is. The anthropology of Christianity, in comparison, appears much less preoccupied with the question as to what kind of object of study Christianity is. Why, then, would we need to have one answer to the question about what Islam is? After all, Islam can be rather different things depending on the questions we ask. This is not to join the argument that there are many "Islams." What I mean is that Islam, like any major faith, is not simply something—it is a part of people's lives, thoughts, acts, societies, histories, and more. Consequently, it can be many different things—a moral idiom, a practice of self-care, a discursive tradition, an aesthetic sensibility, a political ideology, a mystical quest, a source of hope, a cause of anxiety, an identity, an enemy—you name it. The second part of an explanation, then, is that there is too much Islam in the sense that the anthropology of Islam has a preoccupation with defining its field of study, a preoccupation that may not be very helpful for understanding the significance of Islam as a part of people's lives.

These two peculiarities are both related to the way "Islam" in the anthropology of Islam has become more than just a subject matter. The privileging of Islam as the key to the lives of people of Muslim faith allows "Islam" to emerge as a class of its own, a paradigm of study that is attractive and accessible for a growing body of graduate courses, PhD theses, funding applications and research papers. The anthropology of Islam appears to have become more than simply a subfield of the anthropology of religion that focuses on Islam. The anthropology of Islam is a project concerned with methodological debates of its own, guided by a sense about Islam not only being a religion different from, say, Hinduism, but a different kind of an issue altogether—one that requires a disciplinary approach of its own.

In this process, two key topics have emerged as guiding paradigms of much of the recent anthropological study of Islam: the concept of Islam as a discursive tradition and a focus on the cultivation of moral affect grounded in that tradition. These topics have provided direction for a number of innovative studies that often share a focus on Muslims who consciously and consistently aim to be pious, moral, and disciplined; their debates about how to do so; the challenges they face; and the challenges they pose to a liberal secular ideology of subjectivity and normativity. Some of this research is very good and has provided significant progress for our theoretical understanding of embodiment, power, and ideology. The problem with this line of studies, however, is that they are somewhat out of balance. There is a certain tendency to project Islam as a perfectionist ethical project of self-discipline, at the cost of the majority of Muslims who—like most of humankind—are sometimes but not always pious and who follow various moral aims and at times immoral ones. The ideals and aspirations people express and the everyday lives they live are characterized by complexity, ambiguity, reflectivity, openness, frustration, and tragedy. They argue for discipline at times and for freedom at others, but often live lives that lack both. If we want to account for the significance of Islam in people's lives, we have to account for it in this wider context.

In this essay I argue for an existential and ethnographic approach that accounts for the motivations, experiences, complexities, and ambiguities of everyday lives. To understand the complex logic of lived experience, we will have to take the inherent ambiguity of people's lives as the starting point, just as we have to locate their worldviews in both the local contexts they are physically acting in as well as the global connections, both imagined and enacted, they locate themselves in. These are not merely exceptions from some kind of normality; on the contrary, they are the normality of people's lives—even those who at times argue for holistic and perfectionist ideologies.

My critique is empirical and methodological more than it is theoretical, and so are the suggestions I present at the end of this essay. What concerns me is the question how we can study and understand people's lives in a way that credits the importance of religious and other traditions, ideologies, and expectations without losing sight of the complexities of life experience, the powers to which people are subjected, and the active reimagination and reinvention of traditions and ideologies that constantly take place in everyday life.

With this critique I take issue especially with a research program that has become very productive and influential in recent years. Characterized by the keywords piety, ethics, and discursive tradition, this program is often associated with the work of Talal Asad and his influential intervention in the anthropology of Islam.[2] My critique, however, is not directed at the work of Asad and his concept of Islam as a discursive tradition, which is a good concept, and although I do have some reservations about it,[3] my intent is not to engage in a conceptual critique here. Instead, I offer some points of—hopefully constructive—criticism about what has been accomplished by a much wider research program that has taken discursive tradition as its keyword. This is a research program that has achieved some significant insights but also created some problems that need to be tackled. In the following I argue that most of the key insights and issues of this research program, notably ethics and the cultivation of affect, are highly productive but may need to be balanced by a more existential approach that foregrounds the many concerns and pursuits of everyday life. Some issues, however, notably the juxtaposition of the Islamic and the secular/liberal, are flawed and may need to be revised in favor of an approach that is more perceptive of the situational, pragmatic, and incomplete nature of discursive power.

I open the enquiry with a more theoretical discussion of two key issues, first, the search to understand what Islam *is*, and second, the current turn to a study of Islam through the notions of tradition, ethics, and piety in juxtaposition with secular and liberal powers. I then return to the everyday world that is the site of my fieldwork in Egypt in order to point out some key issues that I see as helpful for reaching a better understanding about what it actually means to live a life that, among other things, can be a Muslim life.

What Islam *Is*

Many of the first and groundbreaking anthropological approaches to Islam between the 1960s and 1980s tried to explain what Islam actually is. The answers— the blueprint of a social order,[4] the locally embedded specific version of a greater symbolic order,⁵ or a multitude of culturally specific "Islams"—were unsatisfactory.⁶ Interestingly, some of the best works from this period did not even try to explain what Islam is; instead they offered some good accounts about what it means to live as a Muslim in a specific historical and cultural situation.⁷ Since then, however, Talal Asad has come up with a very powerful solution that has helped to fortify the question about what Islam is as a standard part of teaching, PhD theses, and theoretical sections of research papers.

According to Asad, Islam is a discursive tradition created by the generations of Muslims debating the correct form of practice with a view to its past, present, and future. While extremely popular among anthropologists, this view has not remained uncontested. For example, Gabriele Marranci has argued that Islam is essentially an emotional category, that Islam is about the feeling of being a Muslim.⁸ But this is not the key point for me. What concerns me is the question, What is it about Islam that makes it so important to understand what it *is*? Why is it not sufficient to say that Islam is a religion? Asad has a good theoretical point against the study of Islam as a religion: the category of "religion" in the social sciences, he points out, is the outcome of a very specific European development in Christianity and carries the very likely risk of leveling the specific features of religious traditions around the world—notably the Muslim notion of *dîn* (religion), which is both vaster and narrower than the social scientific category.⁹ It is vaster, because it involves many more fields of life, and narrower because it is a normative notion. There is a very common assumption among Muslims that *dîn* is a true religion revealed by God, including Islam, Christianity and Judaism, but excluding Hinduism, Buddhism Bahaism, and other religions. From this point of view, an anthropology of "religion" that posits Islam as belonging to the same class of things as Buddhism would be rather beside the point.

But if Asad is rightly skeptical of the heuristic value of the term *religion*, his students are very confident about the heuristic value of another general notion: tradition. Nowadays, Asad's name is regularly mentioned in articles and conference papers whose authors explain that they "understand Islam as a discursive tradition." As mentioned before, it is not my intention in this context to discuss the premises and implications of the notion of discursive tradition. What I want to focus on is that those who argue that Islam is a discursive tradition do not argue that, for example, Christianity, Marxism, human rights, or anthropology are also discursive traditions—although this certainly can be argued and has been taken into consideration in the context of the anthropology of Christianity.¹⁰ They are not involved in the general study of discursive traditions but in the study of Islam in particular, and they find it important for the purposes of their analysis and argumentation to specify what Islam is. The label "Islam as a discursive tradition" as it is commonly used these days is thus less often about an actual inquiry into discursive traditions,[11] and more often about an attempt to find a frame that allows one to look at Islam as a whole.

What, then, does *Islam* explain that makes it so important to know what it is? Evidently it is important, otherwise it wouldn't keep us so busy. Islam is the name of the religion founded by Muhammad on the Arabian Peninsula in the seventh century AD. In the literal meaning of the Arabic word, *Islam* means submission, that is, submission of the human to God. In its archaic meaning, Islam is an act and therefore has no agency. Agency, if any, lies with the human believer who submits their will and acts under the supreme agency of God. And yet Muslims today speak of Islam less as an act of the believer and more as an entity external to the believer. What is important is that at some point, probably long before even the oldest Western anthropologists were born, a gradual conceptual shift began that turned Islam from an act and a disposition into a corpus of norms, procedures, attitudes, and eventually into system that itself prescribes acts and attitudes, a system that, metaphorically or literally, is granted agency that is God's: commanding, prohibiting, knowing, describing, sanctioning. So the Orientalists and later the anthropologists of Islam already encountered an abstract notion of religion as a corpus and, to an increasing degree, also as a system and as an agent (and this encounter has further contributed to Muslims' increasing objectification of Islam during the past century).[12] Although most of them were not believers in Islam, and some of them were even openly hostile to it, they nevertheless found it very easy to deal with it as something, an entity, a thing.

Why is it so convenient to deal with the adherence of people to Muhammad's message as an entity? The fact that Muslims themselves commonly do so is not a sufficient answer, for the typical answers given by anthropologists differ a lot from the typical answers given by Muslims (that is, Muslims not trained in anthropology). For Muslims, Islam is neither a blueprint nor a multitude nor a discursive tradition. For Muslims, Islam is the true Religion of God.

To use an extremely old-fashioned anthropological term, *Islam* is a very abstract and powerful fetish: an entity imagined and created by humans that, because people ascribe power to it, begins to have power over them. As a fetish, Islam is in a way even more powerful than God, because God is always surrounded by secrets and mysteries, and His motivations and plans are beyond human understanding, while Islam can be studied, analyzed, explained, and interpreted. And every study, every explanation, every analysis and interpretation makes it more solid, more factual, and more powerful over those who engage it—regardless of whether they believe in it or not.

From a social scientific point of view, the question of what Islam "is" is a bad one, because the logic of the question already loads the category of Islam with expectations. Expectations that by knowing what it "is" we will know what will happen to people who believe in it. No matter what our answer to the question of what Islam *is*, by pursuing the question we will willingly or unwillingly contribute to the power of our belief in the fetish of Islam, making it more solid and encompassing. For a Muslim proselytizer, this makes good sense. But for us as social scientists concerned with the human condition and human agency, there is good reason to be cautious about a question that reinforces, instead of investigates, the growing imagination of a world religion as an entity with agency.

The focus on Islam as a peculiar entity of its own kind is part of a history of exceptionalism in the study of cultures and societies in which Islam is the dominant religious tradition. Even in variants that are radically critical of Orientalism, it carries an Orientalist heritage: an assumption that Islam is something significantly different from the West. Instead of being the backward other of European modernity, Islam may now be taken up as the pious other of secularism, the resisting other of neocolonialism, or the methodological other of comparative social science. Elevated to such a position of significant alterity, the religious traditions of Muslims gain particular brilliance and importance for the sake of highlighting their particularity through their difference. But at the same time, the faith and lives of Muslims in their own uniqueness, their specificity in their own right—and not just comparatively—become opaque, reduced to their Islamicness. To study Islam as "something" makes it much easier to enter sophisticated theoretical debates, but it also makes it much easier to overlook the ways Islam actually matters in the lives of people who adhere to it.

The problem, then, lies not with the answer but with the question. If we should give any anthropological answer at all to the question of what Islam is, we must first realize that this is an empirical question. The answer depends on the situation at hand, the people involved, the dynamics evolving, and the questions we as researchers are asking. This is not to say that the question or the answers to it should be bare of theoretical directions. That would be a sure recipe for bad research. But it is to say that our theoretical directions should have a different focus. If we want to understand what it means to live a Muslim life, then we need a grounded and nuanced understanding of what it means to live a life—more urgently than we need a sophisticated theory about what Islam is.

But the problem is not settled yet. The two questions of what Islam is and what it means to live a Muslim life are commonly intertwined. And they are intimately bound together in what may be the most influential and productive research program in the anthropology of Islam at the moment: the study of piety, ethics, and tradition.

Piety, Ethics, and Tradition

The tremendous significance of Talal Asad's work for the contemporary anthropology of Islam lies less in that particular short essay in which he develops the notion of discursive tradition than in his wider body of work and its reception,[13] that is, the way this work has been taken up and developed by a generation of anthropologists who have made creative use of his critical enquiries about religion and the secular in order to study the dynamics of doctrinal debate among Muslim activists, the power of Islamic ideals of morality and piety, the connections between everyday religiosity and religious scholarship, and the relationship between Muslim practices of piety and secular architectures of power. For the anthropology of Islam, these works have come to constitute what Imre Lakatos has described as a research program, that is, a shared set of problems, methods, and terminology that provides productive fields of research. According to Lakatos, a research program is seldom proven false, because its key premises and theories can always be protected through ad hoc theories. Instead, the key criterion by which the success of a research program can be judged is its capability to produce new problems and solutions. This is a pragmatic criterion and a useful one for inquiring what is and what is not accomplished by the research program of ethics, piety, and tradition.[14]

Although this research program is most prominently associated with the work of Saba Mahmood and Charles Hirschkind,[15] it is far from unified, of course, and different lines of inquiry regarding ethics and piety have been developed in the works of, for example, Michael Lambek, Heiko Henkel, Lara Deeb, and Stefania Pandolfo.[16] The insights provided in these works have been taken up in recent years by a veritable flood of publications marked with the keywords of piety, tradition, and ethics. This emerging field of study, albeit far from unified, is marked by a shared preoccupation with Muslims' pious practice, aligned with a framing of the enquiry as one about "Islam as a discursive tradition." While some authors have been making rather free and eclectic use of these themes,[17] in other cases there is a tendency to develop a canon of references and concepts to the degree that, especially in northern America, one may speak of the emergence of something like an orthodox canon.[18]

The research program of piety, ethics, and tradition has made it possible to recognize much better how Muslims' engagement with their religion is neither the outcome of blind adherence nor the result of coercion but an active and dynamic process of engagement with ideals of good life and personhood—a point that has been truly important in a decade overshadowed by the global "war of terror," as it perhaps should more accurately be called. But this research program has also magnified some of the problems inherent in the anthropological turn to Islam as the key to the lives of Muslims. These are problems that many in the field are acutely aware of, and many share the sense that it is necessary to look beyond the elegant but narrow confines of piety and tradition to include the messier but richer fields of everyday experiences, personal biographies, and complex genealogies.[19] Part of the problem is the specific focus on moral and pious subjectivity, part is the wider master narrative in which the study of Islam as ethics and tradition is commonly embedded.

The first part of the problem—moral and pious subjectivity—is primarily one of balance, whereby the privileging of pious pursuits in isolation from wider paths of life has contributed to accounts of religious experience that are based more on what people argue for and less on how they actually live. All I want to add to this problem are some practical suggestions on how a more balanced approach could be accomplished while building on the important insights about ethics and subjectivity. I will return to this point toward the end of this essay. The second part of the problem—the wider master narrative—is a more fundamental one and may require more substantial rethinking, which is why I try to tackle it in some more detail in the following.

Compelling Pursuits

The turn to look at a creed as a discursive tradition offered an important step forward by focusing our attention on the fact that religion is not about gods, books, and institutions but about the ways people worship gods, read books, and act in institutions. This may appear to be a trivial insight, and yet it seems to be necessary to keep reminding colleagues, students, intellectuals, publicists, and politicians about it. Also, the turn to the cultivation of affect has been an important step forward in the way of understanding what it means to believe in something and to live a life guided by that belief. And the critical theorization of the secular has offered ways to think about modern power and subjectivity in ways that go beyond the self-celebratory tendency of modernist secularism. The question for me, then, is: how can we go on from here? How can we overcome the problems of this line of research without losing sight of the insights it has to offer? How can we account for the ways people express perfectionist ideals in pursuit of living a complex, imperfect life? How can we tell about the motivations and pressures that make some ideas so compelling? How can we tell about the ways a meaningful world is imagined and the ways it both shapes and is shaped by people's expectations and lives?

This is an ethnographic problem as much as it is a theoretical one, and for the sake of an answer I will start by taking a look at the situation in three sites in Egypt where I have been conducting fieldwork since 2002.

In present-day Egypt, Islam has become omnipresent. Like many other places around the world, Egypt has been swept by a veritable religious euphoria since the 1970s. Religion is continuously visible, audible, and palpable. And it has become characterized to an unprecedented degree by an enormous emphasis on individual learning, knowledge, and practice, guided by the perfectionist aim to create a pious character that is "committed" (*multazim*, a term borrowed from the nationalist/modernist notion of engagement) to religion as a complete framework of emotions, will, and acts.[20]

In a village that I call Nazlat al-Rayyis in northern Egypt, a strong sense prevails that people have become more religious and that this is a very good thing. People greet each other with the Islamic greeting "peace be upon you" (*as-salamu 'alaykum*) rather than with the confessionally neutral "good morning/evening"; a lofty new mosque is being built in the outskirts of the village (although the work has temporarily stopped as a result of the global financial crisis); the bar in the village closed decades ago; and all adult women now wear the headscarf (*higâb*) as a part of a covering dress that reveals only hands, feet, and face. In a village that was once a socialist and communist stronghold, the Muslim Brotherhood has become the most important political force and the most important religious one, along with the Salafi piety movement that promotes a rigorous moral and religious discipline.

In Alexandria, Egypt's second-largest city whither the upper and middle class Cairene head for summer vacation, the cosmopolitan heritage and easy-going holiday atmosphere of this port city has been challenged by the spectacular rise of various Islamic movements, most importantly the Salafi movement, which controls a large part of the mosques, especially in the eastern districts of the city. Men sporting long beards and short-hemmed trousers and women wearing a full veil (*niqâb*) covering their entire bodies have become more and more common in the streets of the city. But also those who do not join the Salafi movement generally show a strong sense of emotional commitment to the religion of Islam. There is a very wide consensus about the need for Muslims to fear God, to fulfill their religious duties, to shape their lives and societies accordingly and to defend their faith, their Prophet, and their Muslim brothers and sisters.

In Cairo, Egypt's gigantic capital, a similar image prevails. Buildings, public transportation, shops, and homes are covered with posters, stickers, and graffiti calling people to pray and fast, to mind their manners and to cultivate their characters, to fight the Jews and to feed the poor, for women to cover themselves and for men to teach Islam to their families. Religious literature dominates the newsstands and bookstores. Broadcasts and cassette recordings of the Koran and sermons are routinely played in cafés, buses, shops, and homes. While various social niches, especially in Cairo and Alexandria, continue to encourage worldviews and lifestyles that are at odds with the wave of Islamization, most of the upper- and middle-class citizens have come to embrace the wave of the Islamic revival, albeit in ways that do not challenge the sources of their wealth or their pursuit of consumerist pleasure.[21]

This image is far from harmonious. While there has been a significant increase in religiosity as well as a general turn to a specific kind of religiosity, this does not mean that Egypt has become a generally more pious, moral, or happy country. There are many ambiguities and contradictions, and some of them are sharp. In the village, young people express a nihilistic sense of boredom and frustration in spite of the great promises of modernist progress and religious hope they have embraced. The village has become a local center of drug trade in recent years as marijuana and hashish have swept the black market in tremendous quantities and at low prices, and an increasing number of young people have become habitual consumers. In Alexandria, the rising commitment to religion has also become a breeding ground for violent confessional clashes between Muslims and Christians that have cost many lives (mostly of Christians) in recent years. While public moral discourse focuses very strongly on the rigorous prohibition of adultery, both Alexandria and Cairo have become centers of prostitution for wealthy Egyptians and Arab Gulf tourists, often arranged for in the form of very short-term Islamic *'urfi* marriages.

Yet most of the ambiguities surrounding the Islamic revival are actually of a much less dramatic and bleak nature than those listed above. Rather than dark cracks in a perfectionist image of hope, they present themselves as a complex patchwork of different kinds of hope, different senses of living a good life. The same people who repent their sins and think about the afterlife also debate the previous evening's football match, tell jokes, feel tired, and glance at the opposite sex, even with religious stickers decorating the walls and the voice of the Koran in the background. They entertain ideals of obsessive romantic love that defies all norms. They search for a place in life, try to be responsible toward their families, and dream about new possibilities for themselves. They try to make money and to move up in society, often by any means possible. And at different moments, they hold different points of view and outlooks on life, arguing for them in very different tones. What happens, then, to the power of guidance, the purity that was the very reason and the justification for the ubiquitous everyday presence of religious objects and signs?

Writing on cassette tape sermons, Charles Hirschkind has fittingly described their presence as an "ethical soundscape" that fills and structures the noisy and crowded spaces of Cairo.[22] The sensory presence of Islam as an overwhelming and compelling idiom of life, morality, and politics is in fact almost omnipresent. It is present in the sounds of prayer calls, sermons, and recitations, in the visual presence of religious decoration, graffiti, stickers, and the minarets that mark the skyline. It is present in the bodily motions of prayer and invocation, the strain of wearing covering dress in hot weather, the weariness caused by fasting, the exchange of greetings, phrases, and handshakes, and the smell of certain perfumes preferred by Salafi activists. But this sensory presence is seldom clearly differentiated from other, very different kinds of sounds, images, and surfaces that mark the everyday life of the big city and the provinces alike. Rather than a competition between pious and secular sensory regimes, an unpredictable coexistence of different nuances, moments, and registers characterize daily life in Egypt.

A kiosk at a bus station in Cairo, decorated with verses of the Koran and stickers with moral and pious messages, has the radio turned on, playing the newest mellow love song produced by a Saudi-owned and Lebanon-based music corporation. A minibus arriving at the bus station from the countryside has been decorated by its owner with two kinds of stickers, neatly organized next to each other:

"Don't forget to invoke God"
    Photo of Nancy Ajram [Lebanese female pop singer]
    "This is due to the grace of my Lord" [a pious phrase against envy]
    Photo of Haifa Wehbe [Egyptian-Lebanese female pop singer]
    "I seek refuge in the Lord of the dawn . . ." [a chapter of the Koran believed to protect from evil and envy].

Zapping through satellite television the way many Egyptians do, one can quickly shift from a Salafi sermon to a video clip, a news program, an Egyptian soap opera, a Hollywood film, a football match, or a talk show. Yet one thing that unites almost all programs (with the exception of some state channels) is their commercial nature and their aggressive advertisements for commercial text message services that have become the financial backbone of television channels of various kinds.

Whenever one goes for a walk on the seafront of Alexandria and on the Nile promenades of Cairo, the scenery is without exception dominated by lovers (*habbîba* in Egyptian Arabic). Pairs of young people walk or sit on the promenades, talking to each other, sometimes holding hands, always closely together, always keeping as much polite distance as possible from other pairs. In another minibus, this one driving up and down the seafront in Alexandria, religious stickers admonish youths about dating: "Didn't he know that God sees?" "Would you accept it for your sister?" "Where is your life?" Indeed, the idea of young unmarried people dating, sitting shoulder to shoulder, holding hands, and possibly kissing is a cause of considerable moral and religious unease among Egyptians. But at the same time, the same Egyptians also consider the meetings of lovers as a natural part of life, write and consume love poetry and songs, enthusiastically celebrate Valentine's day, and proudly identify themselves as the romantic people.[23] Some of them do decide to become "committed" and to give up all the ambivalence, stop writing love letters and looking the opposite sex in the eyes and instead dedicate themselves to the purpose of purified piety. But for many of them this remains a passing period in their lives, one part of a complex and often troubled biography. And sometimes even the most energetic Salafis fall madly in love.

It may seem as if different worlds stood here side by side: the world of Islam as a regime of divine protection, order, and justice; the world of commercial media with its reliance on consumerism, advertisement, and sexual attraction; the world of romantic love with its celebration of passion. But these are not different worlds. They are constituent parts of people's life worlds—life worlds that can never be explained by any single principle but that need to be understood in their complexity and openness, in their many hopes and frustrations.[24] While the conservative ethics of the religious revival may appear completely opposed to, for example, the liberal celebration of romance and sexuality in pop music, film, video clips, and youth culture, in fact one cannot be understood without the other, nor are they clearly distinct in people's lives.[25] An attempt to understand what exactly is going on must take these different, highly compelling pursuits as parts of an essentially complex and often contradictory subjective experience and practice.

I argue that we need to take these ambiguities seriously and to consider the ways people live them and their attempts to make sense of their lives. To understand what is going on, it is helpful indeed to look at the ways people cultivate emotional affects; the ways sensual experience structures daily life; and the ways people try to solve, circumvent, or cope with complex moral dilemmas. It is not helpful, however, to work with idealized oppositions, such as revivalist piety versus liberal secularism, because most people adhere to something of both (and something of many other things as well) to different degrees at different times. Nor is it helpful to hold the aspirational aspect of pursuing piety too high without taking into consideration the troubles and disappointments that are often an inevitable part of aspirational projects.

I suggest that one good way to provide a better account is to take seriously Michael Jackson's argument about the primacy of existential concerns.[26] This means we should take as our starting point the immediate practice of living a life, the existential concerns and the pragmatic considerations that inform this practice, embedded in but not reduced to the traditions, powers, and discourses that grant legitimacy to some concerns over others and structure some considerations while leaving others diffuse. Following this existential line of enquiry, it is also important to realize that the ways people try to find a place in life are ambiguous and often tragic in their outcomes. As Robert Orsi has shown in his work on American Catholicism, the same aspects that provide hope, recognition, and inclusion can also be a source of frustration, intimidation, and exclusion.[27] This ambiguity appears to be characteristic of our attempts to live good lives and an anthropology committed to understanding the human condition is well advised to take it seriously.

This is, in fact, something that has been taken seriously by anthropology for a long time. The current preoccupation with ethics and subjectivity is paralleled by other approaches to subjectivity that are more concerned with ambivalence.[28] Both were preceded by an engagement with the issue of multiple identities, an engagement that, whatever its shortcomings may be, provided important insights that appear to have been partly forgotten by the research program of piety and ethics.[29] The existence and importance of multiple voices, too, has been recognized for quite some time.[30] And since the complexity of human characters is common knowledge and therefore also known by anthropologists, there is good reason to assume that this history could be taken much further back in time. Good ideas are usually quite old. There is thus no need to reinvent the wheel to account better for what it means to live a life of which Islam is a part. The theoretical directions are largely available.

In this light, what a good anthropology of being a Muslim needs most is a commitment to a sensitive and dialogical fieldwork and an eye for the biographical and historical depth of people's trajectories and societies, along with a theoretical analysis that is committed to doing justice to the people it tells about, which is far from a trivial task. In the end, this is more than a theoretical problem: it is a matter of an emotional commitment to anthropology as a dialogue and an encounter.

Grounds of Commitment

I have critically noted that there may be too much research on committed activists and too little research on the majority of Muslims who are not that committed. The empirical focus on the committed activists seems to be related to the theoretical focus on Islam as a key to understanding Muslim lives. Although I am critical of this theoretical focus, this does not mean that I would argue that we should stop doing research on committed activists. But I do argue that thinking about the existential primacy of people's search for a place in life and the tragic quality this search often takes also offers us a different image of activist religious commitment. The problem with many of the numerous ethnographies about Muslims that have been published in recent years is that they take committed activism as the paradigmatic, normal standard of religiosity instead of looking at committed activists as what they are: committed activists who are willing to go very far beyond ordinary expectations for the sake of an important cause in a way most people are not. This is a characteristic feature of activism and should have a prominent place in the study with and of activists.

In my own ethnographic encounters with people who for a period of time have tried to live a dedicated and activist religious life, two related motivations feature very centrally. One is the search for a solution to a personal crisis; the other is the desire to find something truly important to pursue in a way that gives one's life a single and permanent purpose. Both appear to be quite general human pursuits, and yet neither of the two is very typical of everyday human experience, in which there are usually several important purposes in life.

To understand what these activists are after, it is therefore important to ask why, on what grounds, and with what expectations some people embark on the search for dedicated perfection while others do not, and why some go on while others stop after a while. Muslims do not simply want to be good Muslims. Neither the will to be pious nor the choice for piety rather than other forms of activism is self-evident. Strikingly, many of those who join the Salafi movement do so because the ritual and moral rigor of Salafism promises order in a confusing life. At other times or in other contexts, they might have joined other religious or political groups, but for similar reasons. The questions I find worth asking, then, are: What makes a specific direction of activism attractive in a specific situation? What are the anxieties people try to overcome and what are the promises they are offered? What does their actual work of dedication look like? What consequences does it have? How do the experiments of activist dedication, which are often temporary, become a part of people's biographies?

To pursue these questions, it is helpful to be open to both the generally human, the historically and culturally specific, and the individually idiosyncratic. For the sake of illustration, take the account of Mustafa, who became a dedicated Salafi in his early twenties after experiencing a period of strong disorientation but stopped after less than a year. Today, he looks back at his Salafi period with a mixture of fondness, distance, and regret. He remembers his short period of dedicated piety as a happy time but is neither willing nor able to return to it.

To understand Mustafa's story, it is important but not sufficient to look at Salafi Islam's success in northern Egypt in establishing itself as the most powerful religious voice and therefore Mustafa's likeliest choice in the search for a clear difference between right and wrong. Having chosen the Salafi path, Mustafa's dedication took a specific direction with emphasis on gender segregation, abstinence from alcohol, drugs, and cigarettes, and viewing life as the application of divine Law. This had very specific consequences for the way he dealt with his mother and some of his friends, for example. But the emotional work this experiment did for him was also of a more general nature: Mustafa later compared it to me with his time in the army, which, he said, similarly provided him the clear structure he was missing. To understand his account, we therefore also need to take seriously his idiosyncratic experience, his family history, and the characteristic way he sometimes marches and sometimes stumbles through life. And considering this idiosyncratic level also helps to make intelligible the more general features of his quest.

Take, for the sake of comparison, the way Mustafa describes his motivations to become a Salafi and the way John Steinbeck has the literary figure of Jim Nolan describe his decision to join the Communist Party in his novel *In Dubious Battle*.

> Nilson touched the desk here and there with his fingertips. "Even the people you're trying to help will hate you most of the time. Do you know that?"
>
> "Yes."
>
> "Well, why do you want to join, then?"
>
> Jim's eyes half closed in perplexity. At last he said, "In the jail there were some Party men. They talked to me. Everything's been a mess, all my life. Their lives weren't messes. They were working toward something. I want to work toward something. I feel dead. I thought I might get alive again."[31]

> In the time when I started to get back to myself I had lost many things. I started to search. Where is the right way? ... I didn't have a basic method

that I could follow to solve my problems and to face the world. I had no principle to follow. I had no law that I could apply and that would allow me to tell right from wrong. . . .

I took to asking about everything in my life: Is it *halâl* or *harâm*? Even if I didn't have awareness about it, no clear textual proof. But my feeling was: If only I could know whether this is *harâm* or *halâl*? . . . For a while I lived a better life like I hadn't lived it since the death of my father. It was even better. I got to know a lot of people, and I felt that the life I live is good. (Mustafa, interview in 2006)

Would Mustafa have been attracted to communism instead of Salafism if he had lived in a different time? Interestingly enough, his father was. But for Mustafa, the answer is probably no. Communism and Salafism are different solutions, not because they stand on different sides of the secular-Islamic divide but because they appeal to slightly different kinds of sensibility. Both the real person Mustafa and the literary figure Jim Nolan search for a way to feel alive, to do something meaningful, to have a basis and direction of life. But while the communist creed that provides the sense of existential hope on the pages of *In Dubious Battle* is oriented toward a struggle against someone, a search for meaningful existence through collective action, the Salafi creed that provided Mustafa a temporary firm hold in a time of crisis was heavily focused on individual discipline and salvation. There may be more similarity between activist careers in communism and militant Islamism, but Mustafa had his reasons to stay away from both.

The point that I am trying to make is that when we look at Islamic—or any other—activism, it is necessary but not sufficient to look at the particular activist movement and the tradition to which it lays claim. This look needs to be supplemented by a look at both the idiosyncratic and the comparative levels. This is likely to require more work, but it is also likely to give us a much deeper view of the motivations and the consequences of activist commitment.

Conclusion: The Ambiguity of Grand Schemes

In a way, my approach bids farewell to the project of an anthropology of Islam, at least if the anthropology of Islam is meant to be an anthropology that is marked not only by its subject matter but also by its own set of theoretical concerns. Such anthropology is too likely to be trapped in the pitfalls of exceptionalism, too preoccupied with Islam to make really good sense of what it may mean to be a Muslim. I am hesitant, however, to relegate the issue to the anthropology of religion.

Doing so, we would still face an analogous problem of an excessive privileging of religious identity and action in people's lives. We would still risk drawing an arbitrary dividing line between religious pursuits and other pursuits, a line I wanted to question by taking up the comparison of Salafi and communist activism.

I think that to understand the significance of a religious or any other faith in people's lives, it is perhaps more helpful to look at it less specifically as a religion or a tradition and instead take a more fuzzy and open-ended view of it as a grand scheme that is actively imagined and debated by people and that can offer various kinds of direction, meaning, and guidance in people's lives.[32] What characterizes grand schemes of this kind is their appearance of being external and superior to everyday experience, a higher and reliable measure and guideline of life—which can be both personified as gods, prophets, saints, and heroes as well as abstract in the form of books, knowledge, ideologies, and attitudes. What makes them so powerful is precisely the ambiguity that is central to their assumed externality: by virtue of their apparent perfection they can be called and acted upon, and yet the contradictions and setbacks of everyday experience seldom shake their credibility.[33] Even if one's attempt to live a life guided by a grand scheme is frustrated by failures and tragedies, the grand scheme as a guideline of life can remain valid and credible. By virtue of their inherent ambiguity of apparent perfection external to daily life and to the existential significance of the everyday, such grand schemes can never be accounted for alone. They must always be understood as connected in at least two dimensions: first, in their relation to everyday concerns and experiences; and second, in their relation to other compelling grand schemes that also promise to provide meaning and direction to those everyday concerns and experiences.

In the case of my fieldwork in Egypt, such grand schemes include commitment to Islam, romantic love, capitalist wealth and consumption, education and social mobility, development and modernization, and nationalist, pan-Arabic and pan-Islamist politics, to name just a few. This is not to say that the promise of a good life and eternal salvation (with the converse threat of eternal damnation) that is central to people's adherence to Islam today is no different from romantic love or from social mobility. It is very different, and herein lies its appeal and its power. But the ways people "live Islam," as Magnus Marsden has put it, may not be so dramatically different from the ways they live capitalism and love.[34] In all these cases, we are talking about great hopes, deep anxieties, and compelling promises about grand schemes and powerful persons that will lead to practical solutions, promises that people try to follow and to put in practice. Some do it more consistently than others. Some attempts actually help people to live a better life as they understand it; others result in tragedy. Most are ambivalent, providing both satisfaction and suffering. Many attempts are short-lived and almost all of them are partial. In all cases, the grand schemes are forever unrealized and yet always apparently within reach, promising a hold, a direction in a difficult, complex, and often frustrating life. Looking at these attempts and their consequences with an eye for the richness and the openness, but also the limitations and power relationships of the human condition is, in my view, the most promising way to understand the significance of the adherence to Islam as a part of human lives.

Notes

This is a shortened and lightly modified version of a working paper originally written in 2010 and intended as an intervention in a debate that was then ongoing and has continued since. Early versions were presented at the Helsinki Collegium for Advanced Studies and at the Zentrum Moderner Orient in Berlin in the spring of that year.

1. Gregory Starrett, *Putting Islam to Work: Education, Politics, and Religious Transformation in Egypt* (Los Angeles: University of California Press, 1998); Michael Lambek, "The Anthropology of Religion and the Quarrel between Poetry and Philosophy," *Current Anthropology* 41 (2000): 309–320; and Saba Mahmood, *Politics of Piety: The Islamic Revival and the Feminist Subject* (Princeton, NJ: Princeton University Press, 2005).

2. Talal Asad, "The Idea of an Anthropology of Islam" (Occasional Paper, Center for Contemporary Arab Studies, Georgetown University, Washington, DC, 1986).

3. Samuli Schielke, "Hegemonic Encounters: Criticism of Saints-Day Festivals and the Formation of Modern Islam in Late 19th and Early 20th-Century Egypt," *Die Welt des Islams* 47, nos. 3–4 (2007): 319–355.

4. Ernest Gellner, *Muslim Society* (Cambridge: Cambridge University Press, 1981).

5. Clifford Geertz, *Islam Observed* (New Haven, CT: Yale University Press, 1968).

6. See Abdul H. El-Zein, "Beyond Ideology and Theology: The Search for the Anthropology of Islam," *Annual Review of Anthropology* 6 (1977): 227–254. For critiques of these earlier approaches, see Asad, "Idea of an Anthropology of Islam"; Daniel Martin Varisco, *Islam Obscured: The Rhetoric of Anthropological Representation* (New York: Palgrave Macmillan, 2005); Gabriele Marranci, *The Anthropology of Islam* (Oxford: Berg, 2008).

7. For example, Michael Gilsenan, *Recognizing Islam: Religion and Society in the Modern Middle East*, rev. ed. (London: Tauris, 2000 [1982]); Lila Abu-Lughod, *Veiled Sentiments: Honour and Poetry in a Bedouin Society* (Cairo: American University in Cairo Press, 1996 [1986]).

8. Marranci, *Anthropology of Islam*.

9. Talal Asad, *Genealogies of Religion: Discipline and Reasons of Power in Christianity and Islam* (Baltimore, MD: Johns Hopkins University Press, 1993).

10. Gil Anidjar, "The Idea of an Anthropology of Christianity," *Interventions* 11, no. 3 (2009): 367–393.

11. See, however, Armando Salvatore, *The Public Sphere: Liberal Modernity, Catholicism, Islam* (New York: Palgrave Macmillan, 2007).

12. On this point, see Starrett, *Putting Islam to Work*.

13. Asad, *Genealogies of Religion*; Talal Asad, *Formations of the Secular: Christianity, Islam, Modernity* (Stanford, CA: Stanford University Press, 2003); Talal Asad, *On Suicide Bombing* (New York: Columbia University Press, 2006); Talal Asad, "Free Speech, Blasphemy, and Secular Criticism," in *Is Critique Secular? Blasphemy, Injury, and Free Speech*, ed. Talal Asad, Wendy Brown, Judith Butler, and Saba Mahmood (Berkeley, CA: Townsend Papers in Humanities, 2009), 20–63, http://escholarship.org/uc/item/84q9c6ft.

14. Imre Lakatos and Alan Musgrave, eds., *Criticism and the Growth of Knowledge: Proceedings of the International Colloquium in the Philosophy of Science* (Cambridge: Cambridge University Press, 1970).

15. Mahmood, *Politics of Piety*; Charles Hirschkind, *The Ethical Soundscape: Cassette Sermons and Islamic Counter-Publics* (New York: Columbia University Press, 2006).

16. Lambek, "Anthropology of Religion"; Heiko Henkel, "'Between Belief and Unbelief Lies the Performance of Salat': Meaning and Efficacy of a Muslim Ritual," *Journal of the Royal Anthropological Institute* 11 (2005): 487–507; Lara Deeb, *An Enchanted Modern: Gender and Public Piety in Shi'i Lebanon* (Princeton, NJ: Princeton University Press, 2006); and Stefania Pandolfo, "'The burning:' Finitude and the Politico-Theological Imagination of Illegal Migration," *Anthropological Theory* 7, no. 3 (2007): 329–363.

17. For example, Starrett, *Putting Islam to Work*; Salwa Ismail, *Rethinking Islamist Politics: Culture, the State and Islamism* (London: I. B. Tauris, 2003); and Dorothea Schulz, "Promises of (Im)mediate Salvation: Islam, Broadcast Media, and the Remaking of Religious Experience in Mali," *American Ethnologist* 33, no. 2 (2006): 210–229.

18. For example, David Scott and Charles Hirschkind, eds., *Powers of the Secular Modern: Talal Asad and His Interlocutors* (Stanford, CA: Stanford University Press, 2006); and Ovamir Anjum, "Islam as a Discursive Tradition: Talal Asad and His Interlocutors," *Comparative Studies of South Asia, Africa, and the Middle East* 27, no. 3 (2007): 656–672.

19. For example, Abu-Lughod, *Veiled Sentiments*; Catherine Ewing, "The Illusion of Wholeness: Culture, Self, and the Experience of Inconsistency," *Ethos* 18 (1990): 251–278; Magnus Marsden, *Living Islam: Muslim Religious Experience in Pakistan's North-West Frontier* (Cambridge: Cambridge University Press, 2005); Filippo Osella and Benjamin Soares, "Islam, Politics, Anthropology," *Journal of the Royal Anthropological Institute* 15 (2009), S1: S1–S23; Adeline Masquelier, *Women and Islamic Revival in a West African Town* (Bloomington: Indiana University Press, 2009); Annelies Moors, "'Islamic Fashion' in Europe: Religious Conviction, Authentic Style, and Creative Consumption," *Encounters* 1, no. 1 (2009): 175–199; Sindre Bangstad, *Sekularismens Ansikter* (Oslo: Universitetsforlaget, 2009); and Lara Deeb, "Piety Politics and the Role of a Transnational Feminist Analysis," *Journal of the Royal Anthropological Institute* 15 (2009), S1: S112–26.

20. Verena Klemm, "Different Notions of Commitment (*iltizam*) and Committed Literature (*al-adab al-multazim*) in the Literary Circles of the Mashriq," *Middle Eastern Literatures* 3, no. 1 (2000): 51–62.

21. Wâ'il Lutfi, *Zâhirat al-du'ât al-gudud*, 2nd ed. (Cairo: Dâr al-'Ayn li-n-nashr, 2009 [2005]).

22. Hirschkind, *Ethical Soundscape*.

23. Aymon Kreil, "La St. Valentin au pays d'al-Azhar: éléments d'ethnographie de l'amour et du sentiment amoureux au Caire," in *Sacrées familles! Changements familiaux, changements religieux*, ed. Martine Gross et al. (Paris: Erès, 2011), 71–83.

24. Michael Jackson, ed., *Things as They Are: New Directions in Phenomenological Anthropology* (Bloomington: Indiana University Press, 1996); Michael Jackson, *Existential Anthropology: Events, Exigencies, and Effects* (Oxford: Berghahn Books, 2005).

25. Samuli Schielke, "Ambivalent Commitments: Troubles of Morality, Religiosity and Aspiration among Young Egyptians," *Journal of Religion in Africa* 39, no. 2 (2009): 158–185.

26. Jackson, *Existential Anthropology*; Knut Graw, "Divination and Islam: Existential Perspectives in the Study of Ritual and Religious Praxis in Senegal and Gambia," in *Ordinary Lives and Grand Schemes: An Anthropology of Everyday Religion*, ed. Samuli Schielke and Liza Debevec (New York: Berghahn, 2012).

27. Robert A. Orsi, *Between Heaven and Earth: The Religious Worlds People Make and the Scholars Who Study Them* (Princeton, NJ: Princeton University Press, 2005).

28. T. M. Luhrmann, "Subjectivity," *Anthropological Theory* 6 (2006): 345–361; and João Biehl, Byron Good, and Arthur Kleinman, eds., *Subjectivity: Ethnographic Investigations* (Berkeley: University of California Press, 2007).

29. Ewing, "Illusion of Wholeness"; James M. Wilce Jr., ed., "Communicating Multiple Identities in Muslim Communities," special issue of *Ethos* 26, no. 2 (1998): 115–119; and Toon van Meijl, "Multiple Identifications and the Dialogical Self: Urban Maori Youngsters and the Cultural Renaissance," *Journal of the Royal Anthropological Institute* 12 (2006): 917–933.

30. See, for example, Abu-Lughod, *Veiled Sentiments*.

31. John Steinbeck, *In Dubious Battle* (New York: Bantam Books, 1961 [1936]), 6.

32. Samuli Schielke and Liza Debevec, eds., *Ordinary Lives and Grand Schemes: An Anthropology of Everyday Religion* (New York: Berghahn, 2012).

33. Gregory Simon, "The Soul Freed of Cares? Islamic Prayer, Subjectivity, and the Contradictions of Moral Selfhood in Minangkabau, Indonesia," *American Ethnologist* 36, no. 2 (2009): 258–275.

34. Marsden, *Living Islam*.

Part IV

Transgressive Acts: Heresy and Blasphemy

Famously, Émile Durkheim sociologically characterized religions as concerned with conceptual distinctions and categorizations and with reproducing social order by affirming conceptual boundaries. Seen in this way, transgressive religious forms and acts such as heresy, ritual pollution, and the violation of taboos may also be construed as both conceptual (or cognitive) and social contestations: they challenge not only doctrinal but also social order.

The contributions in this part focus on one particular kind of transgression that has attracted a lot of attention in recent years—blasphemy. Whereas heresy involves utterances about God or the sacred deemed to be false by those in (religious) authority, blasphemy involves utterances judged to be sacrilegious, offensive, or insulting. Thus, the prerequisites for an act to be qualified as "blasphemous" include not only a particular doctrine of words and of their power to affect the self, the sacred, or the religious community but also a religious authority that is qualified and allowed to determine whether a particular act counts as blasphemy. As such, the phenomenon of blasphemy appears to be particularly associated with revealed monotheistic religions such as Judaism, Christianity, and Islam; but even among these traditions, the differences are enormous, as are the changes between premodern and modern times. In ancient times, the notion of blasphemy was a rather diffuse one: the Old Testament injunction not to use the Lord's name in vain (Exodus 20:7) includes not only swearing and cursing but also perjury or the giving of false testimony. In ancient Greece, *blasphemia* (injurious or impious speech, slander) referred primarily to the use of inauspicious words rather than to offense against the gods; while in the Roman Empire, blasphemy was generally seen as an offense to be punished by the gods rather than men.

The premodern polytheistic and decentralized Hindu tradition, by contrast, lacked both the doctrinal basis and the authority structure for a major concern with blasphemy. On the contrary, mutual criticisms, including derogatory and insulting language about each other's traditions' doctrines, deities, and or founders appear to have been fairly common in religious disputes. In both the Hindu and the Buddhist traditions, it seems, heretic, sacrilegious, or blasphemous acts and utterances were generally seen as resulting from ignorance or misunderstanding rather than from sin or rebellion. It was only in 1860 that the British colonial rulers in India introduced legal provisions against blasphemy, or perhaps more correctly speaking, hate speech: section 295A of the new Indian Penal Code spoke of "deliberate and malicious acts, intended to outrage religious feelings or any class by insulting its religion or religious beliefs."

In his *Blasphemy: Impious Speech in the West from the Seventeenth to the Nineteenth Century* (2002), Alain Cabantous provides a fascinating overview of blasphemy in early modern Europe. His study argues that during this period, blasphemy (which he characterizes as "an intolerably meddlesome interference or admixture of the vilest and most profanatory this-worldliness inside the space of the sacred") was not primarily the work of religious dissenters but of other socially and spatially marginal or isolated groups, like seafarers and soldiers. In modern secular states, however, religious power is either marginalized, relegated to the private sphere, or subordinated to worldly or political powers; hence, blasphemy has acquired a rather different status. In such contexts, blasphemy debates involve novel struggles over the effects of words and the limits of jurisdiction. In a secular public space that relegates the religious to the private sphere, accusations of blasphemy risk being excluded a priori as illegitimate intrusions. The globalized and transnational contexts of international migration and communication in which accusations of blasphemy occur, however, considerably complicate matters. This becomes abundantly clear from what is undoubtedly the most famous blasphemy case in recent history, the 1989 Rushdie affair, in which complaints by Muslims against Salman Rushdie's 1988 novel, *The Satanic Verses*, quickly spread across various countries and culminated in a fatwa by Iranian Ayatollah Khomeini condemning the author to death. More recently, several other blasphemy affairs have gained international attention. Some of these are discussed in the contributions in this part.

In "Eventual Blasphemies," S. Brent Plate explores the event-like character of blasphemy, in particular of blasphemous images. Further developing the argument of his *Blasphemy: Art that Offends* (2006), Plate contends that artworks such as the famous 2006 cartoons of Muhammad in the Danish daily *Jyllands-Posten* and Chris Ofili's *Holy Virgin Mary*, a portrait of a dung-smeared Madonna, are not in and of themselves blasphemous. First, they are deemed to be blasphemous from within religious and political power structures; second, there typically is a time lag between the display, performance, or publication of an artwork and the accusation of blasphemy. Because artworks only retrospectively become blasphemous, he argues, they function like an *analepsis* or flashback; at the same time, however, blasphemous images also operate *proleptically*, that is, in anticipation of particular responses. Emphasizing the mediated character of artworks and the reactions to them, Plate stresses that the blasphemous character of artworks or the rejection of particular works as blasphemous is not a simple question of cause and effect but involves a "messy network" across media, political structures, and others.

Some of these messy networks are described in more detail in the other contributions to this section. Thus, Anne-Marie Korte's "The Political Gesture of 'Blasphemous' Art" on the Russian art collective Pussy Riot's "punk prayer" raises the question why the use of religious scenes or imagery by female—or feminist—artists like Madonna and Lady Gaga seems particularly prone to provoke accusations of blasphemy or sacrilege. The controversy generated by such deliberate interplays of corporeal (and, possibly, transgressive) sexuality and religious themes, Korte suggests, points to the interrelation of religious, sexual, and ethnic identities. She adds that performances like those by Madonna and Pussy Riot contest the demarcation line between the religious and the secular and challenge an antecedent relegation of both religion and sexuality to the private sphere. Following Plate's earlier analysis of the composite character of blasphemy accusations, Korte refuses to reduce such accusations to mere category mistakes or to the authoritarian abuse of political power. Moving beyond Plate, however, she raises the question of why it is that specifically gendered corporeality and nonheteronormative sexuality become so easily the target of blasphemy and sacrilege accusations.

In "On Silencing and Public Debates about Religiously Offensive Acts," Christoph Baumgartner attempts to tease out some hidden dimensions of public blasphemy debates with the tools of speech act theory. After discussing the effects that religiously offensive acts may have, Baumgartner provocatively reconstructs the dismissal of religious "squeamishness" in favor of freedom of expression as in fact amounting to the exclusion of protesting religious voices from the community of respectable and legitimate participants in public debate. Thus, his discussion explores anew the question of exactly what kind of speech acts the participation in public debate amounts to. Baumgartner calls attention to the specific gestures that may performatively institute authoritative norms and set the "grammar of public debates," and thus informally but effectively exclude the voice of believers from public discussion. He then proceeds to analyze different modes of such "silencing," all of which destroy the felicity conditions for equal participation in public debate. Preventing this destruction, he argues, requires others who do have access to public debate to articulate counterspeech in support of the voices that risk being silenced. This analysis takes us far beyond the narrow and reductionist debate whether the freedom of expression should be restricted for the sake of religious sensibilities.

Martijn de Koning's "Offending Muslims" tallies with some of Baumgartner's findings. Employing analytical tools developed by Victor Turner, de Koning analyzes two Dutch films, Ayaan Hirsi Ali's *Submission* (2004) and Geert Wilders's *Fitna* (2008), as well as the 2006 Danish Muhammad cartoons as rituals of antagonism, that is, as performances. These performances, he argues, reduce the multidimensionality of people's lives and ideas to a simple opposition between freedom of speech and religious rage, and as such, they aim at performatively creating the very antagonism between political supporters and the enemies they represent. More specifically, they may be seen as performative acts intended to produce the "angry Muslims" they are ostensibly about. In his own fieldwork, de Koning found that many Dutch Muslims did not in fact regard these films as offensive; moreover, de Koning argues, although the image, or specter, of angry Muslims permeated the public debate surrounding these films, Muslims themselves hardly participated in these debates. Following Turner, de Koning analyzes events surrounding these two films as a form of social drama, which includes the distinct stages of breach, crisis, redress, and final reconciliation or schism. Following Judith Butler's critique of Turner, he argues that such performances also involve a struggle over political authority and legitimation.

CHAPTER 14

Eventual Blasphemies

Setting the Offensive Work of Art in Time

S. Brent Plate

Dung-smeared Madonna.
Crucifix in urine.
Cartoons of Muhammed.
Ant-covered Jesus.

A handful of words invoke visual images, cultural and political engagement, theological battles, and media flare-ups. Perhaps not everyone recognizes all of these phrases, but most readers will recognize at least one, if not two or three. These condensed verbal images conjure international uproars that traverse social and political institutions, cultural values, and religious experiences. They also, of course, traverse the move from images to words. Simple sayings call to mind simple uses of color and contrast, line and form that trigger responses. You don't have to believe in magic to register the power of images on human life.

But, how did we get here? What are the processes that take place that allow this verbal-visual affect to occur? To allow shared memories across nations and languages and times? Clearly, the memories are not the same for each of us, though we might be collectively looking in the same direction.

Further developing and modifying some of the research initiated in my *Blasphemy: Art that Offends* (2006), this essay expands on an understanding of blasphemous images. (I note here I am not discussing legal and political definitions of blasphemy, nor blasphemous literature or other forms of controversial arts.[1]) These images emerge through their existence as *media events*: particular meetings of art and its reactions across time and space; their relation to political and religious power struggles; as well as to religio-cultural establishments of dividing lines between categories of sacred and profane.

More properly, blasphemous images are *eventual*: a series of relational events taking place over time; ongoing, unfolding, and unspecified as to any particular result. We can point to the cause, so we think, but we are never able to predict the effects. Indeed, the cause is only understood once the effect emerges, just as we do not know we have a sickness until we start coughing, itching, or blowing our nose. To understand the blasphemous nature of images it is necessary to understand the visual cultural environment in which blasphemous images eventually emerge. Blasphemy needs to be properly framed within the responses to an artwork, the mediated dissemination of them, issues of power struggles in religious and political environments, and not simply a formal analysis of the art itself.

One way to put this is to say that the proper question to ask is not *what* is a blasphemous image but *when* is it a blasphemous image?[2] We think of these images as existing in space, and indeed they are. Yet, blasphemy occurs in time, over time, through time. Blasphemy is eventual, projected toward a future, unfolding in the now, and pointing to the past. Using the controversy surrounding David Wojnarowicz's short film, *A Fire in My Belly* (the "ant-covered Jesus") as a key indicator, in the following I outline the myriad dimensions of the eventuality of blasphemy. Ultimately this leads me to chart a two-sided understanding of blasphemy taking into account the proleptic and analeptic dimension of blasphemous events.

The Event of Blasphemy

Blasphemy is a contested, fluid, and dynamic category of meaning. Taboo, offensive images serve as powerful components in the making and shaping of societies since they reveal a general public's lusts, longings, fears, and repulsions. Legal scholar Leonard Levy, in one of his mammoth studies of the topic suggests, "Blasphemy is a litmus test of the standards a society feels it must enforce to preserve its unity, its peace, its morality, and above all its salvation."[3] Blasphemy, and the *accusation* of blasphemy, is a culturally symbolic marker that helps define societies and religious traditions.

The term blasphemy, and visual images accused of blasphemy, has had an ambiguous history within Western religious traditions. I have offered an abbreviated history of its functions in Islam, Judaism, and Christianity before, and will not repeat that here.[4] What I will reiterate is that a blasphemous image is not a category of *being* in itself, but an entity that proffers a confusion between the sacred and profane, challenging accepted norms in particular times and places. Furthermore, no work of art is blasphemous in and of itself; it must be deemed so from within religious or political power structures, whether small or large scale, and there are many examples in which an image has appeared without comment in one setting only to explode with controversy in another.

Chris Ofili's *Holy Virgin Mary* is a case in point. I was living in the United Kingdom when the *Sensation* exhibition opened at the Royal Academy of Arts in London in 1997. During that exhibition Marcus Harvey's "portrait" of British child murderer Myra Hindley came to the controversial fore, as the image was created from children's handprints. The image was used as something of a logo for the show as a whole. The British press and many in the public were offended by the juxtaposition created in the work, though that didn't stop hundreds of thousands of people attending the exhibition. Ofili's then recent work was nowhere mentioned. When *Sensation* went to the Brooklyn museum two years later, Harvey's work was barely mentioned (mainly because people in the United States did not know of Hindley's murders), but Ofili's piece made top billing, because of—at least at first—then New York Mayor Rudolph Giuliani's outbursts.

At heart, a blasphemous image needs an artist, an artwork, and an accuser. The context for accusation includes everything from religious dogmatic assertions to media coverage to political posturing made by authorities seeking to appear as defenders of social decorum and morality. The blasphemous event is not an instantaneous, singular thing but an ongoing intersection of competing and complementing gestures by artists, scholars, critics, and religious and political leaders.

The blasphemous images that each of the opening phrases call to mind have been translated, crossed national borders, and pushed through media outlets where they are read, gazed upon, and heard through radio and television, newspapers, word of mouth, and the sprawling tentacles of the Internet. Blasphemous images move through information, misinformation, and disinformation, packaged into data packets, whether typeface, sonic amplification, or the bits and bytes of digital media. By this I mean to indicate that the blasphemous image is impossible without media. And by *media* I evoke the plural, suggesting there is no singular thing, gadget, device, or even artwork but multiple operations and events, networked across space and time.

Copious commentaries on Chris Ofili's *Holy Virgin Mary* (the "dung-smeared Madonna") discuss its controversial 1999 appearance at the *Sensation* exhibition at the Brooklyn Museum of Art. In brief, the controversy erupted when Mayor Giuliani protested, "You can't do things that desecrate the most personal and deeply held views of people in society." To which Ofili countered: "As an altar boy, I was confused by the idea of a holy Virgin Mary giving birth to a young boy. Now when I go to the National Gallery and see paintings of the Virgin Mary, I see how sexually charged they are. Mine is simply a hip-hop version." Struggles over funding ensued, a court case followed, and pundits filled op-ed pages, especially in the *New York Times*.[5]

Discussions of Andre Serrano's *Piss Christ* mention it in the midst of the controversy that emerged during the Senate hearings in 1989 when US Senator Jesse Helms decried the photograph of a crucifix submerged in urine—calling it "blasphemy and insensitivity toward the religious community." Meanwhile, Helm's colleague Alphonse D'Amato performed his own desecrating gesture by tearing up a copy of Serrano's photograph on the floor of the US Senate.

And discussions of the "Danish cartoon controversy" note the global uproar by Muslim communities when twelve caricatures appeared in February 2006 in the politically conservative Danish newspaper, *Jyllands-Posten*. Editors stood up for their right of freedom of expression and commissioned a number of cartoonists/caricaturists (not "illustrators," and here is where the provocation began) to draw images of Muhammad as the artists saw him. Most were silly, hardly salient—a couple were so poor in quality and execution that the paper should have been downright embarrassed in retrospect for even printing them—while several of the images were nasty, aggressive, and violent depictions.

Each of these controversial, "blasphemous" works are well-trod in scholarly work. Eleanor Heartney, in *Postmodern Heretics*, points to the Catholicism of Ofili and Serrano and suggests it is the "incarnational consciousness" of such artists that spurs them toward exploration of the body and its workings. Cynthia Freeland in *But Is It Art?* also points to Serrano's Catholicism, following Lucy Lippard's takes on Serrano, and suggests, "Perhaps Serrano grew up with and looks back upon a somewhat more vital kind of encounter with the spiritual in fleshly form than what he sees in the culture around him."[6] And Talal Asad, among others, takes the Danish cartoon controversy as a point of departure for thinking through the relations of blasphemy, free speech, and cultural critique.[7]

So why should I bring them up again here? Let me add one bit of information about each situation that is usually mentioned but seldom extrapolated upon:

> Ofili's mixed media work is dated 1996, whereas the controversy began three years later.
> Serrano's photo dates from 1987, with 1989 being the time for congressional contestation.

And the controversial images of Muhammad were initially published by the same paper five months earlier, in September 2005, and then republished by the Egyptian paper *Al-Fagr* in October 2005, but nothing much happened after these initial publications.

In each case, critical responses from religio-political leaders, and later from scholars, come to the artwork only by beginning with the consequent controversy. The thing itself, the image, lies bounded by layers of mediated reaction and are sorted through to get to the instigator of the affair. There is a lag time, a delay, between artwork and accusation, and it is this temporal disjuncture, the historical distance between creation and controversy, that constitutes the eventual nature of blasphemy.

Blasphemy's Analepsis

Implicit in all this is the function of media in the creation of the blasphemous event. There is the medium of the artwork itself: Serrano's piece would have had a radically different response if it was a three-dimensional piece of an actual urine-filled vat with crucifix. Senator D'Amato could still have torn up a picture of that on the US Senate floor, but the impact would have been diminished. The *New York Times* was enormously important in establishing the blasphemous event of Ofili's *Holy Virgin Mary*, while the Danish cartoon controversy was of course impossible without the newspaper postings of the images. The passing of time between the Ofili affair, 1999, and the cartoon controversy, 2006, also made blogging and other Internet-related channels strongly instrumental for the latter event. There is also the medium of the institution of the museum—and here I mean media in a broad sense of formal "channels" for the transmission of art and information—which functions in a variety of ways to shape and create responses to the work of art. Blasphemy is mediated, the message always transposed, transfixed, and transfigured through its mediation.

Ultimately, blasphemy comes into existence in the midst of the work of art, and in this way, functions analeptically; the blasphemous artwork is only possible to grasp from a posterior perspective. The artwork itself thus functions like an analepsis, a flashback. It is placed in the midst of narratives about blasphemy which are written by critics, scholars, and religious leaders, and they refer back to the image. Such a flashback becomes part of a story because it is taken up into the narrative unfolding in a particular sense of a "present." Yet the image is not fully comprehensible, and perhaps no longer even approachable, without the posterior, mediated narrative.

To expand upon this lag time, which becomes the eventual nature of blasphemy, I here linger for some time on one more recent example, charting the details of what I am thinking of as the move from an "artwork" to the "*work* of art." Work takes on a verb form instead of a noun. It names an activity, influence, and affect. This is probably best understood when the English *work* is translated into the distinct German terms *arbeiten* and *das Werk*. In English, we can make the distinction between the *artwork* (*das Werk*), the initial material object that is aesthetically experienced, and the "work of art" (*arbeiten*; the responses triggered by particular images). Blasphemy's eventuality emerges in an oscillation between those two senses of *work*.

The Work of Art: Rewinding the Story

In 2010, another blasphemous event emerged in the United States, noted in the opening phrase, "ant-covered Jesus." This regarded the Smithsonian Institution's National Portrait Gallery, which caved under well-placed protests to remove David Wojnarowicz's artwork, *A Fire in My Belly* from the Gallery's exhibition, *Hide/Seek: Difference and Desire in American Portraiture*. The National Portrait Gallery itself is federally funded, though the exhibition was produced with all private money. The story was well-trod in all the major media outlets in the United States. Here I play the story backward, ultimately rewinding twenty-plus years to see what the religio-cultural-political soup of art and accusation reveals. In the midst of the hoopla is a deeply religious artwork made by an artist struggling with and through religion.

> **January 13, 2011:** The Museum of Modern Art, NYC, acquires Wojnarowicz's unfinished film, *Fire in My Belly* (1986–87), including both the "original" thirteen-minute version and a seven-minute version (fig. 14.1).
>
> **December 8, 2010:** New York City's PPOW Gallery issued a statement criticizing the decision by the National Portrait Gallery.[8] The Gallery has represented Wojnarowicz's work since 1988, four years before his death. They also posted the thirteen-minute and a seven-minute version of the artwork.
>
> **December 7, 2010:** The *New York Times* issued an editorial calling the Smithsonian's decision "an appalling act of political cowardice."[9] This was one of many such editorials, statements, and blogs that began to appear on

EVENTUAL BLASPHEMIES

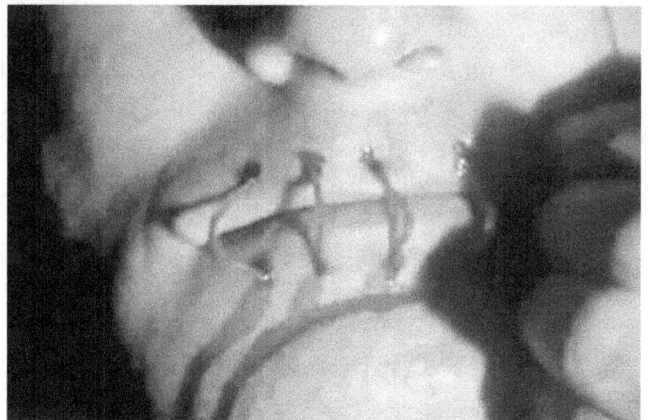

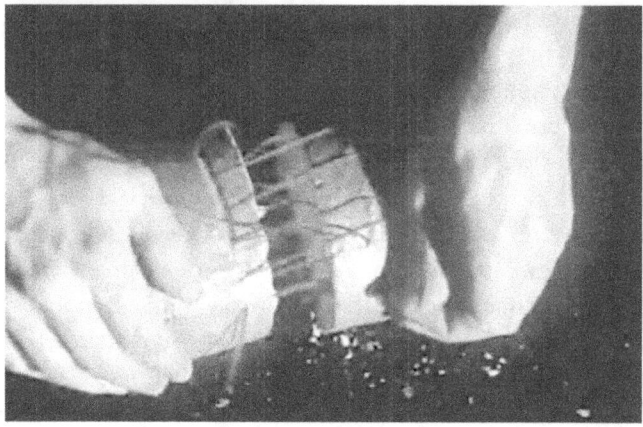

FIGURE 14.1   Stills from David Wojnarowicz, *A Fire in My Belly* (1986-87).

December 2, including the American Association of Museum Directors rebuttal to the Smithsonian.[10]

December 6, 2010: The Smithsonian releases a second statement, standing behind their first one (November 30) and their decision to remove the video.[11]

December 1, 2010: Street-level demonstrations in Washington, DC, centered on and, seemingly, organized by the nearby, tiny Transformer gallery, as protestors walked from one gallery to the other that evening holding signs and images of Wojnarowicz. The Transformer gallery began to show the banned work in its front window.

Afternoon, November 30, 2010: The director of the National Portrait Gallery issued a very brief statement stating they did not intend to offend anyone, and they were removing Wojnarowicz's video from the show.[12]

Earlier in the day, November 30, 2010: Bill Donohue posted a news release with the title "Smithsonian hosts anti-Christian Exhibit" at his Catholic League website. He condemned the Smithsonian, cocurator David C. Ward, and Wojnarowicz, finally saying he will be writing to congress asking them to "reconsider future funding" to the Smithsonian.[13] And Brent Bozell, founder and president of the right-wing Media Research Center sent letters to key members of Congress, urging them "to hold Congressional hearings to investigate the Smithsonian Institution for its attack on Christian values and common decency."[14] House Majority Leader Eric Cantor (R.-Va.) called the exhibition "an outrageous use of tax payer money." Other congresspersons followed.

Also on November 30, 2010: At least two versions of the video began to circulate around the Internet: one eleven-second version cut down to show only ants scurrying across a mass-produced Crucifix, apparently the key focus of Donohue's "hate speech" comment; the other, a four-minute version, approximately the length that National Portrait Gallery had on display. However, the four-minute version that emerged on the Internet contained a striking soundtrack by Diamanda Galás.

Monday, November 29, 2010: Penny Star's article at the conservative news site, CNS News (an outlet of Bozell's Media Resource Center), seems to have been the touchstone for the controversy. While Donohue has received "praise" for bringing the video to light, it was Star's article that raised the issues. Her online article began: "The federally funded National Portrait Gallery . . . is currently showing an exhibition that features images of an ant-covered Jesus, male genitals, naked brothers kissing, men in chains, Ellen DeGeneres grabbing her breasts, and a painting the Smithsonian itself describes in the show's catalog as 'homoerotic.'" Though the reductionist rhetoric up front is not without its problems, her article was much better researched than many of her detractors. She actually attended the exhibition.[15]

October 30, 2010: The exhibition *Hide/Seek: Difference and Desire in American Portraiture* opens at the National Portrait Gallery, a division of the Smithsonian Institution. It was curated by Jonathan D. Katz and David C. Ward. Some good reviews appeared soon after the opening, and National Public Radio reported that a spokesperson for the Smithsonian claims that the museum had only received one complaint up until the late November controversy began.[16] The exhibition contains a wonderful array of artworks around the theme of sexual difference. Huge names in modern art—Warhol, Mapplethorpe, Haring—meet older masters such as late nineteenth- and early twentieth-century artists Thomas Eakins and George Wesley Bellows, and mid-century painters Georgia O'Keefe and Jasper Johns.[17]

Sometime leading up to October 30, 2010: David Wojnarowicz's work *Fire in My Belly*, is edited into a four-minute version for the *Hide/Seek* exhibition by cocurator Jonathan Katz, along with filmmaker and photographer Bart Everly, and mixed with audio from an ACT UP march.

Pause: This initial rewind teaches us a few things. First, that the cause and effect of religious-artistic controversy is a messy network that streams across various media, religious institutions, political structures, art museums, and living rooms. To understand the *production* of art, we must look well beyond the confines of an artist's studio; art is not only produced by artists, but also by galleries and churches, journalists and rabbis, art critics and fellow artists, and cultural-political institutions and leaders alike. The Museum of Modern Art in New York, one of the largest institutions of its kind in the world, only purchased this work of art twenty-five years after its creation, and after a particular exhibition that garnered a particular amount of attention. Media make news, and don't merely report on it. Penny Star, Brent Bozell, and Bill Donohue gave birth to a new artistic event, in and through the media.

Media also create the work of art. To understand the *meaning* of art, and especially the religious meaning, we must look to the artist's intention and formal elements of an artwork, but also to the reception of art, the ways meanings are remade and recycled and reproduced to create ever new, and often unintended meanings. To suggest otherwise is to fall into a similar literalist interpretation that Fundamentalists have taken toward the Bible: The artist said it, I believe it, that settles it. This does not mean there is no image, no more or less "original" artwork, only that to get to the artwork we have to start much further afield. So, with the accusation in place, some thinking about the artwork is helpful. Some more rewinding is in order.

Going back, then, two decades:

July 22, 1992: David Wojnarowicz dies from AIDS-related complications at the age of thirty-seven. He was born in 1954 and spent most of his life in and around New York City. He worked primarily in photography, film, and video. He was openly gay and outspoken about the AIDS crisis, especially after his friend and lover, photographer Peter Hujar, died from the disease.

August 8, 1990: Wojnarowicz is awarded a nominal one dollar for damages to his career. This was the outcome of his five-million-dollar lawsuit against Donald Wildmon (US District Court Case, *David Wojnarowicz v. American Family Association*),[18] Methodist minister and founder of the American Family Association, after the association mailed tens of thousands of pamphlets that spoke out against the homoerotic themes of Wojnarowicz's work and included many details from the artist's photo collages. The suit also included charges of copyright infringement for reproducing imagery without permission. The American Family Association was ordered to cease all distribution and to publish and distribute a correction. Many saw this as a victory for Wojnarowicz, as no one had taken on such a legal battle before. An artist actually went to court against a group on censorship.

November 8, 1989: The National Endowment for the Arts rescinded funding for a catalog and an exhibition on the topic of AIDS, *Witnesses: Against Our Vanishing*. Wojnarowicz contributed an essay that attacked several public and religious figures for supporting policies he believed helped the spread of AIDS. Of Catholic Cardinal John O'Connor, he wrote: "This fat cannibal from that house of walking swastikas up on Fifth Avenue should lose his church tax-exempt status and pay retroactive taxes from the last couple centuries." The NEA eventually reversed their decision and funding was reinstated, though not for the production of the catalog. Nonetheless, the controversy at this time—along with other right-wing criticisms (Senator Jesse Helms led the way) against the artists Andres Serrano, Karen Finley, and Robert Mapplethorpe—brought Wojnarowicz into national media attention beyond the art world. He had entered the Culture Wars.

1986–87: David Wojnarowicz edited *A Fire in My Belly*, a work in progress. He was working on a thirty-minute version but ended up with a thirteen-minute unfinished work. A seven-minute version appeared posthumously, but Wojnarowicz himself scrapped the project and the work remained incomplete in his life.

Wojnarowicz's film work became a four-minute version for the National Portrait Gallery show, and then an eleven-second cut was distributed for publicity. The thirteen-minute version that Wojnarowicz edited is silent. It is easy to see the unfinished parts in the thirteen-minute version, as the "chapter breaks" toward the end get shorter and shorter, as if he was still trying to fill in the gaps with imagery. The most popular video to stream across the Internet in late 2010 contained a soundtrack by vocal performance artist Diamanda Galás. The lyrics for "This Is the Law of the Plague" are taken from Leviticus 15, whose meaning is reappropriated in an age of AIDS. Her music and Wojnarowicz's video were actually both being composed at a similar time in the mid-1980s, and in the controversy the two of them have been linked, producing yet another interesting version of the work. Galás herself offered a (slightly discombobulated) response to the NPG controversy.[19]

The Artwork and Its Mechanical Reproductions

Much of the imagery of *A Fire in My Belly* was shot on Super-8 film and comes from time Wojnarowicz spent in Mexico in the 1980s. Mexican Day of the Dead ceremonies mix with Aztec statues; scenes of professional wrestling merge with cock fights and bull fights; strong crucifixion imagery merges with street scenes from Mexican cities and towns; a man masturbates, mummified bodies appear to come alive, butchers carry cow carcasses, and through it all a sombrero-wearing marionette dances, attempting some comic relief until the puppet is finally shot and burned. It contains many disturbing images, no question about that.

Perhaps most striking are the surrealist images and connections: a loaf of bread, having been cut in half, is sewn back together. With the juxtapositions of a crucifix and blood, it is hard for anyone with some exposure to Christianity not to think: "the body of Christ, broken for you." Except here that brokenness is attempting to be mended. The stitched-together bread is mirrored in another in which a human mouth is stitched shut. That image is later recycled in Wojnarowicz's iconic image of his own stitched mouth, from the 1990 film *Silence=Death*.

One other surrealist borrowing is the ants, and it is the "ant-covered Jesus" that became the rallying cry for the Right. Eleven seconds of this was enough to get the artwork/exhibition/Smithsonian Institution labeled "anti-Christian." In *Fire in My Belly*, ants roam across a Day of the Dead altar scene, and a crucifix.

Salvador Dalí used images of ants throughout his paintings, perhaps best seen in his 1931 *Persistence of Memory* and his infamous 1929 collaboration with Louis Buñuel, *Un Chien Andalou*. When Dalí was a child he found a wounded bat, which he kept, only to return later to find the bat being devoured by ants. Ants are scavengers, feeding off the dead and decaying.

Indeed, the main theme of *A Fire in My Belly* is death. More specifically, it is the vulnerability, penetrability, and perpetually possible disintegration of the human body. Thus, at its core it is a deeply religiously inflected artwork. Religious rituals and myths have long accompanied death, and in the film, we see the Day of the Dead, Aztec sacrifice, mixed with the death of Jesus. This is a meditative piece, similar to that of many religious traditions for many ages, which does not mean these images are pleasant and easy to look at—Wojnarowicz's is no warm and fuzzy pop spirituality.

And then there is the history of Christian, gruesome images of tortured, dying, suffering, and dead bodies, including Jesus's own body. (See Matthias Grünewald's *Small Crucifixion* in the publicly funded National Gallery in Washington, DC; and Hans Holbein's *Dead Christ*). That Christ on the cross is actually dead, and that ants might eat this dead body is both the most orthodox Christian statement and the most scandalous one. Wojnarowicz knew this, and struggled with his Catholic faith throughout his life.

Within the rewinding of the story, the emphasis on the mediated creation of the work of art, it is crucial to pay attention to the artwork. In the midst of discussing the *eventuality* of blasphemy, I do not want to mistake the fact that there is something to the power of images, some *thing* that triggers responses. So, while an artwork's responses ultimately establish blasphemy, some analysis of *what* is seen seems to be in order. Simply put, what lies at the heart of much blasphemy is a breach with the human body, of vulnerability, of bodily fluids and sexualized relations, of Eros and Thanatos. Blasphemy is an event that unfolds from the semi-porous membranes of the human body, coming into being through a series of concentric circles of bodies and power. Here is the artwork becoming the *work of art*.

Blasphemy's Prolepsis

As I have talked about blasphemous art in various contexts, I have continually come up against reactions from people who take the modern romantic notion of the artist who has this strong intentionality, and who is seemingly in control of the reactions of their artwork. While I think this notion overall needs to be given up, I also realize that artist's intentions cannot simply be ignored. There *is* something in the production of the artwork that produces the work of art.

Thus, the blasphemous image can also be said to operate *proleptically*. The artist's artwork is proleptic when we take into consideration the intentions of the artist as well as any symbolic dimensions of the artwork.[20] Any responsible artist (or author) must admit to giving up control of the reception of their work once it is published, made public. Even so, this does not entail that the artist does not work with an anticipation of what might emerge from the responses. In so doing, there is a movement from the artwork to the work of art, its ongoing life.

One response to one of my presentations on blasphemy came from a scholar of biblical studies. He said, "You should chart the various *types* of blasphemy, and create a typology of these." Another, from a social scientific background, pushed me to outline the various "conditions" that take place in which blasphemous images and accusations emerge. Both, from differing perspectives, miss the point, however diffuse the point may be. The eventual nature of blasphemy entails that it cannot be simply predicted. That there is no type, genre, or condition that makes it predictable. (One might imagine some algorithmic equation or complexity theory output that would be programed to account for the blasphemous event, though considering there is not much money involved, chances are slim that it would come into being.) Here we come upon the movement of art in the evolution of culture—artworks in culture.

Conclusion

Here is one more example that gets at the shifts, changes, and media along eventual blasphemies: a 2008 exhibit in Vienna that evoked a strong international response and also had an interesting twist. The exhibition was called *Religion, Flesh, Power* and highlighted the work of prominent, octogenarian Austrian artist Alfred Hrdlicka (who died in 2009). Hrdlicka's drawings of the Last Supper, apparently intended by him as a tribute to Pier Paolo Pasolini, prominently display homoerotic themes, and the meal is turned into an orgy with Jesus and the disciples acting it out. Meanwhile, notes accompanying the exhibition suggest that his work focuses on the carnality of religion and on the search for "God as a human experience." In this case, the work of art evolved into a national dialogue on the relation of art and the church, and the protests decrying Hrdlicka's *Last Supper* as blasphemous led to its removal.

A couple things to note in this case. First, the drawings in question date from 1984, giving it over two decades of lag time, twenty-four years between artwork and accuser. Second, what is curious is that the exhibition in question was actually on display at the diocesan Dommuseum next to St. Stephansplatz in Vienna. In the midst of a conservative Catholic diocese in a conservative country, this piece was initially allowed to be shown. Cardinal Christopher Schoenburn, archbishop of Vienna, eventually succumbed to protesting religious groups and ordered the piece be taken down. His response was, however, mixed and he issued a statement to the Reuters News service: "Hrdlicka is one of Austria's most notable living artists who, probably more than any other living artist, has devoted himself to the suffering and downtrodden human being and has appealed for 'compassion' with the 'Passion.' . . . I still hold the opinion that we must welcome the fact that artists who do not share our faith, or are still searching for belief, occupy themselves so intensively with biblical subjects."[21]

The final note on this case brings us back to the mediated nature of the protest, the analeptic elements of the event. Tracing the protests over time and space reveals that they originally came from conservative Christian groups in the United States and Germany. The exhibition curator, amazed by the reactions from around the world, said, "I've even seen Web postings from extremists who have threatened to come to Vienna and blow up its museums with Molotov cocktails."[22] Through blogs and email campaigns, religious groups were mobilized to respond, even though they'd certainly never heard of Hrdlicka nor seen the image in question in person. These groups had websites that posted graphic, detailed displays of the orgiastic Last Supper, something not found in the mainstream press.

I used to end my discussions of blasphemous images with this quote by George Bernard Shaw: "New opinions often appear first as jokes and fancies, then as blasphemies and treason, then as questions open to discussion, and finally as established truths." This is a useful way to look at the eventual nature of blasphemy, how the artwork becomes the work of art, but as I reexamine it, it seems to be quite an intellectualist approach. In Shaw's realm, blasphemy is about questions, opinions, and truth; but through what I've noted so far, blasphemy is actually about visceral, bodily reactions.

Blasphemy surprises. And in the midst of visual images of blasphemous actions and scenarios, I come back to the power of what we might still call art. This is a problematic term on many levels, and we would be excused in abandoning all hopes of its revival. But there might be, if only analeptically, the possibility for something like art to break through the mundane existence and offer new ways of being. Optimistically, I would still make a claim that art piques our emotions, pushes our perceptions, and provokes our sensibilities. In a sense, that is what art *is* because that's what art *does*. But it is only definable, after the fact. The implication here is that if it doesn't *do* that, it isn't art.

Every society has its taboos, and the uses of blasphemy allows us to look to the forbidden symbols and activities of our past, in order to enquire about our own present list of taboos. In so doing we come up against the structures and strictures of our current culture, enabling a certain charting of the permissible and forbidden that defines contemporary life, living in *medias res*, in the middle of the work of art.

Notes

1. For more on such approaches, see Talal Asad, "Reflections on Blasphemy and Secular Criticism," in *Religion: Beyond a Concept*, ed. Hent de Vries (New York: Fordham University Press, 2008), 580–609; and David Nash, *Blasphemy in the Christian World* (New York: Oxford University Press, 2007).

2. There is thus some affinity with Nelson Goodman's questions about "when is art?" in his *Ways of Worldmaking* (Indianapolis: Hackett Publishing, 1978), 57–70.

3. Leonard Levy, *Treason Against God* (New York: Schocken, 1981), xiii.

4. I gave brief overviews of Jewish, Christian, and Muslim understandings in Brent S. Plate, *Blasphemy: Art that Offends* (London: Black Dog Press, 2006). For more on Western religious dimensions in general, see Leonard W. Levy *Blasphemy: Verbal Offense Against the Sacred, From Moses to Salman Rushdie* (Chapel Hill: University of North Carolina Press, 1995); and Nash, *Blasphemy in the Christian World*. On Islamic dimensions, see Asad, "Reflections."

5. This is discussed in detail in my introduction to *Religion, Art, and Visual Culture*, ed. S. Brent Plate (New York: Palgrave Macmillan, 2002), 1–6.

6. Cynthia Freeland, *But Is It Art?* (Oxford: Oxford University Press, 2001), 20.

7. Asad, "Reflections," 580–609.

8. Press release, PPOW gallery, http://www.ppowgallery.com/press_release.php?id=87 (site discontinued).

9. "Bullying and Censorship," *New York Times*, December 6, 2010, http://www.nytimes.com/2010/12/07/opinion/07tue4.html?partner=rss&emc=rss.

10. Associations of Art Museum Directors, http://aamd.org/newsroom/documents/20101203_NationalPortraitGallerystatementFINAL.pdf (site discontinued).

11. "Smithsonian Stands Firmly Behind 'Hide/Seek' Exhibition," Smithsonian, December 6, 2010, http://newsdesk.si.edu/releases/smithsonian-stands-firmly-behind-hideseek-exhibition.

12. Statement on the *Hide/Seek* exhibition, National Portrait Gallery, http://www.npg.si.edu/docs/hide-seek-statment.pdf (site discontinued).

13. Press release, November 30, 2010, Catholic League, http://www.catholicleague.org/release.php?id=2033 (site discontinued).

14. Media Research Center, http://www.mrc.org/Press/uploads/LBB Reid Letter.pdf (site discontinued).

15. Penny Starr, "Smithsonian Christmas-Season Exhibit Features Ant-Covered Jesus, Naked Brothers Kissing, Genitalia, and Ellen DeGeneres Grabbing Her Breasts," CNS News, November 29, 2010, http://cnsnews.com/news/article/smithsonian-christmas-season-exhibit-features-ant-covered-jesus-naked-brothers-kissing.

16. Elizabeth Blair, "Smithsonian Under Fire for Gay Portraiture Exhibit," NPR, December 1, 2010, http://www.npr.org/2010/12/01/131730255/smithsonian-under-fire-for-gay-portraiture-exhibit.

17. *Hide/Seek: Difference and Desire in American Portraiture*, exhibition website, http://www.npg.si.edu/exhibit/hideseek/index.html (site discontinued).

18. Often misreported as a US Supreme Court case.

19. Jonathan L. Fischer, "Diamanda Galás Responds to the Smithsonian's Removal of David Wojnarowicz's Work," *Washington City Paper*, December 3, 2010, http://www.washingtoncitypaper.com/blogs/artsdesk/visual-arts/2010/12/03/diamanda-galas-responds-to-the-smithsonians-removal-of-david-wojnarowiczs-work/.

20. I am indebted to my colleague Darren Middleton for insights on the analeptic/proleptic nature of blasphemous art.

21. Cardinal Christopher Schoenburn, in a statement to the Reuters news service. Sylvia Westall, "Vienna Cardinal Explains Stand on Erotic Last Supper Painting," Reuters, April 9, 2008, http://blogs.reuters.com/faithworld/2008/04/09/vienna-cardinal-explains-stand-on-erotic-last-supper-painting/.

22. "Furor, Debate, over Jesus Orgy Drawing," Today, April 11, 2008, https://www.today.com/popculture/furor-debate-over-jesus-orgy-drawing-1C9425700.

CHAPTER 15

The Political Gesture of "Blasphemous" Art
Facing Pussy Riot's Punk Prayer

Anne-Marie Korte

"Mother of God, Put Putin Away!" With their punk prayer, performed in the Cathedral of Christ the Saviour in Moscow on February 21, 2012, Pussy Riot openly defied the tightening bonds between the Putin-led government and the leaders of the Russian Orthodox Church. This act was part of a series of political protests against the Putin regime, flash concerts in urban guerrilla style, that the Moscow-based political art collective Pussy Riot had practiced in the foregoing six months at several public locations in the capital city. The entire performance in the Cathedral (singing, shouting, jumping, and kneeling) actually lasted no more than forty seconds; the performers were immediately stopped and removed from the—at that moment almost empty—church by guards and church personnel. The impact of this brief "political gesture," however, was incredibly large: in the Russian media the performance was compared to "the effect of an explosion of a bomb."[1] The punk prayer was followed by extremely critical and unprecedented repressive reactions by the leading figures of the Russian government and the Russian Orthodox Church. Three female members of the group were arrested and charged with "hooliganism motivated by religious hatred" as stated in the Russian Criminal Code.[2] The prosecutors officially accused them of maliciously humiliating the feelings and beliefs of the Orthodox Christians and "disparaging the spiritual foundation of the state."[3] On August 17, 2012, the three women were found guilty and were sentenced to two years in prison.[4]

During their trial and defense and subsequently during their stay in the camps the women were closely followed by the international media and they were widely supported by statements and public acts of solidarity from mainly foreign, that is, North-Western scholars, politicians, and artists. Vigils, protest actions, conferences, and research groups have been organized in response to the case. With the help of these parties a number of texts, letters, and comments of the accused women were circulated via the electronic media and through publications created for this purpose.[5] Research shows that the Western media coverage of this case outside Russia is strongly framed in terms of the accused and convicted women being victims of repressive state and religious regimes and courageous heroines defending the freedom of speech and human rights, in particular the rights of women and LGBT persons.[6] In particular the fact that the accused women—trained as art students in Moscow—referred to Russian philosophers and (dissident) writers, theologians and biblical scholars, and Western gender studies specialists evoked comments and debates on their motives, intentions, and sincerity. Within Russia the Pussy Riot members received rather marginal public and intellectual support; polls show that the great majority of the Russians assented to the accusation and sentence, and many intellectuals and opinion makers openly loathed and ridiculed the performance.[7] Within a year after the conviction of the Pussy Riot members a bill explicitly prohibiting religious insult—which did not exist before in postcommunist Russia—was adopted by the Federation Council (Russia's Upper Chamber of Parliament) with reference to the Pussy Riot case.[8]

In this contribution I raise the question why at present the use of religious scenes, imagery, or ritual by female—or feminist—artists like Madonna, Lady Gaga, and Pussy Riot seems particularly prone to provoke accusations of blasphemy or sacrilege.[9] The controversy generated by such deliberate interplays of corporeal (and, possibly, transgressive) sexuality and religious themes, I will argue, is suggestive of the interrelation of religious, sexual, and ethnic identities and of the public fights over them in modern (post)secular societies. Performances like those of Madonna and Pussy Riot contest the demarcation line between the religious and the secular and challenge an antecedent relegation of both religion and sexuality to the private sphere. Following Brent Plate's analysis of the composite character of blasphemy accusations (see his contribution in this volume), I refuse to reduce such accusations to mere category mistakes or to the authoritarian abuse of political power. Moving beyond Plate, however, I will investigate why it is specifically gendered corporeality and nonheteronormative sexuality that so easily become the target in contemporary accusations of blasphemy and sacrilege.

"Blasphemous" Feminist Art in Cultural and Religious Identity Politics

Among a number of contemporary works of art recently accused of blasphemy or sacrilege in the context of cultural and religious identity politics in Western societies, religiously connotated feminist artworks and performances seem to stand out and to fulfill a particularly provocative role.[10] *Feminist artworks* here refer to objects or acts that are created by artists, performers, and activists who have explicated their aim to contribute to the emancipation of women and to the furthering of the rights of ethnic and sexual minorities. In their work they consciously bring together emancipatory stances and core religious imagery, taken from their own, in most cases Christian, upbringings. In the context of contemporary public debates on the rights of minorities, where freedom of speech and freedom of religion are often considered to be the central oppositional axis, these feminist artworks seem to make paradoxical statements; not only by suggesting that both these rights could be affirmed simultaneously in the fight for gender and racial justice but also by displaying an uncanny mixture of art and politics, religion and secularity, and of sincerity and mockery. Probably this hybridity contributes greatly to the disputed status of these works of art.[11]

Apart from this hybridity, these artworks also have particular common traits in their disputed imagery. They connect naked or otherwise explicitly gendered and sexualized human bodies, often recognizable as those of the artists themselves, to iconic sacred scenes of Western Christian culture and art, such as the suffering Jesus on the cross, the Last Supper, the Virgin Mary with the child Jesus, or the Pieta (Mater Dolorosa). Well-known examples are *Ecce Homo* by Elisabeth Ohlson (Sweden), *I.N.R.I.* by Serge Bramly and Bettina Rheims (France), *Yo Mama's Last Supper* by Renee Cox (USA), *Our Lady* by Alma López (USA), *Blood Ties* by Katarzyna Kozyra (Poland), and *Passion* by Dorota Nieznalska (Poland).

More recently, songs and acts consisting of social, political, and religious critique—performed "provocatively" by pop and punk artists such as Madonna, Lady Gaga, and the Russian art collective Pussy Riot—also have become publicly contested for comparable reasons; although, as will be discussed extensively in this contribution, in this last case significant differences occur in comparison to the other mentioned works and performances. All these works of visual or performative art have been accused—more or less formally—of offense in terms of blasphemy or sacrilege, which contributed to both their notoriety and their controversiality by causing huge media attention. Conservative religious interest groups and religious leaders and representatives are not the only ones who have targeted these artworks and performances; secular politicians and civil authorities also have declared them offensive, and both parties have tried or even succeeded in stopping, prohibiting, or banning their public exhibitions or performances.

In the overall research project from which this case study is taken, I aim to clarify why at present precisely these "religiously embodied" feminist works of art so easily fall prone to controversy, public upheaval, and legal pursuit, in particular to accusations of blasphemy and sacrilege. The case of Madonna's crucifixion scene in her *Confessions on a Dance Floor* show (2006) has been the core example of my earlier research, and the disciplinary fields that inform my analysis are (Christian) theology, religious studies, and gender studies, all informed by a cultural analysis perspective. My formative supposition is that the controversy that these feminist works of art and performances evoke is related to the identity politics of ethnic and sexual minorities and of religious communities, interest groups, and lobbyists involved in a fight over shifting positions of privilege and marginalization in modern Western societies. The deliberate and ostentatious interplay of gendered corporeality and (homo)sexuality with religious themes forms the symbolic arena of this fight.[12] The clashes that these works of art engender are positioned on the fault line of religion and secularity, and their controversiality is deeply embedded in the ideological debates over this demarcation. I think it of great importance to relate the accusations of blasphemy and sacrilege that these clashes bring along, as well as the (meta)discourse on blasphemy that they engender, to the particular identity political fights that have yielded them.

At first sight, the manifestation and spread of the blasphemy discourse during the past two decades seem to belie the fact that in the course of the twentieth century the legal prohibition of blasphemy and sacrilege in most European countries (as well as in the United States, Canada, and Australia) has gradually been waived, diluted, or become obsolete. This paradoxical state of affairs has given rise to discussion—initiated by philosophers, historians, theologians, and scholars of religion—on the reappearance and meaning of (accusations of) blasphemy and sacrilege in contemporary public debate. Cultural historian David Nash, who specializes in the European history of blasphemy, argues that blasphemy's history unsettles both the historiography of Christian religion and the twentieth-century secularization theory engrafted in this history. Blasphemy's present manifestations in Europe disturb the idea of a progressive rationalization and privatization of religion. "Blasphemy's illumination of conflict models and incidents showed that belief was capable of ebbing and flowing and appearing at pressure points in the interaction of individuals and societies."[13]

Contemporary accusations of blasphemy—in particular in contexts where they seem to increase in amount and where they invoke heated public debates, as occurs in the here involved cases—could be seen as signposts of current identity political fights.[14] As condensation points, they refer to the multiple discourses, associations and effects that are involved in charges of blasphemy. From an intra-religious or theological perspective, the blasphemy ascribed to these contentious works of art consists of violating the interdiction of representation of the divine and of trespassing against God as giver of this rule. This argumentation can be found in the public opposition of a range of religious institutions and organizations to the exhibition or performance of the above-mentioned works of art. In their rejection, they accuse the artists of acts of blasphemy and sacrilege, and they argue in particular against the personal hubris of the artists to identify or to compare themselves with Jesus, Mary, or the saints.

On a more general level of mythic conception and cultic practice, the disputed status of these works of art is related to the problematic role and meaning of gendered corporeality in the religious imagination of the main monotheistic religions, Judaism, Christianity, and Islam. As classic feminist theology argues— where in these religions God is seen as transcendent, sovereign, male, and not bound to material existence—women are conceived to be totally "other" than this God.[15] To connect female and nonwhite corporeality to the established symbols of divine reality, in particular to Jesus as God incarnate or to the Virgin Mary as the Mother of God, thus easily generates the judgment of blasphemy or sacrilege. Here not concrete acts of hubris or mockery but more general perceptions of and demarcations between the sacred and the profane determine the actual offensiveness.

On the level of social and cultural differences and tensions in modern societies, these accusations of blasphemy and sacrilege could also be considered as core disputes about values and norms in multicultural and multireligious societies, as clashes between various understandings and imaginaries of what is esteemed most valuable. Cultural philosopher Bruno Latour has coined the term *iconoclash* to address these situations, using a neologism that combines the aspects of clash and iconoclasm.[16] Iconoclash names an object, image, or situation that embodies or creates an unsettled—and unsettling—clash between different scientific, religious, or artistic worldviews. Characteristic of these iconoclashes is that they create ambiguity and hesitation of interpretation, because they counter images with images and combine aspects of image-breaking with those of image-making, a procedure and effect almost inherent to what counts as artistic work and profession in modern Western societies.

I subscribe the general observation that the increased recourse to (the discourse of) blasphemy and sacrilege to oppose or ban culture, critical statements, and performances reflects power struggles and cultural identity politics—also addressed as culture wars—in postsecular, neoliberal, and multireligious societies. However, I do not consider the accusations of blasphemy and sacrilege only to be rearguard actions, relics of old times, or simply mistakes of categories. Following scholar of religion Brent Plate, author of the comprehensive book *Blasphemy: Art That Offends* (2006), I want to emphasize the (co)incidental and composed character of blasphemy accusations in their relation to political and religious power struggles. The discourse of blasphemy emerges between the production and reception of artworks or performances and needs to be studied by "taking into account the proleptic and analeptic dimension of blasphemous events."[17] As a scholar of religion, Plate defines blasphemy as fundamentally consisting of acts of transgression, "crossing the lines between the sacred and the profane in seemingly improper ways."[18] He proceeds that although there are no specific formal qualities that blasphemous images and acts share, sexuality, nudity, and bodily fluids seem to register in a great many of them. According to Plate, they collectively point toward modern society's dis-ease with the human body itself, "that most intimate and yet most foreign of entities."[19] Concurring with Mary Douglas's symbolic anthropological interpretation in *Purity and Danger*, Plate observes that "impure mixings" with these ingredients abound in contemporary contentious imagery.

Although highly relevant to understanding the staging and impact of current public discourse on blasphemous art, these observations do not yet touch upon the pressing question of why gendered corporeality and nonheteronormative sexuality are the very targets of accusations of blasphemy and sacrilege in so many contemporary cases. They do not clarify why precisely the interplay of iconic religious imagery with female corporeality and (homo)sexuality is perceived as endangering the distinction between the sacred and the profane. As theologian Sarah Maitland has shown, pointing to the famous accusations against Jesus, Paul, Dante, Galileo, and Darwin, blasphemy and sacrilege in consecutive periods of Western cultural history have often been located in areas other than those of gendered corporeality and (homo)sexuality, as indicated by the fights over the operation of salvation, the shape of the cosmos, and the definition of the civic state that have been at stake in these accusations.[20] Contentious imagery has its own history and genealogy, which means that the current prominence of instances of "blasphemous" imagery featuring gendered corporeality and sexual diversity should be addressed in its particular details, imagery, and resonance.

Over and against art critics and other scholars who claim that allusions to female bodies and (homo)sexuality will per definition work provocatively in the context of iconic religious imagery because of the strong and potentially conflicting affective registers that are involved,[21] I esteem a more fruitful approach that explores these contested works of art in relation to concrete historical processes of shifting gender positions and changing stances toward sexual diversity in Western modernity and to the social, cultural, and religious power struggles that these changes engender and embody. For instance, as theologian Margaret Miles has shown, in the Renaissance period when the first collective shift of women from the private to the public sphere took place in Europe, female nakedness and sexuality became the focus of a newly explicit public and controversial figuration in the arts.[22] Feminist historians and art critics have suggested that nineteenth- and twentieth-century movements of women's emancipation and the strong political and cultural opposition that these movements have met created a similar impulse to explore gendered corporeality and sexuality in artistic imagination and cultural expressions.

Also, the modern transformations of religion with regard to the distinction between the public and the private sphere should be incorporated in this analysis. In her seminal lecture *Sexularism*, historian Joan Scott points to the nineteenth century's increasing sexualization of women—the reduction of women to body and sexuality—as an inherent part of the upcoming modern ideal of secularity in which the political and the religious, and the public and the private, became opposed along patterns of strengthened gender dichotomy, conceived as a natural distinction rooted in physical bodies.[23] According to Scott it has to be acknowledged that the "domestication" of women, or their increasing assignment to the private sphere, as well as the simultaneous "feminization of religion" took place in the context of the fast expansion of the modern Western political and cultural ideal of secularity. "The public-private demarcation so crucial to the secular/religious divide rests on a vision of sexual difference that legitimizes the political and social inequality of women and men."[24] In modernity's secular ambitions, in its struggle with the hegemony of religious institutions and worldviews for liberal ends, "feminized" religion, women's religiosity, and female sexuality have become intertwined in their position as the "other" of secular reason and modern citizenship, when in the processes of secularization in the West, women became more and more exclusively associated with both religion and the private sphere. As Scott argues, "the assignment of women and religion to the private sphere was not—in the first articulations of the secular ideal—about the regulation by religion of female sexuality. Rather feminine religiosity was seen as a force that threatened to disrupt or undermine the rational pursuits that constitute politics; like feminine sexuality it was excessive, transgressive, and dangerous."[25]

It is my contention that the many instances of alleged blasphemous imagery featuring gendered corporeality and nonheteronormative sexuality that make up the so-called culture wars of the past two decades are related to a particular social and cultural shift in modern and predominantly secularizing societies regarding the public meaning of both religion and sexuality. This shift concerns the position and public perception of both religion and sexuality as identity markers in their mutual interrelatedness. At stake is an oscillating relationship of religion and sexuality as modern individual and collective markers of identity. Significant for this instability is the emergence of a dichotomous public discourse in which a secular position is equated with acceptance of gender equality and sexualities in the plural and a religious position with rejection thereof. The cultural shift this implies could be seen as a reshuffling of prominence, power, and visibility in relation to the former established social and personal meaning of both religion and sexuality. Until late into the twentieth century, in Western countries religious identity counted as a primary marker of one's social position, while sexual preference and behavior were privatized to the degree of invisibility. Most recently the affirmation of sexual diversity, in all its (public) manifestations, for many has come to count as a core value of modern Western life, while religious identity has become far more privatized, or is supposed to be so.[26] The many current cultural conflicts gravitating around religiously founded normativity, gender roles, and sexual diversity thus are not only indicators of changing views of sexuality and procreation and their role in the formation of individual and collective identity, but also of the fundamentally changing role of religion in modern society, which has become private and public both in new ways.[27]

The analytical perspective developed above helps to clarify why contemporary works of art and performances that openly combine "feminized" religion, women's religiosity, and female (homo)sexuality while intending to make critical feminist statements—works such as the ones I referred to above—are potentially transgressive in multifaceted ways and run the risk of being accused of offense, insult, and defamation, not only by conservative religious groups and leaders but also by secular politicians and civil authorities. The Pussy Riot case seems of particular interest in the context of the questions outlined here. After discussing how and why this particular case has become framed in terms of blasphemy and sacrilege, I will return to these initial questions and discuss the Pussy Riot case in comparison to the alleged blasphemous feminist artworks and performances that I already referred to.

Pussy Riot's Punk Prayer and the Accusation of Blasphemy

When the five members of the Pussy Riot formation performed their punk prayer in Moscow on February 21, 2012, they introduced a novel theme to the series of political protests against the Putin regime that they had started, in their own words, in the wake of the Arabian political uprisings of 2011. "After the Arab Spring, we had come to understand that Russia needed political and sexual emancipation, audacity, the feminist whip and a feminist president."[28] The group then consisted of about a dozen persons, both men and women, young and well educated, and it had its origins in an earlier art activist collective called "Voinia" (war). This time Pussy Riot addressed the renewed and tightening relationship between church and state in contemporary Russia, performing a *punk moleben* or punk prayer (as the group labeled its act) in the Russian Orthodox Cathedral of Christ the Saviour near the Kremlin.[29] Another novelty was the fact that only female members of the group performed this time (while some male members were present to support and record the act[30]). The choice for a "women only" performance has not been explained by the group; it could have been a theatrical statement related to the punk prayer's liturgical focus on the Virgin Mary and its explicit feminist stances (see the lyrics below), or to the deliberate choice to perform on the *soleas*, the platform right in front of the Cathedral's high altar and the *ikonostasis*, where normally only male priests appear. Exactly on this spot, clad in brightly colored dresses, leggings, boots, and balaclavas, the women danced, kneeled, and crossed themselves, singing and shouting their "prayer" until the security guards intervened, and the women were removed from the sanctuary (fig. 15.1).

FIGURE 15.1 Pussy Riot performs a punk prayer in the Cathedral of Christ the Saviour in Moscow. Photo by Sergey Ponomarev.

This short scene was filmed by some of the other group members, and within a few hours afterward the collective released a video clip on YouTube and on several social media sites, where they also had published their earlier performances. The clip shows the performance of the punk prayer in the Cathedral of Christ the Saviour as well as the termination of this act, mixed with footage of the same act performed two days earlier in a lesser well-known church in Moscow.[31] In this compiled clip the complete anti-Putin punk prayer can be heard and seen. It is partly performed in the style of a solemn hymn to the Virgin Mary, musically taken from what is in Russia the very cherished Mary Vespers of Rachmaninoff, and partly in the form of a shouted punk rap.

"Bogoroditsa, Putina progoni!"
[Virgin Mary, Put Putin Away! (Punk Prayer)]

Virgin Mary, Mother of God, put Putin away,
Put Putin away, put Putin away!
(End chorus)

Black robe, golden epaulettes
All parishioners crawl to bow
The phantom of liberty is in heaven
Gay pride sent to Siberia in chains

The head of the KGB, their chief saint,
Leads protesters to prison under escort
In order not to offend His Holiness
Women must give birth and love

Shit, shit, the Lord's shit!
Shit, shit, the Lord's shit

(Chorus)
Virgin Mary, Mother of God, become a feminist
Become a feminist, become a feminist!
(End chorus)

The church's praise of rotten dictators
The cross-bearer procession of black limousines

A teacher-preacher will meet you at school
Go to class—bring him money!

Patriarch Gundyaev believes in Putin
Bitch, better believe in God instead!
The belt of the Virgin can't replace mass meetings
Mary, Mother of God, is with us in protest!

(Chorus)
Virgin Mary, Mother of God, put Putin away,
Put Putin away, put Putin away!
(End chorus)[32]

The complete song features sharp criticism of the complicity of the Russian Orthodox Church in the authoritarian regime in Russia, referring to high-profiled incidents and public issues at that moment. It denounces the corruption in the church establishment, ridicules the luxurious lifestyle of Patriarch Kirill, and decries the close connections between the church and the state security police. It points to the dire consequences of the current repressive regime for women, homosexuals, and for those who take part in political opposition, groups who are all bereft of their freedom of speech, act, and choice. This harsh criticism is articulated in punk style shouted verse lines, alternated by a high-pitched sung chorus in which the intercession of Mary as Mother of God is invoked. In the chorus Mary is called "to be with us in protest" and "to put Putin away."

On the evening of the very day of the performance and its release on YouTube, the Russian Orthodox Church issued its first public condemnation. On national television, Archpriest Vsevolod Chaplin denounced the Pussy Riot action in Moscow's most prestigious church. The next day he wrote a blog post on the *Orthodox Politics* website in which he argued that the art collective had violated statutes on anti-extremism, that their action was criminal, and that they had offended the feelings of believers. He also argued that politicians who did not condemn the Pussy Riot action "may stop counting on the support of the Orthodox Church" and declared that the legal standards surrounding acts that offend religious feelings should be strengthened. Chaplin had already been the ROC's spokesman in previous incidences of artistic expression that were perceived as anti-church or anti-Orthodox and that had led to court cases, such as the exhibitions "Beware, Religion!" (2003) and "Forbidden Art" (2006) at the Sakharov Museum. In these cases, he had propagated the position that these exhibitions were a criminal provocation meant to incite religious hatred.[33] Chaplin's comments also proved to be agenda-setting for the criminalization of Pussy Riot's punk prayer by calling it an insidious attack on the church, the state, and the nation in one malicious act. His comments were soon followed by a fast-growing number of official complaints against the group. Already the next day the prosecutor's office received an official complaint from the rector of a local Orthodox school stating that the Pussy Riot action was a "sacrilegious concert" that offended his feelings as an Orthodox believer and that the women should be arrested for "hooliganism" and for the inciting of religious hatred. Similar complaints against the women were to follow, each documenting the perceived blasphemy and sacrilege of the action and the offense against the religious feelings of the complainants. Finally, on March 3, 2012, at the eve of the presidential elections, Nadezhda Tolokonnikova and Maria Alekhina were taken into custody, while Yekaterina Samutsevich was arrested on March 16. They were jailed for over five months, put on trial, found guilty, and were ultimately sentenced to two years' imprisonment in a correctional colony (fig 15.2).[34]

The prosecution defined their offense in terms of infractions that strongly correspond to the type of complaints stated earlier that had also been repeatedly expressed in the official media campaign against Pussy Riot. The women were accused, in particular, of intending to openly express "disrespect for the Christian world and church canons," to "desecrate" the church, and to "inflict deep wounds

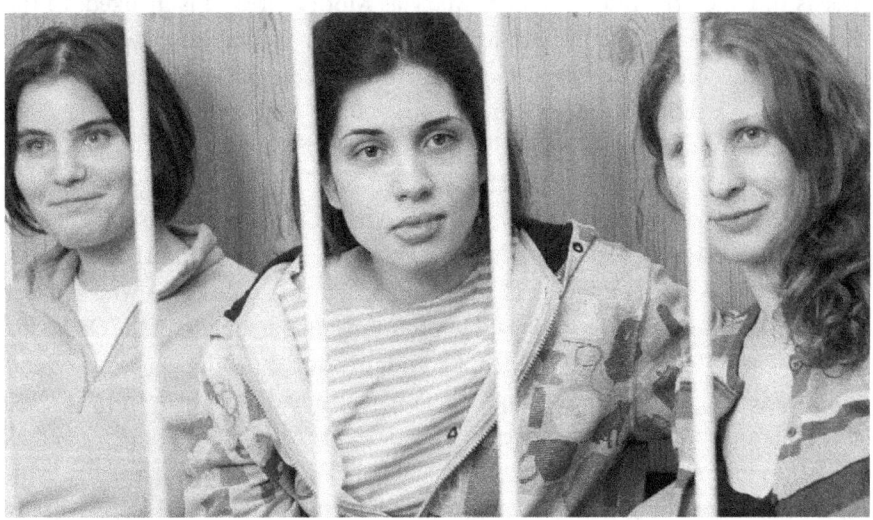

FIGURE 15.2   Pussy Riot members Maria Alekhina, Yekaterina Samutsevich and Nadezhda Tolokonnikova in court. Photo by Maxim Shemetov.

on Orthodox Christians." They were accused of committing a "maliciously conscious and thoroughly planned action of humiliation of the feelings and beliefs of multiple adherents of the Orthodox Christian confession and diminishment of the spiritual foundation of the state."[35] Furthermore, according to the prosecution, the offensive lyrics and the indecent manner of the performance made the three women's behavior "vulgar, impudent, and cynical," which supported the charge of hooliganism.[36] The witnesses for the prosecution (church personnel, guards, and visitors) all attested that they felt hurt, outraged, or threatened by the shouting, movements, clothing, and gestures of the three women and by their appearance in front of the *iconostasis*.[37]

The three Pussy Riot members responded in much detail to the charges of religious hatred and blasphemy both in their speeches at their defense and in their open letters to President Medvedev and Patriarch Kyrill.[38] On one hand, they rigorously denounced and ridiculed these charges and stated that the accusations as such reflect and affirm the corrupt and intimidating Putin regime the women oppose; on the other hand, they offered a series of refined and eloquently formulated arguments to prove that they had not intended to perform a blasphemous act at all. They claimed their act not to be anti-religious, but a necessary critique of the misuse and corruption of the Russian Orthodox tradition in the new alliance between the Putin regime and the Russian Orthodox Church and the building of a new national Orthodox identity that annexes Russian Orthodox religious culture for its own power play. Referring to biblical texts and hermeneutics, the works of philosophers, novelists, Russian dissidents, and of contemporary feminist and political theoretics, they elaborated on this position, suggesting that their own stance might be closer to original intentions and prophetic aspects of the Christian faith than that of their opponents. They showed to be worried in particular about the fact that core Christian values such as conversion, self-critical transformation, humility, and vulnerability become perverted by those in power and are made an instrument of subordination and dependence, which turns "sons of God" into "slaves of God."[39]

Although many commentators both in Russia and abroad have esteemed the accusation of religious hatred and blasphemy a sheer pretext for the intimidation and elimination of political opponents (as they often also perceive Pussy Riot's punk prayer to be an instrumental, deliberate, and deeply ironic or parodic recourse to religious images and forms[40]), a substantial number of theologians and philosophers want to suspend judgments of the intentions, authenticity, and sincerity of both parties with regard to faith and religious practice. They prefer to critically unpack and reconsider the discourse of "motives of religious hatred" and "the intention to perform blasphemy" that are center stage in the charges against the women.[41] They follow several routes of exploration. They challenge the actual legitimacy of the accusation of blasphemy, both more in general and in regard to this particular case. They position the punk prayer and the ensuing lawsuit in its broader political and theological context, arguing that Pussy Riot, if its position is taken seriously, rather exposes the blasphemy committed by the Putin regime in its collaboration with the Russian Orthodox Church. Generally, they affirm and elaborate the arguments that are given by the women themselves, reinforcing and augmenting their points of view regarding their loyalty to the Christian tradition and their appropriation of Russian Orthodox ritual and aesthetics. More concretely, they argue that Pussy Riot well-chosen statements here refer to the holy fool figure in the Russian Orthodox faith tradition to legitimize their performance in the cathedral and that Pussy Riot rightly reclaims the ritual and aesthetics of the Russian Orthodox (folk) tradition to counter the misuse that the current Russian rulers make of this ritual and aesthetics, particularly concerning Mariology.

What I find very remarkable is that in these explorations and argumentations, which ultimately (aim to) support the members of the Pussy Riot group and their performance in the Moscow cathedral and directly focus on the accusation of blasphemy (and offering generally speaking very adequate and enlightening analyses of the political motives and interest that have produced the charge of blasphemy), interest in and critical analysis of gender aspects seem to be missing completely. By this I mean that no attention is paid to the fact that the accusations were only directed at the women of the group, to the openly feminist aspects of their act, the particular details of their performance related to the presentation of the female body, or the feminist theoretical references in their defenses. Nor are the actual details of their enactment of religious ritual addressed in this context, although, as noticed, this aspect of their behavior in the cathedral ("vulgar, impudent, and cynical") counted for the prosecution as a direct proof of the alleged "hooliganism." I aim to add this gender-critical perspective to this debate by relating the punk prayer to the previously mentioned recent cases of alleged blasphemy in Western Europe and the United States where feminism and female-embodied religion are at stake.

Pussy Riot's Punk Prayer in the Context of Recent Cases of "Blasphemous" Feminist Art

As announced, I find the Pussy Riot case of particular importance for the research interest that I outlined in the first part of this contribution. At first sight, there seem to be many similarities and points of affinity between the Pussy Riot performance and its subsequent trial, and the above-mentioned recent cases of "blasphemous" feminist art. In all cases we find an explicit and primary appeal to feminist cultural and religious criticism by the artists; a deliberately provocative reworking of key religious imagery and gesture from the faith tradition the artists have been raised in; a pronounced bodily performance of the artists as the actual medium of the entire scene; a central role of social and mass media in both the publicity and the rise of controversy concerning this scene, generating a great number of supportive as well as declining reactions; and very articulated public defenses by the involved artists themselves in reaction to the critique, controversy, and the accusations of blasphemy.

In my earlier research I attempted to find decisive factors that determine the controversiality of feminist artworks that have been prone to blasphemy accusations in contemporary Western countries in recent times. Next to the historical setting, the social and political context, the actual events, and the comments of the artists, I also studied the specific features of each of the accused works, such as their iconographical religious details, gender strategy (gender bending and confusion, minimalizing of gender aspects, exaggerated or ironic use of gender details), the role of and position of the female body and its sexual connotations, and the impact of the appearance of women of color in these scenes. I concluded from a comparative study of these details that neither the staging of (or allusion to) core or iconic religious scenes as such nor the exposition of the nude or otherwise emphasized female body contributes most to the accusation of blasphemy; the decisive factor seems to be the personal presence, visibility, and recognizability of the artist (and other, often closely related persons) as part of the work of art or the performance. In my view, this finding confirms my contention that the many instances of alleged blasphemous imagery featuring gendered corporeality and nonheteronormative sexuality that make up the so-called culture wars of the past two decades in the West are related to a specific shift in the former established social and personal meaning of both religion and sexuality, in which the affirmation of sexual diversity, in all its (public) manifestations, for many has come to count as a core value of modern Western life, while religious identity has become far more privatized, or is supposed to be so.

However, with regard to this most decisive factor the Pussy Riot case differs significantly from these other mentioned cases. When compared to the alleged blasphemous feminist works of art in Western countries that center on the reworking of iconic, often cited, and reproduced Christian images, it becomes clear that during the punk prayer performance no religious imagery has been shown, and that the artists have not been involved in reenacting sacred scenes.

FIGURE 15.3   Pussy Riot at Lobnoye Mesto on Red Square in Moscow, January 20, 2012. Photo by Denis Bochkarev.

No controversial personal identification of the artists with Jesus, Mary, or the saints took place, and even more important, no individual recognizable presence at all was involved (fig 15.3).

Absence of individuality and recognizability is the most significant feature of the Pussy Riot performances: the use of the colored balaclava that hides the face completely, and the uniformity of the style of the very brightly colored simple and functional clothing. This characteristic outfit makes a great difference with the appearance of Western feminist art activists, but this is a strategy or policy that also makes them distinguishable from the (originally Ukraine) Femen activists who use their bare bodies as instruments of protests. The strict anonymity of the Pussy Riot performers could be interpreted as a protective strategy in the context of a political regime that is extremely oppressive and actually continues to put its dissenters away in working camps and penal colonies. It has also been identified as a tribute to the fact that the group wants to propagate a radical critical vision on Russia's current political and religious regime but in a form that is not depending on its individual messengers: the uniformity of their outfit affirms this communal embodiment. Also, their anonymity has been interpreted as contributing directly to their aim to mobilize political protest: both their clothing and their seemingly uncultivated songs are easy to copy and to identify with.

The most significant attribute of Pussy Riot's performance is the balaclava. This head- and facial covering has a long history in leftist political activism and since the seventies it also has been part of the outfit of punk music bands. The group, which positions itself in the punk tradition, adopted this feature and changed its color from its originally black to a range of very bright colors; in this style it became Pussy Riot's brand or logo. The choice for facial covering differs remarkably from the style in the Western feminist engaged works of art and performances accused of blasphemy that have been found provocative because of the personal presence and recognizability of the artists/performers. It is this difference that I see as central for this analysis. Not only does the unique selling point of the group lie in this characteristic attribute but also the originality of their performance and of the resonance that this performance has experienced.

It is crucial to recognize that the Western media's interest in the Pussy Riot case emerged and immediately increased substantially when shortly after the detention and accusation of the three female members their masks went off and their faces became visible. Their identity as young and very attractive women could be perceived as well as, for the first time, their individuality. The circulation of their faces on the Internet and in the conventional media has been extensive. As research of the media coverage and circulation of the Pussy Riot affair turns out, reaction to their act has been remarkably positive in the Western media. The political protest can easily be understood to incorporate both the most cherished values of Western countries and a strong critique of the Putin regime and the political climate in Russia, a critique that reinforces these core values of (individual) freedom, freedom of speech, equality, and autonomy (particularly for women), as well as recognition of sexual minorities, political freedom, and democracy (as the opposite of dictatorial and suppressive governing). Severe criticism of religious institutions and prescriptions that denounce these rights and values obviously belongs to this stance. It has been suggested that the combination of young attractive women in the role of political activists versus a brute regime, the fearlessness of their public appearance, and the eloquence of their defense has highly contributed to the acceptance of their performance and has advanced the positive evaluation of their intentions.

A positive recognition and even applauding of this act and the public appearance of this punk formation are, however, all but self-evident. The reactions in Russia, as sketched above, are predominantly very averse. The majority of the Russian people loathe the punk prayer act and esteem the persecution and conviction of the three women just and deserved. However, the controversy that the "blasphemous" feminist works of art and performances in Western countries in the past decade have caused also shows that feminist activist art in many cases is not openly embraced as an embodiment of core Western values, on the contrary. Also, as the history of feminist protest movements and their leading figures in Western countries shows, the publicly protesting female person has predominantly been associated with derailed, nonfeminine, nonrational, and disturbed women. The pronounced use of the female body as means of political protest adds to the negative appreciation of this type of protest. A general lack of sympathy and support for women protesters follows from this perception, as well as a particular criminalization of women protesters.[42]

When we turn to the position of the political protesters in Soviet and Russian political history it becomes clear that the balaclava attire of the Pussy Riot group, which masks their individual visibility and their personal recognizability, is also not quite in continuation with the long tradition of political dissidence in the former Soviet Union to which their actions in many other aspects belong. Russian dissidents (artists, novelists, journalists, priests, and other intellectuals) have predominantly operated as individuals and are also known and admired—and thus also persecuted—because of their individual work and unique position. They are seen as the most important bearers of protest and counterweight over and against the sovereign and oppressive state apparatus, and in this tradition also some women have stood out. The credibility of and the high esteem for these dissenters are immediately linked to the exposition of their personal life, vicissitudes, and performances as well as to their status as witness and martyr.

Pussy Riot's act thus does not fit in the most accepted models of political protest and in the usual role ascribed to women in these protests. As the reception of the Pussy Riot in Western perspective demonstrates, in the actual Western perception, built on a strong polarization between Western values and Russian political culture, both Pussy Riot's feminist ambitions as well as their criticism of the political system can be acknowledged. From a Western perspective, the accusation of blasphemy is only instrumental; it regards the suppression of an obvious religion-critical stance or, more nuanced, the suppression of a parrhesia-like stance, of frankly and openly speaking the truth in extremely oppressive conditions.

Also, from a Russian perspective, Pussy Riot's punk prayer does not quite fit in the accepted models of political protest. The centrality of balaclavas and the anonymity that they bring along adds to the idea that a gross disturbance of appropriate behavior has been brought about, and the lack of irony and parody in the punk prayer itself forms an unprecedented form of political-religious critique. The familiar ironizing form of religious critique (from the secular state's perspective) of the Soviet period is here replaced by a serious criticism of (new) religious legitimation of state politics and the misuse of religion for political ends, while simultaneously the need is expressed to purify and recapture Russian Orthodox religious tradition and to retrieve its contribution to the contemporary struggle for freedom and justice.

Pussy Riot member Yekaterina Samutsevich in her court statement very eloquently analyzed Putin's "need to exploit the Orthodox religion and its aesthetics": "Apparently, [Putin] felt the need for more convincing, transcendental guarantees of his long tenure at the helm. It was here that the need arose to make use of the aesthetics of the Orthodox religion, historically associated with the heyday of Imperial Russia, where power came not from earthly manifestations such as democratic elections and civil society, but from God Himself."[43] According to Samutsevich, "the authorities took advantage of a certain deficit of Orthodox aesthetics in Soviet times, when the Orthodox religion had the aura of a lost history, of something crushed and damaged by the Soviet totalitarian regime, and was thus an opposition culture. The authorities decided to appropriate this historical effect of loss and present their new political project to restore Russia's lost spiritual values, a project which has little to do with a genuine concern for preservation of Russian Orthodoxy's history and culture."[44]

Samutsevich sees her performance in the Cathedral of Christ the Saviour with the song "Mother of God, Put Putin Away" not only as an act of protest against this manipulative turn to "Orthodox aesthetics" during election time. She also claims her performance to be an "unauthorized" alternative use of "Orthodox aesthetics." She states, "In our performance we dared, without the Patriarch's blessing, to combine the visual image of Orthodox culture and protest culture, suggesting to smart people that Orthodox culture belongs not only to the Russian Orthodox Church, the Patriarch and Putin, that it might also take the side of civic rebellion and protest in Russia."[45]

Conclusion

My analysis has revealed the deeply hybrid and ambiguous character of Pussy Riot's punk prayer, which I consider constitutive of its aim and function as feminist political protest. This performance critically addresses the oppressive Russian regime (in the tradition of Russian dissident activism) and the new alignment with and legitimization by the Russian Orthodox Church that this regime seeks, showing in particular the intimidating consequences for "the others" of these patriarchal sovereigns: women, homosexuals, political dissidents, and people unable to appropriate the "grace" and favors of the neoliberal economy in its corrupt manifestations. In this act of protest, political analysis and theological arguments, secular and religious points of view, public and private interests, and rational and affective interpellations all come together and cannot be clearly separated from each other. Moreover, this complexity is underlined by the very style and composition of this gesture of protest, with its many deliberately chosen multimedia details of time, location, bodily appearance, and movements, arrangements of sound and music, and its ingenious ritual and symbolic allusions, all of which force the audience to distinguish between sincerity and deception. It is precisely this deliberate entanglement of views, positions, and styles that should be acknowledged in the punk prayer protest, in the accusations that it gave rise to, and particularly in the defense of the Pussy Riot members in which they reflect on their performance, its original intentions, and its actual impact on Russian society and abroad.

To conclude, what is so challenging as well specific in Pussy Riot's criticism that this act could become a landmark event in the history of the suppression of political opposition in Putin's Russia? The observation that the Pussy Riot formation with their punk prayer has created disorder and has deliberately disturbed the peace, and that the persons present in the church at that instant, in particular the faithful, have been unsettled and shocked by this unexpected event, is certainly not incorrect or purely fictitious. However, the charge of hooliganism out of religious hatred and the indictment of blasphemy are unwarranted and reflect a malign identification of the current political order and exercise of power with the defense of the sacredness of Russian Orthodox culture and tradition.

My analysis confirms that the punk prayer performance is not born out of religious hatred. This act is too creative, too complex, and too elaborated regarding religious content and meaning to be possibly reduced to (be motivated by) "religious hate"; this has been affirmed by the rich speeches the accused women have given in court in which a nuanced discussion of religion and blasphemy is made part of their defense. An unusual and uncanny appeal to Russian Orthodox ritual and aesthetics can be found in the prayer. By its appeal to Mary, Russia's patroness and Holy Mother, to chase Putin away and join the feminists, this act forms a paradoxical and scandalous prayer indeed. Also, the enactment of this prayer in the cathedral, in front of the iconostasis, in brightly colored clothes, combined with a confusing mixture of respectful and disrespectful gestures, and fitting and unfitting singing and shouting, reflects the deep ambiguous status and meaning of this performance.

The punk prayer act is also brave because it is ingeniously composed and counters oppressive political positions and tendencies at the heart but in a counterintuitive way. By choosing to seek recourse to Mary with an explicit Hail Mary prayer in cathedral, the women not only appropriated a traditional religious ritual (allowed for women and lay people to do in this Church) but also completely transformed this prayer and acted in a novel way by invoking Mary's help to chase Putin away and begging Mary to become a feminist. They confined their act just to this prayer, expressed in a very noisy, colorfully clothed and strongly gestured performance to attract a maximum of attention. But they stayed anonymous and did not place themselves in the role of Mary or Jesus (as is considered the central act of transgression in the alleged blasphemous Western feminist religious works of art and performances). Their most salient deed of transgression was that they performed their prayer immediately in front of the *iconostasis*, where in religious services only priests and pastors abide. This, in my view, underscores that the invoking of Mary is pivotal in this act. The appeal to Mary is both an act of parrhesia (a venue to speak openly uncompromising truth about current affairs) and an act of faith (a vision of hope expressed with a longing in which all the senses and means of expressions are involved).[46]

Notes

1. Vera Shevzov, "Women on the Fault Lines of Faith: Pussy Riot and the Insider/Outsider Challenge to Post-Soviet Orthodoxy," *Religion and Gender* 4, no. 2 (2014): 122; Catherine Schuler, "Reinventing the Show Trial: Putin and Pussy Riot," *TDR: The Drama Review* 57, no. 1 (Spring 2013): 7–17; and Olga Voronina, "Pussy Riot Steal the Stage in the Moscow Cathedral of Christ the Saviour: Punk Prayer on Trial Online and in Court," *Digital Icons: Studies in Russian, Eurasian and Central European New Media* 9 (2013): 69–85.

2. Geraldine Fagan, "RUSSIA: Pussy Riot, Blasphemy, and Freedom of Religion or Belief," *Forum 18 News Service*, October 15, 2012, http://forum18.org/archive.php?article_id=1754.

3. Fagan, "RUSSIA: Pussy Riot." At the time of the Pussy Riot trial, Russia did not have blasphemy laws; instead, the courts deployed a variety of other laws in their argumentation. Anya Bernstein, "An Inadvertent Sacrifice: Body Politics and Sovereign Power

in the Pussy Riot Affair," *Critical Inquiry* 40, no. 1 (Autumn 2013): 220–241; Rachel L. Schroeder and Vyacheslav Karpov, "The Crimes and Punishments of the 'Enemies of the Church' and the Nature of Russia's Desecularising Regime," *Religion, State and Society* 41, no. 3 (2013): 284–311.

4. "Russia: Pussy Riot Inspired Blasphemy Law Threat to Free Expression," *Article 19*, July 1, 2013, http://www.article19.org/resources.php/resource/37143/en/russia:-pussy-riot-inspired-blasphemy-law-threat-to-free-expression (last accessed April 24, 2017).

5. Pussy Riot, *Pussy Riot! A Punk Prayer for Freedom: Letters from Prison, Songs, Poems, and Courtroom Statements, Plus Tributes to the Punk Band That Shook the World* (New York: Feminist Press at the City University of New York, 2013); and Emily Neu and Jade French with Pussy Riot, eds., *Let's Start a Pussy Riot* (London: Rough Trade, 2013), 12–43.

6. Tabitha M. van Zinnen, "Pussy Riot's *Punk Prayer*; Blasfemie, parrèsia en de strijd om vrijheid" (MA thesis, Faculty of Humanities, Utrecht University, 2013), https://dspace.library.uu.nl/handle/1874/281546. As Anya Bernstein observes: "Most Euro-American coverage of this famous trial focused on familiar dichotomies between free speech and blasphemy, the secular and the sacred, or even rationality and obscurantism, and in general seemed bewildered by what appeared as a disproportionate reaction of the Russian state to this affair." Bernstein, "Inadvertent Sacrifice," 221. For a contrary position, see "Rod Dreher's Brave Stance Against Pussy Riot and in Support of Blasphemy Laws," *Forbes*, August 22, 2012, http://www.forbes.com/sites/markadomanis/2012/08/22/rod-drehers-brave-stance-against-pussy-riot-and-in-support-of-blasphemy-laws/ (last accessed June 9, 2014).

7. See "Pussy Riot, Putin's Russia, and the Orthodox Church," *Free Speech Debate*, August 9, 2012, https://freespeechdebate.com/en/case/why-pussy-riots-church-protest-was-mere-political-dissent/; Masha Lipman, "Putin's Religious War against Pussy Riot," *New Yorker*, July 24, 2012, https://www.newyorker.com/online/blogs/newsdesk/2012/07/putins-religious-war-against-pussy-riot.html; and Bernstein, "Inadvertent Sacrifice."

8. "Russia: Pussy Riot Inspired Blasphemy."

9. This contribution is a sequel to and partly a reworking of a series of publications on recent cases of "blasphemous" feminist art: Anne-Marie Korte, "Madonna's Crucifixion and the Female Body in Feminist Theology," in *Doing Gender in Media, Art and Culture*, ed. Rosemarie Buikema and Iris van der Tuin (New York: Routledge, 2009), 117–133; Anne-Marie Korte, "Madonna's kruisigingsscène: Blasfemie of theologische uitdaging?," in *Tijdschrift voor Theologie* 49 (2009): 125–140; Anne-Marie Korte, "Blasphemous Feminist Art: Incarnate Politics of Identity in Post-secular Perspective," in *Transformations of Religion and the Public Sphere: Postsecular Publics*, ed. Rosi Braidotti et al. (New York: Palgrave Macmillan, 2014), 228–248; and Anne-Marie Korte, "Pussy Riot's *Punk Prayer* as a Case of/for Feminist Public Theology," in *New Horizons of Resistance and Visions. Yearbook of the European Society for Women in Theological Research*, ed. Ulrike Auga, Sigridur Gudmarsdottir, Stefanie Knauss & Silvia Martinez Cano (Leuven: Peeters, 2014), 31–53.

10. For comprehensive and critical overviews of contemporary art accused of blasphemy, see S. Brent Plate, *Blasphemy: Art that Offends* (London: Black Dog, 2006); Elizabeth Burns Coleman and Kevin White, eds., *Negotiating the Sacred: Blasphemy and Sacrilege in a Multicultural Society* (Canberra: ANU Press, 2006); Elizabeth Burns Coleman and Maria Suzette Fernandes Dias, eds., *Negotiating the Sacred II: Blasphemy and Sacrilege in the Arts* (Canberra: ANU Press, 2008); Jojada Verrips, "Offending Art and the Sense of Touch," *Material Religion* 4, no. 2 (2008): 204–225; and Eleanor Heartney, "The Global Culture War," *Art in America* (October 2011): 119–123.

11. Eleanor Heartney, "Thinking Through the Body: Women Artists and the Catholic Imagination," *Hypatia* 18, no. 4 (2003): 3–22; Eleanor Heartney, *Postmodern Heretics: The Catholic Imagination in Contemporary Art* (New York: Midmarch Arts Press, 2004); Eleanor Heartney, "Kiki Smith: A View from the Inside Out," in *After the Revolution: Women Who Transformed Contemporary Art*, ed. Eleanor Heartney et al. (Munich: Prestel, 2007), 189–207; and Bettina Papenburg and Marta Zarzycka, eds., *Carnal Aesthetics: Transgressive Imagery and Feminist Politics* (London: I. B. Tauris, 2013).

12. Luce Irigaray and Karen I. Burke, "Beyond Totem and Idol, the Sexuate Other," *Continental Philosophical Review* 40 (2007): 353–364; Wendy Brown, *Regulating Aversion: Tolerance in the Age of Identity and Empire* (Princeton, NJ: Princeton University Press, 2008); Linda Alcoff and John Caputo, eds., *Feminism, Sexuality, and the Return of Religion* (Bloomington: Indiana University Press, 2011); Nikita Dhawan, "The Empire Prays Back: Religion, Secularity, and Queer Critique," *Boundary 2* 40, no. 1 (2013): 191–222; and John Anderson, "Rocks, Art, and Sex: The 'Culture Wars' Come to Russia?," *Journal of Church and State* 55, no. 2 (2013): 307–334.

13. David Nash, "Blasphemy and Sacrilege: A Challenge to Secularization and Theories of the Modern?," in *Negotiating the Sacred II: Blasphemy and Sacrilege in the Arts*, ed. Elizabeth Burns Coleman and Maria Suzette Fernandes Dias (Canberra: ANU Press, 2008), 16.

14. For discussions of blasphemy and sacrilege in their contemporary forms, see, for example, David A. Lawton, *Blasphemy* (Philadelphia: University of Pennsylvania Press, 1993); Leonard Levy, *Blasphemy: Verbal Offense Against the Sacred, from Moses to Salman Rushdie* (New York: Knopf, 1993); Anthony Fisher and Hayden Ramsay, "Of Art and Blasphemy," *Ethical Theory and Moral Practice* 3, no. 2 (2000): 137–167; Plate, *Blasphemy*; David Nash, "Analyzing the History of Religious Crime: Models of 'Passive' and 'Active' Blasphemy since the Medieval Period," *Journal of Social History* 41, no. 1 (2007): 5–29; Jean-Pierre Wils, *Gotteslästerung* (Frankfurt am Main: Verlag der Weltreligionen, 2007); and Elizabeth Burns Coleman, "The Offenses of Blasphemy: Messages in and through Art," *Journal of Value Inquiry* 45, no. 1 (2011): 67–84.

15. See, for example, Rosemary Radford Ruether, *Sexism and God-Talk: Toward a Feminist Theology* (Boston: Beacon Press, 1983); Carol P. Christ, *Laughter of Aphrodite: Reflections on a Journey to the Goddess* (San Francisco: Harper and Row, 1987); Judith Plaskow, *Standing Again at Sinai: Judaism from a Feminist Perspective* (San Francisco:

HarperSanFrancisco, 1991); Rachel Adler, *Engendering Judaism: An Inclusive Theology and Ethics* (Boston, MA: Beacon Press, 1999); and Marcella Althaus-Reid, *Liberation Theology and Sexuality* (Aldershot, UK: Ashgate, 2006).

16. Bruno Latour, "What Is Iconoclash? Or Is There a World Beyond the Image Wars?," in *Iconoclash: Beyond the Image Wars in Science, Religion, and Art*, ed. Bruno Latour and Peter Weibel (Karlsruhe: Zentrum für Kunst und Medientechnologie, 2002), 12.

17. See Plate's contribution in this volume, "Eventual Blasphemies: Setting the Offensive Work of Art in Time."

18. Plate, *Blasphemy*, 43.

19. Plate, 47.

20. Sara Maitland, "Blasphemy and Creativity," in *The Salman Rushdie Controversy in Interreligious Perspective*, ed. Dan Cohn-Sherbok (Queenston: Edwin Mellen Press, 1997), 124.

21. David Freedberg, *The Power of Images: Studies in the History and Theory of Response* (Chicago: University of Chicago Press, 1989), 374–377; and Verrips, "Offending Art and the Sense of Touch," passim.

22. Margaret Miles, *Carnal Knowing: Female Nakedness and Religious Meaning in the Christian West* (New York: Vintage Books, 1991), 176–179.

23. Joan W. Scott, *Sexularism: Ursula Hirschman Annual Lecture on Gender and Europe, RSCAS Distinguished Lecture 2009/01*, April 23, 2009, 12–13.

24. Scott, 4.

25. Scott, 4.

26. Stefan Dudink, "Homosexuality, Race, and the Rhetoric of Nationalism," *History of the Present* 1, no. 2 (2011): 259–264; Fatima El-Tayeb, "'Gays Who Cannot Properly Be Gay': Queer Muslims in the Neoliberal European City," *European Journal of Women's Studies* 19, no. 1 (2012): 79–95; and Adi Kuntsman, *Figurations of Violence and Belonging: Queerness, Migranthood and Nationalism in Cyberspace and Beyond* (Oxford: Peter Lang, 2009).

27. Mariecke van den Berg et al., "Religion, Homosexuality, and Contested Social Orders in the Netherlands, the Western Balkans, and Sweden," in *Religion in Times of Crisis*, ed. Gladys Ganiel, Heidemarie Winkel, Christophe Monnot (Leiden: Brill, 2014), 116–134.

28. Pussy Riot, "The History of Pussy Riot," in Neu and French with Pussy Riot, *Let's Start a Pussy Riot*, 22; Pussy Riot, "Art or Politics?," in Pussy Riot, *Pussy Riot!*, 15–16.

29. According to Vera Shevzov the Russian term for this prayer, *moleben*, points to a deliberate choice for this particular form of liturgical prayer. "Technically, a *moleben* is a short communal prayer service (in contrast to individual prayer), led by a priest, often following the Divine Liturgy. Such services (or at least certain prayers in them) are often addressed to the Mother of God (as well as to Christ or a particular saint). Structured on the model of Matins, a *moleben* involves supplication or thanksgiving, and is regularly performed in Russian Orthodox churches during periods of local,

regional, or national hardship and crisis, such as drought, war, and civil strife. Believers might also request such a service for personal or familial hardship or illness. Accordingly, a *moleben* that petitions for divine help can be served for virtually any occasion. For instance, in view of Russia's demographic crisis, Russia's Orthodox churches in recent years have held such prayer services for a decrease in the number of divorces, for those who desire to have children, and for the health and well-being of pregnant women. The fact that the group chose to call their performance a *moleben* suggests that they assumed the priestly role in their 'prayer.'" Vera Shevzov, "Women on the Fault Lines of Faith," 127–128.

30. See the original footage of the performance on YouTube, https://www.youtube.com/watch?v=PN5inCayfnM.

31. For the finished video, see "Russian Riot Grrrl Protest," YouTube, March 6, 2021, https://www.youtube.com/watch?v=yZKaBh9pX64. The video went viral with over 200,000 views.

32. Authorized lyrics in Pussy Riot, *Pussy Riot!*, 13–14.

33. The accusations and sentences in these earlier cases had resulted only in large fines, not in lengthy terms of imprisonment. Schroeder and Karpov, "Crimes and Punishments of the 'Enemies of the Church,'" 285.

34. Schroeder and Karpov, 292–293.

35. Schroeder and Karpov, 297.

36. "Prosecutor's Statement," in Pussy Riot, *Pussy Riot!*, 52–54.

37. "Excerpts from the Court Transcript," in Pussy Riot, *Pussy Riot!*, 49–52.

38. See Pussy Riot, *Pussy Riot!*, 15–48, 87–118.

39. Reference to the Russian philosopher Nikolai Berdyaev, in "Closing Courtroom Statement by Masha," in Pussy Riot, *Pussy Riot!*, 106.

40. See for instance Alexander Kissler, "Vaginal Turmoil," *European*, August 23, 2012, http://www.theeuropean-magazine.com/alexander-kissler—3/805-dissidence-and-blasphemy-in-russia.

41. Tom Beaudoin, "'Punk Prayer Service' in Moscow Cathedral," *Rock and Theology*, April 10, 2012, http://www.rockandtheology.com/?p=5316; Colin Jager, "Rethinking Secularism: Pussy Riot's Punk Prayer," *Immanent Frame: Secularism, Religion and the Public Sphere*, September 18, 2012, http://blogs.ssrc.org/tif/2012/09/18/pussy-riots-punk-prayer/; Slavoj Žižek, "The True Blasphemy," *Symptom*, October 8, 2012, http://www.lacan.com/thesymptom/?page_id=2364; Timothy Beal, "Pussy Riot's Theology," *Chronicle of Higher Education*, August 17, 2012, http://chronicle.com/article/Pussy-Riots-Theology/134398/; Nicholas Denysenko, "An Appeal to Mary: An Analysis of Pussy Riot's Punk Performance in Moscow," *Journal of the American Academy of Religion* 81, no. 4 (2013): 1061–1092; and Sergei Prozorov, "Pussy Riot and the Politics of Profanation: Parody, Performativity, Veridiction," *Political Studies* 62, no. 4 (2013): 1–18.

42. Alison Young, *Femininity in Dissent* (London: Routledge, 1990); and Lizzie Seal, "Pussy Riot and Feminist Cultural Criminology: A New 'Femininity in Dissent'?"

Contemporary Justice Review: Issues in Criminal, Social, and Restorative Justice 16, no. 2 (2013): 293–303.

43. "Closing Courtroom Statement by Katya," 88.
44. "Closing Courtroom Statement by Katya," 88.
45. "Closing Courtroom Statement by Katya," 89.
46. See also Shevzov, "Women on the Fault Lines of Faith."

CHAPTER 16

On Silencing and Public Debates about Religiously Offensive Acts

Christoph Baumgartner

In public controversies over for example Salman Rushdie's novel *The Satanic Verses* or the "Muhammad cartoons" that were published by the Danish newspaper *Jyllands Posten*, many believers claimed that the publication of such pieces was wrong and constituted a moral or religious insult. It has been argued that such "religiously offensive acts" violate religious taboos,[1] are blasphemous, offend religious sensibilities, or produce negative stereotypes of particular religions or believers and discriminate against them on the basis of their religion. Others defended such acts in the name of the right to freedom of expression, tolerance, and, in some cases, the claim that such acts would foster the acceptance of liberal democratic values by believers. This was especially the case in France, Denmark, Germany, and the Netherlands, countries that provide the social and cultural context of this contribution. Although there are significant differences between controversies about concrete instances of religiously offensive acts in these countries, these societies currently share the characteristic that members of Islamic traditions are construed as minority to which a specific "culture" is ascribed that is seen by many as distinct from and in tension with the socially predominant customs, practices, and normative ideals and values.[2] This fosters an antagonistic framing and a strong polarization of debates about religiously offensive acts and many participants are highly emotionalized and defensive when it comes to values, principles, and norms they consider essential for their understanding of modernity, democracy, freedom, and religion.

In this essay I want to delineate and analyze an argument that addresses public debates about religiously offensive acts. According to this argument, there are circumstances in which the voices of believers who protest against religiously offensive acts may be silenced and effectively filtered out from public debate because the protestors are denied the status of competent interlocutors and their contributions construed as not worthy of consideration or even as illegitimate. As a result, believers who aim to participate in public debate about the future development of society (such as concerning the public treatment of religious symbols) can be informally excluded from it. As I will show, gestures and other expressive acts can have an important function in this process inasmuch as they are perceived as representing and instituting authoritative norms, values, and common practices by which social ties are knotted together and which set the "grammar" of public debates. In specific constellations, certain types of gestures can function as catalysts that accelerate mechanisms of closure that informally but effectively exclude voices that protest against religiously offensive acts from public debate.

Although I present the "phenomenon of silencing" as a moral and political problem, the question that I address in this article is distinct from the ethical and legal issue whether freedom of expression should be restricted in view of religiously offensive acts. My argument goes beyond the rather narrow scope of this specific moral and legal right and directs our attention to other issues related to political philosophy, but also to assumptions and ideals concerning the self-understanding of pluralistic societies. Moreover, the analysis of various modes of silencing carves out shortcomings of narrow understandings of freedom of expression and points to informal and more complex conditions that enable people to contribute to participate in public debate about matters concerning religion.

In order to be able to clearly distinguish the phenomenon of silencing from other problems that are discussed in relation to religiously offensive acts, I will briefly delineate the two most influential arguments in current debates about such acts in the following section: the argument according to which acts such as the publication of Muhammad cartoons offend believers' deep-rooted religious sensibilities and the damaged-status-argument that claims that such acts can lower the social status of believers in the eyes of their fellow members of society. Next, I will turn to the main topic of this essay; I will delineate three different modes of silencing and suggest an explanation that enables us to understand under which circumstances efforts of believers to participate in public debate about religiously offensive acts can be bound to fail. In the final section, I will offer brief concluding remarks from the perspective of political ethics, especially concerning the suggestion that believers should respond to religiously offensive acts with "counterspeech."

Arguments against Religiously Offensive Acts

Probably the most common complaint against acts such as the publication of the Muhammad cartoons or the exhibition of *Piss Christ* is that they offend religious sensibilities of believers. In public debate, the term *offense* is used rather vaguely, often denoting believers' emotional reactions to perceived breaches of religious taboos or to an alleged "lack of respect" toward their religion. In philosophical discourse, however, Joel Feinberg developed a specific notion of offense. According to Feinberg, we speak of offense if a person suffers a disliked mental state (for example, disgust, shame, hurt), if she attributes this suffering to the wrongful conduct of another person, and if she resents the other person for causing her to experience the disliked mental state.[3] This notion of offense helps to better understand many manifestations of protests of believers against the production and publication of certain texts, pictures, films, et cetera.

Offense

Believers experience and express negative (disliked) emotional reactions such as anger, grief, hurt or feelings of humiliation and ascribe these feelings to (in their eyes) wrongful conduct of others. This is illustrated by a statement of Shaukat Sultan Khan, spokesman of the president of Pakistan, who in February 2006 described the effect that the Muhammad cartoons had for numerous pious Muslims: "It is like shoving pork down our throat."[4] It does not require much imagination to understand that the emotional reaction of somebody who is forced to swallow something that he deeply considers abominable consists in a disliked mental state and that the person who suffers this resents those he considers responsible for his suffering. This example, however, must not bring us to understand the offense that can be caused by acts that denigrate religious beliefs, symbols, or practices as merely unpleasant and rather superficial sensorial or emotional experiences. Feinberg points to this by distinguishing between mere offensive nuisance on the one side and profound offense on the other.[5] According to Feinberg, experiences of offensive nuisance are relatively shallow and inseparable from direct perceptual experiences. They are "affronts to the senses"; merely *knowing* that the offending conduct occurred without directly perceiving (seeing, smelling, hearing) it does not suffice to cause offensive nuisance.[6] Furthermore, and importantly, an act of ordinary offensive nuisance "is thought wrong ... because it produces unpleasant states in the captive witnesses"[7]—it does not result from perceived acts because these acts are thought wrong on independent (for example, moral or religious) grounds. Exactly this, however, applies to profound offense where something offends because it is evaluated wrong; profound offense results from a violation of values, norms, or principles that are essential for somebody's identity—it "offends *us* and not merely our senses or lower order sensibilities."[8] Accordingly, profound offenses are aptly characterized as deep, shattering, or serious.

Feinberg's conceptualization of offense and his distinction between mere offensive nuisances and profound offense makes it possible to better understand the kind of suffering on which the claims of believers who protest against religiously offensive acts are based. It is inadequate to simply dismiss their complaints as expressions of religious squeamishness or incapacity "to put up with insults, mockery, and ridicule," that is, according to Flemming Rose, the cultural editor of *Jyllands Posten*, an important capacity of members of democratic societies.[9] Believers often form and maintain their identity in close relationship to religious beliefs, practices, symbols, traditions, and religious sensibilities that result from this are by definition "higher-order sensibilities."[10] Related to this is in some cases a specific vulnerability of pious believers in view of their religion. What is at stake for them in experiencing vilifications and mockery of beliefs, practices, or symbols of their religion are not merely unpleasant feelings, but they experience themselves being injured.[11]

An important characteristic of offense in the sense that I described in this section is that the offending act must be taken by the offended person to wrong her, that is to violate a certain (moral or religious) claim—whether in fact it does or does not do so.[12] People other than the offended and the offending persons need not to be involved. This is different in the case of group libel and religious racism respectively.

Group Libel, Damaged Status, and "Religious Racism"

An important ethical criticism of the publication of both Salman Rushdie's novel *The Satanic Verses* and the Muhammad cartoons claims that such acts can damage the social standing of believers. Bhikhu Parekh develops this position by tying in with libel, which is public, untruthful and damaging remarks that go beyond fair comment.[13] Unlike in the case of offense, the problem with libel is not that it makes the affected person feel, for example, sad, angry, or disgusted. Rather, libelous acts and objects lower the person affected "in the eyes of *others*, damage his *social* standing, and harm his *reputation*."[14] This reference to other people, who are as it were the audience of libel, is decisive: If the same statements are made in private, the targeted person may be offended. Her social standing, however, will not be affected. In that sense libel is not a matter of disliked mental states, but it damages social relations in a way equivalent to discrimination and social exclusion. These characteristics of libel also apply to utterances that target groups, for example ethnic or religious groups. Accordingly, anti-Semitic or racist expressions (including images and films) can be seen as instances of group libel.[15] Acts such as the publication of a drawing that depicts Muhammad as a terrorist do not constitute (group) libel in a strict sense, since what is expressed by such a drawing does *not directly* address individuals or groups. Nevertheless, they share important features with group libel since certain religious practices, symbols, or persons such as Moses, Jesus, or Muhammad are often taken as representations of the followers of the respective religion. Accordingly, acts that ridicule or vilify religious practices or symbols, or make them appear inferior or dangerous, can serve as powerful tools that indirectly construct and communicate negative stereotypes of the entire religious group whose practices, symbols, and so on are the object of ridicule or vilification. This is especially important with respect to religious minorities who already are in a relatively vulnerable social position. Against this background Tariq Modood states that acts such as the publication of *The Satanic Verses* and the Muhammad cartoons represent instances of anti-religious, or more specifically anti-Muslim racism.[16] Unlike the conventional concept of racism that refers to people in terms of skin color or ethnicity, the notion of anti-religious racism takes into account that the "otherness" that is ascribed to certain people and even the "groupness" under which they are subsumed is often construed by reference to their religion. Thereby, it provides a conceptual tool that makes it possible to theoretically deal with the problem that especially people who already are in a relatively weak social position can be denigrated not only because of their ethnicity but also because of their membership in a religious minority.[17] In this respect, denigrating images of religious practices, symbols or persons can contribute to negative stereotyping and to social marginalization of believers.

The claim that particular instances of religiously offensive acts represent anti-religious racism and damage the social standing of the believers concerned is dependent on a number of empirical assumptions. First, images of religious symbols, persons et cetera can only take effect in the sense outlined above if they are perceived as representations of followers of a particular religion in a quite generalizing manner. Second, acts and images that criticize a religion in a provocative manner are not *as such* racist but only in circumstances where there already are negative prejudices and attitudes against members of a particular religion. In such circumstances, images such as the Muhammad cartoons can tie in with existing resentments against Islam or Muslims and contribute to their perpetuation and intensification. For this reason, the Muhammad cartoons are considered both offensive and racist by several authors, whereas the church-critical and anti-militarist paintings by George Grosz in the 1920s or Andres Serrano's photograph *Piss Christ* may have offended the religious sensibilities of devout Christians but were not considered instances of "anti-Christian racism."

Offense of religious sensibilities and group libel are among the most important objections against acts such as the publication of the Muhammad cartoons. Both criticisms address such acts themselves and the consequences that result (albeit indirectly) from them. In the following sections I will widen the scope of my analysis and include public debates about such acts. I will focus on the European part of the controversy about the publication of the Muhammad cartoons in 2005 and their republication by a number of mass media. This widening of the scope of the analysis will enable me to address the phenomenon of silencing as a problem that is related to the problem of offense and the problem of the damaged status, but that will have to be treated as a distinct problem.

Participation in Public Debate and the Phenomenon of Silencing

The publication of the Muhammad cartoons was from the outset framed in terms of concerns about freedom of expression in general and the possibility to address issues concerning Islam in public debate in particular. In an article that was published along with the Muhammad cartoons on September 30, 2005, Flemming Rose referred to what he described as several incidents of self-censorship by authors, artists, and translators in Europe which where, according to Rose, caused by fears and feelings of intimidation in dealing with issues related to Islam.[18] Such self-censorship motivated by fear, Rose argued, was incompatible with democracy and free speech, and the goal of the publication of the cartoons "was simply to push back self-imposed limits on expression that seemed to be closing in tighter."[19] In other words, the stated aim of *Jyllands Posten* was to promote free speech and to further public debate in democratic societies about issues such as freedom of expression, freedom of religion, and cultural and religious diversity, but also possible relations between Islam and violence.

Participating on Par with Others in Public Debate

The argument I want to present in this contribution shares the concern for an open public debate. However, it points to aspects that differ significantly from what Flemming Rose and supporters of *Jyllands Posten* have argued in the context of the Muhammad cartoons controversy. It carves out shortcomings of an understanding of freedom of expression and public debate that one-sidedly emphasizes the liberty to utter one's opinions and points to the significance of the various conditions that are necessary for the specific form of communication that public debate is to succeed. Briefly stated, I argue that in particular circumstances there can be a danger that voices of believers who object to and publicly protest against religiously offensive acts and in so doing attempt to participate in public debates about issues such as freedom of expression, toleration, and respectful treatment of religion are silenced. Thereby I refer to silencing as the phenomenon that an effort of a person or group to participate on par with others in public debate fails because of conditions that result from actions of people other than those whose contributions are muted. As will become clear later, gestures and other expressive acts can function as catalysts that foster specific modes of silencing.[20] They do so inasmuch as they are perceived as carrying messages that reflect attitudes and emotional or mental states of authoritative people, groups, or institutions in society, having the power to represent or institute norms, values, traditions, and common practices by which social ties are knotted together (see below).

But what does it mean to fully participate, that is to participate on par with others in public debate? What are the conditions that allow for such participation? And is it (morally) significant to be able to do so, and if so—why?

The concern for an open public debate is decisive for democratic societies since legitimate democratic power is constituted and controlled by the people. Legitimate democratic power presupposes self-government and that members of the political community can have the warranted conviction that they are effectively involved in the making of political decisions, rules, and laws to which they are supposed to obey.[21] In order to make this possible, matters of common interest need to be publicly discussed and all members of society, certainly those who are affected by a certain matter or political decision, must be able to fully participate in public debate about it. Participating can take different forms, including deliberation (providing reasons for or against certain views), but also mere statements of one's opinion (for example, in opinion polls) or various forms of symbolic expressions and interventions (protest marches or gestures such as flying or burning a flag). Artifacts and tangible objects such as statutes, monuments, and pictures can also function as contributions to public debate, since they express some proposition or attitude of a person, group, or institution. Nondeliberative acts and artifacts such as the aforementioned are often used in order to put certain topics on the political agenda and introduce them into forums where deliberative forms of public debate take place. This was the case with both the Muhammad cartoons and public protests against them, even though the Muhammad cartoons controversy was in part orchestrated by people with political interests both in Denmark and in countries of the Middle East, Indonesia, and elsewhere.[22]

In many cases, Jeremy Waldron points out, the nondeliberative but enduring and tangible or pictorial expressions have the potential to influence the debate about certain matters of public interest even more fundamentally and subtly than spoken and deliberative contributions because they become a "permanent or semipermanent part of the visible environment in which our lives, and the lives of vulnerable minorities, are lived."[23] Our visible social environment, again, codetermines the framing of public communication by representing and co-determining how people in a particular cultural and historical context imagine their social surrounding. It includes symbolic references to what is considered valuable by powerful members of society or even part of a society's self-understanding (e.g. in the case of public monuments), and the "public culture" that shapes the context of debates about social and political developments (see below). Accordingly, Waldron points out, that "racist or religious defamation is not just an idea contributed to a debate. In its published, posted, or pasted-up-form, hate speech can become a world-defining activity, and those who promulgate it know very well—this is part of their intention—that the visible world they create is a much harder world for the targets of their hatred to live in."[24]

In relatively large and complex societies public debate is mainly carried out via mass media; newspapers and other print media, television, and the Internet enable communication across distance, and spatially and temporally dispersed interlocutors and their contributions are (ideally) knit together to one public debate via media.[25] Because of the above-mentioned normative significance for democratic politics, public debate must be open in a twofold sense. First, it is necessary that *all matters* that are considered of common interest can be publicly discussed. Second, *everyone who is affected* by a certain matter or political decision must be able to contribute to public debate about it and hence to influence the outcome through their ideas and arguments. These formal requirements are grasped by the right to freedom of expression, which is, therefore, a necessary condition of democracy.[26] There are, however, also informal preconditions; in order to fulfill the political function of public debate, participants must also be both able and willing to listen to each other and to understand the views that the respective other puts forward in public debate. They must identify and recognize each other as interlocutors participating on par in one and the same debate. Charles Taylor even argues that democracies can only function effectively and legitimately if the members of society can positively relate themselves to a common identity and thereby create a certain degree of cohesion and a sense of common belonging.[27] If, however, a subgroup of society cannot share in the dominant "common identity" or is (whether formally or informally) excluded from it, members of this group will consider that they are not listened to by their fellow members of society and that they cannot participate as equals in public debate. This again, will make them feel alienated from the process of democratic self-government; political decisions "consequently lose their legitimacy for the excluded."[28]

Against this background, authors such as Wojciech Sadurski interpret freedom of expression in the context of public debate as the right to "equal opportunity to speak and to be heard."[29] This does not mean that others are obliged to listen attentively to what somebody says, but it includes the right to have the opportunity to win the attention of willing listeners, "rather than be confined to a space from which my voice will not even reach [them]."[30] However, even if one construes freedom of expression as a right to equal opportunity to speak and to be heard and enables all members of society to convey their message to the audience they want to reach, there are further conditions that determine whether somebody succeeds in his effort to participate on par with others in public debate. On a fundamental level, presuppositions for public communication concern what Bernhard Peters refers to as "public culture": stocks of shared knowledge, norms, values and conventions, rituals, and symbols and meanings that are relevant for a public, that is "a loosely bounded mass of lay persons connected by continuous processes of cultural transmission and communication."[31] Public debate, Peters argues, is reliant on public culture since the latter includes beliefs, values, rituals, and symbols that build contexts of meaning, dispositions for attentiveness, and components for frameworks within which certain events and decisions are interpreted or justified. On the basis of a public culture it becomes possible for different people to understand statements, events, or decisions, in order to evaluate and weigh them and to communicate about them. One could object that people actually do fail to understand the contributions of others quite frequently, which seems to show that there is no "public culture" in Peters's sense, or—if there is one—that it is quite inefficient when it comes to processes of public communication. However, Peters does not claim that public culture guarantees that people understand each other, and that public culture does away with all kinds of hermeneutic and epistemological problems. Certain statements and events may sometimes be unclear, Peters points out, but they do not remain unintelligible, and can in principle be explained if they fit in with components of the respective public culture from which the shared context of meaning emerges that is required for successful public communication. In that sense, public culture is "the quintessence of facilitative and restrictive conditions of communication within a community. Public culture works like a sluice, opening and closing communicative opportunity."[32]

In the context of my discussion, it is especially important that components of public culture concern the respective community itself. These "collective interpretations" or "collective self-images" refer, for example, to the history and the current state of the respective community and to cultural, historical, or political achievements. Furthermore, they include criteria that are used to ascribe group membership to certain people and to exclude others. These collective self-images are linked with (mostly positive) self-evaluations and collective ideals on the one hand and with contrasting images of other groups and "definitions of the relations to other collectivities (as friendly or hostile and so on)" on the other hand.[33] The normative models can refer to different areas of life such as well-being, culture, morality, or politics. In the latter case, they include what Bert van den Brink calls "informal conceptions of democratic life": normative assumptions that predetermine "how citizens interpret their civic bonds in practice, who they regard as competent citizens, who they regard as incompetent, how much unity and how much diversity they think a democratic polity needs or can endure, and so on."[34] Informal conceptions of democratic life are usually rooted in dominant traditions and often represent and reproduce social power relations. They are expressed and in so doing imparted in public debate as well as in socially prevalent practices, rituals, and traditions, and they are incorporated in and shine through the visible (and audible, tangible etc.) social environment. Moreover, van den Brink points out, informal conceptions of democratic life strongly influence the way in which citizens who are differently situated within the informal power relations of society think of themselves and others in view of democratic citizenship.[35] In so doing, they influence the dominant "grammar" of public debate and determine who is recognized as competent and "respectable" contributor and what passes for a valuable contribution. This brings us to a further aspect that is important for an understanding of the preconditions of full participation in public debate which result from the normative and political character of this specific form of public communication.[36]

At first glance, and in an unspecific sense, participation in public debate could be understood as purely communicative speech act: somebody tells others his views concerning a matter of public interest. In order to succeed, it is essential for such communicative speech acts in the sense of *telling* that the hearer recognizes the speaker's intention. Even if the person who tries to communicate something (p) formulates (p) clearly, and puts it forward by using proper media—communication fails if the addressee does not recognize the speaker's intention to tell him or her (p).[37] In the case of *purely* communicative speech acts, hearer's recognition of the speaker's intention is also sufficient: as soon as the addressee recognizes my intention to tell him (p), I have succeeded. This is not the case when it comes to a different type of speech acts, which are called "communication-plus" by Mary Kate McGowan.[38] Such speech acts can only succeed if the speaker has a specific authority that is recognized by the addressee. McGowan illustrates this by means of the example of an order: "Suppose that I try to order my boss to give me a raise. Although the boss recognizes my (misguided) intention to order her to give me a raise, I nevertheless fail to do so exactly because I lack the requisite authority."[39]

Certainly, participating in public debates in democratic societies is very different from the speech act of ordering a raise. However, in certain contributions to public debate people do not merely want to tell others their views, but they put in normative claims, for instance concerning free speech and self-censorship (as *Jyllands Posten* did) or the respectful public treatment of what one considers sacred (as protestors against the publication of the Muhammad cartoons did). In doing so, contributors claim the authority of somebody who is, as member of a democratic society and on par with others, legitimately engaged in the process of self-government and in the ongoing process of developing and reshaping of society. This distinguishes public debate from other forms of public communication that do not share the normative significance for democratic politics. In order to succeed, the specific authority of the speaker as having a say in matters concerning the society in question must be recognized by the other participants of public debate. Otherwise, the speaker may be able to use his right to freedom of expression, he may even use media which are suited to convey his claims and arguments, and he may also relate to the public culture in his contributions. Nevertheless, without being recognized as somebody who has a say in matters concerning the development of society, the speaker cannot succeed to fully participate as peer in public debate, but his utterances will remain meaningless— very much like the effort of a subordinate employee to order a raise from his boss. This demonstrates that the act of participating in public debate can fail even when pure communication in the sense outlined above succeeds, because such acts "do more than just communicate propositions and there are further conditions required for doing that something more."[40]

Summing up the considerations about the normative significance of public debate and the conditions that allow for full participation in it we can conclude the following. Public debate in the sense that formed the background of *Jyllands Posten*'s concerns about self-censorship is an important means that allows members of society to exercise democratic self-government and to have a share in the ongoing development and reshaping of society. A necessary condition of public debate is the right to freedom of expression. On a more fundamental level, two further requirements have been identified. First, that people who aim to participate must be able to positively relate to the public culture including the dominant informal conceptions of democratic life since otherwise they cannot tie in with a shared context of meaning that is required for the mutual address and understanding in public communication. Second, participants in public debate must recognize each other as interlocutors who participate as equals in one and the same debate. This includes that all participants must recognize the authority of the respective others to codetermine the future development of society. Otherwise, an effort to participate as peer in public debate is bound to fail, and the person in question will be subtly and informally, but nevertheless effectively, prevented from influencing the outcome of public debate. Together, these requirements can be referred to as felicity conditions of equal participation in public debate of democratic societies.

Obstacles to Participation in Public Debate: Three Modes of Silencing

The phenomenon of silencing that I want to explore in the following can take effect in different modes. Above, I referred to silencing as the phenomenon that an effort of a person or group to participate on par with others in public debate fails because of conditions that result from actions of people other than those who are silenced. In other words, silencing occurs if the felicity conditions of equal participation in public debate are not in place because of actions of other people.[41]

A first possible mode of silencing, *formal silencing*, results from formal (for example, legal) limitations of freedom of expression or from restricted access to media that are necessary in order to be able to contribute effectively to public debate. If I am legally prohibited to express certain views in public, I am silenced with regard to these specific views, and the same applies if I am barred from the use of mass media. It is possible that there are legitimate instances of silencing, such as in cases of justified restrictions of freedom of expression (certain forms of hate speech and so forth). However, in Western European societies, such formal silencing did not occur in the controversy about the Muhammad cartoons or similar debates. Neither the publication of the cartoons nor (nonviolent) protests against it were legally forbidden in Denmark or any other European country, and both the cartoons and protests against their publication received much attention in mass media such as newspapers, television, or the Internet.

A second mode of silencing results from unacceptably high social costs that at least some people subjectively anticipate as the price they would have to pay for certain contributions to public debate. The situation of some artists and writers in Denmark (as it was described by Flemming Rose), which provided the stated reasons that brought (according to Flemming Rose) the editors of *Jyllands Posten* to publish the cartoons, can be seen as an example of this silencing through subjectively unacceptable social costs: Here, a number of potential participants in public debate refrained from exposing their views about Islam to public debate because they felt intimidated in dealing with such issues.[42] Unlike in the case of formal silencing, the legal scope of freedom of expression allows for the participation in question, here, but the level of free exercise of the liberty to publicly express one's views is reduced since potential contributors see themselves forced to shy away from participating in public debate about a certain matter, for instance because they fear retaliation.[43] In so doing they respond to an external and often informal censorship regime, not because they consider it right and legitimate but rather because of some sanctions ranging from social pressure to intimidation and threats.[44]

There are situations in which the power of this silencing through subjectively unacceptable social costs effectively approximates that of formal silencing. In such cases, Robert Audi points out, "making the exercise of a freedom costly shades into narrowing its scope."[45] Audi's analysis of a reduced level of free exercise of a liberty concerns circumstances in which the effort to exercise a freedom is unacceptably costly because the agent has to resist the pressure of a culturally, socially, or politically dominant and powerful group. "Consider someone who declines to participate in state-sponsored patriotic activities; here, and surely even in absenting oneself from state- or community-sponsored voluntary prayer sessions, one might conspicuously separate oneself from most others."[46] In such cases, Audi points out, only a courageous few will be able to resist the social pressure to participate in patriotic or religious activities, even if they consider these activities wrong, and even if they are legally permitted not to participate.

The situation of critics of Islam in countries such as Denmark and other Western European countries is structurally different from the people mentioned in Audi's example. If the felicity conditions of criticism of certain Islamic traditions in public debate are in danger of "destruction," it is not because of socially predominant pro-Islamic sentiments and expectations (like the state-sponsored patriotic and religious activities in Audi's example). Rather, the costs that could be perceived as effectively reducing the level of free exercise of freedom of expression for critics of Islam, like they are construed in Rose's sketch of the situation of some Danish artists, are related to concrete and illegal threats of violence. The problem related to this is not so much the question of how to understand this mode of silencing, since it is quite clear why people could eschew situations they consider dangerous. However, in light of the problem of religious racism sketched out above, the kind of dismantling of felicity conditions of full participation in public debate that is described in Robert Audi's example appears to be relevant for potential protestors against the Muhammad cartoons rather than for those who aim to criticize aspects of Islamic traditions they consider problematic. As I described above, Tariq Modood and others argue that the publication of the Muhammad cartoons and similar acts of expression that foster negative stereotypes of Muslims in society contribute to a social climate where Muslims are construed as alien and not welcome. In such circumstances, Muslims find themselves exposed to expressions of religious racism. This again can damage an essential precondition of peoples' effective ability to fully participate in public debate, namely the assurance that they can count on being treated respectfully and as fully recognized members of society.[47] If people cannot reasonably count on this, they have substantial disincentives to take efforts to participate in public debate—because they will be afraid of being submitted to ridicule, denigration, or group libel in public, and also because the members of the target group of religious racism "will become convinced that it is not worthwhile for them to make their points publicly."[48]

There is evidence that Muslims are often met with suspicion and hostility in several European countries, especially in controversies that concern ostensible incompatibilities between what is construed as the "modern Western culture" on the one side and "Islam" on the other.[49] In such contexts, it might well be reasonable to assume that Muslims who are already socially marginalized will be strongly discouraged from actively engaging in public debate about matters in relation to which they themselves are often portrayed as fundamentalist or anti-democratic. However, members of the Muslim community are also met with sympathy and solidarity by many of their non-Muslim fellow members of society, and Flemming Rose rightly observed that after the publication of the Muhammad cartoons, "many Muslims participated in a public dialogue—in town hall meetings, letters to editors, opinion columns, and debates on radio and TV."[50] The reason for the seeming paradox between the latter phenomenon (lively participation of Muslims in public debate) and the thesis that widespread anti-Muslim sentiments could result in Muslims' backing out of public debates about issues related to their religion can be found in the specific quality of the roots of the discouragement of participation in public debate sketched out above. The mode of being silenced under consideration here is based on disliked mental states (for example, feelings of fear, shame, denigration, or frustration) that people expect if they participated in public debate about certain matters. These mental states might have been experienced in earlier situations. Nevertheless, they do not take effect in some direct or "objective" sense but are assessed by potential participants in relation to other factors such as religious or moral considerations, expected social or economic consequences, and the expected impact of the person's (imagined) participation on the development of society. If a person assesses her social environment, which is constituted by fellow members of society, norms, customs, expectations, enduring artifacts (for example, buildings, monuments), symbolic gestures (political demonstrations, public acts of officials), and other (for example, pictorial, verbal, or written) expressions of attitudes that she considers relevant for her own sense of well-being, and if she truly comes to the conclusion that her participation in public debate would be burdened with high social costs, then it can be reasonable for her to conclude that the felicity conditions of her participation in public debate are not in place. In that case, the person feels herself affected by an informal, yet powerful censorship regime that exercises its disciplinary power through informal social sanctions.

This silencing effect of a social stigmatization of certain views or people was already pointed out by John Stuart Mill in his famous defense of freedom of expression. Contrasting "merely social intolerance" with legal restrictions on freedom of expression Mill argued that "our merely social intolerance kills no one, roots out no opinions, but induces men to disguise them, or to abstain from any active effort for their diffusion,"[51] which accords quite precisely with the mode of silencing that I just delineated. One could object that apart from cases of structural racism, where members of certain groups are systematically disrespected and discriminated against, the actual and effective power of particular social environments depends to a significant degree on the weight that is given to possibly suppressive elements. In light of this it may appear wrong to speak of silencing in the sense of the definition above, because it seems to be contradictory to claim that silencing results from actions of people other than those who are silenced while at the same time proposing that a specific mode of silencing is dependent on how those who are silenced perceive their social environment. This problem can be solved, however, if it is recognized that people who submit to an informal censorship regime that exerts its power through (expected) social sanctions and disliked mental states respectively do not do so because they agree with it, but because they estimate the (expected) social, economic, and emotional costs of rejecting it unacceptably high. They see themselves, as it were, bound to back out of public debate since they consider themselves unable to stand to the negative consequences that they expect from efforts to participate in public debate. It is true that this situation is brought about not only by acts of people other than those who are silenced but also by the contribution of others (especially those in power) to the construction of such situations is both necessary and substantial. There are, most likely, also cases where people strongly overestimate the social costs of public participation, which might lead to unreasonable instances of silencing through subjectively unacceptable social costs. However, the possibility of such cases cannot be seen as an argument against this mode of silencing in my view. Rather, it shows that the concept of silencing through subjectively unacceptable social costs can only be applied to a range of cases that can be recognized by many people who are well informed about the relevant circumstances.

A third mode of silencing concerns cases where a person's effort to participate as peer in public debate fails because the framing of the debate and the underlying public culture (including informal conceptions of democratic life) preclude that the person's authority to competently and legitimately codetermine the development of society is recognized. Unlike in the case of formal silencing, a person experiencing this mode of silencing enjoys full freedom of expression and has access to the relevant mass media, and unlike somebody who is silenced in the sense of silencing through subjectively unacceptable social costs, the person affected from this third mode of silencing does not expect that exposing her views to public debate will result in significant informal social sanctions. Nevertheless, the effort of persons to fully participate in public debate can fail because specific discursive patterns bring about that particular (groups of) members of society are denied the status of competent interlocutors and that certain types of contributions appear as not worthy of consideration or even illegitimate in the eyes of others. This mode of silencing can be referred to as *silencing through communicative disablement*.

To understand this mode of silencing in the context of debates such as that about the Muhammad cartoons it is useful to refer to the above-mentioned concept of a public culture and the requirement that in order to be able to participate on par with others, a person's authority to codetermine the ongoing development and shaping of society must be recognized by other members of society.

Above I pointed out that the concept public culture refers to a stock of knowledge, beliefs, meanings, symbols, rituals, or values that are shared by a large part of a group of people living together in a society. Public communication among these people is facilitated by public culture since the latter provides a shared context of meaning within which statements, events, and decisions can be understood and evaluated. The counterpart of this communication-enabling function of public culture, however, is that it also limits communication processes in various ways. For the Muhammad cartoon controversy, it could be argued that such a limitation could have resulted from a possible incompatibility of different notions of religion and religious or moral insult on different sides of the debate. Saba Mahmood, for instance, explained that certain moral claims against the cartoons remained elusive, or even incomprehensible for most participants of the debate, because they were based on a specific form of piety and religious subjectivity that did not accord with the understanding of religion that dominated the debate.[52] For some Muslims, Mahmood points out, religion is embodied practice and their relation to Muhammad a relationship of intimacy and similitude.[53] Such people experience the kind of moral injury brought about by the publication of the Muhammad cartoons as profound violation which emanates "from the perception that one's being, grounded as it is in a relationship of dependency with the Prophet, has been shaken."[54] This sense of violation, and the underlying notion of religion, differs from the (implicitly normative) understanding of religion in the context of modern democratic societies that formed the basis of the predominant framing of the public debate about the cartoons in terms of a conflict between the principles of (a specific understanding of) blasphemy and freedom of expression. In large parts of the debate, Mahmood points out, both the cartoons and Muslim's anger against their publication were interpreted on the basis of a "modern concept of religion . . . as a set of propositions in a set of beliefs to which the individual gives assent."[55] Modern believers in that sense, it was claimed, should be able to take a critical distance to their religion, especially to symbols, forms, and images that are, according to this view, not to be confused with the "real essence" of religion. Muslims who protested against the cartoons, however, were construed as fundamentalist or incompetent in a specific and politically relevant sense: they appeared to "exhibit an improper reading practice, collapsing the [according to that "modern" understanding of religion, ChrB] necessary distinction between the subject (the divine status attributed to Muhammad) and the object (pictorial depictions of Muhammad)."[56] This means that the insult that constituted the main problem of the cartoons in the eyes of a particular group of pious Muslims remained to a large extent unintelligible for other members of society.

This hampering of communication can be reformulated with reference to public culture. As Charles Taylor has demonstrated, the default understanding of religion in modern Western cultures accords with the notion of religion that Saba Mahmood identified as underlying the dominant framing of the Muhammad cartoons controversy.[57] This "secular" understanding of religion as set of beliefs to which a person gives assent underlies not only practices of worship but is also part of the broader social imaginary that determines practices such as economy and public debate; in other words, it is an integral part of the public culture that provides contexts of meaning within which public communication in Western societies takes place. In view of this, it could be argued that contributions to public debate, which are not based on such a secular understanding of religion but are premised, for example, on the form of religion as embodied practices that Saba Mahmood identified in certain traditions of Muslim piety, cannot smoothly tie in with the dominant public culture. As a result, they can be misinterpreted, or ignored.

But does this form of hampering, if not failure, of communication constitute an instance of silencing in the sense outlined above? If it is true that the incongruity of forms of religious subjectivity on different sides of the debate hampers full participation of groups of pious Muslims (and quite likely also members of other religions) in public debate, does this result from actions of people other than those whose effort to participate in public debate on par with others fails? It could be argued that this is not the case, and that the incongruity of important concepts, meanings, and other elements of different public cultures is a given that cannot reasonably be traced back to particular actions. However, in the case of controversies such as the one about the Muhammad cartoons I suggest an interpretation of distortions of public debate that goes beyond Mahmood's observations and that is based on analyses of the dynamics of the debate as a whole, and that points to the activation of exclusionary elements of a public culture and informal conceptions of democratic life respectively. This activation occurs especially through acts that function as expressive gestures that carry messages, albeit often unintentionally, which are taken as reflections of authoritative attitudes and emotional or mental states of people, groups, or institutions.

Processes of public communication are enabled by public culture. However, the relationship between public culture and public communication is not unidirectional. On the one hand, the elements that constitute a public culture, can be invoked as valid, authoritative beliefs or values and thereby provide cornerstones of shared contexts of meaning and dispositions of attentiveness, appreciation, and rejection. On the other hand, as Peters points out, they can also "be questioned, criticized, contested and, in response, defended or supported."[58] In that sense, public culture is always subject to a process of both reproduction and transformation under the influence of social interactions that are enabled by public culture itself, which puts people who are able to seamlessly tie in with important elements of public culture in a privileged position. Certain constellations of public debate, however, can effectively impede the questioning or examination—and hence the possible transformation—of predominant beliefs, norms, and other elements of public culture. In this regard, Peters identified various forms of "closure": "The exclusion of participants from the sphere of deliberation, the denial of respect, either because viewpoints are seen as unreasonable or evil, or because the speakers are suspected of questionable motives or false consciousness. There are more ways, however, in which discussions can be restricted or closed. Orthodoxies or unquestioned authority can be maintained, unusual arguments or viewpoints ignored, misunderstood or distorted."[59]

In the Muhammad cartoons controversy such forms of closure were activated from the very beginning of the debate by positioning both the cartoons and Muslims' protests against them in a framework characterized by a publicly construed opposition between enlightened defenders of democracy and freedom of expression on one hand, and fundamentalist, anti-democratic religious extremists on the other hand. Carsten Juste, for instance, editor in chief of *Jyllands Posten* in 2005, claimed that Muslims who publicly represent Islam in Denmark were voices from "a dark and violent middle age" and beset by a "sickly oversensitivity" to critique.[60] Shortly after the publication of the cartoons, eleven ambassadors and delegates representing Muslim countries in Denmark sent a letter to the Danish Prime Minister Rasmussen. They protested against what they described as "an on-going smearing campaign in Danish public circles and media against Islam," and asked for a meeting. Rasmussen turned down this request. "Free speech goes so far," he stated, "and the Danish government has no influence on what the press writes." Furthermore, he claimed that it was "so obvious what our basic principles are that there is no basis for having a meeting."[61] Rasmussen's refusal to even meet the representatives, and listen to them, was seen as a gesture of hostility and lack of understanding. Much like Carsten Juste's statement, Rasmussen's refusal publicly expressed that in Denmark complaints against acts that were perceived as offensive or disrespectful by members of the Danish Muslim community were considered illegitimate from the outset, and not deserving further consideration.[62] The ostentatious republication of the cartoons by several major newspapers in Europe could be construed as a gesture that expresses a similar message. The framing of the controversy in terms of modern and enlightened Westerners versus fundamentalist and anti-democratic Muslims was certainly not a product of mere fantasy or Islamophobic resentments; reactions to the publication of the cartoons actually did include violent protests and attacks on Danish embassies and death threats against cartoonists and editors provided some evidence for a supposed adequacy of such an approach. The problem, however, that is important for the understanding of *silencing through communicative disablement* is that gestures such as the prime minister's refusal to even listen to the concerns of Muslim representatives, the republication of the cartoons by many media "in the name of freedom of expression," but also violent protests against the cartoons strongly influenced the hermeneutic framework within which all kinds of reactions to the cartoons were interpreted. This made it very easy to construe large parts of the opposition against the cartoons as evidence of an ostensible "clash of civilizations" and a fundamental incompatibility of liberal democracy and Islam.[63] An interpretation of all kinds of protests of believers against the publication of the Muhammad cartoons as expression of anti-democratic attitudes is remarkable inasmuch as the vast majority of Muslims and other opponents of the cartoons in Europe used perfectly legitimate means to express their discontent, including writing letters to the editor, demonstrating, or suing newspapers that had published the cartoons.[64] So how could this be possible?

The abovementioned concept of public culture enables us to understand the processes that made it possible and even likely to construe objections against the cartoons in public debate as anti-democratic and fundamentalist interventions. The predominant framing of the debate in terms of modern and enlightened Westerners versus fundamentalist and anti-democratic Muslims activated and reinforced elements of public culture which concern collective self-images of the (traditional) community and contrasting images of other groups. On the basis of these collective images, the abovementioned forms of closure of public debate could take effect. This again fostered ways of dealing with protests against the cartoons that placed these protests (and the protestors) outside the realm of public debate about the future development of society.[65] In this process, the function of gestures and acts that are taken as symbolic expressions of hostility or lack of understanding of what is construed as "foreign" can be compared to the role of the (semi)permanent visible social environment that Jeremy Waldron identified as important factor in processes of social interactions. Both visible and tangible objects and acts that are taken as gestures of authoritative attitudes, values, and predominant customs shape the realm and the grammar of public debate and hence the felicity conditions of certain forms of participation. Since participation in public debate is a politically relevant act, these felicity conditions are strongly influenced by dominant informal conceptions of democratic life that is by ideas and ideals concerning democratic citizenship, social unity, and legitimate forms of diversity. In the case of the Muhammad cartoons controversy as well as in other debates about matters concerning the role and status of certain religious traditions in liberal-democratic and pluralistic societies, the debate was dominated by ideals of democratic citizenship that included mainly secular and liberal-individualistic norms, ideals, and values. Far from being religiously neutral, these normative elements are in a tense relationship to forms of religion that differ from the secular understanding of religion as a system of propositional beliefs. Mahmood's argument is in line with this, but the decisive point is that a framing of the debate in terms of modern and enlightened Westerners versus fundamentalist and antidemocratic Muslims can activate elements of public culture that make the protestors appear in the eyes of their fellow citizens as not being contributors to but enemies of democratic debate. To put it in terms of the philosophy of language: in certain circumstances, the dynamics of debates such as those about the publication of the Muhammad cartoons can make it hard if not impossible for protestors against such religiously offensive acts that their fellow citizens recognize their intention, competence, and authority to participate as equals in public debate about the development of democratic society. If this is the case, the felicity conditions of participation in public debate are not in place, and an effort to participate as equal in public debate cannot succeed. This can be understood as silencing through communicative disablement if and inasmuch as it results from acts or social circumstances that are outside of the control of those whose efforts to participate in public debate are bound to fail. The considerations above do not show that this was actually the case in the Muhammad cartoons controversy; they indicate, however, that in cases like this controversy, silencing through communicative disablement is a real threat to the possibility of some citizens to participate as equals in public debate and to codetermine the development of the society of which they are a member.

"Counterspeech"? Concluding Remarks from the Perspective of Political Ethics

In this essay I explored possible distortions of public debate about acts that are perceived as offensive by numerous believers. I argued that in certain cases these distortions can prevent the felicity conditions of particular forms of participation in public debate such as peaceful but passionate protests against religiously offensive acts from coming into place. This phenomenon of silencing can take different modes of which I discussed formal silencing, silencing through subjectively unacceptable social costs, and silencing through communicative disablement. I did not argue that these modes of silencing actually took effect in the controversy about the Muhammad cartoons. However, analyses of this and other debates that were carried out by social scientists and scholars from media studies indicate that in Western European societies both silencing through subjectively unacceptable social costs and silencing through communicative disablement are possible threats to democratic culture rather than fictitious scenarios.[66]

In light of the above, the often-heard suggestion that believers should fight religiously offensive acts with counterspeech (including public protests and petitions to politicians and other authorities) turns out to be insufficiently precise and needs to be specified. If it is possible that people, who claim to be profoundly offended by certain acts or who see themselves as target of religious racism mediated by, for example, images that denigrate their religion, can be silenced in public debate, then it does not suffice to prompt these people to express their discontent in public. For the problem of the phenomenon of silencing through communicative disablement does also exist for the courageous few who have the fortitude to stand possible social pressure and who are not discouraged by possibly extraordinary social costs of their counterspeech.

In order to deal with the phenomenon of silencing from a political or ethical perspective, I suggest understanding the prevention of equal participation in public debate in the sense of the second and the third mode of silencing as being structurally similar to the destruction or pollution of public goods such as certain environmental goods (for example, clean water or fresh air). Such goods can be destroyed through accumulated actions of many people who often do not even know that they contribute to the pollution of, for instance, fresh air or, as I suggest, to the dismantling of felicity conditions of equal participation in public debate.[67] Accordingly, the ascription of responsibility to particular individuals is difficult, if not impossible. Moreover, it is far from clear that actions which can possibly contribute to the second or the third mode of silencing, such as the publication of the Muhammad cartoons or public criticism of protests against religiously offensive acts as expression of religious squeamishness or religious fundamentalism, are to be considered illegitimate in and of themselves. An obligation not to contribute at all to circumstance that can result in the phenomenon of silencing in the sense outlined above, can hardly be justified within the normative framework that provides the basis of liberal democratic and pluralistic societies. However, since every citizen of a democratic society has a right to participate as equal in public debate about the future development of society, there is an obligation to guard the felicity conditions of equal participation in public debate from being dismantled as a cumulative result of numerous actions that all contribute a little, in itself seemingly insignificant bit. In light of the above, the addressee of such an obligation cannot be every single individual—otherwise virtually all criticism of peaceful but passionate protests against religiously offensive acts would be illegitimate. Rather, I suggest construing the prevention of a dismantling of felicity conditions of equal participation in public debate as collective civic responsibility of society as a whole. This includes the requirement that all members of society articulate counterspeech if felicity conditions for full participation of others are under pressure. Such a demand can be understood as exercise of solidarity with those who are in danger to be silenced. The good that is protected, however, is public debate in general, and the necessary social arrangements that permit all members of society to participate as equals in public debate about the development of society.

Notes

1. In this essay I use the expression *religiously offensive acts* in a broad sense, denoting acts that are experienced as vilification or denigration of religion or religious beliefs, symbols, traditions, or figures by a significant number of believers.

2. See, for example, Talal Asad, *Formations of the Secular: Christianity, Islam, Modernity* (Stanford, CA: Stanford University Press, 2003), 159–180; Wolfgang Benz, *Die Feinde aus dem Morgenland: Wie die Angst vor den Muslimen unsere Demokratie gefährdet* (Munich: C. H. Beck, 2012); Jan Willem Duyvendak, Ewald Engelen, and Ido de Haan, *Het bange Nederland* (Amsterdam: Uitgeverij Bert Bakker, 2008); Martha Nussbaum, *The New Religious Intolerance* (Cambridge, MA: Harvard University Press, 2012); and Sipco J. Vellenga, "De islam in de beklaagdenbank: Het integratiedebat in Nederland," *Nederlands Theologische Tijdschrift* 62, no. 1 (2008): 1–23.

3. Joel Feinberg, *Offense to Others: The Moral Limits of Criminal Law*, vol. 2 (New York: Oxford University Press, 1985), 2.

4. Simon Weaver, "Liquid Racism and the Danish Prophet Muhammad Cartoons," *Current Sociology* 58, no. 5 (2010): 682. For the claim that (Christian) believers ascribe their feelings of hurt, anger, and grief to (in their eyes) wrongful conduct of others see also Anthony Fisher and Hayden Ramsay, "Of Art and Blasphemy," *Ethical Theory and Moral Practice* 3 (2000): 141–144.

5. Feinberg, *Offense to Others*, 50–60.

6. See Feinberg, 14–22; 57–58. Feinberg also speaks of "affronts to one's lower order sensibilities" in that context.

7. Feinberg, 58.

8. Feinberg, 59.

9. Jytte Klausen, *The Cartoons that Shook the World* (New Haven, CT: Yale University Press), 6. In view of Rose's statement it is noteworthy that Joel Feinberg points out: "The sacred is something not to joke about or treated lightly, something beyond mockery, presumption, and indignity. Something or other is sacred, in this sense, to almost everyone, atheist and theist alike. The person to whom nothing at all is sacred is the person who can laugh at anything—the suffering of children, the victims of genocide, and libels on his loved ones, as well as mockery of his gods." Feinberg, *Offense to Others*, 193.

10. Feinberg, *Offense to Others*, 16.

11. This is shown by research of Saba Mahmood, who reports on devout Muslims who expressed a "sense of personal loss," "a sense of grief and sorrow," and "hurt, loss, and injury" on hearing about or seeing the Muhammad cartoons. Saba Mahmood, "Religious Reason and Secular Affect: An Incommensurable Divide?," in *Is Critique Secular? Blasphemy, Injury, and Free Speech*, ed. Talal Asad, Wendy Brown, Judith Butler and Saba Mahmood (Berkeley: University of California Press, 2009), 74–75. One of the people she

interviewed expressed this as follows: "I would have felt less wounded if the object of ridicule were my own parents. And you know how hard it is to have bad things said about your parents, especially when they are deceased. But to have the Prophet scorned and abused this way, that was too much to bear!" (75). Saba Mahmood provides an elaborated explanation of the sense of moral injury that was felt by devout Muslims in view of the Muhammad cartoons. She emphasizes that an adequate understanding of this sense of moral injury can be adequately understood if the relationship of a Muslim with the Prophet Muhammad is conceived as relationship of intimacy and as predicated upon an assimilative model (where the being of a devout Muslim is grounded in a relationship of dependency with Muhammad; "one wants to ingest, as it were, the Prophet's persona into oneself") rather than upon a communicative or representative one (where *Muhammad* refers to a particular historical figure and the Prophet's words and life are normative as commandments) (75). That this is (mutatis mutandis) not a specific feature of Islamic piety is indicated by a striking similarity between Mahmood's reports and a statement of a correspondent in a Melbourne newspaper in the controversy about the exhibition of Serrano's *Piss Christ* in Melbourne: "Think of the one person you love more than anyone else in this world, the person you look to for guidance and support, the person who is with you in good times and bad. Now take an image of that person, immerse in urine, take a picture, hang it in the National Gallery, and call it art." Fisher and Ramsey, "Of Art and Blasphemy," 142.

12. See Feinberg, *Offense to Others*, 2.

13. See Bhikhu Parekh, *Rethinking Multiculturalism: Cultural Diversity and Political Theory*, 2nd ed. (New York: Palgrave Macmillan, 2006), 313.

14. Parekh, *Rethinking Multiculturalism*, 313.

15. See Parekh, 313.

16. For the following, see Tariq Modood, *Multicultural Politics: Muslims, Ethnicity, and Racism in Britain* (Minneapolis: University of Minnesota Press, 2005).

17. See Modood, 104. This process does not exclusively apply to Muslims, of course. Rather, Modood points out similarities between what he calls the current racialization of Muslims and the older but still effective history of racialization of Jews in the course of which "a faith group turned into a 'race.' More precisely, the latter did not so much replace the former but superimposed itself. No one denied that Jews were a religious community with a distinctive language(s), culture(s), and religion but they also came to be seen as a race." Tariq Modood, "Obstacles to Multicultural Integration," *International Migration* 44, no. 5 (2006): 56. With reference to the cartoons that depict Muhammad with a bomb in his turban or as grim man holding a sword with two women wearing burqas behind him, Modood points out: "If the message was meant to be that non-Muslims have the right to draw Muhammad, it has come out very differently: that the Prophet of Islam was a terrorist. Moreover, the cartoons are not just about one individual but about Muslims per se—just as a cartoon portraying Moses as a crooked financier would not be about one man but a comment on Jews. And just as the latter would be racist, so are the cartoons in question." Tariq Modood, "The Liberal Dilemma: Integration or Vilification?," *International Migration* 44, no. 5 (2006): 4.

18. See Klausen, *Cartoons that Shook the World*, 13–20; and Flemming Rose, "Why I Published Those Cartoons," *Washington Post*, February 19, 2006, http://www.washingtonpost.com/wp-dyn/content/article/2006/02/17/AR2006021702499.html.

19. Rose, "Why I Published Those Cartoons."

20. I refer to *gestures* in the sense of actions and other forms (for example, pictures, films, or monuments) that express attitudes, thoughts, or feelings and that are received as being more than spoken or written expressions. This goes beyond a narrower understanding of gestures as *bodily* movements that are expressive of thoughts, attitudes, emotions, and so forth. See Adam Kendon, "Gestures," *Annual Review of Anthropology* 26, no. 1 (1997): 109–128.

21. Robert Post, "Religion and Freedom of Speech: Portraits of Muhammad," *Philosophy and Public Affairs* 14, no. 1 (2007): 74. See also Robert Post, "Democracy and Equality," *Annals of the American Academy of Political and Social Science* 603 (2006): 24–36.

22. See Klausen, *Cartoons That Shook the World*.

23. Jeremy Waldron, *The Harm in Hate Speech* (Cambridge, MA: Harvard University Press, 2012), 37.

24. Waldron, 74. Against this background Waldron proposes a "political aesthetics" that investigates the subtle power of our visible social environment in general and such things as monuments, cenotaphs, and public architecture in particular. For an art historic analysis of public monuments and their possible effects as permanent political propaganda, see Sergiusz Michalski, *Public Monuments 1870–1997: Art in Political Bondage* (London: Reaktion Books, 1998). On the use of symbolic expressions and artifacts (such as memorials or statutes) in the context of social conflicts and different ways of settling them, see Marc Howard Ross, *Cultural Contestation in Ethnic Conflict* (Cambridge: Cambridge University Press, 2007).

25. See Charles Taylor, *Dilemmas and Connections: Selected Essays* (Cambridge, MA: Harvard University Press), 124–145.

26. Post, "Religion and Freedom of Speech," 76.

27. See Taylor, *Dilemmas and Connections*, 124–145. In a similar vein, Bernhard Peters argues that members of public debate need to identify themselves as politically relevant public sphere and "create a *collective public identity*." Bernhard Peters, *Public Deliberation and Public Culture: The Writings of Bernhard Peters 1993–2005*, ed. H. Wessler (New York: Palgrave Macmillan, 2008), 9.

28. Taylor, *Dilemmas and Connections*, 129.

29. See Wojciech Sadurksi, *Freedom of Speech and Its Limits* (Dordrecht: Kluwer Academic Publishers), 73–98, and Asad, *Formations of the Secular*, 184.

30. Sadurksi, *Freedom of Speech*, 97. Sadurski quotes a number of court decisions in First Amendment cases in the United States that show that the understanding of freedom of expression as a right to equal opportunity to speak and to be heard is supported by judicial doctrine as well.

31. Peters, *Public Deliberation and Public Culture*, 70. For the following, see also Peters, 69–76 and 219–221. That the elements of a public culture are "relevant" to a public

means that they are at least to a great extent accessible to, known by, addressed to, and circulating among a public.

32. Hartmut Wessler and Lutz Wingert, "Study of the Public Sphere: Bernhard Peters' Interest and Contribution," in Peters, *Public Deliberation and Public Culture*, 1–13, 5.

33. Peters, *Public Deliberation and Public Culture*, 72.

34. Bert van den Brink, "Imagining Civic Relations in the Moment of Their Breakdown: A Crisis of Civic Integrity in the Netherlands," in *Multiculturalism and Political Theory*, ed. Anthony Simon Laden and David Owen (Cambridge: Cambridge University Press, 2007), 354. See also Danielle S. Allen, *Talking to Strangers, Anxieties of Citizenship since Brown v. Board of Education* (Chicago: University of Chicago Press, 2004).

35. Allen, *Talking to Strangers*, 355.

36. Following Bernhard Peters I understand public communication in the sense of "freely accessible communication, without formal restrictions or special conditions for participation" such as specific expertise or membership in a particular association. "In public communication, all interested lay persons are free to participate, to listen or to read and to speak their mind." Peters, *Public Deliberation and Public Culture*, 76. For the distinctions between different kinds of speech acts that I delineate in the following, see Jennifer Hornsby, "Illocution and Its Significance," in *Foundations of Speech Act Theory*, ed. Savas L. Tsohatzidis (London: Routledge, 1994), 187–207; and Mary Kate McGowan, "On Silencing and Sexual Refusal," *Journal of Political Philosophy* 17, no. 4 (2009): 487–494. Both authors do not refer to the example of public debate, however.

37. See McGowan, "On Silencing and Sexual Refusal," and Hornsby, "Illocution and its Significance," 193.

38. McGowan, "On Silencing and Sexual Refusal."

39. McGowan.

40. McGowan.

41. Silencing, as it is understood here, does not presuppose that the person who is silenced, actually possessed the necessary possibilities to participate in public debate earlier and that she is more or less actively bereaved of possibilities that she actually had.

42. Rose, "Why I Published Those Cartoons."

43. For the distinction between the legal scope of liberty and the level of free exercise of it, see Robert Audi, "The Separation of Church and State and the Obligations of Citizenship," *Philosophy and Public Affairs* 18, no. 3 (1989): 267.

44. I borrow the concept of "censorship regimes" from Philip Cook and Conrad Heilmann. According to Cook and Heilmann the common goal of censorship regimes "is to create a fit between what they allow to be expressed and what is actually expressed by censees. In pursuing this goal, censors will normally have an implicit or explicit view on the content and mode of permitted and proscribed expressions. A censorship regime may object to certain kinds of content that offend against public decency or religious orthodoxy, or a censorship regime may object to how views are expressed." Philip Cook and Conrad Heilmann, "Two Types of Self-Censorship: Public and Private," *Political Studies* 60 (2012): 3. Censorship regimes can differ substantively in the means and the

manner of their enforcement. "Different censorship regimes may rely on their power to suppress expression, for example by closing down newspapers or preventing access to the internet, while others may use their moral or institutional authority to enforce" (4).

45. Audi, "Separation of Church and State," 267.

46. Audi, 267.

47. See Waldron, *Harm in Hate Speech*, 81–89.

48. Sadurski, *Freedom of Speech and its Limits*, 109.

49. See Benz, *Die Feinde aus dem Morgenland*; José Casanova, "Immigration and the New Religious Pluralism: A European Union/United States Comparison," in *Democracy and the New Religious Pluralism*, ed. Thomas Banchoff (Oxford: Oxford University Press, 2007), 59–83; Modood, "Liberal Dilemma," 5; Nussbaum, *New Religious Intolerance*.

50. Rose, "Why I Published Those Cartoons."

51. John Stuart Mill, "On Liberty," in *J. S. Mill: Utilitarianism and on Liberty*, ed. Mary Warnock (Oxford: Blackwell Publishing, 2003), 112.

52. See Mahmood, "Religious Reason and Secular Affect." In her analysis of the cartoon controversy and of a specific form of the relationship between pious Muslims and Muhammad, Saba Mahmood offers an alternative understanding of the kind of injury that was caused by the publication of the cartoons. I will focus on but one specific aspect of her analysis. For a critical discussion of Mahmood's position, see Andrew F. March, "Speech and the Sacred: Does the Defense of Free Speech Rest on a Mistake about Religion?" *Political Theory* 40, no. 3 (2012): 319–346; and Yolande Jansen, "Postsecularism, Piety and Fanaticism: Reflections on Jürgen Habermas' and Saba Mahmood's Critiques of Secularism," *Philosophy and Social Criticism* 37, no. 9 (2011): 977–998.

53. See Mahmood, "Religious Reason and Secular Affect," 72.

54. Mahmood, 78

55. Mahmood, 72.

56. Mahmood, 73. See also Christian F. Rostbøll's claim that in the Muhammad cartoons controversy, "Muslims were seen as insufficiently enlightened because they take their religion too seriously. . . . The underlying norm was that one ought to keep a critical distance to one's commitments, particularly if these are religious commitments." Christian F. Rostbøll, "Autonomy, Respect and Arrogance in the Danish Cartoon Controversy," *Political Theory* 37, no. 5 (2009): 626.

57. See Charles Taylor, *A Secular Age* (Cambridge, MA: Harvard University Press, 2007).

58. Peters, *Public Deliberation and Public Culture*, 110.

59. Peters, 115. Peters refers to public deliberation here, but the same applies to nondeliberative forms of public communication.

60. Klausen, *Cartoons That Shook the World*, 13.

61. Klausen, 34–37, 186.

62. Jytte Klausen points out that the response of Dutch officials to Geert Wilders anti-Islamic video *Fitna* was much more balanced and contributed to a de-escalation of the controversy. See Jytte Klausen, "Nederland slimmer dan Denemarken," *NRC Han-*

delsblad, March 8, 2008, http://vorige.nrc.nl/nieuwsthema/film_wilders/article 1884628.ece/Nederland_slimmer_dan_Denemarken.

63. A tendency to construe opposition against the cartoons as evidence of an ostensible incompatibility of liberal democracy and Islam was identified in an analysis of the media treatment of the debate about the cartoons in Denmark and France that was carried out by social scientists Carolina Boe and Peter Hervik. See Carolina Boe and Peter Hervik, "Integration through Insult?," in *Transnational Media Events. The Mohammed Cartoons and the Imagined Clash of Civilizations*, ed. Elisabeth Eide, Risto Kunelius and Angela Phillips (Gothenburg: Nordicom, 2008), 213–234. See also Klausen, *Cartoons that Shook the World*.

64. See Carolina Boe and Peter Hervik, "Integration through Insult?," 214.

65. See Peters, *Public Deliberation and Public Culture*, 104. Increasing closure of public debate is supported also by a "fixation" of existing collective self-images including predominant notions of culture, religion, citizenship, and so forth. This results in a strong conservative-assimilationist impulse: People who want to fully participate in the public debate about social institutions and developments first have to assimilate the predominant customs, including the forms of addressing religion that they may consider offensive. "Either you assimilate and are with us or you belong to a backward culture and thus exclude yourself from participation in our democratic game." Van den Brink, "Imagining Civic Relations," 359–360. Van den Brink refers here to the Dutch debate about immigration and Islam after the murder of Theo van Gogh in November 2004.

66. See Benz, *Die Feinde aus dem Morgenland*.

67. See Waldron, *Harm in Hate Speech*, 97.

CHAPTER 17

Offending Muslims

Provocation, Blasphemy, and Public Debate in the Netherlands

Martijn de Koning

On August 28, 2004, the Dutch daily newspaper *NRC Handelsblad* announced that the film *Submission*, a joint effort of the by then well-known politician of Somali origin Hirsi Ali and the filmmaker Theo van Gogh, was going to be "a new provocation by Hirsi Ali."[1] The word *new* drew attention to earlier provocative actions by Hirsi Ali, such as when she commented that the Prophet Muhammad, by today's standards, was a pedophile. The film was intended to critique violence against Muslim women by Muslim men, which, Hirsi Ali claimed, was legitimized or even incited by the Koran. *Submission* was aired on national television and managed to elicit many angry responses, although few Muslims actually saw it. Later that year, Van Gogh, who had taken to speaking of Muslims and their Prophet as "goat fuckers," was assassinated by a young Moroccan-Dutchman.

On November 27, 2007, another newspaper, the *Telegraaf*, reported that the populist anti-Islam politician Geert Wilders would be making a "provocative" film,[2] displaying the Koran in a "*Submission*-like" style. The film *Fitna*, the title of which was translated by Wilders as "beproeving,"[3] was to expose the evil character of the Islam's holy book. The Koran, Wilders pontificated, is a fascist text that incites its believers to violence and hatred. Being one of the most outspoken Dutch politicians on issues concerning security, immigration, Islam, and Muslims in the Netherlands, Wilders has long warned against the "tsunami of Islamization" that would result from showing leniency toward Islam.

These two films are not isolated incidents. In the years between the launching of *Submission* and *Fitna*, the Danish newspaper *Jylland Posten* published a number of cartoons satirizing the Prophet Muhammad. Protests in European, Middle Eastern, and South Asian countries made headlines. In 2012, a trailer of the film *The Innocence of Muslims*, broadcast via YouTube, depicted the Prophet Muhammad as violent and a sex maniac.[4] Protests in Egypt and Libya sparked off even more protests in other parts of the world. The visual rhetoric in all of these cases led to a heated debate about freedom of speech and blasphemy.

In this essay I offer a different interpretation of these controversies by focusing on the events that followed the announcement of *Submission* and *Fitna*. I argue that both films are performances, conducted by two Dutch politicians, which stimulated a series of events and debates to take place in which the multidimensionality of people's lives and ideas was reduced to a simple opposition between freedom of speech and blasphemy. Taking this opposition as a performative act by politicians seeking support, polarization, and the creation of a common enemy cannot be understood without understanding Dutch secular politics.

Muslims, as I will show, to a large extent played only a walk-on part. They hardly took part in the debates themselves, but the image of "angry Muslims" is repeated throughout these episodes by Hirsi Ali and Wilders as well as their political opponents. First, I examine the content of the films. I show how both films work with a similar logic designed to create controversy and how Hirsi Ali and Wilders performed their role as controversial politicians who opened up new avenues of debate. Through their films, Hirsi Ali and Wilders unsettled and challenged the accepted norms of public debate protected by other politicians who deemed the films provocative. Then I explain how the various responses were reduced to a simple dichotomy between free speech and blasphemy by invoking the image of the threatening angry Muslim—an image that enabled secular liberalism to discipline and organize itself against so-called radical Muslims and against Wilders and Hirsi Ali as they all threatened the secular-liberal status quo.

Rituals of Antagonism: *Submission* and *Fitna*

Both films work by using a standard set of symbolic actions that may provoke violence or imply the possibility of violent response. These actions can be seen as *rituals of provocation*, such as were studied by Marc Gaborieau in another context of intercommunal discord: codified procedures of deliberate disrespect, desecration, blasphemy, and the violation of sacred or symbolically charged spaces, times, or objects.[5] First, a selection is made of key symbols representing each community, and, as a second step, the means are chosen by which these symbols might be most effectively desecrated. The third, more ambiguous stage is that of the actual effect that the symbolic actions have. The actions are designed to have a particular effect, and in order for these to "work," they have to tap into deeply felt concerns. The makers, therefore, have to be aware of their audience. What they are doing must resonate with them and create and galvanize (perhaps conflicting) social solidarities, and the audience has to be activated and persuaded to participate in the ritual.

Fitna, *Submission*, the Muhammad cartoons, and the short film *The Innocence of Muslims* contain images of the Prophet Muhammad and the Koran, and they highlight the position of women in Islam. Hirsi Ali's film, directed and produced by Theo van Gogh, was the first example of a member of parliament using a visual method to disseminate a message. According to Hirsi Ali, this was a necessary step in breaking the taboo on discussing the relationship between Islam and domestic violence. Hirsi Ali and Van Gogh projected verses from the Koran onto the semi-naked bodies of four women who represented female Muslims. In so doing they intended to depict the abuse of Muslim women as a direct result of the misogyny of Islam.

In Wilders's film *Fitna*, the Koran itself is targeted. Wilders announced that the film would end with a particular depiction of the Prophet Muhammad and an exposé of the fascist and intolerant nature of the Koran. The film consists of four parts. In the first part, a number of verses from the Koran are shown (with tendentious translations and taken out of context). The second part uses clips featuring "radical" preachers calling for violence, and in the third part a selection of headlines from Dutch newspapers purports to document Wilders's claim of the "creeping Islamization" of Dutch society. The fourth part shows one of the Muhammad cartoons (the face with a bomb as a turban), while the soundtrack features pages being torn from a book—Wilders had hinted in advance that the film would show him tearing pages from the Koran, so that the hint was obvious.

Hirsi Ali's and Wilders's ritual of antagonism, in which they tendentiously target particular key symbols of a specific category of people is carefully constructed and interacts with the political context of the moment. The images of the Koran, terrorist attacks, headlines, women with Koranic verses on their bodies are distortions and reductions of a multidimensional Islamic tradition and symbolize a more abstract idea of the "threat of Islam." Their rhetoric is certainly not shared by all the Dutch political parties (on the contrary, as I will show below). However, it is important to note that since the September 11 attacks, the debates about migration, multiculturalism, and citizenship in both parliament and the media have increasingly been framed in terms of "Islam as a threat."[6] Irrespective of what their real views may be, many politicians of mainstream political parties have implicitly come to take it for granted that the presence of Muslims in the Netherlands is a problem that needs to be addressed, and that the success or failure of integration of (Muslim) immigrants has to be measured by a secular yardstick. The main difference between Wilders and Hirsi Ali and the mainstream political parties is that the latter think Islam can (and should be) changed into something compatible with secular liberalism, whereas the former are convinced that the very essence of Islam is immutable and violent and therefore inherently incompatible with Dutch society.[7]

Both films were designed to evoke responses within the particular political context outlined here. In a double interview with Hirsi Ali and Van Gogh (published in *NRC Handelsblad*), Hirsi Ali stated that she hoped or expected the film to be offensive (although the day after the first screening she had claimed she was unhappy that the newspapers had interpreted the film as a provocation):

"This is going to be worse than 'Muhammad is a pervert.' . . . The whole Muslim world is going to attack me. . . ."

"Can I let you consider another creepy scenario?," Van Gogh says. "What if there are no Muslims who take offence? If they say, 'it is the product of two loose cannons: you and me.'"

Hirsi Ali laughs out loud: "Then I'm going to marry and have children."[8]

In making a film presenting Islam as violent and intolerant, the makers intended to provoke responses that would confirm their claims. Their project would fail if it failed to produce "angry Muslims."

Wilders stated that he intended his film as a new way of pursuing a debate on liberal freedoms: "I want to provoke a discussion. Certain Koranic verses have moved their followers to commit the most abhorrent acts. Where is the imam who stands up in the Netherlands and says, for us, homosexuals are entitled to equal rights and everyone has the right to abandon their faith?"[9]

Wilders and Hirsi Ali also stated that they did not intend to create chaos, but nevertheless their statements mentioned here show that they realized that the films could create new controversies. When we examine their motives, we can see that their intention was also to position themselves as different from mainstream politicians and as heroic champions in the struggle against Islamization.

As De Leeuw and Van Wichelen argue in their analysis of the *Submission* affair, Hirsi Ali attempts to express and demonstrate through this film she is not one of the oppressed Muslim women; she is liberated and, I would add, has the audacity to stand up against oppression.[10] *Submission*, among other public statements and interventions by Hirsi Ali, was a performance depicting her as a liberated (ex-)Muslim woman and politician. Hirsi Ali often lamented the alleged political correctness of Dutch politics aimed at the pacification of Muslims and other minorities and pleaded for a more confrontational style in order to face and solve the problems in Dutch society which she claimed were the product of Islamic culture and compounded by the political correctness of politicians. In her performance she reconciled two apparently contradictory roles: as a citizen belonging to the Dutch moral community with its idealized vision of embracing secular and sexual liberties, and as someone whose place in that community is precarious because she is black and Muslim. Her release of *Submission* was very well timed, taking place two days before a long-awaited debate on a parliamentary investigation of Dutch integration policies and their effectiveness.

Wilders has adopted the role of a hard-liner against (radical) Islam. From 2003 onward he has attacked not only radical Islam but Islam as such, defining it as a totalitarian ideology comparable to communism, fascism, and Nazism. He criticized every accommodation of Muslim demands, interpreting them all as signs of the "creeping Islamization" that threatened the social fabric of Dutch society as well as Dutch identity and culture. In his rhetoric, he frequently uses Arabic terms to support his claims of Muslim duplicity and evil intentions, his favorites being *taqiyya* (dissimulation, hiding one's true convictions), *dhimmi* (non-Muslim subject of protected status but unequal rights), *jihad*, and of course, *fitna*. These are often combined with derogatory terms to describe young Moroccan-Dutch offenders such as "street terrorists" or "Muslim-colonists." He invented a disdainful word for the head covering by which young Muslim women indicate their identity, "*kopvodden*" (head rags), and promised his followers he would fight for a special tax on their apparel, a "*kopvoddentaks*."[11]

Wilders positions himself against the so-called progressive elite, which encompasses most of the political parties, the media, the law courts, and the universities and who, according to him, have hijacked Dutch democracy and society from the "common hard-working people." He presents himself in contrast as a solitary, courageous figure engaged in a dangerous battle against radical Islam, and enjoys likening himself to such men as Winston Churchill, who—unlike the appeaser Chamberlain—was willing to stand up and fight the Nazis. Like Hirsi Ali, Wilders presents himself as both an outsider and an insider, albeit following a different logic. Wilders's role in parliament and his tendency not to leave the political circles of The Hague as well as the fact that he has been a Member of Parliament since 1997 make him very much an insider; but his harsh rhetoric distances him from other politicians and allows him to present himself as the spokesperson for ordinary men and defender of Dutch values and identity.[12]

Setting the Stage: *Submission* and *Fitna* as Oppositional Arguments

Both *Submission* and *Fitna* are performative acts meant to produce angry Muslims by presenting Islam as a religion of violence and anger. An exposition of the content of both films and the ritualized dimensions of these political performances does not, of course, explain the course of events after the announcement and release of the films. The events after the announcement and (in the case of *Submission*) the release of the films produce and reproduce the discourse of "angry Muslims" in several ways but do so almost without Muslims playing an important role in the events (with the important exception, of course, of Mohammed Bouyeri, the young Moroccan-Dutchman who killed Theo van Gogh).

Following Victor Turner, I suggest that the events subsequent to the announcement of *Submission* and *Fitna* can be studied as a social drama consisting of four stages: a breach of a social relationship that is regarded as crucial in the relevant social group; a rapidly mounting crisis in the group's major dichotomous cleavages; the application of a legal or ritual means of redress or reconciliation between the conflicting parties; and the final stage, a symbolic and public expression of reconciliation or irreparable schism.[13]

In this social drama the image of the "angry Muslim" takes center stage in the films, the performances of both Hirsi Ali and Wilders, and the responses of other politicians. It is repeated continuously throughout the whole series of events following the announcements, and it structures the responses by other politicians—including those who disagree with Hirsi Ali and Wilders—and the attempts for reconciliation by making a distinction between radical and moderate Muslims and between appropriate and inappropriate modes of debate of politicians.

As Butler notes, in a critique of Turner's concept of social drama, any analysis of ritual and performance should include a consideration of how political authority and legitimation form part of the performance that takes place within a particular system of sanctions and taboos.[14] This is vital to any understanding of the events because the image of the angry Muslim as invoked by Hirsi Ali, Van Gogh, and Wilders plays such a specific role here: disrupting the political status quo and the usual ways of doing politics in the Netherlands. Olson and Goodnight explore how political acts turn into controversies by using the concept of oppositional arguments. According to them "social controversy . . . flourishes at those sites of struggle where arguers criticize and invest alternatives to established social conventions and sanctioned norms of communication."[15] Making an oppositional argument is the performance of objections against the established status quo, often both in form and content. This perspective allows us to see how the films "disrupt the taken-for-granted realm of the uncontested and commonplace. [It] unsettles the appropriateness of social conventions, draws attention to the taken-for-granted means of communication, and provokes discussion."[16]

As noted above, before being screened both films were announced explicitly as "a new provocation" (*Submission*) and as "provocative" (*Fitna*) in the Dutch press. Amoore and Hall show how particular works of art can be seen as provocative because they are responsible for bringing the unforeseen, unaccountable, unexpected, and unknowable into the public space.[17] They explain that these works of art interrupt the normal state of affairs by making people notice and look again and again, realizing that there are alternative ways of doing politics. Calling something a provocation means that one expects a response, while the nature of that response is yet unclear.

But by whom were these films labelled as provocations? Surprisingly perhaps, this was not primarily by Muslims. The chairperson of the national umbrella organization of Muslims, Contactorgaan Moslims en Overheid (CMO—Muslims-State Interface), when questioned about the film before it was screened, responded that he was not interested and did not intend to watch it. He assumed the film would be "incorrect" and said he found Hirsi Ali's attitude ridiculous. It would be best, he continued, if Muslim representatives simply ignored Van Gogh and Hirsi Ali, for "they just are not worth a response." Another well-known Muslim spokesperson, Haci Karacaer, chairman of the Turkish-Dutch Milli Görüş, declined every request for comments.[18]

In the case of *Fitna*, the Netherlands government issued a press release, which contained the following passage: "According to Mr. Hirsch Ballin (the Christian Democratic Minister of Justice), the participants in the free public debate have to show respect for other people's religion and for that which is held sacred by others. If that boundary is crossed, the government will resist and make clear that 'we owe each other respect,' according to the minister."[19]

Even more telling is the exchange between the Minister of Economic Affairs, Laurens-Jan Brinkhorst (of the left-liberal party D'66) and the Minister of Integration, Rita Verdonk (then still of the conservative liberal VVD but drifting further toward the right). In the daily newspaper *De Volkskrant*, Brinkhorst remarked in regard to *Submission*: "When I saw that film, I thought: 'Oh oh, is this going to end well?' You know what happens when you light a cigarette in an ammunition depot."[20] Brinkhorst found it perfectly understandable that Muslims would be agitated about the film: "I am sorry! Who is calling whom naïve?" His colleague Verdonk, however, insisted that the screening of the film was a matter of free speech, in which the government would not interfere. Later, the Deputy Prime Minister and Minister of Finance, Gerrit Zalm (also VVD) stated that Brinkhorst had not spoken on behalf of the government. Nevertheless several other ministers and the members of the opposition pointed to Wilders's responsibilities as a politician, not to endanger Dutch interests at home and abroad; the Christian-Democrats even called upon him not to show his film.[21]

As these examples show, it was not the Muslim community but the Netherlands government and the Dutch media who responded to these films in terms of transgression and provocation, because they feared the reactions of Muslims at home and abroad. Next to the Dutch electorate and the Muslim community worldwide, Dutch politicians and the media constitute a third group of actors involved in the social drama of the films. Following Olson and Goodnight, we can argue that announcing the films and the films themselves rendered evident and sustained "challenges to communication practices that delimit the proper expression of opinion and constrain the legitimate formation of judgment within personal and public spheres."[22]

To declare the film *Submission* or *Fitna* to be a provocation directed against Muslims constitutes a double and paradoxical performative act by the media and Dutch politicians. First, the declaration expresses and offers a particular kind of solidarity with Muslims who might feel offended by a desecration of their holy traditions. Second, it is a statement of how public political debate should properly be constituted: freely, respectfully and nonconfrontationally. Third, it expresses, confirms, and reproduces the fear that Muslims (in the Netherlands or in the Middle East) will be offended and respond violently against Dutch individuals or institutions (as some Muslims did during the cartoons affair against Danish institutions), or act against Dutch business interests. Fourth, most clearly so in the statements of politicians such as Brinkhorst, it amounts to an implicit denunciation of Hirsi Ali and Wilders as irresponsible politicians who play with fire and threaten national security at home and abroad.

The figure of the "angry Muslim" here serves to make a distinction between responsible and irresponsible politicians, between those who serve the cause of maintaining social peace and cohesion and preventing Muslim anger and those who deliberately threaten national interests by playing with fire. Thus, like the films, which were designed to make Muslims angry, the responses by the Dutch government, however critical of the films, ultimately also reinforced the stereotype of the "angry Muslim" who threatens Dutch interests.

Security Crisis: Freedom of Speech versus Blasphemy

The second stage in Turner's concept of social drama pertains to a "rapidly mounting crisis in the direction of a group's major dichotomous cleavages." In these particular cases, the crisis was quickly framed as marking a dichotomy between freedom of speech and blasphemy in which the image of the threat of the "angry Muslim" was used to either defend freedom of speech or to proclaim that respect and civility should be part of the public debate instead of offending people's religious beliefs.

The course of events following the release of the film was not the same in the cases of *Submission* and *Fitna*. One of the reasons for this is that *Submission* was aired the day after it was announced, while it was months before *Fitna* was released after its first announcement in November 2007. In both cases there was nonetheless much debate about the films. In September and October 2004, the larger national and regional newspapers carried 187 articles about Hirsi Ali and the film. However, if it had not been for another event, *Submission* would have probably just been one more episode in a series of incidents, events, and affairs that have continued to put Muslims in the spotlight. On November 2, 2004, a young Muslim of Moroccan descent, Mohammed Bouyeri, shot *Submission* director Theo van Gogh and cut his throat. With a knife he pinned a letter containing a message for Hirsi Ali to the victim's body before leaving the scene. In the course of the following month, the same set of national and regional newspapers carried more than 500 articles about Hirsi Ali, *Submission*, and the murder, while coverage by television was extensive. The media tended to take for granted that Bouyeri had committed his horrible act because he was, like many Muslims, offended by *Submission*—although Bouyeri himself stated at his trial: "I have never felt offended. I have acted out of conviction."[23]

There was a broad consensus in Dutch society, among those who were supportive as well as those who strongly criticized their makers, that *Submission*, and a few years later, *Fitna*, was offensive to Muslims. But what exactly was it that Muslims themselves found objectionable in these films? There is a widely shared assumption that for Muslims the depiction of the Prophet Muhammad is an unassailable taboo—this assumption lay at the root of the Danish cartoon crisis. Taking a cue from W. J. T. Mitchell, who analyzed offending pictures in other religious contexts,[24] it could be argued that it was not just the very act of depicting the Prophet and by extension the Koran and other things held sacred that caused the escalation, but what was done to the Prophet and the Koran in the film and cartoons. A similar argument about Muslim sensibilities and hurtful forms of blasphemy was put forward by Saba Mahmood. She explained responses to the Danish cartoons as stemming from the profoundly affective relationship that Muslims have with the Prophet Muhammad as a "figure of exemplarity."[25] Following this line of thought, one might argue that Muslims must have felt offended and emotionally hurt by the films *Submission* and *Fitna* too because they also represented acts of aggression against the exemplary figure of the Prophet and his Message.

However, this is not how most young Muslims with whom I worked spoke of the matter. During the years when the *Submission* and *Fitna* affairs were playing out, I was carrying out field research among young Dutch Muslims (most of them of Moroccan background). I encountered a wide range of reactions, from resigned and indifferent to indignant and angry. Several of the Muslim organizations refused to respond; most called upon their members to remain calm and not allow themselves to be provoked. There was a general fear, among the established elite, that radical Muslim groups might profit from the situation. While the dominant tone of reactions was one of resignation, there were also serious death threats against Hirsi Ali and Van Gogh, and later also Wilders.[26]

The two elements in *Submission* that my interlocutors found most offensive were the images of a naked woman with verses from the Koran written on her body, and the connection that the film made between the Koran and domestic violence. Other responses that I recorded were less specific to *Submission* and were made in response to an entire series of similar affairs, from the Danish cartoons to *The Innocence of Muslims*.

In a public debate about the cartoons, films, and blasphemy, one of my key interlocutors in a research project on Salafism laid out an interesting argument. The Danish cartoons, he argued, were transgressive but not really offensive or blasphemous. The reason is that unlike Christianity, which has developed an iconic image of Jesus Christ, Islam has not had a tradition of pictorially representing the Prophet, so that there is no received iconic image of Muhammad. For that reason, the figure represented in the Muhammad cartoons had nothing to do with the Muhammad of Muslim tradition. With regard to *The Innocence of Muslims*, he said that the way Muhammad was represented in that film was completely alien to him, since he had an entirely different notion of what the Prophet Muhammad was like. This led him to conclude that there was no reason to feel insulted at all, because none of the depictions were about the Prophet Muhammad as he knew him.[27]

Another type of reaction among Muslims at the time of *Submission*, *Fitna*, and the Muhammad cartoons also resurfaced during a demonstration against *The Innocence of Muslims* at which I was present in September 2012. Most of the people attending did indeed find *Innocence* insulting but the majority of the slogans and speeches brought two different points to the fore, the first being the argument of the double standards being applied to Muslims. Many Muslims felt they had less freedom of speech than people like Hirsi Ali and Wilders who, they felt, were allowed to say anything about Muslims. The second argument pertained to the so-called war on terror. Many of the slogans and speeches denounced the US attacks on Muslims (for example the drone attacks in Afghanistan, Pakistan, and Yemen). A few of them drew a connection between the depictions of the Prophet Muhammad and the "war on terror," seeing both as aspects of a total war against Islam. The slogan that captured the general feeling best, during the protest meeting in Amsterdam, was "But not our Prophet"—implying that the Americans had already targeted "their" women and children by drone attacks and controlled their governments in the Middle East; the targeting of the Prophet was the last straw. A few of the protesters left the demonstrations because of the furious anti-American slogans, but nevertheless shared the same feeling toward the United States (and extended it to Europe). I found similar opinions in the debates about *Submission*, *Fitna*, and the Muhammad cartoons.[28]

The broad variety of reactions among Dutch Muslims however hardly mattered for how the social dramas of *Submission* and *Fitna* enfolded which, I suggest, shows that the dynamics of these dramas are structured by something else than explanations of why Muslims respond the way they did (or did not at all). A cursory look at the debates in the Dutch media and the political arena shows that they differed considerably from the opinions voiced in Muslim forums that I have highlighted here. Hajer and Maussen have identified three perspectives (or frames) in the media on the murder of Van Gogh: it was understood as an attack on free expression; or as part of the clash of civilizations, the war on terror, and the holy war; or, finally, it was defined as a consequence of failed integration.[29] In the press articles about *Fitna* that I collected, I have found the same three frames. All three frames are marked by an opposition between liberal Dutch society and Muslims who fail to comply with Dutch secular freedoms, in particular the freedom of speech, because their loyalty is with Islam first and foremost, instead of with the Netherlands. Here we see how secularism as a political doctrine is dependent upon a particular conceptualization of citizenship. Instead of maintaining a "religious belonging," citizens should derive their sense of belonging from the nation-state and its values such as tolerance, sexual freedom, nonviolence, and so forth.[30]

Much of these debates have been between non-Muslim Dutch politicians and opinion makers, who differed on the freedom of speech and the right to insult. The obvious exception here is of course Mohammed Bouyeri and his friends, who did refer to the issue of blasphemy in their opposition to *Submission*. In his major overview of blasphemous art, Brent Plate shows that the act of accusing within a particular context evokes the profound power of blasphemy.[31] Pronouncing something to be blasphemous can be seen as an attempt by religious groups to mobilize their own constituency, create unity, and immunize their faith from outside attacks. From the viewpoint of the believer, the accusation of blasphemy toward another person opens up a broad avenue of possible responses, such as the public repentance or the excommunication of the blasphemer. In the case of *Submission*, for the so-called Hofstad Network, the film was the latest of many perceived insults made by Hirsi Ali and Theo van Gogh. In response, they published a text called "The Offense" in which they reasoned that Hirsi Ali and Van Gogh should be killed because they had insulted the Prophet Muhammad. On November 2, 2004, a member of the group, Mohammed Bouyeri, killed Van Gogh, which led to a huge escalation of the "us versus them" opposition that was already ongoing.[32]

The violence against Van Gogh as well as the riots that occurred in several countries during the Muhammad cartoons affair simply confirmed the reaction Hirsi Ali already anticipated, and it therefore also reinforced the stereotypical image of the angry Muslim who resorts to violence. *Fitna* then fueled the expectations that this violence was imminent again. The debate, therefore, quickly became dichotomized between secularism, reason, tolerance, and free speech on one hand and Islam, violence, fanaticism, and censorship on the other hand. Moreover, as had occurred in relation to *Submission*, it was not only Muslims who raised the issue of blasphemy or the related accusations. The Ministers of the Interior and Justice warned Wilders of possible repercussions in the Netherlands and worldwide, and of the personal risks to himself. A letter was sent by the government to all mayors asking them to be extra vigilant to possible tensions. Police forces in several cities foresaw unrest when the film was to be released. Prime Minister Balkenende spoke of a crisis situation and Dutch embassies were warned to take precautionary measures to protect their personnel and Dutch citizens.[33] The chairman of the Netherlands' leading business association (known as VNO-NCW) declared Wilders's film to be a threat to the Dutch image of tolerance and to Dutch commercial interests in the Middle East.[34]

Considerable attention was given in the Dutch media to Syria's Grand Mufti Ahmad Badr al-Din Hassoun, who, on the occasion of a visit to the European Parliament, said that if Wilders tears up or burns a Koran in his film, he will be held responsible for war and bloodshed. Websites were then launched either against Wilders and the film or in support of him. Statements about defending free speech were made on several of these websites and in letters to editors in the newspapers, and an anti-Wilders campaign was launched by Doekle Terpstra, former leader of the Christian National Trade Union Federation (CNV), stating that Wilders was evil and that he should be stopped, accusing him of weakening the social cohesion of Dutch society.[35]

The reactions to *Fitna* show how the issue of blasphemy became connected to security; possible Muslim reactions were presented as a serious threat requiring special measures to ensure safety. Muslim organizations, too, adopted the same security-focused attitude during the *Fitna* affair, stressing to their followers the need for Muslims to remain calm, and liaising closely with the government in order to "prevent *Submission*-like situations" and the possibility of a "lone idiot" committing violent attacks. The organizations moreover successfully raised awareness in policymaking circles at the national and local levels of the very real risk of violence targeting Muslims and their institutions in the heated atmosphere of the *Fitna* affair. Such violence had occurred earlier in the aftermath of the September 11 attacks in America and again following the murder of Van Gogh, when many mosques, Muslim schools, and individual persons were physically attacked. This latter dimension was barely touched upon in public discourse; what remained was the freedom of speech versus blasphemy debate that invoked the specter of the "angry Muslim" haunting the Netherlands.

Dialogue and Radical versus Liberal Islam

Turner's third stage of the social drama is the application of a legal or ritual means of redress or reconciliation between the conflicting parties. In this reconciliation, particular values deemed fundamental to society are repeatedly affirmed in different types of performances. As argued by Brian Goldstone, the rhetorical opposition of angry Muslims and free speech serves as an organizing impetus and legitimizing logic for secular liberalism.[36] Invoking the image of the angry Muslim and labeling the films as provocations already signals, to a certain extent, that an attempt is being made to create order in a crisis situation by separating the sheep from the goats. After the murder of Theo van Gogh, a large governmental project titled Social Cohesion (Maatschappelijke Binding) was launched, which gave all government departments the responsibility of coming up with projects against radicalization and furthering social cohesion. Mainstream Muslim organizations were made partners in these endeavors, but Salafi networks were left out, because these were seen as the main agents responsible for radicalizing Muslim youth.

In this phase the issue of blasphemy also returned. It was not raised by Muslims, however, but by the Netherlands government, which then included the

Christian Democrats—it was the Christian Democrat Minister of Justice Piet-Hein Donner who announced this move. The existing blasphemy law, which had long been dormant, was to be revitalized and the range of punishable actions it covered to be expanded from the original "insult of God." Although the law has its fierce opponents (and supporters, especially among the Christian Democrats), the fact that Minister Donner got his way shows that the concept of blasphemy could be accommodated with Dutch secular liberalism. In the new interpretation, it is not so much God who is protected from injury but people's religious convictions and feelings as well as the social cohesion of society. This was in fact an attempt to offer believers a way to channel the expression of their grievances and to subject them and their religious claims to the rule of law.[37] The attempt to reactivate the blasphemy legislation also reveals how in particular the Christian-Democratic politicians involved believed politics should be conducted: in such a way that it did not offend people's deeply held convictions and beliefs.

It is worth noting that these measures were part of a larger plan to "prevent and counter Islamic radicalization." Thereby the government once again confirmed its conviction of a connection between radical Islam, blasphemy, and violence. The proposed revitalization of the blasphemy law, however, could also be regarded as an attempt to restrain the populist expressions of Islamophobia. The populist Minister of Integration Rita Verdonk denounced the bill and remarked, "I should like to point out that we have a Muslim community in the Netherlands that has a lower level of tolerance than the average Dutch person." She added that she could not believe Donner meant to say that "we" should lower our capacity to deal with criticism; "we," she insisted, have freedom of speech and that should not be curtailed.[38] Donner's statement so shortly after the murder of Van Gogh, gave other politicians the opportunity to stand up and represent themselves as defenders of free speech.

In the period leading up to the release of *Fitna*, the authorities made it easier for people to file complaints against Wilders and his film. This meant that the grievances of people had to be translated and therefore transformed into legal terms of harm or violations of the law.[39] Keeping in mind the fear among politicians and policy makers of unrest among Muslim youth because of the film, I suggest this move can be seen as an attempt to open a channel for the expression of dismay considered to be compatible with the liberal order and to reaffirm the proper place assigned to religion in that order.

Two other attempts to redress the situation are worth mentioning here, as these are some of the few occasions in which Muslims did play an important public role in both affairs: the holding of public solidarity meetings and, after the murder of Van Gogh, the issuing of statements by Muslim organizations and networks condemning his murder. After the announcement of *Fitna*, several meetings were held in local mosques. Churches, in particular, many of them having had long-standing relationships with Muslim spokespersons, were active in expressing their solidarity with Muslims. This time, many Muslim organizations not only took the initiative and started talks with the government but also initiated a pro-Netherlands lobby at embassies of Middle Eastern countries expressing the idea that Wilders's plans did not represent Dutch society as a whole nor the point of view of the government. There was no strong oppositional voice in public among Muslims, however, during the *Fitna* affair; with a few exceptions the efforts of the organizations of Muslims focused mostly on "keeping things calm" behind the scenes by engaging in dialogues with local communities (in particular the churches) and programs for youth and extensive contact with the municipalities.

Reintegration: Back to Normal?

The final phase of the social drama, in Turner's model, consists of either a recognition of reintegration of the conflicting parties or a recognition of schism, a complete separation. At first sight, one may be inclined to argue that there is no recognition of a schism in the sense of a breakdown of social relations. On the contrary, there appeared to be a strong desire to restore cohesion, in particular in the aftermath of the murder of Theo van Gogh which deeply shocked society and caused what has been called a "cultural trauma." It was felt by many to be a fundamental blow to the tolerant image of Dutch society and many people were repelled by it.[40] In the following year, when Hirsi Ali announced her plans for a sequel, *Submission II*, several individual Muslims went to court to get the film banned on the grounds that it would be blasphemous and insulting. They lost the case.[41] The film was never made, however.

Although there were reports about unrest and riots after the release of *Fitna*, in general the reactions among Muslims were very calm, for which they were praised by both Balkenende and Wilders. An interesting dialectic can be noted here. Some opinion leaders (Muslims and non-Muslims) saw the calm reaction of Muslims as a sign of emancipation and a revitalization of the Dutch polder model;[42] Muslims have grown accustomed to the insults and have found a way to put up with them. There is however more to it than that. Hirsi Ali, besides criticizing the Dutch government for its stigmatizing reaction, for example, stated:

> [The government] should show Muslims the words of Junior Minister Ahmed Aboutaleb, a Muslim, spoken in the program *Pauw and Witteman* [a Dutch

television news show]: "Muslims should think about the fear that their religion generates. The majority is silent and that is not good. We have chosen the Netherlands, exactly because of the freedom here. This should be stated publicly. I miss the voice that renounces extremism." That is the appropriate reaction to the basic question raised by *Fitna*.

Fitna has already proven its value. And there are not only the wise words of Aboutaleb; other Muslim groups in the Netherlands are already preparing a counter film. A counter film, not bloodshed! Words should be countered with words, images with images. This proves that provocation works.

Six years ago Aboutaleb was convinced that asking critical questions about Islam was like "pissing in one's own nest." And now he only speaks the right words. Without asking provocative questions, we could never have accomplished this.[43]

Hirsi Ali praises Aboutaleb who "misses the voice renouncing extremism" for his "appropriate reaction" as to how Muslims should respond to the claim about the relation between Islam and violence as made by Wilders. She regards Aboutaleb's reaction as progress compared to his reaction after *Submission*. "Provocation works," according to her, because "now he only speaks the right words." Similar words on the didactic uses of provocation were also spoken in connection with the Danish cartoon affair. In his analysis of the affair, Talal Asad observes that some of the reactions claimed that it was a good thing people felt hurt, because that would encourage them to reexamine their beliefs. Criticizing or offending "questionable" religious thoughts, Asad notes, is claimed to be a form of liberating speech, necessary to free Muslims and subsequently to free society at large.[44] I would add that the insult, provocation or criticism is also a ritual form of teaching a particular group in society to behave in a subordinate manner by way of humiliation.[45]

As such, the films and the enfolding social drama serve to explain, define, and impose authoritative ways of seeing society and idealized norms of behavior upon a particular group. In these cases, for people like Hirsi Ali it was a way of teaching Muslims how to react and to behave in a subordinate manner, thereby confirming the hierarchy in society in which Muslims are still seen as people coming from the outside. It is also a form of including individual Muslims in the group as long as they meet certain criteria that are determined by the dominant groups in society. The murder of Theo van Gogh contributed further (after the Madrid attacks in 2004 by Al-Qaeda) to legitimate the implementation of a counter-radicalization program that focused almost exclusively on Muslims and more in particular on the Dutch Salafi Muslims, the group to which Van Gogh's killer was believed to belong.[46]

Besides confirming and legitimating the separation between an acceptable and unacceptable Islam, *Submission* and *Fitna* had two other consequences for Islam and Muslims in society. First, the aftermath of the *Fitna* controversy during which legal complaints were filed against Wilders proved to be a long-lasting one. A consortium of civil society organizations, including a few mosques, reported Wilders to the police on charges of blasphemy, discrimination, and incitement to hatred. After an initial refusal to prosecute, the appellate court forced the public prosecutor to follow up on the last two of these charges but with seeking acquittal. A highly publicized trial followed in which Wilders was acquitted in 2011. According to the court, Wilders's statements were permissible since they were made in the context of a societal debate on Islam as a religion.[47] As such this verdict confirmed the already existing separation, in Dutch jurisprudence, of Islam from Muslims as a social group in order to assess what is legally allowed and what is not in political speech.[48]

Second, Justice Minister Donner's plans to revive the blasphemy law after the murder of Theo van Gogh were not put into practice at that time because of the strong liberal opposition to them, from the political opposition as well as the government. In March 2008, after the release of *Fitna*, a similar attempt to make offensive speech punishable was made by another coalition government (which not only included Christian-Democrats but also a fundamentalist Christian party). Instead of invigorating the blasphemy law they proposed to expand the criminalization of hate speech. This proposal found insufficient support in parliament, and an alternative proposal, launched in 2012 by opposition parties, to simply abolish the blasphemy law won the day in 2014.[49]

It is difficult to assess the consequences of this stage of the drama for Wilders and Hirsi Ali personally and in their role as politicians, since too many other factors were involved. It is worth noting, however, that Hirsi Ali was stripped of her Dutch nationality and left for the United States to work at a conservative think tank in 2006 after it was revealed that she had lied about her name during her asylum procedure.[50] Her role in Dutch politics has been minor since. Wilders's Freedom Party became the second strongest party during the European elections of 2009 and was one of the most successful parties in the 2010 national elections. The Freedom Party then supported the new government but was not part of it. This, I suggest, can be seen as exemplary for the position of Wilders and his Freedom Party: they are not part of the center of power (Wilders being considered as too much of a firebrand) but neither are they complete outsiders; mainstream parties have occasionally cut deals with them. Wilders has been able to continue to build his party making it to be one of the biggest parties in Dutch politics, in part because of the decline of the political mainstream parties. More recently the party has been getting competition from another radical right-wing populist party.[51]

The overall view of this stage of the drama is more complicated than the two options of either reintegration or schism of Turner's model suggest. I would argue that a situation was created in which both reintegration and schism occurred: the Dutch Muslim population was divided into one with an acceptable Islam (moderate or liberal) and an unacceptable (radical) Islam, between Islam and Muslims in a legal sense, separating Wilders and Hirsi Ali from the "normal" political situation but only excluding the latter.

Conclusion

Turner's work on social drama allows us to develop a more nuanced understanding of the dynamics following particular events, to recognize the interaction between different key players in these events, and to see the complexities of Dutch liberal secularism. Both the films and the debates before and after the release of the films illustrate the performative power of a discourse that connects Islam, the idea of the potentially violent "angry Muslim" and security-related anxiety by invoking, reenacting, and reaffirming moral boundaries of acceptable and expected modes of debate in a secular state.

The dynamics following the announcements of *Submission* and *Fitna* cannot be fully understood by focusing on why Muslims may or may not be offended by it. Turner's work allows us to shift our focus to include the positions Hirsi Ali and Wilders have taken up in the Dutch political field.

Both the use of the film by politicians who present themselves as outside the political mainstream and the films' Islamophobic content are designed to create a response, to generate an oppositional argument. Both announcements of the films challenged the usual political process, required other politicians to react, and forced the public to think about particular conventions that many people considered fundamental to Dutch society: freedom of speech and freedom of religion. The established conventions, freedoms, and politics were disturbed, and many politicians regarded the films to be transgressive as they disrupted the usual consensus-oriented style of politics. Furthermore, government circles feared that they would cause violence and threaten the commercial interests of the Netherlands and the safety of Dutch people in the Middle East. The films opened up new avenues of debate in which Wilders and Hirsi Ali could expand their role of saving Dutch society at large and Muslim women in particular from both angry Muslims and mainstream politicians who, they claimed, sold out the Netherlands to these angry Muslims.

While the debates around *Fitna*, *Submission*, and similar affairs have been reduced to the opposition between secular liberalism versus Islam, my analysis of these cases shows a strong disagreement between secular populists on one hand and secular liberals and Christian Democrats in the Netherlands on the other. Moreover, the secular liberals and Christian Democrats also disagreed on how to deal with questions pertaining to freedom of speech and its limits. It is these internal struggles between secularist factions that have given the *Submission* affair and, to a greater extent, the *Fitna* affair, their specific dynamics enhanced by the killing of Theo van Gogh in 2004.

The performative dimension of the *Submission* and *Fitna* affairs shows how creating a public and a common enemy is an important part of the continuous reaffirmation of and debates about liberal secularism. Just as Paul Brown has suggested in relation to colonialist discourse, liberal discourse expresses a need for order and disorder.[52] In order for the political elite to maintain the status quo, the possibility of a threat has to be created; in this case, the angry Muslim and, for some, the irresponsible politician as well. This works by repeatedly invoking the image of the "angry Muslim"—the same image that has been invoked by Hirsi Ali and Wilders and that has gained plausibility because of events in the recent past. Hirsi Ali's and Wilders's acts of profanity or transgression were seen by their opponents as upsetting both Muslims' religious feelings and the normal state of affairs in politics. Both Hirsi Ali and Wilders threatened the position of mainstream liberal politicians: they were deemed to be dangerous by the political elite because of the violence that might be perpetrated by Muslims. At the same time, mainstream liberal discourse acknowledges the existence of the potential threat by creating a dichotomy between liberal and radical Muslims, the former who need to be taught liberal civility and the latter who violate the place designated to religion and should be subjected to counter-radicalization policies. This latter group contains particular concrete categories of Muslims (in particular Salafi Muslims). As such the political elites recognize that the liberal project is not complete and that it must be continually reproduced. In these affairs Muslims are not so much active persons taking part in the debates but objects functioning as pivotal symbols in the debates—objects over whom power is exercised and battles are fought.

Notes

1. "Nieuwe provocatie Hirsi Ali," *NRC Handelsblad*, August 28, 2004. https://www.nrc.nl/nieuws/2004/08/28/nieuwe-provocatie-hirsi-ali-7699451-a447073.
2. "Provocerende film Wilders," *De Telegraaf*, November 27, 2007.
3. Literally "test" or "ordeal." Wilders refrained from mentioning the standard translation of *fitna* as "discord."
4. Mark Bradshaw, "Innocence of Muslims: A Dark Demonstration of the Power of Film," *Guardian*, September 17, 2012, https://www.theguardian.com/film/filmblog/2012/sep/17/innocence-of-muslims-demonstration-film.
5. Marc Gaborieau, "From Al-Beruni to Jinnah: Idiom, Ritual and Ideology of Hindu-Muslim Confrontation in South Asia," *Anthropology Today* 1, no. 3 (1985): 7–14.
6. Rens Vliegenthart, *Framing Immigration and Integratio: Facts, Parliament, Media and Anti-Immigrant Party Support in the Netherlands* (Amsterdam: Vrije Universiteit Amsterdam, 2007).
7. Martijn de Koning, "Understanding Dutch Islam: Exploring the Relationship of Muslims with the State and the Public Sphere in the Netherlands," in *Muslim Diaspora in the West Negotiating Gender, Home, and Belonging*, ed. Haideh Moghissi and Halleh Ghorashi (Burlington, VT: Ashgate Publishing, 2010), 181–197.
8. "Ze zullen zien dat ik gelijk heb; Een half jaar met Ayaan Hirsi Ali" [They will see that I was right: a half year with Hirsi Ali], *NRC Handelsblad*, August 28, 2004, https://www.nrc.nl/nieuws/2004/08/28/ze-zullen-zien-dat-ik-gelijk-heb-7699553-a1288623.
9. Gerald Traufetter, "'Moderate Islam is a Contradiction': Interview with Dutch Populist Geert Wilders," *Der Spiegel*, March 31, 2008, http://www.spiegel.de/international/europe/0,1518,544347,00.html.
10. Marc de Leeuw and Sonja van Wichelen, "'Please, go wake up!': *Submission*, Hirsi Ali, and the 'War on Terror' in the Netherlands," *Feminist Media Studies* 5, no. 3 (2005): 329.
11. For an enlightening, detailed study of Wilders's discourse, see Jan Kuitenbrouwer, *De woorden van Wilders en waarom ze werken* [The words of Wilders and why they work] (Amsterdam: De Bezige Bij, 2010).
12. For a more elaborate explanation, see, for example, Koen Vossen, "Populism in the Netherlands after Fortuyn: Rita Verdonk and Geert Wilders compared," *Perspectives on European Politics and Society* 11, no. 1 (2010): 22–38.
13. Victor Turner, *Dramas, Fields and Metaphors* (Ithaca, NY: Cornell University Press, 1974), 78–79.
14. Judith Butler, "Performative Acts and Gender Constitution: An Essay in Phenomenology and Feminist Theory," *Theatre Journal* 40, no. 4 (December 1988): 526n9.
15. Kathryn M. Olson and G. Thomas Goodnight, "Entanglements of Consumption, Cruelty, Privacy, and Fashion: The Social Controversy over Fur," *Quarterly Journal of Speech* 80, no. 3 (1994): 249.

16. Olson and Goodnight, "Entanglements," 251.

17. Louise Amoore and Alexandra Hall, "Border Theatre: On the Arts of Security and Resistance," *Cultural Geographies* 17, no. 3 (2010): 314.

18. "Hirsi Ali en Van Gogh Tonen Film," *Trouw*, August 30, 2004, http://www.trouw.nl/tr/nl/4324/Nieuws/archief/article/detail/1735358/2004/08/30/Hirsi-Hirsi Ali-en-Van-Gogh-tonen-film.dhtml.

19. "Zorgen over islamfilm van Wilders" [Concern about Wilders's Islam film], press release ANP (Netherlands Press Agency), November 28, 2007.

20. "Brinkhorst: 'Maken van film *Submission* was onverstandig'" [Brinkhorst: "Making of the film *Submission* was unwise"], *De Volkskrant*, December 13, 2004, http://www.volkskrant.nl/vk/nl/2824/Politiek/article/detail/708634/2004/12/13/Brinkhorst-maken-van-film-Submission-was-onverstandig.dhtml.

21. "Verhagen: 'Wilders, zend koranfilm niet uit!'" [(Christian Democrat leader) Verhagen: "Wilders, do not screen Koran film"], *Elsevier*, Februari 28, 2008, accessed: January 10, 2013, http://www.elsevier.nl/Politiek/achtergrond/2008/2/Verhagen-Wilders-zend-koranfilm-niet-uit-ELSEVIER160139W

22. Olson and Goodnight, "Entanglements," 251.

23. "Ik zeg u, u zult het nooit begrijpen" [I am telling you, you will never understand], *De Volkskrant*, July 13, 2005, https://www.volkskrant.nl/nieuws-achtergrond/ik-zeg-u-u-zult-het-nooit-begrijpen~b4917dbb/.

24. W. J. T. Mitchell, "Offending images," in *What Do Pictures Want? The Lives and Loves of Images* (Chicago: University of Chicago Press, 2005), 125–144.

25. Saba Mahmood, "Religious Reason and Secular Affect: An Incommensurable Divide?," *Critical Inquiry* 35, no. 4 (2009): 836–862, see especially 848. Mahmood's article and her apparent effort to represent offended Muslims in countering liberal arguments have come in for much criticism. One particularly cogent response is Andrew F. March, "Speech and the Sacred: Does the Defense of Free Speech Rest on a Mistake about Religion?," *Political Theory* 40, no. 3 (2012): 318–345. See also Yolande Jansen's contribution to this volume.

26. Martijn de Koning, *Zoeken naar een "Zuivere" Islam: Geloofsbeleving en Identiteitsvorming van Jonge Marokkaans-Nederlandse Moslims* [In search of a "pure" Islam: Religious experience and identity formation of young Moroccan-Dutch Muslims] (Amsterdam: Bert Bakker, 2008).

27. From my field notes, September 2012.

28. For an interesting account of the debates on the Internet, see Liesbet van Zoonen, Farida Vis, and Sabina Mihelj, "Performing Citizenship on YouTube: Activism, Satire and Online Debate Around the Anti-Islam Video *Fitna*," *Critical Discourse Studies* 7, no. 4 (2010): 249.

29. M. Hajer and Marcel Maussen, "Na de moord op Theo van Gogh—Betekenisgeving aan de moord, een reconstructie" ["After the murder of Theo van Gogh—assigning meaning to the murder; a reconstruction"], *S & D. Maandblad van de Wiardi Beckman Stichting, Wetenschappelijk Bureau van de Partij van de Arbeid* 61, no. 12 (2004): 10–18.

30. Brian Goldstone, "Violence and the Profane: Islam, Liberal Democracy, and the Limits of Secular Discipline," *Anthropological Quarterly* 80, no. 1 (2007): 207–237; Talal Asad, *Formations of the Secular* (Stanford, CA: Stanford University Press, 2003).

31. S. Brent Plate, *Blasphemy: Art that Offends* (London: Black Dog Publishing, 2006), 34–50.

32. Martijn de Koning and Roel Meijer, "Going all the Way: Politicization and Radicalization of the Hofstad Network in the Netherlands," in *Identity and Participation in Culturally Diverse Societies: A Multidisciplinary Perspective*, ed. Assaad E. Azzi et al. (Oxford: Wiley-Blackwell, 2011), 220–239.

33. "Balkenende: 'Crisis Door Film Wilders'" [Balkenende: "Crisis caused by Wilders's film"], *De Volkskrant*, January 19, 2008; "Nederland zet zich schrap voor film Wilders" [The Netherlands brace themselves for Wilders's film], *Algemeen Dagblad*, January 17, 2008.

34. "Wilders beschadigt ons land" [Wilders harms our country], *Volkskrant*, March 13, 2008.

35. "Verzetsbeweging tegen Wilders" [Movement of resistance against Wilders], *De Telegraaf*, December 2, 2007; "Benoemen en bouwen" [Naming and building], advertisement, *Trouw* January 2, 2007.

36. Goldstone, "Violence and the Profane," 208.

37. B. A. M. van Stokkom, H. J. B. Sackers, and J.-P. Wils, *Godslastering, discriminerende uitingen wegens godsdienst en haatuitingen* [Blasphemy, religious discrimination and hate speech] (Meppel/Den Haag: Boom/WODC, 2007), 42–48; 87–88.

38. Rita Verdonk, interview, television program *Buitenhof*, November 15, 2004.

39. See Mahmood, "Religious Reason and Secular Affect."

40. Wim de Haan, "Morele paniek of cultureel trauma? Over de betekenis en de gevolgen van de moord op Theo van Gogh" [Moral panic or cultural trauma? On the meaning and consequences of the murder of Theo van Gogh], *Tijdschrift voor Criminologie* 49, no. 3 (2007): 252–264.

41. The Hague Court verdict, March 15, 2005, https://uitspraken.rechtspraak.nl/inziendocument under file number ECLI:NL:RBSGR:2005:AT0303.

42. "Polderende moslims; Beheerste reactie Nedermoslims op *Fitna* is teken van emancipatie" [Muslims seeking compromise: Dutch Muslims' restrained response to *Fitna* is a sign of emancipation], *NRC Handelsblad*, April 5, 2008.

43. "Ayaan Hirsi Ali: '*Fitna* is een blamage voor het kabinet'" [Hirsi Ali, "Fitna is a disgrace for the cabinet"], *Volkskrant*, March 28, 2008.

44. Talal Asad, "Reflections on Blasphemy and Secular Criticism," in *Religion: Beyond a Concept*, ed Hent de Vries (New York: Fordham University Press, 2008). The same claim of "liberating through insult" was made by a Charlie Hebdo cartoonist in the wake of the violent assault of the journal's offices, see Xavier Ternisien, "A 'Charlie Hebdo,' on n'a pas l'impression d'égorger quelqu'un avec un feutre" [At Charlie Hebdo, they don't have the impression they are killing people with a felt tip pen],' *Le Monde*, September 20, 2012, http://www.lemonde.fr/actualite-medias/article/2012/09/20/je-n-ai-pas-l-impression-d-egorger-quelqu-un-avec-un-feutre_1762748_3236.html.

45. See A. Guimarães, "Racial Insult in Brazil," *Discourse and Society* 14, no. 2 (2003): 142.

46. M. de Koning, "Understanding Dutch Islam: Exploring the Relationship of Muslims with the State and the Public Sphere in the Netherlands," in *Muslim Diaspora in the West: Negotiating Gender, Home and Belonging*, ed. Haideh Moghissi and Halleh Ghorashi (Burlington: Ashgate Publishing, 2010), 181–197.

47. Court verdict Amsterdam, June 23, 2011, https://uitspraken.rechtspraak.nl/inziendocument under file number ECLI:NL:RBAMS:2011:BQ9001.

48. This separation was established in the verdict of the Hoge Raad (Supreme Court), the highest court in civil, criminal and tax law in the Netherlands, in the case "Stop het gezwel dat islam heet" [Stop the tumor called Islam], Hoge Raad, 10–03–2009, case file: ECLI:NL:HR:2009:BF0655.

49. The plans were delayed for several years because of elections resulting in new government coalitions. In 2013, the Dutch parliament finally agreed to strike the blasphemy law but the senate accepted a motion that requested the government to inquire if and how religion needs a separate protection in penal law.

50. "Hirsi Ali row brings down government," *Spiegel Online*, June 30, 2006, https://www.spiegel.de/international/dutch-political-crisis-hirsi-ali-row-brings-down-government-a-424458.html.

51. T. Kleinpaste, "The New Face of the Dutch Far-Right," *Foreign Policy*, March 28, 2019, https://foreignpolicy.com/2019/03/28/the-new-face-of-the-dutch-far-right-fvd-thierry-baudet-netherlands-pvv-geert-wilders/.

52. Paul Brown, "'This Thing of Darkness I Acknowledge Mine': The Tempest and the Discourse of Colonialism," in *Political Shakespeare: New Essays in Cultural Materialism*, ed. J. Dollimore and A. Sinfield (Manchester: Manchester University Press, 1985), 48–71.

Part V

Violent Religious Performances: Sacrifice and Martyrdom

The precariousness and ambiguity of religious categorizations, already apparent in the contributions in the preceding part, become particularly acute in the study of forms of violence associated with religion—in particular sacrifice, which involves the death of a living other, and martyrdom, which involves the death of a self. Although this theme had already gained prominence since René Girard's *La violence et le sacré* (1972), it has gained a new political urgency in the twenty-first century, in particular with the rise of religiously motivated suicide bombings. Violent acts may be motivated, sanctioned, or legitimated by an appeal to religion; but in general, both actors and religious authorities are very well aware of the moral and other ambiguities such violent acts may carry. The act of sacrifice is a "making holy," a sacralizing ritual; at the same time, it is an act of violence in which a living animal or human being is killed. Indian traditions clearly display this ambivalence; thus, Wendy Doniger, in *On Hinduism*, has called attention to the ambiguity and the essentially contested character of the concept of *ahimsa* (often, but not entirely correctly, translated as "non-violence") in relation to long-standing Hindu practices of animal sacrifice; similar ambiguities appear in Buddhism. The contributions to the present section explore some of these complex and occasionally troubling dimensions of violence. For the most part, these contributions are primarily descriptive in character; but occasionally, and perhaps inevitably, normative considerations appear in them as well.

In "Sacrifice and the Problem of Beginning," Michael Lambek proposes to analyze the ritual practice of sacrifice as a kind of beginning. Beginnings, he argues, are distinct from origins in that they are acts rather than events; unlike origins, they have specific actors and a precise location in time and in society. With this emphasis on beginning, Lambek argues against the more familiar ideas of ritual as marking a kind of transition that can be found in Van Gennep's famous analysis of rites of passage or in Victor Turner's studies on liminality. Against functionalist approaches to religion and ritual, he argues that ritual is not an expression of something other than itself; against symbolic approaches, he argues that ritual does not involve a kind of symbolic or metaphorical action. Insofar as an act of sacrifice produces a dead body, he argues, it is a *literal* act: it is unequivocal, unmediated, and unambiguous. Further, he sees this literal aspect of sacrifice as grounded in the body. Lambek warns, however, against taking violent gestures like suicide bombings as acts of beginning that transform death into life, arguing that such acts are not explicitly performative and are purely instrumental in aim; more generally, he warns against applying the religious language of martyrdom to politics. Thus, Lambek appears to assume a distinction between religion as nonfunctional by definition and politics as purely instrumental. In this respect, the contributions by Schwartz, Kanie, and Leezenberg reach interestingly different conclusions.

In "The Mass and the Theater," Regina Schwartz complicates the apparently clear-cut distinction between religiously sanctioned sacrifice and illegitimate murder and between the serious performance of religious ritual and the nonserious performance found in the theater. Starting with the spectator's sense of injustice at how the villain Iago emerges victorious at the end of Shakespeare's tragedy *Othello*, Schwartz proceeds to draw some unexpected parallels between religious and theatrical performances. She does this by locating Elizabethan drama in the context of England during the Reformation. In this period, she argues, Reformist objections against the doctrine of transubstantiation as well as claims that the Eucharist represented rather than repeated Christ's sacrifice brought the Mass closer to the theater. This fierce controversy over the agency and materiality of the Eucharist, she argues, is reflected in Shakespearean drama: in plays like *Othello*, the failure of divine justice to prevail leaves us with a "craving for redemption," that is, a need for moral order which she sees as itself religious. She then engages in a reading of *Othello* that not only exposes the crisis of the distinction between sacrifice and murder, that is, between redemptive sacralization and transgressive violence; she also teases out the equally ambivalent role of sacrifice in the play. Her analysis thus resonates with some of the other contributions in this volume that address the ambiguities of sacrifice and martyrdom. Precisely through its staging of murder, Schwartz concludes provocatively, the Elizabethan theater became the first truly Protestant church, which allowed the community to remember sacrifice without the operation of the official church, and which challenged the individual to morally distinguish sacrifice from murder. Seen from this perspective, Elizabethan drama involves not so much the secularization of Reformation views on the Eucharist as the sacralization of a craving for justice.

In "Martyrdom, Religion, and Nation in Kurdish Literature," Mariwan Kanie traces the historical variability of the discourse of martyrdom in (Southern) Kurdish poetry as well as the changing role of religion in this discourse. In early nineteenth-century ghazâl poets such as Nâlî, he argues, martyrdom is primarily a literary phenomenon; it involves a passive death and an inner and spiritual form of mystical religiosity, which is familiar from classical Persianate poetry. In contrast, in the works of Hajî Qadir Koyî, written toward the turn of the twentieth century, the notion of martyrdom becomes politicized and turned toward the outside world. Koyî not only attacks the classical form of ghazâl poetry but also the classical ideal of passive martyrdom for the sake of mystical love. Kanie calls attention to the particular and novel linguistic ideology to be found in Koyî's writings: here, he argues, the Kurdish language itself is seen as a victim of injustice. In Koyî's works, one encounters not only the secularization of religious concepts and emotions but also a political redefinition of religion. Koyî reconceptualizes Islam from a mystical interiorized faith toward a more activist and patriotic political ideology; he repeats the specifically modern adagium "love of the fatherland is a sign of faith." Since this shift is conversely marked by the sacralization of the fatherland, one cannot simply speak of a secularization of originally or literally religious concepts and sentiments in his work.

The tensions between inner faith and activist, even violent, political ideology come to the fore in Michiel Leezenberg's "Suicide Terrorism and the Modern Nation-State." Leezenberg argues that suicide bombing cannot be reduced to either blind irrational fanaticism qualified as religious or rational means-ends calculation defined as political. A closer empirical attention to the moments when and the contexts in which suicide bombing occurs reveals that it involves a good deal more strategic calculation than is often assumed; but given the impossibility of predicting, let alone controlling, its consequences, one cannot *reduce* the phenomenon to strategic political calculation. Although at first blush an abuse of religious symbolism for worldly, political aims, suicide bombing also involves the sacralization both of perpetrators (and, possibly, their families) and of the cause for which they sacrifice their lives. Thus, suicide actions undermine any strict and unambiguous boundaries between the illegal and the sacral, and between political action defined as goal-directed and rational and religious performance held to be essentially irrational, disinterested, or even self-destructive.

Furthermore, Leezenberg argues, suicide bombing also springs the conceptual and normative confines of liberal political theory. With a few significant exceptions, liberal accounts all too easily dismiss suicide terrorism, and terrorist violence more generally, as illegitimate if not irrational almost as a matter of definition. Suicide bombing not only openly violates or challenges the state's monopoly on violence; it also defies the very idea of the rule of law, as it escapes the concomitant logic of crime and punishment. It is not, however, as such directed against liberal values; rather, by turning the very lives of both perpetrators and victims into objects of sacralized politics, it appears to target and to challenge primarily the biopolitical power, as opposed to the sovereign power, of the modern state. Thus, suicide missions may be analyzed as challenging the modern nation-state's biopolitical control over as well as quasi-sacral claims to the lives of its inhabitants rather than its sovereign power over its citizens construed as subjects of law. The fact that biopolitics is a specifically modern modality of power may also go some way in accounting for the thoroughly modern character and relatively rare occurrence of this disturbing phenomenon.

CHAPTER 18

Sacrifice and the Problem of Beginning
Meditations from Sakalava Mythopraxis

Michael Lambek

Imagine you are standing at the podium about to deliver a public lecture. Your voice cuts into the silence and you begin. No moment is so sheer, so existentially chilling. Having begun, the lecture will run its course; practice follows its routines, speakers their texts. This is not a metaphor of cast dice. Inadvertent circumstance may disrupt the speaking; practice reshapes itself to meet contingency; writing itself takes turns the author does not expect at the outset. But no event is so autonomous, so simply itself as beginning.

Of course, a paradox about beginnings is that when we stop in the middle of things to think about them, they are always already in the past. Whether by means of myth or by memory, we are often trying to understand a present open to the future that is itself already located imaginatively in the past.

"The problem of beginning" wrote Edward Said, "is the beginning of the problem."[1] Nowhere in theory is this problem fully resolved. If beginning was unrecognizable to structuralism, it has fared little better in practice theory's revisions of that doctrine. Beginning is an embarrassment for social theory—and yet it is a regular part of our experience as we gird our loins, face the day, start our computers, embark on a journey, a book, or a love affair; or as we collectively set our sights, step forward to battle or toward a new world—or imagine our predecessors having done so.

Beginning is a problem not only for theory but for practice itself. This essay addresses the problem of beginning in Sakalava practice and the enactment of beginning in Sakalava historical consciousness, how descendants of the polity of Boina in northwest

Madagascar have imagined the beginning of their monarchy (events that took place around 1700 AD), and how that beginning forms a kind of prototype for other beginnings, how beginning again is always a beginning *from* the beginning. Following the Sakalava lead, my essay is also about sacrifice. That is to say, it is about sacrifice as a kind of beginning—at once a means, an act, and a sign of beginning—and possibly about beginning as a kind of sacrifice.

Sakalava Beginnings

Scene 1: The Curation of the Knife

The village of Bemilolo sits in a pastoral setting of oxbow lakes along the Betsiboka River, a place of abundant rice fields, waterfowl, and fish, about a half day's travel by bush taxi from the port of Mahajanga. Among the houses is a fenced-off enclosure containing a small building. This belongs to Ndramandikavavy, the founding queen of Boina. Her name means "Noble lady who surpasses all women." The shrine contains her material artifacts, notably a knife (*viarara*). The shrine is cared for by local inhabitants who claim descent from the Queen. They form a clan, the Tsiarana ("Peerless"), whose duty it is to attend to their ancestress as well as to matters of cattle sacrifice in royal ritual. On the occasion of the annual ceremony honoring the Queen many other Tsiarana gather in the village, along with members of the royal family (*mpanjaka*), who also descend from her (through a different offspring than the Tsiarana). Ndramandikavavy herself speaks from one of her spirit mediums seated on a raised platform outside the enclosure. The knife is deployed whenever there is a burial service at the royal cemetery nearby (at Betsioko). Cattle sacrificed at a royal burial must have their throats cut with Ndramandikavavy's knife.

Sakalava are concerned with the enactment of *fanompoa*, a word that means service to royalty and, specifically, care of royal ancestors—named personages in the royal genealogy. While care is ongoing, especially *taking care* not to offend them, specific ceremonies are directed to the curation of the ancestors and their property—their bones and relics, tombs, houses, and artifacts.[2] Some of the ceremonies, like the Queen's, are annual events. The largest one, the Great Service (*Fanompoa Be*), held in a temple on the outskirts of Mahajanga, is a new year's ritual. And yet, as different shrines across the countryside hold their own annual services, each serves in part as a necessary beginning, a prelude, for successive ones at other locations. Thus, the Great Service cannot itself begin until other services have taken place. It is as if the problem of beginning is itself continuously displaced, pushed back into a kind of infinite regress. But such deferral cannot be infinite; if there is to be a conceptualization of beginning, there must be a first beginning—or a first step in the act of beginning. How that is indicated—the problem of beginning—is the problematic of this article.

The Queen's knife also figures prominently in the Great Service, although it is not literally the same object as the one in Bemilolo but a different materialization of the same conception. It is carried at the head of the annual procession that marks the climax of the New Year festival, during which the four male ancestors whose relics reside at Mahajanga are paraded around their shrine immediately after their annual bath. Each year the Queen's knife is purified along with the relics of her menfolk; each year Sakalava begin their historical journey.

Why is the knife of sacrifice such a critical element? And why does it belong to the Queen? The Queen herself is markedly absent from the main shrine, which is commonly known as the Shrine of the Four Men (*Doany Efadahy*). These include the Queen's husband and their joint son.[3] The Queen can never appear on the shrine precincts and yet the annual service cannot take place without her permission. More than that, the Great Service begins with a sacrifice of cattle in her name.

I do not want to treat either myth or sacrifice as discrete things that can be isolated and inspected in and of themselves. Rather, I look at sacrifice as it appears in Sakalava narrative about the past, in characters instantiated in the present, and as enacted in performance. Our idea of myth—sacred narrative abstracted from its context—is itself secular and therefore cannot give us much sense of what it might be like in a more holistic universe.[4] For Sakalava, myth is living or lived, quite literally. Ancestral personages are invoked in prayer, accounted for in the observance of taboos (and manifest in symptoms of their violation), and encountered in embodied performances of spirit mediums. Narrative has no intrinsic priority. Conversely, "sacrifice" is not only an act carried out but an idea or image explored in narrative and other kinds of performance. My narrative, now well begun, is therefore about neither sacrifice nor myth *per se*, but rather about a set of Sakalava images and practices from which both sacrifice and myth could be precipitated as analytic constructs—by an earlier generation of anthropologists, perhaps. It is better to say succinctly that my article is about beginnings.

In *The Weight of the Past: Living with History in Mahajanga, Madagascar*, I portray the texture of historical experience among present-day Sakalava—how the past structures and sanctifies the reception of new events in the present as well as how the past is continuously realized—made real—by the work of the present.[5] But it could be said that I took beginnings for granted, colluding in the common anthropological wisdom that the explanation of beginnings lies beyond our reach of competence. Yet if we cannot say *why* things begin, perhaps we can still say *how* they begin, or *what* beginnings are, what it *means* to begin. This is not an offer to replace one myth with another, as Freud does in *Totem and Taboo*, for example.[6] The question is less about origins, or the problem of discovering *what* happened, than it is understanding beginning *as* a problem.

I distinguish between beginning and origin. We often think of myth as stories of creation; myths of origin are about the emergence of something from nothing, of order from chaos, of absence replaced by presence. In contrast, beginnings occur in the midst of life, rarely as a very first beginning, but each time a *new* beginning. Beginnings emerge against what precedes them.

Beginnings are located in time and in society, whereas origins may be situated in a pretemporal or prehistorical horizon. Evans-Pritchard, for example, distinguishes Nuer accounts of past events which "have therefore a position in structure" from "the horizon of pure myth. . . . One mythological event did not precede another, for myths explain customs of general social significance rather than the interrelations of particular segments and are, therefore, not structurally stratified."[7] Beginnings are acts and therefore require specific actors or agents. Origins are events and imply extrahuman forces. Beginnings entail human intention. Beginnings also imply a narrative that leads forward from their present. An origin is the culmination of its narrative.

The acts of Sakalava narrative belong to a human age. Indeed, in northwest Madagascar there are no prominent first acts of creation and it is said that people came to the island rather than originating there. Key acts are ones of planting, burying, and setting down roots rather than of coming up autochthonously through the soil.

Edward Said, to whom I am much indebted, argues that "beginning is . . . an activity which ultimately implies return and repetition rather than simple linear accomplishment . . . beginning and beginning-again are historical whereas origins are divine."[8] He continues, "the designation of a beginning generally involves also the designation of a consequent *intention* . . . when we point to the beginning of a novel, for example, we mean that from *that* beginning in principle follows *this* novel. . . . *The beginning, then, is the first step in the intentional production of meaning*."[9] Thus, beginnings are active, humanly made, not naturally or divinely given.[10] Along the path through the forest, they are the first step into a clearing, the first stroke of the axe to mark the trail.

Scene 2: From the Schwarzwald to Bourg la Reine to Ithaca:
The Rites, Wrongs, and Rings of Passage

The ring of the axe is no idle metaphor.[11] Chopping, cutting, spilling, killing—in a word, sacrifice—is one of the ways that we mark time, one of the clearest acts of beginning. In beginnings, the flux of homogeneous time is overcome, the stream is parted into a before, a now, and a henceforward into a past, present, and future. Beginnings signal the self-conscious insertion or intervention of the human act and the recognition of time's place in human experience. Simultaneously, they make spatial discriminations as beginning is materialized—in the chopping of a tree or the spilling of blood—and localized, marking a place in the extension of space, a point, a path, and a direction.

In *The Rites of Passage*, cutting is described as a symbolic act of separation.[12] Arnold van Gennep understands ritual as both temporally constituted and temporally constitutive, enacted and enacting, moving its subjects along trajectories of successive social statuses. He pictures the life cycle as the successive habitation of a series of rooms. The passage between them is enacted through ritual, as though one paused at each threshold to rearrange one's habit and demeanor—and took a deep breath before stepping through.

Victor Turner developed the model in a series of brilliant analyses, but with hindsight it may be fair to say that this elaboration became a kind of appropriation.[13] Where Van Gennep distinguishes three phases of ritually produced movement—separation, transition, and incorporation—Turner famously focuses on the middle, liminal phase. Turner's exploration of transition is certainly true to an aspect of ritual and temporality, but as a result we have come to think of the liminal phase as primary and the other phases as mere brackets or containers of the precious liminal cargo. The power of this model of transition entails two emphases that I wish to counter. First, the action of separation, the bracing of the shoulders and decisive first step, is displaced or overweighted by the passion characteristic of liminal beings and their rebirth. Second, the intransitive quality of the act is overshadowed by the transitive.

Consider the term *initiation*. Whereas initiation as the prototypic rite of passage has come to connote some kind of drawn-out process, the verb *to initiate* more fundamentally means simply "to begin" or "set going."[14] Think also of the meanings of *initial* and *initiative*.

Furthermore, in the sense of beginning, the verb *to initiate* does not have the strong transitive sense of initiating *someone*, but only a weaker transitive sense of initiating a course of action. The verb *to begin* can also be used in the intransitive sense of simply *beginning*. Here the end or object is intrinsic to the means and thus the action is understood as valuable in itself rather than instrumental.

In other words, the model of ritual as transition (and essentially transitive) is ready for another look. Viewed as wholes, *rites de passage* might sometimes be better characterized by a shift of emphasis as rites of beginning. Indeed, the first phase, the new departure, is critical insofar as it anticipates the point of the entire ritual sequence. As a codification and realization of intention and commitment, it subsumes what follows. Enactment of the remaining phases of the ritual is but fulfillment of what is established in setting forth. Initiation means literally "beginning," and then "admission." "Transformation" and "induction" are secondary meanings, reinforced by the tripartite Van Gennep–Turner model.[15] Turner's elaboration of the middle phase obviates understandings of sheer beginning or final end.[16]

Liminality is a spatial metaphor of waiting and passivity; I would supplement it with a temporal phenomenology of action. Rituals are frequently culminations of what is past and anticipations of what will follow. Often, they are both simultaneously. Sacrifice is both a passionate culmination for the victim and a significant initiative by the person who offers it. It draws a line in blood between before and after. Once you have killed something there is literally no going back for either victim or killer. Sacrifice is thus a materialization of intention and a consummation of resolution.

How much more powerful all this is when victim and sacrificer are one and the same person.

Scene 3: The Shrine of the Four Men

The Great Service sets the Sakalava community on a fresh start every year. But critical to the success of the ceremony of new beginning is its own beginning. In Sakalava fashion, the key acts happen backstage. Each year, ancestral approval for the service must be sought and confirmed; rising in the bodies of spirit mediums, royal ancestors "open the gate" or "clear the path" to move ahead. Thus, intentionality is marked from the outset—both the intention of the living producers of the ritual, who state their aims very clearly in addressing the ancestors, and the intention of the ancestors, who explicitly acquiesce and join in the wish to see the ceremony successfully completed (*vita tsara*).

A week before the public beginning of the new year's festival and consequent to her acquiescence, descendants of the Queen gather at the shrine to make a bovine sacrifice on her behalf.[17] They signify their commitment by offering the beast—and the animal itself, like all Sakalava sacrificial beasts, must indicate acquiescence by not bellowing or struggling when it is thrown.

The skin of the dead beast is then stretched to dry and used to refurbish the shrine's two sacred drums (*mañandria be*, "great ennoblers"). The vitality inherent in the life of the beast and the intentionality of the offering are transposed into the vibrancy of the drums.[18] There is a literature associating percussion with transition,[19] but I emphasize here its significance as beginning and enactment.

Drumming is both energetic and unambiguous. The drummer beats the drum; each movement of the arm is specific and deliberate. The energy of the arm is transferred to and enlarged by the vibrations of the drumskin. The rhythm of the drum continues to emit the intention of the sacrifice. The passivity of the beast silently submitting to the knife is transcended by dynamism, noise, and vitality. The drums are a medium for the active force of the victim.

In contemporary Sakalava sacrifice, "value" moves from the labor of raising the animal through its market price; but also from the intention of the donor through the acquiescence of the beast; and from the throb of life through the spilled red blood to the pulsing of the drums made from the victim's skin; then from the drums that excite and incite to the acts of those who respond to its rhythm, in anticipation, in attention, in dance, and in labor and loyalty, in virtuous acts of commitment to the monarchy, obeisance to the ancestors, and acknowledgment of hierarchy, hence in granting power to Ndramandikavavy. This is a version of the process of the "dissolution of death . . . into authority" analyzed by Maurice Bloch for the neighboring Merina that combines mystification with morality.[20]

The initial sacrifice is described as an offering on behalf of the Queen, but it is also a repetition of her original sacrifice. Those who perform the offering stand in for their ancestor who made the first sacrifice. Just as Ndramandikavavy's original act began the polity, so does it begin the new year, which is also a celebration and reenactment of the polity and includes offerings to the original monarchs by their subjects. Because many of the offerings end up in the hands of the living monarch and because acts of work, offering, and obeisance form the substance of the polity, the celebration is a literal as well as symbolic enactment. But my point here is simply that both the historical polity and the annual enactment begin with the Queen's sacrifice. Indeed, just as the liturgical cycle enacts the beginning of the polity, so the beginning of the polity is equally the initiation of the liturgical order.

However, the Queen's original offering was not composed of cattle. This is a point to which we shall return.

Sakalava emphasize and elaborate the beginning of their service with various deliberate steps before the public display, putting the weight, one could say, more on the intention than on the accomplishment (which is a kind of anticlimax, or at least it was to me). The sacrifice of the Queen's beast forms a preface to the ensuing festival. It is relatively private (concerning only her own direct descendants, mediums, and shrine workers), whereas the festival is public, incorporating thousands of people through numerous forms of attachment. The sacrifice is also quite discreet; most people do not know the connection between the Queen and the drums. But it is absolutely critical. The festival cannot take place without the Queen's acquiescence, as provided in her speech through a medium and performatively accomplished in the sacrifice. Moreover, the drums are one of the most important heirlooms and signs of royal legitimacy; they must be renewed each year, their skins must be those of the Queen's cattle, and their rhythm must punctuate the ensuing events.

These acts are not only the rehearsal of a genealogical charter but also conditions that enable the felicitous performance and the performative effects of the subsequent main ritual events. But they are also performative events in their own right. The Great Service is front-loaded with a series of such events that establish the intention and willingness to proceed. It is as though Sakalava are preoccupied with the sort of infinite regress of intentionality—the ghost in the machine—described by Gilbert Ryle, albeit in the Sakalava case this is located in the external, interpersonal world of the polity, rather than the internal, private one of the mind.[21] Ryle, of course, saw regress as the product of a category mistake. But it may well be that this category mistake is not so easy for humans to avoid, that mind and body and the mind/body problem are part of the human condition, that the Durkheimian problem of social solidarity and moral commitment is formally similar and that the problem of beginning is one of its manifestations. The series of ritual acts productive and demonstrative of intention and commitment, and each a necessary condition for the succeeding one, are Sakalava expressions of the problem.

Scene 4: Morningside Heights (Manhattan)

Some years before he became famous as the author of *Orientalism*, Edward Said wrote *Beginnings*, subtitled *Intention and Method*, from which I have already quoted. In that book Said is interested in creative production. Every work of art has its beginning, its conception, and the way that conception is activated or materialized in a first sentence, note, or brushstroke.

Said does not explicitly consider beginnings characteristic of social practice, and hence he ignores the field of ritual. And yet his account is extremely relevant for social practice. "What sort of action," he asks, "transpires at the beginning? How can we, while necessarily submitting to the incessant flux of experience, insert (as we do) our reflections on beginning(s) into that flux? Is the beginning simply an artifice, a disguise that defies the perpetual trap of forced continuity? Or does it admit of a meaning and a possibility that are genuinely capable of realization?"[22]

Said speaks of the necessity "to acknowledge the mind as providing self-concerned glosses on itself over time, the mind as comprising its own philosophical anthropology";[23] surely these glosses are found in ritual no less than in literature. Indeed, Said argues that beginnings are necessary. "Without at least a sense of a beginning, nothing can really be done, much less ended.... A beginning gives us the chance to do work that compensates us for the tumbling disorder of brute reality that will not settle down."[24]

Said makes a careful distinction between transitive and intransitive beginning. These are "really two sides of the same coin. One, which I call temporal and transitive, foresees a continuity that flows from it. This kind of beginning is suited for work, for polemic, for discovery." However, "In attempting to push oneself further and further back to what is only a beginning, a point that is stripped of every use but its categorization in the mind as beginning, one is caught in a tautological circuit of beginnings about to begin. This is the other kind of beginning, the one I called intransitive and conceptual. It is very much a creature of the mind, very much a bristling paradox, yet also very much a figure of thought that draws special attention to itself."[25] In sum,

> The point of departure ... has two aspects that animate one another. One leads to the project being realized: this is the transitive aspect of the beginning—that is, beginning with (or for) an anticipated end, or at least expected continuity. The other aspect retains for the beginning its identity as *radical* starting point: the intransitive and conceptual aspect, that which has no object but its own constant clarification.... These two sides of the starting point entail two styles of thought, and of imagination, one projective and descriptive, the other tautological and endlessly self-mimetic. The transitive mode is always hungering ... for an object it can never fully catch up with in either space or time. The intransitive ... can never have enough of itself.[26]

Scene 5: The Countryside West of Mahajanga, circa 1700

The Sakalava have reached the country of Boina where they would like to settle and rule. An oracle advises the King, "In order to succeed, you must sacrifice what is dearest to you (*raha tsifoinao*)." The King offers the best cattle from his herds, but they are not acceptable. He offers gold, and then fine Chinese porcelain, but they too are insufficient. Finally, his wife announces, "I am what is dearest to you." And so she sacrifices herself.

This is an extreme distillation of more elaborated and divergent narratives of the founding of the Sakalava polity but sufficient for my purpose here.[27]

We can see now that if Ndramandikavavy is absent from the main shrine it is precisely because its very existence is predicated on her death. Moreover, it is not merely the sacrificers who take the Queen's place in the annual ceremony but the cattle themselves. They are killed not only on the Queen's behalf, nor in her honor, but with her knife and in her stead. The throat that this knife first cut was the Queen's. Each sacrifice is a repetition and recognition of her original act; each victim is identified with her. It is her skin and her life that animate and empower the drums. It is her intentionality that produces and permeates the ensuing ceremony and that infuses the resolution of the celebrants as loyal subjects.

As a character in the Sakalava poiesis of history, Ndramandikavavy symbolizes *determination*.[28] It is her determination that is harnessed to ensure and energize the enactment of the Great Service. It is her determination that is diffused to her descendants and her subjects—the general population (*vahoaka*) who have produced and renewed the polity through their own acts of sacrifice, service, and celebration over the course of three hundred years. Her resolve is evoked in her every appearance and lends itself to every act carried out with her knife and in her name.

Determination is an interesting word, seemingly pulled between free agency and inevitable coercion. Ndramandikavavy's sacrifice is deeply intentional, yet to call it choice trivializes it, as though Abraham or Isaac had a choice. To draw upon Said again, it is "a necessary certainty, a genetic optimism, that continuity is possible *as intended by* the act of beginning. . . . Consciousness of a starting point, from the vantage point of the continuity that succeeds it, is seen to be consciousness of a direction in which it is humanly possible to move (as well as a trust in continuity)."[29]

In fact, Ndramandikavavy extracted a promise from her husband as a condition of her sacrifice, namely that only their joint descendants would rule; his continuity would be equally hers. In its transitive aspect the beginning thus conforms to Malinowski's notion of a charter in that it establishes legitimacy to rule and both specifies and restricts succession to office. Yet it differs from many genealogical charter myths in validating an ancestral couple. The Queen effectively cuts off all the King's collaterals and other descendants. The King and Queen's respective children by other partners form two separate clans, closely associated with royalty but distinct from it. Descendants from the Queen alone are Tsiarana—the Peerless—who maintain and wield the sacrificial knife.[30]

In comparison with the Judeo-Christian-Islamic tradition, and especially the story of Abraham and Isaac, the following points are salient: (a) the victim is a woman; (b) the victim is said to "kill herself" (*mamon teña*); (c) the victim is not an offspring but a spouse and parent; (d) the sacrifice is fully carried out, there is a human death; and (e) there is no direct recipient, no divine being to whom or on whose demand or behalf the sacrifice is given. There is much to say about gender and about mothers and sons, but having begun an essay on beginnings, I must stay on track.[31] Germane to the present analysis is the determined yet voluntary quality of the sacrifice, the completion and finality of the act, and the absence of a divine arbiter or recipient. Thus, whereas biblical sacrifice seals God's promise to look after His people, Sakalava sacrifice seals the people's promise to care for Ndramandikavavy, her son, and his descendants.[32]

Sacrifice as Exemplary Beginning

There are many theories of sacrifice. I do not intend to review them or to adjudicate among them. Nor do I propose to add another theory; I merely provide a redescription. I want to show that sacrifice is an exemplary mode of beginning and hence that beginning affords one way to interpret sacrifice.[33] This is certainly not the most intuitive interpretation, since—for the person, animal, or object destroyed—sacrifice would appear to form most saliently an ending. In a sense, each new beginning signals simultaneously the end of what it departs from and perhaps the death of alternatives not taken. But I suggest more strongly that endings form and substantiate beginnings. I do not suggest that this is the only way to understand sacrifice, but I admit that one way to read my argument is that no theory of sacrifice—no explanation that draws upon forces external to the act itself—is necessary.[34]

Sacrifice as a Literal Act

By *literal*, I mean here univocal, exact, unmediated, and unambiguous, hence where certainty can be distinguished from uncertainty. The body is often the ground for the literal.[35] The body is literally grounded in burial, and authors such as Astuti, Bloch, and Middleton have noted how in Madagascar this—finally—establishes exclusive social identity. Sacrifice is one of the most literal acts possible, both as an action and in terms of its end product, that is, a dead body.[36]

To be sure, the sacrifice of an ox for a human, or a cucumber for an ox, can be understood metaphorically. But these are merely replacements of one object of sacrifice for another and not metaphors for other, more consequential kinds of acts; at bottom, they are still sacrifice. For the ox, his life is no metaphor. Cut flowers die; liquid cannot be put back into its container; like Humpty Dumpty, a sliced cucumber cannot be put back together again. There may be some ambiguity as to whether a given act of killing is sacrificial or what that might mean,[37] but killing in and of itself is always a literal act. For the victim there is no return, nor can the killer withdraw her act.

In this sense, killing is like ritual. One of the things about rituals is that you cannot take them back in protest that you did not mean it. Once done they cannot be undone, at least not without going to the trouble of holding another ritual of a different kind. Sacrifice ensures and epitomizes this quality of ritual action.

Cutting throats and spilling blood are literal acts. The object can be metaphorically displaced—from royal self to human subject, from animal to vegetable—but the act of sacrifice is no metaphor.

The Gift and Its Limits

It is often argued, following Mauss, that there can be no "pure" gift, since the obligation to give is always met with the obligations to receive and to return a gift. The recipient who does not offer a return is beholden to the donor and the donor achieves a higher moral status in that respect. Hence no gift can be said to be characterized by pure disinterest.

What of sacrifice? In Ndramandikavavy's case, while her sacrifice was noble and courageous, no Sakalava would suggest it was undertaken without self-interest. The Queen struck a bargain; she asked for something in return. However, what her sacrifice shares with the idea of the pure gift is the impossibility of a full return. Here lies the source of her power.

Why can there be no equivalent return? To answer that, I must address the question of who her recipients are and how I know her gift was not disinterested.

There is no third party, no deity to receive or be honored by Ndramandikavavy's sacrifice. The instigator is a diviner, and he is responding to the workings of a neutral, amoral destiny. The immediate beneficiary is posited as the King, her husband, but her death is simultaneously his loss. Indeed, it is phrased in those very words as that with which he could not bear to part, *raha tsifoinao*. Yet Ndramandikavavy's quick response actually turns things in a more interesting way; in sacrificing herself, she seizes his role as the offerer of sacrifice and achieves the perdurance of her own name and rule. What the King loses is not just his wife but his agency (which is dearest to him indeed).

By establishing his exclusive right to succession, the Queen makes their son the direct beneficiary. It is only toward him that her sacrifice might be said to be disinterested and yet it is precisely because of her identification with her son that it is most self-interested. It is his—and therefore her—descendants who succeed him. His paternal half-siblings—the other children of her husband—are specifically excluded and disinherited.

More generally, the beneficiaries are all subsequent members of the kingdom of Boina. This has a sharp ideological angle: the Queen's subjects are expected to honor her for effecting the conditions under which her descendants rule over them, as well as identifying with her as an ideal subject.

When Ndramandikavavy rises in the bodies of her mediums it is evident that she went willingly but not selflessly. She retains great attachment to the things of this world, to her son in particular. And she is especially rude to her husband. He shows his wife great affection and puts his arm around her, but she soon gets impatient. After a few minutes, she says brusquely, "What are you still doing around here? No one needs you any longer!" Thus, the conqueror and first king of Boina slips meekly away from his shrill wife and out of the body of his medium. He is, in her eyes, irrelevant. He is eternally beholden. He cannot return her gift.

If the Queen gave up her life on behalf of her husband, it is clear that he in turn has given over his authority to her. In response to supplicants, the King speaks in platitudes and is generally amenable to whatever is proposed; the Queen is forthright, assertive, and tough, expecting people to uphold the standards of the polity for which she gave her life. She inspires respect and fear not only in her husband but also in her human subjects. She is known to be harsh (*mashiaka*) and her devotees are afraid of her wrath.

Ndramandikavavy's sacrifice is a gift that must be received yet cannot be returned in full and hence canceled. The debt to her is in a sense what keeps the polity running. Generation after generation must bow to her authority, respond to the interpellation of the drum; each royal succession must ensure that the promise to her remains fulfilled. Acknowledgment is mandated, but no return could ever be sufficient to cancel the debt.

The Queen's gift cannot be canceled not only because she courageously gave her own life—and no larger gift could be imagined—or because the existence and persistence of the political community are the outcomes of her act; not only for the obvious reason that she is no longer fully present to benefit from a return gift; but also because what she offered was manifestly a *first* gift. Any and all returns—even were they to be equivalent—are quite literally secondary. Only one act in a sequence can be first.

Insofar as her act is original, Ndramandikavavy points to a problematic of the gift literature left largely unaddressed by Mauss and his successors. These are the questions: What constitutes a first gift? Which donor stands out as the original source of the *hau* to which the gift must return? Moreover, if every gift engenders a return, how do we know that any given gift is not always already a return? How is a gift marked as first? Where and how does the chain of reciprocity begin? How can one break it and start anew?[38] We are back to the question of beginnings.

My point is that sacrifice is one way to mark a gift as "first." Indeed, this may be implicit in our understanding of the distinction between sacrifice and gift.

Blood sacrifice or self-sacrifice makes an especially good beginning, a first gift, because it is a gift that does not—indeed, cannot—return to its origins. It is the gift that cannot be returned, or canceled, or withdrawn. The only thing to do with it is to honor it.

Words and Deeds

Ndramandikavavy's sacrifice is not a gift to a transcendental being but dictated by fate. It is in this respect unmotivated and unreceived. Thus, I do not wish to place undue emphasis on sociality, communion, commensality, appeasement, or supplication. A sacrifice is purely what it is and not something else.[39]

Goethe's *Faust* rewrites the New Testament to begin, "First was the act!"[40] Sacrifice (cutting, killing) is manifestly neither word nor object but act. What distinguishes sacrifice from simple giving or killing is that it is explicitly performative, bringing into being a new conventional or moral state.

Performative acts—in Austin's sense—are frequently beginnings and they are spoken in the first person. They can be understood as public expressions and objectifications of resolution. Austin provides examples like: "I . . . take this woman to be my lawful wedded wife . . . ; I name this ship the *Queen Elizabeth* . . . ; I give and bequeath my watch . . . ; I bet you sixpence . . ."[41] Each of these casts intentionality forward—as vow, promise, contract—most generally, as commitment. Henceforward, the state of affairs, the name, the relationship, and the expectation shall be understood in the terms established in the performative act. Thus, the state of marriage is brought into being in the enactment of the wedding service. As Rappaport notes, acts subsequently committed by persons subject to the conditions initiated by means of the performative act are to be judged with respect to those conditions.[42]

In Muslim societies a simple and ubiquitous act of beginning is found in the utterance of the *bismillah*. Trobriand spells are also beginnings and performative acts in this sense. As Malinowski portrays it, Trobrianders utter a spell at each new phase of the *kula*, from felling the tree to make a canoe to meeting the *kula* partners.[43] The utterance of each spell *is* the beginning of each new phase. The spell can be understood to mark a reorientation in the stream of practice and to begin what lies ahead. The *kula* expedition as an ethical enterprise is thereby constituted as a series of marked intentions, each initiated by a performative utterance that constitutes the quality of the time/space and action of what is to follow.[44]

Austin's insight is that such utterances are simultaneously acts. Rappaport describes ritual as comprised of both acts and utterances, but it could be said that he also privileges utterances. Thus, he singles out ultimate sacred postulates, phrases like the *bismillah* which are unquestionable and invariant, and which sanctify the acts and more specific utterances they accompany, as when a political pronouncement includes the phrase "In the name of God . . . ." Yet if utterances are acts, certain highly conventionalized acts may be considered simultaneously utterances.[45] We can speak of sacred acts no less than sacred postulates, and sacrifice is surely among them.

Of course, sacrifice is an act generally composed of both word and deed, but it is one in which the deed speaks more powerfully than the word.

Just as Rappaport describes a hierarchy of postulates with respect to their sanctity, so, I suggest tentatively, we may think of acts.[46] This hierarchy is one of unquestionableness, invariance, precedence, and inclusiveness; one could add irreversibility. As a pure beginning, the first sacrifice sanctifies and establishes the condition for the acts that follow. Indeed, it sanctifies the entire subsequent history of the kingdom, for so long as it is respected. It also establishes the grounds of value or meaning, providing the standard against which other acts can be understood. Subsequent sacrifices of lesser value—ranging from human subjects, through cattle, down to a few coins or drops of rum—can only approximate, rehearse, and evoke the ultimate sacrifice. But like it, they are performative acts that sanctify the conventional and moral states they initiate.

My point is not that in the beginning lies the deed, or lies the deed alone, but rather that in the performative deed lies a beginning.

Execution

Heidegger has written that "to the anticipation which goes with resoluteness, there belongs a present in accordance with which a resolution discloses the situation."[47] The question is, how is resolve disclosed or realized—made real—both for actors and for their public? The irreversibility of blood sacrifice is certainly one way.

A blood sacrifice is an execution. According to the dictionary, *to execute* means: "1. Carry (plan, command, law, will, judicial sentence) into effect; perform (action, operation, etc.); make (legal instrument) valid by signing, sealing, etc.; discharge (office, function). 2. Carry out design for (product of art or skill); perform (musical composition). 3. Inflict capital punishment on."[48] To execute a living being in sacrifice is simultaneously to execute a plan or course of action.[49] In both Malagasy (where the relevant verb is *manapaka*) and English we see how central killing is to the idea of carrying out a definitive and irreversible social act.[50]

Outright killing is not the only form of executive bloodletting. Scarification is one example; defloration is another. In Mayotte a woman's relinquishment of her virginity is marked. Done in the wrong context, it is simply an ending and thus destructive. Done in the right context, it is a beginning, the first moment of adult sexuality and the consummation—as we say—of marriage. The act of submitting to defloration is sacrifice in this sense, a formal, decisive, and irreversible execution and a gift that can never be fully returned. It is no coincidence that it is likened to the act of male circumcision.[51]

Action and Passion

Rituals are decisive deeds, yet they are acts in which people submit to something larger than themselves. In this respect, as Heidegger would put it, "man is not the opener of truth . . . but the 'opening for it.'"[52] Rituals thereby combine action and passion in a heightened manner. These two dimensions correspond respectively to Said's transitive and intransitive modes of beginning.

Whenever I mention Heidegger I am skating on very thin ice, and you may already have concluded that I have fallen in. But I cannot resist allusion to Heidegger's concept of *Gelassenheit*, releasement or letting go, which is not simple "inaction or passivity." As Dallmayr notes, "an engagement in being . . . challenges or decenters the customary focus of action theory on desire, will, or deliberate intentionality . . . instead, the accent is shifted to ontological participation in which the actor is released at least partially from the dictates of an instrumental pursuit of objectives. This shift . . . does not . . . remove moral–political responsibility."[53]

Sacrifice, especially self-sacrifice, exhibits this inextricable connection of action and passion or "resoluteness of released engagement."[54] It is not dying in a simple, passive sense, or killing in a simple, active sense; not accepting the inevitability of death but, as Lienhardt emphasizes for Dinka, converting it into life.[55] Sacrifice is a negation of the act of giving birth and yet strangely like it. It is "giving death," submitting to it, yet bearing it forth; like birth, it is an act at once transitive and intransitive. And it can provide a sharper sense of beginning even than birth.[56] A birth can be undone—through death. But a death cannot be undone.

As Rappaport argues, in lending themselves to a ritual, performers inevitably accept its terms and effects.[57] There is no more complete mode of participation in this sense than allowing oneself to be sacrificed. Self-sacrifice is the limit act of committing oneself to the liturgical order and hence of confirming, establishing, and realizing it through one's very being. This is equally a form of identification with it. Others then realize their own commitment through their attachment to, or identification with, the sacrificial victim or sacrificer. Instances of exemplary acceptance of this kind include Jesus on the cross, Dinka spear masters buried alive, and dying Hindu pilgrims who prepare their bodies as offerings to the gods on the model of Vishnu's act of creation.[58] As the sacrificer is identified with the sacrifice, so is the ending coextensive with the beginning and the transitive with the intransitive.

The sacrificer conjoins in her act the indexical and canonical aspects of ritual and does so more completely than can be imagined through any other means. We see in this fusion a deeper significance for sacrifice than that presupposed by communication or communion with a deity. In submitting to the liturgical order, it becomes a part of her being and she, too, becomes an intrinsic part of that order.[59] Actors and action can then only be described, interpreted, and evaluated with respect to prior commitments—with respect to what has been begun.

Ndramandikavavy simultaneously acts and submits. Such action by means of submission, or subjection through action, is the hegemonic form of belonging in the tributary Sakalava polity; in this sense Ndramandikavavy is an exemplary subject and, like all Sakalava rulers, expected to be simultaneously more powerful than the average citizen but also more bound by taboo and obligation to the ancestral order, more intimately part of it. Equally, we can see in sacrifice an epitomization of the Durkheimian understanding of society in which each member must give up some individuality in order to be transformed, at a higher level, into a moral person.

Social being more generally entails a dialectic of action and passion, of taking in, doing, and becoming what is expected of us (or what is unexpected) and in taking a purchase on what we are becoming and have become and making it ours. The idea of beginning captures this double edge of social subject and agent. In beginning a new project—even as one is the agent of its production or enactment—one throws oneself into it, one subsumes oneself in the practice that it entails, and one is thereby partially consumed by it. And so, if beginning is signified or realized in sacrifice, that is in part because beginning is, in a way, itself an act of sacrifice.[60]

Time and Intention

"We do not live 'in time,' as if the latter were some independent, abstract flow external to our being. We 'live time'; the two terms are inseparable," says George Steiner in his explication of Heidegger's *Sein und Zeit*.[61] If so, what other way to punctuate time than by means of death? Sacrifice *executes* a beginning and in producing a present realizes both the past that it displaces and rehearses and the future that it anticipates. Sacrifice founds beginnings; it is foundational.[62]

My argument here is less functionalist than poietic or rhetorical. Functionalism assumes the prior existence of the whole, whereas I am describing how certain kinds of wholes are brought into being. Having learned about rites of passage in school, Simon Lambek (my son) asked insightfully how sacrifice could be a ritual if it had no closure. This is exactly the crux of the problem and the basis of my critique.

Both Van Gennep and Turner understand rites of passage as transitions. I have been interested more in sheer beginnings, in beginning as an existential problem and also in how people conceptualize, announce, and enact beginning—how they in fact *begin*. In Said's terms, this is to shift the emphasis from transitive to intransitive acts. Understood in its intransitive aspect, beginning, in the form of sacrifice, is neither a gift, nor an instrumental act, nor a referential statement; it is simply itself. Here we approach Wittgenstein's critique of Frazer: it does not make sense to see ritual as an expression of something other than itself; it simply is what it is, a necessary part of the life of a ceremonial animal.[63]

Many rituals have both transitive and intransitive aspects. For example, if a wedding ritual entails marrying in the transitive sense, something one does to or with a partner or to one's growing children as subjects of a ritual performed on their behalf, there are nevertheless moments in marriage festivities when the intransitive mode prevails, where the act of marrying is experienced or understood as just that, "getting" married. Here is a sense of "the blossom breaking from the bud,"[64] sheer potentiality without any object. This constitutes a ripeness, a sense of capacity rather than utility.[65] Such a state of being (*Dasein*) shares features with Turner's compelling depiction of "liminality," but, understood as intransitivity, it is a different way of conceptualizing the ritual act.

Writing as a professor of literature, Said is naturally most interested in beginning as poiesis, the "bringing into being" of a new cultural artifact, a work of literature or art.[66] I have emphasized less poiesis than practice, seeing beginning as the intentional engagement in social endeavors, commitments, or games. This is partly a matter of anticipation of outcome, partly of submission to the rules, craft, or ethics that the practice entails. Aristotle distinguishes poiesis and practice, making and doing, but in beginning—in authoring a book, performing a ritual, or founding a polity, the distinction may be negligible.[67]

Following the Sakalava cue, I have argued that the resolution entailed in beginning is well signified in the act of sacrifice. Problems of uncertainty and alternative come into focus most clearly at beginnings. Sacrifice can—and with a stroke—end them. Sacrifice combines the ethical consequentiality of judgment with the decisiveness of choice. It thereby forms not merely a kind of "natural symbol" of beginnings but a natural means to execute them.[68]

I argue that the story of Ndramandikavavy addresses the problem of regress in Sakalava historicity, providing, retroactively, a founding moment and a coalescence of intention and the continuation of sacrifice—henceforward figured in her name, by means of her knife—continues to make this available in the ongoing life of the polity.

Rites de passage belong to long cycles of generational repetition, and that is an important part of the experience for participants. But Ndramandikavavy's act is portrayed retroactively as original, a "first" act of beginning, an initiation in the literal sense of the term, a particular and deliberate intervention in history. The sacrifices that punctuate ordinary life realize, focus, and display resolution and add weight, direction, and significance to specific acts and utterances and to the projects and states of affairs they initiate, introduce, and inform. Their force is greater insofar as they draw upon the paradigmatic act of intervention, firstness, and resolve, the perduring sacred prototype or ultimate sacred act of Sakalava beginning.

Ethics and Ending

Without beginnings it is hard to see how action could be conceived in ethical terms. Beginnings cast intention forward; in drawing from the past, they render valuable what follows from them and, as performative acts, they set the terms of reference against which actors, events, and practices are to be judged. Who we are as moral persons is in large part a consequence of the beginnings we have enacted or participated in. Some of these happen before we reach adult consciousness, as we are named, baptized, circumcised, and so forth. Later in life we take up charges with fuller consciousness and resolve, and we indicate this to ourselves and to others, just as we realize it *for* ourselves—sometimes retroactively—in beginning. It is through such explicit engagements and undertakings that our specific ethical lives and characters are formed; they provide the basis for both the cultivated dispositions and the ends and means that constitute us as ethical persons. As a powerful and definitive mode of beginning, sacrifice exemplifies these ethical functions.

Once committed and remembered, sacrifice can be intrinsic to who one is, as a person or a society. Who one *is* is thereby understood existentially rather than essentially, through the sheer initiation of being. And yet, despite the emphasis on intention and resolution, this is hardly the continuous "freedom" that Sartre advocates. That is because each act of sacrifice is simultaneously a passion; each turns us irrevocably in a certain direction, locates us on a certain path; and each invites identification and repetition. Each undertaking we initiate must be made with respect to commitments always already engaged, subject positions already assumed, each new beginning with respect to beginnings already begun.

I am describing regulation or channeling in the flow of social and existential value, the mastering of creative and ethical potential—that is, setting its direction and establishing and accepting its consequences. Of course, this does not happen equally effectively everywhere and not without considerable debate. We might contrast an ostensibly relatively orderly tradition, like that of Sakalava, with more chaotic scenes in which society appears to have lost its way. These may be characterized by epidemics of witchcraft which, by inverting or perverting the logic of sacrifice, both demonstrate and effect the collapse of ethical order.[69] The rhythm of regular beginning is displaced by rupture and increasingly frantic attempts at establishing new beginnings. The place of ethics and the formation of ethical persons will be distinctive in these circumstances.

I have been using beginnings as a means to read across the tradition/modernity divide, but I should add that Said himself worked with a distinction between tradition and modernity that has quite different implications. Indeed, he sees beginnings as distinctive of modernity. He argues that contemporary writers and critics can no longer easily imagine themselves within a tradition, "a place in a continuity that formerly stretched forward and backward in time."[70] After Nietzsche, a text has become "an invitation to unforeseen estrangements from the habitual."[71] In a masculine idiom quite foreign to Sakalava, Said distinguishes father-son succession, "dynastic, bound to sources and origins, mimetic," from that of brotherly displacements, "complementarity and adjacency; instead of a source we have the intentional beginning."[72] He contrasts these in Viconian language as "sacred" and "gentile," respectively.[73]

This distinction doubtless owes its formulation to the structuralist contrast between the syntagmatic and paradigmatic no less than to Vico. I find it overdrawn and indeed something of a rehearsal of modernity's own ideology; an ideology—dare I say it—of traditionalism comparable to that of Orientalism. I have demonstrated the relevance of Said's analysis of beginnings precisely for the succession characteristic of tradition, which is not nearly as uninformed by intention, reflection, uncertainty, contestation, or women's agency as Said would appear to imply.

Tradition is neither timeless nor mindless: that is to say, it is not without beginnings. Beginnings are not routine; at least, in Sakalava "service" every effort is made not to take them for granted. Each beginning actively solicits intention and explicitly demands it. Such intentionality, as Rappaport underscores, is transformed through ritual action into commitment. A difference from the situation of the modern writer described by Said is that commitment is not simply to the work at hand, hence fragmentary and fragmenting, but to a wider order within which specific works and beginnings are construed and authorized.

If beginnings *per se* do not serve to distinguish between tradition and modernity, perhaps the gentiles can no longer encode them as sacrifice. Marshall Berman finds modernity's myth of beginning in Goethe's *Faust*.[74] Faust's pact with Mephisto is a precise inversion of sacrifice: you reap the material benefits and postpone the ethical reckoning. It is life lived on credit, or capital.[75] Yet even Faust must sign his contract with a drop of blood. "Blood's a very special ink, you know," says Mephisto.[76]

If endings are beginnings, then beginnings are endings of a sort as well. I end this somewhat recursive discussion with a final word from Said: "Beginning is a consciously intentional . . . activity . . . whose circumstances include a sense of loss."[77]

Notes

1. Edward Said, *Beginnings: Intention and Method* (Baltimore, MD: Johns Hopkins University Press, 1975), 42. Here is the larger context of the phrase: "'Beginning' alternates in the mind's discriminations between thought that is beginning and thought about beginning—that is, between the status of subject and object. Paraphrasing both Hegel and Vico, we can say that formally the problem of beginning is the beginning of the problem. A beginning is a moment when the mind can start to allude to itself and to its products as a formal doctrine."

2. Michael Lambek, *The Weight of the Past: Living with History in Mahajanga, Madagascar* (New York: Palgrave Macmillan, 2002).

3. Strictly, it is *Doany Ndramisara Efadahy*, Ndramisara's shrine of the four men; Ndramisara was diviner and architect of the polity (Lambek, *Weight of the Past*, 93–94, 97) and sometimes identified with the Queen's brother.

4. See also Talal Asad, *Formations of the Secular: Christianity, Islam, Modernity* (Stanford, CA: Stanford University Press, 2003).

5. Lambek, *Weight of the Past*; cf. Marshall Sahlins, *Islands of History* (Chicago: Chicago University Press, 1985).

6. Sigmund Freud, "Totem and Taboo: Some Points of Agreement between the Mental Lives of Savages and Neurotics," in *The Standard Edition of the Complete Psychological Works of Sigmund Freud*, vol. 13, trans. J. Strachey (London: Hogarth, 1958 [1913]), ix–162.

7. E. E. Evans-Pritchard, *The Nuer* (Oxford: Clarendon, 1940), 108.

8. Said, *Beginnings*, xiii.

9. Said, 5.

10. "As consistently as possible I use *beginning* as having the more active meaning, and *origin* the more passive one: thus 'X *is the origin of* Y,' while 'The beginning A *leads to* B.'" Said, *Beginnings*, 6.

11. References here are to dwelling places associated, respectively, with Heidegger, Van Gennep, and Turner (Ithaca, NY, as well as the prototypic end of the voyage). This section owes a good deal to a conversation with Joshua Barker.

12. Arnold van Gennep, *The Rites of Passage*, trans. M. Vizedom and G. Caffee (Chicago: Chicago University Press, 1960 [1908]).

13. See, for example, Victor Turner, *The Forest of Symbols* (Ithaca, NY: Cornell University Press, 1967); and Turner, *The Ritual Process* (London: Routledge and Kegan Paul, 1969).

14. "Initiate *v.t.* 1. Begin, set going, originate. 2. Admit (person), esp. with introductory rites or forms (*into* society, office, secret, *in* mysteries, science, etc.)." *Oxford Illustrated Dictionary* (1975).

15. And further reinforced by the ubiquitous practices of fraternities and sororities on American campuses that served as undergraduate essay topics.

16. The relevance of *both* modes is amply discussed by Rappaport, to whose analysis I am much indebted. Roy Rappaport, *Ritual and Religion in the Making of Humanity* (Cambridge: Cambridge University Press, 1999). Following Rappaport, any ritual *qua* event takes the preceding (analogic) flux of uncertainty and indecision and, in a clear (digital) act, definitively transcends it (95).

17. I observed this event in July 1994. That year the Tsiarana pooled their resources to purchase the animal. There are no rules regarding the sex or age of the bovine offering. Compare the killing of a bull to initiate Merina rituals of blessing, an act Bloch "hesitates" to call a sacrifice. M. Bloch, "The Ritual of the Royal Bath in Madagascar: The Dissolution of Death, Birth, and Fertility into Authority," in *Ritual, History, and Power: Selected Papers in Anthropology* (London: Athlone, 1989), 59, 98.

18. Cf. Malcolm Ruel, "Non-Sacrificial Ritual Killing," *Man* n.s. 25, no. 2 (1990): 323–335.

19. Bruce Knauft, "On Percussion and Metaphor," *Current Anthropology* 20, no. 1 (1979): 189–91; Rodney Needham, "Percussion and Transition." *Man* n.s. 2, no. 4 (1967): 606–614.

20. Bloch, "Ritual of the Royal Bath."

21. Gilbert Ryle, *The Concept of Mind* (London: Hutchinson, 1949).

22. Said, *Beginnings*, 43.

23. Said, 43.

24. Said, 49–50. For example, while weddings are commonly seen, in accordance with alliance or descent theory, as acts of exchange or affinity or the transmission of rights in offspring, property, and services, a characteristic of the weddings I have observed or

participated in, both in North America and among Malagasy speakers in Mayotte, is the sort of optimistic refocusing ascribed by Said to beginnings. Indeed, I would say that "beginning" forms both a central function and a self-interpretation or theme of weddings. Michael Lambek, "Virgin Marriage and the Autonomy of Women in Mayotte," *Signs: Journal of Women in Culture and Society* 9, no. 2 (1983): 264–281; and Lambek, "The Saint, the Sea Monster, and an Invitation to a Dîner-Dansant: Ethnographic Reflections on the Edgy Passage—and the Double Edge—of Modernity, Mayotte 1975–2001," *Anthropologica* 46, 1 (2004): 57–68.

25. Said, *Beginnings*, 76–77.

26. Said, 72–73.

27. The king is Ndramandisoarivo. The identity of the oracle varies from version to version, as does the method by which the Queen dies.

28. Lambek, *Weight of the Past*.

29. Said, *Beginnings*, 47–48.

30. The clan descended from the King alone holds authority over royal burial grounds.

31. For an exposition of the gender of sacrifice, see Michael Lambek, "How Do Women Give Birth?," in *Questions of Anthropology*, ed. Rita Astuti, Jonathan Parry and Charles Stafford (Oxford: Berg, 2007); and Lambek, "Provincializing God? Apprehensions from an Anthropology of Religion," in *Religion: Beyond a Concept*, ed. Hent de Vries (New York: Fordham University Press, 2008), 120–138.

32. The Queen's act draws on symbolism that stretches back earlier, to the kingdom of Menabe, as does the royal genealogy.

33. A precursor of this view is found in Henri Hubert and Marcel Mauss, *Sacrifice: Its Nature and Function*, trans. W. D. Halls (Chicago: Chicago University Press, 1964 [1888]). They highlight the presence and destruction of a victim as well as the Vedic model of the creation of the universe as a sacrifice. Indeed, Malamoud observes both that Vedic creation presupposes a sacrificer, oblation, and model (hence that it is a beginning rather than an origin) and that the rites themselves elaborate the process of beginning and begin with an act of violence, a "first slice" (*une entame*). See C. Malamoud, "Sans lieu ni date: note sur l'absence de fondation dans l'Inde védique," in *Traces de foundation*, ed. M. Detienne (Louvain/Paris: Peeters, 1990), 188, 190. I am very grateful to Anne de Sales for providing the relevant text. Parry offers an exemplary ethnographic exposition of Hindu death as sacrifice and creation. See Jonathan Parry, *Death in Banaras* (Cambridge: Cambridge University Press, 1994), 30–32, 188–190.

34. This is akin perhaps to Lévi-Strauss's argument with respect to totemism or Steiner's with respect to taboo. See Claude Lévi-Strauss, *Totemism*, trans. R. Needham (Boston: Beacon, 1963 [1962]; and Franz Steiner, *Taboo* (Harmondsworth, UK: Penguin, 1956).

35. This is the case despite the fact that the body itself is often grasped by means of metaphor.

36. Rita Astuti, *People of the Sea* (Cambridge: Cambridge University Press, 1995); Maurice Bloch, *Placing the Dead* (London: Seminar Press, 1971); and Kate Middleton, introduction to *Ancestors, Power, and History in Madagascar* (Leiden: Brill, 1999), 1–36.

However, Sakalava leave the death of royalty ambiguous and unspoken. Rotting flesh is separated from enduring bones and the royal ancestors perdure as *tromba* (possessing spirits).

37. Ruel, *Non-Sacrificial Ritual Killing*.

38. See Eric Schwimmer, *Exchange in the Social Structure of the Orokaiva* (London: Hurst, 1973), on the "starting mechanisms" of exchange and on exchange as sacrifice; David Graeber, *Toward an Anthropological Theory of Value* (New York: Palgrave Macmillan, 2001), 176–188, on the *hau* and the meaning of Maori initial gifts; and A. Caillé, *Anthropologie du don* (Paris: Désclée de Brouwer, 2000), for a lively discussion of sacrifice as utilitarian exchange. Like Caillé, my discussion of sacrifice does not include the sense of abnegation.

39. For this reason also, I do not emphasize the feast. In this I follow Sakalava practice—the meat of animals sacrificed at the shrine is divided up and, for the most part, taken to individual households to be cooked and eaten separately. In contrast to commensality, the act of killing is a salient aspect of animal sacrifice virtually everywhere. As an indirect piece of evidence I note that depiction of animal slaughter is practically *de rigueur* in ethnographic film. Of course, consuming the sacrificial object could be seen as the final, incorporative phase of the rite; and, like cutting and spilling, eating and digestion are irreversible acts and processes that cannot be taken back.

40. Johann Wolfgang von Goethe, *Faust: A Tragedy*, trans. M. Greenberg (New Haven, CT: Yale University Press, 1992 (1797)), 1:39.

41. J. L. Austin, *How to Do Things with Words* (Oxford: Oxford University Press, 1962), 5.

42. Rappaport, *Ritual and Religion*, 133.

43. B. Malinowski, *Argonauts of the Western Pacific* (London: Routledge, 1922), 126–127, 334–349.

44. See also Nancy D. Munn, *The Fame of Gawa* (Cambridge: Cambridge University Press, 1986); and S. Tambiah, "Form and Meaning in Magical Acts," in *Modes of Thought: Essays on Thinking in Western and Non-Western Societies*, ed. R. Horton and R. Finnegan (London: Faber, 1973), 199–229.

45. Michael Lambek, "Taboo as Cultural Practice among Malagasy Speakers," *Man* n.s. 27, 2 (1992): 19–42. Examples include sharing kola nuts in Nigeria and acts of limecutting in Sri Lanka; G. Obeyesekere, *Medusa's Hair* (Chicago: Chicago University Press, 1981). Both examples entail cutting.

46. Rappaport, *Ritual and Religion*, 314. Indeed, utterances are acts, a point made not only by Austin but also, from an alternative philosophical tradition, by Hannah Arendt, *The Human Condition*, 2nd ed. (Chicago: Chicago University Press, 1998 [1958]). Systematic analysis would show similarities and differences between sacred postulations, in Rappaport's sense and other kinds of acts. In any case, alongside Rappaport's ultimate sacred postulates (*Ritual and Religion*, 263–276), one could add ultimate sacred acts of which sacrifice may be a prototypic example.

47. Quoted by George Steiner, *Martin Heidegger* (New York: Viking, 1978), 110.

48. *Oxford Illustrated Dictionary* (1975).

49. The executive significance of sacrifice can also be gleaned from its refusal. Evans-Pritchard describes the Nuer leopard skin chief threatening a curse against those reluctant to accept mediation: "He would take an ox and rub its back with ashes and begin to address it, saying that if the injured party were to insist on revenge many of them would be killed in the endeavour . . . he would then raise his spear to slaughter the animal, but this would be as far as people would care to let him go. Having asserted their pride of kin, one of the dead man's family would seize his upraised arm to prevent him from stabbing the ox, saying: 'No! Do not kill your ox. It is finished. We will accept compensation.'" Evans-Pritchard, *The Nuer*, 175.

50. This might be linked to Heidegger's formulation of the violence of being in his *Introduction to metaphysics* and described by Eric S. Nelson as "an originary strife . . . that is intended to contest the reification of identity." Nelson, "Traumatic Life: History, Pain and Violence in Heidegger's *Introduction to Metaphysics*," in *The Trauma Controversy: Philosophical and Interdisciplinary Dialogues*, ed. K. Brown and B. Bergo (Albany: State University of New York Press, 2009), 189–204.

51. Lambek, "Virgin marriage." Ideally, defloration is followed by a liminal period and final incorporation in Van Gennep's sense. Nevertheless, it is evident in the manner in which the defloration is immediately celebrated (with congratulations, ululations, and sexy dancing) that a new beginning for the bride has been achieved. As for circumcision, insofar as cutting the foreskin is a repetition of Abraham's sacrifice of Isaac, it is itself a sacrifice. Circumcision is a mark not only of difference or singularity but also of intentionality, a performative act establishing the kind of person one (or one's child) is intended to be and in respect to which one accepts subsequent conduct to be evaluated. Among Dogon, sacrifice introduces differentiation, "the birth of a discontinuous world," as observed by Luc De Heusch, *Sacrifice in Africa* (Bloomington: Indiana University Press, 1985), 134. Circumcision as sacrifice is linked to menstruation, periodicity, and alternation, but compare Maurice Bloch, *From Blessing to Violence: History and Ideology in the Circumcision Ritual of the Merina of Madagascar* (Cambridge: Cambridge University Press, 1986).

52. Steiner, *Martin Heidegger*, 115.

53. Fred Dallmayr, *The Other Heidegger* (Ithaca, NY: Cornell University Press, 1993), 58.

54. Dallmayr, 58–59.

55. Godfrey Lienhardt, *Divinity and Experience* (Oxford: Clarendon, 1961), 296.

56. In a companion essay (Lambek, "How Do Women Give Birth?") I interpret giving birth as a form of sacrifice. Conversely, Ndramandikavavy's sacrifice is a form of birth—a claim to being mother of her son and an act that gives birth to the polity of Boina. On Sakalava birth, see G. Feeley-Harnik, "Childbirth and the Affiliation of Children in Northwest Madagascar," *Taloha* 13 (2000): 135–172; on action as natality, see Arendt, *Human Condition*, 9.

57. Rappaport, *Ritual and Religion*, 117–124.

58. Lienhardt, *Divinity and Experience*; and Parry, *Death in Banaras*, 30–32, 188–190.

59. Rappaport, *Ritual and Religion*, 119.

60. I wish to emphasize that I am not attempting to romanticize sacrifice or intending to allude to contemporary acts of violence. The suicide bomber is not beginning anything nor transforming death into life. While the act is surely decisive and irreversible, it is neither part of a liturgical order nor explicitly performative and its aim is purely instrumental. On the dangers of applying the religious language of martyrdom to politics, see Galit Hasan-Rokem, "Martyr vs. Martyr: The Sacred Language of Violencem," *Ethnologia Europaea* 33, no. 2 (2003): 99–104.

61. Steiner, *Martin Heidegger*, 78.

62. Sakalava make blood sacrifices beneath the corner posts of new temples, at doorways, and along paths that people must step over.

63. Ludwig Wittgenstein, *Remarks on Frazer's Golden Bough*, trans. A. Miles, ed. R. Rhees (Nottingham: Brynmill Press, 1979 [1931]); cf. Wendy James, *The Ceremonial Animal: A New Portrait of Anthropology* (Oxford: Oxford University Press, 2003).

64. Steiner, *Martin Heidegger*, 137.

65. Cf. C. B. Macpherson, *Democratic Theory: Essays in Retrieval* (Oxford: Clarendon, 1973), 4–5.

66. Giorgio Agamben, *The Man without Content*, trans. G. Albert (Stanford, CA: Stanford University Press, 1999), 69.

67. Compare Arendt, *Human Condition*, for whom the difference between making (work) and doing (action) is highly consequential. Arendt emphasizes the radical unpredictability and irreversibility of action in contrast to the routines of practice. A full theory of action would bring together the philosophical literature on intentionality and ethics; see, for example, Stanley Cavell, *Must We Mean What We Say?* (Cambridge: Cambridge University Press, 1976), with sociological discussions of "social creativity" and social action as in David Graeber, "Fetishism as Social Creativity, or, Fetishes are Gods in the Process of Construction," *Anthropological Theory* 5, no. 4 (2005): 407–438; and H. Joas, *The Creativity of Action*, trans. P. Keast and J. Gaines (Chicago: Chicago University Press, 1996 [1992]).

68. Mary Douglas, *Natural Symbols* (New York: Pantheon, 1970).

69. Filip de Boeck and Marie-Françoise Plissart, *Kinshasa: Tales of the Invisible City* (Ghent: Ludion, 2004).

70. Said, *Beginnings*, 9.

71. Said, 9.

72. Said, 66.

73. Said, 13.

74. Marshall Berman, *All that is Solid Melts into Air: The Experience of Modernity* (New York: Viking Penguin, 1988).

75. Goethe also works with a contrast between inward activism and outward worldliness (Berman, *All that Is Solid*, 46–47), a theme of German culture that entailed

additional contrasts between Christians and Jews as well as between Kantian idealist and Aristotelian practical ethics. Berman argues that Faust's inversion of 'In the Beginning was the Word' was understood as replacing Christ with the Old Testament God who makes the world. It was part of Weber's brilliance to complexify and transform these oppositions.

76. Goethe, *Faust*, 1:54, line 1759.
77. Said, *Beginnings*, 372.

CHAPTER 19

The Mass and the Theater
Othello and Sacrifice

Regina M. Schwartz

There is something unbearable about Iago's triumph in Shakespeare's *Othello*. But where does this sense of the unbearableness of injustice come from? Where does the impossible expectation that it will end, or the corollary belief—that the triumph of evil must mean the world is out of joint and that eventually it will be righted—come from? What is the source of checks upon naked self-interest, relentless aggrandizement, sheer grasping of power? Does it come from some rational understanding that our will cannot be done without compromise with the wills of others, some recognition of the necessity of essentially contractual relations, whether unwritten or written? Or is its source some higher desire to make the world a good place, that is, to partner the creation by securing the world through acts of justice. The experience of watching *Othello* induces a particularly painful craving for justice, in part because it is brought into relief against other justices, strict and absolute, retributive and economic, that triumph disastrously over the justice that transcends these values.

On Sundays, when plays could not be performed, presumably because they would draw their audience from would-be churchgoers, Shakespeare and his contemporaries could attend church, a service made uniform by the Book of Common Prayer, a service that represented one hundred and fifty years of conflict and compromise, a service whose forms and meanings had racked Christendom, creating a new religion and a new church in England out of furious controversies. Among other changes, Reformers sought to dispel the *opus operatum*—that work through which the church could be the sacramental organ of the salvation offered by Christ—by their doctrine of faith alone. All of the concerns of the Reformation came into sharp focus over the Mass, marking a sea change from the premodern to the early modern world: what was at stake in these debates was not only the obvious issue of redemption but also the relation of matter to spirit, the visible to the invisible, the universal to the particular, the self to the other, language to its referent, and how and where power is vested: the authority of scripture, of the inner Spirit, of the priesthood, of the church, and by extension, of civil government. On one end of the spectrum of the Reformation controversies over the Eucharist was the Reformers' objection to the material ingestion of Christ. They charged that transubstantiation was tantamount to cannibalism: "Thy teeth shall not do him violence, neither thy stomach contain his glorious body. By faith he is seen, by faith he is touched, by faith, he is digested."[1] At the other end was the Catholic fear of losing communion with God altogether, of divinity and humanity locked in a tragic separation that left man wallowing in his sin: "in believing in Christ by faith—which is but an apprehension of the understanding—we do no more really eat the body of Christ than doth the hungrye man his dinner when he apprehendeth and desireth it but cannot have it."[2]

The theater made no claims to perform "work"; the theater was not trying to effect transformations. The theater cannot *do* anything to other humans nor can it *offer* anything to God. Ironically, it was the Reformer's very insistence that in the Mass the sacrifice was only *represented* and not repeated that brought the Mass closer to the theater. After all, it was on stage that representations of events, rather than events themselves, were performed. Perhaps it is helpful to think of the Elizabethan theater as a space where a community recalled, represented, and remembered sacrifice, but does not endure it; and whether, in one sense, the Elizabethan theater competed with the Mass, for an audience, and whether in another, deeper sense, it replaced it, becoming the first truly Reformed church.[3]

With *sola fides* as its watchword, much of Reformation theology belies a deep distrust of the senses. Faith is "the evidence of things unseen, the substance of things hoped for." This invisible truth is both profoundly immanent, the inner Spirit, and transcendent, the God beyond the visible. Lies are very often defined as sensory illusions. Cranmer complained of the Catholic Mass: "Is not in the ministration of the holy communion an illusion of our sense, if our senses take for bread and wine what whiche is not so indeed?" Reformers accused priests of creating illusions that they wanted to be taken as reality, that is, they accused them of fraud. And even as anti-Catholic propagandists pejoratively referred to the Mass as fraudulent, they inflicted the same charge on the theater.

Antitheatrical prejudice found common cause with antipopery, equating ritual with magic, magic with the theater, and all of them with lies. "In Stage Playes for a boy to put on the attyre, the gesture, the passions of a woman; for a meane person to take upon him the title of a Prince with counterfeit porte, and traine, is by outward signes to shewe themselves otherwise than they are, and so within the compasse of a lye."[4] This pseudo-Platonic equation of lies with the senses and truth with the invisible is fraught with difficulties. A less debased understanding, one less dependent upon crude binary distinctions between the visible and invisible, would issue in very different valuations—the Mass could provide access to truth and the theater could be a storehouse of truths. Indeed, even Reformers understood the sacraments as the "seal" of faith, and the most common Renaissance theory of drama was that it offered an image of actual life: "the purpose of playing . . . was and is to hold as 'twere a mirror up to nature."[5]

An accumulating body of criticism has also been willing to think synoptically and fruitfully about religious ritual and the theater, sensitive, not only to the ritual origins of drama in ancient Greek religions and the miracle and morality plays of medieval Catholicism but also to the complex relation between the Elizabethan stage and the English Reformation. Two poles have emerged in these speculations: stressing either that theater is virtually a religious ritual ("for Shakespeare, the carnal spectacles of the theater are better than demystifying: they are sacramental"[6]) or that ritual is mere theater ("theatrical seduction . . . is the essence of the church").[7] However, while critics also make far more subtle distinctions between ritual and theater than the propagandists, they can unwittingly fall under the spell of their polemic. According to Stephen Greenblatt, in order to demystify the Catholic practice of exorcism definitively, Samuel Harsnett felt the need to demonstrate not only why the ritual was empty but also why it was effective, "why a few miserable shifts could produce the experience of horror and wonder [in an exorcism]. . . . He needs an explanatory model, at once metaphor and analytical tool, by which all beholders will see fraud where they once saw God."[8]

Harsnett finds that explanatory model in theater, an arena that readily acknowledges its magical mechanisms, admitting arts of illusion as such. In theater he discovers magic, not miracles: divine justice does not prevail, sin is not redeemed. Greenblatt writes that in Lear, the "forlorn hope of an impossible redemption persists, drained of its institutional and doctrinal significance, empty and vain . . . but like the dream of exorcism eradicable."[9] This leads him to the conclusion that, at best, theater generates expectations that are disappointed. But where Greenblatt speaks of disappointed expectations in tones of lament, I celebrate the remarkable expectation itself, so that precisely where he is discouraged, I locate hope. The very frustration of redemption is the way theater performs its moral vision. And this craving for redemption is not a sign that religion is "emptied"; this craving is itself religious.

To see ritual, as Greenblatt does, as "emptied out" because it no longer performs magic is to presume—already unsympathetically—that magic is the function of ritual and that religion is, in turn, reducible to practices claiming to be magical. In light of the fierce energies that contributed to ritual innovation, the extensive controversies over the liturgy in Book of Common Prayer, and the intense conflicts surrounding ritual initiatives like the placement of the altar, all prompted by changing understandings of ritual efficacy—that kind of arch secularism does not hold up.[10] Not *whether* but *which* rituals would be practiced and what they were meant to achieve were the foci of immense energy—emotional, intellectual, and, in light of the extraordinary destruction of images, physical. Surely in finding religion so "emptied" in Shakespeare, Greenblatt has not unwittingly accepted the terms set by propagandists, reducing religion to "mere ritual," ritual to magic, and magic to fraud. Because it was the work of propaganda to equate ritual with theater and both with lies, we might do well, for all of their affinities, to regard the equation as deeply suspect.

Ritual is not "mere theater," in the sense of being false, nor does theater, however deep its affinity to religion, claim the function of a sacrament.[11] While principals may dress in elaborate costumes and perform ceremonial-like acts, clearly religious ritual makes different ontological claims from the theater. The acts performed by the priest are not intended to inspire pity or strike terror (as Aristotle said tragedy does) nor to delight or instruct (as Horace said poetry must) but to change the world. A priest is not a character "personated" by a "player" (the Renaissance terms for acting and actor);[12] rather, he is the authorized and sanctified vicar of God. Ritual summons the holy, *mysterium tremendum*, and its acts are neither imitations of life nor imitations of imitations but acts that enable the sacred to be manifest and transcendence to erupt into immanence. The effect of such acts on the audience—and they are not an audience, but participants—is to be conclusively altered.[13]

And what is theater? If we were to heed antitheatrical prejudice, we would learn that the theater is a seething caldron of disease, depravity, and debauchery, an immoral realm where "players" threaten the serious business of assuming real social roles. "[The theaters] maintaine idlenes is such persons as have no vocation and draw apprentices and other servauntes from theire ordinary workes and all sortes of people from the resort unto sermons and other Christian exercises, to the great hindrance of traides and prophanation of religion established by her highnes within this Realm."[14] But if we were to tune our ears to the defenders of the theater, we would hear that, for them, the relation of the world of theater to the world of reality is a more deeply considered one, and the relation of the drama to ethics—including drama's moral accountability—is equally serious. Hamlet understands the play as the very instrument that allows us to discern morality: "the play's the thing wherein I'll catch the conscience of the king." Hamlet is not sure whether he should trust his senses or the restless purgatorial ghost (the very existence of purgatory was subjected to doubt), but he does trust *conscience*, and trust the play's ability to exhibit it. Furthermore, the notion of redemption is not an empty one to Hamlet; indeed, it is his aching need for justice, for redeeming the crime, that drives the play.[15] If the theater could not fulfill the religious craving for justice, it could and did express that craving with stunning eloquence. Whether or not it was "the purpose of playing," it was the power of performance.

If, by the late Middle Ages, the traditional church rites had, for some, begun to lose some of their former power, one reason was that these rites were perceived to be on a collision course with ethics.[16] Whether the strains of Protestantism indebted to Luther stressed that only faith grounds morality through Christ's merit or with Calvin emphasized the discipline of the church or like Zwingli focused on communal responsibility, all inveighed against the perceived "abuses" of clergy and liturgy—not with secular skepticism, but with the fury of moral indignation. The theater also addressed this felt need for a moral order differently but perhaps as effectively as the church. At precisely the time when the theater was under attack for fostering immorality and that the rituals of Catholicism were under scrutiny for their "falsity and hollowness," the theater was reaching its apex: the old Senecan version of revenge tragedy flowered into Elizabethan moral tragedy, that is, into a tragedy of injustice. When I understand Shakespeare as "religious," then, it is not because his actors satisfied or did not satisfy longings for magic acts, but because he repeatedly addressed the transcendent problem, in his way, that the sacrament also addressed in its way: justice.

When sacraments figured among the important resources, he called upon from the stage business of life, Shakespeare turned them to an ethical purpose. For his audience, a spotted handkerchief would allude not only to a marriage bed, to virginity and fidelity, but also to a spotted altar-cloth, ocular proof of Christ's miraculous gift of his broken and bleeding body in the Eucharist. Such cloths were relics in Catholic Europe, testimonies to the miracle of the bleeding host. Through lenses that empty it of this sacramental significance, the spotted cloth in *Othello* becomes a heathenish cloth in which magic, not God, was woven. But that reading does not suffice, for the handkerchief *also* becomes ocular "proof" of a betrayal that never occurred, a piece of false testimony used wrongfully to indict the innocent. Therefore, if the reference to the religious ritual has been "emptied out," Shakespeare has refilled it. If Shakespeare has "given up on religion," as C. L. Barbar depicts him, surely, he has not given up on justice. It is the imaginary that has such a deep hold on his plays that they scarcely can make sense without it. How could we understand Lear as suffering? Hamlet as tormented? Macbeth as guilt-ridden? Emptied of its sacral significance, sacrifice is meaningless killing, but Shakespeare does not have meaningless deaths in his tragedy. Like the spotted handkerchief, they are not just emptied, but refilled—with moral outrage.

Sacrifice and Murder

Much of the Reformation was spent negotiating two different meanings of death, as murder and as sacrifice. Whether a death is viewed as a murder or an act of sacrifice depends entirely on how it is culturally framed, but in both cases, its definition is at the service of some idea of justice. Death framed as a sacrifice is most often understood as a gift to a deity, as appeasing his ire for our wrongdoing: sacrifice compensates, pays back, pays off, recompenses, redeems. When the gift offered is pure, chaste, unadulterated, without sin, it compensates for the impure, tainted, adulterated, sinful nature of man. Divine justice is understood to be satisfied by this retribution: "Die he or justice must," as Milton's God puts it in *Paradise Lost*. Sacrifice is substitutive and metonymic: the individual dies for the community, on behalf of the community, as Christ dies for mankind. Murder is framed very differently: far from *satisfying* the demands of justice, murder *violates* them, and its object is not heroically embracing or stoically accepting destruction; it is an unwilling victim. In murder, the emphasis shifts away from the community to the individual whose death does not satisfy collective justice, but whose murder threatens collective peace. Hence, a specific retributive justice comes into play—not the substitutive redemption offered by sacrifice but the collective apparatus of the law. In that system, murder does not satisfy justice; it cries out for satisfaction.

During the Reformation, as reinterpretations of the ritual of the Eucharist occurred, the relation between sacrifice and murder—and their relation to justice—was also revisited. When Reformers altered participating in the material godhead through transubstantiation to only *representing* God, merit was conferred on undeserving man by Christ's sacrifice "as if" the communicant were also sacrificed; merit was imputed to man for something he did not suffer. In the process, the satisfaction of justice and gift of mercy were radically redefined.

Retribution was further inflected by two important changes in the theological climate. First, in the eucharistic controversies over sacrifice, agency came to the fore: priests were accused of presuming to act as sacrificers, offering Christ at the altar. For its part, Catholicism never claimed that the priest was the sacred executioner, only that he was the means through which Christ repeated his sacrifice of himself. But Reformers, eager to reduce the power of the priesthood, claimed that the agency of the priest was, at best, irrelevant and, at worst, idolatrous, for man could not offer God—only God could offer himself. For Luther, the church and its priesthood has no agency in the economy of grace. "Once the Mass has been overthrown, I say we'll have overthrown the whole of Popedom." And so he insisted that the Lord's Supper was only a promise and a testament. "God does not deal, nor has he dealt with man in any other way than by the word of his promise. So too we can never have dealing with God in any other way than by faith in that word of promise." Distinguishing the Catholic Mass from the Reformed Holy Supper, Calvin explained that, "here is as much difference between this sacrifice and the sacrament as there is between giving and receiving. And such is the most miserable ungratefulness of man that where he ought to have recognized and given thanks for the abundance of God's bounty, he makes God in this his debtor!"[17] Thomas Cranmer opens his *Defence of the True and Catholic Doctrine of the Sacrament* (1550) with a preface in which he takes pains to distinguish the reformed (that is, original and true) understanding of the Eucharist from the (he thinks) misguided direction it had taken in Rome:

> Our Saviour Christ Jesus according to the will of his eternal Father . . . made a sacrifice and oblation of his own body upon the cross, which was a full redemption, satisfaction, and propriation, for the sins of the whole world. . . . [H]e hath ordained a perpetual memory of his said sacrifice, daily to be used in the Church to his perpetual laud and praise. . . . But the Romish Antichrist, to deface this great benefit of Christ, hath taught that his sacrifice upon the cross is not sufficient hereunto, without another sacrifice devised by him, and made by the priest, or else without indulgences, beads, pardons, pilgrimages, and such other pelfry, to supply Christ's imperfection: and that Christian people cannot apply to themselves the benefits of Christ's passion, but that the same is in the distribution of the Bishop of Rome.

His response to this assessment is not subtle: "O heinous blasphemy . . . O wicked abomination . . . O pride intolerable . . . For he that taketh upon him to supply that thing, which he pretendeth to be unperfect in Christ, must needs make himself above Christ, and so very Antichrist."[18] Only God could perform a sacrifice. Men perform a murder.

To underscore the point, Cranmer returns to what he deems this greatest of offenses at the beginning of Book V of his *Defence*: it is not transubstantiation nor is it a failure to embrace double predestination, it is presuming to repeat the sacrifice. "The greatest blasphemy and injury that can be against Christ, and yet universally used through the popish kingdom, is this, that the priests make their mass a sacrifice propitiary, to remit the sins as well of themselves as of other, both quick and dead, to whom they apply the same."[19] Cranmer claimed that the doctrines of the *Defence* were reflected in the 1549 Book of Common Prayer and we can discern that even as it went through its contested emendations and revisions over the language of the real presence, this much—that the sacrifice occurred once and is now only commemorated in the Lord's Supper—remained unchanged: there are no offertory prayers; the Secret Prayers, offering-prayers that refer to the *munus, oblatio, sacrificium, hostia,* and *mysterium* have been eliminated. This distinction between divine and priestly agency was reflected in the careful wording of the Book of Common Prayer (1559): "And although we be unworthy through our manifold sins to offer unto thee any Sacrifice: yet we beseech thee to accept this our bounden duty and service, not weighing our merits but pardoning our offences. Amen."[20] Reading the sacramental logic unsympathetically produced a contradiction unknown to the Roman Catholic Church: if the act is repeated, then the original must be incomplete, and conversely, if the original were complete, any repetition becomes superfluous.

This harsh emphasis on remembrance alone was somewhat softened, as became evident in the sacred treatment of the wine and bread. John Jewel's understanding of the Eucharist was close to Cranmer's with the exception of his regard for the elements; the bread and the wine needed to be set aside, consecrated, in order to fulfill their sacramental function: "We affirm that bread and wine are holy and heavenly mysteries of the body and blood of Christ, and that *by them* Christ himself, being the true bread of eternal life, is so presently given unto us that by faith we verily receive his body and blood."[21] Richard Hooker's "real receptionist" understanding of the Eucharist enunciated in his *Ecclesiastical Polity* kept the sacramental emphasis on participation: "The fruit of the Eucharist is the participation in the body and blood of Christ."[22] "This bread hath in it more than the substance which our eyes behold, this cup hallowed with solemn benediction availeth ... what these elements are in themselves it skilleth not, it is enough that to me which take them they are the body and blood of Christ."[23] After the accession of James I (provoking the Millenary Petition and the Hampton Court Conference which ultimately issued in the King James Bible and the Canons of 1604), church doctrine inched closer to asserting the vital importance of the bread and wine—almost, but not quite as an offering of sacrifice—reflected in the felt need to legislate, without precedent, the consecration of the bread and wine; and if that supply is supplemented, even the added bread and wine must be consecrated (canon 21). For all of the Reformers' rhetoric against the "grievous error" of making an offering, by 1604, they had rejected it in doctrine far more definitively than in ritual. Nonetheless, that same year, the stage could offer a clearer—more or less satisfying(?)—sacrifice, of Desdemona, whose name includes the *daimon* of sacrifice.

Reformers were not only disturbed by the problem of agency in sacrifice; they were also clearly uncomfortable with its materiality, preferring to speak of spiritual eating and drinking instead of the literal body and blood of God: "Take and eat this, in remembrance that Christ died for thee, and feed on him in thy heart by faith, with thanksgiving."[24] When they denied the material body in the Mass, to substitute a seal of the promise of faith, they were implicitly putting the meaning of death—as sacrifice—at risk. Foreseeing the problem, Calvin was careful to claim that the sacrament's meaning depends wholly on the body of God having been sacrificed: "It must be carefully noted that the most conspicuous, indeed almost the whole power of the sacrament resides in these words, 'which is given for you,' . . . 'which is shed for you.' For otherwise is would be of no avail that the body and blood of the Lord should be administered, had they not once for all been *sacrificed* for our redemption and salvation."[25] His anxiety is palpable. For with the sacrifice remembered rather than repeated, how can justice be effectively satisfied? What is remembered is the suffering of Christ, the suffering of a victim, but a murder, or a sacrificial victim?

Othello and Justice

I discern a crisis over the distinction between sacrifice and murder in *Othello* and will glean allusions to the sacrifice of the Eucharist from the play, not to assert that Shakespeare is more or less Catholic or Protestant, nor to establish his position on the controversy that raged in his day over the Eucharist, but to demonstrate that *Othello* is a play that evokes longing for justice, longing, that is, for some antidote to the rhetoric of devils and hell that fill the stage, some redressing of the fiendish rituals of murderous vows, blasphemous oaths, and monstrous births of plots engendered by hell and night, invocations of whores and sorcerers, and the triumph of a deadly design that unravels as relentlessly as a providential one—but is so antithetical to providence that it springs from one who inverts the divine name, turning the tetragrammaton of Exodus 3, "I am who I am," into "I am not what I am," thereby setting sin loose upon the world. In a play where the tempter embraces divinity as surely as Milton's Satan does: "divinity of hell.... So I will turn her virtue into pitch, and out of her own goodness make the net that shall enmesh them all"; "If then his Providence / Out of our evil seek to bring forth good, / Our labor must be to pervert that end, / And out of good still to find means of evil" (*Paradise Lost* 1:162–165)—it seems especially terrible that the other shoe does not fall, that infernal ends are not frustrated to bring good out of evil. Desdemona has precisely that intention. When Emilia has just described to her a world in which wrongdoing issues in wrongdoing—"the ills we do their ills instruct us so"—Desdemona objects, "God me such usage send, Not to pick bad from bad, but by bad mend!" Mend, amend, make amends, redemption: Desdemona has articulated her intent to turn evil to good with stunning emphasis at the end of Act IV but that is just before, disturbingly enough, we see evil triumph and Desdemona undone.

Shakespeare challenges us to rethink these differences between a sacrifice and a murder. In his tragedies, acts of violence seem to hint toward redemption, but it is not clear that Desdemona's death redeems. Can we see her death as a sacrifice? A remission of sins? A benefit to others? A satisfaction of the demands of justice? Othello himself wants to stage it that way. The murderous Othello stages his "sacrifice" of Desdemona like a priest at the altar and before he kills her, delivers the injunction to confess derived from the communion service: "If you bethink yourself of any crime, Unreconciled as yet to heaven and grace, Solicit for it straight." He tries to stage a ritual death. It is marked by prayers:

OTH.   I would not kill thy unprepared spirit, No, heaven forfend, I would not kill thy soul.
DES.   Talk you of killing?
OTH.   Ay, I do.
DES.   Then Lord have mercy on me.
OTH.   Amen, with all my heart!

And, in the role of priest, he would extract her confession:

OTH.   Therefore confess thee freely of thy sin
       For to deny each article with oath
       Cannot remove, nor shake the strong conceit
       That I do groan withal: thou art to die.
DES.   Then Lord have mercy on me.
OTH.   I say, Amen.

But this is a perverse priest, for the final prayer that would assure Desdemona's redemption is silenced by Othello:

> DES. Kill me tomorrow, let me live to-night…
> But half an hour, but while I say one prayer.
> OTH. Tis too late.

Othello's carefully orchestrated sacrifice quickly turns into a vengeful murder, as even he admits:

> OTH. O perjur'd woman, thou dost stone thy heart
> And makest me call what I intend to do
> A murder, which I had thought a sacrifice.

He has come to her as a divine executor of justice: "vengeance is mine," saith the Lord; "it is the caus," says Othello, bearing the terrible mission of strict justice and retribution, "else she'll betray more men." The performative confusion of Desdemona crying out to the Lord and Emilia crying "My Lord" seems to lure Othello himself into ontological confusion about his divine mission: "I that am cruel, am yet merciful," he pronounces like an old testament deity who punishes the hardened heart but also like the new testament father who demands the life of his Son. But wait, he is murdering all the while, stifling Desdemona's breath *even as* he invokes mercy. Is this sacrifice or murder? If sacrifice, it should redeem and indeed Othello alludes to the eclipse and earthquake that marked Christ's death. But none happen. He expects to see cloven hoofs on the devil Iago—but has to admit it is only a myth. And so his pretensions to being divine judge soon collapse and he assumes another role: the betrayer of divinity. No longer God the Father demanding retribution for sin, Othello becomes the Judas who betrays his master.

Amidst his confused assertions of justice, Othello virtually confesses that he has sold her:

> nay, had she been true,
> If heaven would make me such another world
> Of one entire and perfect chrysolite,
> I'd not have sold her for it.

Like Judas, Othello brought false evidence against the blessed one, and like Judas, he kissed before he killed.

Mark 14: Now the traitor had arranged a signal with them: "The one I kiss" he had said, "he is the man." So when the Traitor came we went straight up to Jesus and said, Rabbi, and kissed him and then he turns him over to his death. The chief priests and the whole Sanhedron were looking for evidence against Jesus on which they might pass the death-sentence. But they could not find any. Several, indeed, brought false evidence against him. But the evidence was conflicting.

False evidence violates justice, but Othello's court of justice does not hesitate to admit it.

In the communion service in the Book of Common Prayer, after the recital of the Lord's prayer, it calls for the rehearsal of the ten commandments, with the communicant praying that each of the sins he has committed be forgiven and that grace help him ward off transgression in the future. It is little wonder that this play incites hunger for some vision of redemption, for in it, each of the commandments is broken. The name of the Lord is used in vain repeatedly; "s'blood" (Christ's blood) is the first word out of Iago's cursing mouth and "zounds" (Christ's wounds), "by the mass" are blasphemous invocations of the sacrifice. The sabbath day is not kept holy—it sees a brawl; a father is not honored—his daughter flees him in the night and disobeys him; what belongs to the neighbor is coveted—Iago covets Cassio's position; false witness is made—Iago uses the handkerchief; and murder is committed: all of the "thou shalt nots" are violated. The only command of the decalogue that is conspicuously not broken is adultery, and it becomes, in this perverse covenant with a God who-is-not-what-he-is, the provocation of wrath. Othello succumbs to a perversion of the violence of monotheism: "For I am a jealous God, you shall have none but me."[26]

With this old covenant broken, we may well long for a new one, one written on the heart, like that of the prophets, not like the one broken when Israel disobeyed the law but a logos incarnated. And the breaking of the old law given in blood may well demand a new gift given in blood, a sacrifice, like that of Jesus. These allusions hover tantalizingly around Desdemona who does her part in tempting us into seeing her own death as a sacrifice. She calls out in her moment of death, "O Lord Lord Lord" as Christ had "Eli Eli." And she withstands her version of the temptation offered to Christ in the wilderness, the gift of all the kingdoms of the world: "all this dominion will I give to you and the glory that goes with it." Just as Jesus need only do homage to Satan to gain the whole world, so in Emilia's test, Desdemona could have the whole world for one infelicity.

DES. Wouldst thou do such a deed, for all the world?
EMIL. Why, would not you?

> DES.   No, by this heavenly light!
> EMIL. Nor I neither, by this heavenly light. I might do it as well in the dark.
> DES.   Wouldst thou do such a thing for all the world?
> EMIL. The world is a huge thing, it is a great price, For a small vice.
> DES.   Good troth, I think thou wouldst not.
> EMIL. By my troth, I think I should, and undo't when I had done it; marry, I would not do such a thing for a joint-ring; nor for measures of lawn, nor for gowns, or petticoats, nor caps, nor any such exhibition; but for the whole world? Why, who would not make her husband a cuckold, to make him a monarch? I should venture purgatory for it.
> DES.   Beshrew me, if I would so such a wrong for the whole world.

The communion service begins with the recitation of the Lord's Prayer, eking out its Eucharistic significance: "Give us this day our daily bread and forgive us our trespasses as we forgive those who trespass against us. And lead us not into temptation and deliver us from evil." Desdemona is not led to temptation, and her dying words suggest that she forgives Othello's trespass: "Commend me to my kind Lord, O farewell!" But is she delivered from evil or to evil? She is the soul of purity who kneels and prays before her murder. Her prayer is drawn from the general confession of the communion service of the Book of Common Prayer: "We [ac]knowledge and bewail our manifold sinnes and wickedness, which we from time to time most grievously have committed, by thoughts, word, and deeds, against thy divine majestie."

> DES.   Here I kneel: If e'er my will did trespass 'gainst his love
>   Either in discourse of thought or actual deed, comfort forswear me.

How can Desdemona's death be figured as a redemptive sacrifice when Othello so resembles a perverse priest or even a sorcerer at a Black Mass? At the opening of the play, he is arraigned and tried in what is virtually a witch-trial scene, "I therefore apprehend and do attach thee, For an abuser of the world, a practiser of arts inhibited and out of warrant," one whose foul charms, drugs or minerals, have bound her in his chains of magic. But his acquittal by the Venetian Senate in this scene does not put an end to the suggestion of dark arts in this play. He calls Desdemona to the same court, demanding ocular proof of her fidelity—the spotted handkerchief he had given to her: but "ocular proof" was the technical term in witch trials for the mark on the body of the witch, the "witch's teat," as it was so misogynistically called. To demand ocular proof is to demand evidence of sorcery. From at least one of the perspectives that reigns in the play, that of Iago, she is indicted. According to Iago, Brabantio, and Roderigo, she *has* had sexual congress with the devil.

According to historians' accounts of witchcraft beliefs, the devil himself presided at the sorcerer's mass as a big black bearded man, or as a stinking goat and occasionally as a great toad, and an infernal Eucharist took place at the witch's sabbath where the blood of the devil is drunk instead of the blood of God. In that context, Cassio drinks a cup that holds the devil in it at an infernal marriage celebration: "O thou invisible spirit of wine, if thou hast no name to be known by, let us call thee devil!" This seems compatible with a Reformer's version of the Mass the work of the devil, a Black Mass, in their rejection of transubstantiation for the invisible spirit. Cassio will even invoke transubstantiation, not upward, of man into god, but downward, of man into beast. "I remember a mass of things," he laments with remorse—and we can be sure the pun on mass was not lost to the audience—"but none distinctly, a quarrel but nothing wherefore. O God, that men should put an enemy in their mouths, to steal away their brains; that we should with joy, revel, pleasure, and applause, transform ourselves into beasts! ... To be now a sensible man, by and by a fool, and presently a beast! Every unordinate cup is unblessed and the ingredience is the devil." This is the Eucharist from hell.

By means of all these perversions and inversions—all the while calling to mind doctrinal Christian solutions even as they are withheld—Shakespeare is teasing us over and over with the possibility of redemption: an aborted mass ministered by a demented priest, a communion cup turned into a vessel of drunken disorderliness and bestiality, a prayer ("Lord, have mercy on me") that is really a plea for life from the hands of a murderer, a vow that is really a curse, a sacrifice that is really a murder, a death that does not make the earth quake or the sun stand still, a light that, once put out, will not rekindle. Shakespeare even assigns the most explicit articulation in the play of that yearning for salvation to a drunk: "There are souls that are saved and should that are not, may my soul be saved," slurs Cassio. Again, Shakespeare is only teasing us with the idea of redemption, for Cassio's high but drunken talk of salvation reduces to ludicrous pettiness:

CASSIO. For mine own part, no offense to the general, nor any man of quality, I hope to be saved.
IAGO. And so do I Lieutenant.
CASSIO. Ay, but by your leave, not before me; the lieutenant is to be saved before the ancient.

This tease about the idea of redemption is sustained from the beginning of the play to the end: an "old black ram"—it was a ram caught in the thicket that substituted for the sacrifice of Isaac, the typological prefiguration of the sacrifice of Christ—"tupping your white Ewe," the Lamb of God. But is there a sacrifice? Othello takes by the throat the circumcised dog—circumcision, the mark of the old covenant, and smote him thus—with the sign of the new covenant? That is, is Othello's suicide a sacrifice? Does it offer, in his self-murder of the self-defined infidel/idolater a restoration of justice, one confirmed by the legal restitution of order? Or rather, are we left aching for justice in the face of the triumph of evil? I would argue that this unmet craving for justice, so carefully incited and sustained throughout the play, gives the tragedy a transcendent dimension, pointing beyond the terrors of plot and experience to another vision of human possibility.

All of this is certainly not to say that Othello is merely a Christian allegory; of course, it plumbs the depths of all-too-human passions (as do powerful religious myths, for that matter). Nor would I want to suggest, despite the frequent dating of the play to 1604, the very year the Convocation was assembled to further emend the Prayer Book in a period fraught with controversy over the Eucharist, that the play became Shakespeare's covert expression of what had been censured on the stage—his stand on the religious controversy. The evidence is conflicting: on one hand, a deranged Othello imagines himself a priest at a sacrifice as he performs a murder; on the other hand, an innocent victim, falsely accused but faithful to the last, cries out to the Lord at her death by a deranged killer, invoking prayers that did precede the Anglican communion service but do not save or redeem her. These do not add up tidily to an argument that Shakespeare is either critiquing or embracing the doctrine of the sacrifice of the Mass. Rather, in a play preoccupied with the problem of evil and the problem of justice, I discern Shakespeare needing to invoke the Mass—not only the Catholic Mass but also its infernal parody— because it addressed the problem of justice forcefully with its promise of the remission of sins through the sacrifice of the eucharist.[27]

Surely something profound was lost when Reformers gave up the sacrifice of the eucharist or, to be more precise, turned it into a commemoration of a sacrifice rather than a reenactment, a commemoration of a moment in the distant past rather than a sacrifice that occurs at the very moment when the communicant ingests the host, a moment when suffering is redeemed, a mysterious moment when our depravity is absolved. Gabriel Biel was one of the most widely read authorities on the Mass at the time of the Reformation—seven editions of his *Exposition of the Sacred Canon of the Mass* were printed between 1488 and 1547; even Luther said it was the best Catholics possessed on the subject—and he summarizes well what was at stake in the loss of the Mass: "In this sacrifice there is the commemoration of and calling on that unique and perfect sacrifice by which heaven was opened, grace is given, through which alone our works can be meritorious, through which alone all the sin of men are remitted, and heavenly glory, lost by our sin, is restored . . . (Lectio LVII, lit. D)."[28]

During most of Christian history, that work of redemption can occur during the Mass because the sacrifice of Christ was both then and now, because ritual temporality is not simply or strictly linear. Although Christ was offered but once in the natural appearance of his flesh, nevertheless he is offered daily on the altar, veiled under the appearances of bread and wine. This offering of him does not, of course, entail any suffering, for Christ is not wounded, does not suffer and die each day (this distinction came to be known as the bloody and unbloody sacrifices of the Lord). But this consecration and reception of the Eucharist is called a sacrifice and an oblation for these two reasons: "first, because it represents that true sacrifice and holy immolation made once upon the cross, and is its memorial; secondly, because it is a *cause* through which similar *effects* are produced."[29]

How frail faith must have felt before the power of rituals, before the sacrifice of the God-man that satisfied justice from the Gospels to Luther. Having dispelled the *opus operatum*, the Reformers threatened to dispel the sacramental organ of salvation, the means for incarnating Christ within each communicant to effect his redemption. With the Church of England's reluctance to offer sacramental deterrence and sacramental remission of sins—that is, sacramental justice—the scene shifted inevitably to the court where evil was fought judicially and, as we have seen, to the theater where evil was fought imaginatively. If sin was a matter for demonstration, for evidence, as it was for Othello as his madness deepened, it also became a means for evoking moral outrage (tragedy) or envisioning moral order (comedy), and so theater became its forum. When the Reformers had replaced the church's transformation with representation and its sacrifice with remembrance, they had left themselves less the power of ritual than (ironically, given its opposition to theater) the catharsis of spectacle. And while the playwright is no priest, he can *represent* sacrifice, and like his Reformed competitors (the church had to close the theaters on Sundays to ensure its attendance), through that representation he can invite his audience to receive a grace he cannot give through a faith he cannot confer.

Reformers were unwittingly closer to the theater they so severely critiqued not only because they foregrounded representation but also because they too evinced the moral outrage—the craving for justice rather than its satisfaction—that became the deep structure of the Reformed ritual. When communion offers, at most, a memory of a past and a promise of a future event but no redemption in the present, then the longing for redemption is left as just that: longing—in memory and in hope. And when the wine only signifies blood and does not become the blood, communion risks the slippery slope toward disillusionment: "the wine she drinks is made of grapes." But if there is no wine that is blood—not even Desdemona's—then there are no redeemers, and this is the matter for tragedy and for tears, after all, and not for religious ritual.

That the theater should flower during the chill of Protestantism's heyday is no mystery. With bodies strewn all over the stage, the theater became the first truly protestant church, where a community convened and remembered sacrifice—without the *operatum* of the church—and where each individual was challenged privately to try to distinguish sacrifice from murder—*the* question for faith and to crave for justice no longer satisfied by the sacrament. Othello's distorted oath, "My life upon her faith," hauntingly suggests theater's distinct performative symbiosis of sacrifice and faith in a world that craves for both, for either, for anything but "what you know you know" as an answer to why our demi-devils ensnare our souls.

In turning from the Mass to the theater, replacing the sacrifice, the reenactment of Christ's offering of his body and blood to make amends for Adam's sin with the representation of a murder, what has Shakespeare done? Are we to understand this as a debasement of a mystery, a secularizing impoverishment of transcendence on the order of turning the holiness of the sacramental cup into Iago's sneering remark about Desdemona: "the wine she drinks is made of grapes"? Is the flowering of the early modern theater consequently a part of an inexorable process of secularization that begins in the period? Is that what we are seeing at work in *Othello*?

I am arguing that this is *not* the case, that to the contrary, the craving for justice this play incites is transcendent—a horizontal (rather than vertical) transcendence perhaps—nonetheless, vertical transcendence is implicated in the world of this play. As every theater attendee knew, the injunction to be just to the other is offered through a vertical revelation. The structure of the Decalogue makes these transcendences inseparable: divinity gives the commands to honor the other, to not kill, steal, or bear false witness against him, and makes these the very mode of honoring the divine. But when transcendence breaks into immanence at Sinai, it is with a law that is broken even as it is given—the law that *Othello* depicts as broken—and it breaks into world with tragic violence, the violence of justice and the violence of law when justice has been violated.

> And Moses turned, and went down from the mountain with the two tables of the testimony in his hands, tables that were written on both sides; on the one side and on the other were they written. And the tables were the work of

> God, and the writing was the writing of God, graven upon the tables... And as soon as he came near the camp and saw the calf and the dancing, Moses' anger burned hot, and he threw the tables out of his hands and broke them at the foot of the mountain. Moses stood in the gate of the camp and said, "Who is on the Lord's side? Come to me." And all the sons of Levi gathered themselves together to him. And he said to them, "Thus," says the Lord God of Israel, "Put every man his sword on his side, and go to and fro from gate to gate throughout the camp and slay every man his brother, and every man his companion, and every man his neighbor." And the sons of Levi did according to the word of Moses; and there fell of the people that day about three thousand men. And Moses said, "Today you have ordained yourselves for the service of the Lord, each one at the cost of his son and of his brother, that he may bestow a blessing upon you this day" (Ex 32:15-29).

There is no law—only a broken one—without justice.

At first it seems as if a principle of justice that precedes the law disqualifies the ancient Israelites for the gift of the law, but a closer look shows that justice does not precede the law: the violation of justice is also the violation of the first command of the law: "thou shalt not make graven images" is offered to them even as they are worshipping an idol. Is this then an impossible justice, for is it an impossible gift if offered to a recipient who cannot receive it? What is at stake in this commandment about idolatry that makes it the condition for the failure of justice? If we understand the image of God as the image of justice, we can read the commandment against idolatry as a demand for justice: anything else is false, a fake, an illusion of justice (an idol) but not the real thing. The biblical name of injustice is idolatry, and the biblical name for justice is divinity.

Because the Exodus narrative acknowledges that humanity, lost in idolatry, cannot receive and cannot deliver justice, the gift is divinely offered again—this time, as a gift that cannot be refused.

> "The time is coming," declares the Lord, "when I will make a new covenant with the house of Israel and with the house of Judah. It will not be like the covenant I made with their forefathers when I took them by the hand to lead them out of Egypt, because they broke my covenant.... This is the covenant I will make with the house of Israel after that time," declares the Lord, "I will put my law in their minds and write it on their hearts. I will be their God, and they will be my people. No longer will a man teach his neighbor or a man his brother, saying, 'Know the Lord,' because they will all know me, from the least of them to the greatest."

In the New Testament, the incarnation achieves the internalization of the law. In the gospel of Matthew, Christ is seen as the fulfillment of the Torah; in the gospel of John, the Logos is incarnate; in the letters of Paul, the gift of the Holy Spirit is the writing of the law in our hearts. For Levinas, the interiorization of justice cannot be identified with the Logos of Christianity: "God is real and concrete not through incarnation but through Law."[30] He explains that for Judaism, "it is precisely a word not incarnate from God that ensures a living God among us."[31] Because humankind is unjust, the just man will suffer; the "God Who hides His face and abandons the just man, this distant God, comes from within," from the intimacy of one's conscience and the moral law. "This is the specifically Jewish sense of suffering that at no stage assumes the value of a mystical atonement for the sins of the world."[32]

In Jacques Derrida's version of this interiorized justice, this horizontal transcendence, he sees a deep paradox, at first it seems as if immanent justice only seems transcendent but is not really: "the inaccessible transcendence of the law [*loi*], before which and prior to which man stands fast, only appears infinitely transcendent and thus theological to the extent that, nearest to him, it depends only on him, on the performative act by which he institutes it." But then he fully embraces the transcendence precisely because it is immanent: "The law is transcendent and theological, and so always to come, always promised, *because* it is immanent, finite, and thus already past."[33] To read the Old and New Testaments synoptically—instead of either agonistically or typologically—might yield another verdict: the suffering of the innocent, including of the innocent God-man, may be less the fulfillment of the law than the symptom of humanity's tragic failure to qualify for the gift of justice and to understand that failure as such is to live under the horizon of (horizontal) transcendent justice.

Notes

Previously published as "Shakespeare's Tragic Mass: Craving Justice," in Regina M. Schwartz, *Sacramental Poetics at the Dawn of Secularism: When God Left the World* (Stanford, CA: Stanford University Press, 2008), 39–58. An earlier version of this essay was published in Christine E. Joynes and Nancy Macky, eds., *Perspectives on the Passion: Encountering the Bible Through the Arts* (London: T & T Clark International, 2008).

1. Edwin Sandys (Archbishop of York), *Sermons* (Cambridge: Parker Society, 1842), 88–89. Sandys also cites Augustine: "Why preparest thou thy teeth? Believe, and thou hast eaten," in John Ev. Tract. I.4 xxv.12

2. Matthew Kellison's attack on Calvinism in *A Survey of the New Religion, detecting many grosse absurdities which it implieth* (Douay: n.p., 1605 [1603]), bk. IV, 230.

3. English Reformation poets lived on the brink of this new world and most embrace, predictably, the Calvinist doctrine of the spiritual—not material—presence of Christ in the Eucharist. But this leaves them with a persistent nostalgia for that material presence, a nostalgia that reaches just shy of the heresy of transubstantiation. Alongside the explicit theological discourse of the period, the poetry, prose, and theater of the period took up these questions. Despite inveighing against the doctrine of transubstantiation in his prose, John Milton describes a whole universe as incessantly and naturally "transubstantiating" into God in his verse; furthermore, his angel eats not "seemingly, nor in mist, the common gloss of theologians" but "with keen dispatch of real hunger, and concoctive heat to transubstantiate" matter into spirit. George Herbert, at the beginning of *The Temple*, composes a visual altar—not a communion table, but an altar—built out of the stones or words of his lyric; this word picture of an altar also forms a capital *I*—he and the sacrifice become one, and in another lyric, he imagines communion as literally ingesting the Bible. For John Donne, the miracle of the Eucharist is the miracle of genuinely combining with the other, soul and body. For him, the longing set in motion by the promise of communion with God is repeated in the longing for consummation with a lover, and he punned endlessly on consume and consummate, communion and common, that is, promiscuous. I have come to understand these writers as hungry for the mysteries wrought by the sacrament—as their Catholic detractors would have it, condemned to apprehend and desire a dinner that they could not have, but in their work, I have also come to see them concocting their own spiritual food.

4. Stephen Gosson, *Plays confuted in five actions* (1582), facsimile ed. (New York: Johnson Reprint Corp., 1972), sigs C5, G6–G7.

5. This derives Donatus on comedy where it is attributed to Cicero ("commoediam esse Cicero ait imitationem vitae, speculum consuetudinis, imaginem Veritatis").

6. Jeffrey Knapp, *Shakespeare's Tribe: Church, Nation, and Theater in Renaissance England* (Chicago: University of Chicago Press, 2002), 33–34. Knapp continues: "Following those Protestants who instead treated the petty materiality of the wafer as proof that the eucharist represented Christ, Henry V suggests that the carnal spectacles of the theater sacramentally highlight, rather than obscure, the operations of the spirit precisely because those spectacles are so conspicuously inadequate to the tales of *Non nobis* and *Te Deum* (4.8.121) they represent." In a similar vein, Stephen Greenblatt spoke of the "emptying out" of ritual as the enabling condition of the "craving" set in motion by theater for effective ritual. Greenblatt, *Shakespearean Negotiations* (Berkeley: University of California Press, 1988), 126–127. Louis Montrose writes of a transfer of the functions of rites of passage from ritual to the theater. Historians concur: "If the opportunity for popular participation in public rituals was . . . largely removed, that especial meaning which sacred ceremonies and popular rites had periodically conferred on the citizens' tangible environment also fell victim to the new 'secular' order." Charles Phythian-Adams, "Ceremony and the Citizen: The Communal Year at Coventry 1450–1550," in *Crisis and Order in English Towns 1500–1700*, ed. P. Clark and P. Slack (London: Routledge and Kegan Paul, 1972), 80.

7. Samuel Harsnett, "A Declaration of Egregious Popish Impostures," where Harsnett identifies exorcism with the theater, quoted in Greenblatt, *Shakespearean Negotiations*, 112.

8. Greenblatt, *Shakespearean Negotiations*, 125.

9. Greenblatt, 125.

10. For instance, on the Laudian effort to restore the communion "table" to the "altar." See Nicholas Tyacke, *Anti-Calvinists: The Rise of English Arminianism c. 1590–1640* (Oxford: Clarendon Press, 1990).

11. Although critics can be given to the same equation of ritual and theater, but for different reasons: for Julia Houston, Cranmer's innovations in the 1552 Book of Common Prayer had the effect of transforming the sacrament precisely into theater; see Houston, "Transubstantiation and the Sign: Cranmer's Drama of the Lord's Supper," *Journal of Medieval and Renaissance Studies* 24 (1994): 113–130.

12. Andrew Gurr, *The Shakespearean Stage 1574–1642* (Cambridge: Cambridge University Press, 1970).

13. Some critics are more sensitive to the distinction: "Playgoing is a little like churchgoing. It is a public act for private ends. It is a private act performed publicly. It is intimate and individual. It is impersonal and communal. It brings us nearer to the apprehension of our own godhood while at the same time it reinforces awareness of the transitory properties of our flesh. Yet likeness is not identity. Playgoing is a surrender to illusion while churchgoing is a ritual embodiment of a higher truth. Through churchgoing we hope to step from one truth to *the* truth. Playgoing holds out the possibility that we can slip through fancy to a lookout upon truth." Bernard Beckerman, "Shakespearean Playgoing Then and Now," in *Shakespeare's More Than Words Can Witness: Essays on Visual and Nonverbal Enactment in the Plays*, ed. Sidney Homan (Lewsbergu, PA: Bucknell University Press, 1986), 142.

14 Louis Montrose, *Helios*—ES IV 322, 58.

15. Stephen Greenblatt, establishing the purgatorial context for Hamlet, is uninterested in the question of conscience despite the play's overriding preoccupation with it. See Greenblatt, *Hamlet in Purgatory* (Princeton, NJ: Princeton University Press, 2002). But what is purgatory without the question of conscience, one might wonder.

16. Miri Rubin, *Corpus Christi: The Eucharist in Late Medieval Culture* (New York: Cambridge University Press, 1991).

17. John Calvin, *Institution of the Christian Religion*, 1536 Ed. (New York: John Knox Press, 1975), 160.

18. Cranmer, *The Work of Thomas Cranmer* (Appleford, UK: Courtenay Press, 1964), 7:55–56.

19. Cranmer, *Work*, 215.

20. Marion J. Hatchett, *The Eucharistic Liturgies of Historic Prayer Books: Historic Rites Arranged for Contemporary Celebration* (Sewanee, TN: School of Theology, 1984), 36.

21. John Jewel, *An Apology of the Church of England*, ed. J. E. Booty (New York, 1963), 33; my emphasis.

22. Richard Hooker, *Ecclesiastical Polity* (London: Everyman, 1907), bk. 5, chap. 57, sec. 6, 322–323.

23. Hooker, *Ecclesiastical Polity*, chap. 57, sec. 12, 330–331.

24. Jewel, *An Apology of the Church of England*, 35.

25. Calvin, *Institutes of the Christian Religion*, 4:17,3; my emphasis. Calvin joined in with vehemence against the Catholic mass attacking the "mass-Doctors" who purport to be the agent of grace instead of Christ: While they have fashioned themselves a god after the decision of their own lust, they have forsaken the living God. Indeed they have worshipped the gifts instead of the giver. In this there is a double transgression: for both the honor taken from God has been transferred to the creature (cf. Romans 1:25), and he himself also has been dishonored in the defilement and the profanation of his gift, when his holy sacrament is made a hateful idol.

26. See Regina M. Schwartz, *The Curse of Cain: The Violent Legacy of Monotheism* (Chicago: University of Chicago Press, 1999).

27. This inadequacy was felt by the radical Reformers themselves, figures like Menno who needed to solve the problem through a God-man whose heavenly, rather than earthly flesh, offered man the chance to be perfected through communion with that flesh.

28. Gabriel Biel, *Expositio sacri canonis missae* (ca. 1488), Brescia ed. 1576.

29. Biel.

30. "Loving the Torah More than God," in Emmanuel Levinas, *Difficult Freedom: Essays on Judaism*, trans. Sean Hand (Baltimore, MD: Johns Hopkins University Press, 1990), 145.

31. Levinas, 144.

32. Levinas, 143.

33. Jacques Derrida, "Force of Law: The Mystical Foundation of Authority," in *Acts of Religion*, ed. Gil Anidjar (New York: Routledge, 2002), 270; my emphasis. While Levinas did not see this internalization of the law as achieved through the incarnation, the England of Shakespeare, having expelled the Jews, without doubt did.

CHAPTER 20

Martyrdom, Religion, and Nation in Kurdish Literature

Mariwan Kanie

This essay analyzes two discourses of martyrdom in Iraqi Kurdistan in two different historical periods, as well as the different roles that religion plays in these discourses. The first discourse of martyrdom is the one that is formulated in the *ghazal*, or lyric love, poetry, of the beginning of the nineteenth century. Martyrdom here is presented as an integral part of a love relationship between a lover, who claims to be ready to sacrifice his life for his beloved and a worshipped beloved who acts carelessly and indifferently to her (or his) lover's determination of self-sacrifice. Through this determination, the poet wants to send a gesture to his, mostly courtly, public that he is a man of high morals who transcends his ego through sacrificing himself for his beloved.

The second discourse of martyrdom, surprisingly perhaps, presents the Kurdish language rather than the poet or poetic ego as a martyr and places this language in the center of a nationalist discourse. This specific form of martyrdom was constructed in the work of the poet Haji Qadir Koyî (1824–98), who spent the last three decades of his life as an exile in Istanbul.[1] Koyî emphasizes that the Kurdish language was once a living and united entity (*gird bû*, "it was a totality"), but lost that wholeness as a consequence of domination by Arabic and Persian as well as the indifference or dispassionate attitude of Kurdish intellectuals. In Koyî's words, the Kurdish language *tê çû*, "it was ruined" or "it had gone to waste." The verb *tê çûn* implies downfall, destruction, or death, in many cases as a result of violence or injustice.[2] It is therefore semantically related to the Arabic terms *zulm* and *mazlûm*, referring to oppression and victim of oppression respectively, which Bernard Lewis explains as follows: "In common usage, *zulm* has come to signify wrongdoing, evil, injustice, oppression and tyranny, particularly by persons who have power and authority."[3] One who undergoes *zulm* is called *mazlûm*; both notions are important components of the work of Koyî. *Zulm* and *mazlûm* are also central notions in the Islamic discourse of martyrdom. Martyrs are often called *mazlûm* and the act of killing called *zulm*; sometimes *mazlûm* is even used as a substitute for *shahîd*, martyr. Besides developing the notion of *tê çû* in relation to Kurdish as a language, Koyî creates the image of the Kurds as a collective *mazlûm* undergoing the act of historic *zulm*. Koyî tells his public that the remedy for this *zulm* consists in the willingness to take up weapons and fight their enemies. He constructs images of the Kurdish princes of the past as brave warriors who were ready to sacrifice themselves for their country. Koyî even reconstructs the image of the prophet Mohammed as that of a battlefield warrior ready to die in defense of his belief. Although Koyî frequently uses religious language and imagery, there is a strong anticlerical if not anti-religious thrust to his work. He looks back to the history of the Kurds in order to invent not only a militant revolutionary tradition but also to awaken the nation to revolutionary action.

To understand these changes, we have to situate them in the historical context of the last decades of the nineteenth century, when language practices were changing and a language ideology was emerging that reformulated language as a tool to achieve different tasks in a social and political context.[4] As part of these new language practices and ideologies, Koyî tries to bring the unjustly ruined Kurdish language back to life, simplifies it, and uses it as an instrument for educating people, giving them a sense of being a nation, and making them aware of their historical existence. Through this language, Koyî calls his public to action and to develop the mentality of a national fighter for the motherland. In this sense, his poetry is a gesture, a message sent to his readers to create their own national political destiny and to conduct possibly violent action in the name of the nation. It is difficult to know precisely who formed Koyî's public, but as he was a private teacher of Kurdish children in Istanbul, his young students could be among his readers. Koyî was also a well-known poet in Iraqi Kurdistan with a network of contacts in religious madrasa schools. It is also a well-known fact that he sent his poems back to his friends in Iraqi Kurdistan, mostly the small elite who could read at that time. When the first Kurdish newspaper appeared in Cairo in 1898, the editor in chief of the paper, who had been one of his students in Istanbul, started to publish his poetry in the newspaper. The poetry of Koyî is a call to action, both individual and collective action, violent as well as nonviolent action. Koyî presents the national self as an action, as a chain of actions including writing in the mother tongue, educating the nation, uniting them, and taking up arms, ready to fight and face martyrdom.

My basic argument is that not only does religion in the two discourses on martyrdom play different roles but that the very notion of religion in each discourse is differently rearticulated. In the first discourse, religion is presented as something concerned with the inner world of the believer and is articulated as an ethical power that through concentration on love tries to transform individuals into morally good persons. In the second discourse, religion concerns the outside world and engages in the mega projects of social, political, and cultural change related to the emergency of nationalism in the Ottoman Empire. Religion here is not only legitimizing these changes but is also involved in creating and shaping them. Religion is politicized, nationalized, and militarized, and consequently plays a constitutive role in creating a national subject. From ghazal poetry to the poetry of Koyî we witness also a shift: while ghazal poetry could be seen as an instrument of the poet to tell his public that he is a moral person, the poetry of Koyî calls his public to action and urges them to create a new world.

Literary Martyrdom

In the Kurdistan of the first half of the nineteenth century, the notion of martyrdom played an important role. However, it did not concern martyrs who actively sought a fighting death in wars and political battles but martyrs of love who passively died in literary texts. The love in literary texts of that period was not only paired with pain and suffering but also with the willingness to die for love: to become the martyr of love. The literary space in which this specific form of martyrdom has emerged was the genre of love poetry called ghazal. Ghazal originally means "talking to a woman about love";[5] it was a dominant form of poetry in Kurdistan, the rest of the Ottoman Empire, and Iran at that time.

There were of course a lot of wars in that period, but these did not find their way into Kurdish literature. When they did, there was no mention of martyrdom. The main reason why these wars did not enter the literary texts has to do with their political framework and their religious understanding. They occurred within the boundaries of the Ottoman Empire and were part of the growing internal conflicts within the empire itself: between the local Kurdish principalities and the central power of the Ottoman sultan, between the principalities themselves and between different factions within the same principalities. This means that those wars occurred among Muslims themselves. Wars and confrontations between Muslims are radically forbidden in traditional Islamic teaching; they have been generally called *fitna*, "revolt," "disturbances," or "civil war." In Islamic thought, *fitna* is the worst thing that can happen to the Muslim community, a schism that not only divides and weakens the community of believers but also threatens their purity of faith. The person who dies in *fitna*, rather than a martyr, may be seen as an apostate and as an instigator of rebellion against the divine law.[6] For this religious reason, there is almost no single Kurdish literary text that describes or deals with those internal wars and conflicts, which occurred in the first half of the nineteenth century.[7]

Thus, in the first half of the nineteenth century, martyrdom belonged to the domain of personal love and not to the domain of politics. It was part of a literary rather than a political game. The three important Kurdish poets of this time, Nalî (1797–1855), Salim (1800–66), and Kurdî (1801–49), wrote intense ghazal poetry in which they demonstrated their readiness to sacrifice their lives for their idealized beloved. Those poets called themselves *shahîdî 'ishq*, "martyrs of love,"[8] or *ahlî shahâdat*, "devotees of martyrdom."[9]

In ghazal poetry, martyrdom is one of the central notions. Likewise, love occurs frequently here; it is a complex phenomenon and contains contradictory characters; it is spiritual and erotic, dangerous and pleasurable, and quiet and deadly at the same time. The roots of love in ghazal poetry go back to the Sufi tradition of love. In this tradition, love is a unifying divine power, which is "able to bring together all contradictory and varied qualities and to reinstate them in God's unity." This unifying power of love is unique for human beings "who alone were created in the full image of God."[10] This Sufi concept of love is present side by side with the Sufi imagery in ghazal poetry, but this does not mean that ghazal poetry and Sufi poetry are identical. There are some important differences—first, the fact that love in the Sufi poetry has God as its absolute object while love in the ghazal poetry has a human being as an object. The beloved in ghazal poetry is mostly an idealized woman, but it could also be an idealized adolescent man. Second, the core of ghazal poetry is not seeking a mystical transcendence in the sense of seeking God, but it is seeking the overwhelming experience of a passionate love for an idealized but cruel, difficult, and dangerous beloved who does not react to the suffering of the poet. As one scholar rightly observes on the ghazal poetry, it is a "celebration of failure," because suffering and pain have come to be regarded as ethical instruments.[11] The point I want to emphasize is that in this ghazal poetry, the Sufi component of the mystical experience is transformed into a "secular" experience of love between man and woman, or man and man. The poems by Kurdî and Salim are examples of this transformation. Neither of them was a Sufi, and in the case of Kurdi some of his ghazal poetry reflects his love for a real young man. Love in Kurdî and Salim's poetry is not a divine spiritual love; it is primarily an earthly, profane, and corporeal love, described in the images, metaphors, and rhetoric of Sufism.

The total love described in ghazal poetry has an essentially irrational character: its origin lies in the heart, which has other rules than reason, namely *dewana'i* or *junûn*, or "madness." In ghazal poetry love and rationality are contradictory to each other. This negation of rationality makes love dangerous indeed. The dangerous quality of love in ghazal poetry is not only related to the uncontrollable emotions of love itself; it also relates to the capacity to demolish social, cultural, and religious taboos. In ghazal poetry love is presented as something more important than religious dogmas and the orthodox form of religion, which is based on a formal understanding of religion.

In short, being in love means starting a journey on a dangerous path that could lead to death. That is why the one who falls in love should be ready to sacrifice his life and become the martyr of love. Thus, in this tradition, the lover needs, as Henry Corbin says, "the courage of love."[12] Through his readiness for martyrdom the poet and lover represents himself as a moral person, someone who goes through his pain and suffers beyond his ego and individuality. The readiness to be a martyr determines the identity of the lover-poet as a moral individual.

Ghazal poetry also contains strong physical and erotic dimensions, which are oriented toward bodily pleasure, both legitimate and illegitimate, which connects love with the domain of the body. Physical passion for the beloved is prominently present in this poetry. The erotic body of the beloved is described in detail: eyes, eyebrows, lips, mouth, breasts, hips, hands, belly. The lips of Salim's beloved are "sweet as sugar," her eyes "taste like wine," and her breasts are "extremely wild."[13] Nalî calls the nipples of the breast of his beloved "sweet buds" and her breasts "purple pomegranates."[14] Likewise, the manner of waking, laughing, and moving of the beloved all become objects of erotic passion.

These physical and sensuous dimensions of love in ghazal poetry are linked not only to the erotic beauty of the beloved but also to the circumstances in which the lover and the beloved find themselves. The poet frequently imagines meeting his beloved in an imagined *mayxana*, a tavern, where music, alcohol, and dance create a Dionysian atmosphere. Wallowing in his sorrows and in his infatuation with the beloved, the poet sips his wine and gives words to erotic desire.[15]

In short, love in ghazal poetry is a painful, dangerous, obstinate, solitary, irrational, erotic, and altruistic experience. It has an enormous power to transform the poet. To admit to love means to be in a process of metamorphosis in which the person undergoes continuous changes and adopts different forms, which goes beyond the borders of the dominant morality of the society and the border of selfishness and narcissism. Love in ghazal poetry requires a lot from the lover: patience, readiness for radical changes, loneliness, pain, and even self-sacrifice. In other words, love requires and produces *shahîds*, or "martyrs." But this martyrdom in ghazal poetry is a literary construction; it is a *literary martyrdom*—that is, a form of martyrdom that is constructed in fictitious literary love relations in which the act of sacrifice is not real but symbolic. In other words, martyrdom is a matter of a fictive self-sacrifice for a fictive beloved, death is symbolic, and even suffering and pain are also a merry language game. In constructing himself as a martyr, the poet places himself in a subject position acting as an active agency and creating his identity as an altruistic, generous, and ethical person.

The form of religion—which underpins the image of the self, the beloved, and the content of love in ghazal poetry—is the Sufi understanding of religion in which the inner and spiritual dimensions of the individual life form the core of the notion of religion. The importance of personal experience, the path to spiritual self-development and the overcoming of the obstacles to spiritual self-realization are the framework of the Sufi notion of religion. Religion here emphasizes strongly the presence of the godly in the person and deals with the depth of the man and search for the transcendental elements and moments in the man's spirit and practices. Religion is then a matter of personal identity through a personal relationship to God. Religion here is primarily *iman*, or "inner faith."

Thus, religion constitutes a disciplined hierarchical way of life in which a spiritual knowledge and a spiritual authority of the guide play an enormous role. The master-disciple relationship is the social model on which the social fabric of society is based and functions. In the first half of the nineteenth century where ghazal poetry was popular and broadly written in the Ottoman Empire, the Sufi orders were the main organization of the religious life. By the eighteenth and nineteenth centuries at least one half, if not as many as three-quarters, of the male Muslim population was attached in some sense to a Sufi order.[16] This means that ghazal poetry reflected the societal order in which Sufism was a dominant form of religious life.

The erotic and sensual dimension of ghazal poetry does not eliminate this understanding of religion. As already mentioned, love is constructed as the divine power, which bridges and unifies the contradictions. Spirituality in this tradition is a domain in which the rational contradictions are not contradictions anymore. Love follows the rules or, more precisely, un-rules of the heart and not that of reason. Like love, religion is also located in the heart, and it is basically the matter of inner feeling and faith.

In short, what underpins the notion of literary martyrdom in ghazal poetry is this Sufi articulation of religion, religion as a field of organizing the inner domain of the individual within a hierarchical relationship, religion as *iman*. In the last quarter of the second half of the nineteenth century, a new and radically different notion of religion would emerge. The new discourse of martyrdom that emerges, namely the martyrdom of Kurdish language in the work of the poet Hajî Qadir Koyî, is based on a new notion of religion.

Language as a Martyr

From the last decades of the nineteenth century and against the background of emerging new notions of language and the spread of the modern notions of progress, nation, and nationalism in the Ottoman Empire, the concepts of love, beloved, martyrdom, and religion undergo a rapid rearticulation in the work of Koyî. In his poetry, love becomes the political love of the nation. The beloved becomes the *watan*, or "fatherland," and the martyr is no longer simply a literary figure dying for the love of the unreachable male or female beloved but a militant activist who risks real pain and death in nationalistic wars. All these new changes went hand in hand with the formation of nationalism as ideology and paired with it the rearticulation of religion itself. Religion becomes a gesture that calls upon the believers for changing the inhabited world, a force behind the dream of progress and an important part of the newly emerged individual and collective identity. In this sense, religion calls the believers for producing a new sense and symbols of love, a new sense of the self, a new image of the world, a new public, and of course a new form of martyrdom. In the work of Koyî all these changes have happened in relation to the change in the notion of language and the emergence of new language practices and a new ideology in the Ottoman Empire. Before elaborating in detail on the notion of martyrdom of language in Koyî's work and its consequences, it is necessary to illuminate the context in which this rearticulation of language has occurred.

Attention to language reform within the Ottoman Empire goes back to the eighteenth century. The empire attempted to solve the communication problems between different parts of the empire, between the state institutions themselves and between those institutions and the public. Simplifying language constituted the heart of this language reform, to find a language for communication simpler than the language of *ulema*, the "clergy," and simpler than that of the traditional state bureaucrats. These attempts brought language to the center of the state's attention and the attention of intellectuals and the public. After undergoing a profound modernization process in journalism, literature, the administration, and the education system, new forms of public languages emerged. These developments concerned primarily changes in language practices and literature but had in the second half of the century profound social and political consequences. They played an important role in the formation of different national movements within the Ottoman Empire.[17] One scholar traces this change in relations to the changing status of the Arabic and Turkish languages in the second half of the nineteenth century and writes: "in this context Arab national identity is generally defined in relation to Turkish national identity, with Arabic and Turkish acting as primary sources of national identification respectively."[18] The new imagining of language as the primary source of national identity brought about, for the first time, a cultural form of nationalism within the Islamic part of the Ottoman Empire. In short, the Turkish and Arabic languages came to be seen as more important than religion in the formation of a national identity.

In this context, Koyî (1824–97), who lived in Istanbul for the last three decades of his life and watched this development carefully, realized that Kurdish did not exist as a national language. There was also nothing akin to the debate on Arabic and Turkish about the status of Kurdish within the empire even among the Kurds themselves. He was also concerned about the general position of the Kurds in the empire, especially after the abolishment of all Kurdish local principalities in the first half of the nineteenth century by the Ottomans in an attempt to centralize the power of the empire.

Koyî thus developed the thesis of the Kurdish language as *tê çû*, "unjustly victimized and ruined," but also as a powerful instrument with which the Kurds could build a new future:

Lefzî kurdî billaw nebû, gird bû
Wa le mabeynî ême da tê çû.[19]

[The Kurdish tongue was not scattered but a united whole,
It has been unjustly ruined in front of us.]

As noted above, the word *tê çû* means literally "lost" or "ruined," not as a result of a natural development but as a result of unjust treatment. Koyî connects this unjust loss and destruction of Kurdish with two factors. First, he mentions the traditional domination of Arabic as the language of religious education and Persian as the language of personal written communication and literature. Second, he blames the negligence of the Kurdish intellectuals themselves, who before the nineteenth century wrote mostly in Persian and Arabic. Comparing Kurdish to Persian, Koyî asserts that Kurdish is in no way inferior to Persian, and he attacks the Kurdish clergy for not writing in Kurdish. Koyî asks the Kurdish intellectuals:

> Ya le gell Farisî çi ferqî heye
> Bo çî ew rast e, bo çî em keçe ye ...
> Axir em 'eqlleyan hebû boyê
> Ger Suleymanî ye we ya Koyê
> Bûne ustadî Farisî û Tazî
> Ta geyştin be fexrekey Razî
> Çunke sermaye mallî xellqî bû
> Weqtê mirdin hemû be hîç derçû.[20]

> [What is the difference with Persian?
> Why is Persian correct, and Kurdish crooked?
> If at last, they (the Kurdish scholars) had thought properly
> Both in Suleimania and in Koya.[21]
> Became masters in Persian and in Arabic
> They even reached the excellence of (Fakhr al-Dîn) Razî[22]
> But because their capital belonged to others,
> When they died all of it passed away like nothing.]

Besides developing the notion of loss or perishing in relation to the Kurdish as a language, Koyî creates the image of Kurds as *mazlûm*. He calls the treatment of the Kurds in history as *zulm*:

> Hîç xîretêk nemawe sed car qesem be Qur'an
> Peyda ebê Ermenistan, namênê yek le Kurdan
> Sertan le qurr hellênin, ehwallman bibînin
> Çon în le destî zullmî bêdînî dûr le îman[23]

> [There is no courage left, I swear a hundred times by the Koran
> If an Armenian state is established, no single Kurd will survive
> Raise your heads from the mud, look at our situation
> How we are under the *zulm* of unbelief, and far from faith]

Elsewhere Koyî invents the image of the Kurds as *mazlûm*.

Her manewe bênewa û mezllûm,
Wek bûmî xerabezar, meş'ûm[24]

[They have remained miserable and oppressed
Ominous, like a grim owl]

When Koyî presents the Kurdish language as *tê çû* and the Kurds as *mazlûm*, he is using the religious semantic field to define the unjust and tyrannical treatment of Kurdish as a language and the Kurds as a nation. Through creating the image of the language as *tê çû*, the treatment of Kurds in history as *zulm* and the image of Kurds as *mazlûm*, the imagery of victimhood or martyrdom underpins the nationalistic discourse of Koyî.

In short, Koyî's entire intellectual project is devoted to bringing this ruined language to life again, to the nationalistic creation or resurrection of Kurdish, and through it, to the invention of the Kurds as a modern nation. It must be mentioned that nationalism by Koyî is not a developed and coherent set of ideas and expectations, but an ideology in the process of being developed, a political vision seeking a new language, which includes the notions of love of fatherland (*watan*) as beloved as well as nationalized religion and martyrdom. Koyî starts this huge project through redefining and rearticulating of these notions as they have been used and constructed in ghazal poetry. Koyî starts to attack the meanings of these notions in ghazal poetry.

Attacking Ghazal Poetry and Creating a Politicized Concept of the Beloved

Thus, one important aspect of the work of Koyî is his moral and cultural aversion against ghazal poetry. Koyî argues that Kurdish poets should not write ghazal anymore and asks Kurdish readers not to read ghazal poetry, believing that it is the exclusive concern with love in ghazal poetry that has caused the poverty and backwardness of the Kurds:

'Işqebazî û heway derwêşî
Mîlletî xiste feqr û bêîşî[25]

[The obsession with love and Sufi music[26]
Condemned the nation to poverty and backwardness]

For Koyî, reading and writing ghazal poetry will keep people busy with unimportant matters. Instead of reading ghazal poetry, Koyî proposes the reading of his own poems, which show the nation the way of power and glory in the modern world, which starts, according to Koyî, with the love for the fatherland and the establishment of an independent state on the soil of that fatherland. Aversion to ghazal poetry and to the love for an idealized individual beloved in this poetry goes along with writing about a new form of love, namely the political love for the fatherland. Koyî writes:

Weten mehbûbeyêk e hucre arayî
Nîşaney dîn û îman e temennayî

[The fatherland is a beloved woman, and a gentle classroom
Desire of the fatherland is a sign of religion and faith]

Koyî constructs for the first time in Kurdish the notion of *watan*, the fatherland, as a political national homeland. Arab and Turkish intellectuals in the Ottoman Empire had already cultivated the notion of *watan* (place of one's birth) as the fatherland and the focus of love and affection. The Egyptian and Turkish modernist intellectuals Rifa'a al-Tahtawi (d. 1873) and Namik Kemal (d. 1888) both wrote about love of the *watan*, but in their works the word was not yet used in the sense of a national Turkish or Arab homeland. The Ottoman Empire was still the fatherland they had in their political imagination. According to Kayali, "the notion of belonging to a nation (much less to a nation-state) had no meaning at the time."[27] He elaborates: "It is reasonable to assume that the Western-oriented segments of the Ottoman elite were drawn to the concept of the nation-state in the late nineteenth and early twentieth centuries, but not in any ethnic sense."[28] For Koyî, in contrast to Tahtawi and Kemal, fatherland does not mean the Ottoman Empire but the territorial ethnic Kurdish areas with clear borders and a defined population. According to Koyî the breadth of this territorial fatherland "is 15 days on foot" and its length "reaches from the high mountains to Esfahan and Shiraz."[29] Koyî asserts that "four million people" are living in this area.[30] This is the first time that the Kurdish fatherland and the Kurdish people are expressed in figures and cartographic elements in Kurdish poetry. When Koyî talks of the love of fatherland, he then speaks of love for this imagined Kurdish fatherland and imagined Kurdish community. Koyî connects the political love for the fatherland with the necessity and urgency of establishing an independent Kurdish state. In several poems, Koyî emphasizes that the establishment of an independent Kurdish state is of great importance for the fatherland. He writes:

Eger wek min xeberdar bin le dewllet
Le heyfan xo dexinkênin be bê pet[31]

[If you just understand, like I do, the importance of having a state
You will want to strangle yourself in misery (for not having attained it)]

The love for the fatherland is then the love for the state to be established, so that the fatherland and the Kurdish nation have an instrument to protect themselves. The political love in the work of Koyî, as a substitute for the love in ghazal poetry, is directly linked to the protecting power of the state, which embraces and protects both the individual Kurds and the whole of the Kurdish nation.

Besides the functionality of the state as an instrument of self-defense, the state, according to Koyî, is an important means for making other nations respect the Kurdish nation. Respect in a modern world is related to power and power needs a state. Koyî speaks of three "tribes" that do not have their own state or homeland and as a result are looked down upon:

Sê qebîle heqîr û bê rûmet in
Kurd û Dom û Yehûdî gumrrah in[32]

[Three tribes are despised and lack respect
Kurds, Gypsies, and Jews have gone astray]

Koyî's attack on ghazal poetry and his associating it with the backwardness of the Kurds, imagined as a nation, has an important consequence for the discourse of martyrdom. His attack on ghazal poetry indicated also the rejection if not the condemnation of literary martyrdom as the core of ghazal poetry. As mentioned earlier, Koyî ridicules the love theme in ghazal poetry and reduces it to a sensual and a sexual love. Dying for this would not only be ridiculous but shameful. As their religion obliges them, he argues, they should instead love their country and struggle for it. The decadent love in ghazal poetry should be transformed into a political national love.

What is important to emphasize once again, is that this new national political love is religiously legitimized. This means that religion is present in the heart of the nationalist project of Koyî, but the religion that legitimizes the new national self-sacrificing political love has been radically reformulated. Koyî starts three processes: the first one is the changing focus of religion from the inner part of individual life to the outside world. This contains changing the focus of religion from emphasizing individual spirituality into civilizing the nation through promoting and cultivating a modern science and achieving progress. The second process is the nationalization of religion in which religion engages in the formation of national identity and national subjectivity; it becomes one of the many faces or gestures of the nation. The third process is the militarization of religion, in that religion gets involved in the militant conflicts of a modern world and plays an important role in creating a new nationalist militant activist. Let me elaborate on these issues.

Religion: From the Inner to the Outer World

As mentioned above, the form of the religion present in the ghazal poetry is Sufism. Two main points in Sufism need to be remembered: First is the role of the spiritual guide, *shaykhs* or *murshids*. Second is the ritual of *dhikr*, or Sufi dance ritual. The notion of religion that is constructed in the poetry of Koyî has been purified of Sufism and especially these two main elements of Sufism are hardly criticized. Koyî does not emphasize the inner world of the believer but the relationship between the individual believer and the outside world. Religion here assists the believer to discover the outside world, change it, and then take an active role in it. In doing so the ritual of *dhikr* and the figures of *shaykhs* or *murshids* are radically criticized and broadly condemned. Koyî presents the *shaykhs* or *murshids* as impostors who try to keep people ignorant and as a result block the way to progress.[33] Koyî criticizes the morality of the religious guides and accuses them of self-interest. Moreover, he says that they are continuously chasing women, even calling them "the worshippers of the vagina."[34] According to Koyî, this religious elite is neither suitable for the establishment of a modern state nor for the well-being of religion itself.[35]

Koyî believes that the religious elite should get another profession besides the implementation of their religious service, learn to earn the money they need, and do something else than reminding people of religious taboos. In fact, this means that Koyî tries to eliminate the religious elite as a social and intellectual group who wants to mediate between the believers and God. It also means that he believes that individual believers have an autonomous conscience, which does not need the mediation of the religious clergy to lead a real religious life. With the same perspective, Koyî criticizes the religious ritual of inner travel, *dhikr*, and considers it as a useless practice and a waste of time.

Koyî comes to the heart of his intellectual attempt to reformulating religion through relating it to six important dimensions of human life. According to Koyî, religion should protect all these six aspects of life and if it fails in protecting each one of them, then religion is diminished. This means that religion has first the function to motivate people to take care of their basic needs—accordingly, to believe in one God—and then to develop themselves into a strong, powerful, and well-developed people through adhering to sword and pen and by their readiness to make sacrifices.

In this reformulation, religion is presented as a coherent totality and contains—beside the belief in God—protecting and developing all aspects of life. Religion is thus related to this worldly set of activities that aim at enriching and protecting the life and have been powerful in the world. In this sense religion is a civilization or a framework of a civilization. This rearticulation of religion is directly related to the domination of the two grand modern ideologies in the Ottoman Empire in the second half of the nineteenth century, namely Positivism and Darwinism.[36] Positivism strengthened, through the emphasis on the capacity of science, the optimistic belief in progress and the emergence of a new civilization, whereas Darwinism stimulated a positive appreciation of power and the perceived need of a strong state. This does not mean that religion simply translates these ideologies to its own language and images, however; religion is deeply engaged in social and political projects of creating a modern sense of the self and the world. These two modern ideologies play an assisting role in this new process of rearticulating religion.

Here religion is no longer the *dhikr* ritual, which assists individuals in their inner spiritual journey to discover their inner selves. Rather, religion organizes the relationship between the individual and the outside world; it assists the individual to discover, change, and develop the world. The clearest example of this change in the orientation of the religion from the emphasis on the inner world to the discovering and improving of the outside world is to be found in these sentences of Koyî:

> Sefer ender weten çi kellik degirê
> Seyrî nakey şemendefer defirrê . . .
> Telixrafiş telêk e bêma ye
> Muxbîrî rûy kullî dunya ye[37]

> [What kind of worth has the travel to the inner world?
> Look how fast the train can ride . . .
> The telegraph is a simple device
> But it can connect the whole world]

Koyî contrasts the train and telegram with the Sufi techniques of traveling to the inner world; he contrasts also the role of science in discovering the world with the role of religious guide in traveling to the inner world. For Koyî traveling in the outside world through the guidelines of science is more important than traveling to the inner world of the individual through lazy religious guides. This does not mean that Koyî sees religion from a secularist position, however; he stresses the importance of religion in reorganizing the world and the formation of the new collective life. Actually, Koyî sees religion as a framework of modern life. Achieving progress through modern science needs a form of religion that emphasizes travel in the outside world, knowledge of this world, and an active engagement in creating it. Thus, Koyî reformulates Islam by emphasizing that it is a religion that motivates Muslims—both men and women—to search for science everywhere in the world:

> Bo çî fermûyetî nebîyî emîn:
> "Îtlubu 'ilmekum welew fî ssîn"
> Nêr û mê lem hedîse ferqî nîye
> Ger mela nehîyî fermû dînî nîye.[38]

> [Why has our trusted prophet said,
> "Search for science even in China"
> In this hadith he does not distinguish between man and woman
> If a mullah denies that, he has no religious mandate.]

Koyî goes even further to emphasize that Islam asks Muslims to seek science from anyone, regardless of their beliefs and religion: Muslims should not ask whether the owners of the science are Jewish, Christian, or Hindu.[39] In other words, to be a good religious person, someone who could enter paradise, one has to seek and acquire modern science instead of traveling to the inner as a Sufi would. Religion should then motivate the people and contribute to building a strong and developed fatherland through cultivating the modern science. Koyî constructs religion as a force that does not see the world as evil, as something to be ignored or detached from in favor of focusing on inner life; rather it should be discovered, appropriated, and enjoyed. In other words, religion should reconcile the individual with the world and enrich his relationship to it.

Nationalization of Religion

Another aspect of the rearticulation of religion in the work of Koyî is the nationalization of religion. By nationalization of religion, I mean redefining religion in the way that promotes the national project: promoting the establishment of the national state, creating a national subject, and shaping a national identity. This means that religion plays a double role: a mobilizing role at the national level and a role in the creation of a national subject. In this sense religion could not be reduced only to an instrument for mobilization in the hands of religious or political leaders but a power to participate in creating a new political subjectivity. It is not an element from the past but a gesture of a new world.

Koyî is actively engaged in the process of the nationalization of religion. In this process he constructs the Kurds as *true Muslims* and the Ottomans, especially the powerful Ottoman Turks, as *false Muslims* who abuse Islam to increase their own interests and power. Koyî connects the ethnic identity of Kurds to their identity as good Muslims. In doing that, he is ethnicizing the religion and making Islam an important dimension of the national ethnic identity of the Kurds.

Nationalizing Islam is also an attempt to delegitimize the Ottoman Empire. Islam was the binding factor within the multiethnic Ottoman Empire that kept the different ethnic and cultural groups together. Nationalizing Islam takes this binding factor away. The antagonism that Koyî creates on the religious level between the Kurds and the Ottomans, in which the Kurds are constructed as true Muslims and the Ottomans as false Muslims, lie at the heart of nationalizing Islam. Koyî presents the Ottomans as morally low people:

> Rêgir û hîz û diz e, jin hellgir û mallanbirr e
> Faîdey çî nêwî kunyey xoy musullman dadenê[40]

> [Bandits, faggots, and robbers they carry off women and steal property
> But nevertheless, they are not ashamed to call themselves Muslims]

Koyî portrays the Ottomans as unbelievers or as people claiming to be Muslim, while in reality they are anything but Muslims. He adds that the Ottomans look down on the Kurds as ignorant people, who are as stupid as apes:

> Ke çî Romî ke ême deynasîn
> Wa dezanê ke ême nesnasîn[41]

[The Ottomans, as we know
See us as monkeys]

Koyî asks God to put the Kurds on the correct path and to pursue the Ottomans until hell. He writes:

Ya îlahî be ayetî munzel
Bê çwar yarî Ehmedî mursel
Bê newayanî mullkî Kurdistan
Her le gawanî ta degate şwan
Le xewî cehl û mestî û xefllet
Be xeber bên be nexmey rehmet
Pakî derçin le karî nabemehel
Romî rafrrênin bo derî esfel[42]

[Oh God, by the verses (of the Koran) that you sent down
By the four friends of the Prophet Mohammad[43]
And by the riches of the land of Kurdistan
Let all people, be they cowherds or even shepherds
Wake up from the sleep of ignorance, intoxication, and carelessness
So that they may be aware of the beauty of mercy
Pass their days purely in work not unworthy
And put the Ottomans to flight until the gates of hell]

It is clear that Koyî's attack on the Ottomans is aimed at all aspects of being Ottoman. He attacks the Ottoman manner of governing, their legal system, and their integrity as Muslims. Thus, he constructs the Ottomans as the absolute other of the Kurds, by showing their disrespect for Kurds. As an alternative to this decadent religious empire, Koyî does not think of reforming the empire, as many Ottoman intellectuals of his time did, for example, the Yong Ottoman intellectuals in Istanbul, Muhammad Abduh in Egypt, and others in the Islamic parts of the Empire: Koyî wants to leave the Empire behind and establish the independent Kurdish state. Nationalizing religion is part of the political imagination that focuses on achieving this aim.

In nationalizing religion, Koyî does not stop in portraying the Ottomans negatively; he also creates the image of Kurds as true Muslims who implement and guard the *shari'a* in a proper way. In this regard Koyî writes enthusiastically about the Kurdish rulers of the local Kurdish principalities as a true Muslims.[44] As I mentioned earlier, all the Kurdish principalities have been destroyed in the first half of the nineteenth century by the Ottoman army. Koyî writes in the memory of those principalities and their princes:

Yek be yek hafîzî şerî'et bûn
Seyyidî qewm û shexî mîllet bûn[45]

[They were the guardians of *shari'a*
They were the lords of their people and the shaykhs of their nation]

Koyî praises the ancestors of the Kurds and claims that they were brave and good believers and they have achieved a lot of victories against the Ottomans. They were also ready to sacrifice themselves and become martyrs in the battlefield. He writes:

Hemû 'alim, hemû şex û mîr in
Zîrek û jîr û ehlî tedbîr in ...
Dan û bexşînyan le la baw e
Xûnî meydanyan le la aw e
Be şeca'et hemû wekû Rostem
Be sexawet hemû wekû Hatem

Le şerra zor def'e qewmawe
Romîyanyan çilon cewab dawe[46]

[Each of them was learned and had spiritual and worldly authority
Each was intelligent, sharp and wise ...
Giving and generosity had been their habits.
Their blood flowed on the battlefield like water.
They were as brave as Rostam[47]
They were as generous as Hatem[48]
On the battlefield, it has happened frequently
That they have beaten the Ottomans]

Koyî thus invents Kurds as true believers, wise and learned, brave and ready to sacrifice their lives for their fatherland. Koyî reinvents the imagined self-sacrifice of the Kurdish princes and their followers in the battlefield against the Ottomans as a nationalistic act. He nationalizes the past as an important component of the newly created national imagined community. Religion plays an important role in creating this new positive self-image through creating a negative image of the Ottomans. Hence religion here is not only an instrument to mobilize people, but also an important device in creating modern national identities. It is not only a force that could be utilized but also a force that has a performative power. In this reformulation of the past, martyrdom is an organic part of the national battle against the Ottomans.

Militarizing Islam

Finally, religion takes a military character in the poetry of Hajî Qadir. In one of his most famous poems, Koyî shows what this militarization of religion means:

> Qesrî dîn, binc û binaxey mehkemî
> Şîr û tîr e, dîrek û taq û xemî
> Musbhet e fermûy hebîbî kîbrîya
> Min nebîyî şîrim le meydanî wexa
> Gullşenî pirr mîwey baxî me'ad,
> Wa le jêrî sayey tîxî cîhad[49]

> [The strong foundations of the fortress of religion
> Are the sword and the arrow
> The God's pleased prophet confidently said:
> "I am the prophet of the sword on the battlefield"
> The promised garden full of fruits and flowers
> Lies under the shadow of the sword of jihad]

This militarization of religion involves two main ideas: first, religion is connected directly to the idea of jihad and martyrdom. Koyî essentializes Islam as the religion of the sword, which carries out jihad against the enemies of Islam, with the martyrs enjoying the promised garden of paradise. Second, Koyî represents the prophet Mohammed, and through him every real believer, as a militant activist. The militarization of religion, which deviates strongly from the mystical experience in ghazal poetry, is an important aspect of rearticulating Islam in the work of Koyî. Nationalism, especially in circumstances of conflicts, needs warriors, not mystics, and one way of creating those warriors is through the militarization of religion. In this sense the militarized and nationalized religion motivates, even creates, individuals who are prepared to fight for the fatherland and to sacrifice their very lives where necessary.

Conclusion

In this essay, I analyzed two discourses on martyrdom in Kurdish literature from two historical periods, namely, the beginning and the end of the nineteenth century. In the first discourse, martyrdom is a literary phenomenon embedded in the so-called ghazal poetry. The second discourse presents martyrdom as a political phenomenon in the work of the poet Koyî. In each discourse religion is located differently. In ghazal poetry, religion concerns the search for inner spiritual fulfillment; in the second discourse, it assists the believer to discover the outer world. They are also articulated differently. In the first discourse religion is mainly present in the form of a specific ritual and habits concerning spiritual practice, namely *dhikr*, whereas in the second, religion consists of a coherent set of doctrines that concern the totality of social, political, and cultural life and thereby challenge the established religious institutions and ritual practices. In the first discourse religion is basically a matter of faith; in the second discourse religion legitimizes the modern sciences, modern identities, and modern political imaginations and to some extent even takes part in creating them. Religion here becomes more assertive and covers areas of social life that previously were covered by tribal custom or other traditions. In the work of Koyî religion covers almost every aspect of life, from the promotion of science and power to the regulation of behavior and protection of the moral and material well-being of the community. In the first discourse, religion emphasizes the individual redemption, while in the second discourse religion is primarily about social and political salvation. While the first discourse concerns itself with local religious practices, the second discourse opens the path for the rebirth of religion as a social and political ideology.

Notes

This essay is based on research carried out in the research project The Sacred and the Secular: Genealogies of Self, State, and Society in the Contemporary Islamic World, funded by the Netherlands Organization for Scientific Research's Future of the Religious Past program.

1. Hajî Qadir Koyî was born in 1824 in the city of Koya in the Kurdish-inhabited part of Iraq. He started his religious education in Koya and later he went to Iran to finish his studies; after finishing, he returned to Koya and became a clergyman. Around 1868/1869 he left Koya for Istanbul, the capital of the Ottoman Empire, where he remained until his death in 1898. Koyî is the first Kurdish poet with a clear nationalistic vision; see M. Mohamed, *Hajî Qadirî Koyî* (Baghdad: Korî Zanyarî Kûrdî, 1976).

2. In contemporary Kurdish usage, *tê çû* is often said of a person accidentally killed or disappeared in war or armed conflict.

3. Roswitha Badry and Bernard Lewis, "Zulm," in *Encyclopaedia of Islam*, 2nd ed. (Leiden: Brill, 2012).

4. Richard Bauman and Charles L. Briggs, *Voices of Modernity: Language Ideologies and the Politics of Inequality* (Cambridge: Cambridge University Press, 2003).

5. Harbans Mukhia, "The Celebration of Failure as Dissent in Urdu Ghazal," *Modern Asian Studies* 33, no. 4 (1999): 864.

6. Louis Gardet, "Fitna," in *Encyclopaedia of Islam*.

7. This is of course not true in the case of an oral tradition and its various genres of epic and historical narrative; the uprisings and tribal conflicts are narrated in numerous orally transmitted accounts. Those killed in these confrontations are never called martyrs. See N. Amîn, *Mîrayetî Baban le nêwan berdashî Rom û 'Ecemda* [The emirate of Baban, crushed between the millstones of Turkey and Persia] (Berlin: Awadanî, 1998).

8. Mustafa Kurdî, *Dîwanî Kûrdî* (Hewlêr: Çapxaney Kûrdîstan, 1973), 32.

9. Abdul Rahman Salim, *Dîwanî Salim* (Hewlêr: Çapxanî Kûrdîstan, 1972), 80.

10. William C. Chittick, "The Pluralistic Vision of Persian Sufi Poetry," *Islam and Christian-Muslim Relations* 14, no. 4 (October 2003): 423.

11. Mukhia, "Celebration of Failure," 864.

12. Tom Cheetham, *The World Turned Inside Out, Henry Corbin and Islamic Mysticism* (New Orleans: Spring Journal, 2003), 10.

13. Salim, *Dîwanî Salim*, 28, 29, 36.

14. Nali, *Dîwanî Nalî* (Baghdad: Korî Zanyarî Kûrd, 1976), 538, 544, 546.

15. Nali, 475.

16. John Bowker, ed., *The Oxford Dictionary of World Religions* (Oxford University Press, 2002), 925.

17. Michiel Leezenberg, "Comparatieve filosofie van het koffieleuten" [The comparative phiosophy of sipping coffee], *Krisis* 8, no. 2 (2007): 25–45, https://krisis.eu/wp-content/uploads/2017/04/2007-2-02-leezenberg.pdf.

18. Yasir Suleiman, *The Arabic Language and National Identity: A Study in Ideology* (Washington, DC: Georgetown University Press, 2003), 37.

19. Sardar Hamid Miran and Karim Sharaza, eds., *Dîwanî Hajî Qadrî Koyî* (Baghdad: Emîndarêtî Gishtî Roshnbîrrî û Lawan, 1986), 240.

20. Miran and Sharaza, *Dîwanî Hajî Qadrî Koyî*, 240.

21. Suleimania and Koya are two important cities of the nineteenth century in Kurdistan; Koyî was from Koya himself.

22. This line contains a pun on *fakhr*, "pride," which is also the first part of Razî's name. Fakhr al-Din Razi (d. 1209) was one of the greatest Iranian philosopher-theologians.

23. Miran and Sharaza, *Dîwanî Hajî Qadrî Koyî*, 241.

24. Miran and Sharaza, 199.

25. Miran and Sharaza, 253.

26. *Hewa* may mean "affection" or "desire" here but also "melody" or "tune."

27. Hasan Kayali, *Arabs and Young Turks: Ottomanism, Arabism, and Islamism in the Ottoman Empire, 1908–1918* (Berkeley: University of California Press. 1997), 3.

28. Kayali, *Arabs and Young Turks*, 9.

29. Miran and Sharaza, *Dîwanî Hajî Qadrî Koyî*, 211. Esfahan and Shiraz are two cities in Iran, former capitals.

30. Miran and Sharaza, 231.

31. Miran and Sharaza, 230

32. Miran and Sharaza, 264.

33. Miran and Sharaza, 185.

34. Miran and Sharaza, 147.

35. Miran and Sharaza, 147.

36. Aziz Al-Azmeh, A*l-'almaniyya min manzur mukhtalif* [Secularism from various perspectives] (Beirut: Markaz Dirasat al-Wahda al-'Arabiyya, 1998), 145.

37. Miran and Sharaza, *Dîwanî Hajî Qadrî Koyî*, 235.

38. Miran and Sharaza, 186–187.

39. Miran and Sharaza, 187.

40. Miran and Sharaza, 179.

41. Miran and Sharaza, 227. The Kurds called the Ottomans commonly Romî ("Roman").

42. Miran and Sharaza, 194.

43. This refers to Mohammad's first four successors, known as the rightly guided Caliphs.

44. Within the framework of the Ottoman Empire there were a lot of independent Kurdish principalities, but in an attempt to centralize power, the empire destroyed all those principalities in the first half of the nineteenth century. See Martin van Bruinessen, *Agha, Shaikh and State: The Social and Political Structures of Kurdistan* (London: Zed Books, 1992); Jalîlî Jalîl, *Kûrdekanî Împiratorîyatî 'Usmanî* (Baghdad: Dozgay Roshinbîrî û Bilawkirdinaway, 1987).

45. Miran and Sharaza, *Dîwanî Hajî Qadrî Koyî*, 213.

46. Miran and Sharaza, 211–212.

47. Rostam is the principal hero of the medieval Persian epic, the *Shahnama*.

48. Hatim was a legendary pre-Islamic Arab knight, proverbial for his generosity and hospitality.

49. Miran and Sharaza, *Dîwanî Hajî Qadrî Koyî*, 203.

CHAPTER 21

Suicide Terrorism and the Modern Nation-State
Antiliberal Protest or Biopolitical Performance?

Michiel Leezenberg

The first decade of the twenty-first century is symbolically demarcated by two suicide actions that were committed by Muslim Arabs and had great social and political consequences but were very different in character. On September 11, 2001, a group of hijackers linked to the Al-Qaeda network flew two airplanes into the World Trade Center in New York and simultaneously carried out similar attacks directed against the Pentagon and the White House in Washington, DC, killing almost three thousand people (mostly civilians) in the process. On December 17, 2010, Tunisian street vendor Mohammed Bouazizi set himself on fire in front of the governor's office in his hometown, in protest against the confiscation of his vending cart and other acts of humiliation he had suffered at the hands of the authorities; on January 4 of the following year, he succumbed to his wounds. His act led to a number of copycat self-immolations across the Arab world in protest at similar forms of government harassment and corruption; but more importantly, it formed the spark that set off the so-called "Arab Spring" or "Arab revolt," which resulted in the ousting of four rulers or governments that at the time seemed solidly entrenched and more generally in a complete dislocation of an Arab political culture long held to be stagnant. This essay explores the significance of these two acts and the complex questions they raise about suicide terrorism.

The phenomenon of suicide terrorism appears to be distinctly modern, indeed surprisingly recent; it also seems to be of a political rather than religious character. But can it be *reduced* to political considerations and to a rational means-ends calculation? Perhaps this very way of framing the question is already misleading as it appears to rest on a tacit—and questionable—opposition between the political as a domain of rational calculation of interests and the religious or sacral as an essentially irrational sphere of ritual and (self-)sacrifice. This question also appears to be predicated on the assumption that modern political movements are driven by a purely secular political rationality that is allegedly lacking among religious movements and sensibilities held to be essentially premodern.[1] But the question should be precisely *to what extent* suicide terrorism may involve the political use or redefinition of religious symbols and, conversely, to what extent it rests on a religious articulation, or sacralization, of modern political demands. On both accounts, it will appear, suicide terrorism springs the confines of liberal and secularist political philosophy. Hence, after some considerations about the normative questions surrounding suicide terrorism, I will discuss, first, to what extent suicide terrorism can be explained as a strategic act based on rational political calculation; second, the individual motivations and collective ideologies involved in suicide terrorism; and third, whether it can be seen as a specific kind of performance.

Recognizing and Defining Suicide Terrorism

Suicide terrorism has often been described as having a particular link with religion, and more specifically with Islam; but the twenty-first century also witnessed the end of another decades-long insurgency involving the extensive and systematic use of suicide bombings: the independence movement of the Tamil Tigers (Liberation Tigers of Tamil Eelam, or LTTE) in Sri Lanka, which was a largely secular movement of Hindu backgrounds. In spring 2009, the Sri Lankan army conquered the LTTE's main stronghold on the Jaffna peninsula and killed its leader, Vellupilai Prabhakaran, on May 18 of that year. The Tamil Tigers, at first sight a purely secular movement of national liberation, have in fact made crucial use of religious symbolism, both for mobilization and for the legitimation of suicide attacks. Attention to the LTTE's systematic use of suicide missions provides a useful counterbalance to the widespread tendency to see suicide terrorism as somehow uniquely and inherently linked to (political) Islam. That conviction fails to explain why suicide terrorism by Muslims is, in fact, a nontraditional phenomenon, as it first emerged only in the 1970s, and may even be said to be anti-traditional, as both Sunni and Shiite jurisprudence strongly condemn suicide. But if the motivations and legitimations of suicide terrorism among present-day Sunni extremists, in particular among so-called salafi-jihadi groups, do not originate in traditional texts or practices, where *do* they come from? Such questions call for a historicizing, comparative, and interdisciplinary approach to this recent, and deeply disturbing, phenomenon.

First, I will highlight some problems of definition. Defining suicide terrorism more precisely may be a first way of getting a firmer conceptual and normative grasp of it. But already here our troubles begin: is suicide terrorism a modern form of religious sacrifice or ritual performance, or rather a goal-directed kind of political action based on strategic calculation and as such essentially secular or political in character? To many, it is none of these; rather, it is the wanton sacrifice of innocent victims, whether for political or religious purposes, and hence a prototypical kind of evil, showing inhuman cruelty and a callous disregard for innocent lives. This strongly normative characterization is perhaps less a definition than a condemnation of the phenomenon. Undoubtedly, we should take seriously the intuitive horror and even revulsion one may feel at suicide attacks; but we should not let it dominate and prejudice the more analytical questions that can—and should—be raised about it.

The main, and general, problem is that the very concept of suicide terrorism, like terrorism more generally, is an ideologically laden concept rather than a neutral analytical tool: it simultaneously criminalizes acts of violence by non-state actors and tacitly legitimizes the state's monopoly of violence; in the kind of conflicts where terrorist violence occurs, however, the legitimacy of state violence is often precisely what is being contested. Mainstream journalistic reporting on suicide terrorism, and on terrorism more generally, tends to focus on its effects on the civilian population; this focus makes it initially plausible to characterize terrorism as the use of violence against civilian targets by non-state actors with the intent of instilling fear or terror and to qualify suicide terrorism as a form of terrorism that is carried out with the actor's intention of dying in the action. Such a characterization, however, would exclude most Tamil Tiger suicide bombings, which generally targeted the Sri Lankan military and political leadership rather than the civilian population. Thus, the statist perspective implicit in the above definition risks the a priori downplaying, ignoring, or delegitimizing of any political aims of non-state actors. More generally, the understandable focus on the—often horrible—consequences of suicide missions, and on their effects on the victims, risks replacing analysis by condemnation. Such a focus also seems mistaken about the intended effects: as will become clear shortly, the desire to instill fear or mass terror does not appear to figure very prominently among the known motivations of suicide terrorists.

Particularly problematic for the previous characterization is the existence of suicide missions such as self-immolation which neither create nor aim at creating any casualties other than the agent.[2] Hence, for analytical if not moral purposes, it is important to focus on actors' intentions at least as much as victims' suffering. The problem of uncovering actors' intentions becomes particularly acute—and intractable—when trying to characterize suicide terrorism: it is often hard to establish whether a suicide mission involves an active intention to die, let alone possibly more complex motivations, and to distinguish actions in which the perpetrators expect and intend to die from acts in which they accept the risk of dying even if their death is not the aim of the action. Our only sources of information in these are the numerous videotaped or written farewell messages and a small number of interviews with failed suicide terrorists willing to talk about their actions. Given such complications, the term *suicide terrorism* as a blanket expression for the kinds of acts under discussion appears to raise more questions than it answers. In the following, I will therefore speak of suicide bombing and suicide missions or suicide assaults in order not to prejudice ethical and other normative questions at stake.

The Morality of Suicide Bombing: Liberal Perspectives

Philosophers have serious difficulties coming to grips with the morality of suicide bombing and of terrorism more generally. Apart from conceptual questions about how to delimit the phenomenon of suicide bombing, its normative implications also appear to spring the confines of currently dominant forms of liberal theorizing. Among liberal theorists, there is a strong tendency to simply dismiss suicide bombing, and terrorism more generally, as illegitimate—and indeed immoral—virtually by definition: suicide missions are all too easily brandished as beyond the pale of international law, if not outside civilization, altogether.[3] Such sweeping condemnations, however, preclude the very asking of questions about rational goals, and about any political motives and moral intentions behind them.

One provocative critique of such liberal assumptions may be found in Ted Honderich's *After the Terror*, written in the wake of the September 11 attacks and the outbreak of the second Palestinian intifada in 2000. Although Honderich does not systematically distinguish suicide terrorism from terrorism in general (which he characterizes as involving the illegal use of political violence), he does, famously, state that the Palestinians have a moral right to terrorism: "those Palestinians who have resorted to necessary [sic] killing have been right to try to free their people, and those who have killed themselves in the cause of their people have indeed sanctified themselves."[4] This quasi-religious reference to self-sanctification sounds rather odd in an otherwise purely secular line of argument; but there are more serious problems with this line of reasoning. Thus,

Honderich unambiguously justifies acts of suicide terrorism by Palestinians, but he equally unambiguously qualifies the September 11 attacks as "wholly wrong," as its perpetrators "violated the natural fact and practice of morality." He specifically condemns them in the name of what he calls the "principle of humanity," which requires us to save people from "bad lives," but also because their action was not goal-rational with respect to their own ends; it was not, he claims, accompanied by any reasonable hope that it would secure a justifying end (presumably, an improvement in the lives of fellow human beings, and more specifically, poor Muslims living under occupation).[5] This suggests that, contrary to liberal sensibilities, the assaults *would* have been justified if it had in fact been motivated by such a hope.

Whether Al-Qaeda members would accept Honderich's principle of humanity is an open question; but in fact, Bin Laden's hope or expectation that the United States would withdraw its troops from Saudi Arabia following a massive suicide bombing was, in fact, not at all unreasonable, in the light of the withdrawal of American and French troops from Lebanon following a 1983 suicide attack, the Soviet Union pullout from Afghanistan in 1989 (which, according to Al-Qaeda mythology, was due primarily to the efforts of a handful of jihadists), and the United States' withdrawal from Somalia in 1993. Indeed, American troops did tacitly pull out of Saudi Arabia in 2003, in the wake of the Iraq war; in this sense, the September 11 attacks may after all be said to have achieved a major political goal proclaimed by Bin Laden. But does that make them morally justifiable? Or if they had led to an improvement in the lives of, say, the Palestinian or Iraqi civilian population, would that have rendered them more legitimate in Honderich's eyes? More generally, Honderich's assertion of a generic right to terrorism in the case of occupation appears to be too coarse-grained to be of much analytical use: it ignores questions concerning the particular circumstances and motivations of individual suicide missions in particular settings as well as tactical questions as to *when* suicide bombing is used and when it is not.

Unintentionally, then, Honderich's argument suggests that, at least analytically, one should try to abstain from moral condemnation for as far as possible in order to understand the particular moral and strategic mindsets that informs them. It has in fact been argued that suicide bombers, in their self-destruction, annihilate the very logic of a liberal, or juridical, law-based moral framework of crime and punishment. Thus, Christoph Reuter suggests that the very acts of successful suicide attackers escape punishment or retaliation: no meaningful threat of retaliation, he argues, can be made against potential suicide terrorists who wish to die anyway. On such an account, the political and emotional effect of suicide bombing resides precisely in its annihilation of the logic of power.

Similarly, Talal Asad suggests that suicide bombers undermine the very separation between crime and punishment that is essential to the functioning of law on which liberal identities and freedoms are identified; instead, he continues, they mark the violent appearance of the limitless pursuit of freedom.[6] One may raise doubts here, however: Reuter disregards the possible deterrent that may be posed by collective punishment or retaliation; it is also unlikely that (political) freedom is the sole or primary aim of suicide bombers, as Asad claims. But the importance of Asad's genealogical exploration lies in inviting more radical questions about the legitimacy of state power and its monopoly of violence. How is it possible, he asks, that we so much more rarely question or condemn the liberal state's threat or actual use of violence? Undoubtedly, such more general questions about—often implicit—liberal assumptions are important and indeed urgent; but it should be kept in mind that suicide bombing occurs not only, and perhaps not even primarily, against the background of liberal states that are legitimized by popular sovereignty and the rule of law. Similar questions can and should be raised about non-liberal states like post–Soviet Russia facing a Chechen independence movement or Bashar al-Assad's Syria facing a countrywide insurgency from Spring 2011 onward. Instead of focusing on liberalism and its concern with law as based on a threat of violence assumed to be legitimate, one may therefore question the self-legitimations of modern states more generally. Do existing (nation-)states, liberal or not, find it easier to legitimize the threat or use of violence than do non-state actors, and if so, why? More specifically, one may ask how and why states may legitimately lay claim to the very lives of their people: after all, a soldier's death in combat is not generally considered suicide, let alone suicide terrorism. Does, then, Horace's famous and oft-quoted line of poetry—*dulce et decorum est pro patria mori* ("It is sweet and appropriate to die for the fatherland")[7]—capture something crucial about the state in general, or about the modern nation-state? In short, suicide bombings appear to escape or explode the confines of liberal ethics and political theory altogether, and in particular to resist reduction to the liberal language of rights and duties and of individuals as subjects of law; instead, they raise questions concerning the modern state's powers concerning matters of life and death. I will return to these questions below.

Suicide Bombing as Strategy

A more fruitful starting point than normative or normatively loaded questions may be a primarily descriptive exploration of the various ways in which and the different causes for which suicide missions have been used over the past decades.

Such an approach quickly refutes the widespread view that they are irrational acts of blind fanaticism: more often than not, they appear to be used as a strategic tool for concrete political goals. To get a more solid grip on these strategic dimensions, let us therefore look at some of the most famous arenas where it has been strategically employed.

Two modern cases of state-backed suicide missions have on occasion been characterized as models for later forms of suicide bombing by non-state actors: the Japanese kamikaze assaults in World War II and the Iranian "human wave" assaults in the 1980–1988 war with Iraq. In fact, however, these cases are exceptional: states only relatively rarely organize suicide missions; and suicidal acts sanctioned or ordered by a state are not generally qualified as "suicide." The vast majority of suicide missions appear to be directed *against*, rather than committed *by* or *for*, the state.

The first major non-state suicide missions, carried out by the Shiite Hizbollah in 1980s Lebanon, have been claimed to have had organizational and martyrological links with revolutionary Shiite Iran; but this claim has not been substantiated. Not much is known, either, about the sources of inspiration of suicide missions as a major tactic among the Tamil Tigers which started in July 1987, four years after the start of open guerrilla warfare in 1983. The style of that first assault (a truck loaded with explosives) has been described as derived from the 1983 Hezbollah truck bombings of French and American targets in Lebanon; but here, too, no conclusive link has been established. It is not even certain that the Tamil truck driver's death was intentional. After this operation, a three-year lull in LTTE suicide operations occurred, possibly because of the temporary presence of Indian peacekeeping troops on the island. From 1990 onward, a new kind of LTTE suicide mission emerged, carried out by individuals carrying explosives on their bodies, and targeting the very leadership of the Sri Lankan state. Thus, in 1993, president Ranasinghe Premadasa was killed in a suicide assault; and responsibility for the 1991 assassination of the then Indian president Rajiv Gandhi has also repeatedly been ascribed to but strongly denied by the LTTE. Strategically, LTTE suicide missions became a highly selective and effective weapon, with which the LTTE, despite being vastly outnumbered by the Sri Lankan army, could strike at the heart of the Sri Lankan government's military, political, and economic power.

A very different situation obtained among the Palestinians. Here, suicide missions first appeared only in the 1970s and were initially carried out by members of secular (and generally Marxist) Palestinian organizations. In fact, one of the earliest suicide attacks against Israeli targets was carried out neither by an Islamist nor by a secular Palestinian movement, but by agents of the Japanese Red Army, who, apparently after receiving training in the Beqaa Valley in Lebanon, launched a deadly automatic gun attack at Lod airport in Tel Aviv in May 1972.[8] The number of suicide assaults increased during the 1982 Israeli invasion and subsequent occupation of part of Lebanon; but these were generally carried out by Lebanese citizens rather than Palestinians; moreover, it was generally not secular or Sunni Islamist Palestinian organizations behind them but rather the Lebanese and Shiite Hezbollah.

It was only after the 1993 Oslo agreement that the number of suicide missions carried out by Sunni Palestinians rose significantly. They were not carried out by members of Fatah, which could now call itself the Palestinian authority, but by its main rivals, Hamas and Islamic Jihad.[9] The number of Palestinian suicide missions rose again after the outbreak of the second intifada in 2000. To recover the strategic intent behind these missions, it may be useful to trace when their numbers peaked. Many of them appear to have been timed to thwart then ongoing peace negotiations between Fatah and the Israeli government; but they also suggest a competition between Hamas and the Islamic Jihad. The American scholar Mia Bloom has, in fact, compared the suicide actions by rival Palestinian groups as a kind of media strategy, or advertising campaign, as part of their fierce competition for status and recruits.[10] This point, if correct, suggests that the strategic intentions involved in suicide missions are rather more variable than is often thought, and that suicide bombing is indeed one option or strategy among many.

Suicide bombing from among the Workers Party of Kurdistan (PKK) in Turkey displays different characteristics again. Despite a cult of martyrdom and leadership that is in many ways comparable to that of the LTTE, and despite a mythology of self-immolation based on events in Diyarbakir prison in the early 1980s, the PKK only started using suicide bombings from the mid-1990s onward, at a time when its insurgency was arguably past its peak, and when it became clear that the mass uprising of the early 1990s had failed to yield substantial results. The violent counterinsurgency operation launched by the Turkish security forces, which involved, among others, large-scale village evacuations, had largely undone earlier territorial gains by the guerrillas. Even then, however, these missions remained relatively few in number. A substantial number of them involved female actors, one posing as a pregnant woman to hide the explosives strapped to her body. It may well be that there are both organizational and ideological reasons for the predominance of women in self-immolations and the predominance of men in subsequent suicide bombings. Initially at least, these missions primarily targeted the Turkish military and civilian state apparatus; but in December 1998, in a television address from his temporary refuge in Rome, PKK leader Abdullah Öcalan threatened to deploy suicide bombers against civilian targets as well: "Those who explode the bombs wrapped around themselves in a manner to harm innocent civilians will explode them in crowds that support this fascist government ... now, I can hardly stop them. But I may not be able to stop them tomorrow; it is not my responsibility to do so anyway."[11]

Öcalan's February 1999 capture, however, was followed less by suicide bombings than by a number of self-immolations, especially in European capitals. These PKK suicide missions peaked during the Öcalan trial and were in fact carried out against Öcalan's explicitly stated wishes.[12] The relatively small number of PKK suicide missions, and the relatively high number of thwarted operations among them, suggest, first, that suicide bombing never became a major PKK tactic and second, that the PKK did not put nearly as much effort into the recruitment, legitimation, and sanctification of suicide bombers as the LTTE. Apparently, strongly developed cults of leadership and martyrdom are in themselves not enough for the successful use of suicide missions: they require special training and organization. Similar conclusions may be drawn from the experience of post-2001 Afghanistan, where suicide attacks were far more numerous than in Turkey, but hardly more successful. It has been argued that, prior to the October 2001 invasion, suicide missions were alien to Afghan society, and that they did not emerge as a major tactic until 2005; moreover, they had a low rate of success, and enjoyed little support among the local population.[13]

Perhaps the most dramatic shifts in suicide bombing as a tactic may be witnessed in Iraq under and after Saddam Hussein. During the 1980s and 1990s, suicide assaults against Baathist Iraq by non-state insurgent groups were few and far between; it was even more rare for them to be carried out on Iraqi territory. Significantly, a December 15, 1981, suicide attack against the Iraqi embassy in Beirut, widely attributed to the Iraqi Shiite Dawa movement, was never claimed: in short, Iraqi Shiites, unlike their Iranian counterparts, did not systematically resort to suicide assaults against Saddam Hussein's regime. This suggests that, among Shiites at least, the choice whether or not to resort to suicide missions cannot be explained from a religious ideology of martyrdom alone. Apart from national loyalties, it was undoubtedly the prospect of harsh—and often collective—retaliation by the Baathist regime that deterred both Iraqi Shiites and other opposition movements. In other words, and against Reuter and Asad, it seems that suicide missions do not wholly escape the logic of power and punishment after all.

Post-Saddam Iraq witnessed a dramatic increase in suicide missions and in political violence by non-state actors more generally. A bloody spiral of internecine violence, especially between Sunni and Shiite militias in Central Iraq, developed from 2004 onward and peaked in 2006 and early 2007. It led Muhammed Hafez to predict in 2007 that Iraq was in the process of becoming a failed state, nominally ruled by a weak central government, and of becoming a safe haven for global jihadists.[14] From 2007, however, both sectarian violence and the number of suicide missions have decreased significantly, due primarily to the American-led security operation, the so-called Surge, and to the increasing political participation of Sunni Arab groups which deprived the salafi-jihadi groups of much of their potential support base. The year 2013 again saw a significant increase in sectarian violence and in suicide missions, partly as a result of the increasingly violent war in neighboring Syria. The meteoric rise (and fall) of the so-called Islamic State, however, falls outside the scope of this chapter, as does its tactical use of suicide missions against rival factions.

Significantly, neither former Baathists nor Iraqi Shiites but overwhelmingly Sunni Arab extremists were behind the overwhelming majority of suicide bombings in post-Saddam Iraq; moreover, a substantial number of them appear to have been carried out by transnational organizations and non-Iraqi actors. Although Iraqi nationals and Shiites were by no means absent among suicide bombers, they appear to form a minority among the identified male bombers, most of whom were claimed to hail from Saudi Arabia. A significant percentage of female suicide bombers, by contrast, were local women whose relatives had been killed by American troops or Iraqi security forces.[15] This suggests that revenge for perceived private or national humiliations by the American army is but one among many motives for suicide bombings in post-Saddam Iraq. Moreover, the notion that such revenge should be achieved by committing suicide is not at all traditional, whether in religious or tribal terms. The gradual shift in targets also appears to hint at the strategic calculations behind suicide assaults in Iraq. Initially, suicide bombings primarily targeted American soldiers; but increasingly, they became directed against the Iraqi security forces and their recruits, and against the civilian population, especially Shiites. This shift primarily seems to reflect an adaptation of tactics to changing aims and circumstances.

Thus, in Iraq and elsewhere, the rise and decline in suicide assaults appears to reflect calculated choice based on strategic timing rather than—ultimately irrational—desperation, a desire for revenge, or blind fanaticism. Can we derive any more general conclusions as to the strategic aspects of suicide bombing from these widely diverging cases? Famously, Robert Pape, basing himself on an extensive database of suicide missions up until 2003, has argued that the phenomenon has little to do with Islamic fundamentalism or with religious ideology more generally but much more with resistance against foreign occupation.[16] Almost all suicide assaults, he argues, have a very "specific secular and strategic goal: to compel modern democracies to withdraw military forces from territory that the terrorists consider to be their homeland"; and as such, he claims, they are often in fact successful. If Pape is right, suicide assaults are indeed generally guided by strategic timing and by rational (and typically territorial-national) political goals rather than irrational and murderous religious fanaticism.

This is an important corrective to the widespread association of suicide bombing with blind hatred and zealotry; yet Pape may be overstating his case: not only can countries like Sri Lanka, 1990s Turkey, or Vladimir Putin's Russia hardly be called democracies; furthermore, none of these states (as distinct, to be sure, from parts of their populations) would see itself as occupying foreign territory. While it is undoubtedly true that opportunities for suicide bombing were far more restricted in repressive states like Saddam Hussein's Iraq than in liberal democracies or even in American-occupied post-Saddam Iraq, suicide missions have also been directed against non-democratic states. Liberal democracies and foreign occupying powers, then, are neither the sole nor even the most obvious targets of suicide missions. A more important question may be whether there is a—domestic or international—public opinion that may be affected or mobilized by suicide assaults. I will return to this point below.

In short, suicide missions, may certainly in part be explained by strategic calculations; but a major constraining factor in this respect is the impossibility to predict or control the possible consequences or reactions. Thus, Stephen Holmes argues that the September 11 attacks involved a strategic miscalculation of the Al-Qaeda leadership, which may not have expected the Americans to retaliate with a full-fledged invasion of Afghanistan.[17] Possibly, the assaults aimed at provoking the Americans into imperial overstretch; if so, they were both rational and successful. By reducing these and other suicide assaults to strategic calculation, however, we seem to be leaving out what is most significant about them; moreover, the consequences of suicide missions are generally too unpredictable and uncontrollable to allow for an explanation in purely instrumental-rational terms: they may delegitimize causes as easily as they may mobilize people.

Ideologies of Suicide Bombing

This brings us to questions of the individual motivations and collective ideologies that have been invoked to justify suicide missions. Next to Palestinian suicide attacks and the September 11 attacks in America, suicide missions have become a major tactic among Muslim insurgents in, among others, Chechnya, post-Taliban Afghanistan, Pakistan, post-Saddam Iraq, and post-2011 Syria. This has created or strengthened a widespread belief that suicide bombing—and terrorism more generally—is somehow inherently linked to Islam as a religion, if not an essentially or exclusively Islamic phenomenon. As noted above, this claim cannot be maintained (prior to the massive wave of suicide assaults in Iraq in 2005 and 2006, the largest numbers of suicide missions were carried out by the non-Muslim Tamil Tigers); but it invites further scrutiny of the various ideological justifications that have been given for suicide missions by the agents themselves, or by the organizations on whose behalf they acted.

The individual motivations of suicide bombers have baffled many observers: whatever the strategic calculations that may be involved at the organizational level, suicide bombing almost defies understanding at the personal level. Hence, it is tempting to explain the mindset of individual suicide bombers in terms of individual or collective pathology. One such explanation is Hans Magnus Enzensberger's essay on "radical losers," which assimilates the psychology of the suicide bomber to that of the lone gunman running amok, like Americans Eric Harris and Dylan Klebold at Columbine high school in 1999 and German Robert Steinhäuser in Erfurt in April 2002.[18] Societally, however, the perpetrators of the September 11 attacks, were not losers at all: they generally belonged to well-off middle-class families and, unlike the majority of their compatriots, had been able to study abroad, where—at least to outward appearances—they had regular social contacts, even girlfriends. This renders Enzensberger's idea of the "radical loser" problematic already at the individual level, let alone at the level of organizations. Worse, Enzensberger proceeds to project this pathological feeling onto Islamic civilization as a whole, ascribing to it a generic jealousy against the successfully modernizing Western world. Unfortunately, Enzensberger does not back this claim by any empirical evidence, but only by references to Bernard Lewis's equally sweeping and equally unsubstantiated claims in popularizing books such as *What Went Wrong?* (2001) and *The Crisis of Islam* (2003).

An empirically more solidly based approach can be found in Farhad Khosrokhavar's 2005 *Allah's New Martyrs*, which explores the motivations and worldview, or what Weber has called "subjective meanings," of individual suicide bombers in detail.[19] Basing himself on extensive interviews with surviving would-be suicide bombers, Khosrokhavar argues that they are often driven by a sense of humiliation and disaffection with modernity. Typical for his analysis is the lone radicalized youth, such as Richard Reid, the "shoe bomber" arrested in December 2001. Reid, a British citizen of partly Jamaican extraction, had converted to Islam in prison. The problem with Khosrokhavar's account, however, is that although a sense of humiliation and unease with the modern world at large may well be a component of the motivations of individual suicide terrorists, such sentiments are too widely shared to explain how and when an individual actually sets out on a suicide mission. Such explanations fail to explain why it is only a very few individuals who engage in suicide bombings, whereas the overwhelming majority of adolescents, whatever feelings of alienation they may have, do not engage in acts of violence, let alone suicide bombings. Perhaps, then, one should be careful to distinguish individual motivations from collective ideologies.

Khosrokhavar has further argued that it was authors like, most importantly, the Iranian Ali Shariati in the Shii context and the Egyptian Sayyid Qutb in the Sunni world, who paved the way for the political redefinition of martyrdom. On his analysis, Shariati's writings turn imam Hussein's martyrdom, which had long been a saint's story that could be mourned in the Ashura rituals or staged in the *taziya* plays, into a goal to be achieved, or a model to be followed, by the Iranian masses. Shariati's Hussein is no longer an imam, that is, a virtually superhuman and historically unique character, but a fully human and indeed revolutionary hero worthy of emulation.[20] Khosrokhavar does not empirically substantiate this claim, but it would imply that the twentieth century has witnessed a secularization, democratization, or if one likes vernacularization, of martyrdom that has transformed it from a religious into a secular or political phenomenon. However, neither in the writings of Ali Shariati (whose appeal among the Iranian Shiite masses was real, indeed massive) nor in Sayyid Qutb's work do we find any explicit justification for suicide missions.

Indeed, any religious or ideological sanction for suicide missions is remarkable for its absence even in the most radical Islamist authors prior to Abdallah Azzam, who was a key character in organizing the Afghan resistance against the Soviet invasion during the 1980s, and Osama bin Laden's mentor. Azzam's redefinition of jihad as armed struggle and as an individual obligation (*fard ayn*) for all Muslims is of crucial importance for the development of a Sunni Muslim ideology that legitimizes suicide bombings. Even Azzam, however, does not openly legitimize suicide missions; instead, he generically speaks of "seeking martyrdom" (*istishhad*) and combines the idea of armed jihad as the only path to paradise with an emphasis on martyrdom as a means of safeguarding the Muslim community or *ummah*: "The life of the Muslim Ummah is solely dependent on the ink of its scholars and the blood of its martyrs."[21]

The political dimension of this kind of martyrdom, however, appears subordinate to its redeeming and eschatological function: "What will cleanse our sins? What will purify our mistakes? And what will clean our dirt? It will not be washed except with the blood of martyrdom, and know that there is no path except this Path."[22] This suggests that the main source of inspiration for suicide missions among present-day Sunni radicals lies in the Afghan jihad of the 1980s and in the particular cult of martyrdom that took shape there rather than in the Palestinian experience or in Iranian-Shiite martyrology, let alone Tamil or Japanese models.

About this Afghan experience, and especially about the character and even number of suicide missions in 1980s Afghanistan, we do not know very much at present. What is most striking, however, is how consistently Azzam employs a revivalist language that is more familiar from secular nationalism. He not only appears to describe the ummah as a nation, but also uses the revivalist language of (national or spiritual) awakening familiar from nineteenth-century nationalism: "The extent to which the number of martyred scholars increases is the extent to which nations are delivered from their slumber, rescued from their decline and awoken from their sleep."[23]

Whether deterritorialized or not, the modern nation-state and its power over the life and death of its citizens have a hold even on primarily religious imaginaries. The same is suggested by Osama bin Laden's ideology of martyrdom, which appears to derive primarily from Azzam's reinterpretation of jihad as armed struggle and as an individual duty. Bin Laden is more explicit on the topic of suicide bombing in his December 2001 statement on the September 11 attacks, which combines religious language with anti-imperialist rhetoric and a quasi-tribal language of honor.[24] He holds the American government, and by extension the population that has elected it, responsible for all evils in the (Muslim) world: hyperbolically, he claims that "every day, from East to West, the entire ummah of 1,200 million Muslims is being slaughtered without anyone noticing." He describes the September 11 attacks as a response to the alleged American and Zionist injustices against Muslims in Palestine, Iraq, Somalia, and Southern Sudan; that is, he legitimizes them as an act of defense. He is careful not to claim responsibility for the assaults but also avoids condemning the nineteen perpetrators for either their own or others' deaths: he denies that there is any evidence against the nineteen Arabs accused of having carried out the assault yet praises their effort in the "jihad against global unbelief," which suggests that he sees them as martyrs rather than suicides.

Despite Azzam's and Bin Laden's predominantly theological vocabulary, one should clearly beware of reducing their justification of suicide bombing to Islamic religious tradition. As noted, Islamic theology and Muslim jurisprudence have always strongly condemned suicide; hence, recent fatwas legitimizing suicide actions for political purposes involve not only a major juridical revaluation, but indeed a *reconceptualization* of martyrdom against the background of the modern territorial nation-state and modern forms of power and resistance.[25] Perhaps in line with the universal juridical dismissal of suicide, both Azzam and Bin Laden rarely if ever mention the notion of suicide missions, preferring to speak of "martyrdom operations" (*amaliyyat istishhadiyyah*), which, moreover, are framed as part of a defensive jihad against foreign occupation. The closest the latter comes to explicitly mentioning and legitimizing suicide missions is through his allusion to the Koranic account of the Trench (85:4), a fiery pit—which he identifies with Hell—into which a tyrant king has Muslims thrown who refuse to renounce their faith. Thus, Bin Laden suggests that the nineteen agents of September 11 were victorious, not by seeking material gains or even their physical safety, but by sticking to their faith and to their principles.[26]

Similar ideological innovations may be found in the few known statements by Abu Musab al-Zarqawi, the most famous leader of the salafi-jihadi insurgency in post-Saddam Iraq. Like Bin Laden and Azzam, al-Zarqawi prefers to speak of "martyrdom operations." His avowed aims were not only to drive the Americans out of the country but also to establish a Sunni Islamic state there; a crucial part of the latter was the use, novel for Iraq, of suicide missions against Shiite civilians. Violence against Shiites, however, can only be legitimized as jihad if one is prepared to qualify them as apostates or unbelievers; on this point, there appear to have been disagreements between al-Zarqawi and the Al-Qaeda leadership, or at least Ayman al-Zawahiri.[27] In one internal report, al-Zarqawi talks of martyrdom as a means of awakening the Iraqi Sunnis; indeed, he emphasizes the need to introduce a new sense of the importance of martyrdom among them: "If we succeed in dragging [the Shiites] into the arena of sectarian war, it will become possible to awaken the inattentive Sunnis as they feel imminent danger and annihilating death at the hands of these Sabaeans. . . . People cannot awaken from their stupor unless talk of martyrdom and martyrs fills their days and nights."[28] Here, as in Azzam, martyrdom is likewise seen as a prerequisite for a quasi-national (Sunni) religious awakening. This revivalist language of the modern nation-state is especially remarkable in these circles, which otherwise so adamantly reject anything resembling Western ideologies like nationalism.

Given this recurring presence, the language of awakening seems more than a coincidence. Moreover, it is not restricted to Muslim movements: Tamil Tiger ideology surrounding suicide missions similarly involves a blending of political and religious motives. Thus, Michael Roberts argues that the Tamil Tigers' use of suicide bombings initially appears to be driven by a purely secular political rationality, but on closer inspection turns out to be deeply rooted in the lifestyles and religious practices of both Hindu and Christian Tamils.[29] The LTTE, he argues, makes strategic use of religious ritual for mobilizing and legitimizing; but also conversely, the instrumental function of its cult of martyrdom rests on the meaningfulness of symbols selected from Tamil cults. On his account, which he himself admits to be somewhat speculative, this cult goes beyond the LTTE recruits' well-known pledge to swallow a cyanide capsule rather than be captured alive.[30]

More clearly religious in character than this well-known assertion of one's readiness to die is what Roberts calls the new LTTE cult of *mâviran*, "great heroes" or "martyrs," a term that only applies to Tamil fighters who died in combat. Apparently, this martyr cult involves an important conceptual innovation: not only is the political notion of *mâviran* conflated with more familiar religious expressions, such as *tiyaki* and *catci* (respectively, "one who abandons" and "witness/ martyr");[31] the LTTE—or perhaps the population supporting them—also developed an extensive cult of martyrs that includes numerous memorial sites and a ritual calendar introduced in 1989, which marks various days devoted to the commemoration of the *mâviran*. Likewise, the LTTE has introduced the religious innovation of burying martyrs rather than cremating them, as was usual among higher-caste Hindus. This made it possible for their tombs to become places of worship as well as to reinforce the conviction that martyrs do not really die but have their bodies planted as seeds (*vitai*) to be reborn, thus also providing the living fighters with new strength (*shakti*, or "divine power"). In fact, A. J. V. Chandrakanthan describes Tamil nationalism as a new religious movement that employs a new vocabulary derived from ancient Tamil Saivite religion: "I have seen hundreds of shrines erected in Jaffna by the friends and relatives of those LTTE cadres who have died in various actions; and the rituals performed with offering of flowers and lighting of oil lamps are those normally reserved to Saivite deities and saints."[32] Roberts suggests that the LTTE military successes are primarily due to organizational and tactical factors; a comparison with the PKK case in Turkey, however, suggests that not only organization but also a relatively elaborate martyrology as a facilitation of recruitment is required for suicide missions to be successful.

One ideological factor that may be of importance for mobilization and recruitment is a leadership cult, usually matched by a tight hierarchical organization. The sacralization and embodiment of a cause in a leader credited with a superhuman stature may well facilitate the mobilization for and social acceptance of suicide missions conducted in the name of or against nation-states. The carefully cultivated deification of the Japanese emperor Hirohito for distinctly modern strategic purposes during World War II is the most obvious example.[33] Another significant case is the transcendent status of Iranian leader Khomeini during the Iran-Iraq war; since he was often identified with the hidden twelfth imam, his words gained an authority unequalled by any of his contemporaries. A similarly sacralized leadership cult can be seen around LTTE leader Prabhakaran, who himself repeatedly emphasized his readiness to die on behalf of his organization's cause; likewise, pictures of alleged suicide bombers about to set out on their mission having a last supper with the leader formed an important part of Tamil Tiger martyrology.

In PKK circles during the early 1990s, a cult of leadership and martyrdom was developed that was in many respects similar to the LTTE's; but as seen above, the number of suicide missions carried out by PKK activists was far smaller than that by the Tamil Tigers. Complementary to Öcalan's leadership, virtually all PKK cadre remained anonymous or in the leader's shadow while alive; only those who had been martyred were given names and images in PKK-related media. In a virtually complementary logic of physical death and symbolic life, the average PKK guerrilla would remain anonymous while alive, and only acquire a name, identity, and reputation as a guerrilla after his or her death. Thus, the tightly centralized and increasingly personalized rule of Abdullah Öcalan created a climate that sacralized martyrdom—including suicide missions—for the Kurdish national cause. But although the ingredients for a culture or cult of suicide missions were certainly there, this tactic was used far less often and less successfully by the PKK than by the LTTE. A developed leadership cult thus appears to be neither a necessary nor a sufficient condition for suicide missions to emerge: it cannot be found among Sunni Islamist groups employing suicide missions, like Hamas, the Islamic Jihad, and Al-Qaeda. Thus, in his speeches, Osama bin Laden shows few signs of claiming a leadership status for himself; he preferred to call himself a "poor slave," and emphasize the collective character of the jihad.

In short, we know too little about the practical consequences of martyrdom and leadership cults and other legitimizing ideologies to make any generalizations with confidence. In fact, the one detailed exploration we have of the individual ideological views of suicide bombers, Ohnuki-Tierney's 2002 study on kamikaze pilots, displays a remarkable *divergence* between ideology and practice. On the basis of numerous pilots' letters, diaries, and reading lists, she concludes that few of them actually believed in emperor worship, and many of them were highly critical of the Japanese war effort; instead, they were well-read in European romantic literature and mostly shared an aesthetic idealism. It was precisely the Japanese state's nationalist appropriation of seemingly purely aesthetic and politically neutral symbols such as cherry blossoms, she concludes, that practically co-opted young Japanese students, despite their possible ideological disagreements.

There is an equal divergence between ideology and practice among more recent suicide bombers. Indeed, it has been argued that the appeal to ideology as an explanation of suicide missions seems circular if not tautological.[34] In short, explanations of suicide missions in terms of beliefs, ideologies, or individual or collective intentions such as a martyrdom or leadership cult have at best a limited validity. As often as not, religious or political ideologies appear to function as a retrospective legitimation rather than a determining cause. This invites us, in turn, to refocus our thoughts on the actual act, or performance, of the suicide mission itself.

Suicide Bombing as Performance

If, as I have argued, it is generally difficult if not impossible to grasp the agent's intentions, and if neither goal-rational calculation nor ideology provides a fully convincing account, it may be useful to redirect one's analytical attention toward the act of suicide missions themselves. As such, they appear to have a strongly if not irreducibly symbolic dimension: their perpetrators want their act to *communicate* something about themselves or about their cause. This symbolic dimension may be no more defining or essential to suicide missions than their strategic or ideological aspects; but several authors have argued that it has become markedly more prominent in recent years. Thus, Hamit Bozarslan argues that the Middle East has witnessed a qualitative change from a rationally and instrumentally used collective violence by liberation movements like those of Palestinians and Kurds to more individualized forms of sacrificial violence that are at once more nihilistic, more utopian, and more eschatological. By and large, he argues, the hope or expectation of concrete political goals has been replaced by a desire to destroy one's own body for the sake of demonstrating one's moral integrity and loyalty to a cause held to be sacred, transcendent, and non-negotiable.[35] This suggests that the September 11 attacks are only the most famous instantiation of a rather broader tendency: in the 1990s, Bozarslan argues, the Middle East witnessed a sacralization of violence, which as a result became less political and more religious, or moral, in character. This increased religiosity is one important aspect to be explained in all accounts of suicide bombing, and perhaps of political violence more generally.

Bozarslan's analysis, which applies especially well to the Palestinian movement and to the Kurds in Turkey, appears tempting; it also ties in well with influential claims by authors such as Olivier Roy and Faisal Devji, that present-day violence by radical Islamist movements like Al-Qaeda has become deterritorialized and depoliticized as well as primarily moral rather than political in character.[36] Such analyses becomes less plausible, however, when one takes into account the use of suicide bombing by the Tamil Tigers during the 1990s, which reflects neither an increasing religiosity nor a clear political failure; nor does it account for the new forms of suicidal violence in Pakistan and Afghanistan in the wake of the US-led

2001 invasion, and by Salafi-jihadi insurgents that gradually emerged in Iraq after the ousting of Saddam Hussein in 2003 and, more recently, in the more violent arenas of the Arab Spring. It would seem rather far-fetched, for example, to call the so-called Islamic State deterritorialized or depoliticized. There is no good reason to believe that these groups had given up on concrete political goals like ousting American troops, establishing an Islamic state, or provoking increased tensions between different population groups. Clearly, sacrificial violence and rational-instrumental calculation need not clash with each other; on the contrary, both appear to be enduring features of the experience of the modern nation-state.

Next, I will briefly explore the semiotics involved in the performance of suicide bombings.[37] Suicide missions may be said to form particular kinds of communicative acts or signs, which may signify or represent particular claims or ideas, express something about their perpetrators, or performatively create or change social realities. Taken as a communicative utterance, the suicide mission transforms the very body of the perpetrator, or rather its physical destruction, into a sign of the truth and seriousness of a cause. Crucial to such utterances is not so much that they are addressed toward democracies, as Pape holds;[38] rather, they appear to presuppose—indeed require—a public or audience that may be influenced by such signs: a suicide mission that does not kill anyone is not necessarily a failure; a mission that does not attract any attention is.

Osama bin Laden, for one, is quite explicit about this semiotic: in his December 2001 message on the agents of the September 11 attacks, he calls the assaults a "great sign," by which the perpetrators told America and its allies "that they are living in falsehood"; thus, for him, it is actions, not words, which are truthful. More importantly, he describes the assaults as the act of cleansing and restoration of Muslim dignity against alleged American arrogance and its humiliation of the world's poor; they have, he claims, "erased the shame from the foreheads of the ummah," by exposing American weakness and cowardice.[39] Furthermore, suicide missions not only assert the courage of their actors and the justness of their cause; they may also performatively help to bring about what they signify. Thus, Bin Laden appears to have believed that the September 11 attacks themselves helped to widen the civilizational opposition between the capitalist or liberal West and the Muslim world; and in post-Saddam Iraq, suicide missions could both signify and constitute a violent antagonism between Sunnis and Shiites, or even create such an antagonism where it had not existed before.

One symbolic aspect that calls particular attention to the subjectivity of the perpetrators is constituted by "final messages" like the poems, letters, and diary entries written by Japanese kamikaze pilots in their final days, and the videotaped messages of Sunni Islamist suicide bombers. It is tempting to construe the last words of suicide terrorists as involving the uninhibited speaking of the truth; but it is not clear whether "truth" is the right coinage involved here in the first place. Typically, the utterances surrounding suicide attacks involve not factual assertions that may be true or false but rather self-presentations or normative challenges. Also, given the complex hierarchical and ideologically driven organizations behind them, suicide missions are generally too ideologically laden to allow for characterizations in terms of speaking the truth or asserting a limitless individual freedom, as Asad attempts to do.[40] In fact, the videotaped suicide message may be more appropriately seen as a complement to the videotaped confession of captured criminals or terrorists used by states for propaganda purposes; but once again, they provide an inversion or mirror image, and by the same token a challenge, of state powers that usually go unquestioned.

This brings us again to the crucial background factor constituted by the modern nation-state. As is well known, Talal Asad has done much to trace the rearticulation of the category of religion against the background of the modern nation-state;[41] but, as noted above, he tends to focus his genealogical critique too narrowly on liberal secular states. As is well known, nationalism has been characterized as a "civil religion"; perhaps we can say, more specifically, that the sacral character of the modern nation-state resides precisely in its claim to the lives of its citizens, especially in the sacrifice of those fighting for the fatherland. In itself, this idea of patriotic sacrifice is nothing new, witness Horace's line already quoted above; but perhaps the modern state rests on particularly modern forms of religion and power, just as suicide bombing may be said to express particularly modern forms of resistance and agency.

It has been argued that modern states involve a specifically modern "biopower," or "biopolitics," which cannot be reduced to liberal notions of sovereignty, rights, and laws: biopower concerns the population as a whole, conceptualized in terms of life, health, and security, rather than as a corporate body of rights-bearing citizens.[42] Now if indeed the modern state rests on the specifically modern modalities of power associated with biopolitics and with national identity, then suicide may be said to constitute a specifically modern form of resistance against precisely these power modalities, rather than against the state's sovereign power as conceived in liberal theories. It may be argued that, in its gesture of sacrificing others and sacralizing selves, suicide bombing forms the ultimate challenge, not so much of the state's sovereign monopoly of violence, but rather of its biopolitical ability to decide over the life and death of its population. This would imply that the suicide bomber is the complement, if not the opposite, of what Giorgio Agamben has called the *homo sacer*, the individual deprived of all rights and subjected to the modern state's power over his bare life.[43] Like Asad's argument discussed above, however, Agamben's sweeping characterization of the allegedly generic biopolitical powers of the sovereign liberal state seems both too broad, in downplaying the relatively rare occurrence of suicide bombing and its specific tactical and ideological motivations, and too narrow, in de-emphasizing its possible occurrence in non-liberal settings. Likewise, discussions of biopower have hitherto focused on power rather than on resistance and on the biological categories of race, life, and death rather than on the cultural dimensions of nation and religion. Against such analyses, it should be emphasized that suicide bombing is not merely an act of resistance against the state's (sovereign or other) power; it also occurs in contexts where the state is weak or nonexistent, as in post-Taliban Afghanistan and in post-2011 Iraq and Syria. Moreover, a positive ideology or symbolism may also be implied or asserted in them. If elaborated along these lines, such an account might go a long way in actually *explaining*, first, our intuitive awe and horror at its sacrifice of human lives in defiance of the nation-state's claims over the very lives of its citizens; and second, the non-liberal or antiliberal attitude to subjectivity and state power often involved in or expressed by suicide missions: they appear to think of individuals less as rights-bearing citizens than as objects for sacralization; they claim or arrogate a biopolitical power over life and death rather than defying the sovereign power of the state.

Conclusions

Suicide bombing displays a wide variety in articulation, organization, and legitimation; this variety, together with the—often unanswerable—question whether an individual act qualifies as a suicide mission at all, should guard us against any overhasty generalizations. Hence, instead of drawing conclusions, I will make some very tentative suggestions and raise some outstanding questions.

To begin with, one cannot emphasize strongly enough how recent a phenomenon suicide bombing is. Before the 1970s, suicide bombing by non-state actors is virtually nonexistent; and there is a marked increase in suicide missions following the collapse of the Soviet bloc countries and the end of the Cold War in 1989. Several factors may be adduced to account for this shift. First, there is a worldwide ideological or discursive shift from the political language of class struggle and social justice to (Islamic and other) moral or religious discourses of good and evil, purity and pollution, and humiliation and redemption. Second, the 1990s increase in numbers of suicide missions by movements with aspirations to statehood may well reflect the simultaneous decrease in state support for terrorist organizations. Third, following the 1989 withdrawal of Soviet troops from Afghanistan, many Arab mujahideen returned to their home countries, which not only led to new problems of demobilization but also gave a fresh impulse to Salafi-jihadi ideas and tactics in the Arab world, including the new Sunni cult of martyrdom and new symbolic contestations of the state and the superpowers.

A second major point is that suicide bombing appears to be a thoroughly modern phenomenon also in conceptual terms. Of course, there are premodern forms of suicide for political reasons, most famously the Japanese practice of seppuku or hara-kiri; but this practice involved a very specific warrior code and a historically specific form of loyalty to feudal leaders. In the twentieth century, this code was appropriated—and transformed—by the Japanese state for the purpose of defending the fatherland; it worked through military conscription rather than through any samurai tradition, and involved a subjectivity that was constituted and shaped by the modern state's disciplining institutions.[44] Similar points may be raised concerning Tamil Tigers and suicide bombers in the Middle East. Suicide bombing, in other words, is not—and should not be construed as—the persistence or atavistic reemergence of some premodern religious fanaticism in a modern political world assumed to be rational, secular, and disenchanted; rather, it is a radically novel phenomenon that contests the very boundaries between the religious and the political as well as the worldly and the transcendent.

Third, and this point follows from the preceding, suicide bombing may involve religious dimensions of sacralization and self-sacrifice; but ideologically, it often appears predicated on a nationalist vocabulary of martyrdom. It contests—and hence presupposes—not only the modern nation-state's monopolization of legitimate violence; it also reproduces and appropriates the modern nation-state's reconceptualization of martyrdom.[45] One interesting question that deserves further exploration in this context is how and when symbols, rituals, and myths that are available in most if not all religious traditions become re-signified so as to allow for or encourage suicide bombing in a way they did not do so before. Moreover, the discourse legitimizing suicide bombing may have become markedly more religious and moralistic in character, but that does not allow us to describe the movements using this discourse as deterritorialized and depoliticized. If my argument holds, suicide bombing involves the defiance not so much of the state's sovereignty as of its biopolitical control over the lives of its inhabitants. In this respect, too, there appears to be a greater continuity between (allegedly purely secular) nationalist liberation movements and (allegedly purely religious) transnational organizations using suicide bombing as a tactic than might appear at first sight. This should cause no great surprise: suicide bombing, whether legitimated in nationalist or in religious terms, both presupposes and challenges the modern state's quasi-sacral claims over the lives of its inhabitants.

Notes

1. A critique along these lines is perhaps most famously formulated by Talal Asad, *Genealogies of Religion* (Baltimore, MD: Johns Hopkins University Press, 1993); extending this critique, Peter van der Veer, in *Religious Nationalism: Hindus and Muslims in India* (Berkeley: University of California Press, 1994), argues that religion is actually constitutive of modern nationalism and the nation-state.

2. See in particular M. Biggs, "Dying without Killing: Self-Immolations, 1963–2002," in *Making Sense of Suicide Missions*, ed. Diego Gambetta (Oxford: Oxford University Press, 2005), 173–208.

3. See, for example, the lemma "Terrorism" in the *Stanford Encyclopedia of Philosophy* and the references given there; http://plato.stanford.edu/entries/terrorism/ (all links referred to in this chapter were still active in late 2019).

4. Ted Honderich, *After the Terror* (Edinburgh: Edinburgh University Press, 2002), 151.

5. Honderich, 117–119.

6. See Christoph Reuter, *My Life Is a Weapon: A Modern History of Suicide Bombing* (Princeton, NJ: Princeton University Press, 2004), 2; and Talal Asad, *On Suicide Bombing* (New York: Columbia University Press, 2007), 97.

7. Horace, *Odes*, III.2.13.

8. Once again, it is not possible to determine whether the agents in fact expected and wished to die in this attack.

9. These data are primarily from Luca Ricolfi's chapter on Palestinian suicide missions in Gambetta, ed., *Making Sense*, 80–81; see also the appendix to Ami Pedahzur, *Suicide Terrorism* (Cambridge: Polity Press, 2005): 241–253.

10. Mia Bloom, *Dying to Kill: The Allure of Suicide Terror* (New York: Columbia University Press, 2005), chap. 2.

11. Quoted in Doğu Ergil, "Suicide Terrorism in Turkey: The Workers Party of Kurdistan," in *Countering Suicide Terrorism* (Herzliya: Interdisciplinary Center Herzliya, 2001), 115.

12. See Bloom, *Dying to Kill*, chap. 5.

13. Christine Fair, *Suicide Attacks in Afghanistan, 2001–2007*, UNAMA report, https://carnegieendowment.org/2007/10/19/suicide-attacks-in-afghanistan-event-1067.

14. Muhammed Hafez, *Suicide Bombers in Iraq: The Strategy and Ideology of Martyrdom* (Washington, DC: United States Institute of Peace, 2007), 83; see also International Crisis Group, *In Their Own Words: Reading the Iraqi Insurgency*, ICG Middle East Report no. 50 (February 2006), https://www.crisisgroup.org/middle-east-north-africa/gulf-and-arabian-peninsula/iraq/their-own-words-reading-iraqi-insurgency.

15. Hafez, *Suicide Bombers*, appendix 2; cf. Aliza Marcus, "How Baida Wanted to Die," *New York Times*, August 12, 2009, http://www.nytimes.com/2009/08/16/magazine/16suicide-t.html.

16. Robert Pape, *Dying to Win: The Strategic Logic of Suicide Terrorism* (New York: Random House, 2005).

17. S. Holmes, "Al-Qaeda, September 11, 2001," in Gambetta, *Making Sense*, 131–172, esp. 171–172. As argued earlier, however, the assaults *were* successful, in achieving the explicitly stated aim of forcing an American troop withdrawal from Saudi Arabia.

18. Hans Magnus Enzensberger, *Schreckens Männer: Versuch über den Radikalen Verlierer* (Frankfurt: Suhrkamp, 2006); shorter English version available at http://www.signandsight.com/features/493.html. A similar argument may be found in Avishai Margalit, "The Suicide Bombers," *New York Review of Books*, January 16, 2003, http://www.nybooks.com/articles/15979.

19. Farhad Khosrokhavar, *Suicide Bombers: Allah's New Martyrs* (London: Pluto Press, 2005).

20. Khosrokhavar, 29.

21. Abdallah Azzam, "Martyrs: The Building Blocks of Nations," Religioscope, February 1, 2020, http://www.religioscope.com/info/doc/jihad/azzam_martyrs.htm.

22. Azzam, "Martyrs." Koran 3.142 reads, "Do you really think that you will enter Paradise, before Allah has decided from amongst you, those who fight in His Way and those who are patient?"

23. Azzam, "Martyrs."

24. One should resist the temptation, however, to see this as a mere expression of rural Arabic tribalism; it equally appeals to urban Arabs and non-Arab Muslim radicals. Moreover, tribal conflicts are also symmetrical and horizontal in kind rather than vertical and marked by the enormous power asymmetry involved in the confrontation between guerrilla movements and states.

25. For a case study tracing the historical development of the notion of martyrdom in nineteenth- and twentieth-century Kurdish literature, see Mariwan Kanie's contribution to this volume.

26. Osama Bin Laden, *Messages to the World: The Statements of Osama bin Laden*, ed. and introduction by Bruce Lawrence (London and New York: Verso, 2005), 153–154.

27. Although the authenticity of these texts has been questioned, they are in line with Al-Qaeda vocabulary and tactics known from more reliable sources, so I see no good reason to doubt their origins.

28. Quoted in Hafez, *Suicide Bombers*, 76.

29. Michael Roberts, "Tamil Tiger 'Martyrs': Regenerating Divine Potency?," *Studies in Conflict and Terrorism* 28 (2005): 493–514. For a more detailed discussion of Tamil conceptions and expressions of martyrdom, see Peter Schalk, "The Revival of Martyr Cults among Ilavar," *Temenos* 33 (1997): 151–190, also at http://www.tamilnation.org/ideology/schalk01.htm.

30. This indication of Tigers' commitment to their cause also figured in the mythology surrounding LTTE leader Prabhakaran, who himself boasted of carrying a cyanide capsule and reportedly asked his followers to kill him if he were ever to suggest giving up the armed struggle.

31. Schalk, "Revival."

32. Quoted in Roberts, "Tamil Tiger 'Martyrs,'" 504.

33. See also Emiko Ohnuki-Tierney, *Kamikaze, Cherry Blossoms, and Nationalisms: The Militarization of Aesthetics in Japanese History* (Chicago: University of Chicago Press, 2002).

34. S. Kalyvas and I. Sanchez-Cuenca, "Killing without Dying: The Absence of Suicide Missions," in Gambetta, *Making Sense*, 209–232, esp. 216.

35. Hamit Bozarslan, *Violence in the Middle East: From Political Struggle to Self-sacrifice* (Princeton, NJ: Markus Wiener, 2004). A comparable hypothesis is formulated by Pénélope Larzillière, who argues that (Palestinian) suicide terrorism arose from the failure of secular nationalism and that present-day martyrs are a sacralized form of the earlier secular national hero. The religious language employed by suicide terrorists and their organizations, she argues, should be seen as a compensation for political failure. See Larzillière, "Le 'martyre' des jeunes Palestiniens pendant l'Intifada al-Aqsa: analyse et comparaison," *Politique étrangère* 66 (2001): 937–951. These analyses, however, are predicated on the assumption that nationalist discourse is unambiguously secular, which is precisely what can *not* be said of nationalist cults of martyrdom, unknown soldiers, and the like.

36. See Olivier Roy, *Gobalized Islam* (New York: Columbia University Press, 2004), 55–57; and Faisal Devji, *Landscapes of the Jihad* (New York: Columbia University Press, 2005), 132–134.

37. Here, I do not use the term *semiotics* in the structuralist sense dealing with systems of signs abstracted away from individual actions. Rather, I assume the semiotic tradition that sees no reality beyond the individual utterance; likewise, the concept of a "semiotic ideology" should be seen as a generalization of the anthropological concept of a linguistic ideology, which involves the individual utterance in context rather than an abstracted sign system as the central object of investigation; see Webb Keane, *Christian Moderns: Freedom and Fetish in the Mission Encounter* (Berkeley: University of California Press, 2007), 16–21.

38. Pape, *Dying to Win*.

39. Bin Laden, *Messages*, 145–157.

40. Asad, *Suicide Bombing*, 91.

41. See in particular Talal Asad, "Secularism, Nation-State, Religion," in *Formations of the Secular* (Stanford, CA: Stanford University Press, 2003), 181–201.

42. The notion of biopower was coined by Michel Foucault in *The History of Sexuality*, vol. 1, *An Introduction* (New York: Random House, 1978), 133–160; see also Foucault's 1978 lecture course, *Security, Territory, Population* (Basingstoke: Palgrave Macmillan, 2007), 11–16 and 64–66. Much of the vast subsequent literature on biopower, however, displays

a tendency to reduce biopower to state sovereignty, against Foucault's explicitly stated intent of abstracting away from the state, sovereignty, and the law. See Foucault, *History*, 1:87–91; *Security*, 109–110.

43. On the *homo sacer*, see Giorgio Agamben, *Homo Sacer: Sovereign Power and Bare Life* (Stanford, CA: Stanford University Press, 1998); for an application of this notion to suicide bombing, see Nicholas Michelsen, "Liberalism, Political Theology, and Suicide Bombing," *Millennium: Journal of International Studies* 42 (2013): 198–223; and, more famously, the brief remarks on suicide bombing as an act of resistance against "sovereign biopower" in Michael Hardt and Antonio Negri, *Multitude* (Harmondsworth: Penguin Press, 2004), 45, 54; for an earlier, argument that (private and nonpolitical) suicide amounts to an act of resistance against biopower, see John Seery, *Political Theory for Mortals: Shades of Justice, Images of Death* (Ithaca, NY: Cornell University Press, 1996).

44. Cf. Ohnuki-Tierney, *Kamikaze*, 125–156.

45. This is not simply a process of secularization, however, as nationalist martyrdom contains an irreducibly sacrificial and hence sacral element; moreover, the very category of religion underwent a far-reaching transformation in the process of nation-state formation; see Van der Veer, *Religious Nationalism*; and Asad, *Formations*.

Part VI

Secularism and Postsecularism

Several of the earlier contributions in this volume, in particular those dealing with transgressive and violent gestures, indicated how religious practices may raise questions of a normative nature. This part zooms in on one such normative question that is particularly hotly debated in the early twenty-first century: the question of secularism. As noted in the introduction, it seems useful to separate the concept of the secular from the historical thesis of secularization and the normative position of secularism; yet, in practice, the three are often closely linked, if not inextricably intertwined.

The contributions in this part not only address the interrelation between conceptual, empirical (or historical), and normative issues; they also engage with the three distinct normative positions outlined in the introduction. The authors included here implicitly or explicitly address the liberal doctrines that try to salvage (part of) the secularization thesis, in particular Habermas's influential notion of the postsecular. They also discuss communitarian critiques of the liberal-secular assumption of an autonomous, rational individual in the wake of MacIntyre's and Charles Taylor's influential arguments concerning religious tradition and community. Finally, they tackle the genealogical critique of the concept of the secular as shaped by a history of post-Enlightenment Western power, in particular as it has been developed by Talal Asad and his followers. In doing so, they resonate with contributions elsewhere in this volume, thus demonstrating the potential fruitfulness of combining conceptual analysis, empirical or historical study, and normative questioning in the study of contemporary religious practices.

Yolande Jansen tackles two influential, and at first blush very different, recent postsecular views in "Good Religion, Bad Religion." In very different ways, both the liberal Jürgen Habermas and the antiliberal Saba Mahmood have formulated influential versions of a "postsecular" view that argues for the legitimacy of religious beliefs or performances in the public sphere. At first sight, Habermas's plea for a "learning process" that should make Islam compatible with liberal democracy appears to assume precisely the normative secularity criticized by Mahmood. It turns out, however, that both emphasize the dimension of *piety* in religion, that is, the nonreflective, practical, habitual, and nondoctrinal dimension of faith as opposed to the explicit dogmatic and doctrinal (not to say doctrinaire) aspects of belief. In taking for granted the idea of piety as an unreflective and unintentional "way of being," Jansen argues, both Habermas and Mahmood ignore the political contexts in which piety may emerge. Thus, both presume ahistorical, culturalized, and essentialized concepts of piety and fanaticism—and of religion, secularity, and public reason. On Jansen's own account, fanaticism is a relational concept that is legitimized by a specific political-discursive context. This allows her to criticize Habermas's distinction between "genuine religious faith" as a source of energy rather than a mere doctrine and "religious fanaticism" as a literalist, totalizing, and dogmatic claim to truth-possession. Focusing on the Abu Zayd case in Egypt, she also argues that Mahmood, despite her criticisms of Western liberal secularism, uncritically recreates a secularity-piety divide: in her claim that "secular critics" are unable to understand Islam as a "discursive tradition" of nonreflective and apolitical piety, she ignores the political context and motives of Abu Zayd's Islamist critics.

Jansen largely accepts the genealogical epistemological critique of secularism offered by Asad and Mahmood, among others; but she rejects the new opposition between secularist hermeneutics and discursive traditionality that such criticisms construe. This argument also applies to Asad's influential construction of Islam as a "discursive tradition." In this respect, her analysis interestingly converges with Schielke's discussion of everyday religious practice.

In his contribution, "Human Rights, Muslim Communities, and the Unintended Secularization of Canada," Ali Hassan Zaidi exposes some of the ironies and paradoxes of secularism and its contestations, arguing that Muslim communities in Canada have inadvertently contributed to the secularization of Canadian multicultural society, precisely through their struggle for recognition as Muslims. He describes how Canadian Muslims have successfully appealed to the Canadian Charter of Rights and Freedoms for the right to wear a hijab in school or to pray in the workplace; they have brought their religious identity into the public domain, challenging the idea that public space is inherently secular. Yet, in doing so, they paradoxically appealed to a secular charter of rights, which regards religion as a strictly private affair. In other words, insofar as multiculturalism recognizes religious group rights, it reduces public discourse on religion to identity politics. Thus, Zaidi exposes the paradoxical character of Muslim minority communities' appeal to liberal conceptions of human rights, which rest on individualist and secularist assumptions; by doing so, they transform their public reasoning from a discourse on the sacred to a discourse of rights.

Communitarian and genealogical critiques of liberal secularism have assumed rather different shapes and have informed rather divergent normative positions in the Arabic-Islamic and in the Indian context. On Asad's and Mahmood's accounts, secularism has a distinctly Western and post-Enlightenment genealogy. Although the normative implications of this critique are rarely spelled out, it appears to inform a normative view of Islam as not only a distinct "discursive tradition" but more specifically as a viable, and ultimately historically stable, *moral* tradition. Similar genealogical criticisms of liberalism voiced in an Indian context, however, have taken a rather different normative stance. Thus, in his 1994 essay, "Secularism and Toleration," Partha Chatterjee offers a genealogically inspired critique of Indian secularism that nonetheless attempts to safeguard a form of secularism against the increasingly vocal manifestations of Hindu nationalism. On a more theoretical level, Chatterjee takes a stance against the anti-Western and anti-secularist communitarianism to be found in authors like Ashis Nandy.

In "The Distinctiveness of Indian Secularism," which concludes this volume, Rajeev Bhargava tackles these questions from a framework that can be characterized as broadly liberal and secular, but with a difference. Bhargava reacts against both Chatterjee and Nandy; in doing so, also presents an interesting sidelight on communitarian and genealogical claims emerging from other non-Western contexts and traditions. His response to such communitarian and genealogical criticisms is especially interesting because of its acknowledgment of the limitations of Western liberal secularism. Noting the different contents that secularism acquires in different geographical and historical settings, Bhargava argues for a historicizing and transnational approach, which helps us to see Indian secularism as distinct but not unique or incomparable. Western secularism, he argues, is widely understood as involving the exclusion of religion from the state; conversely, it leaves the state powerless, or at least without any legitimate means to intervene, in religious matters. It is also based on an individualistic construal of values like freedom of religion and on a view of faith as primarily an inner phenomenon. In

India, by contrast, the emphasis lies on practices rather than beliefs and on communities rather than individuals. Moreover, the Indian state is explicitly allowed to interfere in religious matters by the constitution, witness its attempts to reform Hindu laws or to suppress the caste system. Because of these local particularities, Bhargava argues for what he calls a "contextual secularism"; Indian secularism, he states, is not only based on a past shared with the West but also has a distinct historical trajectory of its own. Thus, his position also implies a rejection of the oversimplified idea that secularism can be genealogically unmasked and delegitimized as a mere ploy of Western power. As such, Bhargava's essay is very much part of an ongoing debate with, among others, Partha Chatterjee, Ashis Nandy, and Faisal Devji in the Indian context, as well as with Charles Taylor, Alisdair MacIntyre, Jürgen Habermas, and Talal Asad, among other philosophers, in a more theoretical setting. It remains to be seen whether and how the terms of this debate have been affected by recent events in India and in the Islamic world, like the Hindu nationalist Bharatiya Janata Party's landslide victory in India's 2019 parliamentary elections and the 2014 emergence of the so-called Islamic State in Iraq and Syria and its proclamation of a defiantly antiliberal (but, as it turned out, ephemeral) caliphate. Elsewhere in Asia, Europe, and the United States, broadly comparable—if generally less dramatic—contestations of secularism have emerged; jointly, these may force us to take challenges and alternatives to liberal secularism more seriously than has long been the case in Western political theory.

CHAPTER 22

Good Religion, Bad Religion
Beyond the Secularity-Religion and Secularity-Piety Binaries

Yolande Jansen

A substantial part of Habermas's recent work is explicitly dedicated to rethinking the place of religion in the public sphere, and in this recent work he has started to talk in terms of "postsecular societies." His use of this term not only gives a sociological diagnosis in terms of the emergence of such societies; it also offers a tentatively positive, or in any case ambivalent, normative evaluation of postsecularism.[1] Both the notions of secularism and of postsecularism carry complicated sets of meanings in Habermas's work, but I would like to single out initially the understanding of postsecularism in which this implies the idea that neither secular citizens nor the liberal state can or should "expect *all* citizens to justify their political positions independently of their religious convictions or worldviews," as they would expect when defending a secularist position.[2]

Postsecular Encounters:
Habermas and Mahmood as Critics of Secularism

In the work of the anthropologists Talal Asad and Saba Mahmood, what comes under scrutiny is not so much secularism as a political doctrine but the ways in which this is grounded in what Asad has called "the secular," a cultural "concept that brings together certain behaviors, knowledges, and sensibilities in modern life."[3] They have critically scrutinized this discursive and elusive "secular"—and the related concept of (universal) religion—and suggest that it should be disrobed of its self-evidence and pretended cultural-historical and political neutrality. They criticize the ways in which "the secular" affects political conceptions of secularism, both methodologically and ideologically, and especially focus on the ways that it tends to distort the perception of Muslim societies and the contestable policy choices that are based on these distortions, both in the past and today. Particularly the secular interpretation of religious practice as a *sign*—and specifically as a sign of fundamentalism, docility, and sensitivity to authoritarianism—is, according to Asad and Mahmood, not only a misunderstanding of Islamic resurgence; it also puts Muslims in Western contexts at risk because it causes them to be treated as outsiders by dominant constituencies and even as potential enemies within. Worldwide, it causes them to be treated as potential fanatics or even terrorists.[4]

According to Mahmood, contemporary secularism, against its usual interpretations, is not so much about the banning of religion from politics, but about the refashioning of religious subjectivities and so, actually, about the "regulation of religious life . . . in the name of enforcing and protecting religious freedoms" and thus implies a form of "normative secularity."[5] For example, influential American policymakers think that tensions between contemporary Islamic movements and liberal democracy arise because these movements do not follow "historical-hermeneutic" methods of Koran interpretation. These policymakers think that traditionalists in the Muslim world believe that the Koran is the actual word of God and want to preserve orthodox norms and values and conservative behavior, especially by observing Islamic rituals closely. In the terms of one of the reports Mahmood analyzes, traditionalist mentalities are "willing to accept authority with few questions," and this is "causally linked with backwardness and underdevelopment, which in turn are the breeding ground for social and political problems of all sorts."

Mahmood further argues that ironically, this American ideological project finds its unexpected "allies" in those secular liberal Muslim reformers such as Nasr Abu Zayd who are critical of the rise of Islamism and who, in articulating this criticism, rely on the discourses of Western modernity, for example by urging the secularization of the Islamic world and by stressing the need for hermeneutical instead of fundamentalist approaches to religious doctrines. Quite frequently, these ideas are framed in terms of the need for the equivalent of Protestant Reformation in the Muslim world.[6]

Given Habermas's view of postsecularism, we might expect that some of the problems addressed by the second group of critics of secularism, such as Mahmood and Asad, would be addressed by this revision from within political philosophy. But this seems hardly the case. When addressing the place of Islam both in European societies and more generally in world politics, Habermas does so in a language that is precisely the one that Mahmood criticizes, presenting "hermeneutical" and "reformist" approaches to Islam as key to a required transformation of Muslim societies. In his "Notes on a Postsecular Society," Habermas asserts that, while Catholicism and Protestantism have gradually adapted to liberal democracy and in the course of a learning process finally accepted it during the 1960s, Islam lags behind in going through an analogous learning process. He proposes that for Islam, a similar learning process is desirable to the one that caused the "change in epistemic attitudes following the Reformation in the Christian churches of the West,"[7] when religious consciousness became reflexive.

I will return to the specifically Protestant model that Habermas proposes and to his precise phrasing of this proposal; first, however, an observation: Habermas seems to be a third "ally" to the pedagogical project of normative secularity criticized by Mahmood. In what follows I will scrutinize this constellation surrounding secularism as it appears in Mahmood and Habermas. I do so not only because comparing their views is productive in itself for understanding the stakes of postsecularism but also because their views can plausibly be considered as nuanced and well-argued versions of two transnationally represented clusters of ideas that are relevant today to evaluations of Euro-American-Islamic relations. Habermas reaches a broad audience in public fora in Europe, but his work is also broadly discussed, even seen as a model, among liberal or reformist thinkers in the Muslim world.[8] Moreover, Habermas's position is a sound representation of the attitude that many moderate Europeans take: they don't like a "drawing a line in the sand mentality" as to the appearance of religion in politics generally, but they do think that some forms of religion need to be curtailed in order that they do not threaten liberal democracy.

Mahmood's critique of secularism reaches a broad audience as well, perhaps especially among Anglo-American cultural scholars and social scientists. For example, Judith Butler's cover blurb argues that Mahmood's *Politics of Piety* "will reorient the way in which cultural theorists and moral philosophers across the disciplines regard religious practice, the account of moral agency, and questions of embodiment." Sociologist Brian Turner suggests that Mahmood has initiated a change of perspective for all research concerning Islamic resurgence because of the way she has introduced and interpreted the notion of *piety* as an alternative to interpretations in terms of fundamentalism.[9] Mahmood herself puts forward the idea that the anthropological material from her research among pious Islamist women speaks back to the legacies of secularism and liberal humanism and argues that the epistemology needed to understand pious women implies a broader critique of neo-Kantian interpretations of subjectivity that dominate Western progressive discourses, feminist ones in particular. Over the last few years, quite a lot of substantial criticisms of Mahmood's analysis of piety have appeared.[10] I will discuss what their critique implies for my qualified argument that we should take the "piety argument" more seriously within political theory than has been done so far.

Piety, Politics, and Islamic Fundamentalism

Mahmood's critique of liberal secularism and the advocacy of hermeneutics stands in the context of what she considers secularist misunderstandings of contemporary Islam as explained in her *Politics of Piety*. The title of the book summarizes the theoretical perspective Mahmood is proposing: To analyze the specificity of contemporary Islamic religiosity in terms of piety and not to overlook the ways in which piety is *political*.

Mahmood puts forward that some of the most important movements participating in the Islamic Revival in the Middle East are badly understood if we interpret the religious assiduity they advocate in terms of submission, docility, and lack of agency. It is also a misunderstanding to suggest that members of these movements are driven by the idea that the Koran presents a set of dogmas to be taken literally, without interpretation, historicization, or insight in the larger coherence (or incoherence) of the text. During research among women participants in the Egyptian Mosque Movement, which is one of the most important organizations in the Islamic Revival, Mahmood came across self-interpretations in terms of *da'wa*, which she translates as "piety."[11] For the women inspired by *da'wa*, religion is not a belief or a set of dogmas. It is also not (primarily) an identity or a sign of anti-Westernness. Instead, religious practices, rituals, are performed as "a means to the training and realization of piety in the entirety of one's life." One of her respondents, for example, opposes *din* ("religion") to custom and explains that for her, wearing a veil is a religious "duty" [*fard*], part of her striving to "behave in a truly modest manner in our daily lives, a challenge that far exceeds the simple act of donning the veil." The practice is not a means to signal a belonging or tradition but contributes to the "formation of an ethical disposition," in terms of Islamic "virtue," and an "entire manner of existence."[12]

Interpretations of such religious intentions in terms of literalism or fundamentalism presuppose that practices and beliefs are based on reified dogmas or doctrines. Instead, Mahmood argues, for the pious women, reading the Koran and carrying out religious rituals is not something mechanical, and religious intentions are important: the rituals are carried out with the intention of "living modestly." Rather than encouraging dogmatic attitudes, the *telos* of living modestly gives space for reflexivity, albeit within conservative frameworks. But piety is not just a matter of reflexivity either; it is an ethos that works *through* disciplining the body, which becomes the necessary "means through which the virtue of modesty is both created and expressed."[13]

Mahmood argues that the Islamic Revival speaks back to Western traditions of interpreting ethics and religion, especially insofar as these are driven by what she calls the "humanist legacy," especially in its (Neo-)Kantian formulation.[14] These traditions seek the grounds of moral and religious practice and organization in reason, and they tend to abstract from contexts, traditions, and practices. Mahmood proceeds in the footsteps of Foucauldian critiques of Kantianism, especially Judith Butler's, and criticizes interpretations of normativity as stemming from a subject that can determine its own norms rationally and then determine its actions on that basis.[15] "For the pietists," she writes, "bodily behavior is at the core of the proper realization of the norm, and for their [secularist] opponents, it is a contingent and unnecessary element in modesty's enactment."[16] Mahmood instead interprets subjectivity as always embedded in and formed by power relations. Transformations of existing norms or resistance to them are enabled through the openness caused by processes of resignification that (always) accompany the (local) performance of norms.

Mahmood also puts forward that poststructuralist interpretations of normativity themselves do not yet provide the right framework for understanding piety, arguing that, for example, Judith Butler's understanding of agency still remains attached to liberal modernism by its focus on the rearticulation and especially the subversion of norms. Instead, she focuses on "the variety of ways in which norms are lived and inhabited, aspired to, reached for, and consummated."[17] Anticipating my further critique, I would like to put forward that rearticulation and subversion of norms can and should be among "the variety of ways in which norms are lived," so the self-distinction of Mahmood from Butler is perhaps a little quick and too focused on taking a distance from progressive notions of subjectivity. This is in line with the fact that Mahmood, who finds support in late-Foucauldian ethics, interprets this ethics as a form of (Aristotelian) virtue ethics for its concentration on locality and practice. It may be significant, in this respect, that Mahmood hardly refers to one of the key concepts in Foucault's later work, namely *parrhèsia*, by which he means candidly speaking the truth in the presence of power. Instead, ethics, for her, takes a rather "private" turn: it refers to "those practices, techniques, and discourses through which a particular subject transforms herself in order to achieve a particular state of being, happiness, or truth."[18]

If we now ask how the anthropological material as Mahmood interprets it speaks back to the humanist and secularist legacy, it helps to see that Mahmood's critique of Kantian interpretations of normativity is highly influenced by earlier criticisms made of Kant's notion of religion. In 1993, Talal Asad had famously traced the emergence of the concept of universal "religion" as abstracted from specific religious practices and disciplines to early modernity and finds its apogee formulation in Kant, who distinguishes an atemporal essence of "religion" from the diverse historical confessions.[19] According to Asad, the idea that religion could and should be separable from its historical forms—that is, of revealed religions and the religious practices they prescribe—implies that religion becomes something interior, a belief, a moral disposition that can lead to certain actions, but that is not itself grounded in practice, training, or mind-body interaction. Asad stresses the modern character of this idea and of the ensuing interpretation of religious practice as representation, sign, or symbol of an interior mental state. He opposes to this interpretation the ways in which, in medieval discourses and religious practices, interiority and exteriority were experienced as intricately related, producing each other in and through religious performance and training. Such intricacy of bodily practice and the "mind's part" of religion—that is, belief, the inseparability and mutual dependence of mind and body in religion as a social practice—is what Mahmood captures in the term *piety*. Thus, according to Mahmood and Asad, modern understandings of both morality and religion, which form the philosophical kernel of secularism, have resulted in contestable, rationalist conceptions of both morality and religion.

Critique of Islamic Secular Hermeneutics

Mahmood connects her understanding of piety to a critique of reformist approaches of Islam proposed by Muslim liberal secularists, especially of those who favor a hermeneutical approach of the Koranic teachings. Her criticism is directed against those who argue that the Islamist emphasis on religious assiduity is a way to discipline and depoliticize the masses by religious elites, for example, by the Egyptian thinker Hasan Hanafi. The central focus of her criticism is the dependence on secularist discourses and conceptual frameworks that underlie such arguments for "reform." Her main antagonist here is the Egyptian thinker Nasr Abu Zayd, whose work she reads in ways indebted to the anthropologist Charles Hirschkind.

In a 1995 article, Nasr Abu Zayd advocates for a historically grounded hermeneutics of the Koran. Abu Zayd argues that this hermeneutics should be "objective" (*maudu'i*) and "scientific" (*'ilmi*), meaning that we should acknowledge that we can only know the sacred text through the ways in which it has been passed on to a historically changing humanity. According to Abu Zayd, this hermeneutics is closely related to secularism (*al-'almaniyya*), which essentially is nothing but "the true interpretation and scientific understanding of religion." The word of God, the Koran itself, is only interpretable as a human language which acquires its meaning in historical, geographical, and psychological contexts. It cannot be approached directly, as a nonlinguistic, nonliterary text, but will always "belong to a specific cultural structure and produced in accord with the rules of that culture."[20]

Such a hermeneutical reading of the Koran, Mahmood argues, places it back into its historical period and formulates this literary hermeneutics as a correction of what it sees as fundamentalist, absolutist, or authoritarian readings of the Koran; as a result, it misses out on the possibility of conceiving of Islam as a "discursive tradition" and of understanding contemporary Islamic piety as part of such a tradition. A discursive tradition does not interpret its foundational texts (such as in this case the Koran and the *hadith*) in a fundamentalist way in the sense of taking the word of God literally, dogmatically, or without any consideration of temporality and change. But there *is* continuity: tradition should be understood in terms of a historically evolving set of discursive practices that, through pedagogies of reflection upon the past and engagement with sacred texts, link "practitioners across the temporal modalities of past, present and future through pedagogy of practical, scholarly, and embodied forms of knowledge and virtues deemed central to the tradition."[21] The hermeneutics going along with passing on such a tradition takes the interpretation of religious sources to be part of a life-world, a living tradition, an ethical practice. It is not concentrated on "unmasking" religious authority but on seeking counsel in religious sources about "the practicalities of daily living," where the Koran can be read as "a source that can guide one through the problems of contemporary existence."[22]

Discursive traditionality is precisely the option that is ruled out beforehand by those methodologies that can only distinguish between objectifying, historicizing ways of reading and fundamentalist ones, Mahmood argues. This is why secular hermeneutics fails to understand, and hence tends to delegitimize, a contemporary Islamic piety, even though this way of being might be challenging problematic Neo-Kantian conceptions of subjectivity. Moreover, the secular project is *politically* aimed at "creating the conditions for the emergence of a normative religious subject who understands religion ... as a congeries of symbols to be flexibly interpreted in a manner consonant with the imperatives of secular liberal political rule."[23] The secularist argument thus unfolds against the backdrop of colonial and postcolonial government.

On Mahmood's Interpretation of Abu Zayd's Hermeneutics

Like Mahmood, I think it is important to open up possibilities for understanding religious performance beyond the binary of secularism and literalism/fundamentalism and to criticize accounts of religious performance in terms of an inherent dogmatism. The insistence on the agency of pious Muslim women is important, even as the critique of epistemologies that can only conceptualize either-or choices between active norm-challenging forms of agency (often wrongly identified with subjectivities that develop exclusively within liberal democracies) and passive norm-conforming forms of agency. I will return in my conclusion to the importance of this argument, which tends to be downplayed in some of the often vehement critiques of Mahmood's binaries and political conclusions. First, I will focus on her construction of one of these binaries, one that is politically crucial in my view.

My main point is that Mahmood mistakenly abstracts from the complexities of the political-historical context, when she analyzes the relationship between contemporary secular liberalism and piety and ascribes too much explanatory power to the epistemological level at which secularism and piety are being played out against each other. Thereby, she culturizes these notions herself, abstracting from the historical contexts in which they take their full meaning. Secularism, but also piety and discursive traditionality, can be ethical ideals; but they will always be tainted with this-worldly complexities that the distinction between secular readings of Islamic practices and readings in terms of discursive traditionality can never account for on their own. To explain this point, I would first like to look in more detail at the Abu Zayd debate. I will contest the idea put forward by Mahmood, in line with what Hirschkind had argued before, that we can and should separate the discussion about the presuppositions on the relation between religion and reason from the political struggles surrounding Abu Zayd.[24] This argument affects Mahmood's theoretical point itself, for it implies a critique of the ways in which Mahmood implicitly presents us with a secularity-piety divide that only displaces the binaries that she wants to level.

Mahmood assembles the work and views of many geographically dispersed intellectuals under the heading of Reformism, whose respective ways of thinking she explains by reference to a scheme that opposes secularist modernism to a more sensitive understanding of Islamic resurgence in terms of discursive traditionality. Abu Zayd himself gives a more complex account of the many Reformist voices and places them in a long Islamic tradition of thought that can hardly be seen as just "applying" or "conforming" to superficial Western schemes surrounding history and secularity and that should be read in partly intra-Islamic, partly

Euro-Islamic interactional terms.[25] I am not sure Abu Zayd himself would have assumed the categorization of being a secularist thinker without qualification, and I am not convinced that opposition against literalism and authoritarian readings of the Koran in the specific context in which he did so necessarily drives him into a camp of thinkers unable to understand Islamic piety in terms of a discursive tradition. Abu Zayd in his later work conceptualized the Koran in terms of "its living status as a discourse" without withdrawing from his earlier views on hermeneutics; I infer from this that for him, hermeneutics and discursive traditionality are not necessarily on a tense footing.[26]

Moreover, the arguments put forward stand in a highly politically salient context. In 1995, Abu Zayd fled to the Netherlands after he had been denied tenure at al-Azhar university in Cairo earlier that year, because of an unfavorable report by a committee appointed to assess his work. After a nationally mediated debate about the role that his hermeneutical, literary interpretation of the Koran played in this evaluation, an Islamist lawyer started a lawsuit against Abu Zayd to have him forcibly separated from his wife because of apostasy. Later in 1995, Abu Zayd received tenure after all; but in the meantime, he had fled to the Netherlands awaiting the result of the lawsuit against him. He remained because in 1996, the Egyptian appellate court controversially ruled in favor of the lawyer and declared the marriage "null and void."[27] These Islamist claims against Abu Zayd's presumed apostasy were less independent from the intellectual debate about his academic qualities than Hirschkind allows for. In their concentration on critiquing the underlying discursive and conceptual mechanisms in Abu Zayd's reasoning, neither Hirschkind nor Mahmood find it relevant to make clear where the Egyptian authors taking a critical perspective on Abu Zayd's hermeneutics stood politically. Hirschkind paraphrases and, apparently, endorses the committee's criticism of Abu Zayd in terms of the "polemical and often disparaging tone with which Abu Zayd addressed the work of respected earlier and contemporary scholars, was seen as unfitting for one who was supposedly writing within the same tradition of moral inquiry."[28] But this was argued foremost by Abd al-Sabur Shahin, who was the only one of the three professors who authored the report on whether Abu Zayd was qualified to be a professor to deny that he was. Abd al-Sabur Shahin was not just a university professor, but also an Islamist preacher in Cairo at the time, and a partner in a project for Islamic banking that had been involved in a financial scandal and that Abu Zayd had criticized. He was the source of the apostasy accusation, which he put forward during one of his sermons. The struggle around Abu Zayd considerably complicates the picture of pious Islamic traditionalism as a deeply religious way of being that is only political insofar as it is forced to counter the disciplinary powers of the nation-state.

Abu Zayd's plea for a hermeneutics of the Koran clearly has an ideological-critical aspect. It stresses the human origins of the Koran and that its words and rules are subject to human error. More specifically, it stresses that the rules it proposes should be interpreted in the context of how they transform the rules from pre-Islamic societies.[29] In any case, the cultural and human status of the text also leads him to criticize the "principle of divine sovereignty": "The principle of divine sovereignty simply results in the sovereignty of religious men—in the end, nothing but human beings with their own biases and ideological inclinations."[30] Perhaps here Abu Zayd deploys a notion of religious critique that does not reflect enough upon the modernist aggression inherent in the gesture itself of tearing away veils of religious ignorance. Mahmood, however, interprets this quote in a manner that does not allow any ambivalence. Let me quote in some length her comment on the above quote from Abu Zayd:

> Critical reading of the text here assumes a sovereign subject who reconciles the claims of scripture against those of reason, wherein reason is defined in accord with protocols of empiricist historiography. Given the progressivist and empiricist conception of history that animates the interpretive method of Abu Zayd, Hanafi, Soroush, and others, this form of critical reading is the nadir of man's attempt to grapple with the divine—all others who do not agree with this method stand in a false relation to this quest.[31]

Here, Mahmood appears to suggest that religious critique, and particularly critique of the notion of divine sovereignty, immediately results in authoritarian, aggressive, and unbounded claims to *a* sovereignty based on the claims of reason, and that is intolerant toward those who do cherish more religious notions. Thus, she turns around the accusation of dogmatism, and even fanaticism, by suggesting that the humanists accuse everyone holding a different view of not holding true beliefs. Such an interpretation risks making full circle between a critique of secularism and a delegitimation of anyone criticizing religious authority posing as absolute and unquestionable. What makes Mahmood's reading rather ironic is that while interpreting the piety movement in terms of a discursive tradition, she fails to problematize the very modern notion of "divine sovereignty" (*hakimiyya*). The notion of *hakimiyya* is central to the work of Sayyid Qutb, who took it from Abu 'l-A'la Mawdudi, but it is not a traditional Islamic notion. Modernist Islamism has adopted it in its competition with the modern sovereign state, and the concept is related to other modernist political concepts in the work of Sayyid Qutb.[32]

In sum, Mahmood's interpretation of Abu Zayd's work forms an insufficiently historicized interpretation of it, when she argues *that it uses* the wrong epistemological framework for understanding Muslim piety and is taking religious claims too much at face value. We need a second layer, taking Mahmood's critique of secularism at the level of epistemology seriously, but then bringing our interpretation of both secularism and piety back to a more politico-historical, context-sensitive level. This would help to overcome the binary that Mahmood (and Hirschkind) implicitly construct between either secularist, destructive interpretations of Islamic religious traditions in terms of fundamentalism or respectful interpretations of these traditions in terms of discursive traditionality. It might also lead us to question the fact that Mahmood uses the notion of piety itself in close connection to the Arabic *da'wa*, sometimes even as its translation. *Da'wa* literally means "call" or "appeal" and is associated with God's call to "true religion," Islam. In contemporary Islamist discourses, *da'wa* is primarily understood as a religious duty for all adult members of Islamic society to urge *fellow Muslims* to greater piety.[33] If we translate this *social* duty as "piety," we risk losing sight of the intrinsic moral, social, and political sides of *da'wa*, because piety's first connotation is a rather interiorized and individual(ist) religious ethos. Mahmood's emphasis on the "politics of piety" does not remedy this initial confusion.[34]

This could also lead us to rethink the relation between readings of piety in terms of a way of being and those interpretations that emphasize the communicative context. As I already mentioned, Talal Asad, in his reading of the French law prohibiting religious signs in schools and public services, uses this distinction to criticize the hijab's interpretation in terms of a *sign*, stressing that for the wearer, wearing a hijab may form part of a way of being in the first place.[35] Now like Asad, I do think that this is a relevant and legitimate (self-)interpretation, and one that can back up a claim to freedom of conscience and religion by the wearers.[36] However, at the same time, I do not think it is a secularist misunderstanding of piety at the epistemological level which leads some of the French fellow citizens (and policymakers) to privilege the communicative context. In the French (and closely related Algerian) context, piety and claims to piety have been connoted with and distorted by images and experiences of political violence during the Algerian war of independence and the extremely violent Algerian 1990s, and readings of the hijab in terms of signs (and the semiotic insecurities resulting from that reading) are at least partly the understandable result of that context. Only contextual work can help to evaluate the balance between those dimensions of practices related to the hijab that could be interpreted as forming part of "ways of being" and other dimensions that might be interpreted (and historicized) in terms of communication and that cannot be dismissed as totally irrelevant to their "real" signification as religious practices.[37]

A more sober critique of secularism, adopting the epistemological critique à la Mahmood (and Asad) but without the binaries between secularism and piety or secularist hermeneutics and discursive traditionality should be useful in Western debates about secularism as well, especially with regard to the implicit relationship between orthodoxy, piety, and fanaticism still haunting contemporary political thought. This is so because for many secularists neither the appearance of religious practices in public nor the free exercise of religion for the members of religious groups, nor even religious talk in public deliberation is really the problem. Rather, it is the idea that some forms of piety can be related to religious fanaticism, which in turn can motivate violent political action; hence, it is about politics becoming "faithful" in a specific sense that European intellectual traditions have mostly reflected on in terms of fanaticism.[38]

A look at the greater complexities of this aspect of secular thought in the European tradition, which is far more complex and layered than Mahmood's implicit portrayal in terms of Neo-Kantianism acknowledges, will be helpful here. It is important to recognize this because then we could show that Euro-American traditions have resources for self-reflection and ambivalence toward both religious politics and secularism. I will try to bring a few of these complexities to light by reading Habermas's reflections on postsecularism as a contemporary example of this tradition of thinking about political religion, or religious politics, which has lost sight of some complicated distinctions that this tradition had made at earlier stages.

Habermas's Notes on a "Postsecular Society"

Many of the political-theoretical debates surrounding secularism have increasingly turned out in favor of concessions to religious performance in public spheres, both in terms of religious expression in political deliberation and religious practice in public spaces. For example, Jürgen Habermas has long had the reputation of holding strongly secularist views, but as early as in 1988, in his *Postmetaphysical Thinking*, he stressed the legitimacy, even the "indispensability," of religious language in modernity, and this is why he has started to talk in terms of postsecularity. Yet I will try to show that Habermas draws a new boundary for religion, and that, although he does not often explicitly refer to fanaticism, the substance of where he draws the boundary between legitimate, or even indispensable, and problematic, or even illegitimate, forms of religion within a liberal democracy is historically connected to the concept of fanaticism, whose genealogy is intimately linked to secularity.[39] I will argue that Habermas's new boundary disregards important insights from research into the history of fanaticism as a political concept instead of a neutral, universal, and ahistorical one, and that this should have led Habermas to be more ambivalent toward defining "postsecularism" the way he does.

Here is what Habermas writes about Islam in the context of his plea for postsecular thinking:

> Dieser schmerzhafte Lernprozess steht dem Islam noch bevor. Auch in der islamischen Welt wächst die Einsicht, dass heute ein historisch-hermeneutischer Zugang zu den Lehren des Koran nötig is. Die Diskussion über einen erwünschten Euro-Islam bringt uns jedoch erneut zu Bewusstsein, dass es letztlich die religiösen Gemeinden sind, die selbst darüber entscheiden werden, ob sie in einem reformierten Glauben den "wahren Glauben" wiedererkennen können.[40]

> [Many Muslim communities still have this painful learning process (of Reform) before them. Certainly, the insight is also growing in the Islamic world that today a historical-hermeneutic approach to the Koran's doctrine is required. But the discussion on a desired Euro-Islam makes us once more aware of the fact that it is the religious communities that will themselves decide whether they can recognize in a reformed faith their "true faith."]

In a passage a little further on, Habermas writes that this "change of mentality" requires a "becoming reflexive" of religious consciousness following the example of the "change in epistemic attitudes following the Reformation in the Christian churches of the West."[41] Such a transformation is a condition for serious participation in liberal democracy, or even for not forming an imminent threat to it. For intimately connected to the idea that a process similar to Reformation is necessary is the idea that nonreformed religion is characterized by claims of an absolute truth. And these, we have already seen, are connected to religious authoritarianism, obscurantism, and fanaticism. Habermas's postsecular narrative thus remains close to the liberal secular narrative. He remains within the Neo-Kantian interpretation of presumably nonreflexive religion in the way that Mahmood analyzes; he even identifies Islam in general with it. (Please note that the German original is more generally about Islam than the official English translation of the passage suggests.) In his general view of Islam, Habermas thus seems quite clearly dependent on earlier European imaginaries: Voltaire's *Mahomet ou le fanatisme* is famous in this regard, but it is also important to know that Kant, although he does not treat Islam systematically, says some occasional things about it in his anthropology; in fact, in the part on mental diseases: "Fanaticism [*Schwärmerei*] . . . the most dangerous human deceptive screen [*Blendwerk*]," leads to extremities such as "putting Muhammad on the throne."[42]

Apart from the fact that Habermas generalizes about Muslims in terms of how their presumed orthodoxy would determine their identities in a liberal democracy, the idea that Islam should follow a track along a Protestant model testifies to a rather unreflected Eurocentrism in Habermas's thought; here he defends precisely the kind of ideas about importing models from the West that students of colonial and postcolonial thinking are wary of. His remark also testifies to an important lack of knowledge about the history of reform-thinking within Islamic traditions by locating the emergence of such thought in the quite recent debates about Euro-Islam. Abu Zayd tells an Islam-specific and extensive story about the history of reform in the context of Islam and shows that Islam has its own specific traditions of "reform."[43]

We can drive the argument a little further and suggest, along the track of Asad and Mahmood, that the most problematic aspect of Habermas's view is the idea that "reform" should be desirable unequivocally. Mahmood's critique of secularist interpretations of piety in terms of fundamentalism can help to clarify further how Habermas's view of Islam is related to a problematic nexus in his general understanding of religion and an ambivalence in his postsecularism.

The transformation of Habermas's thought mentioned earlier results at least in part from his reflections on the criticisms that have been leveled against secularism in contemporary liberal political theory in general, more particularly against how it excludes religious attitudes and practices closely related to the ones that Mahmood catches with the term *piety* in the Islamist context. The debate about religion in the public sphere has mostly been held in the context of American political theory, in the context of the Rawlsian idea that it belongs to the "duties of civility" to consider oneself obliged to be able to explain how the principles and policies on fundamental questions one advocates can be supported "by premises we accept and think others could reasonably accept."[44] In the course of this debate, objections against this view were raised saying that this requirement excludes from deliberation about justice those citizens whose "comprehensive doctrines" stand in the way of translating their religious concepts of justice into secular language. Although this is not the case for all religious citizens, it is for a substantial number among them, namely for those who cannot or do not want to substitute every religious argument they might have for a particular concept of justice with a moral, universalizable one.

Habermas acknowledges the exclusionary effects of Rawlsian secularism and also thinks that this is an *unjust* and *unnecessary* exclusion in a constitutional democracy. Habermas supports the objections against Rawls by putting forward that his critics rightly stress the "central role that religion plays—that is, its seat—in the life of a person of faith. A devout person conducts her daily existence *on the basis* of her faith. Genuine faith is not merely a doctrine, something believed, but is also a source of energy that the person in faith taps into performatively to nurture her whole life."[45] Habermas contrasts faith as "doctrine" with faith as "a source of energy" for life. Thus, he chooses a philosophical language close to one that Mahmood deploys to express the insight that faith is not something mental in the first place but rather forms part of the complex of meanings and practices that precede, as "world disclosure," the formation of specific mental beliefs. A little further on, Habermas uses the term "to lead a devout life" to designate such an understanding of religion. And a little further, in his discussion of the Protestant reaction to Kantianism exemplified by Schleiermacher, Habermas makes clear that post-Kantian thought developed possibilities at an early stage for understanding religion as a source of communication with the world fundamentally different from what could be achieved by understanding and reason and as a valuable source of morality in itself. Here he explicitly uses the notion of piety to explain the distinction between the dogmatic content of religion and the "piety [*Frömmigkeit*] that inspires and sustains the personal conduct of the believer."[46]

Yet there is something peculiar about Habermas's formulation about "genuine faith" as a source of energy and not merely a doctrine. It nearly imputes a certain dilution of genuineness on the person of faith who *can* (or at least wants to) translate her faith-based conceptions of justice into secular political doctrines, and who is, on the rationalist account of politics, the less problematic citizen. This distinction reminds us of the distinction between "true" faith and "reformed" faith from the quote about Islam's desirable transformation that I analyzed at the beginning of this section. It sensitizes us to an ambivalence on Habermas's part about the requirement to take a historical-hermeneutical or reflexive approach to one's religious truths.

The fact that he still deems this transformation desirable is consistent with how he, typical for contemporary secularists, translates the specific dissonance between faith as doctrine and as a source of energy into another one, when, in his further comments in the passage just quoted, he says that the "*totalizing* trait [*totalisierender Zug*] of a form of faith that permeates the pores of daily life" can make it impossible to translate religiously rooted political convictions into another "cognitive" domain.[47] Here "genuine faith" as a source of energy becomes implicitly connected to a "totalizing trait," which is a term having an immediate political ring to it, and which Habermas later on casually connects with a "reference to dogmatic authority of an inviolable core of infallible revealed truths." By thus proposing a conception of religion whose genuineness is an immediate cause of its being totalizing, Habermas places himself in the tradition of modernist thinking in which "deep belief" is, on one hand, venerated as *genuine* and *authentic* (and as at least one possible way of being guided by something other than cold, dispassionate and ultimately destructive rationality) and, on the other hand, something to be kept outside the core domains of politics precisely for its tendency toward irreflexive claims to truth-possession, that is, fanaticism: "once this boundary between faith and knowledge becomes porous ... reason loses its foothold and succumbs to irrational effusion [*Schwärmerei*]."[48]

It is important here to argue, à la Mahmood, that when it comes to religious piety, our tapping into a source of life on one hand and literalist and fanatical truth-possession in the name of a doctrinal totality on the other hand do *not automatically* go hand in hand and might even be on a tense footing, because literalism and ethical transformation might not even go together very well. The notion of discursive traditionality could be of help here. However, the question remains: To what extent and in which contexts does piety not leave room for dogmatism and, moreover, can piety have its own problematic politics, independently of the question if and how it goes together with dogmatism? The problematic political sides of Egyptian Islamism, and Salafism in particular, have been misrecognized by Mahmood in her culturalist understanding of the mosque movement.[49]

I do not think, however, that the criticisms of Mahmood's politically naïve and culturizing account of piety stand in the way of recognizing the validity of her central claim concerning the misunderstanding of piety from within a secularist framework, which remains a useful point to make in the context of debates about secularism and postsecularism. For example, Habermas's casual but intrinsic link between piety and fanaticism suggests that he, in the manner of the secularism that Mahmood criticizes, remains within the secularist epistemic frame for understanding piety, linking piety implicitly and automatically to potential political violence against those who do not possess the truth, or at least to their misrecognition of the truth, more so than "secular," or reflexive, doctrines and views.[50] Another critique of Habermas should be that, by suggesting that established religious traditions within Europe have achieved this kind of secularity while other religious traditions still have to begin doing so, he might be overestimating both secular and religious constituencies in Europe as well as spreading prejudice about Islam and Muslims; talking about Islam, he loses sight of the ambivalence toward "genuine faith" that he displays when talking about it in general terms.

Conclusion

We need to revise further Habermas's notion of postsecularism on two accounts. We should ask what it means when political philosophers keep debating secularism and religion in the public sphere when they are mostly addressing dogmatism, and indeed fanaticism, be it religious or political or both. Fanaticism is a complicated concept with a complicated history; it connotes both religion and piety but also secular millenarian and totalitarian doctrines and perhaps even other principles. Although the concept came up in early Christianity to denounce religiously abject doctrines and practices especially when they had politically deviant strands, modern English and French uses of the concept have generally not been confined to religious contexts. In the modern era, the concept has been mediating between religion, psychology, and politics. Conceptual historians Reinhart and Conze define fanaticism as "an aggressive form of affect of special strength and endurance, mostly in the service of an idea."[51] So they include the many references to fanaticism in terms of modern millenarian, iconoclastic, and revolutionary discourses that tend to go along with a politics wanting to realize a better world, perhaps even by violent means.[52]

Thus, if fanaticism is the problem, it consists of less *and* more than religion (or piety), of something different, unless we want to sweep away modern political history. Using the language of "secularism" is misleading here, even if we focus on belief instead of on religion. In the opposition that secularists, including Habermas, uphold between "secular" thinking on one hand and totalizing, irreflexive truth claims on the other, no account is given of the secular history of fanaticism, and we can see how deeply problematic the language of secularism is, *even* if we take seriously the project of distinguishing between these two kinds of intentions, or rather intensities, in politics.

However, we also need to criticize the idea that we can identify problematic forms of political thinking on the basis of the perceived *irreflexivity* and *intensity* of the beliefs motivating them alone. Reinhart and Conze warn us that fanaticism is a concept that one mostly uses to "designate the enemy—and therefore a word belonging to religious and political polemics [which is] linked to historical movements."[53] The problem with the language of secularism is that it locates the cause of violent political action in a strong belief, instead of in specific political-historical contexts, which may be at the basis of strong beliefs that something is radically wrong with the world as it is, which in turn may prompt the thought that something needs to be radically changed, through violent means if necessary. Presenting the intensity or irreflexivity of beliefs as the root cause of violence, however, has always been a political act obfuscating more political-historical and material perspectives. As the Italian-British sociologist Alberto Toscano argues, fanaticism always implies a discourse of "fanaticization"; we have to take into account the political imaginaries and realities surrounding its construction as well.[54] What liberal theory needs much more to take into account is the *content* of the doctrines or attitudes we are talking about instead of their literalist, pious, or secular, protestant, or reflexive forms.

Both Habermas and Mahmood, each in their own ways, deal with questions of secularity and postsecularity by including piety in their notion of religion, thus criticizing the concentration on doctrine in usual understandings of religion and opening up new spaces for rethinking the legitimate place of religion in politics. Taking seriously the notion of piety, either Mahmood's or even Habermas's more ambivalent version of it, can help us problematize the still prevailing understanding of religion in terms of doctrines or beliefs that form a legacy of modern European intellectual history in which mentalist, either Protestant or secular-modern, understandings of religion have long been the most accepted ones—though not the only ones, not even within Protestantism, as Asad and Mahmood tend to suggest.

Taking the piety argument seriously would for example help us see the problems of the translation of *religion* into the Rawlsian notion of the "comprehensive doctrine." This notion, which comprises both religious and (secular) metaphysical totalizing views of the good and of truth in the Rawlsian system, has the advantage of including secular comprehensive views as possibly problematic, instead of concentrating on religion alone. In that sense it forms a powerful antidote against the secular-religious divide in political philosophy. Yet the notion has a disadvantage which unfortunately more or less balances this advantage. As was the case in the rationalist interpretations of religion, talking about comprehensive *doctrines*, we lose sight of the habitual, practical, nondoctrinal dimensions of faith, which are precisely the dimensions that complicate the rationalism implicit in the history of secularism, and which have been a central stake for postsecularism to overcome, as we can learn from Mahmood's, Habermas's, and Asad's arguments.[55]

At this point, I find myself not to be entirely in agreement with comparative political theorist Andrew March, who has written a powerful critique of

Mahmood's interpretation of the Danish cartoon affair.[56] In her interpretation of that affair, Mahmood tries to make the affective dimension of Muslim veneration for Mohammed understandable to a secular public. She thinks this public has difficulty doing so, because it tends to conceive of religion as a doctrine that you can either have or not have (very similar to her protest against understanding piety in terms of literalism). In his reaction to that claim, March argues against Mahmood and others: "In their eagerness to set up secularizing Western Protestantism as a foil and an explanation for the failure of many to understand Muslim injury, it seems to me that scholars following Asad's lead have set up an utterly unconvincing opposition between habitus, affect, and embodiment on the one hand and a concern with proposition, truth, and belief on the other. In doing so they exclude so much that is central to Islamic discursive traditions of piety and morality."[57] By concentrating on the piety side of Islamic belief, March suggests, Asad and other scholars, especially Mahmood, lose sight of the fact that there *is* after all also a dogmatic and doctrinaire part of Islamic belief; in so doing, they even tend to give their own overly secular interpretation of the actions and emotions of Muslims and thus evade to talk about theological content.[58] March's point converges with my point, where I ask about the *actual* relations between dogmatism and piety; March argues that dogma *can and does* form part of Islam and that this is neglected by Asad et al. Yet Asad et al. do not argue for an opposition between habitus and belief, as March suggests, but rather, in the phenomenological vein, for the inclusion of dogma as part of a discursive tradition that merges habitus and belief instead of separating them as the rationalist tradition has done. Moreover, March too easily and quickly relativizes the claim that this insight has been lost from sight in secularist discourses about religion and the problems of "truth claiming." This tradition has been so absorbed by the idea that metaphysics and religion imply an unreflexive "truth-claiming" of deeply static, even unmovable transcendental grounds or foundations of our empirical being that the correction in terms of piety and anti-rationalism cannot just be rejected as a foil, constructed by some mistaken belief in the wrongness of Western secularity.

I would like to add that the inclusion of piety as a way of being—instead of merely a doctrine, and, by extension, a more general reflection on how ways of being relate to beliefs (partly available in Taylor, *Secular*, and Habermas, *Naturalism*)—is only one step in the right direction. By concentrating on piety and how this is misunderstood from within secularist, rationalist frameworks, both Habermas and Mahmood tend to either circumvent the troubles posed by religion in context or reduce these troubles to dogmatism or fanaticism.[22] I have already mentioned that by taking piety more or less for granted as a way of being, they tend to leave unmentioned the political context of piety and the earthly ways in which individuals are never just or even mainly religious or pious.[59]

Second, the piety argument should lead us to more fully problematize the relative deliberative immunity of the pious, precisely insofar as they make strong and dogmatic truth claims on the basis of their piety and claim exemption from the need to explain themselves to nonbelievers—except that we should not presuppose they do so. If we take seriously the piety argument, this is only a bigger reason to resist patriarchal, exclusionary, or otherwise problematic claims in the name of religion instead of taking them as the logical expression of that which religion quite naturally does and is. A reply to this argument could be that I am reintroducing a harsh version of secularism through the backdoor, but I submit that I do not, because I question the religious-secular framework in the first place. Religion is much less exceptional than the secular-liberal tradition tends to lead us to believe.

A first "bad" legacy of secular liberalism, I argue, one that both Habermas and Mahmood want to remedy, is liberalism's attempt to develop an a priori criterion for the exclusion of metaphysical or religious arguments from the public sphere. However, they tend to forget to address also the second "bad" legacy, which has been the formalist focus on intensities and the reflexivity of beliefs to evaluate the validity of certain arguments and attitudes in politics. If we took the piety argument more seriously, we would see that piety's arguments can go in many political directions, and there would be no excuse to leave patriarchal, exclusionary, or neoliberal sides of piety unquestioned, just because they fit our ideas of what religions are. Political philosophers in the liberal tradition have tended to limit themselves to defining the formal dimensions of political deliberation causing that they have perhaps become a little too wary of also acting as social critics or as historians of social formations. Asad and Mahmood, following in the footsteps of Foucault, have tended to be much more sensitive to the historical dimensions of both religious and secular formations, yet they lose sight of this historicity in their opposition against Western secularism which impoverishes the force of their analysis.[60]

In sum, the idea that religion quite naturally goes together with exclusionary, fanatical, or patriarchal politics should be criticized much more thoroughly than has been done in those debates that remain within the secularity-religion framework. Religion—insofar as it is at least partly practice, attitude, openness to the world—can include protests against inequality or injustice; it can lead one to leave the social causes of inequality and injustice unquestioned as well as inspire, even teach, strong criticism of such injustice and inequality.[61] This point may sound like an "old saw" for religious persons, theologians, and anthropologists; nevertheless, it has to be made, both in contemporary Euro-American and in Islamic public spheres, which have all been heavily affected by the conceptual history of secular liberalism. Furthermore, even a boundary such as *fanaticism* is actually a relational concept, in which we always have to take into account who accuses whom of being fanatical: the political-discursive context can only determine the legitimacy of certain epithets, and contemporary political theory has lost sight of this. There is no "good religion" or "bad religion"; everything depends on more than religion.

Notes

The research on which this essay is based was part of the project The Sacred and the Secular: Genealogies of Self, State, and Society in the Contemporary Islamic World, funded under the Future of the Religious Past program. An earlier version of this essay was published as "Postsecularism, Piety, and Fanaticism: Reflections on Saba Mahmood's and Jürgen Habermas' Critiques of Secularism," *Philosophy and Social Criticism* 37 (2011): 977–998. I would like to thank Sudeep Dasgupta, Elizabeth Shakman Hurd, Michiel Leezenberg, Jonas Jakobsen, Sindre Bangstad, Irena Rosenthal, Martin van Bruinessen, and Robin Celikates, for their helpful comments, and Michael Koch and Jasmijn Leeuwenkamp for their meticulous editing work.

1. Jürgen Habermas, "Die Dialektik der Säkularisierung," *Blätter für deutsche und internationale Politik* 53 (2008): 33–46; translated into English as "Notes on a Postsecular Society," http://www.signandsight.com/features/1714.html.

2. Jürgen Habermas, *Between Naturalism and Religion: Philosophical Essays* (Cambridge: Polity Press, 2008), 128.

3. Talal Asad, *Formations of the Secular: Christianity, Islam, Modernity* (Stanford, CA: Stanford University Press, 2003), 25.

4. See Saba Mahmood, *Politics of Piety: The Islamic Revival and the Feminist Subject* (Princeton, NJ: Princeton University Press, 2005); Saba Mahmood, "Secularism, Hermeneutics, and Empire: The Politics of Islamic Reformation," *Public Culture* 18 (2006): 323–347; Talal Asad, *Genealogies of Religion: Discipline and Reasons of Power in Christianity and Islam* (Baltimore, MD: Johns Hopkins University Press, 2003); and Asad, *Formations*. See also Elizabeth Shakman Hurd, *The Politics of Secularism in International Relations* (Princeton, NJ: Princeton University Press, 2009).

5. Mahmood, "Secularism," 327.

6. Mahmood's examples include Nasr Hamid Abu Zayd, Abdul Karim Soroush, and Hasan Hanafi. Soroush has sometimes been called the "Luther of Islam."

7. Habermas, "Dialektik," 10.

8. See Ramin Jahanbegloo and Danny Postel, "Ideas Whose Time Has Come: An Interview with Iranian Philosopher Ramin Jahanbegloo," *Logos* 5, no. 2 (2006), http://www.logosjournal.com/issue_5.2/jahanbegloo_interview.htm. See also Nasr Hamid Abu Zayd,

Reformation of Islamic Thought: A Critical Historical Analysis (Amsterdam: Amsterdam University Press, 2006). On Habermas's eightieth birthday (June 10, 2009), the German newspaper *Die Zeit* even carried the headline "Weltmacht Habermas" (World-Power Habermas), a title that in all its exaggeration touches upon the influence of Habermasian ideas and frameworks today.

9. Brian Turner, "The Price of Piety," *Contemporary Islam* 2 (2008): 1–6.

10. See, for example, Sindre Bangstad, "Saba Mahmood and Anthropological Feminism After Virtue," *Theory, Culture and Society* 28 (2011): 28–54; Andrew March, "Speech and the Sacred: Does the Defense of Free Speech Rest on a Mistake about Religion?" *Political Theory* 40 (2012): 318–345.

11. This is in fact a rather idiosyncratic and tendentious translation of *da'wa*, which is commonly rendered as "call," "exhortation," or, more recently, "propaganda." I will return to this point below.

12. Quoted in Mahmood, *Politics*, 51. Attempts to explain religious piety to secular persons have recently often adopted (existentialist) terminology in terms of "ways of being, manners of existence" and are not confined to Islamic discourse. In 2005, during a conference on *laïcité* in Paris, the Jewish-American sociologist Adam Seligman eloquently castigated the scholars gathered in a republican room at the École Normale Supérieure for their conception of religion in terms of identity, and he argued that for many religious people, religion was a "way of being" instead (personal notes, YJ). Talal Asad uses the same wording in his comments of the headscarf law; see Asad, "Trying to Understand French Secularism," in *Political Theologies*, ed. Hent de Vries and Lawrence Sullivan (New York: Fordham University Press, 2006), 493–526, esp. 501. As I will show, the same register is also dear to Habermas in his reflections on religious expression in the public sphere. Interestingly, we find this notion also in Sayyid Qutb's *Milestones*: "Islam is not a 'theory' based on 'assumptions,' but is rather a 'way of life' working with 'actuality.'" Sayyid Qutb, *Milestones (Ma'alim fi al-Tariq)*, (New Delhi: Islamic Book Service, 2006), 25.

13. Mahmood, *Politics*, 23.

14. Mahmood, 5.

15. Similar interpretations of (Neo-)Kantian ethics return frequently among this strand of criticism of liberal secularism. Mahmood states that "the Kantian model of autonomous reason [is] underlying the secular concept of religion." Mahmood, "Secularism," 345. This is in line with Hirschkind when he writes about "the Kantian demand that reason be exercised autonomously and embodied in the sovereign subject"; see Charles Hirschkind, "Heresy or Hermeneutics: The Case of Nasr Hamid Abu Zayd," *Stanford Humanities Review* 5 (1995): 36. From a philosophical perspective, this is an overly schematic representation of Kantian normativity, but I will take it for granted for the moment that similarly schematic interpretations of subjectivity and normativity did indeed influence modernist versions of liberalism. I do not take into account, then, the intra-philosophical critiques of Kantianism ranging from Hegel to Kierkegaard, Heidegger, and Wittgenstein.

16. Mahmood, *Politics*, 24.

17. Mahmood, 23.

18. Mahmood, 128. For a more extensive critique of Mahmood's reading of the late Foucault, see Karen Vintges, "Muslim Women in the Western Media: Foucault, Agency, Governmentality and Ethics," *European Journal of Women Studies* 19 (2012): 283–298.

19. Immanuel Kant, "Perpetual Peace," in *Political Writings* (Cambridge: Cambridge University Press, 1991), 114; quoted in Asad, *Genealogies*.

20. Nasir Hamid Abu Zayd, *Naqd al-khitab al-dini* [*Critique of Religious Discourse*] (Cairo: Maktabat Madbuli, 1995), 193; quoted in Mahmood, "Secularism," 339.

21. Mahmood, *Politics*, 115.

22. Mahmood, "Secularism," 336.

23. Mahmood, 344.

24. See Charles Hirschkind, "Heresy or Hermeneutics: The Case of Nasr Hamid Abu Zayd," *Stanford Humanities Review* 5, no. 1 (1996): 35–49; and Abu Zayd, "The Case of Abu Zaid," *Index on Censorship* 25, no. 4 (1996): 30–39.

25. See Abu Zayd, *Reformation of Islamic Thought*; see also Michiel Leezenberg, "How Ethnocentric Is the Concept of the Postsecular?," in *Exploring the Postsecular: The Religious, the Political, and the Urban*, ed. Arie L. Molendijk, Justin Beaumont, and Christoph Jedan (Leiden: Brill, 2010).

26. See Abu Zayd, *Reformation of Islamic Thought*, 99.

27. For a close reading of the court ruling, see Kilian Bälz, "Submitting Faith to Judicial Scrutiny Through the Tamily Trial: The Abu Zayd Case," *Die Welt des Islams*, 37 (1997): 135–155. It is an understatement, and to my mind a morally and politically dubious one, to write, as Mahmood does, that Abu Zayd "migrated" to the Netherlands; Mahmood, "Secularism," 337

28. Hirschkind, "Heresy," 45. I appreciate Hirschkind and Mahmood's courage to go against received opinion. My problem is that they paint a picture of the Islamist side that fails to provide essential information; moreover, Hirschkind and Mahmood suggest a consensus about these issues among Islamic scholars that is nonexistent, and this risks to make them into partisans of those who present themselves as *the* legitimate voice of the Islamic tradition.

29. See also Abu Zayd, *Reformation*, 93–100.

30. Abu Zayd, *Naqd*, 56, quoted in Mahmood, "Secularism," 339.

31. Mahmood, "Secularism," 339.

32. John Calvert, "Sayyid Qutb and the Power of Political Myth: Insights from Sorel," *Historical Reflections* 3 (2004): 509–528.

33. Mahmood discusses this in *Politics*, 57.

34. The traditional notion of *da'wa* turned into a modern Islamist one in early twentieth-century Egypt, when it was advocated for example by Rashid Rida (1865–1930), who inspired the early Muslim Brotherhood and the Salafi movement. Rida taught that *da'wa* is an obligation for each individual, instead of only for religious teachers, as was the traditional interpretation.

35. Asad, "Trying," 501.

36. See Yolande Jansen, "Secularism and Security: France, Islam, Europe," in *Comparative Secularisms in a Global Age*, ed. Linell Cady and Elizabeth Shakman Hurd (Basingstroke, UK: Palgrave Macmillan, 2010), 94–115.

37. We can trace the interwovenness in French and Algerian cultural memory of Islamic claims with piety and political violence through, for example, the artistic work of Gillo Pontecorvo, Yasmina Bachir-Chouikh, Tahar Djaout, and Boualem Sansal.

38. For example, an implicit link between pious religious practices and the potential for violence has played a more important role in the context of the French headscarf debates than is usually acknowledged. The motive that constituted the broad consensus for banning the scarves from school was not a wish to generally ban religious expression from the public sphere, although this was a motive for some secularist die-hards. The consensus, though, was based on a shared suspicion of the politics that might be "*derrière le voile*" (behind the veil); see Jansen, "Secularism and Security."

39. Charles Taylor traces strands of this genealogy in *A Secular Age* (Cambridge, MA: Harvard University Press, 2007); see the entries on fanaticism in the index.

40. Habermas, "Dialektik," 44–45.

41. Habermas, 10.

42. Immanuel Kant, *Anthrolopogie in pragmatischer Hinsicht*, in *Sämtliche Werke*, ed. F. Rosenkranz and F. W. Schubert (Leipzig: Voss 1838 [1764]), 7.2:25. For a longer explanation on Voltaire's interpretation of fanaticism in Islam, see Dominique Colas, *Civil Society and Fanaticism: Conjoined Histories* (Stanford, CA: Stanford University Press, 1997). For a more detailed interpretation of how Kant and Hegel saw Islam generally as a religion by its very nature bordering on fanaticism, see Alberto Toscano, "Fanaticism: A Brief History of the Concept," *Eurozine* 2006, https://www.eurozine.com/fanaticism-a-brief-history-of-the-concept/; and Alberto Toscano, *Fanaticism, on the Uses of an Idea* (London: Verso, 2010). See also Michiel Leezenberg, "How Ethnocentric Is the Concept of the Postsecular?," in *Exploring the Postsecular: The Religious, the Political, and the Urban*, ed. Arie L. Molendijk, Justin Beaumont and Christoph Jedan (Leiden: Brill, 2010). Leezenberg also gives an account of modernist and secularist strands in Habermas's notion of postsecularity. See also Anna Blijdenstein's *Liberalism's Dangerous Religions: Enlightenment Legacies in Political Theory* (2021, University of Amsterdam). Blijdenstein further elaborates on the Enlightenment conceptual history of "fanaticism" and other concepts related to Judaism and Islam, and then uses her analyses to trace the genealogies of contemporary liberal political theoretical assumptions about religion and religious freedom.

43. There were many longtime interactions between European Enlightenment thinking and critical Islamic intellectuals such as Mohammed Abduh (1849–1905), Rifaat Al-Tahtawi (1801–1883), Namik Kemal (1840–1888), and Taha Hussein (1889–1973); see Bassam Tibi, "Europeanizing Islam or the Islamization of Europe: Political Democracy vs. Cultural Difference," in *Religion in an Expanding Europe*, ed. Timothy Byrnes and Peter Katzenstein (Cambridge: Cambridge University Press, 2006), 209–224. Locating the emergence of reform in the debates about Euro-Islam is especially problematic, because Bassam Tibi, who invented the term *Euro-Islam*, is not an uncontested authority on Islam but a strongly

secularist and contested political thinker. See, for example, Hakan Yavuz's illuminating comments on Tibi in "Islam and Europeanization in Turkish-Muslim Socio-Political Movements," in Byrnes and Katzenstein, *Religion*, 225–254.

44. John Rawls, "The Idea of Public Reason Revisited," *University of Chicago Law Review* 64 (1997): 786.

45. Habermas, *Naturalism*, 127.

46. Habermas, 233. Habermas bases this distinction on the Augustinian distinction between *fides quae creditur*, the faith whose content is believed, and *fides qua creditur*, faith in the sense of the act of believing. Habermas nicely explains how piety, as a Schleiermacherian transcendental notion of religiosity, can be based on a sharable human experience of "absolute dependence on an other," in contrast to autonomy, within a post-Kantian notion of subjectivity.

47. Habermas, 127; italics mine.

48. Habermas, 243. The German term *Schwärmerei* has more ambivalent, less immediately political connotations than *fanaticism*. The translator uses "irrational effusion" for *Schwärmerei*, but inserts the German term as well, for good reasons. "Irrational effusion" better connotes the reference to an affective, deeply religious experience, that is, *piety* in the German *Schwärmerei*, than *fanaticism*, but it loses the fact that *Schwärmerei* and *fanaticism* have been treated as equivalent for centuries; see Werner Conze and Helga Reinhart, "Fanatismus," *Geschichtliche Grundbegriffe: Historisches Lexikon zur politisch-sozialen Sprache in Deutschland* (Stuttgart: Ernst Klett Verlag, 1975), 303–327. Precritical, metaphysical *Schwärmerei* is what Habermas generally ascribes to contemporary Islamic philosophy on the same page (243). For the link between fanaticism and totalitarianism in historical perspective, see Colas, *Civil Society*, and, more critically, Toscano, *Fanaticism*.

49. On the political, "worldly" aspects of the mosque movement, see Asef Bayat, *Making Islam Democratic: Social Movements and the Post-Islamist Turn* (Stanford, CA: Stanford University Press, 2007). On the question of how Mahmood's neglect of these aspects leads her to culturize and essentialize piety, see also Bangstad, "Mahmood."

50. Habermas argues that the recognition foundation of the modern constitutional state implies an "ethos of citizenship" which requires that citizens deliberate about what is reasonable. This necessitates each citizen respecting every other citizen as her equal in principle, and neither a generalized rejection of the ultimate motives of religious actors by secularist majorities nor a generalized rejection of the ultimate motives of secular persons by religious persons in possession of "truth" can be reconciled with that basic principle of equal respect. So the burden is on both sides: reflexivity toward one's proper truths is necessary both for religious and nonreligious persons.

51. Conze and Reinhart, "Fanatismus," 303; my translation.

52. Interestingly, as early as 1846, German sociologist Ruge ascribed the tendency toward political violence rather to secular, political forms of *Schwärmerei* than to religious forms.

53. Conze and Reinhart, "Fanatismus," 303; my translation.

54. Conze and Helga Reinhart in "Fanaticism" and Toscano in *Fanaticism* trace the Constantinian aspects of calling another group fanatical and the dangers of justifying fanatical politics by states against those identified as fanatics. For a related commentary on Charles Taylor's understanding of fanaticism in *A Secular Age*, see John D. Boy, "The Fanatical Counterpublic," *Immanent Frame*, March 2009, http://blogs.ssrc.org/tif/2009/03/12/the-fanatical-counterpublic/.

[22] Mahmood wants us to rethink piety, but she does not touch on the juxtaposition of fanaticism and literalism, nor on the idea that these *would* pose threats to liberal democracy: "The fear is that orthodox Islamic practices—from the veil to public prayers to abidance by rules of sexual segregation—are expressions of a *fanatical literalist mentality* and, as such, a *threat to the entire edifice of our liberal political system*. Thus the unequivocal opposition to U.S. occupation of the Middle East is often seasoned with caveats about the necessity to fight the irrationality of Muslim beliefs and practices through cultural, if not military, means"; Mahmood, "Secularism," 345; my italics.

55. But see also William Connolly, *Why I Am Not a Secularist* (Minneapolis: University of Minnesota Press, 2000).

56. March, "Speech," specifically his discussion of Mahmood, "Religious Reason and Secular Affect: An Incommensurable Divide?," *Critical Inquiry* 35 (2009): 836–862.

57. March, "Speech," 328.

58. For a similar critique of authors representing the "postsecular turn" as remaining firmly within the secular framework, see Gregor McLennan, "The Postsecular Turn," *Theory, Culture, and Society* 27 (2010): 3–20.

59. See also Bangstad, "Mahmood."

60. This problem with genealogies of secularism was first criticized by Jose Casanova, "Rethinking Secularization: A Global Comparative Perspective," *Hedgehog Review* 8 (2006): 7–22.

61. See also Jeremy Waldron, "Secularism and the Limits of Community," *Public Law and Legal Theory Research Paper Series*, working paper no. 10–88, 2010.

CHAPTER 23

Human Rights, Muslim Communities, and the Unintentional Secularization of Canada

Ali Hassan Zaidi

Muslim Canadians, as members of a religiously identified community, have been negotiating their presence and integration in secular Canadian society for many decades now. This search for recognition and integration has in many respects been facilitated by official policies of multiculturalism as well as by a political and civic culture that largely embraces ethnic diversity.[1] In those instances where Muslim communities have found resistance to their needs and demands (e.g., state funding for Islamic schools or Islam-based mediation in family disputes) fuller integration has been sought through appeals to human rights instruments, such as the Canadian Charter of Rights and Freedoms which comprises Part One of the Constitution Act of 1982 (previously its predecessor, the Canadian Human Rights Act of 1977) as well as the Multiculturalism Act of 1988 and the provincial Human Rights Commissions.

Appeals to the charter, to official policies on multiculturalism, and to human rights commissions have been effective means by which Muslim communities in Canada have struggled for equality and identity rights. In some cases, these struggles have brought the issue of religious identity into the public domain and challenged the notion that public space is an inherently secular one. The right to pray in workplaces, the right of Muslim women in Canada to wear *hijab* at school or at work, or the right to take a day off from work for a religious holiday have been hard won and important successes. In most cases, the basis of these victories has been to appeal to rights-based principles of equal recognition and freedom from discrimination. These appeals to rights-based mechanisms seek to extend to Muslim communities analogous rights that already accrue to other identity-based groups defined by race, ethnicity, gender, or sexual orientation.

And yet these victories may have given rise to contradictory influences on the secular public sphere. On the one hand, there is a conscious attempt to resist the secularizing influences of the dominant society. In this, one may speak of a process of re-Islamization: an increase in religious observance, and an expansion of the social fields in which religious identities are made relevant.[2] The outward displays of religious symbols and attire, that is to say, the externalization of religion, may bring a sense of piety to the public sphere, and this may affect the religious consciousness of other individuals, even though the women who wear the *hijab* may or may not have any intention to influence the public sphere, for in many cases it is first and foremost an act of self-discipline and only secondarily a matter of promoting Islam (*da'wa*) in the public sphere.[3] As a response to secularization, one cannot deny the possibility that the wearing of the *hijab* may have some effect on some non-Muslim individuals vis-à-vis the sacred.

On the other hand, in the legal and governmental sphere, that is to say at a structural level, I would argue that by pursuing their search for recognition and integration via the regime of human rights, Muslim minority communities have themselves contributed to the secularization of Canadian society in conscious and unconscious ways. Consciously, some Canadian Muslim groups have actively sought to move toward a more secular understanding of religion. But more interesting is the unintentional displacement or erosion of the sacred from the public sphere by groups that are reacting against the secular public sphere. Indeed, contrary to the view that Muslims are merely subject to processes of secularization, the processes of secularization can also emerge from within Muslim communities as the regulatory capacity of religious authorities decreases, since actual practices of Muslims can occur without reference to mainstream *ulama*.[4] This unintentional erosion of the sacred takes the form of the subjectivization and individualization of religious belief and, in vying for equal rights and integration, of the displacement of the Christian heritage of Canada. Canadian Muslims have therefore had contradictory influences on the secular public sphere.

However, the thesis of this paper is that the unintentional secularizing effects have been stronger than the conscious reactions against secularism. That is to say, dominant structures, such as the furthering entrenchment of liberal secularism through human rights instruments, most likely offset the cultural change desired by religiously oriented Muslim groups in Canada, and these structures actually contribute to the secularization of Canadian Muslims by altering the very process of reasoning that underlies their appeals to human rights principles. This paper argues that because of the necessity of adopting rights-based instruments in their quest for personal and religious equality, and in many cases by narrowly regarding religion as a form of identity politics, Muslim communities in Canada have inadvertently contributed to the secularization of Canadian society. Rights-based instruments, such as the Canadian Charter of Rights and Freedoms, are largely premised upon a secular view that regards religion as a strictly personal and private affair not meant to impinge on the public domain in a meaningful way. Appeals to these sorts of rights-based mechanisms thereby tacitly accept the legitimacy of a secular approach to religion. Hence, in negotiating their presence and integration in secular Canadian society, Muslim Canadians have not always been aware of the extent to which they have themselves aided and abetted the secularization of Canada in their search for equal recognition and integration by buying into the assumptions underlying classical liberal human rights discourses.[5]

Misappropriations

On February 8, 2007, Québec Premier Jean Charest announced the establishment of the Consultation Commission on Accommodation Practices Related to Cultural Differences in response to public discontent concerning reasonable accommodation. The commission came to be known as the Commission on Reasonable Accommodation and it was headed by two respected scholars: the sociologist Gerard Bouchard and the well-regarded political philosopher Charles Taylor. Part of the mandate of the commission was to "formulate recommendations to the government to ensure that accommodation practices conform to Québec's values as a pluralistic, democratic, egalitarian society."[6] The commission had become necessary because of a series of incidents and media reports that had captured the spotlight and created a perceived crisis of accommodation vis-à-vis "the Quebec way of life." Among the incidents and reports was a series of cases brought before the Quebec human rights commissions.

As Bouchard and Taylor note, for approximately twenty years, from 1985 to 2006, court and human rights commissions cases for reasonable accommodation did not receive much media attention; yet when these cases suddenly appeared in the spotlight from 2006 to 2007, the media focused on the place of religion in the public sphere and the debate encompassed a broader concern with the integration of immigrants and minorities.[7] Consequently the commission adopted a broader approach to their problem by reviewing "interculturalism, immigration, secularism and the theme of Quebec identity."[8]

While the struggles for reasonable accommodation and the ensuing victories have in some sense brought the religious back into the public domain, they have also conceded the de facto authority of rights-based instruments precisely because most Muslim community groups seem not to have deeply appreciated the liberal-humanist secular assumptions underlying human rights discourses. For example, the charter and the Multiculturalism Act are each infused with secular assumptions that reduce the public significance of religion, aside from its purely ceremonial use, or else treat it as just another variable of ethnic identity. Both the charter and the Multiculturalism Act mention the rights of religious groups, yet such groups are treated no differently than any other identity-based group. Even more, as a philosophy, multiculturalism finds it much easier to deal with the notion of ethnicity and with ethnic groups, in which religious affiliation is subsumed as simply another element of identity, such as race, gender, language, or sexual orientation. Indeed, Canada's version of multiculturalism, unlike, for example, that of the Netherlands which explicitly recognizes and funds religious communities *qua* religious communities, largely reduces religion to just another component of ethnic identity, such as mother tongue or cuisine. Thus, it is quite likely that in their search for equal recognition and integration many Muslim communities in Canada have been uncritically appropriating the assumptions underlying classical liberal human rights discourses, and in so doing have inadvertently contributed to the secularization of Canadian society.

By relying upon human rights discourse and upon Canada's multiculturalism policies and by accepting the de facto authority of rights-based instruments, Muslim communities have also been confronted by an ethical dilemma when others assert their human rights, also in the name of identity: either Canadian Muslims accept the inherent legitimacy of all identity-based struggles or else they fall prey to a double standard of seeking recognition of their own human rights but denying them to other minority groups. Clearly, this dilemma is most obvious when it comes to same-sex marriage in Canada. The rejection of same-sex marriage by most Muslim community groups leads to a double standard: they fight for their rights in the name of their religious identity but deny identity rights to gays and lesbians. Or else it leads to the emergence of self-declared Muslim "progressives" who seek equal rights for all communities, even if it means breaking with the majority of Muslim groups and radically reinterpreting or reinventing Muslim tradition.[9]

Secularization

Do the public displays of religiosity undermine the classical secularization thesis? After all, rather than being marginalized into the private sphere, since the late-1970s expressions of religiosity have reasserted themselves in the public sphere in a way unimagined by proponents of the secularization thesis.[10] Similarly, Abdul Karim Soroush regards public expressions of religiosity as evidence that secular liberalism has failed as a project, and more broadly as evidence that modern dichotomies of secular public space and private religious space no longer hold.[11]

Yet the definition of secularism is not as straightforward as implied by concepts such as separation of church and state, state neutrality, or removal of religion from the public space, even though these concepts do contain an element of truth.[12] Indeed, Bouchard and Taylor define secularism as comprised of four principles: moral equality of persons; freedom of conscience and religion; state neutrality toward religions; and separation of church and state.[13] Similarly, for Casanova, classical secularization theory actually has three propositions: religious decline, differentiation, and privatization. Casanova argues that while differentiation of spheres is still defensible the other two propositions are not.[14]

But neither of these conceptions of secularization captures the extent to which religious motivations increasingly become detached from otherworldly expectations and shift to this-worldly expectation and actions. From this latter point of view, secularization in Western societies is more encompassing because it involves lowering of the horizon of thought from otherworldly to this-worldly concerns; that is to say, a broader conception of secularization recognizes that in most liberal democratic Western societies basic human purposes are no longer associated primarily with the glorification of God and the salvation of the soul in the heavenly hereafter.[15] Instead, religion has become just one of many social spheres responsible for providing identity, meaning, and purpose in everyday life. Heaven is increasingly brought down to earth through temporal worldly means, that is, through rationalized institutions grounded in scientific and technical knowledges.[16] A long line of sociological scholarship relocates the sacred from the otherworldly, transcendent realm to the this-worldly, secular realm of everyday human activity. But whereas Durkheim famously regarded the social as the sacred, the reenvisioning of the sacred in contemporary times is perhaps most evident in the inviolability that is attached to the individual and to human rights. The individual, rather than the group or the community, becomes the locus of most rights, and human rights are regarded as securing "temporal salvation" for the individual. In his poignant article on human rights and the triumph of the individual, Michael Elliot argues that "just as salvation in the Christian faith is closely linked to the heavenly fate of souls, recognition of and respect for human rights is believed to be integral to the fate of humanity on earth."[17]

The liberal conception of human rights thus sacralizes the individual, that is, makes the individual the sacred. Hence, liberal human rights discourses are secular not only because they largely cast religion to the private sphere, but more subtly in that they *sacralize* the individual. Human rights discourses relocate sacredness from the realm of the divine to the realm of human everyday life.

Human Rights and Secularism

In this section, I want to bring together the two threads that I have been pursuing so far: The Bouchard-Taylor Commission on Reasonable Accommodation and the broader understanding of secularization as sacralization of the individual, which we find epitomized in human rights discourses. Bouchard and Taylor argue that one of the principles of secularization is that the liberal, democratic state must remain neutral toward all religions, although it cannot be indifferent to certain core values, especially basic human rights, the equality of all citizens before the law and popular sovereignty, because these are the constituent values of the political system and they provide its foundation. A democratic, liberal state cannot remain neutral toward them and must assert and defend them. The state must remain neutral toward the fundamental reasons that citizens put forth for their upholding of certain beliefs and values; that is, citizens can agree on the principle of equal respect and dignity without agreeing on the fundamental reasons that underlie that principle.[18]

Bouchard and Taylor cite the example of human rights and freedoms, which a Christian believer may defend by putting forward the idea that God created human beings in His image, whereas a humanist atheist or agnostic would assert that we must acknowledge and defend the equal dignity of all rational beings, while an indigenous person who embraces a holistic conception of the world will maintain that living beings and natural forces are in a complementary, interdependent relationship and that we must consequently grant equal respect to each one, including human beings. These three individuals agree on the principle of human rights and freedoms without agreeing on the fundamental reasons that justify it.

However, does not the very neutrality of the liberal democratic state on the fundamental reasons for protecting human rights already imply a form of secularization? Since human rights are already heavily premised on individual rights, this assumed neutrality actually is not as neutral as it claims to be. Is it not the case that the process of secularization reduces the concern with other-worldly notions of the sacred to a concern with the this-worldly sacralization of the individual?

Let us take seriously the point raised by Bouchard and Taylor that an overlapping consensus can emerge on the practice and implementation of human rights, notwithstanding the different fundamental reasons for doing so, and consider what fundamental reasons Muslims may put forward for their support for human rights. In order to derive an Islamic conception of rights, one may turn to various classical sources, not least the Koran, which refers to the rights of God over individuals, from which stem the rights that spouses have over one another, the rights parents have over their children, and so on. Similarly, in the *Sahifat a-Sajjadiyya*, a collection of devotional prayers and writings attributed to Ali ibn al-Husayn, the great-grandson of the Prophet Muhammad and the Fourth Imam of the Shia, there is a very short treatise called *Risalat al-Huquq*, the Treatise of Rights. In this treatise, the Imam enlists the rights that others have over a person. He begins by listing the rights that God has over a person, the rights that one's own soul, organs, and body have over a person—remember that the notion of sin is the doing of wrong, *zulm*, against oneself—the rights that parents, spouses, children, kin, neighbors, and others in a widening circle have over an individual. Hence, we may infer from this that the classical Islamic sense of rights really emphasizes the rights that others have over us. All of these rights stem from the very basic idea that human beings are defined first and foremost by their relationship to God, and both their responsibilities and rights derive from that relationship.[19] This does not mean that only believers have rights, for indeed because of the primordial nature of human beings as *khalifat Allah* (vicegerents of God) and *'abd Allah* (servants of God), every person is endowed with certain basic rights, even if they rebel against God and their own nature. As Seyyed Hossein Nasr argues, all the rights that we have issue from fulfilling our responsibilities. From an Islamic perspective, as is suggested by the Koran and the *Risalat al-Huquq*, responsibilities—or in contemporary terms, the rights of the other—precede the rights of the self.[20] Hence, notwithstanding the fact that most of the Muslim countries have been signatories to the Universal Declaration of Human Rights, and Muslim and Arab diplomats were active contributors to the drafting of the standards of human rights,[21] there is an important difference in the underlying fundamental reasoning between Islamic conceptions of rights and liberal conceptions of rights.

So far, I have simply agreed with Bouchard and Taylor that, yes, it is possible to reach a consensus on the necessity of human rights despite different fundamental reasons. But Bouchard and Taylor do not go any further to reflect upon the consequences or implications of that consensus for a minority group. Whereas the synthetic ability of Muslim-majority cultures may be strong enough to render liberal, secular human rights discourses compatible with religion-based conceptions of rights and obligations, without necessarily yielding to secularization and individualization that accompanies human rights discourses in the West, the synthetic capacity of minority groups living in Western societies seems to me to be much less secure over the long haul. The predicament of being a minority religious community in a largely secular context determines the way that human rights discourses can be appropriated. In view of the hermeneutic perspective in which the whole determines the meaning of the part (the whole has priority over the particular element, even though the former is constituted by the latter), the appropriation of human rights discourses by Muslim communities in the West, and in Canada in particular, becomes much more problematic because it has the potential to alter the fundamental reasons per se.

The point here is that this overlapping consensus on human rights does have crucial consequences for the fundamental reasons given by Muslim minority communities in the West. In a social context in which the fundamental reasons put forward in the name of religion holds little or no sway in public institutions, would not the fundamental reasons of a minority community be liable to shift toward the fundamental reasons provided by secular advocates of human rights?

Given the unique history of Canada, and the desire to recognize the contributions and distinctiveness of First Nations, and the Anglophone and Francophone heritages, perhaps Canada's constitution goes further than any other to recognize group rights. For example, Section 25 on Equality Rights in the Charter of Rights and Freedoms states that one of its aims is to ameliorate the conditions of disadvantaged individuals or groups, including those that are disadvantaged because of race, national or ethnic origin, color, religion, sex, age, or mental or physical disability. Moreover, in Section 27, the charter states that it should be interpreted in a manner that is consistent with the preservation and enhancement of the multicultural heritage of Canada. Similarly, the Multiculturalism Act of 1988, Section 3, states that it is designed to promote the full and equitable participation of individuals and communities of all origins, recognize the existence of communities whose members share a common origin, foster recognition and appreciation of diverse cultures, and promote reflection and evolving expressions of those cultures.

Yet, both as official policy and as philosophy, multiculturalism finds it much easier to deal with the notion of ethnicity and with ethnic groups, in which religious affiliation is subsumed as simply another element of identity—such as race, gender, language, or sexual orientation—than to deal with religious identity in its own right. Does this mean that the struggle for equality, in the name of a religious identity, has the effect of equating the sacred with a particular group identity? If so, then it would appear that rather than contributing to a more universalistic approach to the sacred and the transcendent, Muslim communities in Canada have inadvertently been part of a process that reduces the sacred to identity politics.

Identity Politics as Secularization

In this section I turn to three issues that have dominated Canadian public discourse and that tie directly into my argument that Canadian Muslims have unintentionally contributed to the secularization of Canadian society: funding for religious schools; faith-based family arbitration; hierarchy of individual rights over group rights.

Funding for Religious Schools

In 1984, the Province of Ontario implemented full funding for Catholic schools, alongside secular public schools. Until then, Catholic school boards received public funding only for primary and middle schools but not for high schools. The decision to fully fund only one religious denominational school system was justified on the basis of the unique history of the Anglophone and Francophone communities, which also differed in religious affiliation (predominantly Protestant versus Catholic), and the constitutional right, enshrined in the British North America Act (1865), for religious minorities (that is, Catholic-minority communities in Protestant-majority areas and vice versa) to educate their children in their own religious traditions.

Not surprisingly, this funding arrangement drew the ire of many religious communities (such as the Jewish, Hindu, and Muslim communities) in Ontario, who also sought public funding for their own religious schools. Until the late-1980s, the argument for inclusiveness and equal rights as expressed by Muslim and other religious groups often took this form: "if funding for other religious schools is not provided, then Christianity ought not to be privileged in public schools either." Specific objections were raised against Catholic school funding, and against the daily recitation of the Lord's Prayer in public schools, which it was argued violated the rights of non-Christian students who had to stand for the recitation of the Lord's Prayer at the beginning of each school day.

Since the equal representation of every religious denominational prayer brought up the unwieldy prospect of every religious group clamoring for its prayer to be recited in public schools, most school boards deemed it easier, fairer, and more in keeping with the increasingly secular basis of Canadian society to remove the Christian prayer. Not surprisingly, in view of these other requests for funding, the province of Ontario decided that it was not feasible to fund all other religious groups and instead essentially prohibited the teaching of religion in public schools, with the Christian Lord's Prayer officially taken out of the daily routine across all public-school boards in Ontario in the late 1980s.[22]

Hence, in the name of identity, minority rights, and inclusivity, Muslim community groups in Canada were thus part of a secularizing process that further eroded a particular expression of the sacred in the public realm. It was not until after September 11, when people suddenly realized that the exclusion of religion from public schools meant that a whole generation of students had grown up without being educated about Islam, or any other religion for that matter, that serious attention was paid to reinstituting expressions of the sacred in public schools.

The removal of religion from public schools, even while Catholic schools continued to be funded, did not entirely appease religious communities that still sought public funding for their own schools. One of the leading Muslim groups in this struggle was the Canadian Islamic Congress (CIC), which joined other religious communities to argue for public funding of all faith-based schools.[23] The CIC regarded itself as the Muslim equivalent of the Canadian Jewish Congress, which is politically and socially active. Yet what the organizers of the CIC did not seem to realize is that the Canadian Jewish Congress is made up largely of reformed, secular Jews, whereas the Muslim members of the CIC would not likely self-identify as secular Muslims but as Muslims who consciously desire to bring religion into the public sphere. This is an important detail because it reinforces the argument that, in attempting to increase its influence in Canadian society, a Muslim organization is inadvertently contributing to the secularization of Canada by following the modus operandi of a secular Jewish organization.

The lack of funding of non-Catholic, religious schools even received attention by the Office of the UN High Commissioner for Human Rights which expressed its concern in 1999 and again in 2005 about the discrimination on the basis of religion in the funding of public schools and urged the province of Ontario to rectify this discrimination. In 1996, appellants representing Jewish and independent Christian schools argued in *Adler v. Ontario (AG)* in front of the Supreme Court of Canada that the lack of funding for independent religious schools was an infringement of the guarantee of freedom of religion. The Supreme Court ruled that the funding of Catholic schools and the lack of funding of independent religious schools did not violate the Charter of Rights and Freedoms.[24] The issue once again became a "hot" topic in 2007 when the provincial Progressive Conservative Party ran on a platform to fully fund all faith-based schools in Ontario. The party lost badly in the election and the leader of the party failed to even gain a seat in the legislature. In 2012, Reva Landau, a Toronto resident who personally believed that no religious school should be publicly funded, nevertheless challenged the discriminatory funding of schools and brought a case to the Superior Court of Ontario. The Canadian Civil Liberties Association intervened in the case and supported Landau. In the end, the Superior Court of Ontario ruled that, although the system of dual funding does discriminate against other religious groups, in light of Canada's particular history it is indeed constitutional.

More importantly for the discussion on secularization, the provincial Progressive Conservative Party's promise to fully fund all faith-based schools had come with the proviso that such schools would also have to adhere to the standards of a common provincial curriculum, including mandatory education in the teaching of evolutionary theory, sex education, and sexual orientation. In effect, funding religious schools would also come with regulating them by a secular education system, not unlike the recommendation to allow faith-based family arbitration which I discuss below.[25] The practice of funding one public secular school board and a separate Catholic school board had already been dismantled by constitutional amendment in a number of provinces, most notably in Quebec and Newfoundland and Labrador, both of which replaced the dual structure with one secular public school system.[26]

Faith-Based Family Arbitration

The Archbishop of Canterbury Rowan Williams caused much furor in England when he broached, in a lecture given in 2004, the possibility of "crafting a just and constructive relationship between Islamic law and the statutory law of the United Kingdom."[27] The debate that emerged had a year earlier already been witnessed in Ontario, when a newly established Muslim institute, the Islamic Institute of Civil Justice (IICJ), proposed making use of the existing Arbitration Act of Ontario to arbitrate family disputes. While this institute was new, Syed Mumtaz Ali, then IICJ president and a retired lawyer, had actually been working for twenty years to bring about Muslim personal law under the auspices of Canadian multiculturalism, which he felt had been unfairly and unjustifiably relegated to resolving issues pertaining to Anglophone, Francophone, and Aboriginal groups. His motivation to bring about the use of Muslim personal law was based in a deep religious sense of worship, and also in a radical disjunction between religious and secular laws. In 1994, Ali wrote:

Muslims of Ontario are also trying to persuade the government to extend some form of autonomy in respect to Muslim personal/family law which they need as an expression of worship and love of Allah—the two elements inherent in its obedience. For Muslims, the *sine qua non* of action is that it be undertaken with the intention of submitting oneself to Allah's Will such that the action is done for the sake of Allah alone. When Muslims are forced to resolve their conflicts under a system that is governed by different motives, Muslims place their spiritual and social lives in dire peril because they are thus made to submit to that which is other than what Allah has ordained for those who wish to submit to Him.[28]

Since this initiative for faith-based arbitration was misperceived as providing new accommodations to Muslims, instead of actually extending existing provisions for faith-based arbitration to Muslims, there was much public controversy. As a result of the furor on the so-called Sharia in Canada debate, the premier of the province of Ontario convened a study by former Attorney General Marion Boyd, who presented her report in December 2004. In her executive summary on the possibility of faith-based family arbitration and law, Boyd writes, "The report concludes that tolerance and accommodation of minority groups who seek to engage in alternative dispute resolution must be balanced against a firm commitment to individual autonomy. . . . It is important to seek solutions that respect not only the *rights of minority groups* within Ontario, but also help individuals within that minority exercise their individual rights with ease."[29]

But even this report did little to quell the controversy, and opponents of the faith-based arbitration only grew more vociferous. Subsequently, in order to quell the controversy and in the face of a looming provincial election, the government of Ontario decided to remove all religious-based family arbitration tribunals. Although the IICJ's parent organization, the Canadian Society of Muslims (CSM), had been pursuing Islamic family mediation as an alternative to the civil court system for many, many years and had done so through the proper channels, in the end, other overtly secular-oriented Muslim groups—such as the Muslim Canadian Congress (MCC) and the Canadian Congress of Muslim Women (CCMW)—helped to ensure the defeat of the Islamic family mediation proposal by politicizing and sensationalizing the debate and raising the specter of Sharia-based corporeal punishments in Canada.

The MCC regarded the proposal for Islamic family law as emergence of Islamic fundamentalism and feared that it would compromise the secular nature of Canadian society. The MCC intentionally chose a name that closely resembled the name of the CIC in order not only to cause confusion but also to challenge the legitimacy of the CIC. The CCMW opposed the family law proposal because they feared that such tribunals would compromise the equality of women. CCMW has repeatedly stated that the rights of religious groups cannot supersede the rights of individual women, nor did they accept the possibility that faith-based arbitration might have provided an opportunity for a reconciliation of religious notions of equity with liberal-individualist conceptions of human rights. Based on their statements in this debate, it is safe to assume that the CCMW considers creating space for the sacred as less important than the concern with equality of women or, at least, that the space for the sacred should not be made on the backs of vulnerable women.

In some sense, the furor created by MCC and CCMW activists replicates the situation in Muslim majority societies where secular Muslims suspect that Islamist groups who participate in liberal, democratic elections are using democratic means to further their own antiliberal, antidemocratic agendas, and that as soon as such Islamists gain power, they will cast aside all liberal democratic pretenses. So, too, the fear and suspicion by MCC and CCMW is that the advocates of alternative family dispute resolution will cast aside the Canadian legal and constitutional framework.

Such fears and suspicions do not recognize the extent to which religiously oriented Muslim groups undergo a process of secularization by engaging with the legal, constitutional, and institutional framework. They have to come to accept the legitimacy of the framework; they recognize it as the standard.

Hierarchy of Rights

Are human rights necessarily individualistic or can they accrue to groups? Or is it possible that rights can be asserted in the name of groups? I have already referred to the protection of group rights enshrined in Canada's constitution. However, one of the most interesting developments over the past few years has been the calls to rank rights or to create a hierarchy of rights. The quest for greater recognition and integration by minority groups, and especially by Muslim communities, is propelling Canadian society to be much clearer about its fundamental values, one of which is the inviolability of individual rights over and above group rights. In other words, Canadian society is beginning to develop a hierarchy of rights that was not clearly stated in its constitution.

Among the various international declarations or bills of rights, perhaps the Canadian Charter of Rights and Freedoms is one of the best examples, if not the best, of trying to balance the rights of individuals with the rights of communities and groups. But the delicate balance between group and individual rights that was envisioned in the Canadian Charter of Rights and Freedoms is being challenged by demands for a hierarchy of rights that would privilege individual rights, particularly rights of gender equality, ahead of group rights, that is, the rights of religious minorities such as Muslims and Orthodox Jews.[30]

The question of individual rights versus group rights was implicitly examined when gay marriage was legalized in Canada in 2005, and opponents were concerned that religious communities would be compelled to perform such marriages in their houses of worship even if they did not agree to it. Opponents of gay marriage were concerned that the sanctity and rights of the individual could be viewed as the trump card that supersedes all other rights, including the right of religious freedom. The concern was allayed somewhat by referring to group rights as enshrined in the Canadian Charter of Rights and Freedoms, although there is a theoretical possibility that a gay or lesbian couple could challenge a religious institution to perform their wedding ceremony.

However, in light of the faith-based arbitration issue, calls for a clearer statement on a hierarchy of rights have been growing. Many of these calls point to Article 28 of the Canadian charter which mentions that none of the rights enshrined therein ought to be interpreted to detract from the fundamental equality of men and women. Article 28 was in fact specifically included to address the concerns of women's groups that some group rights could minimize their individual rights.

For instance, as a reaction to the "Sharia in Canada" debate, in 2005 the Quebec council on the Status of Women put forth a proposal to amend the Quebec Charter of Rights and Freedoms so as to enshrine the primacy of gender equality over rights of religious communities.[31] This council also recommends that public employees be forbidden to wear religious symbols that convey a sexist image or convey patriarchal domination. Perhaps it should come as no surprise that this kind of recommendation is coming first of all from Quebec where the French-speaking majority have come to *perceive* the demands of Muslim minorities as beyond the limits of reasonable accommodation in a secular society.

What does this need to delineate clearly the hierarchy of individual and women's rights over the rights of religious groups imply for the expression of religion in the public sphere? Is it perhaps the clearest statement that secularization underlines liberal discourses of rights? For example, Bouchard and Taylor state in their report on reasonable accommodation that "the subjective interpretation of religion concurs with the broader category of freedom of conscience, which seeks to ensure that individuals are free to adopt the religious, spiritual or secular beliefs or fundamental reasons of their choice."[32]

The privileging of individual rights over against group rights would again seem to confirm the individualization of belief and practice. In other words, the secular-liberal basis of Canadian society is being further clarified by having to take a specific stance on the rights of individuals over and above the rights of groups. Canadian liberal secularism is being forced to be clearer about itself, and it is consistently choosing the path of the sacralization of the individual. Does the individualization of belief not contribute to the secularization of belief, especially when we regard the secular as emphasizing the inviolability of the individual?

Conclusion

Although Muslim community groups in Canada have struggled to bring Islam into the public domain, they have also been part of the process that further reduces expressions of the sacred in the public domain or else reduces it to identity politics.

To what extent are manifestations of Islamic identity regarded as religious in nature—that is, as evocative of the search for the sacred—by non-Muslims and to what extent are such manifestations regarded as just another form of ethnic identity, of identity politics? It seems to me that the manifestation of religious identity in the public sphere is in fact a reduced conception of the religious, the otherworldly, the sacred. The manifestation of religious identity in the public sphere, that is, the externalization of religion, is akin to the manifestation of other forms of ethnic, racial, and sexual identities in the public sphere.

The fundamental reasons themselves, or perhaps the fundamental reasoning itself, becomes altered in the very process of appealing to liberal human rights. In their appeals to the charter for recognition and integration in Canadian society, Muslim minority communities may lose sight of the Divine Source and sacred nature of rights and obligations and may appropriate the sacralization of the individual underpinning the liberal privileging of the individual over the collective. Recent debate and commission findings have tended to come down decisively on the side of individual rights over group rights, thereby contributing to the subjectivization of religion.

Notes

1. Some of the legitimate criticism made by anti-racist activists is that multiculturalism largely conceals the structural inequality in Canadian society by privileging cultural displays over economic integration and racial equity. See Jasmin Zine, "Unsettling the Nation: Gender, Race, and Muslim Cultural Politics in Canada," *Studies in Ethnicity and Nationalism* 9, no. 1 (2009): 151 and 160–161.

2. Sindre Bangstad, *Global Flows, Local Appropriations: Facets of Secularisation and Re-Islamization Among Contemporary Cape Muslims* (Amsterdam: Amsterdam University Press, 2007), 10–11.

3. I am grateful to Arzu Unal and Jeanette Jouili for bringing this important point to my attention. See also Sajida Alvi, Homa Hoodfar, and Sheila McDonough, eds., *The Muslim Veil in North America: Issues and Debates* (Toronto: Canadian Scholar's Press, 2003).

4. Bangstad, *Global Flows, Local Approriations*, 10.

5. Although I will focus on Muslim communities in Canada, it will be evident that my reflections also apply to many other Muslim-minority contexts. Indeed, we need not think only of Western Europe or Australia but can also think of South Africa (see Bangstad, *Global Flows, Local Appropriations*).

6. Gerard Bouchard and Charles Taylor, *Building the Future: A Time for Reconciliation*, report of the Commission de consultation sur les pratiques d'accommodement reliées aux différences culturelles (Quebec City: Gouvernement du Québec, 2008), 17, https://numerique.banq.qc.ca/patrimoine/details/52327/1565995.

7. Bouchard and Taylor, 53.

8. Bouchard and Taylor, 17.

9. See, for example, Scott Siraj al-Haqq Kugle, "Sexuality, Diversity, and Ethics in the Agenda of Progressive Muslims," in *Progressive Muslims: On Justice, Gender, and Pluralism*, ed. Omid Safi (Oxford: Oneworld, 2003). In Canada, two organizations have voiced their support for same-sex rights: Salaam Canada, a Muslim gay rights group, and the Muslim Canadian Congress (MCC), a self-declared progressive, secular-oriented organization.

10. José Casanova, *Public Religions in the Modern World* (Chicago: University of Chicago Press, 1994).

11. Michiel Leezenberg, "Enlightenment and Philosophy in Islam: An Interview with Abdolkarim Soroush," *ISIM Review* 20 (Autumn 2007): 36–37, https://openaccess.leiden univ.nl/handle/1887/17190.

12. Bouchard and Taylor, *Building the Future*, 135.

13. In the aftermath of the 2017 mass murder of six Muslim men at a Québec City mosque by a right-wing extremist, both Bouchard and Taylor repudiated the aspects of their report that proposed a ban on religious symbols in the public sphere. Their report and the proposal for banning religious symbols in the public sphere were cited by the governing party, Coalition Avenir Québec, when it proposed a ban on religious

dress by schoolteachers and principals as part of Bill 21, which designated the province as officially secular.

14. Casanova, *Public Religions*, 7.

15. Michael A. Elliot, "Human Rights and the Triumph of the Individual in World Culture," *Cultural Sociology* 1, no. 3 (2007): 343–363.

16. Elliott, 352.

17. Elliott, 352.

18. Bouchard and Taylor, *Building the Future*, 34.

19. Seyyed Hossein Nasr, *The Heart of Islam: Enduring Values for Humanity* (San Francisco: HarperOne, 2004), 276.

20. Nasr, 276–278.

21. Susan Walzer, "Universal Human Rights: The Contribution of Muslim States," *Human Rights Quarterly* 26 (2004): 799–844.

22. John L. Hiemstra and Robert A. Brink, "The Advent of a Public Pluriformity Model: Faith-Based School Choice in Alberta," *Canadian Journal of Education* 29, no. 4 (2006): 1157–1190.

23. The CIC is now defunct. It was active from 1998 until 2014, when it was dissolved. The issue of funding for religious schools came up many times on the CIC's *Friday Bulletin/Friday Magazine*. In the initial years of the organization, the *Friday Bulletin* was the primary marker of its public presence.

24. See the Supreme Court's judgment, https://scc-csc.lexum.com/scc-csc/scc-csc/en/item/1446/index.do.

25. For a taste of the debate on funding faith-based schools, see Michael Swan, "Funding Debate Could Hurt Catholic Schools," *Catholic Register*, September 5, 2007; Tony Gosgnach, "Renewed Effort to Defund Ontario Catholic Schools," *Catholic Register*, September 1, 2007.

26. See Kate Jaimet, "Experts Split on School Reforms; Quebec Experience Leads to Different Conclusions on How Simple Secularization Would Be," *Ottawa Citizen*, September 11, 2007, A9.

27. The archbishop's arguments were later restated in Rowan Williams, "Civil and Religious Law in England: A Religious Perspective," *Ecclesiastical Law Journal* 10 (2008): 262–282.

28. Syed Mumtaz Ali, *The Review of the Ontario Civil Justice System: The Reconstruction of the Canadian Constitution and the Case of Muslim Personal/Family Law* (Toronto: Canadian Society of Muslims, 1994).

29. Monica Boyd, "Dispute Resolution in Family Law: Protecting Choice, Promoting Inclusion," report for the Ministry of the Attorney General, Canada (Toronto, 2004), 1 (my emphasis), http://www.attorneygeneral.jus.gov.on.ca/english/about/pubs/boyd/fullreport.pdf.

30. In some sense, this is similar to the shift in the position of the American Anthropological Association (AAA) regarding human rights over the past fifty years or so. Initially,

the AAA made it clear that the universalism that was implicit in the Universal Declaration of Human Rights (UDHR) was a threat to the cultural values of different societies. Since the 1990s, however, the AAA has come to regard the UDHR as a key instrument against the violation of vulnerable populations. What needs protection, the AAA now argues, are concrete individuals and not so much the abstraction of cultures.

31. Lynda Hurst, "Sharia Law Out of Question, Quebec Insists," *Toronto Star*, March 26, 2005. See also Janet Keeping, "Why Gender Equity Trumps Religious Rights," *Calgary Herald*, October 2, 2008. The main point of Keeping's article is that freedom of religion should not override the rights of women.

32. Bouchard and Taylor, *Building the Future*, 176.

CHAPTER 24

The Distinctiveness of Indian Secularism

Rajeev Bhargava

Although the election of a government coalition led by the Congress Party has opened new opportunities for secular space, only someone with a blinkered vision would assert that the growth of militant Hindu nationalism has been stalled and deny that secularism in India continues to be in crisis.[1] However, an ambiguity lying at the very heart of this claim has not been dispelled altogether: Is the crisis primarily the result of external factors as when a good thing is undermined by forces always inimical to it, when it falls into incapable or wrong hands, when it is practiced badly? Or is it rather that the blemished practice is itself an effect of a deeper conceptual flaw, a bad case of a wrong-footed ideal? Madan, Nandy, and Chatterjee have all argued that the external threat to secularism is only a symptom of a deeper internal crisis.[2] Secularism in their view has long faced an internal threat in the sense that the conceptual and normative structure of secularism is itself terribly flawed. In different ways, each argues that secularism is linked to a flawed modernization, to a mistaken view of rationality, to an impractical demand that religion be eliminated from public life, to an insufficient appreciation of the importance of communities in the life of people and a wholly exaggerated sense of the positive character of the modern state. In what follows, I argue against this view. I do not wholly dispute their claims about modernity, nation-state, or rationality and the importance of religion and community—in limited but significant ways their critique is valid. But I disagree both with the general implications of their claim as well as with their understanding of Indian secularism as necessarily tied to a flawed modernist project. In particular, I contend that these critics fail to see that India developed a distinctively Indian and differently modern variant of secularism.

Ideals are rarely, if ever, and never simply transplanted from one cultural context to another. They invariably adapt, sometimes so creatively to suit their new habitat that they seem unrecognizable. This is exactly what happened to secularism in India. Indian critics of secularism neither fully grasp the general conceptual structure of secularism nor properly understand its distinctive Indian variant. Indian secularism did not erect a strict wall of separation but proposed instead a principled distance between religion and state. Moreover, by balancing the claims of individuals and religious communities, it never intended a bludgeoning privatization of religion. It also embodies a model of contextual moral reasoning. All these features that combine to form what I call contextual secularism remain screened off from the understanding of these critics.

Although I do not agree with these critics that the conceptual and normative structure of secularism is flawed, I do agree that it faces an internal threat. However, I have a different understanding of the nature of this threat. Isaiah Berlin has reminded us that the history of ideas is replete with great liberating ideas slowly turning into suffocating straitjackets. One reason for this is that we forget that they need continual interpretation: no idea can flourish without its defenders finding better and better ways of articulating and formulating them. An idea faces an internal threat when its supporters—out of akrasia, willful, or unwitting neglect, ignorance, confusion, or delusion—cease to care for it, or when its own proponents mistakenly turn against it. I have no reason to doubt secularism is threatened by forces fiercely opposed to it. But my focus in this essay is on the internal threats to secularism. The principal contention of my paper is that one such internal threat is the failure to realize the distinctive character of Indian secularism.

The Conceptual Structure of Secularism

To identify the conceptual structure of secularism, it is best to begin by contrasting it with doctrines to which it is both related and opposed. These anti-secular doctrines favor not separation but a union or alliance between church/religion and state. A state that has union with a particular religious order is a theocratic state. Such a state is governed by what it claims are divine laws directly administered by a priestly order claiming divine commission. Major historical examples of theocracies are ancient Israel, some Buddhist regimes of Japan and China, the

Geneva of John Calvin, and the Papal States.[3] The Islamic Republic of Iran, as run by Ayatollahs or at least as Khomeini aspired to run it, is an obvious example. A theocratic state must be distinguished from a state that establishes religion. Here religion is granted official, legal recognition by the state and although both benefit from a formal alliance with one another, the sacerdotal order does not govern a state where religion is established.

Just as a theocracy is not always distinguished from the establishment of religion, so a distinction is not always drawn between the establishment of religion and the establishment of a church of a religion—that is a religious institution with its own distinct rules, function and social roles, personnel, jurisdiction, power, hierarchy (on the ecclesiastical levels) and a distinct and authoritative interpretation of a religion.[4] But clearly not all religions have churches. Yet a state may establish such a church-free religion, that is, grant it formal, legal recognition, and privilege. Put differently, the establishment of a church is always the establishment of a particular religion, but the converse is not always true. The establishment of a particular religion does not always mean the establishment of a church. A majority of Hindu nationalists in India may wish to establish Hinduism as state religion but they have no church to establish. Such an establishment may be expressed in the symbols of the state as well in the form of state-policies that support a particular religion. Early Protestants may have wanted to disestablish the Roman Catholic Church, but they could not have wished the state to derecognize Christianity as the favored religion. Alternatively, they tried to maintain the establishment of their preferred religion by the establishment of not one but two or even more churches.[5] The establishment of a single religion is consistent therefore with the disestablishment or non-establishment of a church, with the establishment of a single church, or with the establishment of multiple churches. This issue is obscured because in church-based religions the establishment of religion *is* the establishment of the church and the establishment of Christianity is so much a part of a background understanding that it does not need even to be foregrounded and discussed.

Finally, it is possible that at least theoretically there is the establishment of multiple religions, with or without church. I know of no historical instance of the multiple establishments of religions. Possibly, Ashoka in India came closest to it. It may also have been an aspiration of the Mughal King Akbar. Perhaps another example is the fourteenth-century Vijayanagar kingdom that granted official recognition not only to Shaivites and the Vaishnavites but also the Jains.

We can see then that there are five types of regimes in which a close relationship exists between state and religion.[6] First, a theocracy where no institutional separation exists between church and state and the sacerdotal order is also the direct political ruler. Second, states with the establishment of a single religion; these are of three types: (a) without the establishment of a church, (b) with the establishment of a single church, and (c) with the establishment of multiple churches. Third, states with the establishment of multiple religions.

Historically, where a single religion is established by the establishment of a single church—the unreformed established Protestant churches of England, Scotland, and Germany as well as the Catholic churches in Italy and Spain—the state recognized a particular version of the religion enunciated by that church as the official religion, compelled individuals to congregate for only one church, punished them for failing to profess a particular set of religious beliefs, levied taxes in support of the favored church, paid the salaries of its clergy, and made instruction of the favored interpretation of the religion mandatory in educational institutions or in the media. In such cases, not only was there inequality among religions but also among the churches of the same religion, and while members of the established church may have enjoyed a modicum of religious liberty (an established Protestant church would certainly allow it), those belonging to churches or religions not established did not enjoy any or the same degree of liberty. When members of the other church or religious groups possessed strength or outnumbered the other, then such a multireligious or multidenominational society was invariably wrecked by interreligious or interdenominational wars. If they did not, then religious minorities not only failed to enjoy full religious liberty but were not even tolerated. They faced persistent religious persecution, as in the case of the Jews in several European countries until the nineteenth century. One exception to this, however, was the Millet system of the Ottoman Empire which had Islam as the established religion but three other religious communities—Greek Orthodox, Armenian Orthodox, and Jewish—were treated as equals and given a respectable degree of autonomy. States with substantive establishments have not changed their color with time. Wherever one religion is not only formally but substantively established, the persecution of minorities and internal dissenters continues today. One has to cite the example only of Saudi Arabia to prove this point.[7]

In instances of multiple established churches, the state officially respects more than one denomination without preferring one over the other.[8] In the past, such a state levied a religious tax on everyone and yet gave individuals the choice to remit the tax money to their preferred church. It financially aided schools run by religious institutions but on a nondiscriminatory basis. It may have punished people for disavowing or disrespecting the established religion, but it did not compel them to profess the beliefs of a particular denomination. A state that respects multiple established churches treats members of all churches nonpreferentially. It gives liberty to each church to conduct its religious affairs but is largely indifferent to the freedom of members within the group. The state of New York, which in the middle of the seventeenth century allowed every church of the Protestant faith to be established, furnishes perhaps the earliest example of "multiple establishment." The colonies of Massachusetts, Connecticut, and New Hampshire show a similar pattern.[9]

States with multiple established churches are better than states with a single established church. For example, such states are likely to be relatively peaceful. Members of different denominations are likely to tolerate one another. There may be general equality among all members of a religion (though historically this has not always been the case, women and blacks have been the usual victims). The state grants each denomination considerable autonomy in its own affairs. But states with multiple established churches have their limitations. For a start, they may continue to persecute members of other religions and atheists. Second, they are indifferent to the liberty of individuals within each denomination or religious group. They may do absolutely nothing to foster a general climate of toleration that prevents the persecution of dissenters within recognized communities or of other religious communities. Closed and oppressive communities can thrive in such contexts. Third, they may not have legal provisions that allow an individual to exit his religious community and embrace another religion or to remain unattached to any religion whatsoever. Fourth, such states give recognition to particular religious identities but fail to recognize what may be called nonparticularized identities, that is, identities that simultaneously refer to several identities or transcend all of them. Fifth, such states are unconcerned with the nonreligious liberties of individuals or groups. Finally, such states are entirely indifferent to citizenship rights. States that establish multiple religions face similar problems but are better than states with multiple church establishments in one important respect—there is peace, toleration, and perhaps equality among all religious communities

An important difference between a theocracy and states with multiple established churches is easily discernable. Because they do not identify or unify church and state but install only an alliance between them, states with an established church are in some ways disconnected from it. They do so in different ways. For one thing, there is a sufficient degree of institutional differentiation between the two social entities; both the church and the state are distinct enough to have separate identities. This difference in identity may partly be because of role differentiation. Each is to perform a role different from the other: the function of one is to maintain peace and order which is a primarily temporal matter; the function of the other is to secure salvation which is primarily a spiritual concern. In a theocracy, both roles are performed by the same personnel. In states with established churches, there may even be personnel differentiation. State functionaries and church functionaries are largely different from another. Thus, disconnection between church and state can go sufficiently deep. Yet there is a more significant sense in which the state and the church are connected to one another: they share a common end defined largely by religion. By virtue of a more primary connection of ends, the two share a special relationship with another. Both benefit from this mutual alliance. This is also true of states that establish multiple churches. There is finally another level of connection between church and state. The policies of the state directly favor the church and its religion. They flow from and are justified in terms of the union or alliance that exists between the state and the church. The institutional disconnection of church and state goes hand in hand with the first- and third-level connection of ends and policies.

To sum up: I have referred to three possible levels of connection. A primary, first-order connection refers to the connection of ends, purposes, or values. A second-order connection may exist at the level of roles, functions, powers, or more generally, institutions. A third-order connection exists at the level of state-policy. In theocracies, church and state are connected at all three levels (common end, no institutional separation, common policy). In states with established churches, the two have first, primary, and third-order connections but at the very best only partial second-order connection. In principle, it is not impossible for states with established churches to be entirely disconnected from them at the second level. In short, what differentiates a state with established church-based religion from a theocracy is the second-order disconnection of church and state.

Secular States

How are secular states different from theocracies and states with established religions? Because it is also a feature of states with established churches, the mere institutional separation of the two is not and cannot be the distinguishing mark of secular states. This second-level disconnection should not be conflated with the separation embedded in secular states, because although necessary, it is not a sufficient condition for their individuation. This is an important clarification. Because institutional disconnection is a necessary condition for secular states, especially in states with a long tradition of strong establishments or theocracy, and because much of the struggle for the creation of a secular state is directed at this institutional disconnection (for instance, in virulent anticlericalism), it is not uncommon to identify secularism with church-state separation. But by itself this separation does not install a secular state and is not the distinguishing feature of political secularism.

To grasp this point at a more general theoretical level, let me distinguish three levels of disconnection to correspond with the three already identified levels of connection. A state may be disconnected from religion at the level of ends (first level), at the level of institutions (second level) and the level of law and public policy (third level).[10] A secular state is distinguished from theocracies and states with established states by a primary, first-level disconnection. A secular state has free-standing ends, either substantially, if not always completely, disconnected from the ends of religion or conceivable without a connection with them. States with established religions have something in common with secular states—at least a partial institutional disconnection. But secular states go further in the direction of disconnection; they break away completely. They withdraw favors or privileges that established churches had earlier taken for granted. Finally, a state may be disconnected from religion even at the level of law and public policy. Such a state maintains a policy of strict or absolute separation. The dominant self-understanding of western secularism is that this third-level disconnection is crucial. When a state is disconnected from religion at all three levels, then we may say that a "wall of separation" has been erected between the two. On the wall of separation conception of secularism, the state must have nothing to do with religion. Religion must be outside the purview of the state, and in this sense, it must be privatized. But there are two other modes of relating to religion at this third level. The state may either be strictly neutral, a stance that may in some circumstances implicate it with religion, or it may even go beyond neutrality, connect with it in yet another way, a point to which I return in detail below.

To sum up: A secular state is to be distinguished not only from theocracy but also from a state where religion is established. A non-theocratic state is not automatically secular because it is entirely consistent for a state not to be run by priests inspired by divine laws but to have a formal alliance with one or more religions; nor is a state separated from church necessarily secular, because church-state separation is compatible with the establishment of religion. A secular state goes beyond the separation of church and state—it refuses to establish religion or if it has been established earlier, to disestablish it. Therefore, a secular state follows what can be called the principle of non-establishment. Furthermore, the non-establishment of religion means that the state is separated not merely from one but from all religions (I refer to this as feature a). Thus, in a secular state, a formal or legal union or alliance between state and religion is impermissible. Official status is not given to religion. No religious community in such a state can say that the state belongs exclusively to it; nor can all say that it belongs collectively to them and them alone. This does not mean that a secular state is anti-religious, but it does imply that it exists and survives only when religion is no longer hegemonic. No one is compelled to pay tax for religious purposes or to receive religious instruction. No automatic grants to religious institutions are available.

What are the ends of a secular state? I have said that at the most general level, secular states aim to end religious hegemony, oppression, and domination and to do so by separating them from their structure. Broadly there are two reasons for this separation. First, states may do so simply for self-aggrandizement, for example, when states (political rulers) wish to maximize their own power and wealth. These states are not motivated by values such as peace, liberty, or equality. They may claim to uphold ethical standards but at root they have no commitment to any moral values. I shall call them self-aggrandizing amoral secular states. Usually, such states are imperial and autocratic. A good example of such a predominantly secular state, despite the not infrequent allegation of its biases or Christian character, is the British colonial state in India that—motivated almost exclusively by power, wealth, and social order—had a policy of tolerance and neutrality toward religious communities. This is not surprising, given that empires are interested in the labor or tribute of their subjects and not in their religion. In multireligious societies, for purely instrumental reasons, they may display characteristics of states that establish multiple religions or have a hands-off approach to all religions.[11]

The Values of a Secular State

There is another kind of secular state, one guided also by some moral values or principles. I shall call such secular states value-based secular states. This brings me to more explicitly articulate the connection of a non–self-aggrandizing secular state with several important and substantive values. The first of these values is peace or rather the prevention of a society from its regression into barbarism, not an uncommon tendency where there exist two or more incompatible visions of the good life. The second value is toleration, that is, the state does not persecute anyone on grounds of religion. We must eschew the tendency within Western modernist discourse to conceive of civil strife as a result purely of a clash of interests. The development of secularism in the West and elsewhere cannot be properly understood without fully comprehending the fear of cruelty and disorder that marks the conflict of ultimate ideals. This is equally true of the American and the French experience as it is of India. Consider the United States. One might say that the first amendment, the pivot of American secularism, is a product of the widespread feeling of vulnerability experienced in different religious denominations such as the Anglicans, the Presbyterians, and the Quakers, each dominant in one particular area but vulnerable in others and each viewing the other as extremely odd, if not fanatical.[12]

The third value is that a secular state is constitutively tied to the value of religious liberty that has three dimensions. The first refers to the liberty of members of any one religious group (feature b). It is a brute fact that in most religious communities, one or two interpretations of its core beliefs and practices come to dominate. Given this dominance, it is important that every individual or sect within the group be given the right to criticize, revise, or challenge these dominant interpretations. The second aspect of this important liberty in a secular state (feature c), is that it is granted non-preferentially to all members of every religious community. It is entirely possible that non-preferential treatment by the state of groups that accord religious liberty to its members is also found in states respecting multiple establishment. But religious liberty is not part of the core principles of multiple establishments. However, it is a constitutive feature of the secular state. The third dimension of religious liberty (feature d), unthinkable in states with multiple establishment, is that individuals are free not only to criticize the religion into which they are born but, at the very extreme, to reject it and furthermore, given ideal conditions of deliberation, to freely embrace another religion or to remain without one.

Religious liberty, when understood broadly, is one important value of a secular state. To understand another crucial ingredient, it is necessary to grasp the point that liberty and equality in the religious sphere are all part of the same piece with liberty and equality in other spheres. It is not a coincidence that the disestablishment clause in the first amendment to the American constitution institutes not only religious freedom but also the more general freedom of speech, peaceful assembly, and political dissent. It is entirely possible that a state respecting multiple establishments permits *religious* liberty and equality but forbids other forms of freedom and equality. For instance, a person may be able to challenge the authority of the religious head of his own denomination but not be free to challenge the authority of the state. This is impossible in a secular state which is committed to a more general freedom and equality. Thus, the second value to which a secular state is constitutively linked is the equality of free citizenship.

The value of equal citizenship has two dimensions: one active, the other passive. It is a feature of democratic polities that these two roles of citizens coincide and therefore a democratic government must be continuously justifiable from both points of views.[13] To be a passive citizen is to be entitled to physical security, a minimum of material well-being, and a sphere of one's own in which others ought not to interfere. Although a part of this idea of passive citizenship goes back to ancient Rome, the radical emphasis on material well-being and on privacy is a result of a profound transvaluation of values that has taken place under conditions of modernity.[14] This lies at the root of the idea of the right to life, liberty, material welfare, and perhaps education—crucial elements if ordinary people are to lead their ordinary lives with dignity. Any citizen of the state must be entitled to these benefits. This is partly an extension of the point implicit in the defense of religious liberty but in part it adds something substantial of its own. The benefits of citizenship—resources that enable a dignified ordinary life—must be available to everyone and there is no room here for discrimination on grounds of religion (feature e). This equal treatment is entailed by equal (passive) citizenship. State agencies and the entire system of law must not work in favor of one religious group. If the state works to protect the security and well-being of some individuals or groups but fails to secure these meager but important benefits to others, then the principle of equal (passive) citizenship is violated. Likewise, since citizenship is conditional upon education, no one must be denied admission to educational institutions solely on grounds of religion (feature f).

The active dimension of citizenship involves the recognition of citizens as equal participants in the public domain. Such active citizenship rights can be denied in two ways: when they are brutally excluded from the political domain (they are politically dead) or when their recognition in the public domain betrays the social acceptance of a belief in the intrinsic superiority of one group as when there is communally weighed voting or efforts to dilute the votes of religious minorities through the use of gerrymandering techniques.[15] Groups singled out as less worthy are demeaned and insulted, encouraged to feel that patterns of disrespect existing in society at large enjoy official sanction. In contrast to this, equality of citizenship to which secularism is tied conveys a community wide acknowledgment of equal respect for everyone in the political domain (feature g).

A simple comparison between different types of state-religion political orders shows that at least in multireligious societies and relative to theocracies and states with established religion, a secular state gives maximum liberty and equality, conceived individualistically or nonindividualistically to all its citizens. This point can be made with reference to Table 24.1.

Indian Secularism

Which of the different religion-related political orders mentioned above is found in India? We may answer this by examining the relevant articles of the Indian Constitution. The state in the Indian constitution appears to possess all the features of a secular state. Feature a is specified in Article 27 which rules out

TABLE 24.1 Benefits and rights available to citizens under different regimes of state-church relations.

Values Form of State	Peace with Justice	Religious Liberty			Citizenship Identification			Passive Citizenship Benefits/Right			Active Citizenship Rights		
		Dominant Group		Others	Dominant Goup		Others	Dominant Group		Others	Dominant Group		Others
		Elites	Others		Elites	Others		Elites	Others		Elites	Others	
Theocracy	A	P	A	A	P	A	A	P	A	A	A	A	A
States with substantive singular establishment	A	WP	A	A	P	P	A	P	A	A	A	A	A
States with substantive multiple establishment	WP	WP	A	WP	P	P	A	P	WP	A	A	A	A
States with formal singular establisment	P	P	P	P	P	P	A	P	P	P	P	P	P
States with formal multiple establishment	P	P	P	P	P	P	WP	P	P	P	P	P	P
Anti-religious 'secular' state	A	A	A	A	P	A	A	P	P	P	A	A	A
Value-based secular state	P	P	P	P	P	P	P	P	P	P	P	P	P

A – Absent; WP – Weakly Present; P – Present

the public funding of religion and Article 28(1) under which "no religious instruction is to be provided in any educational institution wholly maintained out of state funds."

Articles 25, 27, and 28 guarantee religious liberty and meet the conditions specified by features b, c, and d. Under Article 25(1), "all persons are equally entitled to freedom of conscience and the right freely to profess, practice and propagate religion" (features b and c). The phrase "freedom of conscience" is meant to cover the liberty of persons without a religion (feature d). Under Article 27, "no person is compelled to pay any taxes, the proceeds of which are specifically appropriated in payment of expenses for the promotion or maintenance of any particular religion or religious denomination." Finally, under Article 28(3), "no person attending any educational institution . . . shall be required to take part in any religious instruction or to attend any religious worship that may be conducted in such institution."

Equality of citizenship is guaranteed by Articles 14, 15(1), and 29(2) of the Indian constitution. Article 15(1) states that the state shall not discriminate against any citizen on grounds only of religion, race, caste, sex, place of birth, or any of them (feature e). Article 29(2) declares that no citizen shall be denied admission into any educational institution maintained by the state on grounds only of religion, race, caste, or place of origin (feature f). Articles 16(1) and 16(2) of the Indian constitution affirm an equal opportunity for all citizens in matters relating to employment or appointment of any office under the state. It further affirms that no citizen will be eligible or discriminated against in respect of any employment or office under the state on grounds of religion, race, or caste. The clause on universal franchise as well as Article 325, which declares a general electoral roll for all constituencies and states that no one shall be ineligible for inclusion in this roll or claim to be included in it on grounds only of religion, race, or caste, embody the value of equal active citizenship. Thus feature g is specified in the articles on equality of active citizenship.

The implications of accepting that the state in the Indian constitution is meant to exhibit features a to g are not always spelled out. First, the constitution rules out theocracy and the establishment of religion. The term *secular state* is usually contrasted simply with theocracy. This is misleading, if not false, because the absence of theocracy is compatible with the establishment of religion. The secular credentials of the state cannot be derived from the mere absence of theocracy.[16] Second, the Indian state is not meant to be merely tolerant (in the sense specified earlier). Indian secularism must not be confused with a generally professed Hindu tolerance. It is frequently claimed that Indians have a natural, traditional affinity with secularism. In view of our traditional obsession with subtle and not so subtle hierarchies, this claim must be taken with a pinch of salt if not pepper. Of course, this should not detract from the important point that tolerance, even within a hierarchical framework, provides a foundation for the development of modern secularism. Elements of this foundation can certainly be found within India. Third, the secularism of the Indian constitution is neither a simple-minded single-value idea nor overinflated and hyper-substantive; rather, it is a complex, multivalued doctrine.

A further point concerns the precise form of secularism to be found in the constitution. Broadly speaking, secularism is taken to be the view that religion must be separated from the state for the sake of extensive religious liberty and equality of citizenship. This view can be interpreted differently. For Donald Smith, the secular state involves three distinct but interrelated relations concerning the state, religion, and the individual.[17] The first relation concerns individuals and their religion, from which the state is excluded. Individuals are thereby free to decide the merits of the respective claims of different religions without any coercive interference by the state—the libertarian ingredient in secularism. The second concerns the relation between individuals and the state, from which religion is excluded. Thus, the rights and duties of citizens are not affected by the religious beliefs held by individuals—the egalitarian component in secularism. Finally, for Smith, the integrity of both these relations is dependent on the third relation, the relation between the state and different religions. Here he argues that secularism entails the mutual exclusion of state and religion. Just as political power is outside the scope of religion's legitimate objectives, just so it is not the function of the state to promote, regulate, direct, or interfere in religion. This interpretation is in line with the dominant American interpretation of secularism as erecting "a wall of separation" between religion and state. On the classical American view of disestablishment, there can be no support for religion even on a non-preferential basis. Even partial aid to educational institutions run by religious organizations will constitute some form of establishment. Moreover, a state that disestablishes all religions is one that has no power to interfere in the affairs of religious institutions. For better or for worse, the state is powerless to bring about changes in religion. So, for Smith, secularism means the strict exclusion of religion from the state or disconnection at all three levels (ends, institutions, policy) for the sake of the religious liberty and equal citizenship of individuals. This is also the dominant understanding of Western secularism.

Departures from Mainstream Western Secularism

Does Indian secularism erect a similar "wall of separation" for the sake of individualistically construed values? Is it a Western idea on Indian soil? Articles 15, 16, 25, 29(2), and 325 support this interpretation. Although there is no direct reference to disestablishment, Articles 27 and 28(1) imply strict separation. By giving the president of the republic the option of not taking an oath in the name of God, Article 60 confirms the strictly neutral character of the Indian constitution. From the discussion so far, it appears that the state in India is constitutionally bound to follow Smith's model of Western secularism. However, further examination of the constitution reveals this impression to be mistaken. First, Article 30(1) recognizes the rights of religious minorities and therefore, unlike other articles applicable to citizens qua individuals, it is a community-based right. Indeed, another community-specific right granting political representation to religious minorities was almost granted and was removed from the constitution only at the last minute. Second, Article 30(2) commits the state to give aid to educational institutions established and administered by religious communities. Also permitted is religious instruction in educational institutions that are partly funded by the state. These are significant departures from the "wall of separation" view of the secular state. Even more significant are Articles 17 and 25(2) that require the state to intervene in religious affairs. Article 25(2)(b) states that "nothing in Article 25(1) prevents the state from making a law providing for social welfare and reform or the throwing open of Hindu religious institutions of a public character to all classes and sections of Hindus." Article 17 is an uninhibited, robust attack on the caste system, arguably the central feature of Hinduism, by abolishing untouchability and by making the enforcement of any disability arising out of it an offense punishable by law. Both appear to take away the individual freedom of religion granted under Section 1 of Article 25 and to contravene Article 26.

These features of the Indian constitution depart from the stereotypical Western model in two ways. First, unlike the strict separation view that renders the state powerless in religious matters, they enjoin the state to interfere in religion. Second, more importantly, by giving powers to the state in the affairs of one religion, they necessitate a departure from strict neutrality or equidistance. This power of interference may be interpreted to undermine or promote Hinduism. Either way it appears to strike a powerful blow to the idea of non-preferential treatment.

In short, some articles in the Indian constitution support an individualist interpretation and others a nonindividualist one; some conceive separation as exclusion, others as non-preferential treatment; and some depart altogether from separation understood as exclusion or neutrality. At the end of the day, a confusing, somewhat contradictory picture on secularism emerges from a reading of the constitution. Critics could hardly fail to notice this and for many of them, Articles 17, 25(2), 30(1), and 30(2) compromise the secularity of the Indian state. For Donald Smith, any intervention in Hinduism—for example, the legal ban on the prohibition of Dalit entry into temples or any protection of the rights of communities—seriously compromises secularism. For others, like Chatterjee, the presence of these features in the Indian constitution shows why the Indian state cannot be really secular. The Indian constitution does not give an unambiguous criterion for maintaining the secularity of the state and, quite simply, given Indian conditions, it could never have.

By accepting community-based rights for religious minorities and endorsing state intervention in religion, did the constitution depart from secular principles?

I do not think it did. Rather, it developed its own modern variant. This distinctiveness of the Indian secularism can be understood only when the cultural background and social context in India is properly grasped. At least four such features of this sociocultural context call for attention. First, there exists the mind-boggling diversity of religious communities in India. Such diversity may coexist harmoniously, but it invariably generates conflicts, the most intractable of which, I believe, are conflicts over values. Second, within Hinduism in particular and in South Asian religions more generally, a greater emphasis is placed on practice rather than belief. A person's religious identity and affiliation are defined more by what she or he does with and in relation to others, than by the content of beliefs individually held by them. Since practices are intrinsically social, any significance placed on them brings about a concomitant valorization of communities. Together, these two features entail intercommunity conflicts which are further exacerbated if fueled by competing conceptions of democracy and nationalism. Third, many religiously sanctioned social practices are oppressive by virtue of their illiberal and inegalitarian character and deny a life of dignity and self-respect. Therefore, from a liberal and egalitarian standpoint, they desperately need to be reformed. Such practices frequently have a life of their own, independent of consciously held beliefs, and possess a causal efficacy that remains unaffected by the presence of conscious beliefs. Furthermore, a tendency to fortify and insulate themselves from reflective critique makes them resistant to easy change and reform. It follows that an institution vested with enormous social power is needed to transform their character. Fourth, in Hinduism, the absence of an organized institution such as the church has meant that the impetus for effective reform cannot come exclusively from within. Reform within Hinduism can hardly be initiated without the help from powerful external institutions such as the state.

In such a context, India needed a coherent set of intellectual resources to tackle interreligious conflict and to struggle against oppressive communities, not by disaggregating them into a collection of individuals or by unrecognizing them (and therefore, not by privatizing religion) but by somehow making them more liberal and egalitarian. A political movement for a united, liberal, and democratic India had to struggle against hierarchical and communal conceptions of community but without abandoning a reasonable communitarianism. Besides, the state had an important contribution to make in the transformation of these communities; for this reason, a perennial dilemma was imposed on it. The state in India walked a tightrope between the requirement of religious liberty that frequently entails noninterference in the affairs of religious communities, and the demand for equality and justice which necessitates intervention in religiously sanctioned social customs. Secularism in India simply had to be different from the Western liberal model that does not recognize communities and dictates strict separation between religious and political institutions.

If we abandon the view, such as Donald Smith's, that political secularism entails a unique set of state policies valid under all conditions which provide the yardstick by which the secularity of any state is to be judged, then we can better understand why, despite deviating from the ideal, the state in India continues to embody a model of *secularism*.[18] This can be shown even if we stick to Smith's working definition of secularism as consisting of three relations. Smith's first relation embodies the principle of religious liberty construed individualistically, that is, pertaining to the religious beliefs of individuals. However, it is possible to make a nonindividualistic construal of religious liberty by speaking not of the beliefs of individual but rather of the practices of groups. Here religious liberty would mean distancing the state from the practices of religious groups. The first principle of secularism can then be seen to also grant the right to a religious community to its own practices. Smith's second relation embodies the value of equal citizenship. But this entails—and I cannot substantiate my claim—that we tolerate the attempt of radically different groups to determine the nature and direction of society as they best see it. In this view, then, the public presence of the religious practices of groups is guaranteed and entailed by the recognition of community-differentiated citizenship rights. Smith's version of secularism entails a charter of uniform rights. But it is clear that the commitment of secularism to equal citizenship can dictate community-based rights. In principle, this could easily accommodate a reasonable demand for community-specific political rights. In India, for reasons outlined earlier, this meant community-specific social rights, such as the right to administer and maintain educational institutions. What this shows is that Indian secularism is concerned as much with intrareligious oppression as with interreligious domination. Smith's third principle pertains to non-establishment and therefore to a strict separation of religion from state, under which religion and the state both have the freedom to develop without interfering with each other. Separation, however, need not mean strict noninterference, mutual exclusion or equidistance, as in Smith's view. Instead, it could be a policy of principled distance, which entails a flexible approach on the question of intervention or abstention, combining both, dependent on the context, nature, or current state of relevant religions. This theoretical interpretation of separation sits much better with its own best practice but perhaps also with the practice of other Western secular states, something that is never properly recognized by Western theories of secularism. But what is this idea of principled distance?

Principled Distance

Principled distance is one particular way of unpacking the metaphor of separation. It accepts a disconnection between state and religion at the level of ends and institutions but does not make a fetish of it at the third level of policy and law. Principled distance must be distinguished both from strict neutrality. It rests upon a distinction between equal treatment and treating everyone as an equal drawn by the American philosopher Ronald Dworkin.[19] The principle of equal treatment, in the relevant political sense, requires that the state treat all its citizens equally in the relevant respect, for example, in the distribution of a resource of opportunity. The principle of treating people as equals entails that every person or group is treated with equal concern and respect. This second principle may sometimes require equal treatment, say equal distribution of resources but it may also occasionally dictate unequal treatment. Treating people or groups as equals is entirely consistent with differential treatment. This idea is the second ingredient in what I have called principled distance. Moreover, it is to admit that a state may interfere in one religion more than in others, depending on the historical and social condition of all relevant religions. For the promotion of a particular value constitutive of secularism, some religion, relative to other religions, may require more interference from the state. For example, suppose that the value to be advanced is social equality. This requires in part undermining caste hierarchies. If this is the aim of the state, then it may be required of the state that it interferes in caste-ridden Hinduism much more than say Islam or Christianity. However, if a diversity-driven religious liberty is the value to be advanced by the state, then it may have to intervene in Christianity and Islam more than in Hinduism. If this is so, the state can neither strictly exclude considerations emanating from religion nor keep strict neutrality with respect to religion. It cannot antecedently decide that it will always refrain from interfering in religions or that it will interfere in each equally. Indeed, it may not relate to every religion in society in exactly the same way or intervene in each religion to the same degree or in the same manner. To want to do so would be plainly absurd. All it must ensure is that the relationship between the state and religions is guided by nonsectarian motives consistent with some values and principles.

Contextual Secularism

A context-sensitive secularism, one based on the idea of principled distance, is what I have elsewhere called contextual secularism. Contextual secularism is contextual not only because it captures the idea that the precise form and content of secularism will vary from context to context and from place to place but also that it embodies a certain model of contextual moral reasoning. This it must do because of its character as a multivalue doctrine. Some conflict-ridden human situations are such that their morally defensible resolution is dictated by single-value doctrines, that is, those that give priority to a value held to be supreme. For example, bodily integrity may be viewed as such an important value that nothing can justify its violation. I may be prevented from torturing someone no matter what my reasons for doing so: neither self-interest nor pursuit of truth may justify it. Other human situations are different because they genuinely involve a value conflict, and the resolution of this conflict cannot be read off the values themselves. Single-value doctrines do not suffice here because they always dictate a unique outcome antecedently favorable to the protection of one value. In these situations, multivalue doctrines are more appropriate. They take on board these conflicts and admit that no general a priori procedure can antecedently arbitrate between competing value claims. Rather, whether a value will outweigh others or which, if at all, will override others will be decided entirely by the context. Frequently, such situations necessitate a tradeoff or compromise albeit one that is morally defensible.

By explicitly accepting that secularism is a multivalue doctrine, we recognize that its constitutive values do not always sit easily with one another. On the contrary, they are frequently in conflict. Some degree of internal discord, and therefore a fair amount of instability, is an integral part of secularism. For this reason, it will forever require fresh interpretations, contextual judgments, and attempts at reconciliation and compromise. No general a priori rule of resolving these conflicts exist; no easy lexical order, no preexisting hierarchy among values or laws that enables us to decide that, no matter the context, a particular value must override everything else. Almost everything then is a matter of situational thinking and contextual reasoning. Whether one value overrides or is reconciled with another cannot be decided beforehand. Each time the matter presents itself differently and will be differently resolved. If this is true, then the practice of secularism requires a different model of moral reasoning than the one that straitjackets our moral understanding in the form of well-delineated, explicitly stated rules.[20] This contextual secularism recognizes that the conflict between individual rights and group rights, between claims of equality and liberty, or between claims of liberty and the satisfaction of basic needs cannot always be adjudicated by a recourse to some general and abstract principle. Rather they can only be settled case by case and may require a fine balancing of competing claims. The eventual outcome may not be wholly satisfactory to either but still be reasonably satisfactory to both. Multivalue doctrines such as secularism encourage accommodation—not the giving up of one value for the sake of another but rather their reconciliation and possible harmonization, to make each work without changing the basic content of apparently incompatible concepts and values.

This accommodation may be accomplished in several ways.[21] First, by placing values at different levels. Second, by seeing them as belonging not to water-tight compartments but as sufficiently separate so that an attempt is made to make a value work within its own sphere without frontally conflicting with another value operating in a different sphere. This endeavor to make concepts, viewpoints, and values work simultaneously does not amount to a morally objectionable compromise. This is so because nothing of importance is being given up for the sake of a less significant thing, one without value or even with negative value. Rather, what is pursued is a mutually agreed middle way that combines elements from two or more equally valuable entities. The roots of such attempts at reconciliation and accommodation lie in a lack of dogmatism, in a willingness to experiment, to think at different levels and in separate spheres and in a readiness to take decisions on a provisional basis. It captures a way of thinking characterized by the following dictum: "Why look at things in terms of this or that, why not try to have both this and that?" In this way of thinking, it is recognized that although we may currently be unable to secure the best of both values and therefore be forced to settle for a watered-down version of each, we must continue to have an abiding commitment to search for a transcendence of this second-best condition. Such contextual reasoning was not atypical of the deliberations of the Constituent Assembly that was convened to draft India's Constitution, in which great value was placed on arriving at decisions by consensus. Yet the procedure of the majority vote was not given up altogether. On issues that everyone judged to be less significant, a majoritarian procedure was adopted. It is by virtue of this kind of reasoning that the Indian constitution appears at once federal and unitary, and why it favors both individual and group-specific rights. It is frequently argued against Indian secularism that it is contradictory because it tries to bring together individual and community rights, and that Articles 25 and 26(b), which have a bearing on the secular nature of the Indian state, are deeply conflictual and at best ambiguous. This is to misrecognize a virtue as a vice. In my view, this attempt to bring together seemingly incompatible values is a great strength of Indian secularism. Secularism in India is not understood to be a mechanical doctrine with a uniform, technical application. Therefore, the demand that the relevant articles in the Indian constitution give us an unambiguous criterion for evaluating separation or the complaint that the best of Indian secularists have an inconsistent understanding of the relationship between state and religion remains wide off the target and altogether fails to grasp the conceptual structure of secularism in India.

If secularism embodies contextual reasoning, it must be understood that this is not private-moral reasoning applied to politics but rather public-political reasoning infused with a moral character.

Back to Preliminaries

Western theories of secularism have tended to see secularism as a single-value doctrine. For them, the state is to be separated from organized religion for the sake of the fullest possible liberties of individuals including their religious liberty. More recently, this separation is seen to serve individual autonomy. Alternatively, as in France, they are guided solely by the value of equal citizenship. However, a history of the secular idea shows secularism to be a multivalue doctrine, tied to several important values. The Indian variant of secularism more explicitly recognizes it to be a multivalue doctrine. Furthermore, Western theories of secularism, quite in contrast to the internally variegated practice of Western states, have tended to unpack the metaphor of separation to mean either exclusion or neutrality. To my mind, this has been a very limiting interpretation of what is meant by separation.

Thus, a proper study of Indian secularism shows not only that it shares a past with the West but also that it has its own distinctive past. Indian and Western secularisms have their own distinctive prehistories as well as a common history. Apart from and beyond these histories, the Indian version has advanced the idea of secularism because, from the very beginning, by virtue of an integral link with nationalism and democracy, it has had to be explicitly tied to citizenship rights, including to the rights of religious minorities. By doing so, it has never tried to completely annul particular religious identities.

To discover its own rich and complex structure, Western secularism can either look backward, to its own past, or else look sideways, at Indian secularism that mirrors not only the past of secularism, but in a way, also its future. Doing so will certainly benefit the secularisms of many Western societies. For example, French secularism needs to look beyond its own conceptions of *laïcité* in order to take into account its own multicultural and multireligious reality. It cannot continue to take refuge in claims of exceptionalism. I feel that a good hard look at Indian secularism could also change the self-understanding of American liberal secularism.

I have argued that a recognition of its multivalue character, in particular its links with community-specific rights and ordinary life with dignity, is one distinctive feature of Indian secularism. Its other distinctive feature is its commitment to the idea of principled distance. I have also argued that the multivalue character of secularism makes it inherently unstable and necessarily ambiguous but that this instability is inescapable and, given the context in which it is meant to work, this vagueness is a virtue. I also argued that Indian secularism both encapsulates the history of Western secularism and mirrors its future. Therefore, by examining the Indian version, the West can learn about its own history as well as see its own future direction. Interestingly, at an earlier time, Indian secularism was similarly positioned when it could see its own future in the trajectory of Western secularism. The situation has now reversed. It is now the mainstream Western countries that have much to learn from attending to the distinctiveness of Indian secularism.

Ironically, this need to attend to the distinctiveness of Indian secularism is as pressing in India as it is in the West. Several critics of Indian secularism have identified it with one or the other Western versions and have ignored its special character. This has been a source of gross misinterpretation and several problems. For example, it is frequently argued that secularism is purely a Christian, Western doctrine and therefore cannot adapt itself easily to the cultural conditions of India, infused as they are by religions that grew in the soil of the subcontinent. This necessary link between secularism and Christianity is exaggerated, if not mistaken. It is true that a time-honored conception of secularism is derived almost wholly from Christianity. The idea that—in order to achieve religious integrity, peace, or toleration—the state must be strictly separated from different denominational churches is part of Christianity and its internal history. It is also true that the separation of church and state is an integral feature of a legitimate form of secularism; however, as I have shown, it is a necessary but not a sufficient condition for the development of secularism even in societies with church-based religions. It is clearly not a necessary condition for the development of all forms of secularisms. This is so even when the term *church* is interpreted to mean institutions that are authoritative centers in which power is wielded by specialized religious personnel and that have been integral, in this sense, to many religions (including, for example, Hinduism where certain kinds of Brahmins enjoyed political privilege and social power). Moreover, as I have argued, the mutual exclusion of religion and the state is not the defining feature of secularism (the idea of separation can be interpreted differently), nor are religious integrity, peace, and toleration (interpreted broadly to mean to live and to let live) uniquely Christian values. Most non-Christian civilizations have given significant space to each. Therefore, none of them are exclusively Christian. It follows that, even though we find in Christian writings some of the clearest and most systematic articulations of this doctrine, even our time-honored conception of secularism is not exclusively Christian. More importantly, this older, Christian secularism must not be confused with its modern counterpart. This Christian secularism is a sufficient but not necessary part of the background condition of modern secularism. Modern secularism may be emboldened by its presence, but it can also be nourished by other traditions of peace and tolerance. Moreover, it means more than just the separation of state and church.

One might argue that secularism is not just a Christian doctrine, but is it not Western? I have argued that the answer to this question is both yes and no. Up to a point, it is certainly Western. More specifically, as a clearly articulated doctrine, it has distinct Western origins. Although elements that constitute secularism assume different cultural forms and are found in several civilizations, one cannot deny that the idea of the secular first achieved self-consciousness and was properly theorized in the West. This Western theorization was linked to the birth of secular states in Western as much as in non-Western societies. For example, one particular form of secular state was installed in India by the Queen's Proclamation of 1858 which guaranteed the government's noninterference in Indian religions following the Indian Rebellion of 1857.[22] One might then say that the middle history of secularism is almost entirely dominated by Western societies. However, the same cannot be said of its later history. Nationalism and democracy arrived in the West after the settlement of religious conflicts, in societies that had been made religiously homogenous, or had almost become so (with the exception of the Jews, who continued to face persistent persecution). The absence of religious diversity and conflict meant that issues of citizenship could be addressed almost entirely by disregarding religious context; the important issue of community-focused rights to religious groups could be wholly ignored. This could not be done in India. Both national and democratic agendas in India had to face issues raised by deep religious difference and diversity. In India, nationalism had to choose between the religious and the secular. Similarly, the distribution of active citizenship rights could not be conceived or accomplished by ignoring religion. It could be done either by actively disregarding religion or by developing a complex attitude toward it. It also had to balance claims of individual autonomy with those of community obligations and claims of the necessity of keeping religion "private" with their inescapable presence and often valuable presence in the public. In addressing these complex issues, the very idea of the secular was taken further than had been evolved in the West. In the course of doing so, it also began to embody a form of contextual moral reasoning with which the notion of principled distance is associated. This distinguishes it from other variants of modern secularism that are grounded in more abstract, theoretical, and context-insensitive conceptions of rationality. Mainstream theories or ideologies in modern, Western societies have taken little notice of these features. Hence, they are struggling to deal with postcolonial religious diversity of their societies. The later history of secularism is more Indian than Western.[23]

Some may still argue that the Indianness of Indian secularism is derived entirely from its strong link with homegrown traditions and that therefore India had worked out its own conception of secularism that is neither Christian nor Western. For example, secularism for many means *sarva dharma sambhava*, or "religious coexistence," "interreligious tolerance," or "equal respect for all religions." Each of these interpretations of *sarva dharma sambhava* points to a crucial ingredient of secularism, but it not only fails to capture its full richness and complexity, it also ignores its relationship with extremely significant, internally constitutive values of secularism. I take religious coexistence to be equivalent to peace; to identify the secular state with a state that maintains peace between religions and allows different religions to coexist does little justice to the rich history and conceptual structure of secularism as a multivalue doctrine. The same is true of the interpretation of Indian secularism as interreligious toleration. There are many good reasons why these two ideals should not be conflated, but I shall mention only one: The mainstream idea of toleration is that it enjoins us to refrain from interfering in the affairs of others, even when one has the power to do so, even when one finds the beliefs and practices of others morally repugnant. In this sense, toleration is entirely consistent with a total refusal to respect the religion of others. It is also compatible with gross inequality and hierarchy. One may tolerate the religion of another person even as one treats that person as inferior. Secularism, on the other hand, is grounded in notions of equality—equal concern and respect—and therefore goes far beyond the notion of interreligious tolerance.

It is also inappropriate to identify secularism with equal respect for all religions. However, there is something valuable in this interpretation and something Indian about this idea. The internal plurality of Hinduism has the potential for a space where equal respect can indeed be accorded to all religions. Besides, a respect for other religions is entirely consistent with the development of their critique and the identification of local faults within them. Respecting other religions as equals does not entail their blind acceptance or endorsement. Indeed, it is precisely because respect is consistent with difference and critique that the idea of equal respect for all religions is closely linked with the proposal for an interfaith dialogue. It is also this idea of respect or care for something that allows one to critically intervene in it. Indian secularism does in a way respect all religions but by embodying the idea of respectful transformation of religions. In doing so, it inherits a venerable tradition of religious reform.

Yet even an important ingredient of secularism cannot become the whole of it. Indeed, to equate the two is to do gross injustice to secularism. This equation implies that one ignores the nonreligious part of human existence that all modern states must confront and that are also an integral part of modern secularism. For example, the idea of equal respect for all religions is entirely consistent with the equal unavailability of active citizenship rights to all members of society. It is also consistent with a total indifference to the freedom of individuals within each religious group. A fruitful dialogue on equal footing is entirely possible between religious groups that sanction gender and caste-related injustices or remain indifferent to them. But sensitivity to such issues is the hallmark of modern secularism. If so, it would be a terrible mistake to identify secularism with equal respect for all religions or modern Indian secularism with *sarva dharma sambhava*. As political attitude and practice, *sarva dharma sambhava* is more in tune with states that establish multiple religions than it does with states that are secular.

I have argued that it is wrong to identify Indian secularism with Western secularism or with *sarva dharma sambhava*. No doubt, Indian secularism is somewhat related to both. At the heart of such identification is a failure to notice that we developed a version of secularism that was at once modern and Indian. Those who identify Indian secularism entirely with homegrown traditional conceptions are able to grasp the prehistory of Indian secularism (even though they do not see it as prehistory), but they entirely bypass its connection with a larger common transnational history as well as with its later history toward which Indians contributed significantly. On the other hand, those who identify the Indian variant with Western conceptions fail to notice both the prehistory and the later history of secularism. Like Western theorists, they focus only on the middle history of secularism, one developed almost exclusively by Western societies. This limited vision is shared by both advocates and opponents of secularism. For example, Indian critics of Indian secularism claim that it has privatized religion. Nothing could be further from the truth. Indian religion has a public presence that is ratified by the Indian constitution. The constitution gives official recognition to religious communities to maintain their own educational institutions. Such institutions foster particular religious identities and are sometimes even funded by the state. There could not be a more suitable illustration of the point that, far from privatizing religion, the Indian constitution continues to support its publicization.

To be sure, there is an important sense in which religion is meant to be depoliticized by the Indian constitution. Indian secularism would not be a version of secularism if it did not support some forms of depoliticization of religion. But this depoliticization of religion must not be confused with its depublicization. Indeed, the constitution even allows a contextual politicization of religion, for example, in cases where such politicization advances the cause of equality and freedom. If justice ever required the local politicization of religion, then any defensible version of secularism must support it. For example, if the minority community in Gujarat is mobilized against the present government, then, even though it relies, at least implicitly, on distinctions and classifications made on the basis of religion, such mobilization would entirely be consistent with secularism. It is noteworthy that separate electorates for Muslims were rejected in postindependent India, not by an appeal to a secularism of a strict separationist variety but on highly contextual grounds. The abandonment of separate electorates was supported because they were believed to have started the awful habit of treating Hindus and Muslims as distinct and congealed political entities, bolstered sectarianism and ghettoized minorities, and strengthened the resolve of every community to care only for their own interests. In short, separate electorates were rejected keeping in mind not some general moral necessity of separating religion and state but because they had "sharpened communal differences to a dangerous extent and prevented the development of a healthy national life." The implication is that if they were compatible with or somehow fostered a healthy national life, then they could easily have been endorsed.

I have focused in this paper on internal threats to secularism. I have argued that a continuous failure to recognize the distinctiveness of Indian secularism strengthens this threat. I believe this problem afflicts the self-understanding of secularism in both India and several Western countries. Western secular states need to improve the understanding of their own practices and to have a better theoretical self-understanding. Rather than get stuck on a model they developed at a particular time in their history, they would do well to learn from the original Indian variant. Likewise, both the self-proclaimed supporters of secularism and some of its misguided opponents could learn from examining the original Indian variant. It is my conviction that many critics of Indian secularism will embrace it once they understand its nature and point.

No idea lives forever. But no good idea should be lost because its supporters are intellectually too lazy to properly defend it.

Notes

1. This article was originally published shortly after the Indian National Congress returned to power upon winning a plurality of votes in the 2004 elections, thereby replacing a right-wing coalition led by the Hindu-nationalist Bharatiya Janata Party (BJP) that had governed since the 1999 elections. Congress led coalition governments for two consecutive periods but lost decisively to the BJP in the 2014 elections.

2. See Rajeev Bhargava, ed., *Secularism and Its Critics* (New Delhi: Oxford University Press, 1998), especially the contributions by T. N. Madan, "Secularism in its Place"; Ashis Nandy, "The Politics of Secularism and the Recovery of Religious Toleration"; and Partha Chatterjee, "Secularism and Tolerance."

3. The *Catholic Encyclopedia* (New York: Robert Appleton Company, 1912) defines theocracy as a form of political government in which the deity directly rules the people or as the rule of priestly caste. The rule of Brahmins in India in accordance with the Dharam Shastras would be theocratic.

4. The whole question of the separation of church and state, I maintain, emerges forcefully in what are predominantly church-based, single-religion societies. The issue of religion-state separation arises, however, in societies without churches or with multiple religions or when the hold of religion in societies has considerably declined, that is, when religion is considered by the majority to be largely insignificant.

5. Leonard W. Levy, *The Establishment Clause* (Chapel Hill: University of North Carolina Press, 1994), 7.

6. The three types of state-church regimes discussed here are all ideal types.

7. Malise Ruthven, *A Fury for God* (London: Granta Books, 2002), 172–178.

8. Levy, *Establishment Clause*, 12.

9. Levy, 11.

10. This would also open up the possibility of distinguishing forms of secular states.

11. Faisal Devji commented that colonial secularism, which meant the strict neutrality of the colonial state with respect to all religions, was also a project of values, in particular the value of a civilizing mission. See Faisal Devji, "Comments on Rajeev Bhargava's 'The Distinctiveness of Indian Secularism,'" in *The Future of Secularism*, ed. T. N. Srinivasan (New Delhi: Oxford University Press, 2007). There is no doubt some truth in this, and it is consistent with my own remark that state neutrality under British rule was always attacked for having a hidden Christian agenda. Yet to forget the instrumental reasons behind the posture of neutrality would be a mistake. To me, the secularity of the colonial state was amoral and self-aggrandizing. The difference, if any, between Devji and me is one of emphasis rather than substance.

12. On this point see, Michael McConnell, "Taking Religious Freedom Seriously," in *Religious Liberty in the Supreme Court*, ed. Terry East Land (Grand Rapids, MI: William B. Eerdmans, 1993), 497–510.

13. Charles R. Beitz, *Political Equality: An Essay in Democratic Theory* (Princeton, NJ: Princeton University Press, 1989), chap. 5.

14. See Charles Taylor, *Sources of the Self* (Cambridge: Cambridge University Press, 1989).

15. This idea is closely related to the notion of social death to be found in Oscar Patterson's writings. See Beitz, *Political Equality*, 109 and 110.

16. Partha Chatterjee's piece on secularism exemplifies this error. Thus, he mistakenly concludes that since the Hindu right does not want the laws of the state to be in conformity with the general spirit of the *Dharmasastra*, it is at peace with the institutional procedures

of modern Western secularism. See Chatterjee, "Secularism and Tolerance." Arguably, the Hindu Right may wish the de facto, somewhat disguised establishment of its own variant of Hinduism.

17. Donald Eugene Smith, *India as a Secular State* (Princeton, NJ: Princeton University Press, 1963), 3–8.

18. For an interesting critique of Smith's interpretation of Indian secularism as derived from the American model with an "extra dose of separation," see Marc Galanter, "Secularism, East and West," in Rajeev Bhargava, *Secularism and Its Critics*, 234–267.

19. Ronald Dworkin, "Liberalism," in *Public and Private Morality*, ed. Stuart Hampshire (Cambridge: Cambridge University Press, 1978), 125.

20. See Charles Taylor, "Justice After Virtue," in *After MacIntyre*, ed. John Horton and Susan Mendus (Cambridge: Polity Press, 1994), 16–43.

21. Here I rely on Granville Austin, *The Indian Constitution: Cornerstone of a Nation* (New Delhi: Oxford University Press, 1999), 311–325.

22. On this issue, see Devji, "Comments on Rajeev Bhargava." Devji wishes to trace the distinctiveness of Indian secularism to the colonial period of which, he says, the republic's constitution is in many ways a juridical culmination. This claim is ambiguous. It could mean either that much of what makes Indian secularism distinctive was generated before India's independence from colonial rule or that the distinctiveness of Indian secularism is a product largely of colonial forces. I have no disagreement with the first claim. However, I disagree strongly with the second. As I have argued in this essay, the idea of a secular state, that is, a state strictly neutral with respect to all religions was a characteristic of colonial modernity and came into existence in India under British rule, specifically with the Queen's Proclamation of 1858. This idea was inserted within a cultural background suffused with the prehistory of secularism, and once installed, it was transformed into something entirely different by the efforts of those struggling against the filth in their own traditions as well as against colonial rule. The product of these struggles, the model of the secular state in the Indian constitution was vastly different from anything that existed in pre-British India or under British colonial rule. Thus, the distinctiveness of Indian secularism is not traceable to colonial sources.

23. By implication, the history of secularism must include the history of other non-Western societies that have sought to install and maintain secular states.

Contributors

Umut Azak is associate professor in the Department of International Relations at Istanbul Okan University. Her research focuses on the history of secularism and memory politics in Turkey. She is the author of *Islam and Secularism in Turkey: Kemalism, Religion and the Nation State* (I. B. Tauris, 2010).

Christoph Baumgartner is associate professor of ethics in the Department of Philosophy and Religious Studies at Utrecht University. His recent work includes "Liberal Political Philosophy of Religious Difference after Saba Mahmood," *Sociology of Islam* 7, no. 4 (2019).

Rajeev Bhargava is director of the Parekh Institute of Indian Thought at the Centre for the Study of Developing Societies in New Delhi, where he has worked since 2005. His writings include *What Is Political Theory and Why Do We Need It?* (Oxford University Press, 2012) and *The Promise of India's Secular Democracy* (Oxford University Press, 2010).

John R. Bowen is Dunbar-Van Cleve Professor at Washington University in St. Louis. He is the author of the collaborative work *Pragmatic Inquiry* (Routledge, 2021) and of *On British Islam* (Princeton University Press, 2016) and is currently writing a five-country study of *Proving Halal*.

Judith Butler is Maxine Elliot Professor in the Department of Comparative Literature and the Program of Critical Theory at the University of California, Berkeley. Her most recent works include *Senses of the Subject and Notes Toward a Performative Theory of Assembly* (Harvard University Press, 2015) and *The Force of Nonviolence* (Verso, 2021).

Rokus de Groot is professor emeritus of Musicology at the University of Amsterdam and a composer. His work includes "From Past to Present and from Listening to Hearing: Final Indefinable Moments in Bach's and Stravinsky's Music," in *On Religion and Memory*, ed. Babette Hellemans et al. (Fordham University Press, 2013) and, as composer, "For Dhruba" (2017), an homage to the sarangi maestro Pandit Dhruba Ghosh.

Martijn de Koning is an anthropologist affiliated with the Department of Islamic Studies at Radboud University Nijmegen. He is the coauthor (with Carmen Becker and Ineke Roex) of *Islamic Militant Activism in Belgium, the Netherlands and Germany: "Islands in a Sea of Disbelief"'* (Palgrave Macmillan, 2020). With Nadia Fadil and Francesco Ragazzi, he edited the volume *Radicalization in Belgium and the Netherlands—Critical Perspectives on Violence and Security* (IB Tauris, 2019). He maintains his own blog: http://religionresearch.org/closer.

Sanne Derks is a freelance documentary photographer and anthropologist (PhD) from Arnhem, the Netherlands. Her work focuses on social and environmental issues in Latin America and is published, among others, in the *New York Times*, the *Guardian*, and *El País*.

Wendy Doniger is the Mircea Eliade Distinguished Service Professor of History of Religions at the University of Chicago. She is the author of *The Hindus: An Alternative History* (Penguin Press, 2009) and the translator, with Sudhir Kakar, of Vatsyayana's *Kamasutra* (Oxford University Press, 2003).

Willy Jansen is professor emerita of gender studies at Radboud University Nijmegen. She has published on religious women's groups in Algeria, missions in the Middle East, and gender and ritual in Spain. She is the coeditor (with Catrien Notermans) of *Moved by Mary: The Power of Pilgrimage in the Modern World* (Routledge, 2009) and *Gender, Nation, and Religion in European Pilgrimage* (Routledge, 2012).

Yolande Jansen is associate professor of philosophy at the University of Amsterdam and professor of humanism in relation to religion and secularity at the VU University Amsterdam, appointed by the Socrates Foundation. She is the author of *Secularism, Assimilation, and the Crisis of Multiculturalism: French Modernist Legacies* (Amsterdam University Press, 2014).

Mariwan Kanie is a lecturer at the Department of Arabic Culture at the University of Amsterdam. He specializes in the political and intellectual history of the modern

Middle East and the Kurdish question and is the author of *Ethics and Resistance: Introduction to Foucault's Thought* (in Kurdish) (Andesha Publication, 2017).

Webb Keane is the George Herbert Mead Collegiate Professor of Anthropology at the University of Michigan and the author of *Ethical Life: Its Natural and Social Histories* (Princeton University Press, 2016) and *Christian Moderns: Freedom and Fetish in the Mission Encounter* (University of California Press, 2007).

Anne-Marie Korte is professor of religion and gender at Utrecht University. She coedited (with Angela Berlis and Kune Biezeveld) *Everyday Life and the Sacred: Re/configuring Gender Studies in Religion* (Brill, 2017); (with Christiane Kruse and Birgit Meyer) *Taking Offense: Religion, Art, and Visual Culture in Plural Configurations* (Fink Verlag, 2018); and (with Mariecke van den Berg, Lieke Schrijvers, and Jelle Wiering) *Transforming Bodies: Religions, Powers and Agencies in Europe* (New York: Routledge, 2020).

Michael Lambek holds a Canada Research Chair in Anthropology of Ethical Life at the University of Toronto and is the author of *Ordinary Ethics: Anthropology, Language, and Action* (Fordham University Press, 2010) and *The Ethical Condition: Essays on Action, Person, and Value* (University of Chicago Press, 2015).

Bruno Latour is a retired honorary professor emeritus at Sciences Po, Paris. His recent work includes *Facing Gaia: Eight Lectures on the New Climatic Regime* (Polity Press, 2016) and *Down to Earth: Politics in the New Climatic Regime* (Polity Press, 2018), and he is the editor of *Critical Zones: The Science and Politics of Landing on Earth* (MIT Press, 2020).

Michiel Leezenberg teaches in the Departments of Philosophy, Religious Studies, and Classics at the University of Amsterdam and has published widely on the philosophy of the humanities, Islamic intellectual history, and the Kurdish question. His recent publications include (with Gerard de Vries) *History and Philosophy of the Humanities: An Introduction* (Amsterdam University Press, 2018), *Sexuality and Politics in Islam* (Prometheus, 2017), and *Foucault* (Athenaum, 2021).

Annelies Moors is professor emerita of contemporary Muslim societies at the Department of Anthropology of the University of Amsterdam. She coedited (with Emma Tarlo) *Islamic Fashion and Anti-fashion: New Perspectives from Europe and North-America* (Bloomsbury, 2013).

Catrien Notermans is an anthropologist and associate professor in the Department of Cultural Anthropology and Development Studies at Radboud University, Nijmegen, The Netherlands. She is coeditor (with Willy Jansen) of *Moved by Mary: The Power of Pilgrimage in the Modern World* (Routledge, 2009) and *Gender, Nation and Religion in European Pilgrimage* (Routledge, 2012).

S. Brent Plate is professor of religious studies at Hamilton College (Clinton, USA) and author of *Religion and Film: Cinema and the Re-Creation of the World* (Columbia University Press, 2017) and *A History of Religion in 5½ Objects* (Beacon Press, 2014).

Samuli Schielke is a senior researcher at the Leibniz-Zentrum Moderner Orient in Berlin and associate primary investigator at the Berlin Graduate School of Muslim Cultures and Societies. He is author of *The Perils of Joy: Contesting Mulid Festivals in Contemporary Egypt* (Syracuse University Press, 2012), *Egypt in the Future Tense* (Indiana University Press, 2015), and *Migrant Dreams: Egyptian Workers in the Gulf States* (American University in Cairo Press, 2020).

Regina M. Schwartz is professor of English and religion at Northwestern University and author of *Loving Justice, Living Shakespeare* (Oxford University Press, 2017) and *Sacramental Poetics at the Dawn of Secularism: When God Left the World* (Stanford University Press, 2008)

Yvonne Sherwood has taught literature and religious studies at several British universities, most recently at the School of European Culture and Languages of the University of Kent. She is the coauthor (with Stephen D. Moore) of *The Invention of the Biblical Scholar: A Critical Manifesto* (Fortress Press, 2011) and author of *Biblical Blaspheming: Trials of the Sacred for a Secular Age* (Cambridge University Press, 2012) and *Blasphemy: A Very Short Introduction* (Oxford University Press, 2021).

Thomas A. Tweed is the Harold and Martha Welch Professor of American Studies and professor of history at the University of Notre Dame. He is the author of *Crossing and Dwelling: A Theory of Religion* (Harvard University Press, 2006) and *Religion: A Very Short Introduction* (Oxford University Press, 2020).

Martin van Bruinessen is professor emeritus in the Department of Philosophy and Religious Studies at Utrecht University. He is the editor of *Contemporary Developments in Indonesian Islam: Explaining the 'Conservative Turn'* (Institute of South

East Asian Studies, 2013) and (with Stefano Allievi) of *Producing Islamic Knowledge: Transmission and Dissemination in Western Europe* (Routledge, 2011).

Sander van Maas teaches philosophy and music at Utrecht University College, the University of Amsterdam, and the Conservatorium van Amsterdam. His publications include *The Reinvention of Religious Music: Olivier Messiaen's Breakthrough Toward the Beyond* (Fordham University Press, 2012), *Thresholds of Listening: Sound, Technics, Space* (Fordham University Press, 2015), and *Contemporary Music and Spirituality* (Routledge, 2016).

Ali Hassan Zaidi is an associate professor in the Department of Global Studies and cross-appointed to the Department of Religion and Culture at Wilfrid Laurier University (Waterloo, Canada). He is the author of *Islam, Modernity and the Human Sciences* (2011) and has published in various journals, including most recently the *Journal of Islamic and Muslim Studies*.

Index

Abraham, 42, 65–95, 484
Agamben, Giorgio, 169, 199, 565–6
agency, 62–3, 71, 98–9, 167–8, 199, 230, 239, 259, 264, 353–4, 472, 507–10, 581–3, 586
ahimsa (non-violence), 471
ambiguity, 71, 364–5
Ammerman, Nancy, 287–8, 290
amulets, 256, 258–64
ancestral spirits, 252, 476, 477, 480
"angry Muslims," 374, 445–63
Arendt, Hannah, 168–9, 195, 197–200, 202–4, 211, 213
Asad, Talal, 20, 32–3, 351–2, 378, 460, 551, 565, 579–80, 584, 597–8
Atatürk, Mustafa Kemal, 323–9, 333, 340
Atta, Mohamed, 84
Augustine, 255, 269
Austin, J. L., 8, 42, 74–5, 107, 488
autochthony, 314–18

Bali (Indonesia), 253–4, 258
beginning, 472, 475–501
bhakti, 176, 217, 220, 221–6, 228–32
Biel, Gabriel, 516–7
bin Laden, Osama, 550, 559, 560, 562, 564
biopolitics, 32, 474, 565
blasphemy, 15, 85, 104, 371–3, 375–90, 392–8, 403–4, 407–10, 446, 453, 454, 456–7; blasphemy law, 394, 458, 461, 467
Bolivia, 303–21
Bourdieu, Pierre, 4, 5, 8–10, 107, 284
Bouyeri, Mohammed, 450, 453, 455–6
Bulwer, John, 42, 56–67, 69, 72, 87, 97
Burton, Richard Francis, 183–6

Calvin, John, 62, 506, 508, 510, 523, 625
Canada, 394, 576, 605–22

Cavarero, Adriana, 197, 213
Chatterjee, Partha, 22, 577, 578, 623, 636
commemorations, 107, 143, 146, 323–4, 326, 329, 332, 335, 336, 338–41, 516–7
communitarianism, 26, 30, 33, 38, 577, 637
Cranmer, Thomas, 503, 508–9
cross-dressing, 170, 180, 181, 186, 219, 221, 224, 226, 231
crossing (crossing and dwelling), 276, 292–5
crucifixion, 77, 93–5, 385, 386, 394, 412
culture wars, 384, 396, 397, 405

dance, 151, 221, 276, 303–21
darshan, 217, 223, 226, 230, 231
da'wa, 170, 243, 582, 589, 601, 606
dematerializing, 171, 249, 250, 253, 257
democracy, 195, 407, 417, 422, 424, 435, 436, 444, 449, 580–1, 591–3, 637, 642, 644
Derrida, Jacques, 41, 42, 48, 77, 79–80, 84, 147, 264
Devi, Indira, 226–8
Devji, Faisal, 563, 578, 648, 649
dhikr, 108, 536, 537, 543
divination, 252, 256, 268
divorce, 43, 107, 113, 114, 116
Docetism, 95
drag, 41, 170, 209
Durkheim, Émile, 9, 12, 16, 287, 371, 609
dwelling, 276, 292–4. *See also* crossing (crossing and dwelling)
Dworkin, Ronald, 639

ecstasy, the ecstatic, 226, 276, 286, 287, 288, 291, 294–5, 300
Egypt, 168, 240, 244, 349, 357–60, 363–4, 365, 446, 540, 576, 601
Elizabethan theater, 472–3, 503–7

embodiment, 48, 49, 169–70, 215–17, 219, 220, 224, 226, 228–32, 258, 293, 305, 406, 522, 561, 597
epistemology, 33, 50, 267, 285, 425, 576, 581, 586, 589–90
eroticism, 168, 175–6, 183, 186–90, 228–9, 527–9
establishment of religion, 625–7, 629, 631–5, 649
ethnicity, 304–5, 308–10, 315, 317, 421, 608, 612
everyday. *See* quotidian
everyday life, 240, 275–6, 279–302, 351, 359, 609–10
everyday religion, 279–302
exclusion, 169, 198–200, 276, 292, 304, 305, 313, 361, 373, 421, 434, 593

felicity conditions, 43, 107, 109, 112–15, 120, 122, 123, 125, 374, 428–31, 436–8
folklore, 308–9, 313–14
Foucault, Michel, 4, 6, 8, 10, 11, 13–14, 17, 32, 35, 36, 199, 284, 570–1
Freeland, Cynthia, 378
Freud, Sigmund, 283, 287, 478

Gandhi, Mahatma, 168, 188
gender, 5, 13–15, 36, 41, 167, 170, 176, 179–83, 185, 196–7, 205, 210–13, 219, 227, 281, 284, 363, 373, 392–8, 404–5, 484, 606, 608, 612, 618, 664
genealogy, 6, 10, 13, 27, 32–3, 38, 278, 396, 476, 482, 484, 551, 565, 575–8, 591
ghazal poetry, 473, 524, 526–30, 533–6, 542–3
Girard, René, 471
Goldstein, Daniel, 308–9
Goldstone, Brian, 457

Habermas, Jürgen, 12, 27–30, 196, 576, 578–81, 590–98
hajj, 107, 108
Heidegger, Martin, 55, 60, 67, 71, 73, 489, 490, 491
Hinduism, 168, 169–70, 173–93, 215–34, 372, 491, 578, 625, 636–7, 639
Hindutva, 168, 174, 188

Hirsi Ali, Ayaan, 445–467
homosexuality, 15, 24, 179–83, 186, 209, 383, 384, 387, 401, 410, 448, 618
Hrdlička, Aleš, 387–88
human rights, 576–7, 605–22

iconoclash, 44, 395
iconoclasm, 44, 132, 137, 254–5, 266, 395, 595
icons/image-making, 43, 44, 73, 107, 125, 131–7, 217, 222, 223, 249–71, 322–47, 385, 393, 396, 405, 454
ideologies, semiotic, 44, 249–271
incarnation, 59, 64, 77, 78, 168–70, 215–17, 223, 226, 254–6, 378, 520
indexicality, 106–18, 252, 259, 267, 268, 491
Indian secularism, 577–8, 623–49
intentionality, 4, 5, 386, 480, 482, 484, 488, 490, 495, 499, 500
Isaac (son of Abraham), 42, 69–96, 484, 499, 516
Islam, 106–17, 235–48, 348–66, 579–602, 605–22
Islamic dress, 26, 43, 116, 170, 210, 235–48, 357, 582
Islamism, 326–7, 337, 338, 340, 364, 580, 588, 594
iteration, 41, 170

Jakobson, Roman, 261
John of Damascus, 254–5
justice, 27, 197, 207–8, 472–3, 502–23, 566, 592–3, 637, 647

Kamasutra, 168, 176–80, 182–90
Kemalism, 277, 322–47
Kierkegaard, Søren, 68, 84, 89–92, 94
Knott, Kim, 287–8, 291
Koyî, Haji Qadir, 473, 524–45
Krishna, 176, 179, 215–34
Kubilay, Mustafa Fehmi, 277, 322, 329–41
Kurdistan, Kurdish language, Kurds, 209, 473, 524–45, 562–3

Latour, Bruno, 43–4, 204, 395
Levinas, Emmanuel, 520
Levy, Leonard, 376
liberal political theory, 27, 474, 585, 592

liberalism, 26-9, 278, 446, 448, 457-8, 463, 551, 577, 586, 598-9, 600
lived religion, 51, 85, 275-6, 279, 282, 284, 289, 290, 292-3
Luther, Martin, 68, 506, 508, 516-17

Madagascar, 476, 478, 485
Madan, T. N., 623
Mahmood, Saba, 112, 170, 237-8, 241, 355, 433-4, 440, 443, 454, 576, 579-604
Marian pilgrimage, 303-20
marriage, 12, 107-8, 113-16, 190, 233, 488, 490, 492, 499, 506, 587
martyrdom, 84, 225, 277, 323, 329-32, 338, 340, 408, 471-3, 524-30, 553-4, 558-62, 567, 569-71
mass, 62, 133-4, 472, 502-23
material practices, 169, 253
materializing, 171, 249-50, 253, 257-60
Mauss, Marcel, 12, 284-5, 486-7
Mehdi, 329
Mesguich, Daniel, 77-9, 101-3, 105
Messiaen, Olivier, 141-64
Miles, Margaret, 397
Milton, John, 507, 511, 521
Mirabai, 220, 222-7, 229, 231
Mitchell, W. J. T., 453
Morales, Evo, 312, 315-16
murder, 60, 71, 80, 83, 331, 455, 458-60, 472-3, 507-18
music, 44-5, 87, 141-64, 170, 226, 228, 231-2, 263, 307-9, 385, 528

Nandy, Ashis, 577-8, 623
Nash, David, 394
nationalism, 20-3, 277, 322, 328, 332, 334, 526, 530-1, 533, 542, 559-61, 565, 570, 577, 623, 637, 642, 644

Öcalan, Abdullah, 553-4, 562
offense, 85, 371, 375-474
Ofili, Chris, 373, 377-9
orientalism, 14, 85, 90, 168, 181, 186, 237, 353-4, 482, 494
Orsi, Robert A., 49, 53-5, 64-6, 276, 282, 287-8, 290-2, 301, 361, 377
Othello, 42, 472, 502-23

Palestinians, 127, 206, 549-50, 552-3, 563
Peirce, C. S., 107
Pentecostalism, 16, 25. *See also* Christianity
performative, performativity, 5, 13, 15, 41-5, 74-5, 108, 113-17, 121, 168-9, 196-202, 211-12, 222, 224, 230, 238, 276, 373-4, 446, 450, 452, 462, 463, 482, 488-9, 518-20, 542, 564
piety, 75, 86, 112, 240, 283, 351, 355-66, 576, 579-602, 606
pilgrimage, 276, 293, 303-20, 326-8. *See also* hajj; Marian pilgrimage
Plate, Brent, 372-3, 392, 396, 456
Plato, 50, 64, 131, 504
postsecularism, 28-9, 396
power, 6-11, 14, 20, 31-3, 41, 168-9, 194-212, 238, 249-54, 261, 276, 289-90, 303-20, 331, 355-66, 375-90, 391-410, 423, 429, 474, 503, 535, 550-1, 554, 565-6, 575, 583, 635
Prabhakaran, Vellupilai, 547, 561
practice turn, 1, 7, 11-12, 13, 18-19
prayer, 60-5, 73, 111-12, 359, 373, 391-410, 477, 512-16, 613-14
precarity/precariousness, 60, 74, 196-213, 449
protest, 24, 169, 173-5, 194-212, 377-380, 388, 391-410, 417-42, 446, 455, 546-68
Protestantism. *See* Christianity
provocation, 378, 402, 445-62
public debate, 27, 29, 167, 373-4, 394, 417-442, 17
public space. *See* space, public
public sphere, 167, 169, 194-212, 397, 417-42, 576, 579-602, 606, 619
Pussy Riot, 391-415

queer, 209-10
quotidian, 1-5, 8, 18, 54, 231, 236-40, 276, 279-366, 576, 609-10
Qutb, Sayyid, 558

Rappaport, Roy, 488-90, 495
religious critique, 393, 409, 588
religious language, 21, 267, 472, 525, 559. *See also* signs; writing

Rig Veda, 168, 175, 183, 187–88
ritual, 2, 5–6, 12–13, 108–10, 175, 263, 303–21, 322–47, 404, 447, 471–2, 479–80, 486, 492, 502–23, 536, 548
Roy, Ram Moham, 187–8

sacralization, 277, 322, 473, 561, 563, 566, 610, 619
Said, Edward, 150, 475, 478, 482
salat, 67, 107–116
same-sex marriage, 608, 618
science, 7, 18, 44, 119–40
Scott, Joan W., 397
secularism, 16, 26–33, 167, 277, 322–46, 354, 360, 455–6
secularization, 3, 11, 15–19, 28–9, 239–40, 277, 322, 473, 558, 575, 580, 605–21
self-immolation, 546, 548, 553–4
Sellars, Peter, 44–5, 141–61
semiosis, semiotics, 5, 43–4, 106–17, 167, 170–1, 249–69, 564, 589
sexuality, 5, 13–15, 167, 170, 173–92, 210–11, 215–33, 373, 391–410, 490
Shakespeare, William, 472, 502–520
shamanism, 25, 152
Shariati, Ali, 558
shi'ism. *See* Islam
signs, 8–9, 43, 58, 66, 110, 170, 249–69, 564, 589
silencing, 373–4, 417–42
Silverstein, Michael, 34, 117, 267, 269
Smith, Donald Eugene, 634–6
social drama (Turner), 445–62
social inequality, 10, 276, 303–20, 598, 645
space, 122, 133, 284–9, 293
space, sacred, 276, 279, 372
space, public, 43, 116, 169, 194–212, 222, 231, 372, 377, 579–602, 605–21
Speech Act Theory, 8, 41–3, 107, 120, 130, 373, 426–7
Spinoza, B. de, 15

spirituality, 45, 151–2, 188, 275, 315, 325, 386, 529, 535
state rituals, 277, 322–46
sufism, 22, 43, 108–10, 188, 324, 331, 527–30, 536–8
suicide, 516
suicide bombing, 84, 546–68
Sunna. *See* Islam

Tahrir Square demonstrations, 168–9, 194–212
talak, 107, 113–16
Tamils, 547–8, 552, 557–8, 560–3, 567
Taylor, Charles, 12, 18–19, 21, 30–1, 273, 423, 433, 575, 578, 597, 605–21
temporality, 31, 43–4, 79, 142, 196, 477, 517, 585
theocracy, 624–5, 627–9, 632–4
toleration, 423, 577, 627, 630, 643, 645
transgender, 209–12, 219
transgression, 42, 78–9, 85, 215–33, 169, 175, 472, 513, 575
truth conditions, 120, 129
Turkey, 26, 29, 169, 209, 240–1, 277, 322–46, 553–4, 556, 561, 563
Turner, Victor, 13, 300, 304, 317, 374, 445–62, 472, 479–80, 482, 492

utterance, 41, 43, 63–4, 75, 113, 121, 260, 371–2, 427, 488–9, 564–5

van Gennep, Arnold, 12, 479–80, 492
violence, 6, 32, 50, 168–9, 175, 200–12, 428, 430, 589–90, 595–6

Weber, Max, 9, 16, 112, 283–7, 557
Williams, Rowan, 84–5, 615
Wittgenstein, Ludwig, 3–4, 6, 8–10, 26, 492
Wojnarowicz, David, 381–6
words. *See* signs
writing, 6, 52–5, 66, 170–1, 249–69, 519

The Future of the Religious Past
Hent de Vries, *General Editor*

Hent de Vries (ed.),
Religion: Beyond a Concept

Meerten B. ter Borg and Jan Willem van Henten (eds.),
Powers: Religion as a Social and Spiritual Force

Dick Houtman and Birgit Meyer (eds.),
Things: Religion and the Question of Materiality

Ernst van den Hemel and Asja Szafraniec (eds.),
Words: Religious Language Matters

Martin van Bruinessen, Anne-Marie Korte, and Michiel Leezenberg (eds.),
Gestures: The Study of Religion as Practice

www.ingramcontent.com/pod-product-compliance
Lightning Source LLC
Chambersburg PA
CBHW080344300426
44110CB00019B/2496